Sri Lanka

The travel guide

Footprint

Robert & Roma Bradnock

*Ceylon present. Dear me, it is beautiful!
And most sumptuously tropical, as to
character of foliage and opulence of it.
'What the spicy breezes blow soft o'er
Ceylon's isle' - an eloquent line, an
incomparable line; it says little, but conveys
whole libraries of sentiment, and Oriental
charm and mystery and tropic
deliciousness - a line that quivers and
mystery with a thousand unexpressed and
inexpressible things...*

Mark Twain, *Following the Equator*

Sri Lanka Handbook

Sri Lanka Handbook
Third edition
© Footprint Handbooks Ltd 2000

Published by Footprint Handbooks
6 Riverside Court
Lower Bristol Road
Bath BA2 3DZ. England
T +44 (0)1225 469141
F +44 (0)1225 469461
Email discover@footprintbooks.com
Web www.footprintbooks.com

ISBN 1 900949 70 9
CIP DATA: A catalogue record for this
book is available from the British Library

In USA, published by
NTC/Contemporary Publishing Group
4255 West Touhy Avenue, Lincolnwood
(Chicago), Illinois 60712-1975, USA
T 847 679 5500 F 847 679 2494
Email NTCPUB2@AOL.COM

ISBN 0-658-01085-9
Library of Congress Catalog Card
Number 00-132889

Credits

Series editors
Patrick Dawson and Rachel Fielding

Editorial
Editor: Stephanie Lambe
Maps: Sarah Sorensen

Production
Typesetting: Richard Ponsford and
Leona Bailey
Maps: Claire Benison and Angus Dawson
Colour maps: Robert Lunn and
Kevin Feeney

Cover: Camilla Ford

Design
Mytton Williams

Photography
Front cover: getty one Stone
Back cover: getty one Stone
Inside colour section: BBC Natural
History Library, Eye Ubiquitous, getty
one Stone, Impact Photos, Robert
Harding Picture Library

Print
Manufactured in Italy by LEGOPRINT

Sri Lanka

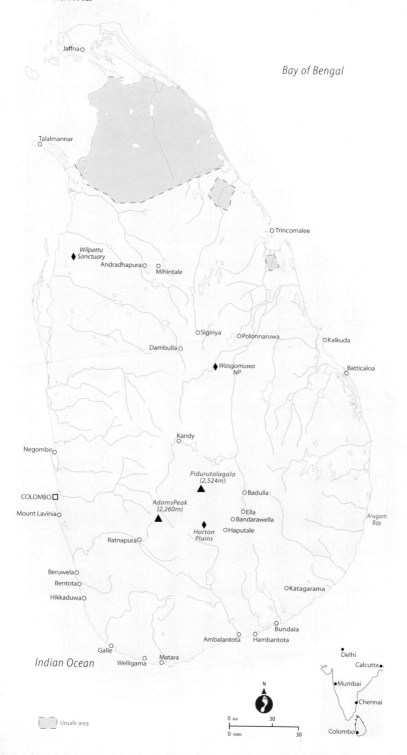

Bay of Bengal

Jaffna

Talalmannar

Trincomalee

♦ *Wilpattu Sanctuary*
Andradhapura   Mihintale

Sigiriya   Polonnaruwa   Kalkuda

Dambulla

♦ *Wasgomuwa NP*

Batticaloa

Kandy

Negombo

Pidurutalagala (2,524m) ▲   Badulla

COLOMBO □

Mount Lavinia

AdamsPeak (2,260m) ▲   Ella
Bandarawella
♦ *Horton Plains*   Haputale

Ratnapura

Arugam Bay

Beruwela
Bentota
Hikkaduwa

Katagarama

Bundala
Ambalantota   Hambantota

Galle
Welligama   Matara

Indian Ocean

□ Unsafe area

N

0 km   30
0 miles   30

Delhi
Calcutta

Mumbai

Chennai

Colombo

Contents

5 A foot in the door

17 Essentials
19 Planning your trip
19 Where to go
19 Planning a route
24 When to go
24 Tours and tour operators
25 Finding out more
26 Language
26 Before you travel
33 Tourist information
36 Rules, customs and etiquette
37 Safety
38 Where to stay
41 Getting around
41 Air
41 Road
43 Train
45 Keeping in touch
47 Food and drink
48 Shopping
49 Special interest travel
50 Holidays and festivals
51 Health
51 Before travelling
53 On the road
56 When you return home
56 Further reading

59 Colombo and the nearby beaches
62 Ins and outs
62 Central Colombo
70 Parks and zoos
70 Essentials
84 Mount Lavinia
88 Beaches near Colombo
89 Negombo

90 Sights
97 Beaches north of Negombo
97 Waikkal
97 Marawila

99 The Western & Northwestern region
102 Along the west coast to Puttalam
102 The road to Kandy
104 Inland from Colombo to Kurunegala
104 Kurunegala

109 Southern Sri Lanka
112 Beaches along the southwest coast
112 Kalutara
114 Beruwela
116 Aluthgama
117 Bentota
120 Ambalangoda
122 Hikkaduwa
130 Galle
137 Unawatuna
140 The Scenic South Coast
141 Weligama
143 Mirissa
144 Matara
147 The Dry Southeast
148 Tangalla
154 Kalametiya Bird Sanctuary
155 Hambantota
157 Bundala National Park
158 Tissamaharama
161 Yala (Ruhuna) National Park
162 Kataragama

164 The heart of the Wet Zone
166 Ratnapura
169 Sinharaja Biosphere Reserve
173 Pelmadulla to the South Coast
173 Uda Walawe National Park

175 The Central Highlands
178 Kandy
179 Sights
183 Essentials
192 Around Kandy
192 West of Kandy
197 Northeast of Kandy
198 East of Kandy
198 South of Kandy
199 The Highlands
200 Nuwara Eliya
207 Around Nuwara Eliya
207 Peaks and plateaus
208 Adam's peak
209 Horton Plains National Park

213 Uva Province
216 Badulla, Ella, Bandarawela and Haputale
217 Badulla
219 Ella
223 Bandarawela
225 Haputale

229 Ancient cities - Cultural Triangle
232 Sites north of Kandy
233 Nalanda and Dambulla

Left: modern Sri Lanka continues to be colourful, a billboard adorns the street.

238 Anuradhapura and
       Mihintale
238 Anuradhapura
239 Sights
245 Essentials
247 Mihintale
251 Sigiriya
255 Essentials
257 Pollonaruwa
259 Sights
263 Essentials
265 Mahiyangana

9

267 **Eastern Region**
270 Eastern Province (North)
270 Trincomalee
271 Sights
273 Essentials
273 Beaches north of
       Trincomalee
275 Eastern Province (South)
275 Batticaloa
276 Gal Oya National Park
277 Arugam Bay
279 Lahugala National Park
279 Monaragala
280 Jaffna and the Northern
       Provinces

10

281 **Background**
283 History
283 Settlement and early
       history
285 Political developments in
       pre-colonial Sri Lanka
286 The Sinhalese move
       south
286 The Kandyan Kingdom
287 Colonial power
288 The moves to
       independance
288 Modern Sri Lanka
289 Government
290 Economy
293 Culture
293 Religion
309 Architecture
314 Art
315 Language
316 Land and environment
316 Geography
317 Climate
318 Wildlife
326 Vegetation

11

329 **Footnotes**
331 Glossary
335 Useful words and
       phrases - Sinhalese
337 Useful words and
       phrases - Sri Lankan
       Tamil
339 Eating out - food and
       menus
341 Sri Lankan specialites
342 Index
346 Shorts
347 Map index
348 Advertisers
359 Colour maps

Inside front cover
Hotel price guide
Exchange rates
Dialling codes
Useful websites

Inside back cover
Map symbols
Weights and measures

Right: *Hindu deities greet those visiting the Buddhist temple of Kelaniya in Colombo.*

A foot in the door

Highlights

For generations of travellers Sri Lanka has conjured up often dreamlike images. White dagobas curving sky-ward create a starting skyline, serene carved stone buddhas lying in permanent silence and elephants in parades glittering in gold. The islands wonderful landscape is invitingly lined with pure white sand. Diving, snorkelling, or just soaking up the seemingly endless warmth and sun are reward in themselves. But beyond the beaches and their waving coconut palms there is much to explore. The ancient temples, shrines and palaces of the northern kingdoms, the tea estates and hill stations of the central hill ranges - culturally rich and scenically beautiful, Sri Lanka's diversity is all within easy reach.

The coast Unawatuna, Mirissa, Bentota, Beruwela - Sri Lanka boasts some of the world's most beautiful beaches. Often no more than the narrowest of silver bands sheltered by crowded coconut palms and backed by green hills which rise in waves to the peaks of the Central Highlands, Sri Lanka's warm sea breezes take the edge off the equatorial heat. If you are looking for beach activities, head for Hikkaduwa or Negombo where you can scuba dive or parasail, watch shark brought in by the fishermen or try your hand at fishing yourself. If you want simplicity and an uncrowded spot you can find a quiet guesthouse, but if you are looking to be pampered, there are five-star hotels scattered all round the southwestern coast of the island.

Head for the hills It was the riches of the coastal lowlands that attracted the Portuguese and Dutch, but the British saw both political gain and economic profit in the mountains of the interior. From the winding roads of the tea plantations stretches an endless vista of closely cropped deep green bushes, the thirst-quenching lifeblood of Sri Lanka's economy for over a hundred years. Hatton, Dimbula, Talawakele - just a few of the tiny settlements that depend on tea for their living. For Nuwara Eliya, the most famous and the highest of Sri Lanka's 'Hill Stations', its situation in a secluded valley at a height of over 2,500 metres suggested it as an ideal spot for rest and relaxation. From here you can trek to the almost magically deserted Horton Plains, an astonishingly bleak and often mist-shrouded plateau now part of the Peak Wilderness Sanctuary or from Ratnapura you can join a thousand pilgrims in their pre-dawn climb to the sacred footprint (*Sri Pada*) or Adam's Peak which is revered by followers of four faiths.

Colonial heritage Scattered across the island is the visible evidence of the three European powers – the Portuguese, Dutch and British – who dominated Sri Lankan political life from the 17th to the mid 20th centuries. If you want to see the colonial influence in microcosm visit Galle on the southwest coast. Here the Dutch captured the beautiful natural harbour from the Portuguese, strengthened the fort and embellished the town with their own public buildings and churches, before being replaced by the British. The narrow streets are lined with two storeyed houses. From the ramparts you can see cargo vessels or the occasional cruise liner entering the harbour across the bay, a reminder of Galle's historic role as Sri Lanka's most important port until the rise of Colombo in the 19th century.

Left: taking a break from Sri Lanka's greatest festival, these revellers join elephants, drummers, dancers, acrobats, pilgrims, torch bearers and a host of others at the Perahera festival in Kandy. ***Below***: a totally tropical treat, one of the island's many wonderful beaches.

Above: a view to be savoured, fields of rice and vegetables in the central highlands.
Left: Polonnaruwa, the island's medieval capital some ten centuries ago. ***Next page***: a step down from the world's second largest land mammal, Nuwara Eliya.

Walk in the wilderness

Call of the wild   In the depths of Sri Lanka's hilly tropical forests is an enormous wealth of animal and bird life. Elephants still roam wild in some of the great national parks and reserves, including the large marsh elephants of the Mahaweli river basin to the east of the Central Highlands which are provided with protected migration corridors by conservationists. At the elephant orphanage at Pinnawela near Kandy you can see rescued elephants, from infants to adults, being fed and bathed, and cared for in natural parkland. Tuskers are particularly prized for their part in ceremonial processions as at the magnificently colourful pageants at various full moon festivals that punctuate the religious year.

Fancy in flight   And keep your eyes skinned for the flash of exotic colour from one of the island's 250 resident species of birds. From kingfishers to bee-eaters and weavers to flycatchers, the forest, coasts and open land contain a wealth of tropical birds. To these can be added the dozens of migrants from the northern winter. The coastal lagoons to the southeast of the island and the great reservoirs attract vast numbers of water birds - sandpipers, egrets, storks and herons - while flamingoes flock to Bundala.

Into the deep   The reefs to the southwest and on the east coast provide the ideal habitat for brilliantly coloured tropical fish and parts still retain extraordinary living coral. Divers and snorkellers are attracted to Hikkaduwa, Bentota and Negombo, but you need to avoid the monsoon months. Between January and August five species of sea turtle return to the warm waters of the south and southwest each year to lay their eggs in the sand. To prevent the collection of eggs which are sought as a local delicacy and to allow vulnerable hatchlings to reach the sea in safety, a number of the projects have been set up, the most exemplary being the Turtle Conservation Project near Tangalla.

A garden of Eden   The highlands nearby also have a different kind of wealth to delight the nature lover. Clear mountain streams tumble down creating numerous delightful leaps and falls with pools at their feet, some of which like Diyaluma, Dunhinda or Ramboda, can be easily reached. Among the forest clad hills, rich in flora, have been created marvellous botanic gardens at Peradeniya near Kandy or Hakgala near Nuwara Eliya but one of the gems of garden design is 'Brief' close to Bentota on the southwest coast. For the natural wonder of a rainforest wilderness, visit Sinharaja Biosphere Reserve which has remained virtually undisturbed and where you can experience something of the excitement of an explorer but go prepared for rain!

A gem of an island   King Solomon may have sent for a prize ruby for his queen from Sri Lanka and Hiuen-Tsang marvelled at the sparkle that lighted the sky, but even today the island remains a legendary source of priceless jewels. The gem bearing rocks which have been washed down the slopes of the Central Highlands to be embedded deep in the soil around Ratnapura are still mined by age-old methods by digging pits and then painstakingly 'panning' in flat baskets. The river gravels have yielded astonishing rubies, topaz, amethyst and other precious and semi-precious stones, but today Ratnapura, the 'City of Gems' is particularly famous for its blue sapphires. It is home to traders who deal in, and artisans who work some of the world's most beautiful gems. The town has different quarters for dealing in cut and uncut stones, polished and unpolished gems. Catch the traders in their white sarongs around the main street where hundreds of people gather in the early morning.

Left: a majestic bird left, the kingfisher.
Below: a preening Indian darter .

Above: up to monkey business. *Left*: buffaloes taking a dip in the Yala (Ruhuna) National Park. *Next page*: taking a rest after decorating the entrance of the home.

Right: a monthly occasion of worship and offerings of flowers, a full moon poya day.
Below: images of Buddha make for a brightly decorated temple in Anuradhapura, Sri Lanka's most sacred town.

Above: a monk checks his mail. *Right*: monks enjoying a beach on the southeast coast.
Next page: a railway track provides the route home.

An island's past and present

Anuradhapura's sacred bo tree, itself grown from a cutting of the tree under which the Buddha gained enlightenment over two thousand five hundred years ago, embodies the still calm at the centre of Buddhist meditation. Under its shelter the fading lotus blooms scattered by today's pilgrims capture the still, meditative essence at the heart of Buddhism. The gleaming white stupas and this same serene stillness of the Buddha's image caught in stone across the island testify to the interweaving of the faith with Sinhalese life. Saffron clad monks, often walking in small groups, add their own touch of vibrant colour.

Buddhism, a living culture

Hinduism, Islam and Christianity too have left their mark on Sri Lanka's culture. Hinduism has been the dominant religion of Tamils in the north for over two thousand years and of many of the tea plantation workers today. But Islam has also been present for over a thousand years. At the tiny fishing village of Kitchimalai, near the coastal resort of Beruwela, a mosque stands proud on the rocky headland. A pilgrimage centre during the month of Ramazan, it remains as a reminder that Islam arrived with the Arab traders across the Indian Ocean over a thousand years ago.

A multi-cultural society

The cultural wealth of the island is encapsulated in the 'Triangle' of Anuradhapura, Polonnaruwa and Kandy which contains five of Sri Lanka's World Heritage sites. Anuradhapura became the centre of power in the fourth century BC and remained the pivot for centuries while medieval Polonnaruwa's imperial fame was brief by comparison. The remarkable remains of stupas and monasteries, royal bathing pools, carvings and frescoes were inspired by Buddhism. At Mihintale, just east of Anuradhapura, is the beautiful site of one of the island's most sacred places. Here the Indian Emperor Asoka's son Mahinda, sent to bring the Buddhist message, met and converted the King Devanampiya Tissa in 243 BC. From its hill top position you can see miles across the forests of the plains below, sparkling lakes glittering in the sun. Nearby, Sigiriya's astonishing hill top fort-palace commands similarly striking views, but Sigiriya's fame rests as much on its wonderfully executed paintings of *apsaras*, or celestial nymphs, painted under an overhang half way up the sheer rock cliff.

Ancient cities

The last bastion of Buddhist political power and the repository of the precious casket which holds the sacred Tooth Relic, Kandy is set around its picturesque lake in the centre of the island. The Dalada Maligawa temple is a constant draw for pilgrims throughout the year but its spectacular 10-day Perahera in July-August, when glittering decorated elephants, colourful dancers, musicians and torch bearers, process down the streets witnessed by throngs of thousands, is unsurpassed on the island.

Colourful Kandy

Like so many other parts of the world, not all is peace and harmony. In the last 20 years conflict in Jaffna and the far north and east has brought tragedy to thousands, a conflict which, though restricted to a relatively small part of the island, continues to leave deep scars on its political and social life. Travel outside the far north and east is as safe as anywhere in the world. Sri Lanka is not just a museum piece or a cut out from a tourist brochure, it is a living island, rich in cultural and political diversity yet facing daunting economic and political challenges. The beach resorts of Sri Lanka still give a wonderful chance to `get away from it all', while the interior offers more – an insight into the islanders' response to the challenge of interweaving of past and present.

A living island

Essentials

2

Essentials

19   **Planning your trip**
19   Where to go
19   Planning a route
24   When to go
24   Tours and tour operators
25   Finding out more
26   Language

26   **Before you travel**
33   Tourist Information
36   Rules, customs and etiquette
37   Safety

38   **Where to stay**

41   **Getting around**
41   Air
41   Road
43   Train

45   **Keeping in touch**

47   **Food and drink**

48   **Shopping**

49   **Special interest travel**

50   **Holidays and festivals**

51   **Health**
51   Before travelling
53   On the road
56   When you return home

56   **Further reading**

Planning your trip

Where to go

The island's superb beaches lie all along its magical coastline to the south and southwest, with sandy coves and estuaries and long palm fringed stretches. Beaches vary in character and facilities so you have a wide choice. There are upmarket resorts such as the colonial **Mount Lavinia** or the modern **Bentota** or **Beruwela**. Further south are the picturesque and quieter beaches at **Unawatuna** or **Mirissa**. For those keen on watersports and marine life, there is the popular **Negombo**, on a sheltered lagoon and conveniently close to the international airport, or crowded 'activity' beaches, notably Hikkaduwa. By contrast, **Nilaveli**, near Trincomalee and the largely deserted Arugam Bay (when accessible) with clear waters and good surfing and diving, offer modest accommodation away on the east coast.

Near the southern tip of the island, the Dutch colonial inheritance is best preserved in the coastal fort at **Galle**, while there are mask makers carrying on an ancient Sinhalese tradition further north at **Ambalangoda**.

But many of Sri Lanka's most beautiful and interesting sights are away from the coast. By venturing a short distance you can explore the richness of the island's cultural heritage. You need only make a couple of short trips and spend a few nights away from your resort hotel to see the Central Highlands, with the last Buddhist capital of **Kandy**, accessible even on a day trip from Colombo. To the north are the other two points of the cultural triangle – the ancient capitals of **Anuradhapura** and **Polonnaruwa** – and the extraordinary royal citadel atop the giant rocky outcrop of Sigiriya, decorated with its world famous frescoes. Close to Anuradhapura is **Mihintale** where the first royal conversion to Buddhism was inspired, while **Dambulla** has impressive paintings in its rock cave.

While visiting Kandy you can also see baby elephants at bath time at the **Pinnawela Elephant Orphanage**. Nearby, are interesting spice plantations and several temples which preserve the late flowering of the Kandyan School of painting as well as craft villages producing fascinating metalwork, carving, pottery and weaving.

The central mountains with spectacular waterfalls and attractive walking trails around **Nuwara Eliya**, surrounded by tea gardens, provide a refreshing break. And while the gemstones of **Ratnapura** will lure some travellers, others will be attracted by the natural wonders of **Sinharaja** nearby or the wildlife at **Ruhuna-Yala National Park** to the southeast with plenty of bird watching along several shallow coastal lagoons.

Planning a route

Despite its small scale there are several alternative ways of seeing the island's great variety of scenery and its historically and culturally fascinating sites. All international flights now arrive at the airport near Colombo, so the city (or Negombo nearby) is the natural starting point for any trip. Hiring a car allows you greater flexibility in your timetable, and in choosing the order in which you visit sites. However, an excellent alternative can be to take the train to Kandy and then to take buses or to hire a car for visiting the rest of the Cultural Triangle and the Central Highlands. Even if you are staying at a beach hotel on the southwest or south coast it is easy to get up to Kandy and to make that a base for further exploration.

The routes outlined below offer different options for seeing some of the most interesting places conveniently within one and three weeks.

Gems of Sri Lanka

★ *The ancient cities of Polonnaruwa, Sigiriya's Lion Rock, Anuradhapura and Mihintale.*

★ *Kandy's Temple of the Tooth, Peradeniya Botanic Gardens and Pinnawela's elephants.*

★ *Kataragama and Hindu pilgrimage.*

★ *The natural wonders of Horton Plains, Adam's Peak, Uva's forests, waterfalls and caves, Yala and Bundala national parks, Sinharaja Biosphere Reserve.*

★ *Nuwara Eliya tea gardens and the Colonial past.*

★ *Galle's Dutch heritage, Brief Gardens near Bentota.*

★ *Turtle Conservation Project, Rekawa near Tangalla.*

★ *Beaches and watersports along the south coast (Beruwela, Bentota, Hikkaduwa, Unawatuna, Tangalla, Negombo), and Nilaveli on the east coast.*

Route 1
6-7 days

Colombo to Anuradhapura, Sigirya, Polonnaruwa and Kandy. From Colombo this route takes you straight to the heart of the `Cultural Triangle' by car. If you allow an extra day at the start, you may choose to stop at the ruins of an ancient kingdom of Yapahuwa (north of Kurunegala) or Dambulla (north of Kandy). Alternatively, take a train to Anuradhapura and visit some of the sites by bus, ending in Kandy.

Day 1 It is about a six-hour drive from Colombo to **Anuradhapura**, Sri Lanka's most important early capital. An early start will allow enough time in the afternoon to visit **Mihintale** 11 km away (where Emperor Asoka's son Mahinda, the Buddhist missionary, met the Sri Lankan king), and possibly also the Anuradhapura Museum. You will find comfortable accommodation in either Anuradhapura or at Mihintale where there is an excellent Rest House.

Day 2 Anuradhapura, with the most holy of Buddhist shrines, the sacred Bo tree, and several famous stupas, can be comfortably visited in the course of the day. The second night could also be in Anuradhapura, or 50 km south at Habarana or Sigiriya.

Day 3 Sigiriya – the magnificent rock palace of Sigiriya is quiet, empty, cool and at its most magical early in the morning, but you might be tempted to climb half way up again to photograph the famous fresco paintings in the late afternoon sunlight. Return to Habarana or continue to a hotel at Minneriya-Giritale, within easy reach of Polonnaruwa (13 km).

Day 4 Polonnaruwa – the second ancient capital is the site of remarkable Buddhist sculptures and a huge artificial lake built by the king in the 13th century. If you leave Polonnaruwa after lunch you can get to **Kandy** the same day. The fastest route takes the new road across the great Mahaweli Ganga colonisation scheme to **Mahiyangana** then climbs into the Central Highlands.

Route 1

Days 5-6 Kandy, once the capital of the Kandyan Kingdom, is an attractive small town. Famous for its Temple of the Tooth and its great Perahera (procession) each July/August, it is an excellent base for further trips into the Central Highlands. Nearby are Kandyan temples, craft villages, the Botanical Gardens at **Peradeniya**, and there is always a chance to see elephants bathing just across the river to the west or at the **Pinnewela** Orphanage. The journey back to Colombo is about a four-hour drive.

Kandy, Dambulla, Sigiriya, Anuradhapura, Mihintale and Polonnaruwa.

Route 2
6 days

Day 1 Taking the early train up to **Kandy** from Colombo is a beautifully relaxing and scenic way to reach the gateway to the 'Cultural Triangle'. Hire a car to go north, passing through spice gardens and the sites near **Matale** and **Dambulla**, and on to Sigiriya. Overnight at **Sigiriya**.

Days 2-5 Continue up to **Anuradhapura**, **Mihintale** and **Polonnaruwa** before returning to Kandy (see Route 1 above).

Day 6 Travel to **Colombo** from Kandy by the fast Inter-City train in the afternoon.

Kandy to Hatton, Adam's Peak, Nuwara Eliya. Kandy is the northwestern gateway to the tea estates of the Central Highlands, and to the highest mountains in Sri Lanka. Although Adam's Peak is not the highest it is the most popular and the most sacred of Sri Lanka's peaks. A popular way to climb is by moonlight (about three hours), arriving at the peak at dawn. One path starts near Hatton, about four hours drive from Kandy.

Route 3
4 days

Day 1 If you intend to climb **Adam's Peak** you can leave Kandy after lunch, travelling via the beautiful Ginigathena Pass to **Hatton** surrounded by tea estates, and on to Dalhousie, where the night walk starts. Hatton, however, has few places to stay so if you don't want to climb Adam's Peak it is better to leave Kandy in the morning and do a scenic drive to Nuwara Eliya.

Route 2

Route 3

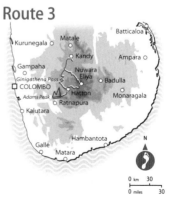

Essentials

Days 2/3 Nuwara Eliya – there are plenty of opportunities to relax in this attractive hill resort, ranging from gentle walks, a day on the golf course or visit the nearby **Hakgala** Botanical gardens which are well-maintained and richly varied.

Day 4 The drive back from Nuwara Eliya to **Kandy** passes through beautiful hill scenery of tea estates and temperate montane forest; you can include a visit to a tea factory and stop at some waterfalls on the way. Alternatively, you can head for Haputale and the Horton Plains (See Route 4).

Route 4
3-4 days
Kandy to Nuwara Eliya, Badulla, Ella, Haputale and the Horton Plains.

Route 4

Day 1 The direct route to **Nuwara Eliya**, Sri Lanka's main hill station gives a cross-section of Central Highland scenery, from the lush lower altitude vegetation around **Kandy** itself to the crisp fresh air of the tea estates surrounding Nuwara Eliya. A comfortable four hours drive, Nuwara Eliya has a wide range of accommodation from small guesthouses to the colonial-style Grand Hotel.

Day 2 Badulla and Ella are two of the most romantic spots in Sri Lanka. **Badulla**, a small hill station with the Dunhinda Falls nearby, is about three hours drive from Nuwara Eliya, and it is easily possible to take in the **Hakgala** Botanical Gardens on the way. After lunch you can drive back to **Ella**, which has one of Sri Lanka's favourite `honeymoon' Rest Houses, for the second night (you have to book in advance). It has superb views to the east over the plains.

Day 3 From Ella it is a short drive down to **Haputale**, another small town with commanding views over the plains to the southwest. You can continue up to **Ohiya** for the **Horton Plains** via Beragala. Popular for day treks or for overnight stay, the Horton Plains are surprisingly bleak and isolated.

Day 4 The route back to **Nuwara Eliya** follows the winding road past the peak of Totapola through Pattipola and Ambewela. Alternatively, you may choose to continue to Ruhunu–Yala National Park (Route 5) or Ratnapura and Sinharaja (Route 6).

Route 5
6-10 days
Nuwara Eliya to Yala, the south coast and Colombo. This longer excursion offers an exciting range of Sri Lanka's most varied landscapes. After passing through the highest areas of the Central Highlands you drop down to the heat of the south–eastern plains and the Yala National Park (check if it is open), and then round the south coast to Colombo.

Route 5

Day 1 An early start from **Nuwara Eliya** would easily allow you to reach **Ella** at lunch time. After a break you can drive down the hill road to the plains at Wellawaya and through the edge of

Ruhunu–Yala National Park to **Tissamaharama**. Alternatively you could take two days over the journey, stopping to see more of the Central Highlands on the way (Routes 3 and 4).

Day 2 Tissamaharama is the natural base from which to explore **Ruhunu–Yala** National Park and the remarkable temple town of **Kataragama**.

Day 3 A drive along the coast road takes you through **Hambantota**, surrounded by extraordinary, glistening white salt pans, an area for bird-watching. The are several striking and scarcely discovered beaches as you drive west through the Dry Zone, and there are several possible stopping places – **Tangalla, Dikwella, Matara, Weligama** or Galle. You could reach Galle comfortably in one day, or you might wish to stop along the way and take three or four.

Day 4 Galle – exploring the old fort town and its neighbourhood provides plenty to see and do in a comfortably relaxed way.

Day 5 You can follow the coast road up through some of the beach resorts and stop to see mask makers at **Ambalangoda**, take a short diversion inland to a small village like **Baddegama** near Hikkaduwa, or visit a turtle hatchery or **Brief Garden** near Bentota.

Day 6 After relaxing on the beach or exploring something of the interior you can take the short drive in through **Mount Lavinia** to Colombo.

To the Central Highlands via Sinharaja and Ratnapura. From Colombo or any of the beach resorts of the southwest you can easily travel inland to see one of Sri Lanka's best forest reserves and the gem capital of South Asia, before heading into the cool interior of the Central Highlands.

Route 6
7 days

Day 1 Sinharaja Reserve is accessible by four wheel drive from any of the popular resorts on the southwest, via Kalawana or Rakwana. Allow two days to explore (NB accommodation is very basic).

Day 2 Exploring **Sinharaja** – you can either stay the second night at Sinharaja or go on to Ratnapura, about 40 km from the Park's entrance.

Day 3 Ratnapura, the `city of gems', is world famous for its precious and semi-precious stones. There are plenty of opportunities to look at the beautiful gems, or buy – if you trust your judgement. After a morning in Ratnapura you can take the very attractive road which skirts the southern edge of the Central Highlands as far as **Belihuloya**, with an enviably placed Rest House beside the rushing waters of the river.

Day 4 Continuing on the same road you can pass from the humid lowlands to the **tea estates** and fresh air of the Central Highlands in half a day. **Haputale** and **Ella** both offer superb views on the way as well as the chance of refreshment, and **Nuwara Eliya** makes for an attractive and comfortable night halt.

Route 6

Essentials

Day 5 Several alternative routes lead to **Kandy**. If you take the shortest you will have a chance to spend the afternoon in the town itself, visiting some of the religious and historical sites, including the Temple of the Tooth.

Day 6 A morning visit to the **Pinnawela Elephant Orphanage**, leaves time to choose between the ancient sites to the west of the city, the **Peradeniya Botanical Gardens** or the **Natturampota Craft village**, just to the east and also see examples of Kandyan wall paintings in temples nearby.

Day 7 After a morning in Kandy you can return to **Colombo** or the coastal **beach resort** from which you started.

When to go

Weather   The best times to visit Sri Lanka are between the main rainy seasons. Because the island lies just north of the equator temperatures remain almost constant throughout the year. However, rainfall varies widely. In the southwest and the Central Highlands the best period is from late October to early March, after the southwest monsoon has finished. However, the north and east are affected by the northeast monsoon during this period and are dry but hot from June to October. The Central Highlands are much cooler throughout the year, but are very wet both during the southwest monsoon (June to October) and the northeast monsoon (October to December).

Festivals   In mid-April, the Sinhala and Tamil New Year celebrations are colourful and feature old traditional games. In May and June the Wesak and Poson Poya (full moon) days are marked with religious pageants. The Esala Perahera (around July-August full moon) is the most striking of all. This is held in Kandy, Colombo, Kataragama and other major temples, when drummers, dancers, decorated elephants, torch-bearers and whip-crackers all add colour and drama to the 10 days of celebrations

Tours and tour operators

You may choose to try an inclusive package holiday or let a specialist operator quote for a tailor-made tour. The lowest prices quoted by package tour companies, from late 2000 vary from about £600 for a fortnight (flights, hotel and breakfast) in the low season, to £1000 plus during the peak season at Christmas and the New Year. For the cheaper hotels, you pay very little extra for an additional week. *Manos*, T020-721680000, www.manos.co.uk and *First Choice*, T0870-750001 www.first-choice.com also allow you to book a return flight with the first night's accommodation, leaving

you free to arrange the rest yourself. *JMC*, T0870-6075085, charges a bit more for a fortnight in a superior hotel (£800-£1,600).

A few specialist operators are listed here. *Abercrombie & Kent*, T020-77309600. *Ace Study Tours*, T01223-835055, ace@studytours.org Cultural study tours, expert led. *Adventures Abroad*, T0114- 2473400 (USA & Canada, T800 665 3998, Australia T800 890 790), info@adventures-abroad.org Outward bound. *Andrew Brock* (*Coromandel*), T01572-821330, abrock@aol.com Special interest (crafts, textiles, botany etc). *Asian Journeys*, T01604-234401, F234866, www.asianjourneys.com Fairs, festivals, culture, religion. *Cox & Kings*, T020-78735001, F76306038, www.coxandkings.co.uk Ancient sites, tourist high spots. *Discovery Initiatives*, T020-79786341, www.discoveryinitiatives.com Wildlife safaris. *Dragoman*, T01728-86113, www.dragoman.co.uk Adventure, camping. *Exodus Travels*, 9 Wier Rd, London, SW12 0LT, T0208-7723822, www.exodus.co.uk *Explore Worldwide*, T01252-319448. *Paradise* T020-7229 7686. *Gateway to India and Asia*, T0870-4423204, F0870-4423205, specialist-travel@gateway-to-india.co.uk *Pettitts*, T01892-515966, F516615 www.pettits.co.uk *Sri Lanka Holidays*, 4 Kingly St, London, T020-74390944 www.srilankaholidays.co.uk Country specialists.

Finding out more

Australia 39 Wintercorn Row, Werrington Downs, NSW, 2747, T47303914, F47292327. *Canada* 1920-925 W Georgia St, Vancouver BC, V6C 312, T6627708, F6627769. *France* 19, rue de Quatre Septembre, 75002 Paris, T42604999, F42860499. *Germany* Allertheiligentor 2-4, D-60311, Frankfurt, T287734, F288371. *India* D19 Defence Colony, New Delhi 110024, T4603124, F4603123. *Ireland* 59 Ranelagh Rd, Dublin 6,

Useful
addresses
Tourist offices
overseas

Essentials

Sri Lanka representations overseas

Australia 35 Empire Circuit, Forrest, Canberra, ACT 2603, T62397041, F62396166.

Austria Herrengasse 6-8, 1010, Vienna, T5337426, F5337432.

Belgium Rue Jules Lejeune, 1050 Brussels, T3445394, F3446737.

Canada Suite 1204, 333 Laurier Ave West, Ottawa, Ontario K1P 1CI, T2338449, F2388448.

France 15 Rue d'Astorg, 75008 Paris, T42663501, F40070011.

Germany Noegarrath Str 15, 53111, Bonn, T694846.

India 27 Kautilya Marg, Chanakyapuri, New Delhi 110021, T3010201, F3015295; also, 9 D Nawab Habibullah Ave, Anderson Rd, Chennai 600 006, T8270831, F 8272387; 34 Homi Modi St, Mumbai 400 023, T2045861, F2876132.

Indonesia 70 Jalan Diponegoro, Jakarta-Pusat, T3141018, F3107962.

Italy Via adige No 200198, Rome, T8554560

Maldives Sakeena Manzil, Medhuziayaaraiyh Magu, Male 20-05, T322845, F321652.

The Netherlands Jacob de Graefflaan, 2517 JM, The Hague, T3655910, F3465596.

Pakistan House No 315C, Khayaban-e-Iqbal, Margalla Rd, F7/2 Islamabad, T828743, F828751.

Saudi Arabia PO Box 94360 Riyadh 11693. T4541745.

Singapore 13-06/12 Goldhill Plaza, 51 Newton Rd, Singapore 308900, T2544595, F2507201.

Sweden Strandvagen 39, Box 24055, S-104 50, Stockholm, T6636523, F6600089.

Thailand 89 Soi 15 Sukhumvit Rd, Bangkok 10110, T2611934, F6510059.

UK 13 Hyde Park Gardens, London W2 2LU, T020-72621841, F72627970.

USA 2148 Wyoming Av, NW, Washington DC 20008, T4834026, F4838017.

Foreign diplomatic representations in Sri Lanka are listed in the Colombo section.

T149-65345, F68043. *Japan* Dowa Building 7-2-22, Ginza Chuo-Ku, T32890771, F32890772. Nitto Ichi Building, 2F, Nanba 1-8-19, Chuo-Ku, Osaka City, T077-4452573, F4450523. *Thailand* 5/105-6/105, Soi Rattanaprahm 2, Sukhumvit Soi 54/2, Bangkok 10250, T3329075, F3328786. *UK* Clareville House, Oxendon St, London SW1Y 4QD, T020-79302627, F079309070 www.lanka.net/ctb

Language

Sinhala and Tamil are the official languages, but English is widely spoken and understood in the main tourist areas though not by many in rural parts. Some German is spoken by a growing number of Sri Lankans in the southwestern beach resorts while Kandy has a few French speakers.

Before you travel

Visas & permits
Ask for a double entry visa if you are intending to visit another country (eg India or the Maldives)

All visitors to Sri Lanka require a valid passport. Nationals of the following 70 countries are issued with a free, 30-day visa upon arrival: Albania, Australia, Austria, Bahrain, Bangladesh, Belgium, Bulgaria, Canada, Cyprus, Czech Republic, Denmark, Finland, France, Germany, Greece, Hong Kong, Hungary, Indonesia, Ireland, Italy, Japan, Korea, Kuwait, Luxembourg, Malaysia, Maldives, Nepal, Netherlands, New Zealand, Norway, Oman, Pakistan, Philippines, Poland, Portugal, Qatar, Romania, Saudi Arabia, Singapore, Slovakia, Spain, Sweden, Switzerland, Thailand, Turkey, UAE, UK, USA, Yugoslavia, plus the five new states of Yugoslavia and the 15 new states of the USSR.

Nationals of all other countries need a prior visa. All tourists should also have a valid visa for the country that is their next destination (if a visa is necessary); check with your nearest Sri Lankan representative before travelling. It may sometimes be necessary to show proof of sufficient funds to support themselves ($15 per day) and a return or onward ticket, although this is rarely checked on arrival. Transit passengers are issued with a Transit Visa.

Visa extensions A three-month extension is available to nationals of all countries upon paying a fee, which varies from country to country. In order to qualify you must also show proof that you have exchanged at least US$15 for each day of your stay up to the time of application (bring all exchange certificates). The fee varies from country to country. From 1st January 2000 the following fees apply: France, Rs 1,840; Germany, Rs 1,510; India, Rs 210; UK, Rs 3,795; USA, Rs 3,185. The most heavily targeted are the Australians who have to pay Rs 6,500. A further three-month extension is possible by paying the same fee again plus a 'Temporary Residence Tax' of Rs 5,000.

No one is allowed to stay longer than 6 months in a calendar year, or change their visa status

Apply in person during office hours, to the Department of Immigration and Emigration, Tower Building, Bambalapitiya Station Road (immediately opposite the station), Colombo 4, T597511. Enter by the side entrance and go to the first floor. Allow one to two hours. It is not necessary to wait until shortly before the expiry of your original visa. Extensions will be granted at any time within the original 30-day period.

Registration Tourists from non-Commonwealth countries who have a visa for over 30 days (and those intending to extend their stay beyond 30 days) may need to register upon arrival at the Aliens Bureau, 5th Floor, New Secretariat Building, Colombo 1, although this does not appear to be always necessary.

What to take

Travel light. Most essentials are available in the cities, items are cheap and laundry services generally speedy. Here are some items you might find particularly useful:

Take twice as much money & half the clothes that you think you will need

Light cotton **clothes** are useful at any time of year. It is a good idea to have some very lightweight long sleeve cotton tops and trousers in pale colours for evenings, as they also give some protection against mosquitoes. It can be cool at night in the Central Highlands and some warm clothing is essential. Dress is usually informal, though one or two clubs and hotels expect guests to be formally dressed at evening meals. In Colombo short-sleeved shirts and ties are often worn for business. For travelling, loose clothes are most comfortable. Comfortable canvas shoes or trainers are good options for protecting feet against cuts and so on. Women should dress modestly. Even on the beach, very revealing swimwear attracts unnecessary attention.

Toiletries, including barrier contraceptives and tampons, are available in the larger towns but you may prefer to take your own supply. Carry personal medicines and inhalers and a copy of a prescription. Camera films are available in all major cities and tourist centres but always buy from a reputable shop since hawkers and roadside stalls may not be reliable - also check the carton carefully as well as the expiry date. To be assured of quality it is best to take rolls of film from home and certainly any specialist camera batteries.

International driving licence, photocopies of essential documents (passport identification and visa pages), spare passport photographs, student (ISIC) card which can be used for discounts on some site entrance fees, hat and sunglasses, sun protection cream (factor 15 plus), Swiss army knife, torch, wet wipes, zip-lock bags. Contact lens cleaning solutions are available in the larger towns and cities but it is best to bring your own. Mosquito nets are standard in all but the very cheapest hotels or those where mosquitoes pose no threat (eg air-conditioned rooms).

Checklist

Budget travellers may also want to take the following: sheet sleeping bag, earplugs, eyeshades, padlock (for room and baggage), soap, string (washing line), towel, washbasin plug. Mosquito mats/coils are readily available in Sri Lanka.

Customs
Duty free
allowances

Import On arrival, visitors to Sri Lanka are officially required to declare all currency, valuable equipment, jewellery and gems even though this is rarely checked. All personal effects should be taken back on departure. Visitors are not allowed to bring in goods in commercial quantities, or prohibited/restricted goods such as dangerous drugs, weapons, explosive devices or gold. Drug trafficking or possession carries the death penalty, although this is very rarely carried out on foreigners. In addition to completing Part II of the Immigration Landing Card, a tourist may be asked by the Customs Officer to complete a Baggage Declaration Form.

You are allowed 1.5 litres of spirits, 2 bottles of wine, 200 cigarettes, 50 cigars or 250 g rolling tobacco, a small quantity of perfume and 250 ml of toilet water. You can also import a small quantity and travel souvenirs not exceeding US$250 in value.

Professional photography or filming equipment must be declared and will be allowed entry on a valid Carnet, Bank Guarantee or a refundable deposit of the duty payable on the items.

It is illegal to buy items made from wild animals & reptiles

Export Up to 3 kg of tea is allowed to be exported duty free. Note that the 'Ceylon Tea' counter at the airport *outer* lobby accepts rupees; export duty is charged at Rs 2 per kilo for excess tea. The following are not permitted to be exported from Sri Lanka: all currencies in excess of that declared on arrival; any gems, jewellery or valuable items not declared on arrival or not purchased in Sri Lanka out of declared funds; gold (crude, bullion or coins); Sri Lankan currency in excess of Rs 250; firearms, explosives or dangerous weapons; antiques, statues, treasures, old books etc (antiques are considered to be any article over 50 years old); animals, birds, reptiles or their parts (dead or alive); tea, rubber or coconut plants; dangerous drugs.

Import of all the items listed above and in addition, Indian and Pakistani currency, obscene and seditious literature or pictures is prohibited.

Money

Currency
It is not possible to purchase Sri Lankan currency before arrival in Sri Lanka

The Sri Lankan Rupee is made up of 100 cents. Notes in denominations of Rs 1000, 500, 200, 100, 50, 20, 10 and coins in general use are Rs 5, 2, 1 and 50, 25 cents. Occasionally you may come across a double alloy Rs 10 coin which, in time, will probably increase in the general circulation. 10 and 5-cent coins are now rarely seen. Visitors bringing in excess of $10,000 into Sri Lanka should declare the amount on arrival. All Sri Lankan Rupees should be re-converted upon leaving Sri Lanka. It is also illegal to bring Indian or Pakistani Rupees into Sri Lanka, although this is rarely, if ever, enforced.

Money
changing
If you cash sterling, make certain that you have been given rupees at the sterling & not at the dollar rate

On arrival at the airport you can change money while waiting for your luggage since you may need some rupees to pay for transport to the hotel. This is generally easy and fairly quick. Larger hotels often have a money exchange counter (sometimes open 24 hours), but offer substantially lower rates than banks. In the larger cities and resorts you will often find private dealers which will exchange cash notes or TCs. Rates are comparable to banks and are entirely above board. There is no black market money changing in Sri Lanka, although it may be useful to carry some small denomination foreign currency notes (eg £10, US$10) for emergencies.

Banking hours Banking hours are generally 0900-1300 Monday to Friday, although some banks in Colombo have extended opening hours. Private banks (eg *Hatton National Bank, Sampath Bank*) are generally more efficient and offer a faster service

Exchange rates

	Rs		Rs
Australian $	42.19	Japanese Yen	0.75
Dutch Guilder	31.22	New Zealand $	32
Euro	68.8	Swiss Franc	45.21
French Franc	10.49	UK £	114.70
Indian Rupee	1.72	US $	80.15

than government owned banks like *Bank of Ceylon* and *People's Bank*. There are several exchange counters at the airport which are open when flights arrive.

Encashment receipts Keep the receipts you are given when exchanging money, as you will need them to prove that you are spending over $15 per day for a visa extension. You will also need at least one to re-exchange any Rupees upon leaving Sri Lanka. All foreign exchange transactions must be made through authorized banks and exchanges and entered on the Customs and Immigration form. Unspent rupees may be reconverted at a commercial bank when you leave Sri Lanka. Changing money through unauthorized dealers is illegal.

Travellers' cheques (TCs) Travellers' cheques issued by reputable companies (eg *American Express*, *Thomas Cook*) are accepted without difficulty and give a slightly better exchange rate than currency notes in Sri Lanka. They also offer the security of replacement if lost or stolen assuming the case is straightforward. Travellers' cheques in £ sterling, US$ and German DM are usually accepted without any problem and the process normally takes less than 15 minutes in private banks and moneychangers (longer in government owned banks). Larger hotels will normally only exchange travellers' cheques for resident guests but will offer a substantially lower rate than banks or private dealers. A 1% stamp duty is payable on all travellers' cheques transactions plus a small commission which varies from bank to bank. Passports need to be shown when encashing travellers' cheques.

Take care to follow the advice given about keeping the proof of purchase slip and a note of travellers' cheques numbers separately from the cheques. In the case of loss, you will need to get a police report and inform the travellers' cheques company.

Credit cards Major credit cards are increasingly accepted in the main centres of Sri Lanka both for shopping and for purchasing Sri Lankan Rupees. Larger hotels also accept payment by credit card but this can sometimes take longer than using travellers' cheques since your credit rating will normally have to be checked. Cash can also be drawn from ATMs using credit cards, although different banks accept different cards (see below). No surcharge should be applied when making purchases but the 1% stamp duty is applicable when obtaining cash against a credit card.

Automated Telling Machines (ATMs) are becoming increasingly common in Sri Lanka, especially in Colombo and other larger towns. ATMs give cash advances on credit cards so it is essential to have your Personal Identification Number (PIN). A small fee (less than the commission charged for changing TCs) will be charged on your bill at home. In Colombo, *ANZ*, *Citibank* and *HSBC* accept Mastercard, Visa and Cirrus, whie ATMs belonging to *Commercial Bank* and *Sampath Bank* give money on Mastercard.

Transferring money to Sri Lanka Thomas Cook, American Express and ANZ Grindlays can make instant transfers to their offices in Sri Lanka but charge a high fee (about 8%). A bank draft (up to US$1,000) which you can post yourself (three to five days by Speedpost) is the cheapest option for which normal charges are between 1.5% and 2%.

Cost of living The Sri Lankan cost of living remains well below that in the industrialized world. Most food, accommodation and public transport, especially rail and bus, are exceptionally cheap. Even the expensive hotels and restaurants here are less expensive than their counterparts in Europe, Japan or the United States. There is a widening range of moderately priced but clean hotels and guest houses and good, inexpensive beach restaurants, making it possible to get a great deal for your money. Budget travellers (sharing a room) can expect to spend about Rs 1,000 (about US$13 or £8) each per day to cover cost of accommodation, food and travel. Those planning to stay in fairly comfortable hotels and use taxis for travelling to sights should expect to spend at least Rs 3,500 (US$45 or £30) a day. Single rooms are charged at about 80% of the double room price.

Carrying money It is best to carry money, preferably as travellers' cheques, in a money belt worn under clothing. Only carry enough cash for your daily needs, keeping the rest in your money belt or in a hotel safe. Keep plenty of small change and lower denomination notes, as it can be difficult to change large notes.

Getting there

Air

The only way to travel to Sri Lanka at present is by air (bar the very occasional cruise liner which calls at Colombo). It is best to book tickets as early as possible, especially during the peak season (mid-December to mid-January and Easter). Take out an insurance, check details and confirm your flight nearer the time. All international flights arrive at Katunayake, 35 km north of Colombo (see 'On Arrival' below for details).

International airlines flying to Sri Lanka include *Aeroflot, Bulgarian Airways, Cathay Pacific, Emirates, Gulf Air, KLM, Kuwait Airways, Malaysia Airlines, Pakistan International Airways, Royal Jordanian, Saudia, Singapore Airlines* and *Thai Airways*. Charter companies (eg *Balair, British Caledonian, Condor, Lauda*) also operate from Europe.

In **South Asia**, there are direct flights to Mumbai (Bombay), Delhi, Chennai (Madras), Thiruvananthapuram (Trivandrum), Tiruchirappalli (Trichy), Male and Karachi. Europe, the Middle East and the Far East are also served by direct flights.

Sri Lankan Airlines (previously *Air Lanka*), Colombo T073-5555 www.airlanka.com the national carrier, flies to over 20 countries worldwide. Flights need to be reconfirmed at least 72 hours ahead. Tickets booked overseas may occasionally be deleted from computer records unless confirmed in person – which is not easy in some cities at weekends. **Overseas offices in India**: Kolkata T295967; Chennai T8275348; Mumbai T2823288; New Delhi T3731473; Tiruchirapalli T460844; Thiruvananthapuram, T462381. **Elsewhere**: Abu Dhabi T212057; Bangkok T2369292; Frankfurt T97573923; Hong Kong T25210812; Karachi T514421; Kuala Lumpur, T2325805; Kuwait T2424444; London T020 85382001; Male T322438; Manama (Bahrain) T224819; New York T8385120; Paris T42974344; Rome T483830; Singapore T2236026; Sydney T92442234; Tokyo T35734261; Zurich T2458090.

Stop-overs and 'Round the World' tickets You can arrange a stop-over in Sri Lanka on a 'Round the World' and other long distance tickets.

If you want to buy your onward ticket to South or South-east Asia in Colombo itself, **George Travel**, 29 Bristol St, Fort, T423447, has been recommended.

Discounts It is possible to get a significant discount from a reputable travel agent especially outside European holiday times, most notably from London. The airlines invariably quote a higher price as they are not able to discount tickets but off-load surplus tickets on agents who choose to pass on part of their commission to passengers. November to March are high season while Christmas, New Year and Easter are the most expensive. Shop around, book early and if using a 'bucket shop' confirm with the airline that your name appears on their list.

Companies dealing in volume and taking reduced commissions for ticket sales can offer better deals than the airlines themselves. The national press carry their advertisements. *Bridge the World*, T020-79110900, F7813 3350 www.bridgetheworld.net *Flightbookers*, T020-77573000, www.ebookers.com *North South Travel*, T01245-492882, donates its profits to charity. *Trailfinders* of London, T0207-9383939, has worldwide agencies. *STA*, in London, T0207-9379962, enquiries@statravel.com with over 100 offices worldwide, offers special deals for under-26s. *Travelbag*, T020-72875558, F020-72874522 www.travelbag.co.uk quotes competetive fares. *Usit Campus*, T0870 2401010, www.usitcampus.co.uk is good for students and has offices in several university cities. *Sri Lanka Tours*, 4 Kingly St, London, T020-74343921 www.srilankatours.co.uk offer deals on flights with Sri Lankan, Emirates and Kuwait Airways.

Travel clubs can be worth joining for good discounts on scheduled flights, eg **Wexas**, 45-49 Brompton Rd, London SW3 1DE, T020-7 589 3315.

Ticket agents

Qantas, *Singapore Airlines*, *Thai Airways*, *Malaysian Airlines*, *Cathay Pacific* and *Air India* are the principal airlines connecting the continents. *STA* and *Flight Centres* offer discounted tickets from their branches in major cities in Australia and New Zealand.

From Australasia via the Far East

From the east coast, it is best to fly from New York via London or pick up a direct charter from UK but this will usually involve a stopover in London. From the west coast, it is best to fly via Hong Kong, Singapore or Bangkok using one of those countries' national carriers. Student fares are also available from *Council Travel*, www.counciltravel.com with several offices in the USA and *Travel Cuts*, www.travelcuts.com in Canada.

From North America & Canada

The following rules apply to charter flights. They are not available to Sri Lankan nationals. The deal must include accommodation. If you take the cheap 'dorm house' option, it may be necessary to change to a more comfortable room. It may be difficult to find a room during the peak Christmas and New Year period so it is worth paying a little extra on booking, to ensure accommodation of a reasonable standard.

Charter flights

Touching down

Sri Lanka's only international airport is at Katunayake, 30 km north of Colombo. It has modern facilities including duty free shops (with a large selection of electrical goods) on arrival; they only accept foreign currency. There are several foreign exchange counters as well as a tourist information counter with limited information although it is worth picking up copies of 'Travel Lanka' and the Ceylon Tourist Board Accommodation Guide. There is a taxi stand and several hotel and tour company booths just after the Arrivals hall. The mid-price *Goodwood Plaza/Orient Pearl* hotels are within a kilometre of the airport. Stringent baggage and personal security checks are often carried out, especially on departure, so be prepared to repack your bags.

Visitors to Departures or Arrivals must buy an entrance permit for Rs 100 at the special booths before entering the terminal, but access is limited due to security controls.

Airport information

Disembarkation Cards are handed out to passengers during the inward flight. Complete parts 1 and 2 and hand them in at the immigration counter on arrival along

Documentation

with your passport. Keep your baggage identification tag safe as this must be handed in when leaving the Arrivals hall.

Public transport to & from the airport

An Expressway between Colombo & Katunayake (via Muturajawela) is under construction

Bus and coach There is a regular intercity bus to Colombo CTB Stand (Rs 20, one hour) leaving from the bus stop immediately outside the Arrivals hall exit, across the first drop-off lane (Departure terminal is further). To ensure a seat it may be worth walking towards the vehicular exit where the bus waits. The bus goes via Katunayake Junction railway station (Rs 5). From the main road (2 km away), there are buses to Colombo (numbers 187 and 240) and Negombo (number 240). You can take a three-wheeler (*tuk-tuk*) to that point (Rs 50). Buses are often crowded but are the cheapest option. Several Negombo hotels and guest houses will arrange a pick-up; see page 96.

Taxi As you leave the Arrivals hall, you will see a pre-paid taxi counter close to the banks. They are not always eager to provide taxis to foreign visitors, preferring to send you outside to the larger travel agents which charge more for a/c cars. Posted fares for non a/c van taxis are Rs 670 to Colombo postal areas 1-3 and 7-15, Rs 793 to Colombo 5 and 6, Rs 915 to Mount Lavinia, Rs 305 to Negombo and Rs 1959 to Kandy. It is worth teaming up with other passengers to share the van. Some taxi drivers may try to persuade you that the hotel you have chosen is closed or full. Insist that you have a reservation. Others may insist that Colombo is dangerous (instant curfews do occur occasionally in the city) and coerce you to be taken to Kandy 'where it is safe'. Ask at the airport information desk for confirmation of the current situation. If you are late arriving and are unsure as to where to stay, choose a hotel in Negombo for the first night and move, if necessary, or go into Colombo or another beach resort the following day.

The more expensive hotels may offer to meet you at the airport but this may not be free – expect to pay about US$25 for two to Colombo. Radio Cabs can be called on the phone from the terminal (see 'Getting around' below). *Ace Cabs*, T501502; *Quick Cabs*, T502888, *GNTC*, T688688. These are a very good option, especially if you share one.

Hire car It is possible to rent a car at the airport, eg *Europcar*, $126 for one week, $234 for two weeks, $18 for each extra day. However, it may not be possible to drive immediately since a Sri Lankan recognition permit must accompany International Driving Permits. These are available from the AA or the Department of Motor Traffic in Colombo.

Train Suburban trains run north to Negombo, south to Colombo from Katunayake Junction, about 500 m from the airport. Enquiries T0315260 (0800-1200, 1300-1630).

Departure tax

A departure tax of Rs 500 is payable for all international departures including those to neighbouring SAARC countries. Even if you have already paid the foreign tax (denoted by FT in the bottom left hand corner of your flight ticket) the departure tax is sometimes demanded.

Sea

Although some cruise ships still visit Colombo, it is almost impossible to travel to Sri Lanka by sea otherwise. It is occasionally possible to get a berth on a cargo or container ship from ports in the Gulf region or South East Asia but impossible to book trips in advance. Sailors in their own vessels may be able to berth in Galle, although it is possible that immigration formalities should be carried out in Colombo. Check with your nearest Sri Lankan representative in advance.

Touching down

Time *GMT + 5½ hours. Perception of time is sometimes rather vague in Sri Lanka (as in the rest of South Asia). Unpunctuality is common so you will need to be patient.*

Voltage *230-240 volts, 50 cycles AC. Some top hotels have transformers to enable visitors to use their appliances. There may be pronounced variations in the voltage, and power cuts are common. Socket sizes vary so you are advised to take a universal adapter (available at airports). Three-pin (round) sockets are still widely used so make sure this is included. The correct adapter is available in the Mount Lavinia Hotel shop for Rs 200. Some hotels do not have electric razor sockets. It is difficult to obtain shaver adapters for Sri Lankan sockets in shops outside Sri Lanka, so a battery operated shaver is recommended.*

Banks: *usually 0900-1300 Monday-Friday. Closed on Saturday, Sunday, Poya days, national holidays,*

30 June and 31 December. Main branches of Peoples Bank are open 0900-1600 Monday-Friday, 1030-1230 Saturday. Top hotels sometimes have 24-hour service. See page 28 and also Colombo banks for details of others open on Saturday mornings and for evening service.

Business hours *Post offices: 1000-1700, Monday-Friday; Saturday mornings.* **Government offices**: *0930-1700, Monday-Friday; 0930-1300, Saturday (some open on alternate Saturday only).* **Restaurants and bars**: *Licensing hours are 1100-1400 and 1700-2300. No alcohol is served on Poya days although alcohol orders may be placed the day before at your hotel. Restrictions do not apply to private clubs.* **Shops**: *0830-1630 Monday-Friday. Some open on Saturday 0830-1300. Shops often close for lunch from 1300-1400 on weekdays, most close on Sunday. Sunday street bazaars in some areas. Poya (Full moon) days are holidays.*

Essentials

Tourist information

There are **Ceylon Tourist Board** (CTB) offices in Colombo and a few major tourist centres. The Tourist information desk at the airport can be very helpful with information on hotels and transport, and will allow you to use the phone. Ask for a copy of *Travel Lanka* there.

Trained Registered English speaking **tourist guides** to sites (and sometimes one speaking a European language, Malay or Japanese) carry Ceylon Tourist Board cards. Fees are about Rs 450 per day depending of size of group for English speaking (Rs 550 for others). Contact Travel Information Centre, T437059 or an approved travel agent or National Tourist Guide Lecturers' Association, 409 RA de Mel Mawatha, Colombo 3, T595212.

Visiting archaeological sites

    Tickets For the major archaeological sites, eg Polonnaruwa, Anuradhapura and Sigirya, the entry ticket is US$15; (children under 12 – half price); a similar student discount, with an ISIC card is sometimes available (eg Polonnaruwa). Dambulla charges Rs 200. Entry fees are much lower for Sri Lankans.

    The **Cultural Triangle Round tickets** cover a single entry (to each) and photography at the major archaeological sites, including Anuradhapura, Polonnaruwa, Sigiriya, Kandy and Nalanda. However, not all parts of these sites are included, eg there is a separate (camera) fee for the Kandy Dalada Maligawa (Temple of the Tooth), Aukana, Issurumuniya Museum (and occasionally Sri Maha Bodhi) at Anuradhapura. The permit is valid for two weeks starting from the date of the first entrance and allows the holder to take photographs (except at the Kandy Temple of the Tooth and Aukana). The tickets are available from Anuradhapura, Pollonaruwa and Sigiriya or less conveniently from Colombo, Central Cultural Fund, 212/1 Bauddhaloka

Mawatha, Colombo 7, T587912 or 500733, F 500731. The ticket price is US$32.50 or Rs 2,340 (US$16 for 5-12 year olds); students carrying ISIC cards usually qualify for a 50% reduction.

The sites are usually open 0600-1800; the ticket office often only opens at 0700. If you are keen to miss the crowds and visit a site early in the day, buying the triangle permit in advance enables you to avoid having to wait for the ticket office to open.

Visiting religious sites Visitors to Buddhist and Hindu temples are welcome though the shrines of Hindu temples are sometimes closed to non-Hindus. Visitors should be dressed decently (skirts or long trousers) – shorts and swimwear are not suitable. Shoes should be left at the entrance and heads should be uncovered. It is best to visit early in the day and to take thick socks for protection against the hot stone.

Do not attempt to shake hands or be photographed with Buddhist *bhikkus* (monks) or to pose for photos with statues of the Buddha or other deities and paintings. Remember that monks are not permitted to touch money so donations should be put in temple offering boxes. Monks renounce all material possessions and so live on offerings. Visitors may offer flowers at the feet of the Buddha.

Mosques may be closed to non-Muslims shortly before prayers. In mosques women should be covered from head to ankle.

Disabled travellers The country isn't geared up specially for making provisions for the physically handicapped or wheel-chair bound traveller. Access to buildings, toilets, pavements and kerbs and public transport, can prove frustrating but it is easy to find people to give a hand with lifting and carrying. Provided there is an able-bodied companion to scout around and arrange help, and so long as you are prepared to spend on at least mid-price hotels or guesthouses, private car-hire and taxis, Sri Lanka should prove to be rewarding.

Some travel companies are beginning to specialize in exciting holidays, tailor-made for individuals depending on their level of disability. For those with access to the internet, a Global Access - Disabled Travel Network Site is www.geocities.com/Paris/1502 It is dedicated to providing information for 'disabled adventurers' and includes a number of reviews and tips from members of the public. You might want to read *Nothing Ventured* edited by Alison Walsh (Harper Collins), which gives personal accounts of worldwide journeys by disabled travellers, plus advice and listings.

Gay & lesbian travellers Homosexuality between men is illegal in Sri Lanka, even in private, and may lead to a prison sentence of up to 15 years. It is therefore wise to be discreet to avoid the attentions of over zealous and homophobic police officers.

Student travellers Full time students qualify for an ISIC (International Student Identity Card) which is issued by student travel and specialist agencies at home (eg *Campus*, *STA*). A card allows certain travel benefits (eg reduced prices) and acts as proof of student status, allowing ticket concessions into a few sites.

Women travellers Compared with many other countries it is relatively easy and safe for women to travel around Sri Lanka, even on their own. There are some problems to watch out for and some simple precautions to take which make it possible to avoid both personal harassment and giving offence. Modest dress for women is always advisable: loose-fitting, non-see through clothes, covering the shoulders, and skirts, dresses or shorts (at least knee-length). Unaccompanied women may find problems of harassment, though this is relatively rare. It is always best to be accompanied when travelling by rickshaw or taxi at night. Do remember that what may be considered to be normal, innocent friendliness in a Western context may be misinterpreted by some Sri Lankan men.

Eco travelling: a few tips

■ Where possible choose a destination, tour operator or hotel with a proven ethical and environmental commitment, and if in doubt ask.

■ Spend money on locally produced (rather than imported) goods and services and use common sense when bargaining – your few dollars saved may be a week's salary to others.

■ Use water and electricity carefully – travellers may receive preferential supply while the needs of local communities are overlooked.

■ Learn about local etiquette and culture – consider local norms and behaviour – and dress appropriately for local cultures and situations.

■ Protect wildlife and other natural resources – don't buy souvenirs or goods made from wildlife unless they are clearly sustainably produced and are not protected under CITES legislation.

■ Always ask before taking photographs or videos of people and don't pose in front of religious images and paintings.

■ Consider staying in local, rather than foreign owned, accommodation – the economic benefits for host communities are far greater – and there are far greater opportunities to learn about local culture.

Essentials

Children of all ages are widely welcomed, being greeted with a warmth in their own right which is often then extended to those accompanying them. In the big hotels there is no difficulty with obtaining safe baby foods, though 'wet wipes' and disposable nappies are not readily available in many areas.

Travelling with children
The biggest hotels provide babysitting facilities

Care should be taken when travelling to remote areas where health services are primitive since children can become more rapidly ill than adults. Extra care must be taken to protect children from the heat by creams, hats, umbrellas etc and by avoiding being out in the hottest part of the day. Cool showers or baths help if children get too hot. Dehydration may be counteracted with plenty of drinking water – bottled, boiled (furiously for five minutes) or purified with tablets. Preparations such as 'Dioralyte' may be given if the child suffers from diarrhoea. Moisturizer, zinc and castor oil (for sore bottoms due to change of diet) are worth taking. Mosquito nets or electric insect repellents at night may be provided in hotel rooms which are not air conditioned. To help young children to take anti-malarial tablets, one suggestion is to crush them between spoons and mix with a teaspoon of dessert chocolate (for cake-making) bought in a tube.

All foreigners intending to work need **work permits**. The employing organization should make formal arrangements. Apply to the Sri Lankan Representative in your country of origin.

Working in the country

Those interested in **voluntary work** should enquire well in advance. In the UK: *International Voluntary Service*, St John's Centre, Edinburgh EH2 4BJ, www.sci.ivs.org or *VSO*, 317 Putney Bridge Rd, London SW15 2PN. Alternatively, students may spend part of their 'year off' helping in a school through '*GAP* ', or teach English through i to i *International projects*, One Cottage Rd, Headingley, Leeds LS64, T0870-3332332 www.i-to- i.com FNotre Dame SFC, St Mark's Ave, Leeds LS2 9BN. In the USA: *Council for International Programs* 1101 Wilson Blvd Ste 1708, Arlington, VA 22209. *United Nations Volunteers* are usually mature, experienced people with special qualifications www.unv.org An international directory can be accessed at www.voluntary work.org Sri Lankan organizations such as the Turtle Research Project, near Tangalla, seek short term volunteers, see page 156.

Rules, customs and etiquette

Greeting 'Ayubowan' (may you have long life) is the traditional welcome greeting among the Sinhalese, said with the hands folded upwards in front of the chest. The same gesture accompanies the word 'vanakkam' among Tamils.

Conduct Cleanliness and modesty are appreciated even in informal situations. Nudity and topless bathing are prohibited and heavy fines can be imposed. Displays of intimacy are not considered suitable in public and will probably draw unwanted attention. Women in rural areas do not normally shake hands with men as this form of contact is not traditionally acceptable between acquaintances.

Hands & eating Use your right hand for giving, taking, eating or shaking hands as the left is considered to be unclean.

Begging The sight of beggars especially near religious sites can be very disturbing. A coin to one child or a destitute woman on the street will make you the focus of demanding attention from a large number before long. Many Sri Lankans give alms to street beggars as a means of gaining spiritual merit or out of a sense of duty but the sum is often very small – a rupee or two. How you deal with begging is a matter of personal choice but it is perhaps better to give to a recognized charity than to make largely ineffectual handouts to individuals. Some people find it appropriate to give food to beggars rather than money. Children sometimes offer to do 'jobs' such as call a taxi, show you the way or pose for a photo. You may want to give a coin in exchange. However, it is not helpful to hand out sweets, 'school pens' and money, indiscriminately to open-palmed children who tag on to any foreigner.

Charitable giving A pledge to donate a part of one's holiday budget to a local charity can be an effective formula for 'giving'. Some visitors like to support self-help local co-operatives, orphanages, refugee centres, disabled or disadvantaged groups, or international charities like Oxfam, Save the Children or Christian Aid which work with local partners, by either making a donation or by buying their products.

Tipping A 10% service charge is now added to room rates and meals in virtually all **hotels/guesthouses** and **restaurants**. Therefore it is not essential to give a further tip in most instances. In many smaller guesthouses staff are not always paid a realistic wage and have to rely on a share of the service charge for their basic income.

Tour companies sometimes make recommendations for 'suitable tips' for **coach drivers** and **guides**. Some of the figures may seem modest by European standards but are very inflated if compared with normal earnings. A tip of Rs 50 per day from each member of the group can safely be regarded as generous.

Taxi drivers do not expect to be tipped but a small extra amount over the fare is welcomed.

Photography There is no separate charge for photography in the Cultural Triangle since this is now included in the ticket price. Photography is prohibited in certain sections of the sacred sites as well as in sensitive areas such as airports, dams and military areas.

It is best to take some film rolls and any specialist camera batteries although colour and black and white films are available cheaply at major tourist centres (check expiry date and seal). Only buy films from a reputable shop. Hawkers and roadside stalls may pass off out-of-date or used films as new.

Safety

Some areas of Sri Lanka such as the Jaffna Peninsula and Batticaloa in the east are no go areas due to the continuing civil war. Permits are not issued for visiting these areas and anyone foolhardy enough to attempt reaching these areas will be sent back by the police or army. Certain archeological sites and national parks require **permits** before visiting. Refer to the relevant sections for details.

Restricted & protected areas

Con-men who aim to part you from your money are now found in most major towns and tourist sites. It is best to ignore them and carry on your own business while politely, but firmly, declining their offers of help.

Confidence tricksters
See page 48

Accommodation touts are common at rail and bus stations often boarding trains some distance before the destination. After engaging you in casual conversation to find out your plan one will often find you a taxi or a three-wheeler and try to persuade you that the hotel of your choice is closed, full or not good value. He will suggest an alternative where he will, no doubt, earn a commission (which you will end up having to pay). It is better to go to your preferred choice alone. Phone in advance to check if a place is full and make a reservation if necessary. If it is full then the hotelier/guesthouse owner will usually advise you of a suitable alternative. Occasionally, touts operate in groups to confuse you or one may pose as the owner of the guesthouse you have in mind and tell you that it is sadly full but he able to 'help' you by taking you to a friend's place.

A new breed of con-men is on the increase especially in towns attracting tourists (Kandy, Galle). One may approach you as you step out on the street, saying he recognizes you as he works in your hotel. Caught off-guard, you feel obliged to accept him as your guide for exploring the sights (and shops), and so are ripe for exploitation. Be polite, but firm, when refusing his offer of help.

A **gem s**hop may try to persuade you to buy gems as a sample for a client in your home country - usually your home town (having found out which this is in casual conversation). A typical initial approach is to request that you help with translating something for the trader. The deal is that you buy the gems (maybe to the value of US$500 or US$1000) and then sell them to the client for double the price, and keep the difference. Of course, there is no client at home and you are likely to have been sold poor quality gems or fakes! Only buy gems for yourself and be sure of what you are buying. This is a common trick in Galle and Ratnapura where various methods are employed.

It is essential to take care that **credit cards** are not 'run off' more than once when making a purchase.

Travel arrangements, especially for sight-seeing, should only be made through reputable companies; bogus agents operate in popular seaside resorts.

In general the threats to personal security for travellers in Sri Lanka are small. In most areas other than the north and east it is possible to travel without any risk of personal violence. However, care is necessary in some places, and basic common sense needs to be used with respect to looking after valuables. **Theft** is not uncommon especially when travelling by train or crowded bus. It is essential to take good care of personal valuables both when you are carrying them, and when you have to leave them anywhere. You cannot regard hotel rooms as automatically safe. It is wise to use hotel safes for valuable items, though even they cannot guarantee security. It is best to keep travellers' cheques and passports with you at all times. Money belts worn under clothing are one of the safest options, although you should keep some cash easily accessible in a purse.

Personal security

Even after taking all reasonable precautions people do have valuables stolen. This can cause great inconvenience. You can minimize this by keeping a record of vital documents, including your passport number and travellers' cheques numbers in a

Police

Essentials

separate place from the documents themselves. If you have items stolen, they should be reported to the police as soon as possible. Larger hotels will be able to help in contacting and dealing with the police.

Dealings with the police can be difficult. The paper work involved in reporting losses can be time consuming and irritating, and your own documentation (eg passport and visas) will normally be demanded. Tourists should not assume that if procedures move slowly they are automatically being expected to offer a bribe. If you face really serious problems, for example in connection with a driving accident, you should contact your consular office as quickly as possible.

Where to stay

The Tourist Board issues a free 'Accommodation List' at the International Airport & at their office at 80 Galle Rd, Colombo 3; the list is not comprehensive

Sri Lanka has a surprisingly uneven range of accommodation. You can stay safely and relatively cheaply (by western standards) in Colombo, Kandy and the popular coastal areas of the south and south-west where there is a choice of quality hotels offering a full range of personal and business facilities (though their food can be bland and uninspired). In smaller centres even the best hotels are far more variable and it may be necessary to accept much more modest accommodation. In the high season (December to March for much of the island) bookings can be extremely heavy. It is therefore best to reserve rooms well in advance if you are making your own arrangements, and to arrive reasonably early in the day. It is now possible to reserve accommodation by email at many hotels and guesthouses.

Taxes
When agreeing a price make sure this includes all taxes & charges

A Goods and Services Tax (GST) of 12.5% which is added to meals, is now applicable to accommodation in the tourism sector for foeigners so expect this additional tax in hotels, especially those graded **C** and above. BTT (Business Turnover Tax) has been abolished so this should no longer appear on bills.

Regional & seasonal variations

Prices are highly inflated in Kandy during the Esala Perahera festival and in Nuwara Eliya during the April holiday season. 'Long weekends' (weekends when a public holiday or Poya Day falls on a Thursday, Friday, Monday or Tuesday) also attract a substantial increase in room rates in Nuwara Eliya.

Many hotels charge the highest room-rate over Christmas and New Year (between mid-December to mid-January). Large reductions are made by hotels in all categories out-of-season in many resorts. Always ask if any is available. During the monsoon rooms may sometimes feel damp and have a musty smell.

Types of accommodation

There are international class hotels in the capital with a full range of facilities where prices and standards are sometimes comparable with the West, as well as excellent 'Resort' style accommodation on beaches or near important cultural sites (minimum around US$65). The choice ranges from these to moderately priced comfortable accommodation in the city or very simple guest houses in small coastal towns and villages or Wildlife Conservation Department bungalows in the parks (about Rs 300-400).

Budget hotels Hotels in general are much more expensive than in India, and it is much less easy to find a choice of good cheap accommodation except in a few coastal resorts popular with backpackers. Some hotels and guesthouses in the **E** and **F** categories have some rooms for Rs 200 and under. Very few towns have cheap youth hostel type accommodation. It is also possible to book rooms in plantation estate bungalows or in private homes in towns or beach resorts; these are a good alternative for those on a low budget as they can be clean and good value.

Hotel Classification

Prices are for a double room excluding taxes during the high (not 'peak') season. A 10% service charge is added in virtually all hotels and guesthouses. Single rooms are rare and single occupancy of a double room rarely attracts a significant discount.

All rooms have attached bathrooms except when specified.

L *US$150+ (Rs 10,000+) Exceptional hotels in the larger cities or in an exclusive locations such as a commanding coastal promontory, beside a lake or on a scenic hill top, with nothing to fault them. They have high class busiess facilities, specialist restaurants and well-stocked bars, several pools and sports.*

AL *US$100-US$150 (Rs 7000-10,000) Major towns have at least one in this category which also reach high international standards; good facilities for business and leisure travellers, but are less exclusive*

A *US$60 - US$100 (Rs 4200- Rs 7000) International class hotel with most facilities: generous group discounts mean even budget package tours may use this category.*

B *US$35 - US$60 (Rs 2450- Rs 4200) Generally very comfortable and particularly good value: except a pool. Several are converted colonial mansions where the 'experience' more than compensates for rather antiquated facilities and furnishings.*

C *US$20 - US$35 (Rs 1400- Rs 2450) Often has a range of fairly comfortable rooms: most should have some a/c rooms, TV and hot water.*

D *US$11 - US$20 (Rs 800- Rs 1400) This may be the highest category available in small towns (though not always the best value). Rooms can vary (most with hot waterm some with a/c and TV). Many **D** Rest Houses are in idyllic locations, but lack investment and are rather run-down.*

E *US$7 - US$11 (Rs 500- Rs 800) Some are bery good value, often noticeably better than **F** category (larger, cleaner rooms, more modern bathrooms etc). Towel, soap and toilet paper are usually provided. A/c often incurs a surcharge.*

F *US$5- US$7 (Rs 350- Rs 500) The backpacker's staple: rooms can be highly variable. Some are attractive, clean and well-kept: others less so, so inspect first. Expect a fan, mosquito net, towel, soap and toilet paper: cheaper rooms may have shared facilities. There may not be a restaurant.*

G *below US$5 (below Rs 350) In places with high demand (eg Colombo, Kandy, Nuwara Eliya), this may provide basic (and sometimes dirty) dormitory accommodation with shared facilities. In backpacker resorts (eg Hikkaduwa, Unawatuna), however, you can find clean but simple private rooms, sometimes with attached toilet and shower.*

Prices above are 'spot-rates' for individual travellers. Tour operators can get large discounts for 'package' clients in the top categories.

National Parks Accommodation The National Park Bungalows at all parks cost a hefty US$24 per person per night for foreigners and you should bring your own food and bedding. If the bungalow is within the park boundaries then you will have to pay park entrance fees for 2 days for an overnight stay. Camping is possible in many national parks at US$5 per night. All accommodation must be booked in advance at the Department of Wildlife Conservation in Colombo.

Government Rest Houses These are sometimes in converted colonial houses, often in superb locations, and often offer good accommodation at a reasonable price, from Rs 800 for a double room). Ceylon Hotels Corporation (the CHC), 411 Galle Rd, Colombo 4, is responsible for management of several of the old Government *Rest Houses* across the island. It is best to book through Central Reservations in Colombo on T503497 or

Full Moon Poya days

		2001	2002
Full Moon Poya days of each month are			
holidays. Buddhists visit temples with	January	9	28
offerings of flowers, to worship and	February	8	27
remind themselves of the precepts. Certain	March	9	28
temples hold special celebrations in	April	7	26
connection with a particular full moon, eg	May	7	26
Esala at Kandy. Accommodation may be	June	5	24
difficult to find and public transport is	July	5	24
crowded during these festivals. No alcohol	August	4	22
is sold (you can however order your drinks	September	4	21
at your hotel the day before) and all	October	2	21
places of entertainment are closed.	November	30/1	19
	December	30	19

F 503504, as occasionally an individual Rest House may accept a direct booking but not necessarily honour it. Prices charged by some on arrival may vary from what is quoted on the phone and from the CHC's 'Official' typed list showing the tariff which only a few managers acknowledge exists. Meals at the *Rest Houses* usually cost Rs 150-200 (though you may find something similar for Rs 30-40 in a local restaurant).

Railway Retiring Rooms For people travelling by rail a few stations have Retiring Rooms which may be hired for up to 24 hours. However, there are only a few stations with rooms and they are generally rather poor at Rs 300 for a double room. Some are open to people without rail tickets and can be useful in an emergency. Stations with rooms are: Anuradhapura, Batticaloa, Galle, Kandy, Mihintale, Polgahawela and Trincomalee.

Facilities **Air-conditioning** Only the larger hotels have central a/c. Elsewhere a/c rooms are cooled by individual units and occasionally large 'air-coolers' which can be noisy and unreliable. When they fail to operate tell the management as it is often possible to get a rapid repair done, or to transfer to a room where the unit is working. Fans are provided in all but the cheapest of hotels.

Insects Mosquitoes may penetrate even the best hotels. In cheap hotels you need to be prepared for a wider range of insect life, including flies, cockroaches, spiders, ants, and harmless house lizards. Poisonous insects, including scorpions, are extremely rare. Hotel managements are nearly always prepared with insecticide sprays, and will come and spray rooms if asked. It is worth taking your own repellent creams. Remember to shut windows and doors at dusk. Electrical devices, used with insecticide pellets, are now widely available, as are 'mosquito coils' which burn slowly to emit a scented smoke. Many small hotels have mosquito nets. Dusk and early evening are the worst times for mosquitoes. Light-coloured trousers and long-sleeved shirts are advisable, especially out of doors. At night fans can be very effective in keeping mosquitoes off.

Laundry This can be arranged very cheaply (eg a shirt washed and pressed for Rs 20 in **C-D** category; Rs 70 in luxury hotels) and quickly (in 12-24 hours). It is best not to risk delicate fibres, though luxury hotels can usually handle these and also dry-clean items.

Toilets Apart from the most expensive hotel (**A** and above), 'baths' do not necessarily refer to bathrooms with Western bathtubs. Other hotels may provide a bathroom with a toilet, basin and a shower. In the lower priced hotels and outside large towns, a bucket and tap may replace the shower, and a 'squat' toilet instead of a Western WC.

During the cold weather and in hill stations, hot water will be available at certain times during the day, sometimes in buckets. Even medium sized hotels which are clean and pleasant do not always provide towels, soap and toilet paper.

Noise Hotels close to temples can be very noisy, especially during festival times. Music blares from loudspeakers late at night and from very early in the morning, often making sleep impossible. Mosques call the faithful to prayers at dawn. Some find ear-plugs helpful.

Getting around

As the civil war erupts sporadically in the north and parts of the northeast and east these areas remained dangerous and closed to visitors in 2000. Conditions have been virtually normal in most places in the rest of the island for the past few years despite occasional bombing, and tourists continue to travel freely in these parts but they may be asked not to use public transport for out of town journeys.

Air

There were no scheduled air services within Sri Lankan in 2000.

Road

Roads in Sri Lanka are generally well maintained but traffic often moves very slowly, especially in Colombo and its surrounds.

Bus Government-run CTB buses are generally yellow and are the cheapest, slowest and most uncomfortable of the options and get very crowded at all times. Private buses offer a higher degree of comfort (if you can get a seat) and cost a little more.

Private intercity buses are often a/c minibuses (sometimes coaches on popular routes). They cost about double the fare of ordinary buses but they are quicker and you are guaranteed a seat since they operate on a 'leave when full' basis. They can be quite cramped, especially if you have big luggage but on the whole they are the best option for travelling quickly to and from the main towns. They are generally non-stop but will let you off on request en route (ask the conductor in advance) although you will still have to pay the full fare to the end destination. If you do want to get off en route it is best to sit near the door since the aisle is used by passengers on fold-away seats. The fare is usually displayed on the front or side window.

In general it is best to board buses at the main bus stand in order to get a seat. Once out on the road it is normally standing room only.

Car hire Travelling by car gives you the maximum flexibility if you want to tour, allowing you to stop wherever and whenever you wish and also see places which are almost inaccessible any other way. Sharing a vehicle can make this occasionally possible for even those travelling on a small budget. They can be a good way of seeing the country and village life if you have time.

There are several **self-drive** car hire firms based in Colombo including some linked to international firms. You have to be 25-65 years old and have an International Driving Permit (contact your local Automobile Association) in order to get a Sri Lankan driving permit through their AA (see page 84). Some hire firms (eg *Avis*) will get this for you for Rs 50.

Essentials

Unwritten rules of the road

The rule of 'might is right' applies.

Never overtake a vehicle in front of you which indicates to the right. It usually means that it is unsafe for you to overtake and rarely means that they are about to turn right.

Flashing headlights mean 'get out of the way, I'm not stopping'. In these circumstances it is best to give the oncoming vehicle space, since they usually approach at great speed. Roundabouts are generally a free-for-all, so take your chance cautiously.

Horns are used as a matter of course, but most importantly when overtaking, to warn the driver being overtaken. It is also used to warn vehicles and pedestrians approaching the main road from a side road since they rarely look.

Most Sri Lankan drivers appear to take unbelievable risks, notably overtaking at ridiculous times (eg when approaching a blind bend). It is essential to be aware of the danger from fool-hardy driving and anticipate the mistakes that Sri Lankan road users might make.

Driving permit Foreigners intending to drive in Sri Lanka need to get a free 'recognition permit' which is issued up to the expiry date of your International Driving Permit. This is a simple process. Just call at the Automobile Association of Sri Lanka, 3rd Floor, 40 Sir MM Markar Mawatha, Galle Face, Colombo 3, T421528, F446074. Open 0830-1630, Monday-Friday.

If you do not have an International Driving Permit but do have your national licence, you must apply for a temporary Sri Lankan Driving Licence from the Register of Motor Vehicles, Department of Motor Traffic, 341 Elvitigala Mawatha, Colombo 5, T694331. Temporary Driving Licences are issued on payment of Rs 600 plus GST per month up to a maximum of 3 months.

Driving conditions Many foreign visitors find the road conditions difficult, unfamiliar and sometimes dangerous. If you drive yourself it is essential to take great care. Pedestrians often walk along, or in the middle of a narrow road in the absence of pavements and cattle and dogs roam at will. There are also barriers and army checks in politically sensitive areas (route to Trincomalee) where it is best to travel in day light.

Car with driver It may actually be safer (and more relaxing) to hire a car with a driver, available through travel agents and tour operators (see page 78). A driver may be helpful in being able to communicate with local people and also make a journey more interesting by telling you more about the places and local customs. It is usual for drivers to make their own overnight arrangements if the hotel you stay in doesn't provide special facilities such as a drivers' dormitory; he may sometimes sleep in the car. They are also responsible for all their expenses, including their meals.

It is best not to depend on the driver for suggestions of hotels, restaurants and gift shops since you may not get an unbiased opinion. Drivers often earn commission from the proprietors so it is you who will end up paying extra for it.

Hire charges vary according to make and can be very high for luxury models. Rates quoted by Mackinnons (*Avis*) are given for a small reconditioned a/c car.

Self-drive Rs 1,500 per day plus Rs 9 per km; Rs 9,600 per week plus 9 per km, or Rs 15,000 per week unlimited kilometres (whichever is cheaper). These do not include fuel (petrol is about Rs 55 per litre; diesel Rs 15), but include insurance though you have to pay up to the first US$ 400 of a claim. You need to leave a refundable deposit of Rs 20,000 in advance (some ask you to leave your return air ticket as surety).

Car with driver A/c car including fuel, Rs 1,600 per day (for 80 km free, then Rs 20 per km) plus Rs 150 per day driver's allowance for out-of-town tour. Clarify driver's hours of duty and '80 km per day free' allowance (ie whether the total distance covered on tour counts rather than the actual distance driven each day).

A **tip** to the driver at the end of the whole tour (if you wish to give one) of about Rs 50 per day in addition to his inclusive daily allowance, is quite acceptable.

Taxis

Taxis have yellow tops with red numbers on white plates, and are available in most towns. Negotiate price for long journeys beforehand. **Radio cabs** (eg *Ace, Quick, Redcabs*) are more expensive having a higher minimum charge, but are fixed price, very reliable, convenient and accept some credit cards. They are a/c, have digital meters and are available 24 hours at the airport, Colombo and Kandy. The cab arrives in 10-15 minutes of phoning (give exact location). However, during busy periods it is best to allow about 30 minutes. They charge nothing extra within 15 km of city limits and offer good discounted rates for return trips of 60+ km. First kilometre Rs 26, extra kilometre Rs 24, minimum charge Rs 50. See Colombo (page 79) and Kandy Transport (page 190) for details.

In tourist resorts, taxis are often Toyota **vans** which can carry up to 10 people. Ask at your hotel/guesthouse for an estimate of the fare to a particular destination. There is usually a 'going-rate', but you will probably have to bargain to reach this. Agree on the fare before getting in.

Tuk-tuks

Although they are the Indian auto-rickshaws made by Bajaj, they are generally called *tuk-tuks* in Sri Lanka. They are for the more adventurous as they move quickly through traffic but compare poorly against taxis for price. Fares are negotiable as they are unmetered but fix a price before starting - around Rs 20 per km. You can offer about 60% of the asking price though it is unlikely you will get to pay the same rate as local people.

Motorcycles

Motorcycles are popular locally and are convenient for visiting different beaches and also for longer distance sightseeing. Repairs are usually easy to arrange and quite cheap. Motorcycle hire is possible for around Rs 500 per day in some beach resorts (eg Hikkaduwa, Negombo) or in towns nearby. It is essential to check all bikes thoroughly for safety. If you have an accident you will usually be expected to pay for the damage. For small-wheeled bikes, sand or gravel roads can be particularly hazardous. Potholes and speed-breakers add to the problems of a fast rider.

Cycles

Cycling is an excellent way of seeing the quiet by-ways of Sri Lanka and particularly enjoyable if you travel with a companion. Foreign cyclists are usually greeted with cheers, waves and smiles. Local bikes are heavy and often without gears but on the flat they offer a good way of exploring comparatively short distances outside towns but try to avoid the major highways as far as possible. Cycling after dark can be hazardous because of lack of street lighting and poor road surfaces. Take bungy cords (to strap down a backpack) and good lights from home, and take care not to leave your bike parked anywhere with your belongings. Bikes may be transported on trains, though you will need to arrive two hours ahead at Colombo Fort station. You can expect to pay between Rs 75-150 per day for cycle hire depending on the resort and condition of the bike. Repair shops are universal and charges are nominal.

Hitchhiking

This is rare in Sri Lanka, partly because public transport is so cheap.

Train

Although the network is restricted there are train services to a number of major destinations and journeys are comparatively short and very cheap by Western standards. Train journeys are leisurely (bar the Intercity between Colombo and Kandy)

Approximate train fares from Colombo (Fort)

To	1st Class	2nd Class	3rd Class
Anuradhapura	Rs 202	Rs 116	Rs 42
Badulla	Rs 289	Rs 166	Rs 60
Bentota	Rs 61	Rs 35	Rs 13
Galle	Rs 113	Rs 65	Rs 24
Hikkaduwa	Rs 95	Rs 55	Rs 20
Kandy	Rs 120	Rs 69	Rs 25
Matara	Rs 155	Rs 89	Rs 33
Nanu Oya (for Nuwara Eliya)	Rs 205	Rs 118	Rs 43

and an ideal way to see the countryside and meet the people without experiencing the downside of a congested bus journey through dusty crowded roads. Should you give in to the temptation of spending many hours riding the rails, take Royston Ellis' *Sri Lanka by Rail* (Bradt, 1994) which makes an excellent, informative companion.

There are three principal 'lines':

1 Northern Line Although the train to Anuradhapura continues north to Vavuniya, tourists are advised not to travel further than Anuradhapura since Vavuniya has been the scene of several recent separatist incidents and the train itself has been a target on occasion. The branch line east goes as far as Polonnaruwa but not to Batticaloa. Although the line to Trincomalee is open at present, it may be subject to regular security checks.

2 Main Line East from Colombo Fort to Kandy and Matale with the ascent starting at Rambukkana. From Peradeniya the Main Line continues to Badulla through the hills, including stops at Nanu Oya (for Nuwara Eliya), Hatton (for Adam's Peak), Ohiya (for the Horton Plains) and Ella.

3 Colombo-Matara Line South originating at Maradana/Fort goes along the coast to Galle and as far as Matara, connecting all the popular coastal resorts. Running initially through the commuter belt south of the city, it can be crowded in the rush hour.

There are also the following lines: On the **Puttalam Line**, there are slow trains north from Ragama (north of Colombo) to Puttalam via Katunayake airport. A broad gauge **Kelani Valley Line** goes from Maradana to Avissawella (previously narrow gauge).

Third class has hard seats; second has some thin cushioning; first class is fairly comfortable. Many slow trains may have second and third class coaches only, with first class only available on some express trains, eg travelling down the southwest coast to Matara, second class is the best available.

Timetables are generally easy to find at most stations. The time of the next train in each direction is usually chalked onto a blackboard.

Reservations Sleeping berth reservation charge in 1st class is Rs 75. In 2nd class and 3rd class 'sleeperettes' (reclining chairs) cost an extra Rs 25 and Rs 18 respectively. Reservation fees for 2nd and 3rd class are Rs 15 and Rs 12 respectively but seats can not generally be reserved in advance. At Colombo's **Fort Station** there are different counters for different destinations and classes. Ask a local person to direct you to the correct counter. The Berth Reservation Office at Fort Station is open 0830-1530, Mondays-Saturdays, 0830-1200 on Sundays and public holidays.

Special a/c trains run to Kandy and Hikkaduwa. There are two daily non a/c, fast, **Special trains** intercity express trains from Fort to Kandy at 0655 and 1535, taking two hours. These must be booked in advance, Rs 72 (extra Rs 50 for observation saloon), Rs 108 for a return within 10 days, the date of which must be specified when booking the outward journey. Reservation fees are extra. A reservation charge of Rs 50 is payable for seats in an 'observation saloon' (not available on all trains), which must be reserved well in advance since these seats are very popular.

There is a daily intercity train to Galle at 1530, two hours, Rs 65 (Rs 100 return) and also to Vavuniya (via Anuradhapura) at 1600, three hours 50 minutes, Rs 150 for first class, Rs 120 for second class.

There are special through trains all the way from Matara to Kandy and Anuradhapura which are routed via Colombo. Extra services are put on during festivals and holidays, eg from January for four months, to Hatton; April holiday season to the hills; May and June full moon days to Buddhist sites, Kandy, Anuradhapura, Mihintale; July/August for Kandy Perahera.

Essentials

Keeping in touch

Letters to Europe cost Rs 20, to the USA, Rs 22. Postcards to most countries beyond **Post** the Middle East cost Rs 14; aerogrammes to all countries (purchased over the counter at post offices) cost Rs 12. Try to use a franking service in a post office when sending mail, or hand in your mail at a counter. Private agencies also act as post offices in some towns.

For valuable items, it is best to use a **courier**, eg *DHL Parcel Service* in Colombo. Documents to UK cost US$24 for first 500 g, to USA and most of EU US$26 for the first 500 g, US$7 for each additional 500 g. Parcels cost about double this rate for the first 500 g, plus US$7 for each additional 500 g. It takes three to four working days to Europe.

Poste restante at the GPO in larger towns will keep your mail (letters and packages) for two months. **American Express** clients may have mail held at offices worldwide. Their website /www.americanexpress.com gives access to a list of offices with phone numbers and hours of opening.

Parcels Air parcel rates to the UK are Rs 761 for the first 500 g, plus Rs 351 for each subsequent 500 g up to a maximum of 10 kg. To the USA the first 500 g will cost Rs 533 with an extra Rs 431 for each subsequent 500 g. For parcels by sea the rates to the UK are Rs 820 for the first kilogramme, Rs 1065 up to 3 kg, Rs 1337 for 3-5 kg and Rs 1751 for 5-10 kg. To the USA it costs Rs 472 for the first kilogramme, Rs 908 up to 3 kg, Rs 1359 fro 3- 5 kg and Rs 2373 for 5-10 kg.

Local calls within Sri Lanka have a maximum charge of about Rs 30 per three minutes, **Telephone** the rate depending on distance. STD codes are listed for each town in the text. Dial the *Directory enquiries T161* local number within the town but use the STD area code first (eg Kandy 08) when *International* dialling from outside the town. However, there are now several private operators *enquiries T134 from* which use a separate code which must be used wherever you call from. These *Colombo, T324144* numbers usually begin with 071, 072, 074, 075 and 077 and are quoted in the text. *from outside*

International phone calls can be made from the Colombo GPO between 0800 and 1900. When you can't dial direct you will need to book an International call at the post office, or by phoning T100 (from Colombo), or T101 (from outside). These operator connected calls are for a minimum of three minutes.

Reverse charge ('Collect Calls') to Australia, UK and USA can be made quickly using the following numbers, avoiding the Sri Lankan operator. *Australia Direct* (*Telstra*) T01-449499. *UK Direct* (*BT*) T01-432999. *USA Direct* (*AT&T*) T01- 430430.

IDD calls IDD dialling is now quite straightforward in Sri Lanka with many private call offices in the main resorts. It is best to use one with a computerised billing system rather than a stop-watch. Peak rate is between 0800-1800 Monday to Saturday; the cheapest rate is from 2200-0600 Monday to Saturday and all day Sundays. Calls to the UK and USA cost around Rs 100 per minute at cheap rate, Rs 140 at peak rate and somewhere in between at other times. Some places may allow you to accept incoming calls but may charge a nominal rate for each minute. Calls made from hotels usually cost a lot more (sometimes three times as much).

Card-operated pay phones There are now IDD card-operated pay phones which can connect you to several countries through satellite (eg Australia, China, India, Italy, Japan, Malaysia, UK); most other countries can be accessed through an operator. Phone cards can be bought from post offices, kiosks near the pay phones and some shops (minimum Rs 100). Pay phones can of course be used for local calls as well. Different companies issue cards which can be used for their own pay phones only and are not interchangeable – yellow and blue *Lanka* and the orange and black *Metrocard* are the most commonly used.

Cell phones The coverage by mobile phones extends from Colombo to Anuradhapura, Galle, Kandy, Kurunegala, Nuwara Eliya, Ratnapura and some west coast towns and is being increased across the island. It may be possible to use international mobile phone sets in Sri Lanka; enquire at home before leaving. The following are operating: *Hutchison* 0786-61111, 078-63333; *Celltel*, T01-541541, 0722-43333; *Dialog GSM* (digital), T077-678678; *Mobitel*, T0717-55777.

Internet and email Internet access is becoming widespread across Sri Lanka (see individual town sections for details). Prices range from Rs 5-10 per minute.

Fax You can send faxes from Communication Agencies in major towns. Charges vary according to country (about Rs 150-200 per minute). Business centres in top hotels charge considerably more. Machines vary so it is best to write clearly in black or blue ink.

Media **Newspapers** *The Daily News* and *The Island* are national daily newspapers published in English; there are several Sunday papers including the *Sunday Observer* and *Sunday Times*. In Colombo and some other hotels a wide range of international daily and periodical newspapers and magazines is available. The *Lanka Guardian* is a respected fortnightly offering news and comment.

Radio and television Sri Lanka's national radio and television network, broadcasts in Sinhalese and English. SLBC operates between 0540 and 2300. BBC World Service (1512khz/19m and 9720khz/31m from 2000 to 2130 GMT) has a large audience in both English and regional languages. Liberalization has opened the door to several private channels and an ever growing number of private radio stations.

The two state TV channels are *Rupavahini* with morning and evening programmes on weekdays, while *ITN* starts at 1800. Both have extended hours at weekends. Most programmes are in English with news at 2130 and 2200 respectively. Many Sri Lankans now watch satellite TV with a choice of several channels: 24-hr *ETV-1* for BBC and *ETV-2* for StarPlus; *MTV; TNL*. These offer good coverage of world news and also foreign feature films and 'soaps'.

The email explosion

As the internet shrinks the world, travellers are increasingly using emails to keep in touch with home. Their free accounts are invariably with **hotmail.com**, **yahoo.com**, **email.com** or **backpackers.com**; usually the less common the provider, the quicker the access.

Sri Lanka has its own set of problems which can be frustrating: very few machines which may also be out-dated; untrained staff and poor technical support; the server may be unreliable; the system may be clogged with users, especially during day; there may be frequent power cuts ... There are exceptions, of course.

New offices are opening weekly and new towns are getting connected. To track down the most reliable and best value internet service, ask other travellers. The length of the queue can be a good indicator. On the web, you can get a list from **www.netcafeguide.com**. Don't always head for the cheapest since they may also have the oldest and slowest equipment.

Hot Tips

- Use the folder facility to save mail
- Keep your in-box clear to reduce loading time
- Avoid junk mail by not giving your address to on-line companies
- Avoid downloading and using scanned pictures and documents
- Save files and back up regularly

The system can be efficient and satisfying but it can also become an expensive habit with more than its fair share of frustrations. As one sending an email to us mused, "many a hard-up traveller will wax lyrical about 'getting away from it all' and escaping 'the pressure of western society'. They will then spend hours and several hundred rupees a week slaving over a computer keyboard in some hot and sticky back street office".

Food and drink

Dishes Rice and curry are the staple main course food of Sri Lanka, but the term 'curry' conceals an enormous variety of subtle flavours. Coriander, chillies, mustard, cumin, pepper, cinnamon and garlic are just some of the common ingredients which add flavour to both seafood and meat curries. Fresh seafood – crab, lobster and prawn, as well as fish – is excellent, and meat is cheap. Coconut milk, vegetables and lentils are often added to a curry and the main dishes are accompanied by spicy pickles, sweet and sour chutneys and fiery hot *sambols* made of ground coconut or onion mixed with red chillies. Milder curries and *mallung*, a dish prepared with grated coconut, shredded leaves, red onions and lime, are alternatives to try. The cupped pancake-like hopper made with a fermented rice flour and coconut milk batter is a breakfast speciality which is often served up with a fried egg in the centre. String hoppers look more like a nest of thin noodles and are eaten with curries at a meal. You can get a traditional 'plate' meal (*thali*) for as little as Rs 50, whereas a meal in a good restaurant could cost Rs 250 and a buffet lunch at a five-star hotel might cost over Rs 450.

Rice forms the basis of many Sri Lankan sweet dishes, palm treacle being used as the main traditional sweetener. This is also served on curd as a delicious dessert. Sadly, it is not easy to get good Sri Lankan food in most hotels which concentrate on western dishes.

Town restaurants offer Indian, Chinese and Continental dishes too. Some foods that are common in Europe are both less readily available and of much lower quality in Sri Lanka, eg breakfast cereals, bread, cheese and chocolates.

Vegetarian food is much less common in Sri Lanka than in India, and in places can be difficult to get.

Fruit Sri Lanka has a wide variety of tropical fruit throughout the year - pineapple, papaya and banana being particularly good. The extraordinarily rich jack (jak) fruit is also available all year. Seasonal fruit include mangosteen (no relation of mangoes), passion fruit, custard apples, avocado pears, durian and rambutan from July to October. In addition to ordinary green coconuts, Sri Lanka has its own almost unique variety – the golden King Coconut (*thambili*); the milk is particularly sweet and nutritious.

Many **spices** are grown in the island and are widely available in the markets and shops. Cinnamon, nutmeg, cloves, cardamom and pepper are all grown, the Kandy region being a major centre of spice production. Many private spice gardens are open to the public.

Drink **Soft drinks** There is a huge variety of bottled soft drinks, including well known international brands (eg Sprite, Fanta, Coke at about Rs 11). The local mineral waters include Soda water (Rs 7), Club Tonic, Ginger Beer (Rs 12) and others at about Rs 11 (Cream Soda, Lemonade, Necto, Orange barley). These are perfectly safe but always check the seal. One of the most popular drinks however is tender coconut (especially the golden *thambili*), very widely available, always pure straight from the nut and refreshing.

Do not add ice cubes to drinks: the water from which the ice is made may not be pure

Alcoholic drinks are widely available, though imported drinks (wines) are very expensive. Local beer (*Lion, Carlsberg* and *Three Coins Pilsner*) is acceptable but can be expensive (Rs 60-80), larger hotel restaurants charging about Rs 125. Spirits are available too, eg Mendis Special (Rs 190) and Double distilled (Rs 250). The local *arrack*, distilled from palm toddy, can be very potent. The matured VSOA and seven-year old arrack are smoother.

Alcohol is not sold on *Poya* days (see page 40). Orders for alcoholic drinks in hotels are usually taken on the previous day!

Shopping

What to buy Handloom cotton and silk, hand painted batik hangings and clothing, silverware, wood carvings, coir and palm leaf articles, leather goods, jewellery and gem stones are good buys. Craft department stores in the larger cities offer a range under one roof - *Lakphana, Lanka Hands, Craft Link, Viskam Nivasa* are some you will come across. There are government *Laksala* shops in many towns. Private upmarket shops and top hotel arcades offer better quality, choice and service but at a price. Vibrant and colourful local bazars (markets) are often a great experience but you must be prepared to bargain. Sri Lankan tea, spices and cashew nuts are worth taking home and also make ideal gifts. Some tea and spice gardens welcome visitors and have retail outlets for their produce.

Bargaining In some private shops and markets bargaining is normal and expected but avoid bargaining at government 'fixed price' shops. It is best to get an idea of prices being asked by different stalls for items you are interested in before taking the plunge. Some shopkeepers will happily quote twice the actual price to a foreigner showing interest, so you might well start by halving the asking price. On the other hand it would be inappropriate to do the same in an established shop with price-tags, though a plea for the 'best price' or a 'special discount' might reap results even here. Remain good humoured throughout.

Tips & trends Gem stones, gold jewellery, silver items are best bought in reputable shops (see also page 48). Taxi (and *tuk-tuk*) drivers often receive commission when they take you to shops. If you arrive at a shop with a tout you may well end up paying absurdly high prices to cover the commission he earns. You may want to take this into account when you tip your driver after a round-island tour! Sometimes drivers are given a rice packet for simply taking you to a shop. If your driver asks you to just take a look at a shop, it may be a good thing to do, as he will have a useful gift to present his wife upon his return! The quality of goods in a shop which needs to encourage touts may be questionable too. Try to select and enter a shop on your own and be aware that a tout may follow you into a shop and pretend to the shopkeeper that he has taken you there.

Batik 'factories', mask and handicrafts 'workshops', spice 'gardens', gem 'museums' across the island attract a traveller's attention by suggesting that a visit will be particularly interesting but the main purpose of most is to get you into their shop where you may feel obliged to buy something in exchange for the free 'demonstration' or visit.

Export of certain items such as antiquities, ivory, furs and skins is controlled or banned, so it is essential to get a certificate of legitimate sale and permission for export.

Special interest travel

Watersports The warm waters along Sri Lanka's palm fringed coast which are dotted with beach resorts ideal for swimming. Some of them hold the added attraction for those keen on windsurfing, waterskiing, parasailing etc, as well as snorkelling and diving. Diving is best avoided during the monsoons. The best time for the southwest of the island is the winter, from November to March when the sea is relatively calm and clear. The far south and the east coast (which is sometimes inaccessible) are better from April to September (but avoid July). Specialist companies will advise you on good reefs. See the box on page 95. The better diving to the northwest and west are out of bounds.

Ayurveda Ayurvedic healing has been practised on the island since ancient times although it was overshadowed by western medicine in the 19th century. With the renewed interest in alternative forms of therapy in the West, Sri Lanka too considers Ayurvedic healing a serious subject for scientific research and has begun exploring its wealth of wild plants. There has been a regeration of special ayurvedic herbal cure centres which are increasingly attracting foreign visitors, particularly to the southwest coast around Bentota. See the box on page 181.

Birdwatching Over 425 bird species have been identified in Sri Lanka, of which 21 are endemics and even within a relatively short distance of Colombo, the bird watcher will be able to spot half of these. The Sinharaja Forest Reserve, the Peak Wilderness Sanctuary and the Ruhuna-Yala National Park are particularly rewarding since they offer diverse habitats, while the reservoirs and coastal lagoons to the southeast (at Bundala and Kumana) attract a large variety of water birds. Local specialist tour operators are listed on page 78.

Buddhism The ancient Buddhist centres hold great attraction for all visitors and certainly for those interested in the living religion. Sri Lanka provides rewarding opportunities to discover more about the practice of Theravada (Hinanaya) Buddhism and meditation. Several centres offer courses on Buddhism in English (and occasionally in French and German). See page 76.

Holidays and festivals

Most religious festivals (Buddhist, Muslim and Hindu) are determined by the lunar calendar and therefore change from year to year. Please check at the tourist office for exact dates. Saturday and Sunday are always holidays.

January: *Duruthu Poya day* – Sri Lankan Buddhists believe that the Buddha visited the island and celebrate with *Colombo's* biggest annual festival at the Kelaniya Temple. *Tamil Thai Pongal* day observed by Hindus.

January-February: *Navam Poya* celebrated at *Colombo's* Gangaramaya Temple, with elephant processions.

February 4: *National (Independence) Day* – processions, dances, parades.

February/March: *Maha Sivarathri* marks the night when Siva danced his celestial dance of destruction (*Tandava*) celebrated with feasting and fairs at Siva temples, preceded by a night of devotional readings and hymn singing.

March: *Medin Poya Day*.

April: *Bak Poya Day* – Good Friday with Passion Plays in *Negombo*, in particular on Duwa Island. **13**: Sinhala and Tamil *New Year Day* marked with celebrations (originally harvest thanksgiving), by closure of many shops and restaurants.

May 1: *May Day*. *Wesak Poya Day* and the day following. celebrating the key events in the Buddha's life: his birth, enlightenment and death. Clay oil-lamps are lit across the island; also folk theatre performances. Special celebrations at *Anuradhapura, Kelaniya* (Colombo) and *Kandy*. **22**: *National Heroes' Day*.

June: *Poson Poya Day*, marking Mahinda's arrival in Sri Lanka as the first Buddhist missionary; *Mihintale* and *Anuradhapura* hold special celebrations. *Bank Holiday* (**30**).

July (**early August**): *Esala Poya Day* – this is the most important Sri Lankan festival with a grand procession of elephants, dancers etc, honouring the Sacred Tooth of the Buddha in *Kandy* lasting 10 days and elsewhere including Dewi Nuwara (*Dondra*) and *Bellanwila Raja Maha Vihare*, South Colombo. *Kataragama* holds purification rituals including firewalking. *Munneswaram (Chilaw) Vel Festival* and in *Colombo* from Sea St Hindu temple, procession to *Bambalapitiya* and *Welawatta*.

August: *Nikini Poya Day* – celebrations at Bellanwila, Colombo.

September: *Binara Poya Day* – Perahera in Badulla.

October: *Wap Poya Day* : **October/November**: *Deepavali*. Festival of Lights celebrated by Hindus with fireworks, commemorating Rama's return after his 14 years exile in the forest when citizens lit his way with earthen oil lamps.

November: *Il Poya Day*

December: *Unduwap Poya Day*, marks the arrival of Emperor Asoka's daughter, Sanghamitta, with a sapling of the Bodhi Tree from India. Special celebrations at *Anuradhapura, Bentota* and *Colombo*. **25**: *Christmas Day*. **31**: *Special Bank Holiday*.

These are fixed according to the lunar calendar, see page 307. According to the **Muslim holy** Gregorian calendar, they tend to fall 11 days earlier each year, dependent on the **days** sighting of the new moon.

Ramadan Start of the month of fasting when all Muslims (except young children, the very elderly, the sick, pregnant women and travellers) must abstain from food and drink from sunrise to sunset.

    Id ul Fitr The three-day festival marks the end of Ramadan.

    Id-ul-Zuha/Bakr-Id (7-8 March 2001) Muslims commemorate Ibrahim's sacrifice of his son according to God's commandment; the main time of pilgrimage to Mecca (the Hajj). It is marked by the sacrifice of a goat, feasting and alms giving.

    Muharram (7 April 2001) when the killing of the Prophet's grandson, Hussain, is commemorated by Shi'a Muslims. Decorated *tazias* (replicas of the martyr's tomb) are carried in procession by devout wailing followers who beat their chests to express their grief! Shias fast for the 10 days.

Health

With the following advice and precautions, you should keep as healthy as you do at home. In Sri Lanka the health risks are different from those encountered in Europe or the USA but the region's medical practicioners have particular experience in dealing with locally occuring diseases.

Before you go

Take out medical insurance. You should have a dental check up if you are visiting for a long period, obtain a spare glasses prescription and, if you suffer from a long-standing condition such as diabetes, high blood pressure, heart/lung disease or a nervous disorder, arrange for a check up with your doctor who can at the same time provide you with a letter explaining details of your disability. Check the current practice for malaria prophylaxis (prevention) for the parts of the country you intend to visit.

Good hotels can often provide a list of recommended doctors. There are many well **Medical care** qualified doctors in Sri Lanka, a large proportion of whom speak English. However, the quality and range of medical care are much lower in rural areas. Traditional systems of medicine are common and local practitioners have a lot of experience with the particular diseases of their region. If you are a long way away from medical help, a certain amount of self medication may be necessary.

Many drugs available in the west are available from chemists. However, always check the **Medicines** date stamping and buy from reputable pharmacies because the shelf life of some items, especially vaccines and antibiotics, is markedly reduced in hot conditions. Many locally produced drugs are not subjected to quality control procedures and so can be unreliable.

Antiacid tablets; anti-diarrhoea tablets; anti-malaria tablets; anti-infective ointment; **Health kit** condoms/contraceptives; dusting powder for feet; first aid kit and disposable needles; flea powder; strong insect repellent (Deet); tampons; travel sickness pills; waspeze or similar spray; water sterilizing tablets (and iodine).

If you require travel vaccinations see your doctor well in advance of your travel. Most **Vaccination &** courses must be completed in a minimum of four weeks. Travel clinics may provide **immunisation** rapid courses of vaccination but are likely to be more expensive. The following vaccinations are recommended:

Typhoid (monovalent) One dose followed by a booster in one month's time. Immunity from this course lasts two to three years. An oral preparation is currently being marketed in some countries and a one dose injectable vaccine is also available but is more expensive than monovalent: Typhim-Vi (Mevieux).

Polio-myelitis This is a live vaccine generally given orally and a full course consists of three doses with a booster in tropical regions every three to five years.

Tetanus One dose should be given with a booster at six weeks and another at six months. Ten yearly boosters thereafter are recommended.

Meningococcal Meningitis and Japanese B Encephalitis (JVE) Immunisation (Japanese or Korean vaccine: effective in 10 days) gives protection for around three years. There is an extremely small risk, though it varies seasonally and from region to region. Consult a Travel Clinic.

Hepatitis A Many travellers contract Hepatitis A. Protection is very strongly recommended. Havrix, Havrix Monodose and Junior Havrix vaccine give protection for 10 years after two injections (10 days to be effective). Alternatively, one gamma globulin injection to cover up to six months' travel is effective immediately and is much cheaper.

Hepatitis B This is a sexually transmitted disease, also passed on from blood transfusions or infected needles. A vaccine is available – three shots over six months. Regular travellers should have a blood test first to check whether they are already immune to Hepatitis A or B.

Rabies Rabies is endemic in Sri Lanka. Pre-exposure vaccination gives anyone bitten by a suspect animal time to get treatment (so particularly helpful to those visiting remote areas) and also prepares the body to produce antibodies quickly; cost of vaccine can be shared by three receiving vaccination together. If you are bitten by a domestic or wild animal, don't leave things to chance. Scrub the wound with soap and water/or disinfectant, try to have the animal captured (within limits) or at least determine its ownership where possible and seek medical assistance at once. The course of treatment depends on whether you have already been vaccinated against rabies. If you have (and this is worthwhile if you are spending lengths of time in developing countries) then some further doses of vaccine are all that is required. Human diploid cell vaccine is the best, but expensive: other, older kinds of vaccine such as that derived from duck embryos may be the only types available. These are effective, much cheaper and interchangeable generally with the human derived types. If not already vaccinated then anti-rabies serum (immunoglobulin) may be required in addition. It is wise to finish the course of treatment whether the animal survives or not.

Small-pox, cholera and yellow fever Vaccinations are not required. You may be asked for a certificate if you have been in a country affected by yellow fever immediately before travelling to Sri Lanka.

Children should, in addition, be properly protected against **diphtheria, whooping cough, mumps, measles** and **HIB**. Teenage girls should be given **rubella** (German measles) vaccination if they have not had the disease. Consult your doctor for advice on BCG inoculation against **tuberculosis**; the disease is still common in the region.

Further Information The following organizations give information regarding well trained English speaking physicians throughout the world: *International Association for Medical Assistance to Travellers*, 745 5th Ave, New York, 10022; *Intermedic 777*, Third Ave, New York, 10017; *MASTA*, T0891-224100, T020-76314408; *TRAVAX*, Glasgow, T0141-94671201 ext 247.

Further information on medical problems overseas can be obtained from the book by Richard Dawood (Editor) (1992) *Travellers' Health: How to Stay Healthy Abroad*, Oxford University Press, fourth edition.

Leeches

When trekking in the monsoon be aware of leeches. They usually stay on the ground waiting for a passerby and get in boots when you are walking. Then when they are gorged with blood they drop off.

Don't try pulling one off as the head will

be left behind and cause infection. Put some salt, or hold a lighted cigarette to it, which will make it quickly fall off. It helps to spray socks and bootlaces with an insect repellant before starting off in the morning.

On the road

Almost everyone suffers upset stomachs. Most of the time, intestinal upsets are due to the insanitary preparation of **food**. Undercooked fish, vegetables or meat (especially pork), fruit with the skin on (always peel your fruit yourself) or food that is exposed to flies (especially salads) are all highly risky.   **Intestinal upsets**

All unbottled **water** is probably unsafe, as is ice. Do not put ice cubes in drinks. If you have no choice but to drink dirty water, strain it through a filter bag (available from camping shops) and then boil or treat. Bringing the water to a rolling boil at sea level is sufficient but at high altitude you have to boil the water for longer to ensure that all the microbes are killed. Various sterilising methods can be used and there are proprietary preparations containing chlorine or iodine compounds.

Pasteurised or heat treated **milk** is now widely available, as is ice cream and yoghurt produced by the same methods. Unpasteurized milk products, including cheese, are sources of tuberculosis, brucellosis, listeria and food poisoning germs. You can render fresh milk safe by heating it to 62°C for 30 minutes, followed by rapid cooling or by boiling it. Matured or processed cheeses are safer than fresh varieties.

This is usually the result of food poisoning, occasionally from contaminated water. There are various causes – viruses, bacteria, protozoa (like amoeba), salmonella and cholera organisms. It may take one of several forms, coming on suddenly, or rather slowly. It may be accompanied by vomiting or by severe abdominal pain and the passage of blood or mucus when it is called dysentery. If you can time the onset of diarrhoea to the minute, then it is probably **viral** or **bacterial** and/or the onset of **dysentery**. If the diarrhoea has come on slowly or intermittently, then it is more likely to be **protozoal**, ie caused by amoeba or giardia and antibiotics will have no effect.   **Diarrhoea**

Treatment The lynch pins of treatment for diarrhoea are rest, fluid and salt replacement, antibiotics for the bacterial types and special diagnostic tests and medical treatment for amoeba and giardia infections. All kinds of diarrhoea, whether or not accompanied by vomiting respond favourably to the replacement of water and salts taken as frequent small sips of some kind of rehydration solution. There are proprietary preparations, consisting of sachets of powder which you dissolve in water, or you can make your own by adding half a teaspoonful of salt (3.5 g) and four tablespoonfuls of sugar (40 g) to a litre of boiled water. For **viral and bacterial diarrhoea rehydration** take **Ciprofloxacin**, 500 mgs every 12 hours. The drug is now widely available and seek medical help. For **protozoal diarrhoea rehydration** the following drugs may help if there are severe stomach cramps: Loperamide (Imodium, Arret) and Diphenoxylate with Atropine (Lomotil). Any diarrhoea continuing for more than three days should be treated by a doctor.

Salmonella infections & cholera

These can be devastating diseases: it would be wise to get to a hospital as soon as possible if these are suspected

Fasting, peculiar diets and the consumption of large quantities of yoghurt have not been found useful in calming travellers' diarrhoea or in rehabilitating inflamed bowels. Alcohol and milk may prolong diarrhoea and should be avoided during and immediately after an attack. Antibiotics taken before and during travel may help to prevent diarrhoea for short periods but these are ineffective against viruses and, to some extent, against protozoa, so this technique should only be used in exceptional circumstances. Some preventives such as Entero-vioform can have serious side effects if taken for long periods.

Heat & cold

Full acclimatisation to high temperatures takes about two weeks. Drink plenty of water (up to 15 litres a day can be needed if taking vigorous exercise), use salt on food and avoid extreme exertion. Tepid showers are more cooling than hot or cold ones.

Insects

Insects can be a great nuisance and some carry serious diseases. To ward off mosquitoes sleep off the ground with a mosquito net and burn Pyrethrum mosquito coils. Sprays and insecticidal tablets, heated on a mat plugged into the wall socket, are effective, as are personal insect repellents. The best contain a high concentration of Diethyltoluamide. Liquid is best for arms and face (take care around eyes and make sure you do not dissolve the plastic of your spectacles).

Aerosol spray on clothes and ankles deters mites and ticks. Liquid DEET suspended in water can be used to impregnate cotton clothes and mosquito nets. New style mosquito nets are wider-meshed and impregnated with permethrin (an insecticide). If you are bitten, itching may be relieved by cool baths and anti-histamine tablets (care with alcohol or driving), corticosteroid creams (great care - never use if any hint of sepsis). Calamine lotion and cream have limited effectiveness and anti-histamine creams have a tendency to cause skin allergies and are, therefore, not generally recommended.

Bites which become infected (common in the tropics) should be treated with a local antiseptic or antibiotic cream such as Cetrimide as should infected scratches. Skin infestations with body lice, crabs and scabies are unfortunately easy to pick up. Use Gamma benzene hexachloride for lice and Benzyl benzoate for scabies. Crotamiton cream alleviates itching and also kills a number of skin parasites. Malathion lotion 5% is good for lice but avoid the highly toxic full strength Malathion used as an agricultural insecticide.

Sunburn & heat stroke

The burning power of the tropical sun is phenomenal. Always wear a wide brimmed hat and use some form of sun cream or lotion on untanned skin. Always use high protection factor suntan lotions, designed specifically for the tropics or for mountaineers or skiers. Glare from the sun can cause conjunctivitis so wear sunglasses, especially on tropical beaches. There are several varieties of 'heat stroke'. The most common cause is severe dehydration. Avoid dehydration by drinking lots of non-alcoholic fluid. Put extra salt on your food.

Other risks & more serious diseases

AIDS In Sri Lanka AIDS is still rare but is increasing in its prevalence as in most countries, but with a pattern closer to that of developing societies. Heterosexual transmission is now the dominant mode and so the main risk to travellers is from casual sex. The same precautions should be taken as when encountering any sexually transmitted disease. The only way to determine whether you have been infected is by having a blood test for HIV antibodies at a place where there are reliable laboratory facilities. The test does not become positive for many weeks. Ensure that needles used for **injections** have been properly sterilised or that disposable needles are used. Hepatitis B is the main risk. Blood for transfusion should be screened for HIV but this cannot be guaranteed and remains a real risk. Be wary of carrying disposable needles yourself; customs officials may find them suspicious.

Malaria Malaria is a serious disease and is prevalent in Sri Lanka. Certain areas are badly affected, particularly by the highly dangerous falciparum strain. Malaria prevention is becoming more complex as the malaria parasite becomes immune to some of the older drugs. Some of the preventive drugs can cause side effects, especially if taken for long periods of time, so before you travel you must check with a reputable agency the likelihood and type of malaria in the countries which you intend to visit and take their advice on prophylaxis. Be prepared to receive conflicting advice. You can catch malaria even when taking prophylactic drugs, although it is unlikely. If you do develop symptoms (high fever, shivering, severe headache, sometimes diarrhoea) seek medical advice immediately. The current advice is:

Protect yourself against mosquito bites - cover up exposed skin at dusk, wear light coloured long-sleeved clothes and mosquito repellent cream or Gel, use a net to sleep under. It is now possible to buy light-weight impregnated nets such as the *Repel Trekker*. Enquire from your local travel shop, or in UK the British Airways Travel Shop or Ikea.

Take prophylactic (preventive) drugs. Start taking the tablets a few days before exposure and continue to take them six weeks after leaving the malarial zone ('Paludrine' is difficult to find in Sri Lanka).

Remember to give the drugs to babies, children and pregnant women also.

Seek up-to-date advice from the Malaria Reference Laboratory, T0891-600350 (recorded message, premium rate) or the Liverpool School of Tropical Medicine, T0151-7089393. In the USA, try Centre for Disease Control, Atlanta, T404-3324555.

Snake bite

Death from snake bite is very rare. If you are unlucky enough to be bitten by a venomous snake, spider, scorpion, centipede or sea creature try (within limits) to catch the animal for identification. The reactions to be expected are fright, swelling, pain and bruising around the bite, soreness of the regional lymph glands, nausea, vomiting and fever. If, in addition, any of the following symptoms occur get the victim to a doctor without delay: numbness, tingling of the face, muscular spasm, convulsions, shortness of breath or haemorrhage. Commercial snake bite or scorpion sting kits are only useful for the specific type of snake or scorpion for which they are designed. The serum has to be given intravenously. If the bite is on a limb, immobilise the limb and apply a tight bandage between the bite and the body, releasing it for 90 secs every 15 mins. Reassurance of the bitten person is very important because death from snake bite is, in fact, very rare. **Do not** slash the bite area and try to suck out the poison; this does more harm than good. Hospitals usually hold stocks of snake bite serum. Do not walk in snake territory with bare feet, sandals or shorts. Also good to make noise (eg by tapping a stick). Snakes are scared of humans.

Other risks & afflictions

Dengue fever is present in Sri Lanka. It is a virus disease, transmitted by mosquito bites, presenting with severe headache and body pains. Complicated types of dengue known as haemorrhagic fevers occur throughout Asia but usually in persons who have caught the disease a second time. Thus, although it is a very serious type, it is rarely caught by visitors. There is no treatment, you must just avoid mosquito bites.

Athlete's foot and other fungal infections are best treated by sunshine and a proprietary preparation such as Tolnaftate.

Influenza and **respiratory diseases** are common, perhaps made worse by polluted cities and rapid temperature and climatic changes.

Intestinal worms are common and the more serious ones, such as hook worm can be contracted by walking barefoot on infested earth or beaches.

Leishmaniasis This can be a serious disease taking several forms and transmitted by sand flies. These should be avoided in the same way as mosquitoes.

Prickly heat A very common itchy rash is avoided by frequent washing and by wearing loose clothing. It is helped by the use of talcum powder and/or Boroline ointment. Allow the skin to dry thoroughly after washing.

When you get home

If you have had attacks of diarrhoea, it is worth having a stool specimen tested in case you have picked up amoebic dysentery. If you have been living rough, a blood test may be worthwhile to detect worms and other parasites.

The information above was compiled for us by Dr David Snashall, Senior Lecturer in Occupational Health, United Medical Schools of Guy's and St Thomas' Hospitals and Chief Medical Adviser, Foreign and Commonwealth Office, London.

Further reading

Art & architecture **Archer, WG & Paranavitana, S** *Ceylon, paintings from Temple Shrine and Rock*; Paris, New York Graphic Soc, 1958. **Arumugam, S** *Ancient Hindu temples of Sri Lanka*; Colombo, 1982. **Basnayake, HT** *Sri Lankan Monastic architecture*; Delhi, Sri Satguru, 1986. A detailed account of Polonnaruwa. **Coomaraswamy, AK** *Medieval Sinhalese Art*; New York, Pantheon, 1956. **Godakumbure, CE** *Architecture of Sri Lanka*; Colombo, Department of Cultural Affairs Monograph, 1963. **Goonatilleke** *Masks and Mask Systems*. **Manjusri, LTP** *Design elements from Sri Lankan Temple Paintings*; Colombo, Archaeological Survey of Sri Lanka, 1977; a fine collection of line drawings from the 18th and 19th century, particularly of the Kandyan style. **Seneviratna, A** *The Temple of the Sacred Tooth Relic* Govt of Sri Lanka (State Engineering Corp), 1987. A well-illustrated survey of the various temples in ancient Sinhalese capitals that held the sacred relic, in addition to Kandy.

Current affairs & politics **Little, D** *Sri Lanka: the invention of enmity*; Washington: United States Institute of Peace Press, 1994; a recent attempt to provide a balanced interpetation of conflict in Sri Lanka. **Moore, MP** *The State and Peasant Politics in Sri Lanka*; London, 1985; an academic account of contemporary Sri Lankan political development. **McGowan, W** *Only man is vile: The Tragedy of Sri Lanka*; Picador, 1983; an account of the background to the 1983 Tamil-Sinhalese conflict.

History: pre-history & early history **Deraniyagala, SU** *The Prehistory of Sri Lanka*; Colombo: Department of Archaeological Survey of Sri Lanka, 2 Vols, 1992; an erudite and detailed account of the current state of research into pre-historic Sri Lanka, available in Colombo and at the Anuradhapura Museum.

History: medieval & modern **de Lanerolle, Nalini** *A Reign of Ten Kings*; Colombo, CTB, 1990. **de Silva, KM** *A History of Sri Lanka*; London, OUP, 1981; arguably the most authoritative historical account of Sri Lanka. **de Silva, RK and Beumer, WGM** *Illustrations and views of Dutch Ceylon*, 1988. Superbly illustrated. **Geiger, W** *Culture of Ceylon in Mediaeval times*; Wiesbaden, Harrassowitz, 1960. **Robinson, Francis** (ed) *Cambridge Encyclopedia of India, Pakistan, Bangladesh, Sri Lanka*; 1989, ed, Cambridge; excellent and readable introduction to many aspects of South Asian society.

Dissanayake, JB *Say it in Sinhala.*

Clarke, Arthur C *View from Serendib* (among many others), New York, Random House, 1977; a personal view from the prolific author who has made Sri Lanka his home. **Goonetileke, Hai** *Lanka, their Lanka*; New Delhi, Navrang, 1984; delightful cameos of Sri Lanka seen through the eyes of foreign travellers and writers. **Goonetilleke, DCRA,** Ed *The Penguin New Writing in Sri Lanka*; India, 1992. **Gunesekhara, Romesh** *Monkfish Moon*; Penguin; evocative collection of short stories of an island paradise haunted by violent undercurrents. *Reef*; Penguin, 1994; the story of a young boy growing up in modern Sri Lanka.

Muller, Carl *The Jam Fruit Tree* (the first of a trilogy) about the free-and-easy Burgers, and *Colombo*. **Obeyesekere, R & Fernando, C**, Eds *An anthology of modern writing from Sri Lanka*; Tucson, Arizona, 1981. **Ondaatje, Michael** Writing by modern novelist, including the amusing autobiographical *Running in the family*; Penguin, 1983. **Reynolds, CHB,** Ed *An anthology of Sinhalese Literature of the 20th century*; London, 1987.

Cordiner, James *A description of Ceylon*, an account of the country, inhabitants and natural productions, London, 1807, now reprinted by Colombo, Tisara Prakasakayo, 1983. **Beny, Rolf** *Island Ceylon*; London, Thames & Hudson, 1971; large coffee-table book with some excellent photos and illustrative quotes. **Brohier, RL** *Changing face of Colombo 1505-1972*; Lake House Colombo, Lake House, 1984; excellent history of Colombo. **Maloney, Clarence** *Peoples of South Asia*; New York, Holt, Rheinhart & Winston, 1974; a wide ranging and authoritative review, perhaps over-emphasising the Dravidian connection with Sri Lanka.

Malangoda, K *Buddhism in Sinhalese Society, 1750-1900*; Berkeley, 1976. **Perera, HR** *Buddhism in Ceylon, Past and Present*; Kandy, Buddhist Publication Soc, 1966. **Qureshi, IH** *The Muslim Community of the Indo-Pakistan Sub-Continent 610-1947*; Karachi, OAP, 1977. **Stutley, Margaret and James** *Dictionary of Hinduism*; London, Routledge Kegan Paul, 1977. *Dictionary of Buddhism.*

Handbook for the Ceylon Traveller; 2nd ed, Studio Times, Colombo, 1983; a good collection of essays from many writers (who live in and plainly love the island) about people, places and everything Sri Lankan. Now dated, but many interesting insights. **Anderson, JG**, ed *Insight Guide to Sri Lanka*; 6th ed, APA, 1995; some excellent text articles and good photographs, some inaccuracies especially with updating since 1991. **Hatt, John** *The tropical traveller: the essential guide to travel in hot countries*; 3rd ed 1992; excellent, wide ranging and clearly written common sense, based on extensive experience and research. **Leestemaker, J**, and others *Trekkers' guide to Sri Lanka*; Colombo, Trekking Unlimited, 1994. A well described selection of popular (and some off-the-beaten-track) treks and walks, pointing out wildlife and interesting features, and with maps to help.

Bond, Thomas *Wild Flowers to the Ceylon Hills*; OUP, 1953. **de Silva Wijeyeratne, G,** and others **Harrison, John & Worfolk, Tim** *A field guide to the birds of Sri Lanka.* OUP. *A bird-watcher's guide to Sri Lanka*; Oriental Bird Club, The Lodge, Sandy, Beds, UK, 1997; a good, illustrated leaflet giving all you need to know about the numerous reserves on the island. **The Pica traveller Sri Lanka**. Pica Press, UK. Covers wildlife in general and also cultural sites. **Henry, GM** *Guide to the birds of Ceylon*; 3rd ed. OUP, India. 1978. **Munro, Ian** *Marine and Fresh water fishes of Ceylon*; Canberra, Australian Department of External Affairs, 1955. **Wijesinghe, DP** *Checklist of birds of Sri Lanka*; Colombo, Ceylon Bird Club, 1994. **Woodcock, Martin** *Handguide to Birds of the Indian Sub-Continent*; Collins, London.

Language

Literature

Essentials

People & places

Religion

Travel

Natural history

Maps The *Road Map of Sri Lanka* (scale 1:500,000), Rs 50, published by the Survey Department, is adequate for those planning to hire a car to see the principal sights around the island. Partly revised in 1993, it doesn't include changes in the last few years. The small insets of places of tourist interest lack detail, however; these places are all covered in this Handbook with far greater information. For more detail the department's four large sheet maps cover the island, 1992 (scale 1:250,000); they are the best available. However, for security reasons most large scale maps and town plans are not for sale without the Surveyor General. You may ask to consult these at the Survey Department, Map Sales Branch, Kirula Rd, Narahenpita, Colombo, T585111, and a few at the Map Sales Centre, York St (opp *Hilton Hotel*), Colombo 1, T435328. *Arjuna's Atlas of Sri Lanka*. Arjuna, 1997 (arjunaco@slt.lk) A comprehensive demographic survey of Sri Lanka. The *National Atlas of Sri Lanka*, 1988, also published by the Survey Department, is a superb large format colour atlas with excellent text and maps. Ceylon Tourist Board, 80 Galle Rd, Colombo 3, T437059, F440001, www.lanka.net/ctb, and some of their offices abroad, give out a Sri Lanka itinerary map plus several city and site guides with sketch maps, free, but these are not particularly clear. Nelles Verlag 1:450,000 *Sri Lanka*, is conventional with four city insets. The new Sarvodaya Vishva Lekha (41 Lumbini Ave, Ratmalana, T722932, F722932) is 1:500,000. It has four fold-outs in a handy format with added advantage of an index, but does not include small towns everywhere. *Sri Lanka* road map by Berndtson and Berndtson is nicely laminated and includes maps of Colombo, Anuradhapure, Polonnaruwa and Kandy.

Colombo Numerous single sheet maps are available. Two booklets are more useful: the *A to Z Atlas and Street Index*, 1:12,500, 1989, Rs 50, from the Survey Department is the most detailed and accurate; *A-Z Street Guide*, 1994, Rs 295, published by Arjuna, Dehiwala, includes Colombo surrounds plus Anuradhapura, Kandy, Nuwara Eliya and Polonnaruwa, but lacks the accuracy of the *A to Z*.

Colombo and nearby beaches

3

Colombo and nearby beaches

62   Ins and outs

62   Central Colombo

70   Parks and zoos

70   Essentials

84   **Mount Lavinia**

88   **Beaches near Colombo**

89   **Negombo**

90   Sights

97   **Beaches north of Negombo**

97   Waikkal

97   Marawila

Colombo has no pretensions. It is the island's only metropolitan city and the country's commercial heart. It is crowded with traffic and sprawling. In the neighbourhood of the fort however some impressive red brick and whitewashed buildings survive giving a visitor a sense of its colonial origins. To the east are the criss-cross of narrow lanes of the heavily congested Pettah district with its more atmospheric and colourful bazars. South, the main Galle road run straight as a die, parallel with the coast but lined with shops and offices. West and north the roads quickly enter the coconut shaded suburbs of a more "local" Colombo.

The pleasant suburb of Mount Lavinia with its narrow strip of beach lure city dwellers out but the bulk of foreigner visitors are attracted to Negombo beach to the north of Colombo because of its convenient closeness to the international airport.

A foot in the door

★ Wander across Galle Face Green in the early evening to watch the city at play, buzzing with hawkers, kite-flyers, impromptu games of cricket and colourful food stalls.

★ Enjoy the quiet stillness of the botanical garden at the Vihara Mahadevi Park and gain an insight into Sri Lankan culture in the National Museum there.

★ Capture the Dutch past at the Wolfendahl Church and the Dutch Period Museum in the Pettah.

★ Marvel at the spectacle of the January festivities at the Raja Mahavihara Temple in Kelaniya.

★ Be transported to the 1870s and Governor Barnes' opulent lifestyle by visiting Mount Lavinia Hotel.

Ins and outs

Getting there Virtually all visitors to Colombo arrive by air at the international airport at Katunayake about 30 km north of the city and 6 km from Negombo. There are regular buses to Colombo which take an hour (Rs 20) as well as pre-paid van taxis and more expensive a/c cabs. Trains leave from the station about 500 m away (see page 44).

Getting around The city is quite spread out so you will need transport. The fort area itself is fairly compact and small enough to walk around and short hops by tuk-tuk should cost no more than Rs 50. Radio Cabs are a reliable alternative and quite afford-able if you can share one. Several streets in the fort area are blocked or have strict security checks so it is often impossible for transport to take the most obvious route.

Orientation Colombo remains the commercial capital of the country although the administrative capital was moved to the new city of Sri Jayawardenepura-Kotte in 1982. The official limits of Colombo itself are quite confined, stretching just over 6 km south from the Kelaniya River and under 5 km east from the coast. However, the built up area now straggles indeterminately along all the major roads radiating from the centre, and it is difficult to tell where the city really begins and ends. Before the new harbour was built the centre of upper class Colombo was 3 km north of the fort at Mutwal. Little remains from that period, and the city has grown south and east.

History Sheltered from the southwest monsoon by a barely perceptible promontory jutting out into the sea, Colombo's bay was an important site for Muslim traders before the colonial period. However, it is essentially a colonial city, whose rise to pre-eminence did not start until the 19th century and the establishment of British power. Before that it was a much less important town than Galle, but when the British took control of Kandy and encouraged the development of commercial estates, the island's economic centre of gravity moved north. The capital, Colombo, offered two easy routes into the Kandyan highlands.

Central Colombo

While the fort is the centre of Colombo's modern commercial activity, the Pettah (in Tamil 'pettai' means suburb and in Sinhalese 'pitakotuwa' means outer fort) is the hub of its traditional markets.

Fort area The **fort**, no more than 500 sq m, lies immediately south of the harbour. Little remains from either the Portuguese or Dutch periods. As the main commercial area of Colombo it is dominated by tower blocks with the area around York Street and Sir Baron Jayatilleke housing many large banks, airline offices and

Colombo Harbour

The growth in shipping passing through Colombo during the early 20th century reflected the advantages of Colombo's position on the Indian Ocean Sea route between Europe, the Far East and Australasia. However, the city also benefited from its focal position on the rapidly expanding transport system within the island. After 1832 the British had encouraged the rapid development of a road network which radiated from Colombo. In the late 19th century this was augmented by an expanding rail network. Since Independence it has retained its dominant position.

The harbour facilities are quite large and it remains the chief port. There are usually a large number of ships waiting to enter the harbour. Colombo's small promontory offered little protection for larger ships, so in the later 19th century the British started work on a series of breakwaters which were to provide an effective harbour round the year. The southwest breakwater, over 1,000 m long, was completed in 1885. It has the pilot station at its head. The northeast breakwater, a rubble embankment 350 m long, was completed in 1902, followed in 1907 by the northwest breakwater. As this breakwater has no land connection it forms an artificial `island'. Overall the breakwaters enclose an area of 3 sq km, more than 8 m deep. There are, however, no beaches and the sea is quite dangerous.

Phone code: 01
Population: 2.1 mn
Altitude: sea level

Colombo & nearby beaches

travel agents. The whole area has adopted a siege mentality following the continuing problem with separatist bombings of government targets.

Marine Drive runs down the coast to the *Intercontinental Hotel* and across the wide open space of the Galle Face. Immediately inland of its northern section is the narrow road now called Galle Buck, an English corruption of the old name Gal Bokka – rocky belly.

Galle Face Green is the area between the mouth of the canal feeding Beira Lake and the *Galle Face Hotel* has been redeveloped with new walls and paved areas. It is very popular with Sri Lankans who come to walk and relax so there are lots of food stalls and hawkers selling knick-knacks kites and children's toys.

Be on guard for the inevitable pick-pockets, especially at night when the whole area really comes alive

From the northern end of Marine Drive, Church Street runs east, past **St Peter's Church** on the right. Part of the former residence of Dutch Governors, the Church **cemetery** contains the tombs of several British residents, including William Tolfrey (1778-1817), an army officer and the first translator of the Bible into Pali and Sinhalese. The nave of the church was originally a reception and banqueting hall, first converted into a church in 1804 and consecrated in 1821.

To the east is the **Grand Oriental Hotel**, from which York Street, one of the main shopping areas, runs due south. Half way down it is Sir Baron Jayatilleke Mawatha, the main banking street. Nearly all the buildings are in red brick. Hospital Street, running west at the south end of York Street, is a lively centre of low-cost restaurants, fruit sellers, and pavement merchants.

Running south from Church Street to the west of St Peter's Church is **Janadhipathi Mawatha** (formerly Queen Street). At the northern end are **Gordon Gardens**, with a statue of Queen Victoria and a stone bearing the Portuguese Coat of Arms. Threats of terrorist violence have led to entry to the Gordon Gardens being restricted, as it lies in Republic Square, alongside the offices of the Prime Minister and Cabinet. The northern end of Janadhipathi Mawatha is normally closed to the public. Colombo is not graced with many fine buildings, but the white-washed **GPO**, on the east side of Janadhipathi Mawatha is a good example of Victorian colonial building heavily inspired by Greek classicism. Opposite it is the **President's House**, (*Janadhipathi*

Mandiraya). The **Standard Chartered Bank**, another imposing commercial structure, is decorated with reliefs of elephants.

The statue in front of the President's House is of the 19th-century British Governor Edward Barnes. An adjutant of the Duke of Wellington during the Battle of Waterloo, in Sri Lanka he is better known for building the Colombo-Kandy road. His statue is the point from which the distances of all towns in Sri Lanka from Colombo are measured. Just to the south again is the **Lighthouse Clock Tower** (1837), now replaced as a lighthouse by the new tower on Marine Drive. Sir Baron Jayatilleke Mawatha runs east, immediately

Colombo

N

0 metres 500
0 yards 500

Related maps
A Fort & Pettah,
page 66
B Galle Face & Union
Place, page 68
C Kollupitiya & ward
place, page 72
D Bambalapitiya,
page 74

■ **Sleeping**
1 Big John Guest House
2 Brighton
3 Ceylon Inn
4 Janaki
5 Rawanlanka
6 Sapphire
7 Trans Asia & Pastry Shop
8 YMBA

Slave Island

The high rise hotels and offices which have occupied the northward jutting peninsula in Beira Lake facing the fort now leave no trace of the earlier uses of what was known as Slave Island. 'Island' was a misnomer, but slaves played a very real part in the colonial history of Colombo.

Brohier has recorded how in the Dutch period this tongue of open land was known as Kaffir Veldt. The Kaffirs – Africans from the East Coast around Mozambique – were brought to Sri Lanka for the first time by the Portuguese from Goa in 1630. When the Dutch ousted the Portuguese they made use of the slave labour force to build the fort

in Colombo, when there may have been 4,000 of them. Their numbers grew, but after an unsuccessful insurrection in the 18th century the Dutch authorities decided to insist that all slave labour must be identifiably accommodated. The Kaffir Veldt was the nearest open space on which special shanty houses could be built, and a nightly roll call would be held to ensure that every slave was there.

In 1807 Cordiner reported that the number of slaves had fallen to 700, but the British did not abolish slavery in Sri Lanka until 1845. Nonetheless, the name Slave Island has persisted.

north of the GPO, with a number of impressive commercial buildings, including a good example of inter-war architecture in the Bank of India.

East of the *Grand Oriental Hotel* is the Central YMCA, next to the Moors Islamic Cultural Home in Bristol Street. Across Duke Street is the Young Men's Buddhist Association. The shrine houses a noted modern image of the Buddha. The Fort Mosque, in a Dutch period building, is to the south on Chatham Street.

The Pettah To the north and east of Fort Station is a busy market area with stalls lining Olcott Mawatha and Bodhiraja Mawatha, making pedestrian movement slow and tedious at times. The central area of Pettah, bounded by these two roads as well as Main Street and Front Street, are quieter with many wholesale outlets. Specialist streets house craftsmen and traders, eg goldsmiths (Sea Street), fruit and vegetable dealers (the end of Main Street) and ayurvedic herbs and medicines (Gabo's Lane). In the market area to the north, Arabs, Portuguese, Dutch and British once traded.

At the southeastern edge of the Pettah is the Fort Railway Station. Half way along Main Street on the left-hand side after 2nd Cross Street is the **Jami-ul-Alfar Mosque** with its interesting white and red brick façade but little of architectural interest inside.

At the end of Main Street, Central Road goes east from a large roundabout, just north of the market. A left turn off Central Road immediately after the roundabout, Brass Founder Street, leads to a right fork, Ratnajothi Saravana Mawatha, formerly Wolfendahl Street. At the end is the **Wolfendahl Church**. Built in 1749 on the site of an earlier Portuguese church, it is prominently placed on a hill, where its massive cruciform shape stands out, commanding a view over the harbour. Its Doric façade is solid and heavy, and inside it has many tombstones and memorial tablets to Dutch officials. It is the most interesting surviving Dutch monument in Sri Lanka.

To its northeast is **Santa Lucia**, the Roman Catholic cathedral, in some people's eyes the most remarkable church building in Sri Lanka. It is a huge grey structure with a classical façade and a large forecourt. Begun in 1876 it was completed in 1910. Inside are the tombs of three French bishops but little else of interest. The Pope conducted a service here during his visit in 1994. **Christ Church**, the Anglican Cathedral, is just to the northwest, the main church in a diocese which dates from 1845.

To the south in New Moor Street is the **Grand Mosque**, a modern building in the style, as one critic puts it, of a modern international airport covered in metallic paint.

Also in the Pettah are three modest Hindu temples, of little architectural interest, but giving an insight into Hindu building style and worship. Perhaps the most striking is that of **Sri Ponnambula Vanesvara** at 38 Sri Ramanathan Road. The *gopuram* (gateway) has typical sculptures of gods from the Hindu pantheon. A Siva lingam is in the innermost shrine, with a Nandi bull in front and a dancing Siva (*Nataraja*) to one side, see page 304.

In **Borella**, 6 km east of the fort, the modest building of the Gautama Vihara contains impressive modern murals depicting the life of the Buddha by the Sri Lankan artist George Keyt.

Fort & Pettah

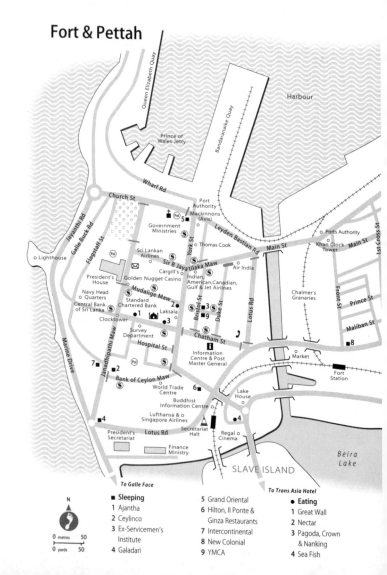

■ Sleeping	5 Grand Oriental	● Eating
1 Ajantha	6 Hilton, Il Ponte &	1 Great Wall
2 Ceylinco	Ginza Restaurants	2 Nectar
3 Ex-Servicemen's	7 Intercontinental	3 Pagoda, Crown
Institute	8 New Colonial	& Nanking
4 Galadari	9 YMCA	4 Sea Fish

A further 13 km northeast across the Kelaniya River is the **Raja Maha Vihara**, the most visited Buddhist temple in Sri Lanka, after the Temple of the Tooth in Kandy. In the 13th century Kelaniya was an impressive city but for Buddhists its chief attraction today is the legendary visit of the Buddha to the site. The *Mahavansa* recorded that the original stupa enshrined a gem-studded throne on which the Buddha sat when he supposedly visited Sri Lanka. Ultimately destroyed by the Portuguese, the present dagoba is in the shape of a 'heap of paddy'. The first city on the site was believed to have been built by King Yatala Tissa. According to legend this was destroyed by a flood from the sea which was a punishment given to the king for mistreating the Buddhist *sangha*. He tried to placate the sea by setting his daughter afloat on a golden boat. Having drifted ashore in the south of the island she married King Kavan Tissa, and became the mother of one of Sri Lanka's great heroes, King Dutthagamenu.

The city is subsequently believed to have been destroyed by Tamil invasions, and was only re-built in the 13th century by King Vijayabahu. The present temple dates from about 1300. There is a famous image of the reclining Buddha, but there are also many images of Hindu deities. *Duruthu Perahera* in January every year, draws thousands of pilgrims from all over the island.

Colombo Centre

Inland and parallel with Galle Road runs RA de Mel Mawatha (formerly Duplication Road), built up all the way south. East of Kollupitiya station, Ananda Coomaraswamy Mawatha leads to the attractive Vihara Mahadevi Park with the museums and art gallery to its south, and further east the most prestigious residential area of Colombo, **Cinnamon Gardens** – widely referred to by its postal code, Colombo 7. Broad roads and shaded avenues make it a very attractive area. A series of rectangular lakes to the east of the park leads to a golden statue of the seated Buddha. The impressive Town Hall, the 'White House' on Kannangara Mawatha, stands in the north-east corner of the park. It was completed in 1927. At the De Soysa Circus roundabout is an equally interesting red-brick building, the Victoria Memorial Rooms built around the end of the 19th century.

N H M Abdul Cader Rd (Sea Beach Rd)

Sea St

o Colombo Central Supermarket

Gabo's Lane

Bankshall St

Jami-ud-Alfar   24hr

Main St

Keyzer St

3rd Cross St

People's o Supermarket

PETTAH

Dutch Period Museum

2nd Cross St

4th Cross St

5th Cross St

Bodhiraja Maw

Saunders Place

3

1

Toilets o

Olcott Maw

Manning Market

E W Bastian Maw

2

D R Wijewardana Maw

Bus stands
1 CTB
2 Bastian Maw
3 Peoples Park/
   Saunders Place

— Barrier

South Colombo

There are some attractive walks and drives to the south of the fort area and Beira Lake. Galle Road runs almost due south across the windswept open space of the Galle Face, gradually moving away from the sea southwards, and separated from it by the railway. The areas of Kollupitiya and Bambalapitiya are busy commercial centres with the large shopping malls of Unity Plaza and Majestic City. Galle Road continues through Dehiwala with its zoo towards the suburb of Mount Lavinia and the coastal resorts further south. Near the busy bazar of Dehiwala, the **Subbodaramaya Temple** is a Buddhist complex with a shrine room dating from 1795. There is the usual dagoba, a Bo-tree and also a 'Seven-Week House' which illustrates the weeks following the Buddha's enlightenment. There are several Buddha statues, some well preserved wall paintings and wood carvings but the most arresting figure is the supremely serene 4.5 m reclining Buddha with eyes set in blue sapphires.

Sri Jayawardene pra-Kotte Built in the shadow of the modern city of Colombo, most government offices have relocated in this new artificially planned capital 11 km southeast, but Colombo still retains its importance as the commercial capital. The decision to put the new 'Parliament' here was based partly on the fact that the site was formerly the almost sacred territory of Kotte, the ancient capital of Sri Lanka under Alakeswara who built a large fortress and defeated the Tamil leader Chakravarthi. Parakramabahu VI (ruled 1412-1467), transformed the fortress into a prosperous modern city, building a magnificent 3-storey temple to hold the Tooth relic which he had placed within several bejewelled gold caskets.

Galle Face & Union Place

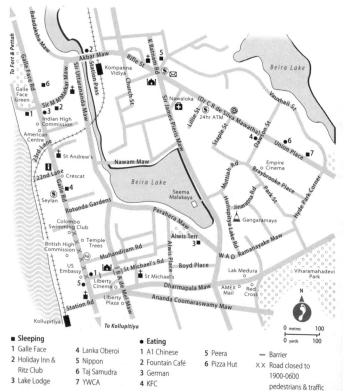

■ Sleeping
1 Galle Face
2 Holiday Inn & Ritz Club
3 Lake Lodge
4 Lanka Oberoi
5 Nippon
6 Taj Samudra
7 YWCA

● Eating
1 A1 Chinese
2 Fountain Café
3 German
4 KFC
5 Peera
6 Pizza Hut

— Barrier
X X Road closed to 1900-0600 pedestrians & traffic

However subsequent weak rulers left the city relatively defenceless and it fell easy prey to the Portuguese. They destroyed the city so that there are no traces of its former glory left. Some panels from the old temple can be seen in the Colombo museum. ■ *Getting there: the drive from Colombo's Fort area through the suburbs takes about 30 mins.*

Parliament Building The impressive new Parliament Building, designed by the renowned modern Sri Lankan architect Geoffrey Bawa, stands in the middle of a lake surrounded by parkland. It is heavily fortified and not open to the public.

The **Gramodaya Folk Arts Centre** has craftsmen working with brass, silver, leather, coir and producing jewellery, pottery, natural silk, lace and reed baskets. There is a craft shop and a restaurant serving Sri Lankan specialities. Ask at the tourist office for details.

Museums

National Museum There is a statue of Sir William Gregory, governor 1872-77, in front of the imposing façade. Opened in 1877, it has a very interesting collection of paintings, sculptures, furniture, porcelain and Kandyan regalia. The library houses a unique collection of over 4,000 *Ola* (palm manuscripts) – an extremely rich archaeological and artistic collection. Very well labelled and organized, a visit is an excellent introduction to a tour of Sri Lanka. Exhibits include an outstanding collection of 10th-12th century bronzes from Polonnaruwa, and the lion throne of King Nissankamalla, which has become the symbol of Sri Lanka. There are interesting details and curiosities, eg the origin of Kolam dancing is traced back to the pregnancy craving of the Queen of the legendary King Maha Samnatha! The ground floor displays Buddhist and Hindu sculptures, including a striking 1,500 year old stone statue of the Buddha from Toluvila. `Demon-dance' masks line the stairs to the first floor. One visitor noted, "These are more 'satire' than 'demon' in nature, with lots of characters of court officials, soldiers and 'outsiders' such as Muslims. Some were very elaborate and capable of moving their eyes etc. It is interesting to see how these evolved as different fashions swept the court." The first floor has superb scale reproductions of the wall paintings at Sigiriya and Polonnaruwa. Other exhibits include ancient jewellery and carvings in ivory and wood. ■ *0900-1700, closed Fri and public holidays. Entry Rs 55, children RS 30 (Bus 114, 138). 8 Marcus Fernando Mawatha, (Albert Crescent), T694767.*

Natural History Museum It has good natural history and geological galleries. ■ *0900-1700, closed Fri and public holidays. Entry Rs 35, children Rs 20. Entered via the National Museum or from A Coomeraswamy Mawatha, T694767.*

Dutch Period Museum Originally the residence of the Dutch governor, Thomas van Rhae (1692-97), it was sold to the VOC before becoming the Colombo seminary in 1696. This ceased in 1796 when it was handed over to the British who turned it into a Military Hospital and later into a Post Office. Now it has been restored and offers a fascinating insight to the Dutch period. The museum surrounds a garden courtyard and has various rooms dedicated to different aspects of Dutch life including some interesting old tomb stones. Upstairs, several rooms have Dutch period furniture on display. These are not always open and you may have to ask the curator to show you around.

■ *0900-1700. Entry Rs 55 for foreigners, camera Rs 135, closed Fri and public holidays. Prince Street, Pettah, T448466. Allow 30 minutes.*

Bandaranaike Museum. Devoted to the life and times of the late prime minister. ■ *0900-1600, closed Mon and Poya holidays, Rs 3. Bauddhaloka Mawatha.*

National Art Gallery Small permanent collection, mainly portraits. ■ *0900-1800, closed Poya days, Sun and public holidays. Free. 106 Ananda Coomaraswamy Mawatha.*

Municipal Council Museum, in the Town Hall courtyard, Pettah, for those interested in the city's history (eg steam-powered rubbish vans).

Gangaramaya Buddhist Temple Museum Rare carvings, gold and silver articles, library, plus elephants! ■ *0500-2300, entry $1. 61 Sri Jinaratana Rd, Colombo 2 (southeast of Beira Lake), T327084, F439508.*

Parks and zoos

Dehiwala Zoo is one of the most attractive in Asia. It is very crowded on holidays. The 15 ha of undulating ground is beautifully laid out with shrubs, flowering trees and plants, orchids, lakes and fountains. There are over 2,000 animals include sloth bear, leopard, civets and other small cats, many kinds of lizard, crocodiles and snakes. Lions, tigers, jaguars, black panthers, and many exotic species such as hippopotami, rhinos, giraffes and kangaroos. The aquarium has over 500 species of fish. The zoo is particularly noted for its collection of birds. Sea-lions perform at 1600 and a troupe of trained elephants, around 1715. The restaurant is quite expensive. ■ *Entry Rs 25 (Sri Lankans) Rs 150 (foreigners), still camera free, video camera Rs 100. A Dharmapala Mawatha (Allan Ave), 10 km southwest from the centre, T7127510830-1800. Getting there: bus No 100, 155 (to Dehiwala Junction and walk the last km) or get 118, also train to Dehiwala Station.*

Vihara Mahadevi Park (formerly Victoria Park), on the site of the old Cinnamon Gardens, was re-named after the mother of the Sinhalese King Dutthagamenu. Early morning is an excellent time to visit (opens 0700). A botanical garden, including named species, it has a range of tropical trees, including a Bo tree, ebony, mahogany, *sal* and lemon eucalyptus which attract a wide variety of birds. There is also an enormous profusion of climbing and parasitic plants as well as rare orchids. The park is particularly colourful in the spring. You may catch sight of elephants which are bathed in the water tank to the southwest.

Essentials

Sleeping Those arriving late or departing early may prefer to find a hotel close to the international airport at **Katunayake** (30 km north of Colombo). Not all offer a free transfer to the airport. Another alternative is to stay at Negombo, some 6 km north of the airport, where the accommodation choice is much wider, see page 91. For Mount Lavinia see page 85.

Expensive A *Airport Garden*, 234 Negombo Rd, Seeduwa, 2 km towards Colombo (request airport pick-up, about Rs 200), T252950, F252953. 120 rooms, bath tubs, set back from main road, pool, watersports on lagoon, plush and convenient. **Mid-range C** *Goodwood Plaza* and *Orient Pearl*, Canada Friendship Rd, 1 km from airport (from terminal, cross the road, and turn right towards Colombo), T252356,

F252562. 32 rooms in each, most a/c, twin hotels (former marginally better) with large rooms off long corridors, some refurbished to a good standard, reasonable restaurants, Colombo and Negombo buses pass the hotel, free airport transfer (driver may insist it is not free). **C-D** *Sirimedura*, 842 Negombo Rd, Ambalanmulla, Seeduwa, 8 km from airport, T236632, F236614. 40 rooms (28 a/c), coffee shop, pool. **D** *Airlink*, 580 Negombo Rd, Seeduwa, 5 km from airport, towards Colombo, T253607, F253664. 11 simple rooms with bath, 2 a/c, 24-hr meals brought in. **Cheap** **F** *Mrs Jayatillake's*, Minuwangoda Rd (5 km from airport), T253031. 3 simple rooms, meals on request.

Fort and Pettah area **Expensive** **L** *Colombo Hilton*, 67 Lotus Rd, Echelon Sq, Col 1, T344644, F544657 hilton@sri.lanka.net 387 rooms fully refurbished, best views in the city, all facilities including 7 restaurants, sports, riding, nightclub (Rs 500 for non-members, ladies free), real sense of luxury. Recommended. **AL** *Galadari*, 64 Lotus Rd, Col 1, T544544, F449875 galadari@sri.lanka.net 446 rooms with good views, all facilities, good nightclub, inefficient reception. **AL** *Transasia*, 115 Sir CA Gardiner Mawatha, Slave Island, Col 2, T544200, F449184 tah_asia@sri.lanka.net 358 rooms, 25 suites ($300+), 3 speciality restaurants, excellent pool, nightclub, "exceptional hotel". **A** *Intercontinental*, 48 Janadhipathi Mawatha, Fort, Col 1, T421221, F326887, colombo@interconti.com 217 fully equipped rooms with good views, good pool, open-air Pearl seafood restaurant, good bookshop. **B** *Grand Oriental*, 2 York St, Fort, Col 1, T320391, F447640. 62 rooms (ask for deluxe), Old colonial era hotel built to accommodate travellers arriving by sea, faded feel but good value, excellent views of the docks from Harbour Room restaurant (no photography), nightclub (Fri and Sat Rs 300, ladies free), friendly staff. Recommended. **Cheap** **E-G** *YMCA (Central)*, 39 Bristol St, Fort, Col 1, T325252. 40 untidy rooms (Rs 400 common bath, Rs 650 attached), dorm (Rs 100), nominal membership, returnable deposit Rs 100, cafeteria serving simple local food. **G** *Ex-Servicemen's Institute*, 29 Bristol St, Fort, Col 1, T422650. 10-bed mixed dorm for foreigners, Rs 185, another for Sri Lankans, fans, safe, TV lounge/bar area, simple meals, friendly. Recommended. There are several **F** and **G** hotels in the area around Fort Railway Station. They are basic and unused to dealing with foreigners. You might try **F** *New Colonial*, opposite Fort Station, T323074. 7 singles (Rs 250) 5 doubles (Rs 450), all common bath, all right for a night if catching an early train.

Galle Face Green area **Expensive** **L** *Lanka Oberoi*, 77 Steuart Place, off Galle Rd, *See map on page 68* Col 3, T437437, F449280 lkoberoi.bc@netgate.mega.lk 600 smallish rooms, most with city views, some with sea or lake views (currently being refurbished) with unimaginative approach. All facilities, 2 restaurants, nightclub (Rs 350, ladies free), good pool (non-residents pay Rs 500), and a pool for crows! **AL** *Taj Samudra*, 25 Galle Face Centre Road, T446622, F446348 taj@sri.lanka.net 400 comfortable rooms some with good views (but some tired and dirty), 6 restaurants (excellent Chinese), nightclub (Thu, Fri and Sat Rs 250, ladies free). Good pool (non-residents against annual fee only), friendly service. **A** *Holiday Inn*, 30 Sir MM Markar Mawatha, Col 3, T422001, F447977 holiday@sri.lanka.net 100 reasonable rooms, executive floor, very good Mughlai food at *Alhambra* restaurant, large pool (open to non-residents, Rs 175). Recommended. **A-B** *Galle Face*, 2 Galle Rd, Col 3, T541010, F541072, gfhrsvn@itmin.com 80 rooms ($35-75 according to view, from none to ocean!), 70 more refurbished, westernized menu, (Edward Lear described it in 1874 as "a very nasty, second rate place, now much improved!"), still retains colonial atmosphere, splendid old lift takes you up but you have to walk down! Friendly (though rather casual) staff, pleasant pool overlooking Indian Ocean (non-residents pay Rs 200), verandah bar best in Colombo for sunset drink, very competent travel desk. Recommended.

Mid-price **C** *Nippon*, Manning Mansions, 123, Kumaran Ratnam Rd, Col 2, T431887, F33260. 30 rooms, mostly a/c, TV extra Rs 300, bar, good Oriental restaurants, old colonial style. **D** *YWCA International Guest House*, 392 Union Place, Col 2, T324181. 20 rooms (breakfast included) in Dutch colonial mansion set in attractive gardens, accepts men, women and couples, large rooms with bath but a bit pricey, good meals available, friendly, clean. **D-E** *Lake Lodge*, 20 Alwis Terrace, Col 3, T326443, F434997. 16 rooms, mostly a/c, breakfast included, some overlooking lake, good Sri Lankan food, quiet but could be cleaner.

Kollupitiya, Ward Place and Bambalapitiya Expensive B *Renuka & Renuka City*, 328 Galle Rd, T573598, F574137 renukaht@panlanka.net Twin hotels with 80 comfortable a/c rooms ($50-55), TV, fridge, IDD phone, 3 bars, pool, basement *Palmyrah* restaurant recommended for Sri Lankan curries. **Mid-range C** *Empress*, 383 RA de Mel Mawatha Col 3, T574930, F574931. 33 grubby a/c rooms with TV but good Korean restaurant. **C** *Janaki*, 43 Fife Rd, Col 5, T502169, F589139. 70 reasonable a/c rooms, be prepared for 'Fawlty Towers' style meal service (!), pool (open to non-residents). **C-D** *Colombo House*, 26 Charles Way, off Bagatelle Rd, Col 3, T574900, F574901 colombohse@eureka.lk 4 large rooms (2 a/c for extra Rs 350), very quiet

Kollupitiya & Ward Place

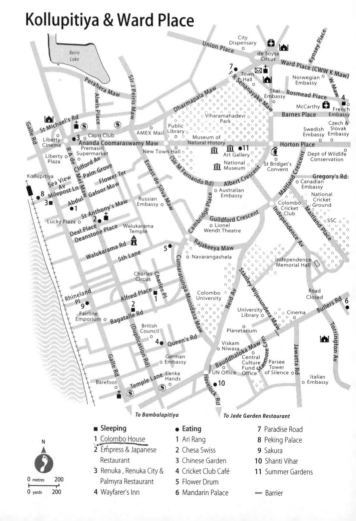

■ Sleeping	● Eating	7 Paradise Road
1 Colombo House	1 Ari Rang	8 Peking Palace
2 Empress & Japanese Restaurant	2 Chesa Swiss	9 Sakura
3 Renuka, Renuka City & Palmyra Restaurant	3 Chinese Garden	10 Shanti Vihar
4 Wayfarer's Inn	4 Cricket Club Café	11 Summer Gardens
	5 Flower Drum	
	6 Mandarin Palace	— Barrier

N

0 metres   200
0 yards   200

location in colonial house set in leafy suburb. Recommended. **D** *Wayfarer's Inn*, 77 Rosmead Place near Town Hall, Cinnamon Gardens, Col 7, T693936, F686288, wayfarer@slt.lk 2 guesthouse rooms (a/c extra), meals on order, nice garden, pool. **Cheap E** *Ottery Tourist Inn*, 29 Melbourne Ave, Col 4, T588727, off Galle Rd. 7 large rooms (Rs 500), breakfasts, rather run down but quiet location, friendly and helpful owner. **G** *Sri Lanka Youth Council*, 50 Haig Rd, Col 4, T581028. 18-bed male dorm, 12-bed female dorm (Rs 125 in bunk beds), 1 **E** triple (Rs 500), discounts for ISIC and IYHA card holders, maximum 3-day stay, can get crowded but friendly and cheap.

Welawatta Expensive B *Sapphire*, 371 Galle Rd, Col 6, T583306, F503575. 40 comfortable a/c rooms, attached bath (TV and fridge available), rooftop Chinese restaurant, private beach restaurant (*La Lavinia*), bar. **Mid-range D** *Brighton*, 57 Ramakrishna Rd, Col 6, T585211. 62 rooms in a modern hotel on the sea front, close to railway line but away from busy road. **D** *Ceylon Inns*, 501 Galle Rd, Col 6, T583338, F583337. Rooms with bath and fan (a/c no longer available), restaurant, pool, rather old fashioned but popular with tour groups. **Cheap F** *Charlemont Beach Inn*, 26 Charlemont Rd, Col 6, T583250. 56 large bare rooms (Rs 360 shared bath, Rs 500 attached), very basic. **F** *Ranwanlanka*, 382 Galle Rd, T508357. Rooms with bath and fan, those at rear quieter with better views, roof garden.

Dehiwala Cheap F *Big John Guest House*, 47 Albert Place, T715027. (Coming from Colombo take the first right after the gaudy 'wedding cake' church), rooms with bath and fan in a private house, rather dark, close to (unappealing) beach, have to walk up to Galle Rd for food. **F** *Peeco Beach*, 56 Peter's Lane (just north of Dehiwala railway station), T723450. Basic rooms and restaurant, close to beach.

Some of the best speciality restaurants are to be found in the upper category hotels. **Eating** The eat-all-you-want **buffets** at the *Hilton* (different each night), *Intercontinental*, *Galle Face*, *Galadari* and *Trans Asia* are worth trying. Particularly recommended at lunchtime (Rs 400-600 plus 20% tax), when you have the added benefit of sitting in cool comfort during the hottest part of the day.

Fort and Pettah *Great Wall*, 77 Chatham St, Fort, Col 1. Chinese. Offers reasonable lunch time set menus for Rs 200. *Nanking*, 33 Chatham St, Col 1. *Nectar*, Mudalige Mawatha, corner of York St, Fort, for snacks, ice creams. *Pagoda*, Chatham St, Fort, Col 1, offers good value Chinese (main dishes Rs 50-95) plus Sri Lankan and Western. Recommended. *Seafish*, 15 Sir CA Gardiner Mawatha, just behind Regal Cinema, south of Fort, T326915. Excellent fish at reasonable prices, hoppers with curry (evenings), though lacking in atmosphere. Recommended. The *Ys* have good, inexpensive food. Cheap 'rice and curry' places abound in the Fort, Pettah and along Galle Rd.

Galle Face and Union Place *Taj Samudra's Chinese*. Excellent and moderately priced. *The German Restaurant* (*Alt Heidelberg*), 11 Galle Face Court 2 (opposite *Galle Face Hotel*), Col 3, has German specialities (Rs 300-450 main course) plus German beer on tap. *Max's San Remo Café*, 199 Union Pl. Continental food with piano music at dinner, lounge cocktail bar, also garden café with fast food, all day for cold drinks, ice creams, good value. Recommended. *Pizza Hut*, 321a Union Place (between Dawson St and YWCA), Col 2, T334760, T305305. Good range of pizzas and pastas (Rs 105-655 depending on size), salads (Rs 60-100), beer (Rs 100), a/c. Also delivery service.

City dwellers take in the sea air on Galle Face Green while eating out off the many street vendors

Kollupitiya *Ari Rang*, 16 Abdul Gafoor Mawatha, Col 3. Japanese and Korean with barbecues at tables, special eel dishes. *Chesa Swiss*, 3 Deal Place, off RA de Mel Mawatha, Col 3, T573433, has excellent Swiss food, though at a price (Rs 1,500+) open 1900-2300. *Chinese Garden*, 32 Dharmapala Mawatha, wide range of Chinese priced by size (Rs 85-355), unimpressive exterior but popular with local people (may have to wait for table). *Cricket Club Café*, 34 Queen's Rd (near Br Council), Col 3, T501384. International range including good Western snacks and desserts in excellent setting (cricket theme) with good though pricey bar. *Da Guido*, 47/4 Dharmapala Mawatha, Col 7, does good Italian. *The Fab*, 474 Galle Rd, Col 3, western food and excellent patisserie. *Flower Drum*, C Munidasa Mawatha, Col 3. Chinese. quiet atmosphere, excellent food, reasonable prices. Recommended. *Fountain Café*, 1 Justice Akhbar Mawatha (Bridge St) opposite Kompanna station, Col 2, excellent Sri Lankan dishes, full meal for under Rs 200; also European food. Open 1100-1830. *Moshi Moshi*, 594/2 Galle Rd (3rd floor), Col 3. Authentic Japanese, pricey though plentiful. *Paradise Road*, 213 Dharmapala Mawatha, Col 7, T686043, beautiful old colonial mansion open daytime for light meals and drinks. *Peking Palace*, 3 Sellamuttu Ave, Col 3. Moderately priced Chinese. *Sakura*, 14 Rheinland Place, Kollupitya, Col 3. Good Japanese. *Saras*, 31 Charles Dr, Col 3. Inexpensive Sri Lankan/Indian. *Summer Gardens*, A Coomaraswamy Mawatha, Col 7, has a selection of cheap Sri Lankan dishes in an open air setting.

Bambalapitiya and Havelock *Beach Wadiya*, next to Bambalapitiya station, Col 4. Offers superb seafood including lobster (Rs 500+), well stocked bar, rustic surroundings. *Gallery 706 and Garden Café*, 706 Galle Road, Colombo 3 (entry via 'Barefoot'), T505559. Exclusive setting for the literary and art set with attached art gallery, wonderful ambience, good food. Recommended. *International Food Hall* at 'Majestic City', Bambalapitiya, Col 4, in the basement. *Crescat*, Galle Rd (next to *Lanka Oberoi*), Col 3. Smart outlets downstairs for a quick bite. *Itzza Pizza & The Delimatz*, RA de Mel Mawatha, Bambalapitiya, good eat-in or takeaway. *Jade Garden*, 126 Havelock Rd, Col 5. Chinese. *Kinjou*, 33 Amarsekera Mawatha, Col 5, opposite BRC grounds (Havelock Rd). Chinese and Japanese. Good Szechuan in plush Japanese surroundings. *Mathura Madras Woodlands*, 185 Havelock Road, Colombo 5, T582909. A/c, choice of good North and South Indian cuisine, good value lunch-time buffets. *Sapid*, junction off Vajira/Galle Rd, Bambalapitiya, Col 4, offers Chinese, Sri Lankan and Western dishes (halal meat). *Station Road Restaurant*, Bambalapitiya, Col 4, 'really good' Sri Lankan and Western dishes (Rs 100), fresh juices.

Vegetarian *Crowns*, next to *Laksala*, York St. South Indian style, simple but good, friendly, cheap. *Palms*, 40 Galle Rd, Col 6. Dosas and other inexpensive Indian vegetarian. *Saraswathie Lodge*,

Bambalapitiya

■ **Sleeping**
1 Charlemont Beach Inn
2 Ottery Tourist Inn
3 Sri Lanka Youth Council
4 Vegelands

● **Eating**
1 Beach Wadiya
2 International Food Hall
3 Itzza Pizza
4 KFC & Station Road
5 Sapid
6 Saraswathie Lodge

25 Charles Drive, Col 3. Cheap vegetarian Sri Lankan food. *Shanmugas*, 53/3 Ramakrishna Road, Colombo 6, near Roxy Cinema, T587629. Good South Indian restaurant boasting 15 varieties of dosa. *Shanti Vihar*, 3 Havelock Rd, Havelock Town, Col 5, T580224. Good, simple 'Indian' veg food, *thalis* and *dosas* (Rs 75), breakfasts too (0700-0900).

Goodies Pastry Shop at *Trans Asia Hotel*, 115 Sir CA Gardiner Mawatha, Slave Island, Col 2. Highly recommended. *Peera*, 217 Galle Rd, Col 3, for cakes, snacks, breads, mainly takeaway.

Confectionery

Alcohol is available in almost all hotels, with the **AL**, **A** and **B** hotels having pleasant, if expensive bars (local beer Rs 150-200 for 625ml). Cheaper options are the numerous bars in the fort area, notably along York St and Mudalige Mawatha, though security concerns mean that they now close earlier than they used to. On *poya days* alcohol is not generally available until midnight. The *Cricket Club Café*, 34 Queen's Rd (near Br Council), Col 3, T501384, is a good place to enjoy a drink (including Australian wines). Cheap-watchers may like to try the *Sri Lanka Ex-Serviceman's Institute* in fort (see 'Sleeping' above).

Bars

Colombo's nightclub scene is largely restricted to the top category hotels, most of which impose a hefty cover charge on non-residents at weekends (Rs 300-500, ladies often free) and expensive drinks (local beer Rs 180+). Some have early evening 'happy hours', though few get going much before midnight. *Valentino* at the Galadari is rated highly. *My Kind of Place* at *Taj Samudra*, *The Library* at *Trans Asia* (members and hotel guests only), *Blue Elephant* at *Colombo Hilton* and *Chapter One* at *Lanka Oberoi* all have their moments, though it really depends upon the crowd on the night.

Nightclubs

MGM Grand Club, 772 Galle Rd, Bambalapitiya, Col 4, T502268. Open 24 hrs, offers banco, blackjack, roulette, baccarat, has VIP 'foreigners only' lounge. *Golden Nugget*, Mudalige Mawatha, Fort, Col 1. *Ritz Club*, 5 Galle Face Terrace, Col 3 (behind *Holiday Inn*).

Casinos

There are numerous cinemas on Galle Rd and RA de Mel Mawatha, though the diet is mainly 'action' or highly edited 'adult' movies. See also under 'Cultural centres' above.

Cinemas

Performances of Sinhala dance and music can be seen at the *YMBA Hall*, Borella, *Navarangashala*, C Munidasa Mawatha, Col 7, and at *Lionel Wendt Hall*, 19 Guildford Crescent, Col 7, T695794. *Lumbini Hall*, Havelock Town, specializes in Sinhalese theatre. Some top hotels put on regular folk dance performances (also western floor shows/live music for dancing); open to non-residents.

Cultural shows

Lionel Wendt Gallery & Theatre, 19 Guildford Crescent, Col 7, T695794. *Tower Hall Theatre Foundation*, 'Sausiripaya', 123 Wijerama Mawatha, Col 7, T687993. *Theatre Information Centre*, (adjoining Elphinstone Theatre), Maradana, Col 10, T433635.

Theatres

Jan-Feb: *Navam Maha Perahera*, Gangaramaya Temple, celebrates the full-moon with processions around Beira Lake-Viharamahadevi Park area. A large number of elephants, torch-bearers, drummers, dancers, acrobats, stilt walkers and pilgrims take part.

Festivals

Most shops are open 1000-1900 on weekdays and 0845-1500 on Sat. You can shop with confidence at government run shops although it is interesting to wander in the bazaars and look for good bargains – *Sunday Bazar* on Main St, Pettah and Duke St, Fort. The top hotels have good shopping arcades selling quality goods but prices are often higher than elsewhere.

Shopping

Shopping complexes *Liberty Plaza* on Dharmapala Mawatha, Kollupitiya, *World Market*, near Fort Railway Station, *Majestic City* and *Unity Plaza* on Galle Rd, Bambalapitiya. *Crescat*, Galle Rd, Col 3 (near Lanka Oberoi), is the city's newest upmarket shopping mall. *Duty Free Complex*, City shop on Galle Rd, Kollupitiya to be paid for in foreign currency and noted in your passport. Shops in the Fort tend to be good but more expensive than equally good quality items in Kollupitiya. Boutiques in Pettah are worth a visit too. *The Philatelic Bureau*, 4th floor, Ceylinco House, Janadhipathi Mawatha, Fort has a good stock of stamps.

Bookshops Good shops in the *Inter-Continental* and *Grand Oriental* Hotels. *Cultural Bookshop*, 34 Malay St, Col 3, has a wide selection. *Lakehouse*, 100 Sir CA Gardiner Mawatha, particularly good for art books. *KVJ de Silva*, 415 Galle Rd, Col 4; *MD Gunasena*, Olcott Mawatha, Col 11; *Vijitha Yapa*, 376 Galle Rd, Col 3.Recommended. Others on Sir Baron Jayatilleke Mawatha, Fort. Second-hand books from *Ashok Trading*, 183 Galle Rd, Col 4 and antiquarian from *Serendib*, 100 Galle Rd. *Children's Bookshop*, 20 Bogala Building, Janadhipathi Mawatha, near Fort clocktower for Sri Lankan music cassettes. *Travel Information Centre*, 78 Steuart Pl, Col 3, has cassettes of words and music on pilgrim sites, booklets on the ancient cities, posters and picture post cards. Books on **Buddhism** from *Buddhist Information Centre*, 380/9 Sarana Rd (off Bauddhaloka Maw), Col 7, T689388. *Buddhist Cultural Centre*, 125 Anderson Rd, Nedimala, Dehiwala, T726234, bcc@sri.lanka.net Open daily 0830-1730 including Poya and public holidays.

Gemstones, silver and gold These should only be bought at reputable shops – eg arcades in the top hotels (*Hotel Lanka Oberoi*. Recommended). *Premadasa*, 17 Sir Baron Jayatilleke Mawatha and 20 Duke St, Col 1; *Zam Gems*, 81 Galle Rd, Col 4 with a few branches; *Janab*, 9 Temple Lane, Col 3. Sea St in Pettah has a number of private jewellers; *Hemchandra*, 229 Galle Rd, Col 3. *Sri Lanka Gem & Jewellery Exchange* is a government institution; 310 Galle Rd, has 34 wholesalers and retailers; the Gem Testing Laboratory on the 2nd floor, will test gems free for foreigners (you have to pay about US$2 for a certificate), Mon-Fri, 0830-1630 (closed for lunch); Customs, insurance, banking facilities.

Handloom and handicrafts Government outlets include *Laksala*, Australia House, York St, Col 1 which carries a wide range. Other branches in Galle Face and Bambalapitiya. Open 0900-1700, except Sat and Sun, Apr-Oct. *Viskam Niwasa* (Department of Industries), Bauddhaloka Mawatha, Col 7 also has high quality craft goods. *Handloom Shop*, 71 Galle Rd, Col 4. *Barefoot*, 704 Galle Rd, Kollupitiya, Col 3, T505559 barefoot@eureka.lk started by Barbara Sansoni, the artist; also bookshop with good coverage of Sri Lanka and books on design, photography, architecture and modern fiction, as well as cards and postcards. *Gallery 706* next door exhibits and sells works of art. *Good Earth*, *The Shoppe*, Crescat Boulevard, Galle Road (next to Lanka Oberoi Hotel). *Ceylon Ceramics Corp* showroom in Bambalapitiya also has terracotta ware. *Lakmedura*, 113 Dharmapala Mawatha, Col 7. For good batiks try *Serendib*, 100 Galle Rd, Col 4, *Fantasy Lanka*, 302 (1st floor), Unity Plaza, 2 Galle Rd, Col 4, *Ena de Silva*, Duplication Rd, Kollupitiya.

Maps *Survey Department*, *Map Sales Branch*, Kirula Rd, Narahenpita and *Map Sales Centre*, York St, Col 1.

Photography Numerous in town. *Hayleys*, 303 Galle Rd, Col 3, offers special 1 hr service.

• •

Sports mad Sri Lanka

Sri Lankans are as sports mad as their neighbours in India. Cricket is very popular, and winning the World Cup One Day competition in 1996 has achieved international recognition for the island as a world class competitor. During test matches groups cluster around radios and TVs and people often try to take holidays just to watch them. Children play - and are taught the game - from an early age. Most large towns have cricket grounds, and during the season between January and April games are played throughout the island.

Cricket is not the only obsession. Football (soccer) is becoming increasingly popular,

and national and international events, such as the Bristol SAARC Cup - a South Asian football festival held annually in March, attracts a lot of interest. Rugby is played in the Highlands, but Sri Lanka has also produced some notable indoor sportsmen, such as the former World Amateur snooker champion M J M Lafir.

At the Sydney Olympics in September 2000, the woman sprinter Susanthika Jayasinghe fulfilled the national expectation by winning the bronze medal in the 200 metres. Satellite TV has brought world sports into Sri Lankan homes, where they have an enthusiastic audience.

• •

Tea and spices *Mlesna Tea Centre*, Liberty Plaza and Majestic City. *Sri Lanka Tea Board*, 574 Galle Rd, Col 3. *YWCA Spice Shop*, Union Pl.

Cricket Colombo has several cricket stadiums. Tests and One Day Internationals are played at the *Sinhalese Sports Club Ground* (SSC), on Maitland Place, Col 7. Next door to the Colombo Cricket Club is the *Nondescript's Cricket Club* (NCC) which has a very attractive colonial style pavilion. North of Colombo, the *Premadasa/Khettarama Stadium* hosts test matches day/night. **Diving** Though diving is possible off Colombo, most of the dive schools operate from coastal resorts, notably Hikkaduwa, *Lanka Sportreizen*, 211 Hospital Rd, Dehiwala, T824500, lsr@sri.lanka.net (also nature and wildlife). *Underwater Safaris*, 25c Barnes Place, Col 7, T694012, F694029, offer diving along the southwest coast, as do *Aqua Tours*, 108 Rosemead Place, Col 7, T695170 (see under 'Hikkaduwa', below). **Football**: Matches at the *City Football League Ground*, Sir CA Gardiner Mawatha, Slave Island, Col 2. **Golf**: *Royal Colombo Golf Club*, Ridgeway Golf Links, Col 8, T695431, offers temporary membership (a full round including club hire costs around Rs 2,000). **Rowing**: *Colombo Rowing Club*, Sir CA Gardiner Mawatha, Col 2 (opposite Lake House Book shop), T433758, offers temporary membership. **Squash**: At the *Lanka Oberoi, Intercontinental, Taj Samudra* and *Trans Asia* hotels. Also at Gymkhana Club, 31 Maitland Crescent, Col 7, and Sri Lanka Ladies Squash Assoc, T696256. **Swimming**: *Colombo Swimming Club*, 148 Galle Rd, Col 3 (opposite Temple Trees, the President's Residence), T421645. Popular ex-pats hangout with pool, tennis, gym, bar, restaurant, initial membership Rs 35,000 (of which Rs 17,500 is refundable), annually thereafter Rs 865; you must be recommended by an existing member. Alternatively, many hotels allow non-residents to use their pool on a daily basis for a fee ranging from Rs 175 to Rs 500 plus service charge/GST. **Tennis**: Available at most top hotels. **Yachting**: *Royal Colombo Yacht Club*, welcomes experienced sailors.

Sports

City tours By car with a driver/guide (for 3) – Half day: 40 km, Buddhist Temple, Hindu Temple, Zoo and residential area. Full Day: also includes Kelaniya Temple. For nature safaris, hiking and bird-watching contact Wildlife and Nature Protection Society, Chaitya Road (Marine Drive), Col 1, T325248.

Tours

Colombo & nearby beaches

☞ Cricket crazy

The cricket crazy traveller may not wish to overlook the chance of watching a Test Match or a One Day International. If you are in town during one, head for the SSC grounds in Maitland Place, Colombo. The best seats are in the Members' Enclosure which is a covered stand with the best atmosphere, where you might meet 'Percy', the local rabble rouser/ cheer leader and a real character. Alternatively, the Phillips Pavilion is an air conditioned room from where you have a good view and can also watch replays on a TV screen but does not have such a good atmosphere. The most expensive seats for 5-days of a Test Match is only Rs 800!

Other Test Match grounds are 'located at the Premadasa/Khetterama Stadium, north of Colombo (which is a day/night venue), at Asgiriya in Kandy near the monastery ("probably the most beautiful Test Match ground in the world"), and one in Galle. Another in Matara is striving to achieve the status.

Tour operators
Only a few are listed here
See also 'Tourist offices' below

Some (eg *Aitken Spence*, *Confifi*, *Jetwings*, *Keells*, *Walkers*) run a number of luxury hotels on the southwest coast and elsewhere. US$80-100 per day includes their hotel and breakfast (if you choose your own hotel, a large reservation fee may be added). *Aitken Spence*, 13 Baron Jayatilleke Mawatha, Col 1, T433755, F446838, ashmpvti.@slt.lk *Confifi*, 33 St Michael's Rd, Col 3, T334461, F333324, confifi@eureka.lk *Cox & Kings*, 315 Vauxhall St, Col 2, T434295. *Gemini Tours & Travels*, 160/2 Bauddhaloka Mawatha, Col 4, T591470, F587974 gemini@eureka.lk *Hemtours*, 75 Braybrooke Pl, Col 2, T300001, F300003, hemtours@sri.lanka.net includes wildlife tours. *Jetwing*, 46/26 Navam Mawatha, Col 2, T345700, F345725. jettrav@sri.lanka.net, recommended for personalized service, good car and driver/guide; also nature and wildlife tours. *Keells*, 130 Glennie St, Col 2, T320862, F447087. *Paradise Holidays*, 160/2 Bauddhaloka Mawatha, Col 4, T/F502110. *Thomas Cook*, 15 Sir Baron Jayatilleke Mawatha, T445971, F436533 thomcook@slt.lk and 245C Galle Rd, Bambalapitiya, T580141, F580275. *Twitter Holidays*, 101 Vinayalankara Mawatha, Col 10, T693361, F698139, delmege@sri.lanka.net includes wildlife tours, *VIP Tours*, 57A Dharmapala Mawatha, Col 3, T448167, F448541. *Walkers Tours*, 130 Glennie St, Col 2, T421101, F439026 leisure@walkers.slt.lk (expensive but recommended for excellent service).

For air tickets to South and Southeast Asia try *George Travel*, 29 Bristol St, Fort, T423447.

Adventure Lanka Sports, T074-713334, F577951 adventur@sr.lanka.net_ has been recommended for good adventure activities such as white water rafting, mountain biking, trekking. Contact Peter for details.

Transport: local
See also page 41
Beware of pickpockets on public transport.
Avoid hotel touts at bus & railway stations

Bus Colombo has an extensive network of public and private buses competing on popular routes. Although the system can get very crowded, it is not difficult to use since the destinations are usually displayed in English. Useful services are those that run from Fort Railway Station down the Galle Rd (including **Nos 100, 101, 102, 106, 133**), **No 138** goes from fort past the Town Hall and the National Museum (Glass House stop, across the road); **No 187** between Fort and the International airport. Local buses have white signs, while long distance have yellow. Details of the 3 bus stations near Fort Railway Station are given below. Ceylon Transport Board (CTB), T581120.

Car hire For general information on car hire, charges and self-drive versus chauffeur-driven, see page 41. Most hotels and travel agents can arrange car hire (with or without driver); see also under Negombo. Also from: *Aset*, 315 Vauxhall St, Col 2, T440480, F447249. Efficient, good 24-hr service; *Aban's Tours* (Europcar), 498 Galle Rd, Col 3, T574160 (international airport, T452388, F575662). *Avis*, 4 Leyden Bastion

• •

Colombo's straggling suburbs – a traveller's woe

Nearly 200 years ago the Rev James Cordiner, describing the road out of Colombo in 1807, wrote that "all the roads, in their commencement from the Pettah, are streets of a straggling village, having houses on each side extending to a considerable distance inland". A recent traveller's description suggests that little has changed, except that today modern traffic has been added to the congestion of narrow streets and straggling village houses: "Leaving Colombo was a hot and rather tedious business. Heavy traffic on the A1 together with chaotic driving – minibuses, buses, cars, bicycles, cattle and

people all conspiring to confuse and disorientate. At least the Indian-made small lorries are smoke-free, as there are strict Government standards on emission, and they look far smarter than their Indian relatives, with often beautifully varnished wooden sides. Obtaining petrol or diesel can be a problem for those self-driving: there are comparatively few filling stations, all of which were overflowing with traffic. Great patience is needed. We were never quite sure when we actually left Colombo as the A1 seemed to be built up for many miles".

• •

Rd, Col 1, T329887, F522351 (24-hr garage T524498) avis@ens.lk A/c Mitsubishi Lancer, Rs 3,200 per day, Rs 19,000 per week, unlimited mileage. Recommended. *Quickshaw's*, 3 Kalinga Place, T583133, F587613 quiktur@lankacom.net *Savoy*, 12 Galle Rd, Col 6, T595595. *Sudans*, 63 1/10 Chatham St, Col 1, T/F431176, F431865.

Motorbike/bike hire *Gold Wing Motors*, 346 Deans Rd, Col 10, T685750, F698787, rental on daily, weekly or monthly terms. *Rent a bike*, T685750.

Taxi Metered taxis have yellow tops and red-on-white number plates. Make certain that the driver has understood where you wish to go and fix a rate for long distance travel. **Radio cabs** are very convenient and reliable (see page 43); *Ace Cabs*, T501502; *Quick Cabs*, 911/1 Galle Rd, Col 4, T502888, 501502, *GNTC*, T688688, *Savoy Comfort*, T595595.

Tuk-tuks The three-wheelers are quick but you need to bargain hard (min usually Rs 20 per km). Fort to Mount Lavinia will cost around Rs 200 depending upon your negotiating skills (see page 43). Radio 3-wheelers are cheaper, charge a fixed price and are reliable.

Train Suburban train halts are Fort, Secretariat, Kompanna, Kollupitiya, Bambalapitiya, Wellawatta, Dehiwala, Mount Lavinia (Rs 4, 30 mins, every 30 mins).

Air Bandaranaike International Airport (or **Colombo**), T452911, is located at Katunayake, about 6 km north of Negombo and 30 km north of Colombo. Aviation Services, T252861. Flight Information, T0732677, at flight times, day and night. The helpful tourist Information counter will give advise, brochures, maps, and the useful monthly *Travel Lanka* magazine. **Domestic Airport**. Just south of Mount Lavinia, the Ratmalana Domestic airport is 1.5 km off the A2. The uncertain political situation has led to the cancellation of internal commercial flights. See also page 30.

Transport: long distance

Bus Most major towns have an Express Service at least every 30 mins to 1 hr. There are 3 main bus stations in Colombo, all close to Fort Railway Station. All 3 are quite chaotic, choking with fumes, with services usually operating on a 'depart when full' basis.

There is a good island-wide network & travel is cheap

    CTB or **Central**, on Olcott Mawatha, southeast corner of Pettah (right from fort station, and across the road), T329604. Part private-part government owned buses,

● ●

Daily trains from Fort Station (unless otherwise indicated)

If you haven't reserved a seat in the 'Observation Car', try your luck at the station. After the train comes in, it is checked for empty seats

To	1st Class	2nd Class	3rd Class	Departure time	Journey
Anuradhapura (Intercity to Vavuniya)		Rs 150		1600	3¼ hrs
Anuradhapura (via Kurunegala)	Rs 202	Rs 116	Rs 42	0545, 1100, 1410, 2130	4¾-5 hrs
Badulla (for the Hill Country)	Rs 289	Rs 166	Rs 60	0555, 0945 (Express with observation car), 1940, 2200	9 (Exp)-11 hrs
Bentota	Rs 61	Rs 35	Rs 13		
Galle (from Maradana)	Rs 113	Rs 65	Rs 24	0830, 1015, 1400, 1535, 1720, 1750	2¾-3¾ hrs
Galle (Intercity via Hikkaduwa)	Rs 122	Rs 72 (Rs 108 return)		1530	2½ hrs
Galle (from Maradana via Hikkaduwa)	Rs 122	Rs 72	Rs 24	0830, 1015, 1400	
Galle (from Fort)	Rs 113	Rs 65	Rs 24	1330 (Sat only)	2½ hrs
Hikkaduwa	Rs 95	Rs 55	Rs 20		
Kandy (Intercity)	Rs 122 (Obs)*❖	Rs 72❖	none	0655, 1535	2½ hrs
Kandy	Rs 120	Rs 69	Rs 25	1030, 1245 (to Hatton), 1655, 1750	3¼ hrs
Matara (from Fort)	Rs 155	Rs 89	Rs 33	0715, 1015, 1405 (Not Sat and Sun), 1605	3½–4½ hrs
Matara (from Maradana)	None	Rs 89	Rs 61	0705	4¾ hrs
Nanu Oya (for Nuwara Eliya)	Rs 205	Rs 118	Rs 43		
Negombo (via airport)	None	Rs 25	Rs 10	0430, 0520, 0600, 0825, 0925, 1345, 1445, 1720, 1735, 1738, 1820, 1855, 2020	1½ hrs
Trincomalee	None	Rs 168	Rs 61	0610	8½ hrs

*Obs = 'Observation Car' (reserved in advance, fee Rs 50).   ❖ Return tickets, valid for 10 days, Rs 208, Rs 108.

● ●

which are the cheapest, oldest and slowest, offer services to almost all island-wide destinations. **Left Luggage**, here (Rs 8 per locker), is sometimes full.

Bastion Mawatha, to the east of Manning Market. Transport Authority, T421731. The buses are privately run, with the cost and journey time depending on whether you get an a/c coaster, a 'semi-luxury' bus, or an ancient bone-shaker. It serves most destinations to the east, southeast and south, including **Kandy** (Rs 70), **Nuwara Eliya** (Rs 110), **Hikkaduwa** (Rs 50), **Galle** (Rs 50), **Matara**, **Tangalla** (Rs 80) and **Kataragama**.

Colombo & nearby beaches

Transport from the international airport

See details about arrival on page 32

Bus To Colombo: Private buses (no 187) run between the airport and Bastian Mawatha Bus Station in Fort regularly between 0600-2200, as do CTB buses (stopping opp Laksala in York St, Fort). This is the cheapest means (about Rs 8) on Nos 187 to Fort (also 240, 300 and 875); it takes about 1 hr.

Taxi To Colombo Fort, about Rs 800; to **Mt Lavinia**, Rs 950; you may initially be asked for considerably more. There is a pre-paid taxi counter which should obviate the need for bargaining, though these do overcharge at times; Airport Express, T 687037/698207, F 699109, a/c, Airport-Colombo, Rs 700.

Radio cabs (see above and in Information for visitors), are cheaper, about Rs 25/km. Tour operators charge considerably more (eg Airwing quotes: Colombo Rs 1,400, Mt Lavinia Rs 1,800).

Commuter trains Between **Negombo** and **Colombo** go via the airport; the station is 500m from the terminal.

To **Negombo**: there are also buses (No 240, Rs 5), taxis (Rs 400) and 3-wheelers (Rs 300). Taxis are available to other destinations, eg **Kandy** and **Hikkaduwa**, the latter for around Rs 2,500 from the airport, though only Rs 1,800 in the opp direction.

People's Park or **Saunders Place**, just to the north of the CTB bus station, which also offers private a/c coasters and bone-shakers to destinations to the North and North-east, including **Anuradhapura** (Rs 75), **Badulla** (Rs 120), **Balangoda**, **Bandarawela**, **Chilaw** (Rs 35), **Embilipitiya**, **Gampola**, **Hatton**, **Ja-ela**, **Kegalla**, **Kurunegala**, **Negombo** (Rs 20), **Nittambuwa**, **Polonnaruwa**(Rs 80), **Puttalam** (Rs 60) and **Ratnapura** (Rs 40).

There are bus stops on Olcott Mawatha outside and opposite the station mini-buses also leave from the bus stops and from the railway station.

Train There are trains to most places of interest on 3 separate lines. Enquiries (Express and Commuter trains), T434215. For foreign travellers, the **Railway Tourist Office**, Fort Station, T435838, is particularly useful. Fort station Superintendent, T421281 Ext 389. **Left Luggage** ('Cloak Room'): Rs 8 per locker.

There are special a/c Hitachi trains for day tours to Kandy and Hikkaduwa. Occasional tours are arranged on vintage steam trains – details from the Railway Tourist Office. Inter-city Expresses to Kandy (with a stop at Peradeniya) costs Rs 72 (return Rs 108), and continues to Bandarawela. These have a 1st Class 'Observation Car' at the end of the train; morning departure from Colombo is recommended for best views, avoiding the hot sun. For the south coast, if you fancy riding in the 'Guard Van', pay an extra Rs 15 on the day to reserve a seat on the 1545 towards Matara.

Airline offices *Aeroflot*, 7A Sir Ernest de Silva Mawatha, Col 7, T671201. *Air France*, Galle Face Hotel, Galle Rd, Col 3, T327605. *Air India*, 108 Sir Baron Jayatilleke Mawatha, Col 1, T325832. *Air Mauritius*, 30-34 Sir Baron Jayatilleke Mawatha, Col 1, T430523. *American Airlines*, 5 York St, Col 1, T348100. *Balkan Airlines*, 321 Union Pl, Col 2, T451304. *Bangladesh Biman*, 4 Milepost Ave, Col 3, T439319. *British Airways*, Trans Asia Hotel, 115 Sir CA Gardiner Mawatha, T320231, F447906. *Canadian*, 11a York St, Col 1, T348101. *Cathay Pacific*, 186 Vauxhall St, Col 1, T334145. *Delta*, 45 Jandhipathi Mawatha, Col 1, T338734. *Emirates*, Hemas Building 9th Flr,75 Braybrooke Place, Col 2, T300200. *Gulf Air*, 11 York St, Col 1, T347857. *Indian Airlines*, 4 Bristol St, Col 1, T326844. *Iraqi*, 20A Bank of Ceylon Bldg, 18A York St, Col 1, T436103. *Japan Airlines*, 61 WAD Ramanayake Mawatha, Col 2, T300315. *KLM*, 29 Braybrooke St, Col 2, T439747. *Korean*, 7th floor, East Tower, World Trade Centre, Echelon Sq, Col 1, T422686. *Kuwait*, 30-34 Cargills Bldg, 30 Sir Baron Jayatilleke Mawatha, Col 1, T445531. *Lufthansa*, 61 WAD Ramanyake Mawatha, Col 2, T300501. *Malaysian*, Hemas, 81 York St, Col 1, T342291. *Middle East*, 24 Flower Rd, Col 7, T343252. *PIA*, 342 Galle Rd, Col 3, T573475. *Qantas*, Trans Asia Hotel, 115 Sir CA G,ardiner Mawatha, Col 2, T348490. *Qatar*, 64 Lotus Rd, Col 1, T341101. *Royal Jordanian*, Hotel Taj Samudra, 25 Galle Face Centre Rd,

Directory

Colombo & nearby beaches

Col 3, T445318. *Royal Nepal Airlines*, 4 Milepost Ave, Col 3, T565391. *Sahara India*, Jetwing House, 46/26 Navam Mawatha, Col 2, T3457000. *SAS*, 16 Janadhipathi Mawatha, Col 1, T326424. *Saudia*, 466 Galle Rd, Col 6, T577242. *Singapore*, 315 Vauxhall St, Col 2, T300750. *Sri Lankan Airlines*, East Tower, World Trade Centre, Echelon Sq, Col 1, T073555, F0735122. *Swissair*, 5th Floor, 41 Janadhipathi Mawatha, Col 3, T435405. *Tarom*, 18A York St, Col 1, T448593. *Thai Airways*, *Intercontinental Hotel*, 48 Janadhipathi Mawatha, Col 1, T438050. *United Airlines*, 06-02 East Tower, World Trade Centre, Echelon Sq, Col 1, T346026.

Banks Usually open at 0900 and close at 1300 or 1500. Some branches open for Sat morning and have an evening service; most are closed on Sun, *Poya* days and national holidays. . There are numerous licensed moneychangers in the fort area, notably on Mudalige Mawatha, offering marginally better rates for cash. Hotels are generally offer a poor rate of exchange for cash and TCs, though they may be convenient for residents. **Local banks** *Bank of Ceylon*, Bureau de Change, York St, Fort, is open 0900-1800 weekdays, 0900-1600 on holidays. They may accept UK cheques backed by Visa cards. Head Office, Tower Building, Colombo 1, cashes TCs, 0900-1900 on weekdays. Katunayake Airport counter is open 24 hrs. *Commercial Bank*, 21 Bristol St, Col 1, accepts Mastercard. *Hatton National Bank*, 16 Janadhipathi Mawatha, Col 1, accepts Mastercard. *People's Bank*, Foreign Branch, 27 MICH Bldg, Bristol St, Col 1, T326427, 0900-1330 on weekdays; *Night Service*, 75 Sir CA Gardiner Mawatha, Col 2, Tue-Fri, 1530-1900, Sat 0900-1330, closed Sun, Mon. Some main branches stay open 0900-1600, accept TCs and sterling but **not** credit cards. *Sampath Bank*, Card Centre, 90 Chatham St, Fort, and 55 DR Wijewardena Mawatha, Col 10, for Mastercard. Ceybank Travel Centre, 189 Galle Rd, Colombo 3, 0830-1930 on weekdays, 0830-1630 holidays. **Foreign banks** *ANZ Grindlays*, 37 York St, Fort, Col 1, T446150, has a 24-hr Visa/Mastercard ATM machine. *Bank of America*, Head Branch, will give cash against Visa or Mastercard. *HSBC*, 24 Sir Baron Jayatilleke Mawatha, Fort, Col 1, and JAIC Shopping Mall, Union Pl, and at 38 Galle Rd, Welawatta, Col 6, have ATM machines that take Visa/Mastercard. *American Express*, 104 Dharmapala Mawatha, Col 7, T681215, F682789. Open Mon-Fri 0900-1700, Sat 0930-1230, foreign exchange, client's mail, travel service, agent Mackinnons Travel, 4 Leyden Bastion Rd (corner of York St, Fort) has exchange. *Card Centre*, 1st floor, 20 Sir CA Gardiner Mawatha, Col 2, T434147. *Thomas Cook*, 15 Sir Baron Jayatilleke Mawatha, Fort, Col 1, T445971. Open Mon-Fri 0830-1700, Sat 1000-1230.

Phone code: T01 **Communications** Directory enquiries 161, International enquires 134. **Couriers DHL** Keells (Pvt) Ltd, 130 Glennie Street, Colombo 2, T541285 tracing@cmb.co.lk.dhl.com Documents to UK, US$24 for first 500 g, to USA and most of EU US$26 for first 500 g, US$7 for each additional 500 g. Approximately double rate for first 500 g on parcels plus US$7 for each additional 500 g. Approximately 3-4 working days to Europe. Open 0830-1700, Mon-Fri, 0900-1300 Sat. **GPO**: the beautiful GPO building on Janadhipathi Mawatha, Col 1, T326203. Open 24 hrs Mon-Sat. Closed Sun and public holidays. Each district has either a *Branch Post Office* or one of the many *Post office agencies*. **Poste Restante** the GPO will keep your mail (letters and packages) for 2 months, T326203. Open 0900-2000, Mon-Sat. You can also ask for mail to be forwarded to another town. *American Express* client mail is held at 104, Dharmapala Mawatha, Red Cross Building; T681215. You can phone either office to check if any mail is waiting. **Internet** Cyber Café, 211 Union Place, Col 2, T334723. Open daily 1000-2200, internet/email use Rs 80 per 30 mins, email address Rs 600 per month, Rs 1,600 per quarter, Rs 3,800 per year. **Telephones** International phone calls (including 'Collect calls') from the GPO via an operator (minimum 3 mins); 0800-1900 (0800-1700 on Sun). Numerous private telephone offices offer more or less standard rates for IDD (International Direct Dialling) calls. *Card Pay Phones* (yellow Lanka Payphones and orange Metrocard) offer 24-hr service and much lower rates than hotels. Phone cards (Rs 100-600) are sold in shops and kiosks near pay phones.

Cultural centres Foreign Most have a library and reading room and have regular music and film programmes. *Alliance Française*, 11 Barnes Place, Col 7, T694162. *American Centre*, 44 Galle Rd, Col 3, T332725. Open Tue-Sat, 1000-1800. *British Council*, 49 Alfred House Gardens, Col 3, T581171. open Tue-Sat, 1000-1800. *German (Goethe) Cultural Institute*, 39 Gregory's Rd, Col 7, T694562. Open 0900-1300, 1500-1700 weekdays. *Soviet Cultural Centre*, 10 Independence Ave, Col 7, T685429. Open weekdays 0900-1700. For courses on **Buddhism** and **meditation**: *Bhikku Training Centre*, Gangaramaya, 61 Sri Jinaratana Rd, Col 2, T327084, F439508 (offers classes in English, French, German); *The Buddhist Centre*, 7 Buddhist Centre Rd (near Hotel Sapphire) Col 10, T695216; *Buddhist Cultural Centre*, 125 Anderson Rd, Nedimala,

Dehiwala, T714256, F723767. 8 km south of town centre, information, instruction and meditation by prior arrangement; *Buddhist Information Centre*, 50 A Coomaraswamy Mawatha, Col 7, T573285; *International Buddhist Research and Information Centre*, 380/9 Sarana Rd (off Bauddhaloka Mawatha, Col 7, T689388.

Embassies & consulates *Australia*, 3 Cambridge Pl, Col 7, T698767. *Bangladesh*, 47/1, Sir Ernest de Silva Mawatha, Col 7, T681311. *Canada*, 6 Gregory's Rd, Col 7, T695841. *China*, 381a Bauddhaloka Mawatha, Col 7, T694491. *Egypt*, 39 Dickman's Rd, Col 5, T583621. *France*, 89 Rosmead Place, Col 5, T698815. *Germany*, 40 Alfred House Av, Col 3, T580431. Mon-Thu 0730-1630, Fri 0730-1400. *India*, 36-38 Galle Rd (next to Galle Face Hotel), Col 3, T421605. Mon-Fri 0900-1730, visas 0930-1200, may need to collect next day 1630-1720 (also in Kandy). *Indonesia*, 400/50 Sarana Rd. off Bauddhaloka Mawatha, Col 7, T674337. *Italy*, 55 Jawathe Rd, Col 5, T588388. *Japan*, 20 Gregory.'s Rd, Col 7, T693831. *Malaysia*, 92 Kynsey Rd, Col 7, T686090. *Maldives*, 25 Melbourne Av, Col 4, T586762. *Myanmar*, 65 Ward Place, Col 7, T696672. *Nepal*, 153 Kynsey Rd, Col 8, T689656. *Netherlands*, 25 Torrington Av, Col 7, T596914. *Norway*, 34 Ward Pl, Col 7, T692263. *Pakistan*, 211 De Saram Place, Col 10, T696301. *Russian Federation*, 62 Sir E de Silva Mawatha, Col 7, T573555. *Saudi Arabia*, 39 Sir Ernest de Silva Mawatha, Col 7, T682087. *Sweden*, 47/1 Horton Pl, Col 7, T688455. *Switzerland*, 63 Gregory's Rd, Col 7, T695117. *Thailand*, 43 Dr CWW Kannangara Mawatha, Col 7, T689037. *UK*, 190 Galle Rd, Col 3, T437336. Mon-Thu 0800-1630, Fri 0800-1300. *USA*, 210 Galle Rd, Col 3, T448007. Mon-Fri 0800-1700.

Emergencies *Accident service*: T691111. *Fire & Ambulance*: T422222. *Police*: T433333. Police stations, south of Maradana Railway Station, Kollupitiya, Bambalapitiya and Welawatta. *Tourist Police*: New Secretariat Building, Bank of Ceylon Mawatha, Fort, T421111.

International agencies *IMF*, 9th floor, Central Bank of Sri Lanka, Janadhipathi Mawatha, Col 1, T438183. *UNDP*, T580691. *UNFPA*, T580840. both at 202 Bauddhaloka Mawatha, Col 7. *UNICEF*, 231 Galle Rd, T584204. *WFP*, T586244. *WHO*, 135 Bauddhaloka Mawatha, Col 4, T502319.

Libraries See also cultural centres above. *Colombo Public Library*, A Coomaraswamy Mawatha, Col 7, T695156. Open daily except Wed and public holidays, 0800-1845, Rs 2 fee.

Medical services Chemists a number on Galle Rd, Union Place, Pettah and Fort. *State Pharmaceutical* outlets at Hospital Junction, Col 7. Main St, Fort. Pharmacy attached to *Keells Supermarket*, Liberty Plaza, Dharmapala Mawatha, Kollupitiya, reasonable prices though expensive Sri Lankan standards. *City Dispensary*, 505 Union Place, Col 2. *Ward Place Pharmacy*, 24a Ward Place, Col 7. **Hospitals** General Hospital, 10 Regent St, T691111, 693184 (24-hr Accident and Emergency). Dental Institute, Ward Place, Col 10. *Poison information*: Extn 350. **Ambulance** T422222. Ministry of Indigenous Medicine, 385 Deans Rd, T597345. Has a list of practitioners. Homeopathy and herbal medicine from Government Ayurvedic Hospital, 325 Cotta Rd, Borella, T695855. Foreigners often prefer to use the more expensive **private hospitals**: Asiri, 181 Kirula Rd, Col 5, T500608; McCarthy's, 22 Wijerama Mawatha, Col 7, T697769; Nawaloka, 23 Sri Saugathodaya Mawatha, Col 2, T544444 (24-hr).

Places of worship Buddhist contact *Buddhist Information Centre*, 50 A Coomaraswamy Mawatha, Col 7, T573285. Or *The Buddhist Centre*, 7 Buddhist Centre Rd, Col 10, T695216. **Christian** *Anglican*: St Peter's, 26 Church St, Col 1, T422510. Christ Church, Sir MM Markar Mawatha, Col 3, T325166. St Michael's & All Angels, 1 Cameron Place, Col 1, T323456. *Baptist*, 120 Dharmapala Mawatha, Cinnamon Gdns, Col 7, T695153. *Dutch Reform*, 724 Galle Rd, Col 3. 363 Galle Rd, Col 6, T580454. Station Rd, Dehiwala, T717122. *Interdenominational*, St Andrew's, 73 Galle Rd, Col 3, T323765. *Roman Catholic*, St Philip Neri's, 157 Olcott Mawatha, Col 11, T421367. St Mary's, Lauries Rd, Col 4, T588745. St Lawrence's, Galle Rd, Col 6, T581549. St Mary's, Galle Rd, Dehiwala. **Hindu** Contact *Ramakrishna Mission International Culture Centre*, Ramakrishna Rd, Col 6, T584029. **Muslim** Grand Mosque, New Moor St; Devatagaha Mosque, De Soysa Circus, Union Place, Col 7; Borah Mosque, Pettah, Col 11; Kollupitiya Mosque, Col 3; Bambalapitiya Mosque, Col 4.

Tourist offices *Tourist Information Centre*, Ceylon Tourist Board, 76-8 Steuart Place, Col 3, T437059, F437953. ctb_ch@sri.lanka.net Open 0830-1615 Mon-Fri, 0830-1230 on Sat, friendly, free literature in English (some in German, French, Italian, Swedish, Japanese), guide service arranged but not much information on transport (Cultural Triangle tickets are not sold here; best bought at sites). Information Counter at Katunayake airport, T452411. *The Railway Tourist Office*, Fort Station, Col 11, T440048, F580507. Offers friendly, invaluable advice to anyone planning a rail journey. They will suggest an itinerary, book train tickets and hotels (keen to persuade you to hire a car with driver); they appreciate feedback after your trip. Special steam train excursions are offered on the *Viceroy Special* (usually groups of 30 are required, at around US$200 a head for a 2-day 1-night trip to Kandy) in conjunction with *JF Tours*.

Useful addresses *Automobile Association of Ceylon*: 40 Sir MM Markar Mawatha, Galle Face, Col 3, T421528, open Mon-Fri 0830-1630, for issue of temporary Sri Lankan driving permit (bring 2 photos, photocopy of your national licence and international driving permit). *Central Cultural Fund* (Cultural Triangle Office), 212 Bauddhaloka Mawatha, Col 7 (to the right and half way to the back of building), T500733, F500731. The 14-day Visitors' Permit is on sale (US$ 32.50) for entry to the sites and photography; information booklets are also available. The permits are easier and quicker to get at the sites (Anuradhapura, Kandy, Polonnaruwa or Sigiriya). *Ceylon Hotels Corporation (CHC)*: 411 Galle Rd, Col 4, T503497, F503504. *Customs*, T421141. *Department of Archaeology*: Marcus Fernando Mawatha, Col 7, T694727, for photography permit. *Department of Immigration*: Bambalapitiya Station Rd (right outside the station), Col 4, T436353. 1st Floor (allow 1-2 hrs). *Forest Department*: Conservator of Forests, Rajamalwatta Rd, Battaramulla (Colombo outskirts), T566631/566626. Issues necessary Entry Permits for *Sinharaja Biosphere Reserve*, accommodation booked on ground floor. *Ministry of Cultural Affairs* (for visiting archaeological sites): Malay St, Col 2, T587912. Open 0830-1615. *Ministry of Tourism* 66 Galle Rd, Col 3, T441477. *National Aquatic Research Agency* (NARA): Crow Island, Col 15, T522000. *Wildlife Conservation Department*: 18 Gregory's Rd, Col 7, for Wildlife Information and Bungalow Reservation T694241, F698556. *Wildlife and Nature Protection*: Chaitiya Rd (Marine Drive), Col 1, T325248.

Mount Lavinia

Phone code: 01
Colour map 3, grid A1

Mount Lavinia, just 12 km south of Colombo Fort, is a pleasant place to stay, away from the noise and congestion of the city. Once a fishing village, the drive along the busy Galle Road scarcely marks it apart from the rest of Colombo. The historic connection with British governors in the 19th century brings many seeking to sample something of that era in the famous Mount Lavinia Hotel here.

Ins & outs   **Getting there** From the International airport, non-a/c van taxis charge Rs 915 to Mount Lavinia. **Getting around** Plenty of buses run along Galle Road to and from Colombo. Trains are not busy outside the morning and evening rush hours and are a pleasant (and cheap) way of travelling to the city centre.

History   Some believe Mount Lavinia takes its name from a corruption of the Sinhalese 'Lihinia Kanda' – *gull rock*. The Mount Lavinia Hotel may contest the origins of the name. Their literature suggests that British Governor Sir Thomas Maitland established the original building in 1806 for himself and his 'lady love', Lavinia. Hence the name. Once an attractive picnic spot, the original *Mount Lavinia Hotel* was Governor Edward Barnes' weekend retreat. He had the bungalow significantly extended in the 1820s (the 'Governor's Wing'), but was forced to sell it since the Government in England neither approved of the expenditure nor his luxurious lifestyle.

Beaches   The beach north of *Mount Lavinia Hotel* has several bar/restaurant shacks mostly run by the hotels immediately behind them. However, the beach itself is quite narrow and has a noticeable amount of litter especially when it gets busy at weekends and holidays. South of *Mount Lavinia Hotel*, the cleaner beach is 'private', for the use of the hotel residents, although non-residents can pay Rs 300 for access as well as use of the pool.

Hotels close to the beach are also close to the railway line, with trains passing at regular intervals from early morning to late at night, invariably using their

Mount Lavinia

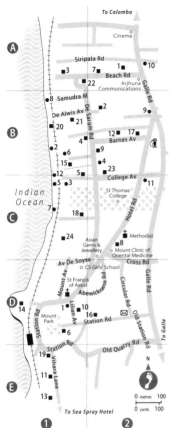

To Colombo

Cinema

Ⓐ

Siripala Rd

Beach Rd

Arjhuna Communications

Samudra M

De Alwis Av

Ⓑ

Barnes Av

College Av

Indian Ocean

St Thomas College

Ⓒ

Asian Gems & Jewellery

Methodist

Mount Clinic of Oriental Medicine

Av De Soysa

Cross Rd

CS Girls' School

St Francis of Assisi

Abewickrama Rd

Ⓓ

Mount Park

Lillian Av

Station Rd

To Galle

Old Station Rd

Old Quatry Rd

Vihara Lane

Ⓔ

To Sea Spray Hotel

N

0 metres 100
0 yards 100

❶ ❷

■ **Sleeping**
1 Beachways Guest House *A2*
2 Blue Seas *B2*
3 Carrington Villa *A1*
4 Cee Cee Inn *B1*
5 Cottage Gardens *B1*
6 Estoril *D1*
7 Falado *A2*
8 Green Shines *C2*
9 Ivory Inn *B2*
10 Jayan's Mount Resort *D1*
11 Lak-Mahal's Inn *E1*
12 Lanka Tour Inn *B2*
13 Mount Breeze Tourist Inn *E1*
14 Mount Lavinia *D1*
15 Ocean View *B1*
16 Ozeanblick *D2*
17 Ratna Inn *B2*
18 Rivi Ras *C1*
19 Sadallaa Tourist *E1*
20 Sea Breeze Tour Inn *B1*
21 Sea Gull *B1*
22 Sunray Beach Villas *A1*
23 Tropic Inn *B2*
24 Windsurf *C1*

● **Eating**
1 Angler *D1*
2 Beach restaurants *B1*
3 Connie's *C1*
4 Crystal *B2*
5 Fisherman's Villa *C1*
6 Frankfurt Lavinia Beer Garden *B1*
7 La Langousterie *C1*
8 La Lavinia & Traveller's Club Beach *B1*
9 Mount Garden *B2*
10 Mount Grill *A2*
11 New Golden Bridge *C2*
12 Sea Spray Club *B1*

horns to alert pedestrians on the track. Also take care when crossing the railway en route to the beach.

Expensive AL *Mount Lavinia*, 102 Hotel Rd, T715221, F715228, lavinia@sri.lanka. net 186 rooms, 'Bay Wing' a/c (US$90 – $110), good value non a/c rooms (US$50) retaining olde worlde ambience, renovated and extended former governors' weekend retreat located on a small, but prominent headland retaining a rich colonial atmosphere, huge public areas and labyrinthine corridors, now fully modernised with all facilities, range of restaurants, terrace bar (good for sunset drinks), nightclub (see entertainment), sports including tennis/mini golf, pool table (Rs 200 per hour), elephant rides (Sun 1000- 1400, Rs 200), impressive terrace pool (open to non-residents Rs 300, Sun Rs 600 including brunch), peaceful private beach (cleaner than public beach to the north). Recommended. **B** *Berjaya Mount Royal Beach*, 36 College Av, T739610, F733030 berjaya@sit.lk 95 large a/c rooms in comfortable, recently refurbished resort hotel, private balconies, restaurants, pool (non-residents Rs 200), *Sea Spray* club on the beach. **B** *Carrington Villa & Haus Chandra*, 37 Beach Rd, T730236, F733173. 28 small a/c rooms, 1 excellent villa for 6 people (US$125), in twin hotels opposite each other, 3 restaurants (cheaper Italian at *Boat Haus Café* on beach), small, but deep pool (non-residents Rs 115), acupuncture school on the first of every month, chauffeur driven Rolls Royce available for hire! Recommended.

Mid-range D *Cee Cee Inn*, 17 Off De Saram Rd, T/F717187. 25 rooms, mostly a/c, in new hotel, clean, attached bath, restaurant, ask manager about renting apartments (Rs 1000). **D** *Cottage Gardens*, 42-48 College Av, T719692. 3 fully equipped bungalows with kitchenette (US$15), set in quiet, attractive garden, friendly, good value. Recommended. **D** *Ivory Inn*, 21 De Saram Rd, T715006. 17 reasonable rooms, restaurant bar. **D** *Oceanview Tour Inn*, 34/4 De Saram Rd, T738400. 23 large rooms with fan

Sleeping
Some of the cheaper guesthouses in Mount Lavinia (excluding those that are family run) are used as brothels

Colombo & nearby beaches

although attached bathrooms grubby, restaurant, very close to beach (and railway line). **D** *Rivi Ras*, 50/2 De Saram Rd, T717786. 50 rooms, some non-a/c slightly cheaper in 2 storey villas with verandahs set in attractive garden, some cheaper thatched huts, excellent *La Langousterie* sea food restaurant on beach.

Cheap D-E *Beachways Guest house*, 2 Beach Rd, T712843. 10 reasonable rooms (Rs 990), some non-a/c (Rs 650) with attached bath, restaurant. **D-E** *The Falado*, 20 Beach Rd, T/F716203. 10 comfortable rooms (Rs 700-850), some a/c (plus Rs 210), used by package companies but usually 4 or 5 rooms free, relaxed atmosphere, excellent restaurant, good value. Recommended. **D-E** *Tropic Inn*, 6 College Av, T738653, F344657. 16 rooms (a/c Rs 1000), some non-a/c (Rs 700), sizes vary so check first, nets, average. **E** *Estoril*, 5/2 Lilian Av, T074-203480. 19 bare rooms (Rs 700), dark, small restaurant, good views from empty rooftop terrace. **E** *Green Shines Beach Hotel*, 49 Hotel Rd, T714515. 5 simple, clean rooms with attached bath (Rs 550 ñ Rs 750) in private house, meals on request, friendly. Recommended. **E** *Lanka Tourist Inn*, 6/4 Off Hotel Rd, T738506. 6 rooms (Rs 550), 1 **D** a/c, restaurant, a bit dark and gloomy. **E** *Mount Breeze Tourist Inn*, 38 Vihara Rd, T718943. 6 good sized, clean rooms (Rs 550) in family guesthouse, roof top garden, very friendly and interesting retired owner, meals on request, good value. Recommendeda **E** *Ozeanblick*, 38 Station Rd, T724249. 33 rooms with attached bath (Rs 612), small balconies but unattractive building and views, swimming pool planned, though a reasonable deal. **E** *Ratna Inn*, 8 Barnes Av, T716653, F732493. 10 rooms (Rs 800) in large colonial guesthouse, quiet and friendly. **E** *Sadallaa Tourist*, 85 Station Rd, T713857. 7 large but basic rooms (Rs 550), quiet, friendly. **E** *Sunray Beach Villa*, 3 De Saram Rd, T716272. 3 rooms with private entrances in family home (Rs 950-1050 including breakfast), attached bath, quiet, friendly, for the mature visitor, discounts for singles, meals on request. Recommended. **E** *Windsurf*, 15a De Soysa Av, T/F732299. 15 large, simple rooms (Rs 750), clean, restaurant, rooftop beer garden, friendly, good value. Recommended. **F** *Blue Seas Tourist Guest House*, 9/6 De Saram Rd, T716298. 12 good clean rooms (US$9 including breakfast) in family run guesthouse, quiet location, very friendly. Highly recommended. **F** *Lak Mahal's Inn*, 8 Vihara Lane. Good value rooms with fan, attached bath, good rooftop restaurant, quiet and friendly. Recommended. **E** *Sea Breeze Tour Inn*, 22/5a De Saram Rd, T714017, F733077. 15 simple clean rooms, fan, attached bath, a bit old-fashioned. **E** *Sea Gull*, 22/2 De Saram Rd. Avoid. **F** *Jayan's Mount Resort* (was *The Bungalow*), 6 Lilian Av, T074-204065. 8 large, simple rooms in private house (Rs 450), cheap for the area but odd atmosphere.

Most hotels and guesthouses in Mount Lavinia have a restaurant, though many serve fairly bland food (family guest houses and private houses tend to be the exception, although lunch and dinner should be ordered in advance). Breakfast is often included. Most hotel restaurants are only open for breakfast, lunch and dinner. For other times head for the beach shacks which are open all day.   **Eating**

Seafood is, naturally enough, the speciality. Expect to pay Rs 200-400 for a main course. One of the best is *La Langousterie* (part of *Ravi Ras* Hotel). Seafood ranging from Rs 220 to Rs 840 (for Lobster Thermidor). *Sea Spray Club*. Drinks and snacks. *Fisherman's Villa*. 3 course meals (Rs 400); also recommended for barbecued seafood. **Away from the beach** *The Angler*, 71 Hotel Rd. Sri Lankan, Chinese and Western dishes. *Connie's*, College Rd. Good Sri Lankan dishes, seafood, pizzas and pastas, cheaper than most; plus breakfast (Continental or Sri Lankan, Rs 120). *Falado*, 20 Beach Rd. Excellent seafood (Rs 250+), steaks (Rs 225), pizzas (Rs 175-240), rice and noodles (Rs 80-120), good value, recommended. *Frankfurt Lavinia Beer Garden*, 34/8 De Saram Rd. German specialities (Rs 300+), foreign and local beers plus a wide range of European and world wines starting at Rs 150 per glass. *New Golden Bridge*, 19 Hotel Rd. Specialises in Chinese dishes (Rs 400); also takeaways and cheap beer.

Bars Almost all restaurants serve alcohol, with beer generally costing R 80-200. The terrace bar at the *Mount Lavinia Hotel* is probably the best setting for an end of day drink, although the beach bars will provide a cheaper option to enjoy the sunset.

Entertainment The more expensive hotels often provide live music over dinner, especially at weekends. Big occasions are often advertised in the local press. *Mount Lavinia Hotel's* **Little Hut**, nightclub on Fri and Sat with a local, friendly crowd (Rs 400 non-residents, ladies free). Some in Colombo are livelier.

Shopping
Better shops in Colombo
Mount Lavinia Hotel has a selection of shops. A few others selling souvenirs run along Hotel Road close to the hotel entrance, although nothing special is on offer.

Transport
At fort, buy ticket from counter number 13 for Mount Lavinia
Road Bus: Numerous buses run up and down Galle Road between Colombo and Mount Lavinia for a nominal fare. Numbers 100, 101, 102, 105, 106, 133 and 134 go to fort. For long distance buses board at Central Bus Stand or Peoples Park (north)/Bastian Mawatha (south and central) in Colombo for inter city services. **Taxi**: About Rs 300 to fort, less if you are lucky. **Tuk-tuks**: Don't expect to pay less than Rs 200-250 (after bargaining) between Mount Lavinia and Fort.

Train Suburban services run regularly between fort and Mount Lavinia (and beyond) approximately every 30 mins (less frequently at weekends and holidays) between 0446 and 2221. Timings of the next train are chalked up on a blackboard, Rs 3.50.

Directory **Communications** Post office: Station Rd. **Telephone**: At the junction of Galle Rd/Hotel Rd is for local calls only. For International phone calls private agents. Charge wildly different rates. One of the cheapest is *Procare Communications*, 339/1 Galle Road, T074-201479, procare@sol.lk Open 0800-midnight, call back available and internet Rs 7 per min, *Arjhuna Communications*, 200-B Galle Rd.

Medical services Ayurvedic and alternative medicine: *Mount Clinic of Oriental Medicine*, 41 Hotel Rd, T723464, offers acupuncture, ayurvedic and Chinese medical massage, including 'milk rice massage'. *Siddhalepa Ayurveda Hospital*, 106 Templer's Rd, T722524, F725465. Herbal and ayurvedic health programmes include herbal/steam baths and massage, large a/c rooms with TV, about Rs 3,000 for 3 days (2 nights) including treatment.

Places of worship Christian: Methodist, Hotel Rd. Service, Sun, 0800. Church of Ceylon, St Francis of Assisi, 80 Hotel Rd, T712472. Sun 0600, 0730, 1700 and Wed 0630.

Beaches near Colombo

Many visitors choose a beach near the international airport for their holiday resort as they are very easy to reach and offer very good value for money.

Negombo, the principle resort on the west coast, is rather characterless but its proximity to the airport tips the balance in its favour since the more salubrious resorts to the southeast of the island add several hours to the transfer time. Some travellers find it an uninspired tourist ghetto but still a relatively pleasant way to begin (or end) a trip.

Routes Travelling by road out of Colombo, at **Dalugama** the A3 leaves the A1 to run north to **Wattala** which is 11 km from the city centre. **A** *Pegasus Reef*, Santa Maria Mawatha, Hendala, by old Dutch canal, 18 km from the airport, T530205, F549790. 150 rooms, 500 m of coconut-fringed beach, good restaurants, pool. Half way to Negombo the road passes through Kadana and **Ja-ela**, at the heart of what used to be one of Sri Lanka's main cinnamon producing areas. Now the road runs through coconut groves, following the line of the Dutch canal up to the Negombo lagoon.

Negombo මීගමුව

Negombo town is rather scruffy and contains little of genuine interest. There are a few shops and a Bank of Ceylon on Main Street leading from the square in front of St Mary's Church towards the train and bus stations. If you follow Main Street west, there are some fine buildings with attractive balconies. At the end of the street is a curious roundabout guarded by a fish, the cricket ground, and opposite it, the remains of the fort. The beach varies, being rather dirty in places and the water not too clear, though the swimming is generally good.

Phone code: T031
Colour map 2, grid C1
Population: 60,000
Altitude: sea level

Getting there Negombo town is easy to get to by taxi (about Rs 350-400), tuk-tuk (Rs 250) or bus on arrival (see transport below). It takes about 20 mins to cover the 6 km. Hotels often arrange transfer on request. **Getting around** The main tourist area is about 4 km north of the town itself. You can walk most of the way along the beach (which gets progressively more inviting), or take a tuk-tuk (Rs 50-75) or the Kochchikade bus (No 905) from the bus station. The journey to Colombo can be irritatingly slow because of heavy traffic during the day. **Ins & outs**

The Dutch had captured Negombo from the Portuguese in 1644, and made it an important centre. The system of canals (which were originally explored in the 15th century) were improved and expanded by the Dutch who saw their advantage in moving spices (cinnamon, cloves, pepper, cardamoms) and precious gems from the interior and along the coast, to the port of Negombo for loading on to ships sailing for distant shores. Today the Negombo Lagoon has become the country's main fishing port and a centre for prawn and shrimp fishing and research. Negombo also has a high reputation for its brasswork. **History**

Sights

The Portuguese originally built a fort on the headland guarding the lagoon in about 1600. Since the area was rich in spices and particularly the much prized cinnamon, it changed hands several times before the Portuguese were finally ousted by the Dutch in 1644. It was the Dutch who built a much stronger structure. However this was largely destroyed by the British who pulled much of it down to build a jail. Today only the gate house to the east (dated 1678) with its rather crooked clock tower survives. The place is still used as a prison and the District Court is tucked away in a corner of the grounds. **Ruined fort**

A more enduring monument to the Dutch is the canal system. You can see this if you follow St Joseph Street around the headland. It skirts the lagoon where mainly fishing boats are moored (witness to its thriving fishing industry). The junction of the canal is just past the bridge crossing the lagoon. Unfortunately at its mouth it is rather dirty and not very appealing. **Canals**

The area is very rich in marine life and although there is much evidence of a motorized fleet in the harbour, you can still see fishermen using catamarans and ancient outrigger canoes to bring up their catch onto the beach every day. The outrigger canoes known as *oruva* here are not made from hollowed-out tree trunks but rather the planks are sewn together and caulked to produce a fairly wide canoe with an exceptionally flat bottom. Look out for them as some are often beached in front of the hotels. You can usually see the fleet early in the morning returning to harbour, each canoe under a three-piece sail. Their catch includes seer, skipjack, herring, mullet, **Canoes & catamarans** pomfret, amber-jack, and sometimes sharks. Prawns and lobster are caught in the lagoon. There are a number of fish markets – one is near the bridge on Duwa Island across the lagoon and there is another beyond the fort. For a trip around the lagoon or canal you should pay no more than Rs 350 and Rs 450 respectively; it is possible to arrange a much lower rate.

Crocodile spotting The **Muthurajawela marsh** in the lagoon is an Estuarine wetland which harbours the **salt-water crocodile** which in ideal conditions can grow up to 9 m in length. They are easier to spot at night (when their eyes reflect a flash light) rather than in daytime amidst the thick vegetation in which they find easy cover. A conservation project, with a Visitor Centre, protects the species.

The reef The nearest reef is 3 km west of the beach hotel area with corals within 10-20 m and the marine life includes barracuda, blue-ringed angels and unusual star fish. Tourists are attracted here for the diving though Negombo offers other watersports as well.

Portuguese influences **St Mary's Church** which dominates the town, is one of many that bears witness to the extent of Portuguese conversions to Roman Catholicism, especially among the fishermen in Negombo District. Started in 1874, the church was only completed in 1922. There are a number of alabaster statues of saints and of the Easter story as well as a colourfully painted ceiling. Easter holds a special

Negombo Town

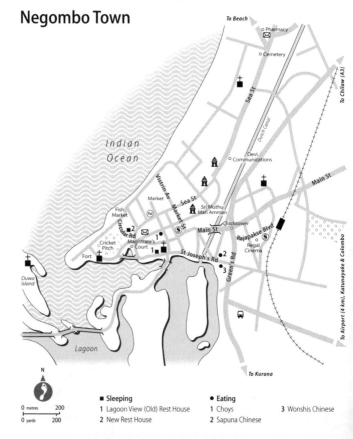

■ Sleeping
1 Lagoon View (Old) Rest House
2 New Rest House

● Eating
1 Choys
2 Sapuna Chinese
3 Wonshis Chinese

European influences: catholicism and canals

The coastal road runs through the region most affected by Portuguese colonialism. Their imprint is clearly visible in the high proportion of Roman Catholics and the number of Catholic churches in the numerous villages through which the road passes. Nearly a quarter of the population immediately inland from Negombo is Christian, increasing in the north to almost 40%.

Dutch influence is also evident in the now unused canal which was built between Colombo and Negombo. Once it was busy with the flat-bottomed 'padda' boats which travelled the 120 km between Colombo and Puttalam. As the Rev James Cordimer wrote in 1807 'the top of the canal (near Colombo) is constantly crowded with large flat-bottomed boats, which come down from Negombo with dried fish and roes, shrimps, firewood, and other articles. These boats are covered with thatched roofs in the form of huts.' The Dutch built canals extensively not just around Colombo but also around Galle in the south, but they were relatively minor works compared to the 1,000 km of irrigation canals already dug by the Sinhalese by the 12th century. The boats on these canals were often pulled by two men in harness but now the canal banks are largely the preserve of people strolling along the waterway. You can hire bikes at several points, including Negombo, and ride along a section of the banks.

place in this strongly Catholic area. There are numerous passion plays usually held on Easter Saturday, the most famous of which is on **Duwa Island** which involves the whole community. If you are short of time, it is worth stationing yourself between the two churches on Sea Street (about 1 km south of Lewis Place). Young girls in spotless white dresses are carried shoulder high by four men between the churches. This takes place in the afternoon but preparations take most of the day.

Temples There are three Hindu temples on Sea Street – the largest, Sri Muthu Mari Amman has a colourful gopuram in the inner courtyard.

Excursions

Colombo It is perfectly feasible to go into Colombo for a day's visit by hiring a car (hotels will often arrange for a driver to take you to the main sights). It is worth returning via **Hendola** by leaving the main road at Wattala. This route follows the course of the old Dutch Canal for much of the way. Keep an eye out for the birds. If you follow the road to Pamunugama which skirts the lagoon along a narrow spit of land it will take you to the heart of Catholic Sri Lanka and you will pass numerous churches and shrines. You cross Pitipani and Duwa Islands which guard the mouth of the lagoon before entering Negombo Town. The road is virtually free from traffic and makes a very pleasant alternative to the bustle of the main road.

Kandy Many hotels will organize a day-trip to Kandy and although this is possible it is not really recommended as it takes about three to four hours and means you have little time to do Kandy justice. A shorter trip takes you to the Pinnawela Elephant Orphanage near Kegalla, see page 196.

Sleeping **Negombo town D-E** *New Rest House*, Circular Road, Negombo Town, T22299. 21 rooms, half with a/c, bar, restaurant, pungently close to the fish market. **F** *Lagoon View (Old) Rest House*, T22199. 4 rooms (Rs 400), fan, nets, attached bath, no real lagoon views, restaurant. *Choys*, 31 Customs House Rd, T22807 is quite pleasant. *Sapuna* and *Wonshis*, St Joseph's Rd, do Chinese.

Many add a large surcharge in the peak season over Christmas/New Year. Resort hotels usually offer watersports

Negombo beach Hotels are spread out along almost 2 km, mostly on Lewis Place (the beach road due north of the lagoon) and further north in Ethukala and beyond. The beach gets progressively better the further away from Negombo you get so the accommodation falls into 2 sections, *Browns Beach Hotel* forming the mid-point at the junction with Lewis Place, Porutota and Cemetery Roads. To its south are most of the cheaper guesthouses while to the north are the more expensive package hotels. Meals are normally included in the price, especially in the peak season (mid-Dec to end-Jan) when a large supplement may be added. Some hotels don't allow Sri Lankans accompanying tourists to stay, partly because the area has been a suspect destination for shady practices.

Expensive A *Blue Oceanic* (Jetwing), Porutota Rd, Ethukala, T79000/3, F79999, (Colombo T345700, F345729) blue1@sri.lanka.net 108 large rooms with tub (US$50 supplement at peak season), not all with good views, typical resort hotel, all amenities, good pool, sports, entertainment, German run Negombo Diving Centre. **A** *Brown's Beach* (Aitken Spence), 175 Lewis Place, T22638, F074-870572, brownsbh@slt.net.lk 140 a/c rooms (US$60) including 25 beachside rooms plus 8 private cabanas (US$85) in busy resort hotel popular with families, full facilities, good reasonable restaurants, large pool (non-residents, Rs 100), night-club (2130, Rs 500, ladies free), Karaoke bar, sports, Barracuda Diving Centre (T77208). **A** *Royal Oceanic* (Jetwing), Porutota Rd, Ethukala, T79000, F79999, roh2@sri.lanka.net 91 a/c rooms with balcony (US$50 supplement in peak season), overlooking beach or garden, tubs, pool (only open to non-residents when occupancy is low), sports, busy resort hotel. **B** *Camelot Beach* (was *Golden Beach*), 345-7 Lewis Place, T22318,

Negombo Beach

To Kochchikade, Waikkal, Dolphin Hotel & Coconut Research Institute (10 km)

ETHUKALA

Indian Ocean

Ethukala Rd

Fortuna Travels

Voice-World Communications

Perera Place

Call-Me Communications

Golden Beach Travel Agents

Suba Communications

Health Centre

Carron Pl

Senaviratna Maw

Rosary Rd

To Town Centre

■ **Sleeping**
1 Beach View *A1*
2 Beach Villa *C1*
3 Blue Oceanic *A1*
4 Brown's Beach *B1*
5 Catamaran Beach *C1*
6 Coconut-Primitive & Ocean Park Restaurant *B1*
7 De-phani *C1*
8 Golden Beach *B1*
9 Golden Star Beach *C1*
10 Goldi Sands *A1*
11 Hellmich Village *B2*
12 Icebear *C1*
13 Oasis Beach Resort *A1*
14 Rainbow *C1*
15 Randiya *A2*
16 Rani *A2*
17 Romantic Garden *B1*
18 Royal Oceanic *A1*
19 Sea-Drift *C1*

20 Sea Joy *C1*
21 Sea Sands *B1*
22 Silver Sands *C1*
23 Star Beach *C1*
24 Sunflower Beach *C1*
25 Sunset Beach *C1*
26 Topaz Beach *B1*
27 Village Inn & Spice Restaurant *A2*

● **Eating**
1 Bijou *B2*
2 Happy Banana & Rodeo Pub *A1*
3 Keith's *A1*
4 Pri-Kin *B2*
5 Seafood *B2*
6 Sea View *B1*
7 Sherryland *A2*
8 Tropicana & Seara Travels *B2*
9 Vasana *B2*

F38235. 72 a/c rooms, new management is improving rooms, exceedingly white and bright! Focus is around pool (non-residents pay Rs 200), 2 bars, restaurant. **B** *Golden Star Beach*, 163 Lewis Place, T33564, F38266. 60 rooms, 25 a/c, popular with European package tours, very close to beach, travel office, pool (non-residents, Rs 75), restaurant, arrack bar in garden, pleasant enough although rooms could be tidier for this price. **B** *Goldi Sands*, Porutota Rd, Ethukala, T79021, F79227, goldi@eureka.lk 70 a/c rooms (rooms could be cleaner), utilitarian package hotel in rather ugly building, restaurant, pool (non-residents, Rs 100).

Mid-range C *Catamaran Beach*, 209 Lewis Place, T22206, F075-310046. 45 rooms including 23 a/c with balconies but no real views, small pool (non-residents, Rs 100), close to beach, snooker, lower end British package hotel. **C** *Hellmich Village*, 14/3 Porutota Rd, T79052 (Germany T02845-5841, F37475). 3 nicely furnished a/c 'cabanas', attached hot bath, quiet, breakfast to order, skin diving. **C** *Sunset Beach*, 5 Carron Pl, T22350, F074-870623, www.jetwing.net 40 small non-a/c rooms (US$50 supplement in peak season) in 3-storey block on the beach, upper floors more spacious, clean, light and airy, pool, package oriented, visitors' book full of praise and useful local information. **C** *Oasis Beach Resort*, 26/10 Porutota Rd, T79526, F79022. 32 a/c rooms (breakfast included) in brick built hotel set around small pool, 2 restaurants, English lessons for Japanese visitors, friendly staff but indifferent management. **C** *Sunflower Beach*, 289 Lewis Place, T/F38154. 66 rooms, some a/c with private balconies and sea views, restaurant/bar, pool (non-residents, Rs 100), unattractive building, popular with packages. **C-D** *The Icebear*, 103 Lewis Place, T33862, F38281 gahicebear@aol.com 2 attractively furnished bungalows (Rs 1950) plus 3 'villas' with spotless shared bath in well kept guest house, pleasant garden, personal attention, good home cooking (all day breakfast Rs 235, dinner Rs 440, snacks Rs 95+), Swiss owned with ducks in the garden although some may have reservations about monkey on a chain, cheap cycle hire (Rs 75 per day). **D** *Coconut-Primitive*, 11 Porutota Rd, T27185. 4 a/c rooms, popular bar and restaurant, relaxed atmosphere. **D** *Rani Holiday Village*, 154/9 Porutota Rd T24803, F38289. 12 very appealing self-contained a/c cottages, 2 bedrooms with attached hot bath, sitting area, fully equipped kitchen, fridge, TV, good value. Recommended. **D** *Romantic Garden Guest House*, 222/2 Lewis Place, T80340. 4 a/c cabanas, 4 with fan, 12 more being added, hot bath, breakfast included, garden fails to inspire romance though! **D** *Topaz Beach*, 21 Porutota Road, T79265, F075-310329. 30 good sized rooms, 7 a/c, views better from 2nd and 3rd floors, restaurant, helpful owner, minor maintenance required but reasonable value. **D-E** *Windmill Beach*, 70 Porutota Road, disorganized and overpriced.

Cheap E *Beach View Tourist Guest House*, Porutota Rd, T79706. 15 rooms (Rs 650), upstairs better, restaurant, unhelpful reception. **E** *De-phani*, 189/15 Lewis Place, T38225. 12 clean, comfortable rooms with nets (Rs 500-650), in friendly family run guesthouse, small balconies (better upstairs), restaurant. Recommended. **E** *Randiya Guest House* 154/7 Porutota Rd, T79568, F074-871437. 9 rooms ($ 10), 1 a/c, breakfast included. **E** *Silver Sands*, 95 Lewis Place, T22880. 15 large, well kept clean rooms, cheaper downstairs (Rs 500), best with large sea facing balconies (Rs 750), nets, good restaurant, helpful owner, reliable taxi service, best value in this class, popular so book ahead. Highly recommended. **E** *Village Inn*, 20a Porutota Rd, T79423. 5 cottages, 2 with kitchenettes (Rs 500-750), worth a look. **E-F** *Star Beach*, 83/3 Lewis Place, T22606, F38266. 10 rooms (Rs 600) with darker downstairs rooms (Rs 400), nets, hot water, restaurant, marvellously antiquated switchboard, on the beach, popular with budget English package groups. **F** *Beach Villa Guest house*, 3/2 Senaviratna Mawatha, T22833, F34134. 14 clean rooms with fan and net (Rs 600), cheaper rooms downstairs (Rs 450), restaurant next to the beach, owner Mr Nissanka organises island tours. **F** *Ceylonica Beach*, run down. **F** *Ocean View*, 104 Lewis Place, T38689. 4 simple

Colombo & nearby beaches

rooms (Rs 450) with 6 more being added, tours available, reasonable value though no ocean views. **F** *Rainbow*, 3 Carron Place, T22601. 8 simple, clean rooms (Rs 500), nets, food has been recommended, not bad value. **F** *Sea-Drift*, 2 Carron Place, T22601. Soon to be 10 rooms (Rs 350-500) in expanding family guesthouse (one of the originals in Negombo), kitchen facilities available, friendly. Recommended. **F** *Sea Joy*, 124/1 Lewis Place, T32667. 4 simple rooms (Rs 400), nets, cheap restaurant (local beer Rs 70), basic but reasonable value. **F** *Sea Sands*, 7 Porutota Rd, T79154. 11 simple rooms with attached bath (Rs 400-450), friendly, reasonable. Recommended. **F** *Srilal Fernando*, 67 Parakrama Rd, Kuran, towards airport (near Kurana Railway Station, RAC Bus Stop), T22481. 5 rooms set around a courtyard, with very clean baths and fan in well-staffed spacious family home, excellent food, good value (from airport: phone for pick-up Rs 300; or take bus during daytime), German spoken. Highly recommended. **F** *Vishwa Guest Rooms*, 91 Pallansena Rd, Kochchikade (1 km from railway station, 4 km north of Negombo on Bus route 905), T27215. 3 rooms in house with large garden, Sri Lankan veg meals, peaceful, walking distance of beach north of Ethukala, the Institute of Oriental Medicine is here.

Talahena C *Blue Lagoon* (Serendib), across the lagoon, 6 km south of Negombo Town, T33004. 28 rooms (US$25), full facilities including restaurant, pool, attractive garden and watersports but unfortunately rather remote.

Eating Seafood is the speciality of many hotels and restaurants; lobsters, crabs and prawns are all excellent. Even though tourist hotels sometimes carry notices advising guests not to venture out (possibly because of the difficult political situation in the past), it is possible to eat out at restaurants which is much the cheaper option.

Mid-range *Alt Saarbrucken*, 35 Porutota Rd, on the beach side, where the Alpine influence is obvious with heavy wooden furniture and pricey fondue. *Bijou*, opposite *Sea Sands*. Swiss owned and moderately expensive (although much cheaper than the tourist hotels), excellent for seafood and noodles. *Coconut-Primitive*, Lewis Place is a very popular bar/restaurant with a good range of freshly prepared food in a relaxed setting (service can be slow at times), pasta Rs 220, seafood Rs 240+, pizzas Rs 175-250. Unique in that prices include taxes and service charge. Recommended. *Edwin*, 204 Lewis Place, T39164. Excellent Sri Lankan meals (9 curries) ordered previous day, Rs 200, devilled prawns, Rs 200. Generous portions, attentive host, very clean kitchen and loos. *Happy Banana* specializes in seafood (most Rs 350), plus Chinese dishes (Rs 300). *Ocean Park* has good Chinese (Rs 90-250), Sri Lankan, and Western meals (pasta Rs 200, vegetarian Rs 175, pizza/steaks Rs 275), served in a pleasant environment *Rodeo Pub*, pastas Rs 200, steaks Rs 300. *Vasana*, Ethukala Rd.

Cheap *Ammehula*, 286 Lewis Place, opposite Camelot Beach Resort. Small but excellent restaurant, seafood speciality (fish is presented to you for inspection), good pancakes (Rs 150), rice and curry (Rs 200) huge portions, very friendly and amusing owner. Highly recommended. *Keith's*, mixed menu at reasonable prices, popular. *Pri-Kin*, offers excellent Chinese dishes (most Rs 150-250), try their soups and prawn dishes. *Sherryland*, set back from the road in a garden, most dishes under Rs 200 with attentive service, lively bar (*Lion* lager Rs 95), good value.

Bars Most hotels have at least 1 bar, or serve alcohol in their restaurant. Some of the larger hotels have nightclubs (open 2130, dress 'smart but casual'). *Coconut-Primitive* has one of Negombo's most popular bars, young crowd, popular with Aussies (*Lion* lager Rs 90, *Two Dogs* alcoholic lemonade Rs 140); *Tropicana* is probably Negombo's cheapest bar (*Lion* lager Rs 70, meals from Rs 200).

The lure of the underwater world

Sri Lanka with its warm coastal waters, its reefs with a wealth of corals and colourful tropical fish and the comfortable resort hotels, has invited divers to return to search for new excitement, once they have been hooked to the pleasures of underwater life. The delights on offer among the varied corals and rocks include invertebrates and a dazzling number of fish – Blue Surgeon, comical Parrot, Butterfly, Lion, several large and small Angels which are not camera shy – to the larger Snappers, Groupers, Barracudas, Jackfish.

Snorkels, masks and flippers can be bought in Colombo (if you cannot carry your own), and specialist diving gear is available for hire. Air tanks can be rented from Colombo, Hikkaduwa and Koggala (and possibly from Trincomalee and Nilaveli when the area is free from political troubles); it is best to only go to a reputable, established company (eg Underwater Safaris, 25 Barnes Place, Colombo; Poseidon Station and Coral Garden Hotels, Hikkaduwa; Browns Beach, Negombo, Bay Beach Aqua Sports, Weligama). The only decompression chamber is at the Naval Base at Trincomalee's Fort Ostenburg. It is best to carry your own underwater photographic equipment and films.

Several beaches in the southwest were adversely affected by 'bleaching' in 1998 but the reefs are recovering slowly. Hikkaduwa's Marine Sanctuary has a sheltered lagoon with a wealth of easily accessed corals. To avoid disappointment seek out clearer waters by taking a boat further out to sea and avoid outlets of rivers. Negombo's reef is 3 km out and really only worthwhile with SCUBA to descend from 15-20m; the better Third reef is 20 km offshore. Ambalangoda, Belapitiya and particularly Hikkaduwa are popular for corals and exploring around wrecks and Galle and Gintota offer opportunities on off-shore rocky islands and wrecks. From April to June, in the far south, Dondra to Tangalla are fine in calm seas while 4 km off Hambantota rewards you with a reef and a shipwreck. For the more adventurous, enquire about the delights off the Great and Little Basses before setting sail.

Colombo & nearby beaches

Festivals

Mar-Apr: *Easter* is celebrated with passion plays, particularly on Easter Sat on Duwa island. **Jul**: *Fishermen's festival*, St Mary's Church; a major regional festival.

Shopping

Handicrafts The curio stalls near the large hotels are handy for getting last-minute presents. Quality varies considerably and they are not nearly so good as buying direct up country. Visit them all before deciding and then bargain hard. **Supermarkets** *Davids*, opposite *Sea Garden*, carries a range of basic goods as well as a selection of teas and spices, good medical supplies and bottled water. *Home Needs*, opposite *Oasis Beach Resort*, has frozen food. **Tailors** *Chandi*, 166 Lewis Place and *Gaffal*, 266 Lewis Place, will make suits etc (silk and cotton) in about 2 days.

Sport

Watersports Deep-sea fishing from *Halcyon Beach Hotel* (US$40 per hr for 4 hrs, for 4 people or US$200 for 6 hrs), 'Leisure' fishing (US$40 per hr for 6 per person), rods (US$10-20). *Serendib Watersports Paradise*, 11 Porutota Rd (next to *Coconut-Primitive*), T/F38397. Arrange diving, including PADI course (US$370 plus extra for logbook and certificate). Government restrictions on the import of high-powered boat engines means that water–skiing, parasailing and 'Bananaboat' may not be available here. Also, Negombo's 3 main diving reefs are 5, 8 and 20 km off-shore; high-powered boats are needed to reach the distant reefs. Fishermen offer boat trips for snorkelling; and to see the lagoon and canal for about Rs 350 and Rs 450 respectively. **Diving** There are PADI qualified diving centres at *Blue Oceanic* and *Brown's Beach* hotels. **Swimming** Most of the larger hotels allow non-residents to use their pools (Rs 75-200). **Tennis and squash** *Brown's Beach Hotel*, *Blue Oceanic* and *Royal*

It is often dangerous to swim, particularly during the southwest monsoon, May-Oct. Warning notices are now posted on the beach

Oceanic hotels allow non-residents to use their tennis and squash facilities (Rs 200 per hour includes racquets, discounts for residents).

Transport
The flat roads make a short trip out of Negombo attractive

Local Transport is well regulated and hotel receptions should display a list of the agreed taxi rates. **Bicycle hire** Available from many hotels/guest houses; about Rs 150-200 per day. **Bus** Frequent buses run along the main beach road from the bus and railway stations. From the bus stand there are regular services to Colombo (number 240), both intercity Express (Rs 25, 1 hr) and the cheaper, slower CTB buses. **Tuk-tuks** Drivers cruise the main beach road from Lewis Place to Ethukala, consistently pestering tourists with 'Hello taxi?' every time you emerge onto the street. Be prepared to be tolerant with them or walk along the beach for short journeys. From Lewis Place to the bus or railway stations expect to pay around Rs 50, and up to Rs 70 from the hotels in Ethukala. When arriving, if you are asked for more than double these prices you can be fairly sure that your named hotel does not pay commission! **Car hire/taxi** Mostly through hotels; inspect vehicles carefully and expect to pay from about Rs 1,500 including driver and fuel for 80 km (some don't accept credit cards). Rates vary widely so shop around, eg return trip to Galle, Rs 2,500-3,900. Cars from *Beach Villa Guest House*, 3/2 Senaviratna Mawatha and *Charisma Tours* just south of *Golden Beach Hotel* (also motor bikes). A/c van (8-seater) US$50 per day from *Edwin Restaurant*, 204 Lewis Place, T39164 (ask for driver Alex). *Nishal Travel*, 274 Lewis Pl, T22725. Mr Lakshman Bolonghe, 146 Lewis Place, T33733, a/c van, good English speaking guide. Mr V Sivanathan, 10/35 Don Bosco Mawatha, Periyamulla, offers excellent service at reasonable rates. **Motorbike hire** Expect to pay Rs 600 per day. Some hotels (eg *Beach View*, Ethukala and *Gold Wing Motors*, 546 Colombo Rd, T22895, rent on daily/weekly terms.

To airport **Bus**: Frequent buses (number 240 to Colombo) stop close to the airport from early morning to late evening but can be crowded. **Taxi**: Rs 350-400 (after bargaining) to/from Ethukala hotels. Expect to pay Rs 500-600 at night. Most hotels/guesthouses can arrange this for you. **3-wheelers**: charge Rs 250.

Long distance **Train** The regular commuter train goes to Colombo via Katunayake (for the airport). Avoid this train during rush hours when it gets very crowded.

Directory **Banks** *Bank of Ceylon* on Main St nearly opposite St Mary's. *Seylan Bank*, Porutota Rd, just north of *Browns Beach Hotel*, open 1000-1800, a very efficient new branch with much better rates than in hotels. *Sampath Bank*, Card Centre, against Mastercard. **Communications** the post office is on Main St towards the fort. There is also an Agency post office on Lewis Place. There are several IDD phone outlets on Lewis Place, some with internet facilities, mostly at Rs 10 per min. The best of the bunch is *Call Me Communication*, 184 Lewis Place, opposite the church. Reliable machine (only one terminal), Rs 5 per min, billed through the computerised phone system. *Sabana Communications*, opposite *Village Inn* is open 24-hrs, internet Rs 7 per min. **Medical services** most hotels and guest houses have doctors on call. *General Hospital*, Colombo Rd, T22261. **Herbal massage** *Kräuter Shop*, 32 Porutota Rd, open daily 0930-1730, offers massages from Rs 750 per 30 mins, also other herbal treatments 'offer relief from various allergies (including mosquito bites!), sunburn and rheumatism'. Food and drinks are available. An ayurvedic *Royal Health Centre*, has opened at 4 Carron Place. **Tour operators** in addition to hotel travel desks, independent travel agents include *Airwing Tours*, 68 Colombo Rd, Negombo, T38116, F38188 airwing@Sri.lanka.net which offers several 'eco' tours for bird-watchers, photographers, trekkers etc (UK T/F0181 5211191). *Jetwing*, Ethukala, opposite *Blue Oceanic Hotel*. *Top Shop*, small travel counter, and *Fortuna Travels*, opposite *Browns Beach Hotel* on Cemetery Rd, T22774, F28239. **Tourist offices** *Ceylon Tourist Board*, 12/6 Ethukala, Lewis Place, 0900-1715, Mon-Sat. **Useful addresses** **Tourist Police** at Ethukala. A new post is to be sited near the Oceanic Hotels during 2000. Police HQ, Sea Street, T24287.

Beaches north of Negombo

Waikkal is quite remote and separate from Negombo so you are dependent on transport to get anywhere. It is around 45 minutes' drive from the airport.

Waikkal
Phone code: 031
Colour map 2, grid C1
12 km N of Negombo

Sleeping A *Clubhotel Dolphin*, Kammala S, sandwiched between the sea and the old Dutch canal, T33129, F01-253504 dolphin@slt.net 76 a/c rooms (US$65), 50 cottages (not all with sea views) being upgraded to a/c, however since this family orientated resort hotel is quite isolated expect to pay over US$100 for full board, popular with European packages, all facilities, plenty of sports and entertainment laid on, excellent swimming pool which zigzags attractively between the rooms, not really geared towards individuals. **A** *Ranweli Holiday Village*, T77359, F77358 ranweli@slt.lk 84 a/c chalets in eco-friendly resort hotel (guests are encouraged to re-use linen rather than add to pollution by daily laundering), reached via hand-punted ferry, peaceful atmosphere, sports, handicrafts, bird watching amongst many activities on offer, well designed and furnished rooms, plants in bathrooms, whole concept well thought out. Highly recommended.

Marawila is one of many villages with large Roman Catholic churches and also produces good quality batiks. There is a growing number of resort style hotels here. The beach is good in places but sometimes gives way to breakwaters constructed of large rocks. It is some 20 km north of Negombo, off the A3.

Sleeping AL *Club Palm Bay*, Beach Rd, T54956, F01-345086 yorkhtl@lanka.com.net Recently opened resort hotel popular with packages. 106 well furnished a/c cottages in attractive setting surrounded on 3 sides by a lagoon, all facilities, sports including fishing and boating, 9-hole golf, huge pool (rivalling *Clubhotel Dolphin* as Sri Lanka's largest), good beach close by. **C** *Aquarius Beach Hotel*, Beach Road, T54888, F078-660555 sport@sri.lanka.net 36 comfortable rooms in German run, sports-orientated hotel with excellent facilities including indoor stadium, pool, all-weather football pitch, currently host to Asian-German sports exchange programme but interested in establishing links with sporting associations in other countries (contact Dietmar Doering asian-german@t-online.de) very close to beach. Recommended. **C** *Sanmali Beach*, Beach Road, T54766, F54768. 20 rooms, some a/c, in understaffed resort hotel, restaurant, small pool, basic maintenance required. **D** *Mario Beach*, Beach Rd, T54555, F54554. 25 large, bare rooms, some a/c, better with sea view, but overpriced despite being the cheapest in the area, restaurant, large pool which could be cleaner. **D** *Palm Haven*, Beach Road, T/F53349 touraan@slt.lk 14 rooms including 4 cabanas, pool, restaurant, most rooms are acceptable but glass partitions in cabanas are potentially lethal. The hotel is up for sale!

The Western and Northwestern Region

The Western and Northwestern Region

102 Along the West coast to Puttalam

102 The road to Kandy

104 Inland from Colombo to Kurunegala

104 Kurunegala

The Western and Northwestern Region is a zone of transition. Around the densely populated suburbs of Colombo in the south, closely packed coconut groves, occasional stands of typical Wet Zone forest and intensive cultivation all contribute to the lushly evergreen landscape. Yet beyond the Wilpattu National Park, which forms the northern boundary of the region, are the arid wastes of the Vanni, leading to the densely populated but still dry Jaffna Peninsula. From west to east the landscape also undergoes a transformation, from the wide shallow lagoons of the sand-fringed coast, to the hills and mountains of the Central Highlands. Fishing villages are strung out along the coconut lined coast, while the hills are still forest clad where plantations have not converted them to endless vistas of close cropped tea bushes.

Along the west coast to Puttalam

From Colombo, the A3 to Puttalam, which is an alternative coastal route to Anuradhapura, runs due north through apparently endless groves of coconut palms. It passes the international airport about 6 km south of Negombo, then remains close to the sea and coastal lagoons.

Beyond Marawila and after crossing the estuary the road passes between the lagoon and the railway through **Madampe** (13 km) known for its Coconut Research Institute, and continues to Chilaw.

Chilaw
Phone code: 032
75 km N of Colombo

Chilaw is a small town with a large Roman Catholic church but little else to warrant a night halt. **Munneswaram**, 5 km east of Chilaw, has Tamil inscriptions and is an important pilgrimage centre. **Sleeping and eating D** *Rest House* across the lagoon, close to the beach, T22299. 17 reasonable rooms (5 a/c), some with balcony overlooking sea, nets, 2 restaurants (1 a/c), but overall pricey. *Seven Eleven*, 5 Corea Avenue, near clocktower. Recommended for reasonably priced Sri Lankan and Chinese food. May also have some **E** rooms by late 2000.

Route The A3 runs due north. A left turn at Battulu Oya leads to Udappawa. Both the road and rail line can be subject to flooding after heavy rain.

Udappawa

This tiny Tamil Hindu village is 12 km north of Chilaw. It is noted for **fire-walking** ceremonies which take place in July and August every year. Experiments in 1935-36 showed that the coals were heated to about 500°C.

Route Marshes and lagoons lie between the road and the sea for much of the route north to Puttalam, which crosses a series of minor rivers and a few major ones such as the Battulu Oya.

Puttalam
Phone code: 032

D *Rest House*, next to the bridge at Battulu Oya and Urban Council Park, T65299. 8 rooms, fan, attached bath, rather basic, restaurant. **D** *Senatilake Guest Inn*, 81/a Kurunegala Rd, T65403. 7 rooms with attached hot bath (a/c Rs 100 extra), restaurant.

Route From Puttalam the A12 goes northeast to Anuradhapura, fringing the Wilpattu National Park which is closed to visitors at present. It crosses much more open terrain, the dryness leading to much less dense forest and sparser cultivation.

The road to Kandy

The route runs from Colombo northeast across the coastal plain. Lush and beautiful scenery continues 65 km, through paddy fields interspersed with coconut and areca nut palms, endless bananas and above all pineapples (roadside stalls sell them graded by size and price). Taking 11 years to complete, the trunk road from Colombo to Kandy was the first modern road to be opened in Sri Lanka (in 1832), when the first mail service ran between the two cities. Although the road route is quicker, the train often gives better views, the last hour being through stunning scenery.

Route Colombo is strung out in a long suburban sprawl up the A1 to the 'Clocktower junction' just beyond Warakapola, where it separates from the A6 which goes to Kurunegala and Trincomalee. The really attractive scenery on the Kandy road does not start until after this point.

Leaving Colombo on the A1 a minor road at 12 km leads off to the right to **Sapugaskanda**
Sapugaskanda temple on a low hill 3 km away. There are beautiful views from
the terrace of the small stupa, but the temple is famous for its murals which
show the arrival of the Burmese saint Jagara Hamuduruvo in Sri Lanka.

Route The A1 goes through **Mahara** (15 km, excellent Rest House). The
small town was once a Dutch cantonment. About 5 km off the main road to the
left, just before Yakkala, is Heneratgoda near Gampaha.

The beautiful garden town is well signed. It is particularly famous as the nurs-   **Heneratgoda**
ery of Asia's first rubber trees introduced from the Amazon basin over a cen-   **Botanical**
tury ago. Several of the early imports are now magnificent specimens. No 6, the   **Gardens**
first tree planted, is over 100 years old, but the most famous is No 2 because of
its remarkable yield. The trees include *Hevea brasiliensis*, *Uncaria gambier*,
rubber producing lianas (*Landolphia*), and the drug *ipecacuanha*. A female of
the Coco de Mer was imported from the Seychelles and bore fruit in 1915.

The road passes by the former estate of Sir Solomon Dias Bandaranaike, aide   **Bandaranaike**
de camp to the British Governor at the time of the First World War. His son,   **family home &**
Solomon Western Ridgway Dias Bandaranaike, became Prime Minister of   **memorial**
independent Ceylon in 1956 but was assassinated in 1959. His widow succeeded him as Prime Minister and his daughter, Mrs Chandrika
Kumaratunge, was elected President in 1994. The family home, where visitors
such as King George V and Jawaharlal Nehru stayed, can be seen nearby. The
Bandaranaike memorial is by the side of the road at **Nittambuwa**, 38 km from
Colombo. A broad walkway, about 10 m wide and 100 m long, leads to a raised
plinth with 6 stone pillars behind it, the whole, surrounded by a coconut grove.

After a further 7 km Pasyala is on the western edge of the central highland mas-   **Pasyala**
sif. The area is noted for its graphite (*plumbago*) mines, betel nuts and above
all, cashew. Passing through **Cadjugama** ('village of cashew nuts'), you will see
women in brightly coloured saris selling cashew nut from stalls lining the road.
The nuts are relatively expensive, but freshly roasted, they are well worth it.

Pasgama at Ellalamulla, 2 km off the road from Pasyala junction, is a unique   **Pasgama**
'village' re-creation– a 'Step into Remoteness'– which endeavours to keep
ancient traditions alive. On arrival, the village headman is called, who must
give you permission to enter (which is never withheld) provided you conform
to the 'no smoking' rule, and then you are shown around by the 'school
teacher'. You can watch artisans and craftsmen at work– their articles are sold
in the shop, though the 'villagers' themselves operate a barter system. You can
taste authentic Sri Lankan dishes in a restaurant with a Vedda theme, while
being entertained by local musicians, and even sip fresh toddy straight off the
palm tree, brought down by a tapper. And, if you are single you can ask for the
good offices of the resident match-maker! If you spend a night in one of the
rustic village houses (with 'modern' toilets) you will be entertained to devil
dances, fire limbos, traditional games and songs. About 60 people, mostly
from neighbouring villages, work at being part of this concept.

Route The road passes through a series of small villages and towns including
Warakapola and, just beyond which the A1 turns east towards Kandy, via
Kegalla.

Warakapola
Phone code: 072
A popular stop en route
to Kandy or Kurunegala
& beyond

Warakapola provides an outlet for locally made cane baskets and mats in its bazar. It is also a popular halt for those with a sweet tooth searching for seasame seed *thalagulis* which are freshly made at *Jinadasa's* shop, among others. Stay at the **F** *Navimana Inn*, Kandy Rd, Warakapola, just south of clocktower junction at Weweldeniya, T51339, 10 rooms (Rs 350). There is a good restaurant/take away with good snacks indoors or on the verandah. Try the excellent breakfast (fish curry with hoppers). A pleasant atmosphere is helped by the small garden.

Ambepussa
Phone code: 035
60 km from Colombo

Ambepussa is just off the road to the west, with a train station. Sleeping at **D** *Rest House* (CHC), pleasantly located, T7299, Reservations T01-503497, F01-503504, 8 rooms, restaurant, bar.

Inland from Colombo to Kurunegala

The road to Kurunegala passes through the densely wooded and often crowded suburbs of Colombo climbing gently from the coastal plain to the low hills around Kurunegala, the site of chena (shifting) cultivation for generations and the major crossroads of inland routes from north to south. The direct road from Colombo to Trincomalee crosses the shortest route between Puttalam and Kandy to the southeast here. Rainfall declines steadily northwest.

Route The first part of this route follows the A1 out of Colombo to the junction with the A6 (Anuradhapura road), just north of Warakapola, 57 km from Colombo. The A6 takes a left turn at the clock tower. It is then relatively quiet and follows the forested banks of the Maha Oya for several miles before crossing it at Alawwa and on to **Polgahawela** ('the field of the coconut'), 75 km from Colombo, where you can turn off to see the **Pinnawela Elephant Orphanage** (see page 104). The area often suffers from drought at the end of the dry season. The Maha Oya flows slowly between sand-banks – with more grit than sand. The grit is used as building material and you can see women digging the river bed by hand before carrying it up the 3-m high banks to stock pile it for small lorries to transport.

Kurunegala කුරුණෑගල

Phone code: 037
Colour map 3, grid C3
93 km from Colombo

Kurunegala is an important crossroads town astride the route from Kandy to Puttalam and Colombo to Anuradhapura. It enjoys a pleasant location overlooked by huge rocky outcrops some of which have been given names of the animals they resemble: elephant rock, tortoise rock etc. According to a legend, when during a drought, the animals threatened the city's water supply, they were magically turned into stone. Situated at the foot of the 325-m black rock Etagala, there are excellent views across the lake from the top. It is also within easy reach of a few sites which are not very often visited.

Ins & outs **Getting there** There are buses from all major centres, eg Intercity from Kandy (1 hr, Rs 30), Colombo (2 hrs, Rs 35), Negombo (2 hrs, Rs 35). Some trains from Colombo to Vavuniya and Anuradhapura stop at Kurunegala; the station is southeast of town. **Getting around** The centre is compact and easy to cover on foot.

Sights Kurunegala was the royal capital for only half a century, starting with the reign of Bhuvanekabahu II (1293-1302) who was followed by Parakramabahu IV (ruled 1302-1326). There is little left of the Tooth relic temple save a few stone steps and part of a doorway. Nearby are three earlier capitals –

Panduvasnuwara (northwest off the A10) with remains of a moated palace and monasteries from the 12th century, Dambadeniya (southwest, mid-13th century), and Yapahuwa (north).

C *Diya Dahara*, 7 North Lake Rd, T/F23452. 2 a/c rooms, No 3 has large balcony overlooking the lake, best-located restaurant in town, good buffet lunch (Rs 350) but very limited evening menu. **C** *Kandyan Reach*, 350 Kandy Road, 1 km from centre, T24218, F24541 athgiri@eureka.lk 10 a/c rooms, 42 more being added, already dirty in parts though rooms are adequate, hot water, restaurant, pool. **D** *Madonna Inn*, 44 North Lake Road, T23276. 7 good-sized rooms, attached bath, nets, restaurant, quiet location close to the lake. **D** *Situ Medura*, 21 Mihindu Mawatha, T22335, F23288. 2 a/c rooms in large traditional mansion, restaurant, little English spoken at reception. **D-E** *Ranthaliya Rest House*, South Lake Rd (1 km from centre), T07-690032. 12 basic, cleanish rooms, 2 a/c, some with view (with a bit of a stretch!), nets, restaurant. **E** *Rajapihilla Rest House*, Rajapihilla Rd, T22299. 12 large, bare rooms, restaurant. **E** *Sun Reef*, 51/1 Kandy Road, T/F22433. 8 clean rooms with attached bath (Rs 650) including 1 larger a/c room (Rs 1000), simple but comfortable, friendly, good English spoken, reasonably priced restaurant, away from town centre but handy for railway station. Recommended. **E** *Wehilihini*, 150 South Lake Road, T33504. 5 rooms with attached bath, restaurant.

Sleeping & eating

Long distance Train: To **Colombo Fort**, 2 hrs. 0122, 0224, 0400, 0559, 1215, 1538, 1705 (1st class, Rs 95, available), 1812; Rs 55 (2nd class), Rs 20 (3rd class). To **Anuradhapura** (Vavuniya train), 3 hrs. 0742 (1st class, Rs 109, available), 1335, 1611, 2343; Rs 63 (2nd class), Rs 23 (3rd class). To **Trincomalee**, 0818. To **Matara**, 0737.

Transport

Banks *Sampath Bank* Card Centre, against Mastercard.

Directory

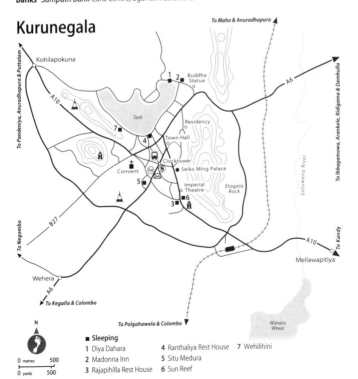

Kurunegala

To Maho & Anuradhapura

To Pandeniya, Anuradhapura & Puttalam

Kohilapokuna

A10

Tank

Buddha Statue

A6

To Ibbagamuwa, Arankele, Ridigama & Dambulla

Residency

Town Hall

Convent

Clocktower

Seiko Ming Palace

Imperial Theatre

Etagala Rock

Getuwana River

To Negombo

B27

To Kandy

A10

Mellawapitiya

Wehera

A6

To Kegalla & Colombo

To Polgahawela & Colombo

Wanaru Wewa

N

0 metres 500
0 yards 500

■ **Sleeping**
1 Diya Dahara   4 Ranthaliya Rest House   7 Wehilihini
2 Madonna Inn   5 Situ Medura
3 Rajapihilla Rest House   6 Sun Reef

Around Kurunegala

Arankele
At Arankele, 24 km north of Kurunegala (west of the Ibbagamuwa-Moragollagama Road), is a 6th century **cave hermitage** up a forested hillside. Ancient Brahmi donative inscriptions have been found in some caves. Excavations have revealed meditation halls, stone-faced double platform structures and ambulatories for the *Tapovana* (forest-dwelling) sect of austere Buddhist hermits here. Typically, the platforms aligned east-west, with the entrance porch to the east, would be bridged by a large monolith. The smaller of the double-platform structure here was probably divided into nine 'cells' or monks' dwellings – the roof being supported on columns.

Ridigama Vihara
The 'Silver Temple', 18 km northeast of Kurunegala, marks the place where silver ore was discovered in the 2nd century BC, during the reign of Dutthagamenu (Dutugemunu). It is an ancient Buddhist temple site with rock cave hermitages and an image house with Kandyan paintings. Among the finds, which mostly date from the 18th century, are Buddha statues (seated and reclining), a door frame beautifully carved and inlaid with ivory, and a curious altar with Dutch (Delft) tiles with Biblical figures gifted by a Dutch consul! There is an attractive artificial lake at the foot of the hills. ■ *Getting there: Head north from Kurunegala on the A6 (Dambulla road). Passing Ibbagamuwa (11.5 km), take the first right (east) after a another 2 km onto the B409. At 7 km, turn right at the junction onto the B264; after 9 km you reach Ridigama. Turn left at the main junction, then right at the clocktower and follow the dirt track for 200 m. Turn left onto the sealed road, then turn right at the T-junction. Follow the road past the lake and go uphill for 1.5 km to the vihara.*

Kurunegala area

Ivory door inlay, Ridigama Vihara
Source: LTP Manjsri's, Design Elements LXXV

Dambadeniya

Dambadeniya, about 30 km south-west of Kurunegala, became prominent in the mid-13th century when the capital was moved there by Parakramabahu II (ruled 1236-1270) together with the Tooth Relic. Little remains of the palace buildings though six ponds are still there. The two-storey temple (originally three) about 400 m south, which has Buddha images, is identified as the Vijayasundaramaya. It has some interesting wall paintings dating from the 18th century, when it was restored. It was used to exhibit the Tooth Relic which was normally housed in another temple near the palace.

North from Kurunegala

Route From Kurunegala two routes go north to Anuradhapura. The eastern route takes the A6 to Dambulla (with a diversion to Arankele) and then A9 to Anuradhapura, see page 237. The quieter western route (106 km) is on the A10 as far as Padeniya, and then forks right onto the A28 to Maho.

Maho Maho, 19 km north of Kurunegala, is a pleasant small town, where you cross the railway and take the right turn along a poor road to see the late 13th-century capital of Yapahuwa. Kaikavala Vihara is only 2 km away.

Yapahuwa The road, 5 km east from Maho, leads to the foot of the rock at Yapahuwa. The **fortress** stands on a very pleasant, shaded site. Bhuvanekabahu I (ruled 1272-1284) moved his capital from Dambadeniya to Yapahuwa seeing the need for stronger fortification against Tamil invaders, and built a palace and a temple where the Tooth and the Alms Bowl relics were housed for 11 years.

A vast granite rock rising 100 m from the surrounding plain, is encircled by a 1 km long path rising to the top. The fort palace built of stone is surrounded by two moats and ramparts and there are signs of other ancient means of defence. The impressive ornamental stairway with some fine lions is still well preserved, and somewhat resminiscent of Far Eastern art. The steps are fairly steep so can be tiring to climb. The ruins at the head of the remarkable flight of granite steps are unique and the views over the palms towards the highlands are not to be missed. The temple (restored in 1886) illustrates South Indian artistic influence in its fine carvings on the pillars, doorway and windows which show dancers, musicians and animals. One of the window frames is now exhibited in the Colombo Museum. The remains of a temple to the northeast, outside the fortification (which was thought at one time to have housed the Tooth relic), has some sculptures visible. There is a small, fairly modern museum on site.

This fortress capital of the Sinhalese kings when abandoned was inhabited by Buddhist monks and religious ascetics. The relics were carried away from the temple here to South India by the Pandyas, and then recovered in 1288 by Parakramabahu III (ruled 1287-1293), who temporarily placed them in safety at Polonnaruwa.

■ *Getting there: from Kurunegala, it is possible to take a day trip to Maho (for Yapahuwa). The train takes 1 hr, leaving Kurunegala at 0630 and 0900, returning from Maho at 1115, 1438 or 1605; fare Rs 25 (2nd class), Rs 9 (3rd class). Three-wheelers can take you to Yapahuwa.*

Southern Sri Lanka

5

Southern Sri Lanka

112 Beaches along the southwest coast
112 Kalutara
114 Beruwela
116 Aluthgama
117 Bentota
120 Ambalangoda
122 Hikkaduwa
130 **Galle**
137 Unawatuna

140 The Scenic South Coast
141 Weligama
143 Mirissa
144 Matara

147 The Dry Southeast
148 Tangalla
154 Kalametiya Bird Sanctuary
155 Hambantota
157 Bundala National Park
158 Tissamaharama
161 Yala (Ruhuna) National Park
162 Kataragama

164 The heart of the Wet Zone
166 Ratnapura
169 Sinharaja Biosphere Reserve
173 Pelmadulla to the South Coast
173 Uda Walawe National Park

At the heart of Sri Lanka's Wet Zone, Sri Lanka's southwest region is the most densely populated part of the island. Small scale farms are scattered under the thick cover of trees in the interior, while the coast is one of the island's most scenic regions, with magnificent bays and palm fringed sandy beaches interspersed with rocky headlands. Most of Sri Lanka's major resort hotels are found between Colombo and Dondra Head, the southernmost point.

Beaches along the southwest coast

Places are described from north to south, following the route from Colombo

On the coastal strip many people depend on fishing with fishermen bringing in their catch at numerous points along the sea. The coconut palms that line the shore also provide a livelihood for many. The A2 south of Colombo runs close to the coast. It is a wholly distinctive drive, contrasting sharply with journeys into and through the hills or across the Dry Zone of the north and east. The railway line hugs the ocean as it goes south making this a very pleasant journey.

Moratuwa   Moratuwa, 23 km from Colombo, is fairly congested. The town is noted for its furniture making and its college.

Panadura   Panadura is situated to the south of wide estuary. For those interested in **batik**
Phone code: 034   it is well worth the small diversion to the workshop and showroom of Bandula
28 km from Colombo   Fernando, 289/5 Noel Mendis Road, just off the A2, T33369, F34036. One of the foremost batik designers in Sri Lanka, Bandula Fernando combines traditional and modern styles to produce some exceptionally vibrant and original batiks. He is also credited with evolving mosaic art in batik, acknowledged as a uniquely individual style of batik. The designs on offer are quite different from those seen elsewhere on the island and are sold at fair prices considering the detail and excellence.

Sleeping   From Eluwila Sub-Post Office, 4 km south of Panadura, a road leads east to Kiriberiya Estate (15-min drive) which has the attractive **C** *Paradies 'Country House'*, T32356, Colombo F652045. 4 large comfortable rooms with period furniture, meals to order, spacious grounds amidst rubber plantations in a peaceful, rural setting, fresh water pool, boats, bird-watching and possibility of pony/elephant rides. Kiriberiya Bus Station is a 3-minute walk away. Pick up from the airport can be arranged.

Kalutara   කළුතර

Phone code: 034   The northern outskirts of Kalutara are 42 km from Colombo Fort. The Portu-
Colour map 3, grid B2   guese built a fort on the site of a Buddhist temple here, the Dutch took it over and the British agent converted it to his residence. The site, by the bridge across the Kalu Ganga, now again has a modern Buddhist shrine, the Gangatilaka Vihara, with a sacred Bo tree outside. It is worth stopping to look at the 74 paintings inside the hollow *dagoba* (others on the island contain relics and are not accessible).

   Kalutara has a huge stretch of fine sand with Wadduwa to the north, which has the area's top resort, Mahawaskaduwa (Kalutara North) where the beach is more scenic, right down to Katukurunda (Kalutara South). The town, however, is busy and rather scruffy.

   The large number of coconut palms along the coast road marks the centre of the arrack industry. The island's best quality mangosteen (introduced from Malaya in the early 19th century) and rubber are economically important. Graphite is also mined. The town is wellknown for its basket making – leaves of the wild date are dyed red, orange, green and black, and woven into hats, mats and baskets. Wild hog deer, introduced by the Dutch from the Ganga Delta, are reputedly still found.

Southern Sri Lanka

Expensive L *Blue Water* (Jetwing), Wadduwa, T/F35067 (Colombo T345700, **Sleeping**
F345729), bluewater@eureka.lk 100 excellent a/c rooms (US$150), in luxurious hotel
with top facilities amidst palm groves, designed by Geoffrey Bawa with spacious public areas, understated décor, ethnic feel (copied but not excelled by other hotels along
the coast), large imaginative pool. Recommended. **AL** *Royal Palms Beach*, Kalutara
North, T28113, F28112, (Colombo T343720, F434524) tangerine tours@eureka.lk 124
superb fully equipped rooms, private balcony or patio with sea or garden views, disco
and pub, sports facilities shared with Tangerine beach Hotel, huge pool (can almost
swim around the hotel). Recommended. **A** *Golden Sun Resort*, (Aitken Spence),
Kudawaskaduwa, Kalutara N, T28484, F28485, (Colombo T304604, F433755)
ashmres@lanka.ccom.lk 100 a/c rooms including 32 cabanas, all sea facing, in attractive gardens onto the beach, full facilities. **A** *Tangerine Beach*, De Abrews Rd,
Mahawaskaduwa, T22640, F26794, (Colombo T343720, F434524) tangerinetours@
eureka.lk 166 a/c rooms, full facilities though reception can be slow, beautifully laid
out with huge lawns and ponds stretching beneath coconut palms to the sea, popular
with package groups. Recommended. **A** *Sindbad*, St Sebastians Rd, Katukurunda,
T26537, F26530 serenlti@sri.lanka.net 105 rooms (33 a/c) in a good location
sandwiched between sea and lagoon, mostly packages, restaurant, pool, ayurvedic
health centre, simple rooms but you pay for the view. **A-B** *Mermaid*,
Mahawaskaduwa, T22613, F28572. 72 a/c rooms, split-level restaurant, bars, sports,
excursions, mainly tour groups, beautiful location in coconut plantation, attractive
lawn runs down to beach. **A** *Villa Ocean View*, Wadduwa, T32463, F070-343054
villaocn@sltnet.lk 142 a/c rooms in either newer wing or 'villas' close to the beach, all
facilities, focus around the pool, rooftop beer garden with real grass, hotel elephant,
popular with package groups.

Mid-range C *Hibiscus Beach* (Aitken Spence), Mahawaskaduwa, T22704, F22705,
(Colombo T304604, F433755) ashmres@lanka.ccom.lk 50 large rooms (a/c extra),
pleasant balcony with sea view, lounge bar overlooks colourful hibiscus garden, pool,
sports, good beach, helpful, friendly staff. Recommended. **C-E** *Garden Beach*, 62/9 Sri
Sumangala Rd, Kalutara N, T22380. 12 spacious and airy rooms (Rs 750-1250), some
a/c, hot bath, restaurant, pool, modest hotel.

Cheap E *New Castel*, Sea Beach Rd, Kalutara North. 3 small, basic, cleanish rooms
with shared bath (Rs 600), overpriced. **E** *Prima*, 173 St Sebastian Road, Katukurunda,
near Sindbad, T/F26127. 16 reasonable rooms (Rs 1000 including breakfast), restaurant, small pool, popular with Germans, not bad value. **F** *Dugong Beach*, 208 Sea
Beach Rd, Kalutara North, T24330. 5 clean rooms (Rs 450) with attached bath, restaurant, quiet, family run, close to beach, good value.

Besides the hotel restaurants, there are numerous places to eat (and buy souvenirs) **Eating**
along the roads leading from Galle Rd to the hotels.

Kalutara is on the Colombo-Matara railway line, though only the 'slow' **trains** stop **Transport**
here. It is probably easier to reach by one of the **buses** that run between Colombo
and Galle.

Medical Services *General Hospital* T22261. **Directory**

The road south passes through **Paiyagala** North and South There are several **Route**
places to stay on Galle Road, including **E** *German Guest House*, Paiyagala
South, and **E** *Palm Woods*, Paiyagala North, T22219, 18 rooms.

Southern Sri Lanka

The Sap Tappers

For most Sri Lankans, wherever the coconut palm thrives, palm toddy is a universal favourite as is the stronger distilled arrack throughout the island. These, and sweet palm juice, treacle or jaggery, are produced from the sap which is collected in earthen pots which you will notice hanging at the base of the long green fronds at the crown of the palms which have been set aside for 'tapping'.

The sap flows when the apex of an unopened flower bunch is 'tapped' by slicing it off and tapping it with a stick to make the cells burst and the juice to flow. This usually starts in about 3 weeks of the first cut. From then on successive flower buds are tapped so that sap collecting can continue for half a year. Fruit production, of course, stops during this period, but

tapping seems to result in an improved crop of nuts where the yield had previously been poor.

The task of extracting the sap from the crown of the palms is left in the hands of the toddy tappers (Duravas). The skilful tapper usually ties a circle of rope around his ankles and shins up the tall smooth trunk two or three times a day to empty the sap pot into one he has tied around his waist. An agile man collecting from a group of palms will often get from tree to tree by using pairs of coconut fibre ropes tied from one tree top to the next, which saves the tapper time and energy wasted in climbing down and up again! Not quite a tight-rope walk but hazardous nevertheless. See also 'The Indispensable Coconut' on page 291.

Beruwela   බේරුවෙල

Phone code: 034
Colour map 3, grid B2
58 km from Colombo

The name Beruwela is derived from the Sinhalese word Baeruala (the place where the sail is lowered). It marks the spot where the first Arab Muslim settlers are believed to have landed around the eighth century. The **Kitchimalai mosque**, on a headland, is worth seeing; it is a major pilgrimage centre at the end of Ramadan since there is also a shrine of a 10th-century muslim saint. Nearby, the fishermen unload their daily catch. The fish market is busy early each morning – you may well see fresh shark or tuna change hands even before the sun is up. You can also go out to the **lighthouse** raised on a small island offshore which offers an excellent view of the coastline from the top.

The beach, sheltered by reefs, has been attractively developed & is very popular with package tourists, particularly from Germany

All the hotels listed below are actually in **Moragalla**, an adjoining settlement to the south of Beruwela, with some of the more upmarket hotels further south at Kaluwamodara. Fishermen offer to ferry holidaymakers across the narrow estuary to Bentota, the next resort.

Expensive AL *Club Palm Garden*, T76039, F76038, (Colombo T334420, F333324) **Sleeping**
palmgdn@eureka.lk 140 a/c rooms in 2 wings enclosing pool and garden, day long entertainment, possibly the best 18 hole crazy golf course in Sri Lanka, almost exclusive package groups, refurbished in 2000. **AL** *Confifi Beach*, T76217, F76317, (Colombo T334420, F333324) confifi@eureka.lk 73 rooms in either a/c garden view or non a/c 'deluxe' with sea view, 2 restaurants, bar, pool. **AL** *Eden*, Kaluwamodara, T76075, F76181, (Colombo T334420, F333324) eden@eureka.lk 158 rooms in the newest and most luxurious of the top class hotels here, grand entrance, superb large pool, full entertainment and sports facilities. Recommended.
AL *Riverina*, Kaluwamodara, T76044, F76047, (Colombo T334420, F333324) riverina@eureka.lk 190 a/c rooms, full facilities including tennis, watersports, good indoor games room, cyber café, ayurvedic centre, well organised hotel. Recommended **A** *Bayroo*, T76990, F76297 (Colombo T439049, F447087) htlres@keells.com 100 good a/c rooms, all with sea views, well laid out, wooded grounds, the current President stays here on occasion, full facilities, not bad value. **A** *Neptune* (Aitken Spence), T76031, F76033, (Colombo T304604, F433755) ashmres@lanka.com.lk 145 a/c rooms (US$105 - $115 all inclusive) in ageing hotel (25+ years old) so a little shabby, pleasant gardens and pool, beautiful beach with safe swimming (life-guard), floodlit tennis, ayurvedic health centre, pleasant layout with shady trees. **A** *Tropical Villas* (Jetwing), T76780, F76157, (Colombo T345700, F345729) tropvilla@eureka.lk 54 tastefully furnished split-level villas with sitting area, focused around small pool (with cascade) and pleasant gardens, personalised service. Recommended. **A** *The Villa Riviera* (Jetwing), was Riviera Beach Resort, T074 288262, F76245 jethot@sri.lanka.net 54 rooms, buffet meals, a little old fashioned but recently refurbished, cosy atmosphere, sea facing rooms. **A-B** *Barberyn Reef*, Barberyn Rd, T76036, F76037 barberyn@slt.lk 74 rooms, 24 cottages without views, some a/c, extensive ayurvedic health centre, safe swimming enclosed by a reef, 95% German clientele. **B** *Swanee*, (Keells), T76007, F76073 htlres@keells.com 52 rooms, some a/c, balcony on upper floors, shady garden around pool, popular with tour groups although a bit grubby around the edges, free shuttle to Club Inter Sport at Bentota.

Beruwela

To Colombo

Beruwela Station

To Barberyn Lighthouse

7
12
11
4

2

MORAGALLA
1

Galle Rd

KALAWILA

KALUWAMODARA

9
10
6
3
8

ALUTHGAMA WEST
5

ALUTHGAMA EAST

Indian Ocean

Aluthgama Station

River Av

Bentota Ganga

BENTOTA

N

0 km   1
0 miles   1

■ **Sleeping**
1 Barberyn Reef &
    Bavarian Guest House
2 Bayroo
3 Club Palm Garden

4 Confifi Beach
5 Eden
6 Neptune
7 Panorama
8 Riverina
9 Sagarika Holiday
    Bungalow
10 Swanee
11 Villa Riviera
12 Ypsylon Guest House
    & Dive Centre

Mid-range C-D *Sagarika Holiday Bungalow*, T/F074-289024. 10 modest chalets, 1 a/c, breakfast included, old fashioned, clean but some rooms are a bit musty, caters mainly for Germans, good location with restaurant on beach **D** *Bavarian Guest house*, 92 Barberyn Road, T/F76129. 6 large modern rooms, hot bath, pool, restaurant, bar, German owned. **D** *Ypsylon Guest House*, T76132, F76334 ypsylon@slt.lk 25 rooms, hot bath, breakfast included, pool, German run diving school (see below).

Cheap E *Panorama*, T77091. 10 simple, clean rooms (Rs 600) in small guest house, restaurant, good value for the area.

Eating   Besides the hotel restaurants, there are numerous places to eat (and buy souvenirs) along the small roads leading from Galle Rd to the hotels.

Sports   **Diving** (best Dec-Mar). German run dive centre at *Ypsylon Hotel*, T76132, F76334, ypsylon@slt.lk PADI Open Water Course (DM570, Rs 22,000), Advanced Course (DM390, Rs 15,000), single dive DM42 (or DM35 with own equipment) plus some introductory pool-based lessons. Recommended. *Confifi Marina*, T42766 at Bentota (T76039 at Palm Garden Hotel). PADI Open water (US$380), single dive (US$32). Also sailing, canoeing or windsurfing (US$5 per hr), snorkelling (US$10), deep sea fishing.

Transport   **Road Buses** ply the route between Colombo and Galle. **Train** Again, Beruwela is on the main Colombo-Matara line, though only the slower trains stop here. The best option is to take one of the express trains, get off at **Aluthgama** (see below) and take a tuk-tuk from there.

Directory   **Tourist Police** Galle Rd, Moragalla, opposite *Neptune Hotel*.

Aluthgama
අලුත්ගම
Phone code: U34
60 kms from Colombo

The rather unattractive Aluthgama town has a busy fish market and is famous for its oysters. The sand spit which separates the river from the sea where most of the hotels are built provides excellent waters for windsurfing and sailing. Many of the hotels referred to as being in Bentota are to the north of the Bentota Bridge and so actually in Aluthgama.

Sleeping Expensive A *Ceysands* (Keells), T75073, F75895, (Colombo T439049, F447087). 84 a/c rooms (US$80 - 100), located on a narrow spit of land between the sea and river reached by shuttle boat, good beach, floating restaurant, good food, marvellous setting, good choice despite looking a little frayed around the edges, discounted use of Club Inter Sport at Bentota. **A** *Robinson Club*, 'Island Paradise', T75167, F75172 (or Germany T0511 955 5848). 72 rooms and 78 bungalow in a maze of rooms

Returning home
from a hog hunt
Source: Kincaid, D
(1938) British social
life in India,
Routledge, London

Southern Sri Lanka

on small spit of land accessible by shuttle boat, exclusively Austro-German clientele, full facilities; up for sale. **Mid-range C** *Nilwala*, Galle Rd (on the river), Kaluwamodara, T75017, F70408. 14 clean a/c rooms, although a/c units are noisy, overlooking river, watersports (eg water skiing Rs 400/hr, boat trips Rs 800 for a 3 hr trip up and down the river), also Eden Roc Divers (see under Bentota below). **D** *Araliya*, Galle Rd, Kaluwamodara, T/F75385. 22 rooms (4 a/c), not all with sea views, watersports, clean but a bit pricey. **D** *German Lanka Guest House*, Manju Sri Mawatha, T075-581530, F074-289006. 5 large, attractive rooms, some on terrace overlooking river, hot bath, nets, restaurant (breakfast included), bar, watersports, German run. **D** *Hemadan*, 25 Manju Sri Mawatha (on the river bank), T/F75320. 11 good clean rooms (some with balcony), Danish owned, quiet, hot bath, restaurant, watersports, boat shuttle to beach. **D** *Terrena*, Manju Sri Mawatha, by the bridge, T/F074 289015. 7 clean rooms with hot bath, breakfast included, Austrian owned, pleasant terrace and garden although location can be noisier than others.

Singharaja Bakery and Restaurant, 120 Galle Road, Kaluwamodara is a good, clean establishment providing excellent Sri Lankan food including short eats, hoppers and curries. Popular as a roadside halt but worth visiting for a cheap and authentic alternative to hotel food,. Recommended. *River Inn Restaurant*, 97 Manju Sri Mawatha, has fine views.

Eating
Numerous restaurants around Bentota Bridge & on the narrow lanes leading down to the hotels

Aluthgama is the main transport hub for Beruwela to the north and Bentota to the south. **Road Buses** running between Colombo and Galle stop here. **Tuk-tuks** will take you to Beruwela and Bentota. **Train** On the main Colombo-Matara line, Aluthgama can be reached by Express trains from Colombo (see above) in around 1½ hrs (2nd class Rs 34, 3rd class Rs 13).

Transport

Bentota ⠀ බෙන්තොට

The **Bentota Bridge** marks the border between the Western and Southwestern Provinces. The resort is built entirely for foreign tourists with a beach complex with shops, bank and post office. A full range of sports is available though it is also gaining a reputation for providing ayurvedic healing centres. Unofficial "guides" offer nearby river and lagoon trips and visits to temples, coir factories and woodcarvers. They are way overpriced.

Phone code: 034
Colour map 3, grid B2
63 km from Colombo
Sea rough during the monsoons; best between Nov & Apr

The splendid 'Brief Garden' at Kalawila was created between 1929 and 1989 by the late Bevis Bawa, the landscape architect, writer and sculptor– the name refers to a court brief! It is an enchanting garden on a hill side with wonderful views. Bawa's private collection of paintings, sculptures, photographs and furniture (many colonial antiques) provides an added incentive to visit the bird-filled 5-acre landscaped garden with cool, shady woodland paths, many mature specimen trees, exotic flowering plants and interesting water features. Highly recommended. ■ *Daily, 0800-1700. Rs 125 includes leaflet. T70462. Getting there: From Aluthgama, the road inland to Matugama, leads to Dharga (8 km), and a 2 km rough track (right at the first fork and left at the second) takes you to the gardens.*

Brief Garden

Most of the accommodation in Bentota itself is close to the train station, on the beach side. Several hotels along this strip of coast are in Aluthgama and Kaluwamodara (listed above) and not strictly in Bentota.

Sleeping

Expensive It is worth visiting the top two hotels here if you are not staying. They are exceptional! **LL-L** *Saman Villas*, Aturuwella, on a rocky headland 5 km south,

T/F75433, (Colombo T/F439792) samanvil@sri.lanka.net 27 magnificent split level suites with sea views set on a rocky headland, member of the Small Hotels of the World Association, all with attractive furnishings (CD systems in sitting area), 'astonishing' open-air bath, superb pool high above sea with good views and access to long beaches either side, expensive but worth it. **L** *Taj Exotica*, T75650, F75160 exotica@sri.lanka.net 162 large a/c rooms (ask for higher floors) in the newest of the top class hotels here in a superb location on a headland, all with sea facing balcony or terrace, good, varied buffets (à la carte disappointing), 'fantastic' pool. **L-AL** *The Villa*, 138/18-22 Galle Rd (1.5 km south of Bentota), Mohotti Walauwa, T75311, F072 269187. 15 luxurious suites, individually and tastefully decorated with antique furniture in a large 1880 villa (extensions by Geoffrey Bawa), superb bathrooms, good beach, small pool, beautiful garden. Recommended. **AL** *Bentota Beach*, south of Bentota Bridge, T75176, F75179, (Colombo T439049, F447087) bbh@keells.com 133 comfortable a/c rooms, design reminiscent of a Dutch fort, luxurious layout in extensive gardens, good beach, full facilities including hotel elephant, location of Club Inter Sport (see below). **A** *Lihiniya Surf*, T75126, F75486, (Colombo T471620, F434364) lihiniya@slt.lk 86 a/c rooms, popular with British tour groups, small pool, tennis, feel of a dated beach-side motel, watersports, PADI diving centre. **A** *Serendib*, T75248, F75313 serenlti@sri.lanka.net 90 a/c rooms in ageing hotel which is still bearing up well, attractive rooms with balcony or terrace, directly onto beach, pleasant gardens, friendly service, full facilities, recommended. **C** *Club Villa*, 138/15 Galle Rd Mohotti Walauwa (next to *The Villa*), T/F75312. 16 beautiful, though simple rooms (3 a/c and 1 **B** suite) in a Dutch style villa, restaurant (good Italian), wonderfully peaceful palm-shaded garden, small pool, beach a short walk across coastal railway line, very friendly staff, superb ambience, 10 more rooms due after acquisition of next door property. Highly recommended. **Mid-range D-E** *Susantha*, Resort Rd, Pitaramba, a short walk behind the railway station (5 mins from beach, across the rail track), T75324, F75590. 12 rooms with bath in a pleasant guest house, restaurant.

Aluthgama & Bentota

To Saman Villas (5 km), Niroga & Galle

0 km 1
0 miles 1

■ Sleeping
1 Araliya
2 Bentota Beach
3 Ceysands
4 Club Palm Garden
5 Club Villa
6 Eden
7 Hemadan
8 Lihiniya Surf
9 Neptune
10 Nilwala & Eden Roc Divers
11 Riverina
12 Robinson Club (Island Paradise) & Club Paradise Ayurvedic Centre
13 Sagarika Holiday Bungalow
14 Serendib
15 Susantha, Palm Restaurant & Ayurvedic Centre
16 Swanee
17 Taj Exotica
18 The Villa

● Eating
1 Aida's Gem
2 Refresh & Tourist Information at National Holiday Resort

Refresh at the *National Holiday Resort* complex, has no sea-view but a garden. Good food all day especially sea-food and rice dishes. Across the Galle Rd, *Aida's Gem*, has a restaurant upstairs (access from the back). Italian pasta dishes (about Rs 250-300 for a meal), tasty curries are cheaper. *Susantha Palm* near the guest house serves simple Sri Lankan and continental dishes for around Rs 200 as well as short eats.

Eating

B *Ayurveda Walauwa*, Galle Road, Warahena, T753372, F75374. 20 rooms in treatment centre (minimum stay 1 week although 2 weeks is advised for best effect), including diagnosis, therapy, diet and treatments (US$980 per week all inclusive for single room, US$840 per person per week for double room). *Club Paradise*, near Robinson Club, Aluthgama, T75354, F071 754448. Similar treatment as Ayurveda Walauwa (US$1100 per week single, US$950 per person per week double). *Bentota Aida Ayurveda and Holistic Health Resort*, 12a Mangala Mawatha, Bentota, T71137, F71140 aida@visual.lk 15 comfortable rooms with TV, small balcony, minimum stay 1 week including treatment and all meals (DM360- DM440). Also one day packages available for non-residents including consultation, massage or herbal bath/sauna (Rs 4,025). *Niroga Ayurveda Health Centre*, next to Saman Villas, T/F70312, chithral@slt.lk 8 rooms, minimum 1 week (from Rs 10,000 depending on treatment). Also 1 day courses possible from Rs 3000 (phone in advance).

Ayurvedic centres

A range of watersports and activities is possible on the lagoon or the open sea. *Club Inter Sport* (Keells), within the grounds of *Bentota Beach Hotel*, T75178, F75179. Watersports include windsurfing (Rs 400 per hr, Instructor Upali recommended), water skiing (Rs 350-500 per round), banana boat (Rs 250), lessons possible. Also tennis, squash, archery, badminton. Sport passes available for discounted activities on 2-day (weekend) or weekly basis. Discounts for residents of any of the Keells hotels in the area. **Diving** (best Nov and Apr). *Eden Roc Divers* at *Hotel Nilwala*, Kaluwamodara, T75017, F70408. Friendly, German run, 1 dive with own equipment, Rs 1600 (with hired equipment Rs 2000), PADI Open Water Course, Rs 20,000, Advanced Course, Rs 14,400 (including certificate fees), recommended. **Swimming**: some hotel pools are open to non-residents (eg *Bentota Beach Hotel* Rs 300 per day). **River safaris** Boat trips up the Bentota Ganga to see the mangrove swamps, birdlife and 'safe' basking crocodiles; avoid the 'zoo'. Most trips last 2 hrs to half a day. These are offered through many hotels and from near the bridge.

Sports

Road Buses passing through Bentota are often already full, so it is better to go to Aluthgama and take a bus that originates there. **Train** Bentota's tiny railway station is on the main Colombo-Matara line but only the 'slow' trains stop here so it is better to travel on an Express train to/from Aluthgama.

Transport

Useful addresses Tourist Police, National Holiday Resort, T75022.

Directory

Induruwa has a pleasant stretch of beach which is being developed. From Bentota to Galle the road is nearly always in sight of the sea. It passes one of several turtle hatcheries along this coast. The exemplary Turtle Conservation Project is at Rekawa beyond Tangalla. See page 156.

The **Turtle Research Project** (Victor Hasselblad Project), just south of Bentota, has a hatchery where visitors are welcome. This project has been running for about 20 years, buying eggs from local fishermen at a higher price (Rs 3-4 per egg) than they would get normally if sold for food. The eggs are buried as soon as possible in batches of 50. After hatching, the baby turtles are placed in holding tanks for two to three days before being released into the sea in the evening under supervision. Depending on the time of year (best November to April), you can see the hatchlings of up to four species (green,

Induruwa
Phone code: 034
68 km from Colombo

hawksbill, leatherback and loggerhead) at any one time. Adult turtles which are kept in separate tanks as exhibits will be held up for you to photograph. ■ *Rs 50 if you come from the direction of the road, Rs 100 from the beach side (strange anti-environmental pricing policy!); donations welcome.*

Several places are close to the railway station

Sleeping and eating Expensive B *Indurawala Beach Resort*, Galle Rd, T75445, F75583, inbeachr@ sltnet.lk 90 a/c rooms, tubs, private balconies with sea view, breakfast included, pool with jacuzzi, full facilities, on good section of beach but large 4-storey block with uninspired architecture, popular with package groups, good value. **C** *Emerald Bay* on the beach, T/F75363. 24 comfortable rooms, 6 a/c (rates negotiable), restaurant, pool, large garden. **Mid-range D** *Long Beach Cottage*, Galle Rd, north of station,T/F75773, (Colombo T727602, Mon-Fri), 5 clean, sea facing rooms with fan (Rs 600), local dishes and seafood to order, pleasant mangrove shaded garden with direct access to a fine beach, free pick up from Aluthgama station, friendly Sri Lankan/German owners, prepare to be photographed for the Visitors' Book! Recommended.

Kosgoda

Phone code: 09
73 km from Colombo

Kosgoda has a **turtle hatchery** similar to Induruwa. This larger operation seems to be more popular with the bus tours (souvenir sellers ply their business outside the entrance). The fishermen are paid a slightly higher premium for the eggs than elsewhere, whilst the eggs are buried in the same batches as they are laid. You can also see a couple of albino turtles, which (it is claimed) would otherwise be highly vulnerable in the ocean. See also, Turtle Conservation Project, Rekawa. ■ *Donations are expected rather than a fixed entrance fee.*

Sleeping AL *Triton*, (Aitken Spence), Ahungalla, 6 km south of Kosgoda, T64041, F64046, (Colombo T304604, F433755) ashmres@lanka.ccom.lk 160 a/c rooms including 18 suites, excellent food, full sports and entertainment facilities, imaginative landscaping merging ponds into swimming pool into sea, you can virtually swim up to reception (pool open to non-residents who stay for a meal), also another, quieter pool for those wanting a more peaceful holiday with separate eating facilities, excellent beach, well run hotel. Highly recommended. **A** *Kosgoda Beach Resort* (Jetwing), between the sea and lagoon, T64017, F64019, or Colombo T345700, F345729, kosgodab@eureka.lk 52 comfortable and attractive a/c rooms including 12 duplexes, open-air tubs, large garden, lovely pool, boating, excellent restaurant, environmentally aware policy. Recommended.

Ayurvedic centre *Lotus Villa*, 162/19 Wathuregama, south of Ahungalla, T64082, F64083 ayulotus@sltnet.lk 14 rooms in exclusive ayurvedic herbal treatment centre. 2 week minimum including all meals, consultations and treatment (DM1730 per person).

Ambalangoda අම්බලංගොඩ

Phone code: 09
Colour map 3, grid C2
85 km from Colombo

Ambalangoda, along the coast road, is the home of **devil dancing** and **mask making** which many families have carried out for generations. It may be possible to watch a performance of folk theatre (*kolama*); ask locally. Ambalangoda is also famous as a major centre for cinnamon cultivation and production. Ask your hotel or guest house about visiting a plantation and factory. The colourful fish market is worth visiting early in the morning.

The masks

Traditional masks worn for dancing, using vegetable colours instead of the brighter chemical paints, are available on the northern edge of the town. Masks sell from around Rs 500 to several thousand rupees. Traditional masks are more expensive. Antique shops often sell newly crafted items which have been 'aged'. It is illegal to take out any article over 50 years old without a government permit.

Dance of the sorcerers

The **Devil Dance** evolved from the rural people's need to appease malevolent forces in nature and seek blessing from good spirits when there was an evil spirit to be exorcised, ie a sickness to be cured. It takes the form of a ritual dance, full of high drama, with a sorcerer 'priest' and an altar. As evening approaches, the circular arena in the open air is lit by torches, and masked dancers appear to the beating of drums and chanting. During the exorcism ritual, which lasts all night, the 'priest' casts the evil spirit out of the sick. There are 18 demons associated with afflictions for which different fearsome sanni masks are worn and although there is an element of awe and grotesqueness about the whole performance, the audience is treated to occasional light relief. These dances have a serious purpose and are, therefore, not on offer as 'performances'.

The **Kolam Dance** has its origins in folk theatre. The story tells of a Queen, who, while expecting a child, had a deep craving to see a masked dance. This was satisfied by the Carpenter of the Gods, Visvakarma, who invented the dances.

The Kolam dances tell stories and again make full use of a wonderful variety of masks (often giant size) representing imaginary characters from folk tales, Buddhist jatakas, gods and devils, as well as well-known members of the royal court and more mundane figures from day-to-day life. Animals (lions, bears) too, feature as playful characters. This form of folk dance resembles the more serious Devil Dance in some ways – it is again performed during the night and in a similar circular, torch-lit, open air 'stage' (originally Kolam was performed for several nights during New Year festivities). Inspite of a serious or moral undertone, a sprinkling of cartoon characters are introduced to provide comic relief. The clever play on words can only be really appreciated by a Sinhalese.

Southern Sri Lanka

There are actually two of these run by the two sons of the late mask-carver, who **Ariyapala Mask** have set up in competition, opposite each other. The smaller one houses the **Museum** museum proper, while the other ("Mask and Puppet Museum") is primarily a workshop and showroom. Some of the exhibits tracing the tradition of mask dancing are interesting and informative. The masks can be very elaborate, eg the *naga raksha* mask from the *Raksha Kolama* has a fearsome face with bulging eyes that roll around, a bloodthirsty tongue hanging from a mouth lined with fanglike teeth, all topped by a set of cobra hoods (see box). You can watch the odd craftsmen at work carving traditional masks from the light *kaduru* (*nux vomica*) wood. The carvings on sale in the showroom are not of the best quality and are quite expensive It is better to take your time to visit some of the smaller workshops around town on foot and compare prices and quality. ■ *426 Patabendimulla, at the main crossing, 0830-1745*

Further reading *The Ambalangoda Mask Museum*, edited by W Mey and others, Ambalangoda, Mask Museum Council, 1987.

Mid-range C *Dream Beach Resort*, 509 Galle Road,T58873, F074-382111 **Sleeping** dream@slt.net.lk 25 large a/c rooms, some with sea-view, balcony, TV, restaurant, pool. **C** *Sun Oriental Resorts*, 786 Galle Road, Randombe, T58317, F58087 ayurvede@slt.lk 25 overpriced rooms, small pool, restaurant, ayurvedic centre. **D**

Southern Sri Lanka

Brass plate of a peacock Source: LTP Manjusri's, Design Elements

Princess Guest House, 418 Main St, Patabendimulla, near Museum, 5 rooms, good home cooking, pleasant atmosphere, good value. Recommended. **D** *Sena's Lake View House*, Duwa, Maha Ambalangoda, about 2 km inland, very quiet, by attractive lagoon (safe swimming), watch wildlife from the balcony at dawn and dusk, excellent 3 hr trip arranged (sail on an outrigger and climb up to a large reclining Buddha). Recommended. **Cheap D** *Shangrela Beach Resort*, 38 Sea Beach Rd, T58342, F59421. 23 rooms (Rs 850 old wing, Rs 1400 new wing) in extension of former family guest house. **D** *Rest House*, Beach Rd, T27299. 15 rooms (Rs 850) of which 7 are in old building (originally a Dutch warehouse for cinnamon and coconuts) and 8 are in the shabby and characterless new wing with no sea views. **F** *Lahiru Guest House*, near Ambalangoda at Ahuvala, rooms with bath, restaurant, guided tours with knowledgeable owner. **F** *Piya Nivasa*, Akurella, south of town, T58146. Light and airy rooms (Rs 300) in a lovely colonial house opposite the beach, good food, welcoming friendly family. Recommended.

Transport   **Road**   Regular buses run between Ambalangoda and Hikkaduwa, 13 km south (Rs 5). **Train**   See Hikkaduwa below.

Meetiyagoda   Meetiyagoda village, 16 km inland, has a moonstone quarry. The semi-precious stone which often has a bluish milky tinge, is polished and set in silver or gold jewellery. The road sign claims that it is the "only natural moonstone quarry in the world".

Seenigama   Seenigama, 6 km along the coast, has a Devil's Temple by the roadside. Sri Lankan travellers pay their respects here bringing most traffic to a temporary halt.

Hikkaduwa   හික්කඩුව

Phone code: 09 Colour map 3, grid C2 101 km from Colombo

Hikkaduwa has become the most popular and developed beach on the southwest coast. It offers reasonably good swimming and surfing as well as a wide range of facilities for snorkelling and scuba diving. It is unique on this coastal stretch in having a vast number (and a full range) of hotels and guesthouses though its popularity with German holidaymakers is reflected in the rising prices (and the food on offer). To some visitors, however, it is the least attractive of the island's resorts.

Ins & outs   **Getting there**   Express trains and private buses are best for those travelling from or via Colombo. **Getting around**   It is possible to walk uninterrupted along much of the beach. Tuk-tuks can be stopped along the Galle Rd (bus drivers are less obliging), but you will need to negotiate the price. Cycles and otorbikes can be hired.

Orientation
Hikkaduwa has "beach boys" who try to befriend tourists; they may be friendly but are generally not to be trusted

There are really four parts to what is known collectively as 'Hikkaduwa'. At the northern end is **Hikkaduwa** proper, the original settlement. The beach tends to be somewhat narrower here, and possibly less appealing, with most of the hotels managing to incorporate the word 'coral' into their name. Further south is **Wewala**, where the beach is a bit wider and more attractive. Along with **Narigama** this is the main centre of 'Hikkaduwa' with numerous beach bars and restaurants. At the southern end is **Thirangama**, which is less frantic, but has good surfing waves and a wider beach.

A major disadvantage here is the very busy main road which runs close to the beach. The traffic moves very fast and makes it a death trap. The local authorities have finally come up with a semi-solution. In an effort to prevent vehicles from overtaking each other at high speed on the Galle Road, in early 2000 a central concrete barrier about 15 cm high was put in place. This resulted in serious damage to many buses and cars which were taken by surprise in the first few weeks!

Sights

The **coral gardens**, a protected reef close to the *Coral Gardens Hotel*, was adversely affected by 'bleaching' in early 1998, leaving little live coral here. However, it is still possible to see reef fish which are fed by fishermen to provide an attraction for visitors who come to the resort because of its reputation.

The **Alut Vihara** (Totagama Rajamahavihara) at Telwatta, dating from the early 19th century, is inland about 2 km north of Hikkaduwa and a very pleasant bicycle ride away. It is the only temple to Anangaya on the island, where lovers make offerings to him. The carvings between the fine *makara* ('dragon') arches leading to the sanctuary hide a cupid with his bow and flower-tipped arrows. The murals too are particularly impressive. It is hardly ever visited by travellers which adds to its charm.

Excursion

Baddegama (11 km inland) is within easy reach of Hikkaduwa by bicycle or motor bike. It is a very attractive road through coconut and banana groves, followed by several small plantations– rubber, tea and spices. About half way the road passes the **Nigro Dharama Mahavira** (stupa) in Gopinuwala. On a hill above the river in the grounds of Christ Church Girls College is the first **Anglican church** in Sri Lanka, built in 1818 and consecrated by Bishop Heber in 1825. It has noteworthy ironwood pillars.

Sleeping at Baddegama C *Plantation Hotel*, Halpatota, 15 min bus (no 186) or car drive inland from Hikkaduwa, T92405 (Colombo T587454). 3 rooms set in small tea estate surrounded by very peaceful wooded garden, excellent bird life, has the feel of an old planter's house although it is relatively new, excellent food (breakfast included), welcoming hosts, guest book repeatedly mentions 'paradise'. Highly recommended. Very welcoming.

Hikkaduwa area

To Plantation Hotel & Baddegama (11km)

To Colombo, Telwatte, Vihara & Ambalangoda

Gonapinuwala

HIKKADUWA

WEWALA

A

NARIGAMA

THIRANGAMA

B

PUTUWATHA

Indian Ocean

Lake Rest

Polgasduwa

N

DODANDUWA

Lagoon

To Galle

0 km   1
0 miles   1

Sleeping

There are innumerable hotels lining the beach here, often with very little to distinguish between them. The sheer number of places to stay can be initially daunting. It is worth spending some time visiting various places and comparing facilities, prices and ambience. Places away from the beach side, understandably, tend to be cheaper than beach front properties with similar facilities. Many prices drop by 50% out of season (May-Oct). Whatever season you visit, it is worth bargaining.

Hikkaduwa Expensive A *Coral Gardens* (Keells), T77023, F77189 htlres@keells. com 154 a/c rooms in attractive building on small promontory though no balconies, nice pool

Related maps
A Hikkaduwa & Wewala beach, page 126
B Narigama & Thirangama, page 129

Above: Lion (Alut Vihara) dated 1802
Right: Images from Telwatta: Brahmon and Indian stag (Purana Vihara) dated 1799
Source: LTP Manjusri's, Design Elements

(non-residents Rs 100)/garden area, excellent restaurants (dinner buffet Rs 600, Sun lunch Rs 500), night-club (Wed, Fri and Sun, Rs 100, ladies free), squash (Rs 250 for 45 mins) diving centre co-owned by Dr. Arthur C Clarke (glass-bottom boats Rs 100), full of German groups, best hotel in town but not the most efficient. **B** *Blue Corals*, 332 Galle Rd, T77679, F074 383128. 60 good, clean, sea-facing rooms (6 a/c), balcony rooms better, small pool, ayurvedic health centre, popular with package groups, smarter inside than exterior suggests. **B** *Coral Sands*, 326 Galle Rd, T77513, F074-383225. 50 good rooms (20 a/c), not all sea facing, restaurant, bar, tiny pool, diving school, reasonable value.

Mid-range C *Coral Rock*, 340 Galle Rd, T77021, F77521. 40 rooms (28 a/c), better sea facing, restaurant (good fish), small pool (non-residents, Rs 100), close to noisy road. **C** *Hikkaduwa Beach*, 298 Galle Rd, T77327, F77174. 52 clean rooms (better 16 a/c on top floor), modern block, small pool (non-residents, Rs 75), hot bath, library, ayurvedic centre. Recommended. **D** *Coral Reef Beach*, 336 Galle Rd (Km 99 post), T77197, F77453. 32 rooms with sea view (breakfast), although a bit spartan, bar, restaurant, Aqua Tours Dive Centre (see below). **D** *Mama's Coral Beach*, 338 Galle Rd, T77137. 12 rooms refurbished in early 2000.

Cheap D-E *Wewala Beach*, 380 Galle Rd, T77167. 25 large, clean rooms (Rs 800-1200 including breakfast) with balconies, restaurant, small pool, reasonable value. **E** *Poseidon Diving Station*, T77294, F76607. 10 simple clean rooms (Rs 325 single, Rs 600 double) attached to the dive school, right on the beach, restaurant. **F** *Ozone Tourist*, 374 Galle Rd. 5 simple, bare but clean rooms (Rs 450), attached bath, fan, friendly, not bad value. **G** *Udaya's Place*, 49 Amarasena Mawatha, near Bank of Ceylon, T77143. 3 simple rooms with attached bath (Rs 200) in family guesthouse, quiet (away from main road), good value.

Wewala Expensive A-B *Lanka Super Corals*, 390 Galle Rd, 1 km from Bus Stand T074-383385, F074-383384 supercor@pan.lk 100 rooms ranging from non-a/c road-facing rooms, to deluxe a/c with hot tub, TV, minibar, sea view, and a range of a/c rooms, good pool (non-residents, Rs 150), 24-hr coffee shop, a bit shabby in places, new wing nicer. **A-B** *Reefcomber*, T77377, F77374, serenlti@sri.lanka.net 54 a/c rooms with terrace or balcony facing the sea though some face the road, nice beach garden, good pool (non-residents, Rs 100), restaurant, popular with package groups, a bit pricey.

Mid-range C *Moon Beam*, T078-76932, Nigama. 11 clean rooms in fairly new hotel, better on upper floors with sea views but overpriced. **C-D** *Blue Ocean Villa*, T77566. 9 large clean rooms, upstairs better, restaurant, hot bath, good choice. Recommended. **C-D** *Imperial*, 500 Galle Rd, T/F074 383109. 3 rooms (Rs 800-1400) and 2 suites (Rs 2000), prices negotiable, clean, reasonable deal. **D** *Blue Note Cabanas*, 424 Galle Rd, T/F77016. 9 very clean rooms with own verandah, well furnished, good restaurant but indifferent management and thefts from rooms reported in early 2000.

Cheap D-E *Casalanka*, Galle Rd, T/F074-383002. 6 rooms (Rs 550) 4 with hot water (Rs 1200) in barracks style block, beachside restaurant, popular backpacker hangout. Recommended. **E** *Richard's Son's Beach Inn*. 8 simple rooms (Rs 500), attached bath, fan, nice block though a little old, beach-side garden, very cheap out of season. **E** *Tandem*, Galle Rd (Km 100 post), T074-383019, F77103 tandem@sltnet.lk 9 reasonable rooms (Rs 850 including breakfast), nets, though not on beach, not bad value. **E** *Whispering Palms*, 382a Galle Road, T77481. 4 clean rooms (Rs 500) in family guesthouse, attached bathroom, nets, good value. **E-F** *Surfing Beach*, T77008. 9 rooms (Rs 350 common bath, Rs 600 attached), basic but clean. **F** *Miga Villa*, T77092. 15 large, clean rooms (Rs 350-500) in beautiful old house, some family rooms, attached bath, friendly family run, excellent value, despite requiring minor maintenance in places. Highly recommended. **G** *El-Dorado*, Milla Rd, 200m inland from Galle Rd, T77091. 6 rooms (Rs 250 shared bath, Rs 350 attached), in small family run guesthouse, use of kitchen, very clean, very peaceful setting away from busy road (but still only 10 mins from the beach), good value, good choice. Highly recommended. **G** *Sam'a Surfer's Rest*, T77184. 6 pretty basic rooms (Rs 300), cold bath, fan, restaurant with pool table, videos, music, laid back atmosphere, little run down but cheap and cheerful.

Narigama Mid-range C *Sunil's Beach*, just south of Marine Gardens, T/F77187. 62 rooms, 5 a/c (Rs 500 extra), modern, bookshop, pool, popular with German groups. **C-F** *Ranmal Rest & Tourist Home*, T/F77114. 19 rooms ranging from cheap non a/c rooms (Rs 400) to very clean luxury rooms with a/c (Rs 2000), upper rooms with balcony (Rs 800), sea facing first floor restaurant with lovely sunset views, good section of beach, good food, pleasant staff, reserve ahead. Recommended. **D** *Golden Beach*, T77060. 10 good, clean rooms (Rs 800) although no views. **D** *International Beach* T77202. 8 rooms in 2-storey block, very clean, nets, reasonable value. **D** *Sahra*, T76093. 6 spotless rooms in Swiss chalet style, nice terrace, friendly, not bad value. Recommended.

Cheap E *New Hotel Harmony*, T76559. 13 large, clean rooms (Rs 550-650), sleepy staff but otherwise not bad value. **E** *Rita's*, T/F77496. 9 clean rooms (Rs 600- 800), better on first floor, popular beach restaurant (with perennial Bob Marley). **E** *Seethani*, T77426. 14 rooms (Rs 600-800), those closer to the beach are better value (and cheaper) than in the newer 2-storey block. **E** *Shilasa*, T/F77969. 4 reasonable rooms (Rs 750) with beachside restaurant. **E** *Sun Beach*, T77356. 11 rooms (Rs 700) with fan and attached bath. **E-F** *Hilda Guest House*, Uswatta, Wawala, 300 m from Galle Road, T074-383204. Rooms (Rs 300-600) in an attractive house 10 mins from the beach with a quiet, pleasant garden, worth a look. **F** *Hansa Surf*, T77039. 17 simple rooms (Rs 450), shady verandah, table tennis, popular with backpackers. **F** *Lotus Garden*, 7 clean rooms, fan, attached bath, nice verandah, friendly. **E** *Trust Inn*, T77409. 8 reasonable rooms (Rs 600 including breakfast, negotiable), although some can be a little musty, good restaurant, friendly and helpful owner. **G** *Jupiter*, 6 very basic rooms (Rs 250), shared squat toilets, beach restaurant, popular, about as cheap and cheerful as you can get!.

Southern Sri Lanka

Thirangama Expensive B *Suite Lanka*, T/F77136. 9 beautifully furnished rooms, plus 4 deluxe a/c rooms and suites, private verandahs, pool, bar, very quiet and intimate. Highly recommended. **Mid-range D** *Ocean View Cottage*, T77237. 3 large, attractive rooms, fairly new and modern, nice terrace restaurant, quiet, pleasant garden, also 2

Hikkaduwa & Wewala beach

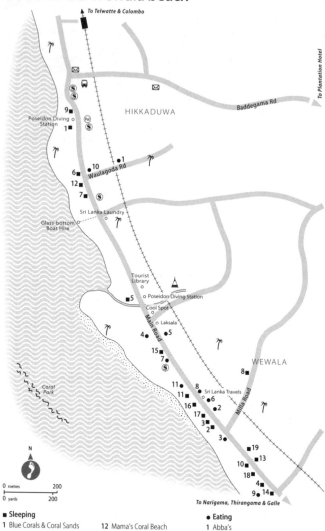

Southern Sri Lanka

■ **Sleeping**

1	Blue Corals & Coral Sands	12	Mama's Coral Beach
2	Blue Note Cabanas	13	Miga Villa
3	Blue Ocean Villa	14	Moon Beam
4	Casalanka	15	Ozone Tourist
5	Coral Gardens	16	Reefcomber
6	Coral Reef Beach	17	Richard's Sons Beach Inn
7	Coral Rock	18	Surfing Beach Guesthouse
8	El-Dorado	19	Tandem Guest House
9	Hikkaduwa Beach		
10	Imperial		
11	Lanka Super Corals		

● **Eating**

1 Abba's
2 Blue Fox Cool Hut
3 Budde's Beach
4 Curry Bowl
5 Farm House
6 Hotel Francis & German Bakery
7 JLH
8 New Moon Beam
9 Ranjith's Beach Hut
10 Red Lobster
11 Refresh

cheaper, clean rooms (Rs 600) across the road. Recommended. **D** *Pearl Island Beach* T76392. 14 small, musty rooms (Rs 850) in 2-storey block, garden, restaurant. **Cheap E** *Elephant Garden Beach Resort*. 2 rooms with clean shared bath (Rs 600) and 3 cheaper wooden cabanas (Rs 500) in quiet setting, nets, restaurant. **E** *Florida*, T077-77345. 8 very clean, modern rooms (Rs 750), restaurant. Recommended.

Most places listed are in Wewala offering plenty of choice, particularly for seafood. **Eating** Prices are pretty much similar wherever you go; you can eat well for under Rs 200, though it is also possible to eat a good rice and curry for under Rs 70. For a change, opt for the cool of the plush a/c restaurant at the *Coral Gardens Hotel* for the excellent Rs 400 lunch time buffet. Crowded places may not necessarily be better; it could just be a mention in guidebooks!

Mid-range *Curry Bowl*. Good food and service, 'delicious garlic toasts', upmarket setting. *Farm House*, 341 Galle Rd, offers a wide range of other services. *Hotel Francis*, T77019. Good international choice (under Rs 200), lobster Rs 1,000, beer Rs 100. *New Moon Beam*, Wewala. Seafood particularly good, lobster Rs 750-1,000, pleasant ambience. *Red Lobster*, Waulagoda Rd. Excellent food, good value, friendly owners. *Refresh*, 384 Galle Road. Good food, large menu, including a good choice of international vegetarian food. Recommended. *Sukhawathi Vegetarian Wholefood*, Thiranagama. Good choice of vegetarian food at good prices (Rs 160 for a main course).

Cheap *Abba's*, Waulagoda Rd. German-style, snacks and meals, good value, quiet setting. *Blue Fox Cool Hut*. Nice setting, really good food, breakfast Rs 90, fish, steak, prawns and chicken Rs 120-170, beer Rs 80. Recommended. *Budde's Beach*. Popular beach-side place, good food, breakfast Rs 82, fish Rs 140, pasta Rs 120, noodles Rs 70, beer Rs 100. *German Bakery*, 373 Galle Rd (opposite *Reefcomber*). Excellent bread and cakes, breakfast all-day 0800-1800, closed Mon. *JLH*. Ideal for breakfast, right by the water. *Rotty Hut*, Thirangama. Tasty rice and curries, excellent rotties, local clientele.

Pop Star Beach, Wewala, nice spot, though food disappointing and portions small. **Nightlife** *Ranjith's Beach Hut*, Wewala, top spot to end the day with a few beers and late night music or table games. Also hires out surf-boards. *Roger's Garage*, friendly owners, popular bar, nightly videos, pool table. *Why Not Rock Café*, Wewala, popular place for late night music and drinks.

There are numerous handicraft, leather work, jewellery and clothing stores along the **Shopping** length of Galle Rd. Bargaining is expected. *Janaka Pharmacy and Curio Shop*, opposite Hotel Super Corals. Small, but good range of woodcarvings and good quality masks at reasonable prices.

Diving The season along the southwest coast is Nov-Apr. *Aqua Tours Diving Station*, at **Watersports** *Coral Reef Beach Hotel* T072-260208. Single dive including equipment, US$26; PADI Open Water Course, US$330. *International Diving School* at *Coral Sands Hotel*, T77436, F77103. *Poseidon Diving Station*, just north of *Coral Sands Hotel*, T77294, F76607 nilucom@sltnet.lk Also at 325 Galle Road, T77447. Single dive including equipment, US$18; PADI Open Water Course, US$320; Advanced Course, US$220. There are several other dive schools. Check whether they are PADI qualified before agreeing to a dive or course. **Snorkelling** equipment, **surfboards** can be hired from a number of places along the main street. **Glass-bottom boats** These can be hired from a number of places just north of the *Coral Gardens Hotel*. Rates are negotiable, though a 30 min viewing trip (without stops for snorkelling) is about Rs 200; from *Coral Gardens* Rs 100. Some travellers find there are too many boats chasing too few viewing spots, turtles are disturbed unnecessarily and that the glass is not as clear as you might expect.

Southern Sri Lanka

Trains from Hikkaduwa

To	2nd class	3rd class	Type	Departure time	Journey
Aluthgama	Rs 21	Rs 8	Slow	0624, 0643 (Mon-Fri), 1223, 1403, 1458 (Mon-Fri), 1531 (not Sat), 1758	
Colombo	Rs 55	Rs 20	Slow	0419 (not Sun), 0519, 0605, 1223	4 hrs
Colombo (via Aluthgama)	Rs 55	Rs 20	Express	0708, 0805, 0927 (not Sat), 1103, 1427, 1508, 1834	2½ hrs
Galle	Rs 11	Rs 4	Slow	0645 (not Sat), 0744, 0822, 1903, 1959, 2021, 2044, 2221	
Kandy (via Colombo)	Rs 123	Rs 46	Express	1508	5¾ hrs
Matara (via Galle)	Rs 36	Rs 13	Express	0932, 1106, 1241, 1626 (not Sat), 1758, 2021	1½ hrs
Vavuniya (via Anuradhapura)	Rs 190	Rs 62	Express	1103	

Tour operators *Sri Lanka Travels*, opposite *Reefcomber Hotel*, T075-451864. Offers 1 to 5 day tours as well as longer island tours on request. Minimum 3- 4 persons. Honest deals. Recommended. *Travel Aid*, opposite *Coral Gardens Hotel*, also offers tours and vehicle hire (see below).

Transport **Road Bus**: To **Colombo**: The old, slow CTB buses between Colombo and Galle via Hikkaduwa (Rs 18) can take up to 3 hrs+. Better option are private minibuses from Colombo's Bastian Mawatha bus station (Rs 50); they take under 2 hrs. Frequent buses run from Hikkaduwa's bus station (at the north end of town) to **Ambalangoda** and **Galle** (both Rs 10). However, it is almost impossible to hail a bus on the Galle Road (even from official bus shelters) so it is worth going to the bus station or taking a taxi or auto for short journeys. **Car and motorbike hire** *Sri Lanka Travels*, opposite Reefcomber Hotel, T075-451864. Motorbike hire, Rs 600/day including helmet and insurance. Car hire $30 per day with or without driver, 100 km free, then Rs 6 per km. Taxi to airport Rs 1600 (not necessarily the cheapest), 3 hrs. **Taxis** wait outside the *Coral Gardens* and *Reefcomber* Hotels (more likely to be minibuses than cars). **Tuk-tuks** are available up and down Galle Rd, for short trips. To Unawatuna, bargain down to Rs 250.

Directory **Banks** Usually open Mon-Fri, 0900-1500. *People's Bank*, *Commercial Bank* and *Bank of Ceylon* all offer foreign exchange (Cash and TCs), whilst the latter also gives advances on Visa cards. The moneychanger just north of *Hotel Lanka Super Coral* charges no commission on cash or TCs, and will outbid the bank rate. **Communications** The *Post office* is at the north end of town, a few mins walk inland from the bus station, 0800-1900 (Sun 0800-1000). Dimasha Agency Post Office, opposite the bus station to the north, sells stamps and arranges international calls, usually 0800-2100. There is a Sub-Post Office at Thirangama. For international phone calls, it is best to use *Lanka Payphones* (yellow) and *Metrocard* (orange) card phones that are found all along Galle Rd. Most stores nearby sell the phonecards. **Internet** *Nilu Communications*, 7 Galle Road, opposite Hikkaduwa Beach Hotel, has 2 reliable terminals, Rs 7 per min. Open 0730-2130. Others generally charge Rs 10 per min. **Libraries** Tourist Library, opposite *Coral Gardens Hotel*, open 1000-1900, has a small selection of paperbacks for sale, and also lends out books (Rs 25 fee, Rs 100 deposit). **Useful addresses** Tourist Police, Police Station, Galle Rd, T77222. Sri Lanka Laundry Service, next to *Hotel Sea View*, open 24 hrs, 7 days a week, same day service.

Dodanduwa has a beautiful lagoon which is popular for bird-watching. Touts on the beach offer boat trips from Rs 100 per person which includes a visit to Polgasduwa and bird-watching. **Kumarakanda Rajamahavihara** (just before Km 103 post) has some murals and statues which some find a little disappointing. It is on the tourist trail so sometimes has a dancing monkey and 'school pen' collectors. The temple is reached by a long steep and narrow flight of stone steps. Donations are expected. The beach opposite has a very small private **Turtle Research Centre** which works to protect this endangered species. You can see eggs and different stages of a turtle's development and a few posters under a shelter. ■ *Rs 50*. **Sleeping** at D *Lake Rest*, inland towards lagoon (from Hikkaduwa take the next road after the turn-off to the vihara). The Sri Lankan house has 10 rooms with fan, net and cold shower and a restaurant. It overlooks the lagoon in a quiet rural setting facing forests and is idyllic. ■ *Getting there: Hire a bike or tuk-tuk to get to and from Hikkaduwa.*

Dodanduwa
05 km from Colombo

Some 15 km south of Hikkaduwa the road crosses the Dutch Canal to enter Galle. Just before entering the town, at **Dadella**, on a bend in the road, is the fabulous new *Lighthouse Hotel* (see under Galle).

Route

Southern Sri Lanka

Narigama & Thirangama

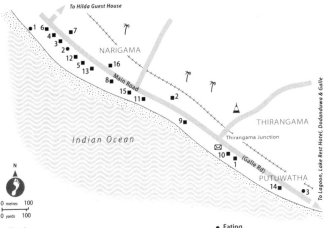

■ **Sleeping**
1 Elephant Garden Beach Resort
2 Florida Guesthouse
3 Golden Beach & Sun Beach
4 Hansa Surf
5 International Beach
6 Jupiter
7 Lotus Garden
8 New Hotel Harmony
9 Ocean View Cottage
10 Pearl Island Beach
11 Ranmal Tourist
12 Rita's Guesthouse
13 Sahra & Seethani
14 Suite Lanka
15 Sunil's Beach
16 Trust Inn

● **Eating**
1 Pop Star Beach & Why Not Rock Café
2 Rotty Shop
3 Sukhawathi

Galle ගාල්ල

Phone code: 09
115 km from Colombo

Galle (pronounced in Sinhala as 'Gaa-le') is the most important town in the south and has retained much of its colonial atmosphere. The crescent-shaped shoreline was once dotted with islands, though some have now been joined up or been altered by the harbour developments. The Portuguese, Dutch and British used the natural harbour as their main port until 1875, when reconstruction of breakwaters and the enlarged harbour made Colombo the island's major port.

Ins & outs **Getting there** Express trains are preferable to a bus journey to or from Galle provided you avoid the rush hour. Taxis charge over Rs 3,000 from Colombo. **Getting around** Galle is so small and compact that most hotels are within 10 mins' walk of the train and bus stations and are very easy to find. To get to the upmarket hotels outside Galle, you will need to hire a taxi or tuk-tuk.

History Galle's origins as a port go back well before the Portuguese. Ibn Batuta, the great Moroccan traveller, visited it in 1344. The historian of Ceylon Sir Emerson Tennant claimed that Galle was the ancient city of Tarshish, which had traded not only with Persians and Egyptians, but with King Solomon. The origin of the name is disputed, some associating it with the Latin '*gallus*', others with the Sinhala '*gala*' (cattle shed) or '*gal*' (rock).

The Portuguese Lorenzo de Almeida drifted into Galle by accident in 1505. It was a further 82 years before the Portuguese captured it from the Sinhala Kings, and they controlled the port until the Dutch laid siege in 1640. The old Portuguese Fort on a promontory was strengthened by the Dutch who remained there unitl the British captured Galle in 1796. The Dutch East India Company, 'VOC' (*Vereenigde Oost Indische Campagnie*) ruled the waves during the 17th and 18th centuries with over 150 ships trading from around 30 settlements in Asia.

A P&O liner called at Galle in 1842 marking the start a regular service to Europe. In 1859, Captain Bailey, an agent for the shipping company took a fancy to the spot where a small disused Dutch fort had stood in a commanding position, 3 km across the harbour. The villa he built and set in a tropical garden (now *Closenberg Hotel*) was named 'Marina' after his wife. P&O's Rising Sun emblem can still be spotted on some of the old furniture.

Marriage (1837) from the Kumarakanda Rajamahavihara, Dodanduwa Source: LTP Manjusri's, Design Elements

Sights

Allow a full day to see the old town enclosed within the fort which was declared a World Heritage Site in 1988. Part of the charm of the fort is being able to wander around the streets. Nothing is very far away and, by and large, there are only a few curio shops. You won't get pestered very much either although on the ramparts you may be offered coral (near the Neptune bastion) and there are usually vendors near the *New Oriental*. However Galle does have more than its fair share of touts who will try to earn commission on accommodation and shopping (especially gems).

The old fort enclosing about 200 house completely dominates the town. The Dutch left their mark here, building brick-lined sewers which the tides automatically flushed twice a day. The fort's main streets run over these old sewers and you can still see the manhole covers every 20 m or so.

The fort

Entry There are two entry points. The more impressive gate is under the clock tower. The ramparts just here are massive, partly because they are the oldest and have been reinforced over the years on many occasions. There are three quite distinct bastions (*Star* in the west, *Moon* and *Sun* in the east). The **clocktower** (1883) itself is quite modern and usually has a huge national flag flying from it. In Queen Street is the second and much older gate.

The **ramparts**, surrounded on three sides by the sea are marked by a series of bastions covering the promontory. The two nearest to the harbour are *Sun* and *Zwart*, followed by *Aurora* and *Point Utrecht* bastions before the lighthouse, then *Triton*, *Neptune*, *Clippenburg*, *Aeolus*, *Star* and *Moon*. Those on the west side are more accessible and stand much as they were built, although there is evidence of a signals post built in the Second World War on top of *Neptune*. The Sri Lankan army still has a base in the fort and so have a use for the *Aeolus* bastion. Under the ramparts between *Aelous* and *Star* bastions is the tomb of a Muslim saint neatly painted in green and white, said to cover an old fresh water spring. The open space between Rampart Street and the ramparts is used as a recreational area and there is often an unofficial game of cricket in progress in the evenings and at weekends. Also on the Green is a small shrine the main one, Sri Sudharmalaya temple, being across the street.

A walking tour around the ramparts is a must. You can try to do it on a clear evening and aim to reach the clock tower at sunset, starting at about 1630 and wandering slowly from the *New Oriental* clockwise.

The views over the roofs of the houses & the sunset out over the sea is unforgettable

An interesting route is to walk south from the hotel, all along Church Street, then east to the 20-m high lighthouse which was built by the British in 1934, nearly on top of the old magazine with its inscription 'AJ Galle den 1st Zeber 1782'. You can get good views from the top. You then return up Hospital Street past the Police Barracks (built in 1927 but failing to blend in with the older parts of the fort). The Government offices on Hospital Street were once the Dutch 'Factory' (warehouse). You then arrive at the square with the district court near the *Zwart* Bastion. Note the sign: 'All vehicles should proceed slowly and noiselessly. Horns or other warning signals should not be given beyond this point. By order'. Turn west along Queen Street which joins Church Street at the post office.

The quiet fort streets are lined with substantial buildings, most with large rooms on the ground floor and an arched verandah to provide shade. The arched windows of the upper floors are covered by huge old louvered wooden shutters the lower ones have glass nowadays. Unfortunately, quite a few of these fine houses are in need of restoration.

The **Dutch Reformed Church** (1754), next to the *New Oriental*, is certainly worth visiting. It was built as a result of a vow taken by the Dutch Governor of Galle, Casparaous de Jong, and has a number of interesting memorials. Inside, the floor is covered by about 20 gravestones (some heavily embossed, others engraved), which originated in older graveyards which were closed in 1710 and 1804 the British moved them into this church in 1853. There is a splendid wooden memorial to EAH Abraham, Commander in Galle, who died 3 May 1766. note the hour glass and skull on top of it. The organ loft has a lovely semi-circular balustrade surrounding the organ while the pulpit, repaired in 1996, has an enormous canopy. Opposite the church, is the old bell tower erected in 1701, while the bell, open to the elements, is hung in a belfry with a large dome on top of it.

The old **post office**, restored by the Galle Heritage Trust in 1992, is a long low building with a shallow red tiled roof supported by 13 columns. It is still functioning although it is very run down inside.

Further down Church Street is the **All Saints Church** though it is not always open. This was built in 1868 (consecrated in 1871) after much pressure from the English population who had previously worshipped at the Dutch Reform Church. Its bell has an interesting history as it came from the Liberty ship 'Ocean Liberty'. When the vicar asked the Clan Shipping Company whether they could help with a bell, the chief officer who had acquired the bell when the Liberty ship was scrapped (and named his daughter Liberty!), willingly presented it to the church in its centenary year, 1968. There is a particularly good view of the church with its red tin roof surmounted by a cockerel and four strange little turrets, from Cross Church Street. The old Dutch Government House opposite the church, is now Walker & Sons.

At the end of Church Street, lies the old **Arab Quarter** with a distinct moorish atmosphere. Here you will find the Meeran Jumma Masjid in a tall white building which resembles a church with two square towers topped by shallow domes, but with the crescent clearly visible. Slender, tubular minarets are also topped by cresent moons. The mosque was rebuilt at the beginning of the 20th century where the original stood from c1750s. The Muslim Cultural Association and Arabic College which was established in 1892, are here. It is still very active and you will see many Muslims in the distinctive skull caps hurrying to prayer at the appointed hours.

On the Old Gate, the British arms are on the outside. On the inside, mono-grammed arms of the Dutch East India Company, VOC arms can clearly be seen with the date MDCLXIX (1669), above it. On the ground floor of this imposing building is the National Maritime Museum (see below).

Modern Galle town This area hasn't much to offer. It is quite good to wander around though and its bustle contrasts with the more measured pace of the fort. It is an easy walk either out of the old gate and along by the sea with its rows of fishing boats neatly drawn up on the beach or through the main gate and around by the cricket ground.

Near the main post office on Main Street, there is however a splendid equestrian statue. You can walk alongside the old Dutch canal; very dirty at low tide. Monitor lizards can often be seen.

On the Colombo Road to the west of Victoria Park, are several gem shops. If you take the road opposite them you can walk up to **St Mary's Cathedral** which was built in 1874 and has a very good view over town. There is little of interest inside, though. SCIA Handicraft Centre factories are nearby (see Shopping below).

Historical Mansion Museum, 31-39 Leyn Bann Street (well signed). The old **Museums** house was restored in 1992 by Mr Gaffar, the owner. There are a number of rooms around a small courtyard containing his potentially worthwhile collection of colonial artefacts, glass, VOC china, record players and much else. There are several intersting and rare items which are simply 'stored' here– most of the exhibits are unlabelled and poorly displayed. The real aim of the

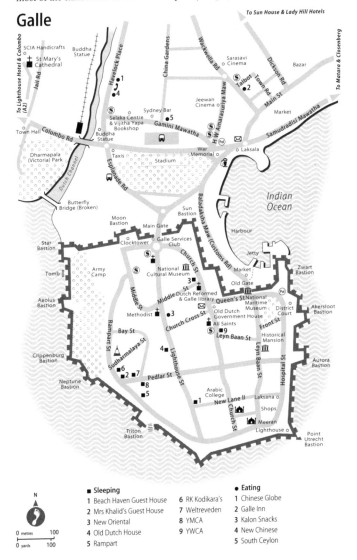

Galle

To Sun House & Lady Hill Hotels

Southern Sri Lanka

■ **Sleeping**
1 Beach Haven Guest House
2 Mrs Khalid's Guest House
3 New Oriental
4 Old Dutch House
5 Rampart
6 RK Kodikara's
7 Weltreveden
8 YMCA
9 YWCA

● **Eating**
1 Chinese Globe
2 Galle Inn
3 Kalon Snacks
4 New Chinese
5 South Ceylon

N

0 metres 100
0 yards 100

'museum', however, becomes apparent when visitors are led to the gems for sale in the adjoining shop (all supposedly guaranteed by the Ceylon Gem Corporation)! You can watch gem cutting and polishing 'demonstration' around the courtyard which has an old well. ■ *0830-1800 (closed on Fri 1200-1400 for prayers). Entry free.*

Mr Gaffar's residence, an unusual rambling mansion, is opposite. He takes pride in having restored the old Dutch building and sometimes shows interested visitors around.

National Maritime Museum, the Old Dutch Gate, Queen Street. The exhibition is housed in the basement of what was originally storehouses (*Pakhus*) and you can really appreciate the strength of the building with 1-m thick walls and huge stone pillars to keep the building from collapsing. There is much of interest inside the museum but regrettably it is not well exhibited. There is a small collection illustrating the island's maritime history including trade, spices, sea products (a pickled cuttlefish), fibreglass whales, models of different styles of catamarans. At the far end there is an interesting exhibit about fishermen about their annual pilgrimage to Kataragama to offer alms. They carry a seahorse for good luck. and perform the *Gara Yakuma* dance on the sea shore in the hope of increasing yields. ■ *0900-1700 Sun-Thu, Rs 55. Entrance under the gate arch.*

National Cultural Museum, Church Street (next to *New Oriental Hotel*), in an old colonial stone warehouse. Exhibits include a model of Galle and the fort's Dutch and Portuguese inheritence. ■ *0900-1700, closed Sun, Mons and public holidays, Rs 35. T32051.*

Further reading *Galle As Quiet As Asleep* by Norah Roberts, 1993. A comprehensive local history of Galle by a former librarian. *Illustrations and views of Dutch Ceylon*, by RK de Silva and WGM Beumer, 1988, has a chapter on the town. *Furniture of the Dutch Period* by RL Brohier. Reprinted 1994. An illustrated booklet.

Essentials

Sleeping **Outside the fort** **LL** *Lighthouse Hotel* (Jetwing), Dadella, just north of Galle, T23744, F24021, or Colombo T345700, F345720, lighthousehotel@lanka.com.lk 60 superbly furnished a/c rooms, about the most expensive rooms in Sri Lanka (US$200), recently joined the Small Hotels of the World Association with consequent price rise though reduced price (Rs 4940) for Sri Lankans, impressive public areas, panoramic views from sea-facing terrace, 2 restaurants including excellent Cinnamon Room for fine dining at a reasonable price for the quality, pools. Highly recommended if you can afford it. **AL-A** *The Sun House*, 18 Upper Dickson Rd, T/F22624, sunhouse@ sri.lanka.net 5 superbly furnished rooms plus an excellent **L** suite, all with different themes in 1860s spice merchant's house, described as a 'five-star boutique hotel' it is highly exclusive with discreet service, fine dining, pool, library, very atmospheric. Highly recommended. No credit cards. Contact also for *Taprobane Island Resort*, Weligama and a highly exclusive private property in Tangalle. **B** *Closenberg*, 11 Closenberg Road, Magalle, Unawatuna Road (3 km, tuk-tuk from fort or bus stand, Rs 100), T24313, F32241. 20 comfortable rooms (US$35) in attractive colonial house built in 1858 on promontory overlooking Galle Bay (see above), modern wing has good sea views, attractive restaurant, plenty of character and quiet ambience. Recommended. **B** *The Lady Hill*, Upper Dickson Road (a little further up from The Sun House), T44322, F34855. 15 well furnished a/c rooms (US$40), with TV and balconies, restaurant, very good pool, rooftop Harbour Bar which affords the best views in Galle of the Fort and the harbour, to the north views of Adam's Peak in the Hill Country! Recommended.

Galle Fort B *New Oriental (NOH)*, 10 Church St, T/F34591. 23 large rooms and 12 very large suites, originally the Army barracks in a building dating from 1684, the oldest registered hotel on the island, now run down and in desperate need of cleaning up and investment, still retains colonial character with Dutch period furniture, public rooms full of old prints and a grand piano which guests can play, ridiculously pricey mediocre restaurant (exhorbitant lager Rs 175), lovely garden with small pool (non-residents, Rs 125) and large mosquitoes, billiards room (only one cue!), excellent views of the Fort. **D** *Rampart House*, 31 Rampart St, T074-380103, F42794. 2 fairly simple rooms (Rs 1200) in 200 year old building overlooking the walls, though rest of mansion is quite impressive, hot bath, nets, good views from verandah restaurant although the jewellery and handicraft showroom is the main focus of business attention. **E** *Weltevreden*, 104 Pedlar St, T22650. 4 clean rooms (Rs 600), quiet lush garden, friendly family, very good food. Recommended. **E-F** *Beach Haven Guest House*, 65 Lighthouse St, T34663, thalith@sri.lanka.net 6 clean rooms (Rs 300-700), good range (1 with noisy a/c), some in separate block with sitting area, very friendly and welcoming, no commission to touts. Recommended. **E-F** *RK Kodikara's 'Beatrice House'*, 29 Rampart St, T22351. 3 rooms (Rs 450) and 2 upstairs with sea views (Rs 750), colonial house with sea facing garden (try the king coconuts in season!), friendly owner, collect from station. Recommended. **E-F** *Mrs Shakira Khalid's Guest House*, 106 Pedlar St, T34907. 4 rooms (Rs 400-700) in very friendly family home, good atmosphere, small shady garden, really excellent home cooked food, no commission to touts. Highly recommended.

Expensive *Lighthouse Hotel*, is highly recommended for a treat, especially in the Cinnammon Room (separate vegetarian menu), fine dining superb attention to detail, order an Irish coffee just to see it being prepared; surprisingly, under US$10 per head. **Mid-range** Consider taking a tuk-tuk to *Closenberg Hotel* across the bay (see above). Tour groups mean service can be slow, from under the pergola there are lovely views over the harbour, pleasant and quiet in the evenings, main courses around Rs 300, beer Rs 120. *Rampart House*, Fort. The verandah is a pleasant setting for a meal but the food is average (main courses around Rs 225, lime soda Rs 100). **Cheap** There are numerous cheap 'rice & curry' places around the train/bus stations, plus: *Chinese Globe*, 38 Havelock Place. *New Chinese*, 14 Havelock Place. *Galle Inn Chinese*, 4 Talbot Town. *South Ceylon*, Gamini Mawatha for good Chinese, Sri Lankan (try pineapple curry or cashew nut curry), Continental plus bakery. *Kalan Snacks*, 21 Lighthouse St, Fort. A very friendly little place for short eats and snacks.
Eating

Galle is known for its lace-making, gem polishing and ebony carving. Several shops accept credit cards and foreign currency. **Bookshops** *Vijitha Yapa Laitiru Bookshop*, 2nd floor, Selaka Building, 34 Gamini Mawatha, next to the Bus Station, carries a good selection of English books on crammed shelves. **Handicrafts** *SCIA Handicraft Centre* on Kandewatte Rd T34304. There are 5 workshops producing polished gems, carvings (ebony), batik and lace, and leather bags etc employing about 50 people (approved by the State Gem Corp and Tourist Board). *Laksana*, 30 Hospital St. Recommended. *Lihinya Trades*, by the lighthouse. Good selection, knowledgeable, helpful owners. Jewellery In **Galle town, on Colombo Rd, west of Victoria Park are several gem shops including** *Star Jewellers*, at 41 Colombo Rd. Nearby is *Sapphire Gem Centre*, 5 Mosque Lane, Kandewatte. also *Universal Gems*, 42 A Jiffriya St (Cripps Rd). In the Fort area, *Ubesiri & Co*, Rampart Hotel, 31 Rampart St, T074-380103, F42794. Modern designs, well displayed. Tea *Hatton Tea Stall*, 31 Main Street. Good quality tea, loose or in more costly gift packs, very helpful proprietor helps you to choose without pressure.
Shopping

Southlink Travels, 2nd floor, Selaka Building, 34 Gamini Mawatha, next to the Bus Station.
Tour operators

Southern Sri Lanka

Trains from Galle

To	1st class	2nd class	3rd class	Departure time	Journey
Aluthgama		Rs 32	Rs 11	1330, 1425 (not Saturday/Sunday), 1705	1-¾ hrs
Anuradahapura (to Vavuniya via Colombo)		Rs 180	Rs 66	1040	7½ hrs
Anuradhapura (via Colombo)		Rs 184	Rs 66	1030	7½ hrs
Colombo (Maradana)	Rs 113	Rs 65	Rs 24	0645, 0905 (not Saturday/Sunday), 1030, 1040, 1445, 1650	2½-3 hrs
Colombo (via all staions, Maradana)	Rs 113	Rs 65	Rs 24	0345 (not Sunday), 0455, 0530, 1140	3½ hrs
Colombo (Intercity)	Rs 122 (Rs 208 return)	Rs 72 (Rs 108 return)		0740	2½ hrs
Kandy (via Colombo)	Rs 232	Rs 133	Rs 48	1445	6-7 hrs
Matara		Rs 25	Rs 9	1015, 1145, 1325, 1835	1½ hrs
Matara		Rs 25	Rs 9	0530, 0730, 0920, 1430, 1715, 2055	2 hrs
Panadura	Rs 84	Rs 42	Rs 15	0550	2½-3 hrs
Trincomalee (via Colombo)	Rs 232	Rs 84		1805	11-12 hrs

Transport **Road** **Bus**: There are regular services along the coast in both directions. Both CTB and private buses operate from the main bus stand. To: **Colombo**: a/c Express recommended (Rs 60), 3 hrs, but avoid Sun as it can be very busy with queues of over an hour before you actually get onto a bus. To **Hikkaduwa** (Rs 5), **Matara** (Rs 15), **Unawatuna** (Rs 5) and **Tangalla** (Rs 15), 2 hrs. **Taxi**: over Rs 3,000 for a trip to or from Colombo. **Train** The railway station is a short walk from the bus station and the fort and town.

Directory **Banks** *Bank of Ceylon*, Lighthouse St. *Hatton National Bank*, HW Amarasuriya Mawatha exchanges currency, TCs and gives cash advances on Visa and Mastercard. *People's Bank*, Middle St. Exchange also at the *Historic Mansion Museum*. **Communications** The huge *GPO* is on Main St. It also has *Poste Restante* and is the only place south of Colombo that offers EMS Speedpost (though you must call before 0900). There is a *Branch Post Office* on Church St, within the Fort. There are numerous IDD. *Lanka Payphones* and *Metrocard* cardphones scattered around, or you can use the various private offices on Havelock Place. **Hospital**: *General Hospital*, T2261. **Useful addresses** **Police Station**: is in the Zwart Bastion.

Route The A2 continues southeast along the coast. Just south of the '74 mile' marker a narrow coastal road, 'Bona Vista' offers excellent views across Galle Harbour towards the fort. It is worth doing a detour for the views. Walk up along the tarred road until you reach the highest point. On a clear day look inland to catch sight of Adam's Peak.

Unawatuna උනවටුන

Unawatuna has a picturesque beach along a sheltered bay, which although rather narrow, is more suitable for swimming than, say, Hikkaduwa, with some coral within safe snorkelling distance of shore (though you may be disappointed by their poor colour). It also has the advantage of not having a terrifyingly busy main road right through the middle of it. Indeed, some find Unawatuna more appealing than its popular neighbour. Although it has developed rapidly, with almost every house displaying a 'rooms for rent' sign, it is still more relaxed than Hikkaduwa, with fewer package tourists. If you are seeking somewhere with a safe beach, a wide range of cheap and clean accommodation, plus a variety of good value beach-side restaurants, then Unawatuna is a good choice.

Phone code: 09
Colour map 3, grid C3
5 km SE of Galle

In addition to whiling away your time on the beach, it is worth spending some time following the paths through the Rumassala Jungle up towards 'Jungle Beach'

Popularity has taken its toll though. Once thought to be 'one of the 12 most beautiful beaches in the world', Unawatuna now struggles to be one of the 'top 50'. (It is worth searching out old postcards of the bay before there was any development.) Beach restaurants have encroached to the point where the actual usable beach is very narrow indeed and the increasing number of visitors means that the beach is sometimes crowded and dirty. The western end of the bay being popular with day trippers at weekends and public holidays. Since the double reef encloses the bay, the coastal water is never fully flushed out but does give the advantage of safe all-year swimming. The resort has been reported as 'sleazy', with some men behaving offensively in public. Others have found coconut sellers and rickshaw drivers become threatening when you do not concede to their demands.

Rumassala kanda (hillock), the rocky outcrop along the coast has a large collection of unusual medicinal herbs. In the *Ramayana* epic, Hanuman, the monkey god was sent on an errand to collect a special herb to save Rama's wounded brother Lakshmana. Having failed to identify the plant, he returned with a herb-covered section of the great mountain range, a part of what he was carrying is believed to have fallen here! (another part is said to have been dropped in Ritigala). This area of forest is now protected by the State to save the rare plants from being removed indiscriminately. The sea bordering Rumassala has the *Bona Vista* coral reef which has some 'living' coral–a feature which is becoming rare along the crowded sections of popular beaches.

Expensive B *Milton's*, Ganahena, T83312, F074-380955. 16 rooms including 9 a/c, attached hot bath, well furnished but upstairs rooms are better, nice terrace restaurant, breakfast included, popular with tour groups, tiny but unofficially 'private' beach, pricey. **B** *Unawatuna Beach Resort* (UBR), T074-380549, F32247 ubr@sri.lanka.net 62 rooms, mostly a/c (10 cheaper non-a/c), best in new annexe, large private garden, pool, various sports including boat trips, good restaurant, resort style hotel now fenced off from the crowded beach.

Sleeping

Mid-range C *Beach Hotel Cormaran*, Ganahena, T/F074-381337. 8 clean a/c rooms (Rs 1500) with balcony/terrace, restaurant, close to main road so can be noisy, fish everywhere including on the reception desk! **C** *Dream House*, T074-381541. 5 very nice rooms in Italian run old colonial style house, very Italian ambience. **C** *Sea View Guest House*, T/F23649. 22 rooms plus a bungalow with 2 bedrooms and kitchen, balconies, restaurant, popular with local weekenders, pricey. **C-D** *Thaproban*, T077-901559, F074-381722. 7 attractive, comfortable rooms (Rs 900-2000) some with balcony, nets, well furnished, restaurant, young friendly management. Recommended. **C-E** *Strand*, Yadehimulla Rd (set back from beach), T24358, F503 -2107891 strand_u@sltnet.lk 6

Southern Sri Lanka

spacious rooms plus 2 bungalows (Rs 550- 1200) and a 2-storey family apartment in 1920's colonial house in large grounds, private balcony/verandah, good food, friendly family, knowledgeable host, a little dark and frayed around the edges but recommended for atmosphere. **D** *Blue Swan Inn*, Yadehimulla Rd, T/F24691. 4 spotless comfortable rooms in English/Sri Lankan run family guesthouse, well furnished, rooftop restaurant. Recommended. **D** *Flower Garden Cabanas*, T/F25286. 9 pleasant cabanas, restaurant, quiet spot in pretty garden. **D** *Lands End*, Yakdehimulla, on the headland, T074 380099. 6 comfortable rooms in excellent location on headland, good restaurant/bar, snooker table. **D** *Sri Gamunu*, Dalawella, south of police station, T/F83202. 16 clean rooms in friendly guesthouse set in nice garden on attractive beach, restaurant, fishing and wildlife trips arranged. **D** *Sun-n-Sea*, Ganahena, at east end of bay, T83200, F83399 muharam@sltnet.lk 8 clean rooms, a/c extra Rs 250, good terrace restaurant overlooking the bay with excellent view, popular, Mrs Perera is a charming owner, friendly, close to main road but recommended.

Cheap D-E *Neptune Bay*, T/F34014, neptunbay@eureka.lk 16 clean rooms (Rs 500-1000), nets, some with balconies with sea views, travel office, reliable internet (Rs 9 per min). **D-E** *Unawatuna Beach Bungalow*,T/F24327. 6 rooms (Rs 1000 with breakfast) in newish building, clean and better upstairs, restaurant. **D-F** *Eterna Guest House*, Ganahena, T074-380029. 8 clean rooms (Rs 450- 900), nets, bit pricey, worth bargaining. **D-F** *Rock House*, Yaddehimulla Rd, T24949 (cheaper rooms), T24948 (others). 20 rooms in 2 blocks with 2 owners (Rs 400-1000), all clean, some new, airy and spacious, good range, good value. **E** *Amma's Guest House*, T25332. 13 rooms (Rs 500-600), upstairs better opening onto a lovely balcony, nets, clean, Arthur C Clarke was one of the first ever guests here, "lovely owner". Recommended. **E** *Araliya*, T83706, F074 380365. 12 clean, large rooms (Rs 650-700) away from the road, restaurant, reasonable value. **E** *Weliwatta House*, T42891. 5 rooms (Rs 500), quiet, good food. **E** *Weliwatta*, T42891. 5 rooms (Rs 500), quiet, good food. **E-F** *Village Inn*, T25375, F074 380691. 13 rooms in chalets and 1 bungalow (Rs 350-800), breakfast available, meals to order, quiet, friendly. **E-G** *Zimmer Rest*, Valledewala Road, T074 380366. 5 rooms (Rs 200 shared bath- Rs 450 attached) plus 2 simple cabanas (Rs 600), peaceful garden, free tea, food on request. **E-F** *Happy Banana*, T074-380152. 5 rooms (Rs 750 including breakfast), upstairs better, good restaurant. **F** *Heaven on Earth*, 4 rooms (Rs 350 shared bath, Rs 450 attached), rather simple but well furnished for the price. **F** *Upul*, T077-903747. 6 rooms (Rs 450) under new English management, upstairs rooms light and airy, clean, friendly. Recommended. **G** *Prema's*, T077-330855. 4 simple rooms with shared bath (Rs 250) in family run guesthouse, friendly. **G** *Royal Kingdom*, 3 rooms, small and quiet. **G** *South Ceylon*, 5 basic rooms with shared bath (Rs 200), good restaurant, meditation, laundry facilities.

Talpe (east of Unawatuna) Expensive C *Club Point de Galle*, 654 Matara Rd, T53206. Airy rooms, fan, attached bath, slightly upmarket, right on beach. **E** *Beach Haven*, Matara Rd, T53362. 25 small rooms, attached bath, fan, pool, restaurant. **F** *Happy Tuna Guest House*, Matara Rd, T53387. 5 small rooms, attached bath, fan, upstairs rooms with balconies breezier.

The Strand, an example of a colonial house

There are numerous restaurants along the beach, serving good cheap meals from as **Eating** little as Rs 80. Almost all serve alcohol (though those at the western end of the bay don't advertise it since the area close to the temple is officially 'dry'). Travellers have reported that some coconut sellers agree Rs 15/16 initially but once you take a drink, the demand goes up to Rs 50/60. Those who refuse to pay are threatened with the small machette they carry to cut the coconuts! **Expensive** *Cocorumba Bar Rendezvous* at the *Unawatuna Beach Resort*. Popular place, wide menu including lunchtime buffet (Rs 450), authentic 'Aussie burgers' Sat night disco. **Mid-range** *Happy Banana*, nice setting, good for seafood, Fri night disco. *Hot Rock*, probably the busiest and most popular partly because of its location, tables and loungers on beach outside, though food not necessarily the best. *Thaprobane*. Good food in a new place in pleasant surroundings. *South Ceylon*. Wide vegetarian menu, different themed international cuisine every night. Highly recommended. *Sunil's Garden*, has the best sound

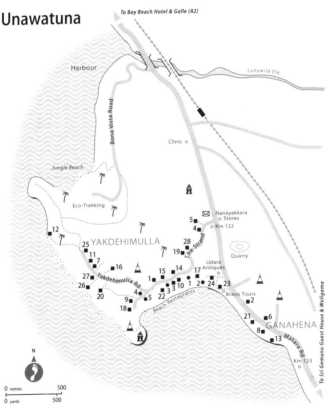

Unawatuna

Southern Sri Lanka

■ **Sleeping**
1 Amma's Guesthouse
2 Araliya
3 Benny's Beach Resort
4 Blue Swan
5 Bruno's Flower Garden Cabanas
6 Cormaran
7 Dream House
8 Eterna
9 Golden Ente & Brinkhaus
10 Happy Banana
11 Heaven on Earth & Royal Kingdom

12 Land's End
13 Milton's
14 Neptune Bay
15 Prema's Guesthouse
16 Rock House
17 Rumassala
18 Sea View Guesthouse
19 South Ceylon & Sonya Health Food
20 Strand
21 Sun-n-Sea
22 Thaprobane
23 Unawatuna Beach Bungalow

24 Unawatuna Beach Resort
25 Upal Guesthouse
26 Village Inn
27 Weliwatta
28 Zimmer Rest

● **Eating**
1 Lucky Tuna
2 Madushani
3 Pink Elephant
4 Sunil's Garden
5 Three Fishes & Hot Rock

system (plenty of Bob Marley!). **Cheap** *Lucky Tuna*. Good cheap rice and noodle dishes. *Madushani*. Small and intimate, beach-side place, friendly.

Shopping The woodworker Chandrasekera sells his exquisite woodcarvings at low prices in a hut near the beach.

Sports & activities **Snorkelling** Most of the beach-side restaurants hire out equipment (mask, snorkel, flippers Rs 75 per hr). **Ayurvedic massages** Dr Esman Sourfah has been practising from his hut on the west end of the beach since mid-1980s (part or whole body massage, 'anti-stress therapy'). He has numerous testimonials from satisfied customers. Also teaches basic principles of meditation.

Tour operators *Bravo Tours*, T078-68664. IDD phone, 2-5 day tours and safaris arranged. *Vista*, IDD calls (discounts on Sun and after 2200), airport minibus (Rs 450 per person, minimum 4), minibus with driver (Rs 1,500 per day), plus a number of tours.

Transport

Touts and tuk-tuk drivers at the station can be very persistent (& threatening). Agree price ahead for the tuk-tuk to take you to your choice of hotel

Road It is very easy to miss Unawatuna when travelling by road. Look out for the Km 122 marker on the (sea) side of the road (or the more obvious sign for *Bruno's Flower Garden Cabanas*, if coming from the north). **Buses** between Galle and Matara will drop you here. **Tuk-tuks** to/from **Hikkaduwa**, Rs 250, after bargaining. **Galle** under Rs 100, takes 15 mins. **Train** The railway station is to the east of the main Galle-Matara Rd, some 500 m north of the Km 122 marker (about 15-min walk to the beach). If coming from Colombo, take the Express to Galle then change onto the slower train that stops here.

Directory **Communications**: IDD calls can be made from a number of private 'travel offices/reisburos' (see above). **Internet** Many outlets at Rs 10 per min, but most suffer from connection problems and are slow. *Neptune Bay* has one of the better systems.

The Scenic South Coast

*Phone code: 09
Colour map 3,
grid C3 & 4*

The scenic coast road from **Unawatuna** *to* **Matara**, *runs close to the sea affording excellent views and links a series of small attractive beaches. The coast between Ahangama and Weligama was best known for its remarkable fishermen who perched for hours on poles out in the bay. Now, Midigama (Km 137) is one of the few remaining places where these 'stilt' fishermen still operate but it is a dying tradition although when visitors with cameras appear, so does the odd 'fisherman'. There is good surf nearby and consequently it is popular with long-term surfers.*

Ins & outs **Getting there** Many visitors to these beaches arrive by car but it is equally feasible to reach one of the resorts by public transport. Slow trains between Galle and Matara stop at Talpe and Ahangama, where there are tuk-tuks. Between Galle and Matara, buses can be flagged down and stopped at any of these settlements. The coast road passes an old wartime air strip beyond Talpe and Habaraduwa before reaching Koggala, 15 km from Galle. Kogalla has a large lake with rocky islets to its north and is a Free Trade Zone with some new light industry.

Sights

Koggala
Phone code: 09

Just by the Confifi Club Horizon hotel gate, a road leads to the **Martin Wickramasinghe Folk Art and Culture museum** which houses the wellknown Sri Lankan writer's personal collection. His family home displays photographs and memoribilia. ■ *0900-1300, 1400-1700; closed Mon and holidays.*

Temple paintings from the Purvarama Vihara, Kataluva: Dice players far right and Sword players right
Source: LTP Manjusr's, Design Elements

East of Koggala, the Purvarama Mahaviharaya (originally 18th century with late 19th century additions) is 3 km along a minor road turning off at Kataluva (Km 132 marker, next to Serendib Guest House); you may need to ask directions locally. The ambulatory has excellent examples of temple paintings illustrating different styles of Kandyan art. Young monks will happily point out interesting sections of the *Jataka* stories depicted on the wall friezes. Note the musicians and dancers on the south side and the European figures illustrating an interesting piece of social history.

Kataluva

Southern Sri Lanka

Essentials

Habaraduwa and Koggala AL-A *Club Horizon* (Confifi), Matara Rd, Koggala, T83297, F83299. 50 a/c rooms, 22 attractive cabanas, 1 suite, restaurant, bar, large pool, health club, tennis, badminton, minigolf, nice beach. **C** *Koggala Beach*, Matara Rd, Habaraduwa, T83243, F83260. 204 rooms (a/c US$10 extra) in one long block, with breezy balcony or terrace, restaurant, pool, access to excellent beach, a candidate for Asia's longest hotel. **E-F** *Sunny South*, Matara Rd, Habaraduwa, fairly basic, attached bath, fan.

Sleeping

Ahangama (4 km east of Kogalla) **C** *Hotel Club Lanka*, Matara Rd, T83296, F53361. 33 rooms, fan, attached bath, restaurant, large pool, set in gardens on a fine beach. **D** *Serendib Guest House*, on opposite side of road. Rooms in a newish house set back from the road.

Midigama (10 km east Kogalla) **F** *Hilten's Beach Resort*. 5 rooms with attached bath (Rs 400, negotiable), 2 with shared bath, restaurant, idiosyncratic owner. **G** *Ram's Shack*. 3 basic rooms with attached bath (Rs 300), 5 with shared bath (Rs 200), restaurant, friendly and entertaining host, popular with surfers.

Weligama ව‍ැලිගම

Weligama's sheltered bay allows diving and snorkelling beyond the usual season experienced along the rest of the southwest coast. Further east, the rocky headland across the bay hides the quiet beach at Mirissa.

Phone code: 041
Colour map 3, grid C3
29 km from Galle,
144 km from Colombo

The tiny **Taprobane** island in the lovely bay was once owned by the Frenchman, Count de Maunay, who built a house on it which is now an exclusive hotel. At the approach to the town there is a 4-m high statue of Kushta Raja, sometimes known as the 'Leper King'. Various legends surround the statue believed by some to be of Bodhisattva Samantabhadra. Look out for the *mal lali* fretwork decorated houses along the road from the centre towards the statue. The area is known for its hand made lace (see shopping). **Devil Dances** are held in neighbouring villages.

Expensive AL *Taprobane Island Hotel*, Taprobane Island (for reservations contact *The Sun House*, Galle, T074-380275, F09-22624 sunhouse@sri.lanka.net Possible to rent the whole house, 3 bedrooms, fully equipped kitchen, hot water, reached at low tide without getting too wet. Recommended. **B-C** *Crystal Villa*, New Sea Road,

Sleeping
NB New Sea Road is New Matara Road

Pelana, T50635, (Colombo T725032, F735031). 5 large, comfortable rooms, plus 2 bungalows with alfresco showers, good garden on the beach, pool, good restaurant. **C** *Bay Beach*, Kapparatota (west end of bay), T50201, F50407. 60 a/c rooms, hot bath, private balcony/terrace, restaurant, bar, disco, pool, access to good beach, watersports, Aqua Sports Diving Centre (see below). **D** *Weligama Bay Inn*, New Sea Road,T50299, (Colombo T503497, F503504). 12 simple rooms in an old airy villa set in large garden, some with sea view, a bit tatty around the edges, balcony/terrace, good restaurant, bar, exchange.

Mid-range D *Bay Inn Resthouse* (CHC), New Sea Rd, T50299 (or T01-503497, F01-503504). 12 simple rooms with attached bath, fan, balcony/terrace, some with seaview, old airy villa set in large garden, good restaurant, bar, exchange.

Cheap D-E *Jaga Bay Resort*, New Sea Rd, Pelana, T/F50033 jagabay@sltnet.lk 17 large, almost spotless chalets plus 3 cabanas with hot bath (Rs 650-850), nets, set in large garden on the beach, very peaceful location, very good restaurant, difficult to stay only one night, recommended. **D-E** *Weligama Bay View*, New Sea Road, Pelana, T51199. 6 large rooms (Rs 750 including breakfast), reasonably clean, good restaurant, popular with Japanese surfing girls, friendly but a bit pricey. Recommended. **E** *Chez Frank*, 158 Kapparatota Rd, near *Bay Beach Hotel*, T50584. Large rooms, restaurant. **E** *Greenpeace Inn*, down track to beach off New Sea Road, Pelana, T52046. 6 attractively furnished rooms (Rs 500) with bath, some nice touches, clean, quiet location, garden, close to beach, friendly. **E** *Hotel Angel*, New Sea Road, Pelana, T/F50475. 6 rooms (Rs 1000 including breakfast) in neo-colonial style building built in 2000, needs some minor finishing touches, but rooms are large, light and airy, garden stretches to the beach, reasonable restaurant, worth a look. **E** *Kantha*, 124 Kapparatota. Just 1 room (Rs 500) with another planned, friendly, good reasonably priced restaurant. **E** *Samaru Beach House*, 544 New Sea Road, Pelana, T/F51417. 5

Weligama

To Ratnapura

Kushta Raja Statue

Old Galle Rd

Main St

New Sea (Matara) Rd

Old Matara Rd

Polwatta Ganga

PELANA

Taprobane

Parei Duwa

Weligama Bay

Matara Rd

Kapparatota

Galle Rd

To Galle

To Matara

MIRISSA

To Matara

N

0 metres 500
0 yards 500

■ **Sleeping**
1 Angel
2 Bay Beach & Aqua Sports
3 Bay Inn Rest House
4 Bay Tourist Inn
5 Bay View
6 Chez Frank
7 Greenpeace Inn
8 Jaga Bay
9 Kantha
10 Paradise Beach Club
11 Raja's Guest House
12 Rest House
13 Samaru
14 Sam's Holiday Cabanas
15 Taprobane Island Resort
16 Udula Beach Inn
17 Weligama Bay View

● **Eating**
1 Crystal Villa
2 Diver's
3 Keerthi's Seafood

spotless rooms (Rs 550-750), 3 more planned, good location on the beach, restaurant, friendly young management, good value. **E** *Udula Guest House*, New Sea Rd, T50721. 7 simple rooms (Rs 500) with attached bath. **F** *Raja's Guest Home*, down track off New Sea Road, opposite 'Mile 91', Pelana, T51750. 4 simple, clean rooms (Rs 300), nets, great location on clean section of beach, pleasant garden, excellent seafood (especially lobster) but other tastes catered for, Raja is an exceptional host. Highly recommended. **G** *Bay View*, 147 New Road, Kapparatota. 3 simple, clean rooms (Rs 300), seafood restaurant, friendly, good value

Eating *Crystal Villa, Divers'* and *Keerthi* are close to the sea, but home cooking in the privately run guest houses is difficult to beat. *Crystal Villa* also has 4 rooms and 2 bungalows.

Shopping Weligama lace is available at several outlets and workshops along the road opposite Taprobane Island.

Sports **Diving** (open Nov-Apr) *Bay Beach Aqua Sports*, is highly recommended. PADI Open Water Course (US$295 plus US$55 for certificate and logbook), Check dive (US$21 including equipment), Wreck diving (US$115 including possible visit to a plane wreck near Koggala's Second World War airstrip), PADI Resort Course (lessons, 2 sea dives but no certification, US$77), also dive safaris, notably to the Great Basses Ridge off Kirinda (similar conditions to Maldives). **Deep sea angling** To fish for marlin, yellowfin and sharks, is also possible. A day's angling in a 24ft *Fjord* with 200Hp engine (including outriggers, *Penn* equipment) is US$500.

Transport **Road Bike** and **motorbike hire**: from *Bay Tourist Inn*, 10 New Matara Rd. **Bus**: between Galle and Matara will let you down on the New Sea (Matara) Rd, though some local buses will drop you at the bus yard on the Old Matara Rd. Buses from Colombo: about 4 hrs; from Galle, about 30 mins. **Train** Weligama is on the Colombo-Galle-Matara railway line, though check to make sure the train stops here if it's an Express.

Directory **Communications**: the Branch Post Office, is on Main St, opposite the railway station.

Route Along this outstandingly beautiful stretch of road from Weligama to Tangalla there is an endless succession of bays with the road often running right by the startling blue sea and palm fringed rocky headlands. The district is known for the manufacture and export of citronella perfume.

Mirissa
මිරිස්ස
Phone code: 041
34 km from Galle
149 km from Colombo

Beyond the headland and 5 km along the coast across Weligama Bay is Mirissa which has a beautiful, small rocky beach which is no longer a secret hideaway. As the word spreads, its popularity increases, but it is still a pleasant place to relax for an extended stay. You can try deep sea fishing, river trips, snorkelling or visit rubber and tea factories or a snake farm (enquire at the *Paradise Beach Club*).

Sleeping **Mid-range C-D** *Paradise Beach Club*, 140 Gunasiri Mahime Mawatha, T51206, F50380 mirissa@sltnet.lk 30 bungalows plus 4 simple rooms and 6 very nice 2-storey family bungalows, restaurant (mostly buffet), set in large rustic garden, pool, tours, located on beach, not bad value but enforced half board tends to be restrictive. **Cheap E** *Mirissa Beach Inn*, T50410, F50115. 9 clean bungalows (Rs 600-750), restaurant, good beach access. **E** *Ocean Moon*, Udupila Junction, T50959. 4 cabanas (Rs 700) on the beach, peaceful, restaurant. **E-F** *Central Beach Inn*, on beach, T51699. 6 simple rooms (Rs 400) and 2 larger cabanas (Rs 650), restaurant. **E-G** *Damith Holiday Wings*, Gunasiri Mahime Mawatha, opposite Paradise Beach Club, T/F51651 damee@sltnet.lk 4 clean rooms (Rs 300- 400) and 4 bungalows (Rs 500-600), restaurant, good internet connection (Rs 90 for 15 mins), worth a try. **E-G** *Giragala Village*, Bandaramulla, to the east of the beach, T50496. 7 outside rooms (Rs 700-750) plus 4 more spartan rooms inside converted house (Rs 300), restaurant, good information about swimming and snorkelling areas in Mirissa. **G** *Amarasinghe's Guest House*, 5 mins inland (follow signs). 6 large rooms (Rs 250) but grotty bathrooms, pleasant, quiet garden away from beach. **F** *Sunshine Beach Inn*. 6 simple, clean, new rooms (Rs 450), nets, restaurant, close to beach. **G** *Mirissa Calm Rest*, Gunasiri Mahime Mawatha, T51610. 3 simple rooms with attached bath (Rs 300), restaurant.

Transport Road Buses between Galle and Matara pass through Mirissa. From **Weligama**, bus (Rs 3) or tuk-tuk (around Rs 100).

Matara මාතර

Phone code: 041
Colour map 3, grid C4
42 km from Galle
157 km from Colombo

Matara (pronounced locally as Maat-re) is a town divided by the Nilwala Ganga with the two Dutch forts standing on either side. As one of the important Dutch posessions on the south coast, it controlled the trade in cinnamon and elephants. Today, the Ruhuna University 3 km east of town, has brought students into the town with narrow streets where in the old marketplace you might still see the local wooden oxcarts ('hackeries') which are sometimes used for races! The seaside promenade retains some interesting old buildings and though the beach is attractive the waters are too rough for comfortable bathing much of the year.

Sights

The Broadway is also known as Dharmapala Mawatha, Colombo Rd or New Galle Rd

Dutch forts The larger **Main Fort**, consisting of a rampart from which guns were fired, is on the peninsula to the south which held most of the old town. There is also a church dating from 1769. It was badly damaged by attackers from Kandy in 1761, who occupied it for a time. Following this, the **Star Fort**, faced with coral, was built in 1763, which has a moated double-wall and six points. The gateway which shows the VOC arms and date, is particularly picturesque. The fort itself is private property now with some modern buildings against the inner wall, and a courtyard which has the old well in the centre, still in use. You can get some idea of the original plan from the northeast point. **Further reading** *The Dutch Forts of Sri Lanka* by WA Nelson, 1984, gives details of a number of forts across the island.

The Buddhist hermitage, *Chula Lanka*, on a tiny island joined by a causeway to the mainland, was founded by a Thai Prince priest.

Polhena, 2 km west (towards Galle), has become dominated by the most exploitative kind of tourism. Hotels vie with each other to gain business and unabashadly claim that others have closed or insist you place your order for dinner in the morning to obviate the opportunity to sample food anywhere else. There is, however, a good coral **beach** here protected by a reef which offers year round safe bathing with good value guest houses. The reef within easy reach offers good snorkelling.

The Archeological Department Museum has closed, with many of the exhibits having been transferred to Kataragama.

Sleeping: Matara

Mid-range D-E *Rest House*, main Fort area, south of bus station, T22299. 14 rooms in 2 wings, those in new block away from the sea are better but old wing due to be refurbished, nets, restaurant, popular with tour groups, worth considering. **Cheap E** *Browns Beach Resort*, 39b Beach Rd, T26298. 7 rooms (Rs 500) more for a/c, no sea view, inefficient staff, restaurant. **F** *River Inn*, 96/1 W Gunasekara Mawatha, next to the prison. Avoid despite pleasant exterior. **G** *Blue Ripples*, 38 W Gunasekara

● ●

Daily Trains from Matara (unless otherwise indicated)

To	2nd class	3rd class	Train	Departure time	Journey
Anuradhapura (and Vavuniya)	Rs 204	Rs 75	Express	0910	9 hrs (10½ hrs)
Colombo	Rs 89	Rs 30	Express	0400, 0725, 0915, 1325, 1540	3½ hrs
Galle			Express	Colombo trains	1 hr
Galle			Slow	0610, 1155, 1430, 1715	1¼ hrs
Hikkaduwa	Rs 36	Rs 13	Express	Colombo trains	1½ hrs
Kandy	Rs 157	Rs 57	Express	1315	7 hrs
Trincomalee			Express	1650	

NB From **Kandy**: the early morning train at 0500 (7¼ hrs) is very busy (2nd and 3rd class only which doesn't gaurantee a seat) but is still recommended if you can get on the train by 0440.

● ●

Mawatha, T22058. 4 simple, grubby rooms (Rs 280), no nets but fairly priced, food available on request, right on river bank where you might sport a monitor lizard.

Broadway Chinese, Broadway Cinema, Dharmapala Mawatha. *Chinese Dragon*, 62 Tangalla Rd, good meals for around Rs 150. *Galle Oriental Bakery*, Dharmapala Mawatha, does good Sri Lankan meals for Rs 50, as well as snacks. A local delicacy is buffalo milk curd served with honey or jaggery. There are numerous outlets. the *Fine Curd Food Cabin* is rec. *Golden Dish*, Station Rd.

Eating: Matara
Lots of Chinese

Many budget travellers prefer to stay in Polhena to the west of the town where there are a number of excellent, good value guest houses.

Sleeping: Polhena

Mid-range D *Polhena Reef Gardens*, 30 Beach Rd (turn off at 98th mile post), T22478. 20 large clean rooms with private balcony, bar, restaurant, best in the area but ridiculously overpriced. **Budget hotels E** *Beach Inn*, Madiha, T26356. 5 hopelessly overpriced rooms (Rs 700-800), on beach, clean but broken toilet cisterns in some rooms. **E** *Royal Sea Winds*, Beach Rd, T24907. 11 overpriced, smelly rooms (Rs 550), 12 new rooms under construction, bar and restaurant aimed for local wedding parties. **E-F** *TK Guest House*, 116/1 Beach Rd, T22603. 11 good, very clean rooms (Rs 350-550), nets, restaurant, well-run, quiet, nice garden, look out for Donald for good value batiks, enquire here about snorkelling (see below). Recommended. **F** *Sunil Rest*, off Beach Rd, T21983. 5 small rooms (Rs 350-400) with 5 more to come in very friendly family guesthouse, nets, restaurant, snorkelling and boat trips organised, cycle, motorbike and even self-drive 3-wheeler for hire! Recommended. **F** *Sunny Lanka Guest House*, Polhena Rd, T23504. 5 very clean rooms (Rs 400) in friendly guesthouse, modern building, nets, good restaurant, snorkelling and day trips arranged (see below), cycle hire (Rs 100 per day), visits to snake farm, friendly. Recommended.

Paying guest You can rent simple rooms in family homes in a beautiful rural setting for under Rs 100. contact HK Shantha, Paluwata, Walgama South, 5 min walk from Polhena.

Shopping **Bookshops** *HB Eramanis Appuhamy*, 87 Dharmapala Mawatha, has some English books. **Handicrafts** You will also find good batiks and citronella oil in town. Shirley Dissanayake of *Art Batiks*, 58/6 Udyana Road is a holder of the President's Honorary Gold Medal 'Kala Booshana' in arts. He produces top quality batiks, only available on site here in his workshop. Beware of imitations! You can buy, or simply watch craftsmen producing musical instruments (particularly drums) at 21 Dharmapala Mawatha.

Watersports **Reef visit** Titus is an excellent snorkelling guide who knows the reef like the back of his hand, having had over 30 years of experience. The reef is also good for first time snorkellers ("after 10 minutes I felt like Jacques Cousteau!"), and there are night trips to see Moray eels. Ask at *TK Guest House* or *Sunny Lanka Guest House*. Highly recommended.

Transport **Local** Very irregular local buses run to the beach at **Polhena** (260, 350, 356). Alternatively a tuk-tuk will cost Rs 50. **Long distance Bus** The Bus Station is in the main Fort area with buses running on a 'depart when full' basis. A bone-shaker to **Colombo** costs Rs 28, and a/c coaster Rs 50, 3-4 hrs. There are regular buses to **Galle**, **Hambantota**, **Kataragama**, **Tangalla**, **Tissamaharama**, and all points along the coast. There is also at least one early morning departure to **Nuwara Eliya**, 8 hrs. **Train** Matara station, the terminus of this railway line is 1 km away from town; tuk-tuks and taxis transfer passengers.

Directory **Bank**: *Sampath Bank*, against MasterCard. **Communications**: the old 1940s *General Post Office* is being moved to a brand new building next door. There is a *Sub Post Office* in the Fort area, plus agency post offices on Station Rd and Dharmapala Mawatha.

Matara & Polhena

■ Sleeping
1 Befriend Inn
2 Blue Ripples
3 Rest House
4 Royal Sea Winds
5 Sunil Rest & Polhena Reef
6 Sunny Lanka
7 TK Guesthouse

● Eating
1 Chinese
2 Chinese Dragon
3 Galle Oriental Bakery
4 Golden Dish

The Dry Southeast

The dry southeast coast offers a striking contrast with the Wet Zone lushness of the southwest. In an astonishingly short space of around 15 km everything changes. Open savanna takes over from the dank forest and rich undergrowth and the increasingly frequent patches of bare earth have a burnt and arid look. The contrast is dramatically illustrated by the gleaming white salt pans of Hambantota. From Matara, the coastal road takes you all the way to one the most visited national parks on the island, passing through some good bird-watching areas.

Most of the places of interest reached from the A2 coastal road are difficult to visit by public transport. The Southern Province is not fully covered by bus services along the major roads so to go north may mean several changes.

Ins & outs

The A2 from Matara crosses the Nilwala Ganga. After 5 km a left turn leads to this modern Buddhist sanctuary which has a 40-m high painted Buddha statue. The interior walls and ceilings underground section of the large vihara are covered in painted friezes with modern depictions of the Buddha's life. *Perahera* at November/December full moon. ■ *Getting there: bus No 349 runs from Matara.*

Weherahena

Dondra or Devinuwara (City of Gods) is a fishing village marks the southern-most point of Sri Lanka. The Vishnu **temple** has an ancient shrine possibly dating from the 7th century AD which may be the oldest stone built structure on the island. The modern temple retains old temple columns and a finely carved gate. The 50-m high **lighthouse** on the southern promontory at Dondra Head was built in 1889. Due to security controls, the lighthouse may not be open to visitors.

Dondra
10 km from Matara

Festivals At the end of July/August is *Esala Perahera*. There are spectacular processions and celebrations and a fair for 12 days at the site of the old Vishnu temple which was destroyed by the Portuguese. Even now, the Buddhist pilgrims continuing the ancient tradition venerate Vishnu of the Hindu trinity.

Expensive A *Club Dikwella Village* (Keells), Bahteegama, 1 km west, T55271, F55410. 70 large a/c rooms in bungalows in 'Little Italy' luxury resort (Italian owned and patronised), guaranteed maximum 15 m distance from beach, all with sea views, pool, ayurvedic massage, tennis, watersports, diving (see below), excellent restaurants, very attractive location on rocky promontory. Recommended. **Mid-range D** *Dikwella Beach Resort*, just past the town, T55326, and **E** *Michael Inn*, opposite. Both have simple rooms.

Dikwella
Phone code: 041
13 km from Matara

Watersports Diving (Nov-Apr): *Club Dikwella Village* T072-642107 (Alex), offers PADI Open Water Course (US$350), single dive including equipment (US$40, every 6th and 11th dive free), snorkelling gear (half day US$2.50, full day US$4), windsurfing and surfboards (1 hr US$10, half day US$25, full day US$40), discounts for expats living in Sri Lanka.

Here is the largest Buddha statue on the island at **Buduraja Mahawehera**. The statues, tableaux and Buddhist temple are in a small complex which has an impressive 50-m high seated Buddha statue with a 'library' at the back. 635 paintings in cartoon strip form depict events from the Buddha's life covering

Wewurukannala
2 km inland from Dikwella (on the Beliatta rd)

every square centimetre of the interior. The artists are from all over the world but retain the same style throughout. There is also a 'Chamber of Horrors' with depictions of the consequences of leading an incorrect life including some frighteningly graphic life-size models. ■ *Rs 5. Expect to be approached by a guide (Rs 50 tip is acceptable). Getting there: the site is quiet and makes an interesting half-day trip from Tangalla or Matara especially if combined with the 'blow hole' at Kudawella.*

Kudawella The natural blowhole at Kudawella, also known as **Hummanaya** due to the 'hoo' sound that you hear, which is particularly strong during the monsoon, is one of the more bizarre attractions in Sri Lanka and worth the detour. The water spray can rise to 25 m when the waves are strong and it can be good fun guessing when the next big one is coming whilst dodging the spray, which engulfs you and your camera equipment! Take care when clambering on the rocks as they are wet and slippery in places. It is best to avoid weekends and go during school hours to avoid the more unappealing elements of exploitative tourism. ■ *There is no entrance charge, although those living along the path to the blow hole may try their luck. You will probably be asked for money for "looking after your vehicle", a situation you should deal with depending on the number and size of those making the demand! Getting there: about 6 km east of Dikwella (117th mile post), immediately after the small bridge a large sign indicates right to the 'Blow Hole'. There are a number of prominent signs (sponsored by Elephant House) along the rough 2 km road, although one is missing at an important right hand turn (look out for a tiny yellow sign in Sinhala). This will take you down to a number of drinks stalls at Kudawella from where it is a few hundred metres walk to the blowhole.*

Tangalla
තංගල්ල
Phone code: 047
40 km from Matara,
198 km from Colombo

Tangalla (pronounced Tunn-gaa-le) or Tangalle, famous for its turtles, is an attractive fishing port with a palm fringed bay with extensive irrigation to north. It also has one of the best beaches in the southern coastal belt and even though there are a growing number of hotels and guesthouses, the beach remains mostly deserted with good sand and safe swimming when the sea is not rough.

There is a **Dutch fort** standing on the slope above the bay. Built of coral with two bastions in opposite corners it was turned into a jail after a report in 1837 declared it was in sound condition and able to safely hold up to 100 men. The exterior has now been covered over by cement.

The beach shelves quite
suddenly & there is often
an undertow, so take
care when swimming if
windy or rough, when it
can be dangerous

Visitors have a choice of three main areas to stay. The settlements of **Goyambokka** and **Pallikaduwa** are on a series of bays to the south of town. Some visitors have reported a terrible smell at the top end of the beach (near *Turtles' Landing*). In Tangalla town, several hotels are near the harbour including the Resthouse. The cove in front of is fairly sheltered so is consequently quite busy. The quietest locations are probably **Medaketiya** and **Medilla** along the long sweep of beach to the north of the harbour (across the bridge from the bus station). Medaketiya Beach, in particular, has a fine, clean sand and is quite idyllic as it is usually deserted. Access to the latter two may be restricted and so may be only possible from Tissa Road.

Sadly, Tangalla is rumoured to be one of the 'child-sex' destinations in Sri Lanka. The authorities have taken successful legal action against a number of offenders operating on some popular beaches.

Essentials

Sleeping

Mid-range C *Nature Resort*, most easterly hotel, T/F40844. 7 cabanas plus 4 bungalows in new resort, light and airy rooms but with serious red ant problem, beach bar, restaurant, pool, attractive gardens with good section of beach, also some cheaper **D** lagoon side bungalows. **C** *Palm Paradise Cabanas*, Goyambokka, 2 km west, T40842, F40338. 20 comfortable cabanas set in a spacious and shady garden, close to the beach, very peaceful, good restaurant, efficient service, well run. Highly

Tangalla

To Nature Resort, Ganesh Garden & Hambantota

MEDILLA

MEDAKETIYA

Medaketiya Beach

Southern Sri Lanka

To Mulgirigala Rock Temple (15 km)

To Ibis, Let's Dive, Palm Beach, Jewel & Panorama Rock Café

Kirama Oya

Tissa Rd

Vijaya Rd

Market

Parakrama Rd

Main St

Halton

Beach Rd

Dagoba

Harbour

Children's Playground

Muhudu Mawatha

Bodhi Mawatha

Naval Base

PALLIKADUWA

Pallikaduwa Rd

GOYAMBOKKA

To Matara

Mahawela Rd

Indian Ocean

N

0 metres 200
0 yards 200

■ **Sleeping**
1 Anila Beach Inn
2 Blue Horizon
3 Catamaran Beach Home & Sarath
4 Dilena Beach Home & Shanika Beach Inn
5 Gayana Guest House
6 Kingfisher
7 Mansion Guest House
8 Namal Garden Beach
9 Palm Paradise, Goyambokka & Calm Garden Cabanas
10 Rest House
11 Rocky Point
12 Saman's Travellers Rest
13 Santana Guest House
14 Sea View Tourist Inn
15 Tangalla Bay
16 Tangalla Beach
17 Touristen Gasthause/ Tourist Guest House
18 Tourist Guest House
19 Villa Araliya
20 Villa Ocean Waves

● **Eating**
1 Bay View
2 Chalet
3 Chanika
4 Sea Beach
5 Sea Food
6 Sun Beach
7 Sun Shadow
8 Turtle's Landing

recommended. **C** *Tangalla Bay*, Mahawela Rd, Pallikudawa, T/F40346, (Colombo F449548). 32 breezy rooms, including some unnecessary a/c (extra US$5) in unlikely 1970s kitsch 'truly eccentric' ship design although it has seen better days ("the lower the rooms, the more it feels like 3rd class on the Titanic"), restaurant likely to improve with the new chef, small pool, popular for weddings, 'a sadly sinking ship'. **D** *Ganesh Garden*, Medilla Beach. 4 rather dark cabanas, a bit overpriced but in a quiet, secluded location, laid back atmosphere, reasonable restaurant. **D** *Ibis Guest House*, 27 Medaketiya Rd, between the beach and a small lagoon. 3 cabanas with 3 **E** to be built plus 2 rooms in brick built bungalows, very peaceful location on beach, restaurant, friendly. **D** *Rocky Point Beach Bungalows*, Goyambokka, near Palm Paradise, T40834. 3 bungalows and 4 rooms, all large, clean with private verandah, pleasant gardens in quiet location overlooking rocky promontory, good food. Recommended. **D** *Touristen Gasthause/Tourist Guest house*, 13 Pallikudawa Rd, T/F40370. 2 bungalows, 4 rooms, 2 with hot water, all spotless plus an apartment, also 1 room with kitchen and a house for rent so you are spoilt for choice, friendly owner, extremely well run. Recommended.

Cheap D-F *Green Jewel Cabanas*, T/F40827. 3 rather run down cabanas (Rs 400) plus 2 overpriced rooms (Rs 900), close to beach and lagoon, restaurant, catamaran service. **D-F** *Tourist Guest House*, Mahawela Rd, opposite *Tangalla Bay Hotel*, T40389. 8 good-sized rooms (Rs 400-1000), clean, friendly, restaurant, nice setting. **E** *Goyambokka Guest House*, Goyambokka, opposite *Palm Paradise*,T/F40838. 4 comfortable, well sized, clean rooms (Rs 700 including breakfast), quiet, pleasant garden, restaurant, good off-season discounts, good value. **E** *Rest House*, on promontory overlooking harbour, T40299. 25 rooms (Rs 600) in 18th century Dutch building, those in new block better, balcony/verandahs, restaurant, overall a bit tatty but worth a visit for tea or a drink to admire the view. **E-F** *Gayana Guest House*, 96 Medaketiya Beach, T/F40477. 8 rooms of varying size (Rs 400-700), some fronting directly onto beach, good restaurant, friendly staff, secure, popular with backpackers, one of the best in this class, Wed evening slide presentation on turtle conservation (see Rekawa), Recommended. **E-F** *Kingfisher*, (was *Lanka German Ranjith* Guest House), Medaketiya. 5 clean rooms (Rs 400- 600), good location close to beach, restaurant, friendly family, worth a try. **E-F** *Namal Garden Beach*, 3a/58 Medaketiya Rd, Medaketiya, T40352. 14 rooms (Rs 400-600), upstairs better with private balcony and sea views, terrace restaurant, rather block-like but reasonable value **E-F** *Palm Beach Resort*, Medilla, north of *Blue Horizon*, T40458. 3 lovely cabanas set in beach garden (Rs 450- 600), price negotiable, friendly owner, good food at the Panorama Rock Café. Recommended. **E-F** *Villa Araliya*, Medilla, T42163. 2 rooms (Rs 400-800 depending on size), furnished in old style but not kept up to its full potential. **E-G** *Blue Horizon*, 'Lakmal', Medilla, 1.5 km north of harbour, T40721. 3 rooms (Rs 250-700), 4 poster beds, very peaceful spot, friendly family, excellent food. Recommended.

F *Anila Beach Inn*, 23 Vijaya Rd, T40446. 7 rooms (Rs 350-500), showing their age, garden restaurant, cycle hire, peaceful. **F** *Calm Garden Cabanas*, Goyambokka, next to *Palm Paradise Cabanas*, T40523. 3 newish cabanas (Rs 750 including breakfast), unfortunately let down by spiritless site. **F** *Mansion Guest House*, Mahawela Rd, Pallikudawa, basic but cheap. **F** *Saman's Travellers Rest*, 75 Vijaya Rd, Medaketiya, T40464. 6 clean rooms (Rs 350) set in lush garden, very good food. **F** *Sarath*, Medaketiya Beach. Good double rooms (Rs 350) with modern bath, very clean, quiet, good food, friendly and helpful host, bike hire (Rs 100 per day). **F** *Villa Ocean Waves*, 67 Beach Rd, T40491. 5 average rooms (Rs 400) in popular local watering hole but surprisingly good restaurant.

G *Catamaran Beach Home*, Medaketiya Rd, Medaketiya. 4 basic rooms (Rs 200 shared bath, Rs 300 attached), but cheap and friendly. **G** *Dilena Beach Home*, Medaketiya. 2 clean rooms (Rs 300) in good location, friendly, nets, good value. **G** *Mansion Guest House*, Mahawela Rd, Pallikudawa, T077-902732. 3 basic rooms (Rs 300), reasonable value. **G** *Sea View Tourist Inn*, Mahawela Rd. 2 rooms (Rs 150 single, Rs 300 double) with shared bath in friendly family home set in large garden. **G** *Shanika Beach Inn*, 69 Medaketiya Beach, T42079. 7 simple rooms (Rs 300), good cheap food.

Mid-range *Blue Horizon* (try the mixed seafood for Rs 350) and *Saman's Travellers Rest* are particularly recommended. Also fine BBQs at the *Palm Beach Resort's* *Panorama Rock Café*. *Chalet*, west of town, 'one-stop-spot' favoured by taxis and tour coaches hence overpriced ('priciest cup of tea on the island'), rather poor quality and service, sells postcards and souvenirs. By contrast, the small *Chanika's*, Mahawela Rd, opposite entrance to *Tangalla Bay Hotel*, an 'exceptional find', does excellent food, delicious and fresh (over 1 kg whole lobster for two, Rs 1,000!), if tired of tamed down "European" dishes, ask for Sri Lankan style, friendly and obliging, delightfully chatty hostess (now also chef at *Tangalla Bay*). *Sun Shadow* has a nice location at the harbour's north end, while *Turtles' Landing* is towards Gayambokka beach to the south.

Eating
Along the beach towards the town, several restaurants & guesthouses prepare very good dishes, especially seafood

Diving *Let's Dive*, Medilla, access from Tissa Road, T077-902073, F40401. German-run dive school. 2 dives, $50; PADI Open Water Course, US$325; Advanced Course, US$210.

Watersports

Road Bus: Tangalla's bus station is in the town centre, close to the bridge. There are regular buses along the coast (via Beliatta) to **Matara** (1 hr), and **Hambantota** (1 hr), with other services continuing on to **Tissamaharama** (2 hrs) and **Kataragama** (2¾ hrs). There are several morning departures for **Colombo** (5 hrs), plus some to **Wellawaya** and the Hill Country. **Tuk-tuks**: From the bus station ferry passengers to beaches nearby.

Transport

Communications: the **Post office**: just off the Main Rd opposite the mosque, is open Mon-Fri 0800-1700. There are several IDD *Lanka Payphones* and *Metrocard* cardphones around town.

Directory

Excursions

The monastic site on an isolated 210 m high rock was occupied from the 2nd century BC and was again used as a place of Buddhist learning in the 18th century. In 1826, George Turnour discovered the *Tika*, commentaries on the *Mahavansa*, here. This allowed the ancient texts, which chronicle the island's history from the 3rd century BC, to be translated from the original Pali to English and Sinhala.

Mulgirigala
Colour map 3, grid C4

Although not a citadel, it is in some ways similar to Sigiriya. At the base of the rock there are monks' living quarters. The fairly steep paved path goes up in stages to the main temple and image house at the top. Along the way there are three platforms.

The first platform has the twin temple, Padum Rahat Vihara, with two 14 m reclining Buddhas, images of Kataragama and Vishnu among others and a Bodhi tree. The wall paintings inside illustrate the *Jatakas* while the ceiling has floral decorations.

The small second platform has a *vihara* with another Buddha (reclining) with two disciples. The murals show Hindu gods including Vishnu and Kataragama and the nine planets, and elsewhere, scenes from the Buddha's life.

The third has four cave temples and a pond with a 12th-century inscription. The Raja Mahavihara with a fine door frame, has several statues and good wall

Tangalla to Hambantota

paintings (though they are not as fine as at Dambulla), some partially hidden behind a cabinet which hold old *ola* manuscripts. A visitor described it as "a fascinating tropical Regency restoration, reminiscent of the Brighton Pavilion! The wooden cases and fittings evoke the English Adam/Chippendale period while the faces of the painted figures and their clothing wear a European look." The little cave temple, *Naga Vihara*, to the far left has a small door with a painted cobra– a cobra shielded the Buddha from rain when meditating, so is considered sacred and worthy of protection. The cave is believed to be a snake pit, so take care.

The final climb is steeper. You pass a Bodhi tree believed to be one of 32 saplings of the second Bodhi tree at Anuradhapura, before reaching the summit with a renovated stupa, image house and temple. Although Mulgirigala is a fairly strenuous climb, it is well worthwhile as there are very good views across the surrounding countryside from the top.

■ *Entrance Rs 100. Guides ask for Rs 50 which is reasonable. Getting there: By car, 16 km north of Tangalla via Beliatta (or 20 km via Wiraketiya on B52).*

Rekawa

The **Turtle Conservation Project** (TCP) operates an 'in situ' conservation policy whereby turtles are allowed to lay their eggs naturally and the hatchlings immediately permitted to make their way to the sea. The nests are protected by local watchers, many of whom are ex-poachers. The project is a community-based enterprise in that the TCP pay a wage to those who patrol and monitor the turtle rookeries. The TCP also organises local educational programmes and turtle awareness programmes as well as conducting extensive research of the Sri Lankan turtle population. Of the seven species of marine turtles in the world, five nest at Rekawa. Over 97% are green turtles. Visitors are encouraged to observe the females

The Rekawa lagoon has been earmarked for developing as an Environmental Education Centre to highlight the mangroves & coastal birdlife

laying their eggs and returning to the sea under the guidance of TCP members. A visit is highly recommended. ■ *Best to contact TCP in advance to visit between 1900-0300 (bring a jumper). Donation Rs 300 helps to sustain the local economy so that egg-stealing is not necessary. 73 Hambantota Rd, T/F40581 turtle@pan.lk No toilets or other facilities. Getting there: 6 km east of Tangalla, then 3 km along Rekawa Road from Netolpitiya Junction. Taxis from Tangalla charge around Rs 650 including waiting.*

Route East of Tangalla the move from the Wet Zone to the Dry Zone is very apparent. The road passes through **Ranna** (12 km) where there is a Buddhist temple on the summit of hill and then **Hungama**, where a road leads to Kalametiya.

Kalametiya Bird Sanctuary This is ideal for watching shorebirds in the brackish lagoons and mangrove swamps. It is a beautiful beach and lagoon, excellent for bird-watching undisturbed save for a few fishermen who might pester you for money. There are no facilities, nor entry fees.

Sleeping Cheap The Fisheries Corporation, **F** *Holiday Resort*, 5 km from 214 km post (turn off on A2, then first left at fork along the track), 3 rooms (1 a/c), reservations T01 522415. Caretaker prepares meals. **G** *Isuru*, opposite, has simple rooms, fishing trips arranged.

Transport Bus Take the signposted right turn, a short distance after Hungama (214 km post) and walk 2 km to the lagoon, 5 km to the *Resort*. Alternatively, get off at the 218 km post and walk 300 m to the sanctuary but it is best to organize your own transport. A 3-wheeler from Ambalantota should cost Rs 150, Tangalla Rs 300.

Route The A2 continues along the coast and beyond the left turn (A18) towards Embilipitiya and after crossing the Walawe Ganga River you reach **Ambalantota** (16 km from Ranna). The attractive coastal area just before the A18 turn-off (and south of Ambalantota) is good for exploring and camping.

Madungala, Karambagala caves & Mahapalessa Hotsprings
24 km inland NE from Ambalantota
The road along the Walawe Ganga river runs through the Dry-Zone where the forest deteriorates to a dirt track for the last 7 km. The **Madungala** hermitage reputedly has remarkable paintings. In fact, all that remains of the old monument is a square white base and some writing engraved in the rock. There is a new concrete dagoba with murals on a hilltop. There are fine views of Ridiyagama Tank and Adam's Peak from there. A walk through the forest takes you to another new dagoba. Nearby, in an open space north of the tank, are the **Mahapalessa** hot springs. Believed to have healing powers, the bubbling water is collected in pools for bathers.

To the south, **Ridiyagama** village is well known for its fine curd and honey. If you approach the hot springs from the A18, take the road to the right (east) at **Siyambalagoda**, cross the Walawe Ganga river and follow the track along the stream for about 5 km. Also close to the A18, are the 100 or so ancient rocky **Karambagala Caves**, once occupied by Buddhist hermits, which were discovered in the scrub land.

Route On the A2 towards Hambantota is **Godaraya** Junction. A turn right (1 km south) has a cave with King Gajabahu's inscription but these are difficult to find amidst the cacti. As this is not on a regular bus route, you need to arrange your own transport (1½ hrs by car). It is possible to cycle but watch out for elephants!

Hambantota හම්බන්තොට

Hambantota is a small fishing port with a large Muslim population who are largely of Malay descent of which many are proud. It is the centre for producing salt from evaporated sea water. The *lewayas*, or shallow pans, are by the road and you can see the salt flats of *Lanka Salt Ltd* stretching away inland.

To protect the salt pans, and access to cinnamon plantations inland, the Dutch built a stockade or 'fort'. Today's circular 'Dutch' fort on a hill overlooking the bay, is a British *Martello Tower* (c1796), one of a twin. the other stands in Simonstown in South Africa! Two-storeyed, the stone Tower had a single entrance (with a retractable ladder) at the first floor level, where the garrison of about 50 was housed, above the stores at ground level. The pierced holes were for firing muskets while a heavy gun on wheels was placed on the parapet of the flat roof, which had circular rails on which the gun could be moved to face attack from any direction. **Further reading** *The Dutch Forts of Sri Lanka* by WA Nelson, 1984, gives details of a number across the island.

Phone code: 047
Colour map 3, grid C6
41 km from Tangalla
238 km from Colombo

Southern Sri Lanka

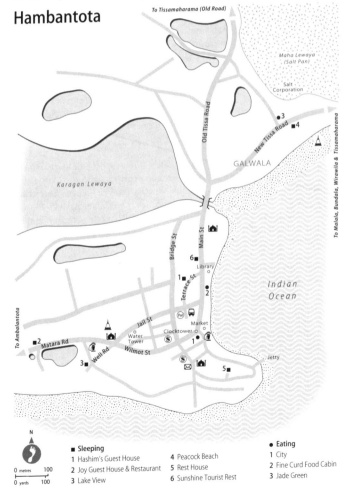

Hambantota

■ Sleeping
1 Hashim's Guest House
2 Joy Guest House & Restaurant
3 Lake View
4 Peacock Beach
5 Rest House
6 Sunshine Tourist Rest

● Eating
1 City
2 Fine Curd Food Cabin
3 Jade Green

Endangered turtles

The green turtle (Chelonia mydas), leatherback turtle (Dermochelys coriacea), olive ridley turtle (Lepidochelys olivacea), loggerhead turtle (Caretta caretta) and the hawksbill turtle (Eretmochelys imbricata) all come ashore to nest on the beaches of Sri Lanka. All these are listed by the World Conservation Union (IUCN) as either threatened or endangered. Despite the measures taken by the government, marine turtles are extensively exploited in Sri Lanka for their eggs and their meat. In addition, turtle nesting beaches (rookeries) are being disturbed by tourism related development, and feeding habitats, such as coral reefs, are being destroyed by pollution and unsustainable harvesting. Many turtles are accidentally caught and drowned in fishing gear each year, while the illegal 'tortoise shell trade' continues to encourage hunting of the highly endangered hawksbill turtle's carapace.

The Turtle Conservation Project with its head office at Tangalla was established in 1993. It is an NGO (non-governmental organization) which pursues sustainable marine turtle conservation strategies through education, research and community participation and aims to increase awareness of the importance of conserving the coastal ecosystems on which the local people depend. It is dedicated to protect in situ hatching of marine turtles wherever possible, and to promote scientifically managed ex situ programmes elsewhere. It has also had volunteers (local and foreign) assist in projects for short periods. The TCP has an impressive research programme and works closely with the University of Peradeniya and several international organisations. Although Rekawa, near Tangalla, has been the centre of activity, five more coastal nesting beaches have been identified where the four rarer species of marine turtle (in adddition to the green) may be protected, following the Rekawa model.

The town, with sand dunes immediately around it, has little to recommend it– the square has its usual clock tower and a curious statue of a 'coolie'. It is sometimes used as a base to visit **bird sanctuaries**. The *Karagan Lewaya* and *Maha Lewaya* are easy to get to, where shore birds (Flamingo, Gulls, Plovers, Terns etc) are attracted to the salt pans. The small bay offers some swimming, but the beaches, where you will see outriggers, are not attractive– the deserted eastern side, though, is great for jogging.

Sleeping　**A-B** *Oasis*, Silsilasagama, 6 km west, off the A2, T/F20651. 40 a/c rooms, plus 10 chalets with small tubs, set in large gardens between the sea and a lagoon, full facilities including a huge pool, good restaurant, service can be a bit slack at times, aimed at package groups, good safaris to Yala. **B** *Peacock Beach Resort*, New Tissa Rd, 1 km from bus stand, at Galwala, T20377, F01-449325. 111 a/c rooms, in secluded but indifferent gardens, pool (open to non-residents Rs 250 but sometimes demand day rate for room), popular with groups, depressing beach front, overall shabby.

Town C-D *Rest House*, T/F20299. 15 large rooms (1 a/c), situated in superb position on a promontory overlooking the harbour, unexciting restaurant (inaccurately described as "the bright spot of Hambantota"). **E** *Lake View*, 12 Well Road, T20264. 10 clean, modern rooms (Rs 600), 4 new, restaurant, not a bad choice. **F** *Joy*, off Matara Rd, T20328. 6 small, basic rooms (Rs 400) in well-run guest house with restaurant. **F-G** *Sunshine Tourist Rest*, 47 Main St (150m north of Bus Station), T20129. 7 simple rooms (Rs 300 shared bath, Rs 500 attached), nets, friendly family guest house, good food available, not bad value but could be cleaner. **G** *Hashim Pushena's*, 33 Terrace Street, up steps from bus stand, look for house number. 3 clean rooms (Rs 300) attached to family home, good food, no commission given, excellent value. Recommended.

In addition to hotel restaurants, *Jade Green* in Galawala, opposite *Peacock Beach Resort*, is smart, modern and western style with prices to match (though you may get hassled by 'safari' touts). *Fine Curd*, Tissa Rd, opposite the Bus Station (beach side) does delicious curd and treacle and inexpensive meals (huge, tasty rice & curry meal plus drink for under Rs 50).

Road Buses 'depart when full' at regular intervals to **Tissamaharama** (1 hr, Rs 10) and **Tangalla** (1 hr 20 mins, Rs 12). Buses go to **Weligata** every 15 mins. Morning departures to **Colombo** (6 hrs). Services along the A18 via **Embilipitiya** to **Ratnapura** (4 hrs, Rs 40). The 'Colombo to Ratnapura and Bandarawela' route description (in reverse) is on page 164. A **jeep** with driver to Bundala National Park should cost around Rs 1200.

Bank *Hatton National Bank* in town, deals in foreign exchange.

Bird sanctuaries and national parks

The area of open scrub around the coastal lagoons (lewayas) offer great opportuniy for bird watching with the added bonus of being able to spot the odd elephant and basking crocodiles by taking diversions off the A2 towards the sea (or in the direction of Tissamaharama). The salt pans attract vast numbers of shore birds. There are lots of stalls on the main road here selling delicious buffalo-milk curd in attractive clay pots.

Getting there It is best to hire a jeep with a driver from Hambantota or Tissamaharama. Expect to pay about Rs 1,200 from Hambantota to Bundala, and Rs 1,500 from Tissamaharama to Yala or Bundala (see below). **Admission** Entry US$12, children under 12 (and students with ISIC cards), US$6, Sri Lankans Rs 20.

Having crossed the bridge over the Karagan Lewaya that divides Hambantota proper from its northerly suburb of Galwala, the A2 splits. The better new road is to the south, though both branches meet again several kilometres further on, having skirted around the Maha Lewaya salt pan. From the second bridge after '246 km', a track to the right goes to Malala Lagoon. Follow the Malala River towards the lagoon and you will reach this bird-watcher's paradise. You will probably see several crocodiles sunbathing undisturbed, and numerous species of Dry Zone and water birds here including flamingo near the mouth of the channel. The bonus is you are free to wander around at leisure since there are no guides (as when visiting a 'Park' such as Bundala) and no hassle.

Bundala Lewaya, which you reach before the village and Bundala sanctuary proper, is outside the park boundary so you can wander freely. On the way you will pass Embilikala Kalapuwa.

The reserve consists of a series of shallow lagoons which are surrounded by low scrub which is really quite dense. Tracks go through the bush and connect each lagoon. The sanctuary skirts the sea and it is possible to see the lighthouse on the Great Basses some 40 km away to the east.

Some 12 km from Hambantota along the A2, at Weligatta, a right turn between 250 km and 251 km is signed to Bundala Bird Sanctuary (now a national park), 2 km away, and Kirinda (33 km). The road to the coast from Weligatta leads to coastal lagoons with a wealth of birdlife. The entrance to the Bundala is about 2 km down this road.

Salt of the earth

The lewayas (shallow lagoons) along the southeastern coast were prized and protected for centuries as they were the unending source of precious salt. The Dutch fort stood guard over the seaward trade while inland, trundling bullock carts faced many a perilous slow journey through the jungles.

Even today, the local people follow the age-old method of trapping sea water into shallow rectangular enclosures where it stands and slowly evaporates in the strong sun to yield up crystallized salt. You will notice the white salt shining stunningly bright, piled up high before being transported.

You are likely to come across elephants (though often difficult to see), jackals, monkeys, rabbits (apparently rare and carry a Rs 1,000 fine for killing!) crocodiles and snakes. The beaches attract olive ridley and leatherback turtles which come to nest here.

Apart from peacocks and other bush birds, there is a good variety of water birds including spoonbills, ibis, pelicans, Painted storks, flamingoes and different egrets, mostly concentrated around the lagoons. Winter migrants include plovers and sandpipers.

You travel around the park in your vehicle or a hired jeep, with a guide (some can't be too knowledgeable when they insist that flamingoes are summer visitors from Australia). Unfortunately, the jeep drivers don't seem to be very willing to stop and let you just observe. Tracking an elephant seems to be the high point of the day. When one is sighted, all jeeps home in on it and follow it so closely that ultimately the animal is angered enough to turn and charge one of the jeeps which sends all the vehicles to burn off down the track. Some visitors find this disturbing.

Sleeping **Cheap** Salt Corporation **E** *Guest House*, turn right off track, passing park entrance, 3 rooms, caretaker will cook (carry provisions), contact T01-590597. Good **F** *Campsite*, along Embilikala Kalapuwa (lagoon), reserve with Wildlife Conservation Dept, T01-694241.

Route Continuing northeast from Weligatta along the A2, at 8 km (past Wirawila), just after the air force base, turn right (east) on the B52. After 6.5 km you reach the clocktower at **Debarawewa junction** (though a sign says this is Tissamaharama). There are a few guest houses along the road to the left (west) from the clocktower but most of the accommodation, and Tissamaharama 'proper', is to the right (east). The alternative route from the north, on the A2 road from **Wellawaya** to Tissamaharama is not very interesting. Shortly after Wellawaya, the road finishes descending the 150 m or so to the flat plain. There are only two or three small towns, the biggest of which is at Tanamalwila, and not much can be seen of the Lunuganwehera Reservoir although there is the occasional glimpse of the Kataragama peak. The turn off to Debarawewa junction and Tissamaharama is to the left (east) at Pannegamuwa on the edge of the Wirawila Wewa.

Tissamaharama
තිස්සමහාරාමය
Phone code: 047
32 km from
Hambantota

Tissamaharama, or 'Tissa', is one of oldest of the abandoned royal cities. King Dutthagamenu made it his capital before recapturing Anuradhapura. The ruins had been hidden in jungle for centuries and today there is little of interest visible. It does not in any way compare with the better preserved Polonnaruwa or Anuradhapura.

The tank at **Tissawewa**, thought to have been created at the end of the 3rd century BC, was restored with two others and attracts a lot of water birds. At dawn, the view of birds roosting on large trees and then moving over the tank is very beautiful.

Numerous **dagobas**, including one 50-m high, built by King Kavantissa (2nd century BC) to hold a relic, had been lost under the sand, having been destroyed by the invading Dravidians. These have now been restored entirely by local Buddhists. Other buildings resemble a palace and a multi-storeyed monastery on the edge of Tissawewa. The *Menik Wehera* and *Yatala Wehera*, are east of the clock tower. The latter, dating from the 2nd century BC, has a moon stone and an 'elephant wall'. It houses a new **museum** with a collection of low-impact, but charming, Buddha and *Bodhisattva* statues. Excavations have been assisted by German archaeological groups.

Visiting Yala & Bundala

It seems as if every other vehicle in Tissamaharama is a jeep and you will be constantly offered a jeep safari to the national parks both from your guesthouse and from jeep owners on the street (opposite *Lakeside Inn* is a good place to find them). The semi-official rate for either park is Rs 1800 although persistent bargaining on a quiet day may get it down to Rs 1500. You will normally be offered a five-hour round trip but remember that Yala is an hour away so only expect three hours within the park itself. Ask whether they will stop when you want them to and if they will turn the engine off for photography. It is also a good idea to ask other tourists if they can recommend a particular driver.

Kirinda

A fishing port on the coast, 7 km south of Tissa, it has a good beach and some Buddhist ruins on the rocks. It is historically linked to the King Dutthagamenu. His mother, having been banished by her father, landed at the village and married the local king. Although popular with scuba divers who are attracted by the reefs at Great and Little Basses off the coast, the currents can be treacherous. If you walk east along the coast towards Yala there is an area of Dry Zone scrubland along the coast, contiguous to Yala itself. It is a good place for bird-watching but keep a look out for elephants! **Sleeping E** *Kirinda Beach Resort*, down dirt track off main road, T047 23405, F0722 32026. Not exactly on the beach, six rooms with fan, attached bath, all looking rather forlorn, eclectic collection of odds and ends decorate the place, restaurant. Buses run between Tissa and Kirinda.

Sleeping

There are plenty of options, so bargain hard. Tissa is plagued by touts who jump on the bus as it draws into town since hotel or guesthouse will pay them a commission. They get a commission for the hotel room they 'fix' and also any 'safari' you may arrange through the hotel. Some of the places are not actually in Tissa proper (despite what the touts may tell you), but in **Debarawewa** (the area around and just to the west of the clocktower). Most in Tissa are along the road to the east of the clocktower, and along the turning to the north just after the bus station, on the Kataragama Road. There is also accommodation at Amaduwa on the coast near Yala National Park (see below), and at Kirinda (above).

Expensive B *Tissamaharama Rest House* (CHC), Kataragama Rd, T37299,

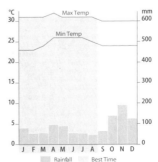

Climate: Tissamaharama

Southern Sri Lanka

F37201, (Colombo T503497, F503504). 57 rooms (34 a/c with balcony), rather basic and box-like, in large concrete building, restaurant (limited menu but tasty curries), open air bar, nice pool overlooking tank, gardens, pleasant staff (but Faxed reservation 'lost'), excellent location but a bit scruffy inside, popular with pilgrims to Kataragama at weekends, virtually empty at other times.

Mid-range C-D *Chandrika*, Kataragama Rd, T/F37143. 20 clean rooms (7 a/c), fairly modern, bar, pricey restaurant, pleasant garden. **C** *Happy Cottage*, off Kataragama Road, T37085. 3 2-bedroomed bungalows with kitchen and living room (Rs 2500) or separate rooms (Rs 550), nothing special, untidy site. **C** *Priyankara*, Kataragama Rd, T37206, F37326. 26 clean a/c rooms, deluxe with hot bath, all with private balcony overlooking paddy fields, bar, good restaurant, pleasant atmosphere, friendly staff, reasonable deal, best in town. Recommended.

Cheap D-E *Austria Lanka Pala*, off Kataragama Rd, Akurugoda, T37648. 6 very clean rooms (Rs 750), 1 a/c (Rs 1000), add Rs 100 for driver's commission, quiet location, well run, friendly. Recommended if you can bargain the price down. **D-E** *Lakeside Tourist Inn*, Kataragama Rd, Akurugoda, opposite lake, T/F37216. 24 clean and comfortable, but rather stuffy rooms (Rs 750) including 7 a/c (Rs 1050), nice sitting areas overlooking lake (no views from rooms), good restaurant. **E** *Refresh*, Kataragama Rd, Akurugoda, T37357. 4 attractive, clean rooms (Rs 700) including 2 a/c (Rs 1000) in nice block, good restaurant, accepts Visa/Mastercard. Recommended. **D-E** *Singha Tourist Inn*, Tissawewa Mawatha, off Kataragama Rd, Akurugoda, T37090, F37080. 7 dark and musty rooms (Rs 650) including 1 a/c (Rs 1150) in block in excellent location on the lake, potential not realised, overpriced.

Tissamaharama

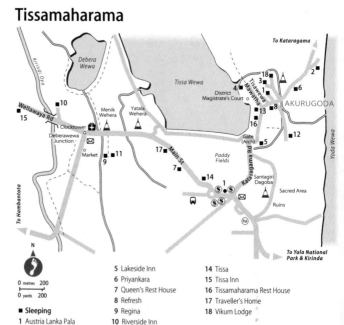

	5 Lakeside Inn	14 Tissa
	6 Priyankara	15 Tissa Inn
0 metres 200	7 Queen's Rest House	16 Tissamaharama Rest House
0 yards 200	8 Refresh	17 Traveller's Home
	9 Regina	18 Vikum Lodge
■ **Sleeping**	10 Riverside Inn	
1 Austria Lanka Pala	11 Sakura	● **Eating**
2 Chandrika	12 Sandakumari	1 Roots Café & Independent
3 Happy Cottages	13 Singha Tourist Inn	Safari Jeeps
4 Lake Lodge		

E *Lake Lodge*, Tissawewa Mawatha, T37287. 3 very basic, run down rooms (over-priced at Rs 550), but good lakeside location, may improve with a new owner in future. **E** *Tissa Inn*, Wellawaya Rd, 1.3 km west of clocktower, Polgahawelana, T/F37233. 12 clean rooms (Rs 600-700), a touch overpriced, pleasant garden, restaurant, rather pushy at selling tours, however still one of the most popular in town. **E** *Vikum Lodge*, off Kataragama Rd, T37585. 10 clean and comfortable rooms (Rs 750), quiet location, good food, friendly. Recommended. **E-F** *Hotel Tissa*, Main St, near bus stand, T37104. 7 very clean rooms (Rs 450-700 negotiable), popular bar/restaurant, good value. Recommended. **E-F** *Regina Holiday Home*, off Main Street, Deberawewa, just east of clocktower, T37159. 5 large, clean rooms (Rs 500) plus a couple of cheaper rooms in old block, nice garden, restaurant. Recommended.

F *Queen's Rest House*, 196 Kachcheriyagama Rd (Main St, east of clocktower), T37264. 6 dark rooms (Rs 450) including 2 a/c (Rs 750), nets useless as they don't fit, restaurant, not really looked after. **F** *Riverside Inn*, track off Wellawaya Rd, 300m west of clocktower, Deberawewa, T37101. 9 dark rooms (Rs 400) set in small garden,.a bit too quiet, rather spooky! **F** *Sandakumari*, off Kataragama Rd (15-min walk along a track, follow the signs), 4 fairly basic rooms (Rs 350), maybe worth a look after promised repairs. **F-G** *Sakura*, off Main St, Deberawewa, just east of clocktower, T37198. 5 clean rooms (Rs 300-500) set in quiet garden plus one separate 'cottage' (Rs 600), good food. Tentative recommendation. **F-G** *Traveller's Home*, 195/4 Kachcheriyagama, T37958, F37915 supuncj@sltnet.lk 3 clean rooms (Rs 300 with separate bath, Rs 500 attached), nets, friendly, good food, good safaris. Recommended.

Festivals

Jun: *Poson* full moon commemorates the introduction on Buddhism with week-long festivities ending with colourful elephant processions accompanied by drummers and dancers.

Transport

Road Colombo, is 6 hrs drive. **Jeeps** for **Yala and Bundala**: the following drivers have been recommended: SP Chandrasiri, T37522, who has testimonials from satisfied customers; Sunil (Bindhu), T072 678735; Metthe of the *Independent Safari Jeep Service*, office in Main Street next to *Roots Café*, T072-687033, who can also arrange camping.

Yala (Ruhuna) National Park රුහුණු - යාල

The 1,260 sq km park varies from open parkland to dense jungle on the plains, scrub land with rocky outcrops and several streams, small lakes and lagoons. The picturesque ocean frontage to the east has wide beaches and high sand dunes while to the north is the Lahugala Elephant Sanctuary.

Colour map 5, grid C5

Ins & outs

Best time to visit: Oct-Dec, early morning & late afternoon

Getting there The entrance to the reserve in the Dry Zone is 20 km from Tissamaharama, bounded by the river and the sea. Kumana (see page 278) to the east is a bird sanctuary, reached from Pottuvil and Arugam Bay. Jeeps from Tissa take 1 hr; from Hambantota (50 km) poor roads can take nearly 2 hrs; from Galle, 4-5 hrs. **Getting around** Walking is not permitted within the park. Buses or jeep tours within the park are at 0630, 1500. Safari tours, about Rs 200 per person in a jeep carrying six passengers, last 2½-3 hrs. Some are disappointed by the difficulty of seeing wildlife. A car can manage the main track but others are best in a 4WD. The compulsory tracker costs US$6 (or Rs 315). Up to 30 vehicles are allowed into the park at any one time. **Admission** Entry permits are available from the park office at Palatupana, open 0600-1800 daily mid-Oct to end-Jul. Entry US$12, children under 12 (and students with ISIC cards), US$6, Sri Lankans Rs 20. If you leave the park (eg to get a meal) you will have to pay again.

Southern Sri Lanka

Southern Sri Lanka

 God Kataragama's antics

Next to the Maha Devala is the temple of God Kataragama's consort Theivaiamma, while further along is that of his mistress Valliamma. M Chandrasoma in his Vignettes of the Ceylon Civil Service 1938-57 describes the procession during the Kataragama Festival. 'The God Kataragama comes out of his abode in the evening, makes his way to his consort's temple and disports himself there making all the noise he can to impress on his wife's mind the fact of his presence. When he has established a convincing alibi, he sneaks quietly down the outer street to the temple of his mistress. Then after a suitable interval, with flute, drum and fanfare, he comes jauntily down the main street and triumphantly enters his temple.'

Elephants are the main attraction and are easily seen especially near water sources from January to May. Other animals seen throughout the park include macaque and langur monkeys, sambhur, spotted deer, wild boar, buffaloes and crocodiles. Bears are occasionally spotted, particularly in June, when they feed on local fruit while the magnificent leopard may sometimes be seen in the dry sandy and rocky areas. Vepandeniya is considered a favourite spot.

There are about 130 species of birds including barbets, hoopoes, malabar pied hornbills, orioles, ceylon shamas, paradise flycatchers, and peacocks. The expanses of water attract eastern grey heron, painted stork, serpent-eagle and white-bellied sea-eagle. In addition a large number of migrant water-fowl arrive each winter to augment the resident population. You may be lucky enough to spot the rare black-necked stork near buttawa on the coast.

The park comprises five blocks and Yala Strict Natural Reserve. The central area was originally a sportsmen's shooting reserve which was established as a protected area in 1938. The archaeological remains of ancient sites suggest that many centuries ago the area was a part of the Ruhuna Kingdom. Akasa Chetiya and Magul Mahavihara date from the second and first centuries BC. Thousands of Buddhist monks resided at the monastery at **Situlpahuwa** where the white Akasa Chetiya dagoba has now been restored.

Sleeping   **Cheap**   Ask about **E-F** *Park Bungalows*, 7 simple bungalows in scenic locations: Old and New Buttawa, Mahaseelawa, Patangala along the coast, Heenwewa facing a tank, Yala and Thalgasmankada on the Manik Ganga River (tourists may only stay in Patangala and Heenwewa). Each has a cook who can prepare Sri Lankan meals but take the ingredients. No electricity. Reservations up to 3 months in advance: Wildlife Conservation Dept, T694241. Also two *Camp Sites*, on the bank of the Manik Ganga River.

Amaduwa, on the coast, is just south of the main gate. The beach here is lovely although the sea is too rough for swimming. The lagoon has shrimp fishers at night who stand in the water with candles on sticks to attract the shrimp. the crocodiles apparently dislike the nets. **A** *Yala Safari Beach Hotel*, T047-38015, F047-20471, or Colombo T345700, F345729, www.jetwing.net   63 rooms, 10 a/c (US$60), restaurant, bar, diving, dining area faces lagoon, safari jeep, 'wonderful, idyllic, peaceful, a real escape from the rat race'.

Kataragama   කතරගම

Colour map 4, grid C4
16 km N from
Tissamaharama

Kataragama (in Uva Province) is well off the beaten track and not often visited by tourists. It is, however, a popular pilgrimage centre throughout the year, even outside of the great festivals. A small town with clean, tree lined roads with rows of stalls selling garlands and platters of fruit (coconut, mango, watermelon) it attracts people of all faiths from across the island.

Barefoot over hot coals

Fire-walking, a part of the Kataragama festival, may hark back to the story of Sita in the epic Ramayana. Ravana, the King of Lanka, abducted Rama's wife Sita, an Indian princess, from the forest and carried her away to his island. After she is finally rescued by her husband, Sita proves her purity (chastity) by walking barefoot over fire and emerging unhurt. In southern Sri Lanka, devotees of Kataragama and Pattini follow her example and seek their blessing as they undergo the purification ritual.

The Hindu and Buddhist sanctuaries are quite separate. Buddhists visit the ancient Kirivehera dagoba, 1 km west of the plain white Hindu temple but also consider the 'Kataragama Deviyo' here sacred. Muslims associate the town with two saints and come to pray at the Khizr Takya mosque nearby.

There is quite a large car park on the south side of the river which is busy with garland and fruit stalls. A short walk takes you to the Menik Ganga. Steps lead down to the water which is quite shallow in places allowing pilgrims to take their ritual bath almost in the middle of the river. It is a very attractive area with large trees on the banks providing plenty of shade. Cross the bridge to enter the main temple complex. The wide street lined with tulip trees leads to the Hindu temple (300 m).

The **Hindu Temple (Maha Devale)** dedicated to Skanda (Kataragama Deviyo) is not particularly impressive. A small gate with a large wrought iron peacock on the reverse, leads onto the rectangle where there is a small area where the pilgrims throw coconuts onto a stone slab to split them before making the offering. Trees in the rectangle are surrounded by brass railings and there are a number of places where pilgrims can light leaf-shaped candles. Here, you can see men in 'ritualistic trances': some are professionals, though, since you might see the same man, a little later, making his way to the Buddhist dagoba, carrying a briefcase and an umbrella!

There is often a long queue to enter the shrine (particularly on *Poya* days) where platters are offered to the priests. The idea seemed to be to 'hide' some money in the platter. Some say, anything less than Rs 200 may be unacceptable and the gift might be refused by the deity. There is certainly evidence that the platters are 'recycled': men on bicycles can be seen returning them to the market, covered in garlands– nobody seems to mind though! There is no image of the god Skanda in the shrine– simply his *vel* or lance. There are separate small shrines to others in the Hindu pantheon, including Vishnu, Ganesh and Pattini, the last also linked to the fire-walking ceremony. Nearby are the two Bodhi trees. Prayers are held at 0430, 1030 and 1830.

The largest draw is the *Esala* (July/August) full moon festival which ends with fire-walking and 'water cutting' ceremonies. Thousands of pilgrims flock to the Hindu temple for the **Kataragama Festival**. They come to perform penance for sins they have committed and some of the scenes of self-mutilation, performed in a trance, are horrific. The water-cutting ceremony, in which the waters of the Manik Ganga are 'cut' with a sword at the moment of the full moon, symbolises the separation of pure from impure.

You may see groups of pilgrims performing the *Kavadi* (peacock) dance when men, women and children hold semicircular blue arches above their heads as they slowly progress towards the temple.

Kirivehera Beyond the Hindu shrine and a meeting hall on the north side of the square, starting from the east gate, there is another tulip tree avenue which leads to the milk-white Buddhist dagoba, about 500 m away. Stalls selling lotus buds line the route but here there is competition with girls shouting out the bargains and pressing people to buy. Clearly those on the shady side of the road won! You can often see the temple elephant shackled to the trees here, being fed a copious diet of palm leaves. The dagoba itself is a very peaceful place and, as usual, beautifully maintained. It is not especially large and its spire is quite squat compared with those farther north.

Archaeological Museum There is a small museum near the Hindu temple, with Buddha statues, moonstones and ancient inscriptions. ■ *Closed on Tue.*

Sleeping & eating

There are numerous guesthouses & hotels for all budgets on the Sella Kataragama Rd

C *Robinson's Rest House*, Tissa Rd, Detagamuwa. Rooms in an attractive building in a pleasant garden. Nearby, *Safari Park*, signed from the road has about 60 rooms and a pool. **C-D** *New Rest House*, off Situlpahuwa Rd, T35299. 18 rooms. **E** *Kataragama Rest House*, near the river, has 23 simple rooms and dormitory, simple Sri Lankan food. Enquire in Colombo (T01-544315) about rooms at the attractive *Bank of Ceylon Guest House* which does Sri Lankan meals. If stopping for lunch *Nandana Hotel*, 40b New Town, near clocktower, does a good authentic rice and curry.

Transport

Road Bus services in all directions including direct bus to Nuwara Eliya, Galle and Colombo.

The Heart of the Wet Zone

Away from the palm fringed coastal belt of the southwest, dense forests and lush vegetation stretch inland to the Central Highlands, at places clearly visible from the coast itself.

Colombo to Ratnapura and Bandarawela

The most attractive route from Colombo to Ratnapura goes via Avissawella through the Wet Zone, before reaching the centre of Sri Lanka's gem producing region. It is a gentle drive to the foot of the hills, with superb views of Adam's Peak and the hills when they are not shrouded in heavy cloud. This is the heart of the Wet Zone and one of the wettest regions of Sri Lanka. From Colombo the A4 runs southeast past Nugegoda. The slower but more attractive route, the B1, heads east, following the left (south) bank of the Kelaniya River, passing Kaduwela and Hanwella.

An alternative route is from the coast south of Colombo. The A8 travels east from Panadura leading to Ratnapura, passing **Horana** on the way. The **D** *Rest House* here is built in the remains of an ancient Buddhist monastery and is good value. On the opposite side of the road is a large Buddhist temple with a particularly noteworthy bronze candlestick, over 2 m tall.

From Ratnapura the main road circles to the south of Adam's Peak, climbing into the hills through Balangoda to Bandarawela.

Kaduwela

(16 km)

Here is a rest house in a beautiful position overlooking the river with a constant succession of varied river traffic. There is a fairly large Buddhist temple and the irrigation tank of Mulleriyawa.

Hanwella

(33 km)

On the site of a Portuguese fort, Hanwella is noted as the place where the last king of Kandy, Sri Vikrama Rajasinha, was defeated. There is an excellent rest house (CHC) on the Kelaniya River. Rooms with bath (US$7) with a beautiful view along the river. Reservations: T01 503497, F01 503504. At Hanwella the road joins the A4 and turns left towards Avissawella.

Avissawella, the ancient capital of the Sitawaka kings and now the centre of rubber industry, is in beautiful wooded surroundings. The ruins of the royal palace of Rajasinha, a Buddhist king who converted to Hinduism can still be seen. He was responsible for starting work on the unfinished Berendi Kovil temple, which still has some fine stonework despite the Portuguese attack. It is just off the Ginigathena road on the opposite bank of the river. There is a district hospital, T22261.

Avissawella
Phone code: 036
(18 km)

The A4 takes a circuitous route into the Highlands. It turns sharply south in Avissawella, passing first through low gaps between the Central Highlands to the east and the outermost ranges of the hills to the west, and periodically crossing rivers that come tumbling down from the Southwest Highlands. It passes through Pusella and crosses the river Kuruwita, running through a landscape that was the site of some of Sri Lanka's earliest settlements and also a gem bearing area.

Route

Palm Garden Travellers Paradise Restaurant on the right of the road is hard to miss. Pleasant gardens, open-sided seating, good for a stop for drinks and simple snacks. The road goes on to Ratnapura.

Kuruwita

At **Batadombalena Cave** nearby, Deraniyagala reported the find of fragmentary skeletal remains, as well as those of several large mammal skeletons, including elephants and cattle, dating back at least as far as 28,000 years ago, and possibly very much earlier. ■ *Getting there: Take the road towards Eratne, turn right after 2 km and follow it to the end (2 km). A path reaches the cave in 5 km.*

Avissawella is one of the gateways to the Central Highlands. The A7 goes east out of the town and then northeast into the hills towards Kandy. Just before Ruwanwella, where the old rest house occupies the site of a former Dutch Fort, the A7 turns east directly into the hills, following the valley of the Maskeliya Oya for 20 km before climbing steeply to the Ginigathena Pass, offering magnificent views at the top including Adam's Peak on a clear day before descending to Kitulgala.

Avissawella to Watawala, Hatton & Nuwara Eliya

On the Kelaniya River provided the picturesque location for David Lean's film, 'Bridge on the River Kwai'. You can stay at the **D** *Kitulgala Rest House* (CHC), on the banks of the river, T7528 (or T01 503497, F01 503504). 18 rooms (US$22) with shower. There is a restaurant, bar, and exchange. It is usually full during pilgrimage (December-April). Stalls on the roadside at the *Rest House* turn off sells local food.

Kitulgala
Phone code: 036

From here on the road runs through tea country. Ginigathena is a small bazaar for the tea estates and their workers. The road winds up through a beautiful valley, surrounded by green, evenly picked tea bushes to Watawala (10 km) where the Carolina Falls are spectacular in the wet season. The air becomes noticeably cooler, and occasionally there are views right across the plains to Colombo and the Kelaniya Valley. Follow the lower road to Hatton (12 km), then through Talawakele and Nanu Oya to Nuwara Eliya (see page 200).

Route

Southern Sri Lanka

Ratnapura රත්නපුර

Phone code: 045
Colour map 3, grid B3
100 km from Colombo

*This town is
aptly named the
'City of Gems'*

The climate of Ratnapura has been likened to a Turkish bath. One of Sri Lanka's wettest towns, even February, the driest month, normally has nearly 100 mm of rain, while May, the wettest, has nearly 500 mm. The vegetation is correspondingly luxuriant. The city however is best known for its gem stones that are washed down the river bed. The gravel beds which contain the gemstones are also the source of evidence of some of Sri Lanka's earliest cultures and of the wildlife that is now extinct. Discoveries of animal bones as well as of a variety of stone tools have made it clear that the area is probably one of the first sites to have been occupied by humans in Sri Lanka. Travel agents can organize visits to gem mines.

The quality of Ratnapura's gems is legendary. In the seventh century Hiuen Tsang claimed that there was a ruby on the spire of the temple at Anuradhapura whose magnificence illuminated the sky. Marco Polo (1293) described the flawless ruby as 'a span long and quite as thick as a man's arm'! Today sapphires are much more important. A number of precious stones are found nearby including sapphire, ruby, topaz, amethyst, cat's eye, alexandrite, aquamarine, tourmaline, garnet and zircon. Several are mined from pits dug into a special form of gravel. Genuine stones are common. Valuable stones by definition are rarer. Advice given to travellers at the beginning of the century still holds:

'As regards buying stones, it is a risky business unless the passenger has expert knowledge or advice. It is absolute folly to buy stones from itinerant vendors. It is far better to go to one of the large Colombo jewellers and take the chance of paying more and obtaining a genuine stone.'

Sights

*Gem traders usually
wear a white sarong &
white shirt to bring
them luck with most of
the trading taking place
early in the day*

Gem market Although people seem to trade gems all over town, there are certain areas that specialize in uncut and unpolished stones, polished stones, cut stones, other streets will only deal in star sapphires or cat's eyes. On Saviya Mawatha (off Main Street) you can watch hundreds of people buying and selling gems every morning.

Views of Adam's Peak Ratnapura is surrounded by rubber and tea estates in a lush and beautiful setting, and gives better views of Adam's Peak than almost anywhere else on the island. It is well worth going to the top of the fort for the views. Driving up to **Gilimale** from the bridge gives you a chance to see the massive curtain wall of the central highlands to the north. The surrounding forests are rich in flowers, one of the most notable being the *Vesak Orchid*, which takes its name from the month of Vesak in which it flowers.

Maha Saman Dewale Some 4 km west of town is the richest Buddhist temple in Sri Lanka. Dedicated to the guardian god of Adam's Peak, it is originally thought to date from the 13th century, but was rebuilt by Parakramabahu VI in the 15th century before being damaged by the Portuguese soldiers. The temple, which has been restored, has an ornamental doorway and fine wall paintings inside. Interesting features include the remains of a Portuguese fort alongside. on the temple wall is a Portuguese soldier sculpted in stone while a slab bearing their coat of arms

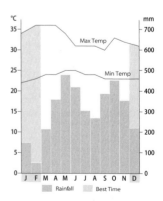

Climate: Ratnapura

was also found here. There is a major *Perahera* procession during the July-August full-moon, when decorated boats sail along the Kalu Ganga.

Ratnapura National Museum Small exhibition of pre-historic fossil skeletons of elephants, hippos and rhinoceros found in gem pits. Also arts and culture of the province (jewellery, gems, textiles and flags). ■ *0900-1700, closed Fridays, Rs 50. On Ehelapola Walauwa, Colombo Rd, near the Bus Depot, T22451.*

Museums

Private museums tend to be primarily retail outlets for gems but at the same time demonstrate the craft of gem polishing. **Gem Bureau and Museum**, Pothgul Vihara Rd, Getangama (2 km south). 0900-1700. Gems from different parts of Sri Lanka. **Gemmological Museum**, 6 Ehelepola Mawatha, Batugedera. Interesting private collection of gems and precious minerals and mining related exhibits including a model of a pit.

Adam's Peak Ratnapura is the base for the much steeper and more strenuous route which leads to Adam's Peak starting at the Carney Estate, 15 km away (buses run during the pilgrim season taking one hour). The climb takes about seven hours. Some pilgrims walk the 25 km from Ratnapura to Adam's peak during the winter months. ■ *Route: Malwala (8 km) on the Kalu Ganga to Palabadalla (11 km. 375 m), then a very steep path to Heramitipana (13 km. 1,100m) and the summit (5 km. 2,260m). See page 208 for the shorter route.*

Excursions

Pompakelle Urban Forest Park is northeast of town, near the swimming pool on Reservoir Road. Signposted trails lead you through the surprisingly large forest– a welcome change of pace from Main Street.

Ratnapura

Southern Sri Lanka

The sparkle of romance

Rubies and sapphires, topaz, aquamarine, amethysts and garnet are just some of the gems which have given Sri Lanka one of its most enduring attractions and which place it among the top five gem bearing nations of the world.

According to legend it was a Sri Lankan ruby that King Solomon gave to the Queen of Sheba, and a wonderful sapphire, the Blue Belle, embellishes the British crown. Marco Polo described the ruby which he saw on the Ruwanveliseya Dagoba in Anuradhapura as 'as big as a man's arm'.

Given the exquisite nature of many of Sri Lanka's gems exaggeration is not surprising. Even today gem mining, cutting and setting are thriving activities in Sabaragamuwa Province immediately to the southwest of the Central Highlands. Washed out from the ancient rocks of the Highlands themselves, the gems are found in pockets of alluvial gravel known as Illama, usually a metre or two below the surface. Ratnapura - the 'city of gems' - is still the heart of the industry, though new

pits are being explored in other parts of the island. Some stones, such as the milky white moonstone, are found only along the south coast near Kataragama.

Traditional gem mining makes use of only the simplest technology. Pits are dug in the gravel. Divided in two, one half is used for extracting water while the gravel is dug out from the other half. When after two or three days a large enough pile of gravel has been excavated it is systematically washed in a stream, sifting the gems and heavy minerals from the lighter material. The work is done in teams, everyone getting a share of the value of any gems found.

The cutting and polishing is carried out largely in Ratnapura itself. Dressed, cut and then polished, the methods and materials used are still largely local. Hand operated lathes, and polishing paste made from the ash of burnt paddy straw have been used for generations and continue to allow the lustre of Sri Lanka's fine gems to shine through.

Kalugas Ella Falls 2 km north from centre are attractive falls offering the opportunity to swim in the river. There are snack bars. Avoid visiting on Sundays when it can get busy.

A **Buddha Statue** overlooks the town. Climb up to it through low woods.

There are impressive **caves** at Kosgalla, 8 km from Ratnapura and at Eratna/Batatota, 19 km away.

Sleeping **Mid-range C** *Ratnaloka Tour Inns*, Kosgala, Kahangama (6 km from town), T22455. 53 rooms, central a/c, good restaurant, exchange, pool, gem museum. **C** *Rest House*, Rest House (Inner Circle) Rd, on a hill 1 km from centre, T22299. 11 rooms (best upstairs), food good value, peaceful, outstanding views and delightful site, but poor garden and service rather slack. **D** *Kalawathie*, Polhengoda Village, Outer Circular Rd, 1.6 km from Bus Stand, T22465. 23 rooms, some a/c, separate dorm (**G**), restaurant, house decorated with collector's pieces (antiques cabinets, palm leaf manuscripts, statues, betel cutters etc), beautiful tropical garden, tours (Dec to May), natural therapy 'Healing arts' practised here including oil baths and massage (about Rs 700), herbal treatments (Rs 450-800), floral baths, tuk-tuk from Bus Stand, Rs 50.

Cheap **E** *Nilani Lodge*, 21 Dharmapala Mawatha, T22170. 10 rooms with balcony, some a/c, in large modern white apartment-style building, restaurant and gem museum and shop on site, tours to mines and cutters– a gem shop with beds!. **E** *Darshana Inn*, 68/5 Rest House (Inner Circle) Rd, just below *Rest House*, T22674. 4 simple and clean rooms, fan, rather damp attached bath (front room, larger and better furnished), restaurant, popular bar, pleasant owner, resident mongoose to deter snakes. **F** *Gemland*, 12 Mudduwa Rd, T22153. 10 rather dingy rooms (some a/c)

To drink or not to drink

Villagers make free use of the sap from the fishtail or kitul palm (Caryota urens) and can sometimes be seen carrying pots of this home. The sap which drains from a cut at the end of the main stalk of the inflorescence is collected in clay pots. This liquid produces not only the fermented toddy (distilled to yield arrack), but also the unfermented treacle produced by heating it (peni) which in turn is used to make the dry brown sugar, jaggery (hakuru). Both forms of sugar are excellent served with curd or when used in preparing sweets. The Sinharaja jaggery is particularly fine.

in a large hotel but with not much going on. **F** *Ratna Gems Halt*. 153/5 Outer Circular Rd, 4 pleasant rooms in family house overlooking paddy fields, meals available. **F** *Travellers Halt*, T23092. 30 Outer Circular Rd, 5 acceptable rooms in family house but no one speaks English. 3-wheeler from Bus Stand, Rs 35.

Jayasiri Hotel & Bakery, 198 Main St, Sri Lankan rice and curry downstairs, Chinese on 1st floor, meals about Rs 75, bustling with activity, friendly staff, full of local colour. *Kanchana*, 189 Main St, Indian veg meals (Rs 25), 1st floor overlooking busy Main St. *Pattaya*, 14 Senanayake Mawatha, T23029, modern a/c upmarket restaurant with a wide choice of Chinese and Thai dishes, average meal Rs 500. *Rainbow*, 163 Main St, good for Rice and Curry 'meals' (Rs 50), large airy room looking onto part of gem traders street market. *Rest House*, food and service can be variable but is usually good value. **Eating**

Bar: *Darshana Inn* has a very popular bar. **Entertainment**

Road There are CTB buses from the main bus stand to the west of the Rest House, or private buses from near the clocktower. There are regular buses to **Colombo** (3 hrs, Rs 20), and buses via **Embilipitiya** to **Hambantota** (4 hrs, Rs 40). Most other buses, including to **Balangoda** (2 hrs, Rs 16), **Belihuloya** (2½ hrs, Rs 20) and **Haputale** (3½ hrs, Rs 25) originate elsewhere and often come through full. The Colombo-Haputale bus passes through Ratnapura at around 0830. For **Galle**, take an a/c bus along the A8 to Panadura and change to a Colombo-Galle bus there. **Transport**

Communications: the main **post office** is on the clocktower square (open Mon-Fri 0830-1900). **International phone calls**: can be made here, or through the IDD *Metrocard* and *Lanka Payphones* cardphone boxes. **Directory**

Sinharaja Biosphere Reserve   සිංහරාජ

Sinharaja is a unique stretch of rain forest on the island which apart from very limited use by tribal peoples has been left largely undisturbed. Designated a Man and Biosphere Reserve in 1978, it is Sri Lanka's first Natural Heritage site. In 1989 it was recognized by UNESCO as one of the international Biosphere Reserves and is a World Heritage Site. The forest reserve has the name meaning 'Lion King' and is believed to have been the final refuge of the now extinct lion on the island.

Getting there It can easily be reached by road. The shortest route leaves the A4 east of Ratnapura at Tiruwanaketiya and runs to *Kalawana* (in a gem-bearing area) which sells provisions, where a left turn leads to *Weddagala* (Veddagala). From Colombo the usual route is via the Kalawana-Weddagala road from the northwest. Visitors' must enter at Kudawa. There are three other options: from the northeast (A 17) via Rakwana-Morningside Estate, Deniyaya-Pallegama road from the southeast, or the **Ins & outs** *Suggested minimum stay, 2 nights; 3 nights give you an opportunity to see a good cross-section of the forest*

Rubber

Third in importance after tea and coconuts as a crop, the first rubber trees were introduced to Sri Lanka from their native Brazil via Kew gardens in London in the last quarter of the 19th century. In the decade after 1904 Sri Lanka experienced a rubber boom, the Wet Zone land between the sea and the Central Highlands being found particularly well-suited. The apparently sparsely populated land, combined with an ideal climate, encouraged widespread planting. In fact the shifting cultivation which had dominated much of the region around Kalutara, now one of the most important centres of the rubber industry, was severely curtailed by the planting of rubber trees, which spread up the valley sides, leaving paddy the dominant crops in the valley bottoms.

The pale cream sap (latex) of the rubber plant is gathered (or `tapped') from a fine cut in the bark, renewed two or three times a week. The latex is collected in a tin cup or coconut shell hung beneath the cut. You can ask to be shown round a rubber estate and the processing plant, where you can see the latex being mixed with water, strained and hung out to dry after having been rolled into sheets.

Hinduma-Neluwa road from the southwest. **Climate** The area receives over 2,500 mm of rain annually, most falling between May-Jul and Oct-Dec. Afternoons can be wet so be prepared! The average temperature is 23.6°C. Best time to visit: December-early April and August-September. **Admission** Entry US$12, children under 12 (and students with ISIC cards), US$6, Sri Lankans Rs 20. Apply in advance (see sleeping below) taking your identity card or passport. Register at Kudawa Forest Dept Office (northwest entrance). Foreigners are charged Rs 55 per day for entry. You have to be accompanied by a guide to enter, Rs 100 per day. They are very knowledgeable but don't always speak English. Don't forget your binoculars.

It rains in Sinharaja most afternoons. It doesn't have the modern sleeping and prestige animal spotting facilities of some of the other reserves or national parks (eg Yala), yet just being in the thick of the rain forest is a unique experience and you are not confined to a jeep.

The animals include sambhur, barking deer, mongoose and the golden palm civet, the purple-faced leaf monkey is common. Although leopard tracks have been seen frequently, it is much more difficult to sight than many of the other animals. Birds include some rare endemics such as red-faced malkoha, Sri Lanka blue magpie, and the white-headed starling and plenty of others including orange minivets, orioles and babblers. Reptiles include the endemic Green pit viper and the Hump-nosed viper.

Lying in the southwest lowland Wet Zone, the reserve's rolling hills with ridges and valleys between 200-1,300m stretch 21 km from east to west. However, it is less than 4 km wide, bounded by the Kalu Ganga in the north and the Gin Ganga in the south. Twenty-two villages surround the reserve and the villagers make free use of the resources within, eg collecting *kitul* sap for jaggery (see box) and leaves and wood for construction and fuel, making the task of conservation and forest management more difficult.

There are three main **nature trails** with good guide leaflets available.

Waturawa Trail, 4.7 km: the path starts 250 m from the Camp and leads through the forest up to the visitors centre. There are 14 observation posts which are marked on the relevant guide. It is about three hours of gentle walking with two good places for spotting birds and watching monkeys. It is a good introduction to the rain forest.

Moulawella Trail, 7.5 km: taking about seven hours this is a fairly strenuous trek. It takes you through primary forest up to Moulawella peak (700 m) and from there you can see Adam's Peak and look over the forest canopy. The walk gives you a chance to see fascinating leaf-shaped frogs, lizards, tropical fish, snakes, crabs and a 300-year-old vine (which features on Rs 10 notes).

Sinhagala Trail, 14 km: this trek takes a full day. It leads through the heart of the rain forest to 'Lion Rock' from where you can look out over the unbroken tree canopy of an undisturbed forest and see the various hill ranges– 'twice as good as Moulawella'.

Cheap *Forest Department Camp*, Kudawa, northwest entrance, simple dormitory style with some partitions, shared western toilets, showers (sometimes 'out-of-order'), rooms sleep 8, cabins 2-3, forest river for washing and bathing, not really aimed at tourists as majority are on research or educational programmes. Rs 220 per night (foreigners), hire of sheet and pillowcases, Rs 25. Reservations are essential. contact Forest Department, 82 Rajamalwatta Rd, Battaramulla, Colombo outskirts, T566626. *Forest View*, Kudawa, on park boundary, T045 5256. 100 m from visitor centre, 3 km from the camp, *Martin Wijesingh's lodge* has simple dormitory accommodation, clean toilet and shower.

Sleeping

You can arrange rice and curry meals (Rs 35) by speaking to the Camp cook. Day visitors should carry food and drink.

Eating

Bus: from Colombo, public buses to Weddagala (direct bus dep 1145), 117 km via Mathugama, 154 m via Ratnapura. Turn off the main road to Kudawa (6 km) with the Forest Department Camp. 4 buses run daily from Weddagala to Kudawa, which has a bad surface. **Cars** may find it unpassable at times. **Walkers** can ask locally for the short cut from Weddagala or use the 4 km track.

Transport

Southern Sri Lanka

Ratnapura to the east and southeast coast

The A4 between Ratnapura and Pelmadulla (18 km) continues across the fertile and undulating low country, while the hills on either side come closer and closer to the road. It is a major gem bearing area. **Pelmadulla** is at the junction of three major routes. The A4 runs east and then northeast, curving round the southern flank of the Central Highland massif. The A18 goes southeast to **Madampe** (13 km), and continues almost due southeast to the South coast at Nonagama near Hambantota. From Madampe the A17 goes south to the coast at Matara.

From Pelmadulla the A4 continues to Balangoda and the caves beyond, through superb lush scenery all the way. This is the heart of the rubber producing area, and there are many rubber estates. Adam's Peak and the Maskeliya Range rise magnificently to the north, although during the Southwest monsoon they are almost permanently covered in cloud.

Pelmadulla to Balangoda

There is little to do in Balangoda but it is a base for excursions into Peak Wilderness Sanctuary and to visit prehistoric cave sites. You can visit the **Kuragala Cave** with the Jailani Muslim shrine nearby. The **Budugala Cave Temple** (25 km) is across a deep gully from the shrine. You take the road to Uggalkaltota, to the east, which follows the downward sloping ridge (buses go most of the way). For Kuragala (altitude 350m), you have to follow a path uphill from Taniantenna on the Kaltota road. For Budugala, the 3 km track from Uggalkaltota is safe for four wheel drive in dry weather.

Balangoda
බලංගොඩ

Phone code: 045
45 km from Ratnapura
145 km from Colombo

From Balangoda, after passing Rajawaka on the Kaltota road, a track leads 4 km down to the south to **Diyainna Cave**, near the village of the same name, which was also inhabited between 8000 and 2500 BC. If you continue along the track southeast towards Uda Walawe Reservoir, you will reach **Handagiriya** on the river bank. It is claimed that the old Buddhist stupa once held the Tooth Relic. This is close to **Bellan Bendi Pelessa**, the plain where large finds of prehistoric skeletons has confirmed it as an open-air site once used by *Homo Sapiens Belangodensis*.

Balangoda

Sleeping Cheap F *Balangoda Rest Inn*, 110 Old Rd (west of clocktower), T87207. 5 good rooms, fan (no net), attached bath, restaurant. **F** *Chamaara Rest*, 7/5 Karawjetiya Rd (west from clocktower, left after library, then left again), T87244. Rather musty rooms, not much English spoken. **F** *Pelmadulla Guest House*, 82/12 Barnes Ratwatta Mawatha, 5 very clean rooms, attached bath, net, no fan, nice quiet setting, friendly family, good meals. Recommended. **F** *Rest House*, Rest House Rd, T87299. 5 large rooms, linen clean though rooms a little shabby, fan, attached hot bath, verandah, large dining hall, good location above town, reasonable value. **G** *Samanala*, in town centre, clean and light rooms in large rundown, modern building, rice and curry restaurant.

Transport Road Bus: Services to Ratnapura (2 hrs). for the south coast, buses go to Tangalla via Pelmadula and Embilitipiya (2 hrs), Rs 40.

Route The densely forested land to the east has now largely been cleared, and the road goes on 14 km to Belihuloya.

Belihuloya
බෙලිහුල් ඔය
Phone code: 045

A small settlement on the Ratnapura-Badulla road, Belihuloya is best known as a picturesque rest point on the banks of a gushing river, among tea estates. There is also a track from here leading up to World's End on the Horton Plains, though from this side it is a long uphill walk (four hours plus).

Sleeping Mid-range C *Rest House* (CHC), near the bridge, T87599 (or T01-503497, F503504). 11 rooms (best in a newer extension) in an over 100-year old building by an attractive though very noisy stream, rooms rather shabby though bed linen clean, attached hot bath, no nets or fan, very overpriced for what you get, good restaurant that's popular with tour groups (set lunch US$10, à la carte Rs 275-325), a 'honeymooners' hotel. **D** *River Garden Resort*, T072 260990. Ratnapura side of the bridge, attractive thatched huts on the hillside, fan, attached hot bath, nicely positioned restaurant and bar, takes Visa/Mastercard, there a 'natural pool' for bathing in the river, but you have to be careful. **E** *Pearl Tourist Inn*, 208 Badulla Rd, T87200. On hill above town, rather smelly rooms, attached bath, fan, restaurant, bar, overpriced.

Eating The rest house restaurant on a pleasant covered terrace serves good food but is a popular lunch stop for coaches and is busy at weekends when service may be slow.

The A4 begins to rise heading northeast. At 16 km you reach the *Non Pareil Tea Estate*, where a dirt track winds 24 km up to World's End. Passing through **Halpe** (6 km), the road continues for a further 7 km to a turn off for the **Bambarakanda Falls**(or Bambaragala Falls) at 237 m in three stages, Sri Lanka's highest waterfall. The falls, which are impressive after the rains, are reached by a sealed road, 5 km off the A4. Just beyond the turn off for the falls is the settlement of **Kalupahana**. **Haldumulla**, nearby, has excellent views across to the sea. It is possible to visit an organic tea garden here, the *Bio Tea Project*, run by Stassen Exports Ltd. Their centre is signposted 3 km off the road. Some km further east from Kalpahana is Beragala, and then a further steep climb of 10 km is Haputale. For details of Haputale, Ella, Badulla etc, see page 216.

To Haputale

From Pelmadulla the A18 runs southeast through Kahawatta Ford. After 10 km at Madampe, the A17, branches off to the right (south) towards Galle and Matara. On the way you go through various towns and villages. **Rakwana** is the chief village of a tea-growing district. Sleeping at *Rest House* with views that are some of the most beautiful in Sri Lanka. There are many beautiful flowering trees in season and wild orchids, notably the large flowered *Dendrobium maccarthaie*. It is possible to reach the **Sinharaja Forest Reserve** from Rakwana by taking the road west to Weddagala. This road climbs to over 1,200m before descending into the valley of the Delgoda Ganga along the northern flank of the reserve.

Pelmadulla to the south coast

The A17 crosses the Bulutota Pass and passes just to the east of Gongala Peak (1,358 m) running down the easternmost edge of the Wet Zone. Just south of Akuressa the road forks, the A24 turning left to Matara down the valley of the Nilwala Ganga, and passing from one of the wettest areas of Sri Lanka to one of the driest in under 20 km. The right fork continues as the A17 to Galle, remaining in typically Wet Zone vegetation and cultivation throughout.

Gongala Peak

From Madampe the A18 runs to **Maduwanwela** (35 km), one of best known *walauwas* of the Kandyan chiefs where small inward-looking courtyards were built on the 'Pompeiian plan'. The A18 continues southeast into the Dry Zone and through areas with over 90% of the land under shifting cultivation.

To Hambantota

At this small village on the edge of a great rice growing area, is a paper mill set up to use rice straw. Intended to be an environmentally friendly development, it is causing some water pollution problems with its waste. Embilipitiya is a convenient base for trips to Uda Walawe National Park. E *Centurion Guest House*, New Town, T301104, 13 rooms.

Embilipitiya
Phone code: 047

In 1972, the 308 sq km park was set up to protect the catchment of the Uda Walawe Reservoir which is at the south end of the Walawe Ganga. Along the river there is thick woodland of old teak trees, but the rest of the area is mainly open parkland traversed by streams, which makes elephant viewing easy.

It has similar wildlife to Ruhuna-Yala with particularly large herds of elephants. Bird-watching is more rewarding than searching for any other wildlife.

Elephants can be seen along the river and near the numerous streams and tanks. The water birds gather in large numbers around the tanks (best around Magam, Habarlu and Kiri Ibban).

Uda Walawe National Park
උඩ වලවේ
Best season: Nov-Apr when the resident population of water birds are joined by migrants from the north

Southern Sri Lanka

You may also be able to stop at the **Palugaswewa** tank, approached from the A18, about 8 km along a dry weather track from Galpaya to the west of the reservoir. **Timbirimankada** 3 km from *Sinnukgala*, at the north end of the reservoir, is particularly good for bird-watching. These are not far from **Handagiriya** village which has a prehistoric site nearby (see page 172). **Ranagala**, which can be reached in dry weather, about 7 km from Sinnukgala is good for bird-watching. elephants too may come to the river here.

Entry US$12, children under 12 (and students with ISIC cards), US$6, Sri Lankans Rs 20. Timbolketiya, to the south of the reservoir, is the nearest settlement on the A18 to the national park entrance. For the entrance and Range Office, take a turn after 'Km 11' post. 4WD vehicles only (Rs 1,000) are allowed to use the dry-weather roads and jeep tracks. These are for hire at the gate.

Sleeping E *Walawe Rest*, Right Bank Canal Rd, Timbolketiya, T047 33201 or T01 589477. 20 mins drive from park entrance, 3 cottages. *Campsites* are near the river at Pransadhara and Wehrankade. Reservations: Wildlife Conservation Dept, T694241.

Route The road joins the A2 on the coast at Nonagama which continues to Hambantota, see page 154.

The Central Highlands

6

The Central Highlands

178 **Kandy**
179 Sights
183 Essentials

192 **Around Kandy**
192 West of Kandy
197 Northeast of Kandy
198 East of Kandy
198 South of Kandy

199 **The Highlands**

200 **Nuwara Eliya**
207 Around Nuwara Eliya
207 Peaks and plateaus
208 Adam's peak
209 Horton Plains National Park

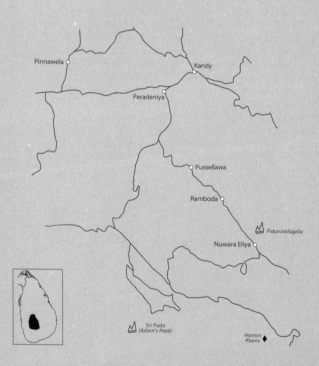

The stunning view over Kandy's 18th-century lake towards the Temple of the Tooth hints at some of the reasons for Kandy's unique character. In the heart of the island's interior, protected for centuries from direct external control by its mountains and forests as well as by a fierce desire by a succession of leaders to protect its independence, Kandy and its region offers rich insights into Sri Lanka's cultural traditions. Designated a World Heritage Site in 1988, the city is at the southern corner of the 'The Cultural Triangle'. The other two ancient capitals which enclose the heritage sites are Anuradhapura and Polonnaruwa.

Kandy නුවර

Population 55,000
Colour map 2, grid C4

Be aware of touts,
see page 183

Kandy is a modest sized city rather congested with traffic, but it stands as one of the most important symbols of Sinhalese national identity. The last bastion of Buddhist political power against colonial forces, the home of the Temple of the Buddha's tooth relic, and the site of the island's most impressive annual festivals, the city is also the gateway to the higher hills and the tea plantations. Its architectural monuments date mainly from a final surge of grandiose building by King Vikrama Rajasinha in the early 19th century, so extravagant, and achieved only with such enormous costs for the people of Kandy, that his nobles betrayed him to the British rather than continue enduring his excesses. The result is some extraordinary buildings, none of great architectural merit, but sustaining a Kandyan style going back to the 16th century, and rich in symbolic significance of the nature of the king's view of his world. Today, Kandy has the reputation of being something of a tourist trap, as it is on the itineraries of most travel groups. Despite this, the clarity of the air and its position on hills around the lake (with its lovely pink blossom in the spring) make it a nice place just to wander around.

History Although the city of Kandy (originally *Senkadagala*) is commonly held to have been founded by a general named Vikramabahu in 1472, there was a settlement on the site for at least 150 years before that. On asserting his independence from the reigning monarch, Vikramabahu made Kandy his capital. He built a palace for his mother and a shrine on pillars. In 1542 the **Tooth Relic** was brought to the city, stimulating a flurry of new religious building – a two-storey house for the relic itself, and 86 houses for the monks. As in Anuradhapura and Polonnaruwa, the Tooth temple was built next to the Palace.

Defensive fortifications probably only came with the attacks of the Portuguese. Forced to withdraw from the town in 1594, King Vimala Dharma Suriya set half the city on fire, a tactic that was repeated by several successors in the face of expulsion by foreign armies. However, he won it back, and promptly set about building a massive wall, interspersed with huge towers. Inside, a new palace replaced the one destroyed by fire, and the city rapidly gained a reputation as a cosmopolitan centre of splendour and wealth. As early as 1597 some Portuguese showed scepticism about the claims that the enshrined tooth was the Buddha's. In 1597 De Quezroy described the seven golden caskets in which the tooth was kept, but added that it was the tooth of a buffalo. The Portuguese were already claiming that they had captured the original, exported it to Goa and incinerated it.

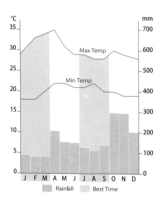

Climate: Kandy

By 1602 the city had probably taken the form (though not the actual buildings) which would survive to the beginning of the 19th century. The major temples were also already in place. Kandy was repeatedly attacked by the Portuguese. In 1611 the city was captured and largely destroyed, and again in 1629 and 1638, and the Tooth Relic was removed for a time by the retreating King Senarat. A new earth rampart was built between the hills in the south of the city. In 1681 there is evidence of a moat being built using forced labour, and possibly the first creation of the **Bogambara Lake** to the southwest, as a symbol of the cosmic ocean.

Vimala Dharma Suriya I had a practical use for the lake for he is said to have kept some of his treasure sunk in the middle, guarded by crocodiles in the water. Duncan suggests that there was also the symbolic link with *Kubera*, the mythical god of wealth, who kept his wealth at the bottom of the cosmic ocean. Crocodiles are often shown on the dragon gateways (*makara toranas*) of temples.

A new **Temple of the Tooth** was built by Vimala Dharma Suriya II between 1687-1707, on the old site. Three storeys high, it contained a reliquary of gold encrusted with jewels. Between 1707-1739 Narendra Sinha undertook new building in the city, renovating the Temple of the Tooth and enclosing the **Natha Devala** and the sacred **Bodhi tree**. He established the validity of his royal line by importing princesses from Madurai, and set aside a separate street for them in the town.

Major new building awaited King Kirti Sri (1747-1782). He added a temple to Vishnu northwest of the palace, but at the same time asserted his support for Buddhism, twice bringing monks from Thailand to re-validate the Sinhalese order of monks. The Dutch, who captured the city in 1765, plundered the temples and palaces. The Palace and the Temple of the Tooth were destroyed and many other buildings were seriously damaged.

Kirti Sri started re-building, more opulently than ever, but it was the last king of Kandy, Sri Vikrama Rajasinha(1798-1815) who gave Kandy many of its present buildings. More interested in palaces and parks than temples, he set about demonstrating his kingly power with an exhibition of massive building works. Once again he had started almost from scratch, for in 1803 the city was taken by the British, but to avoid its desecration was once again burned to the ground. The British were thrown out, and between 1809-1812 there was massive re-building. The palace was fully renovated by 1810 and a new octagonal structure added to the palace, the **Patthiruppuwa**. 2 years later the royal complex was surrounded by a moat and a single massive stone gateway replaced the earlier entrances.

In the west, Sri Vikrama Rajasinha built new shops and houses, at the same time building more houses in the east for his Tamil relatives. But by far the greatest work was the construction of the lake. Previously the low lying marshy land in front of the palace had been drained for paddy fields. Duncan records that between 1810-1812 up to 3,000 men were forced to work on building the dam at the west end of the low ground, creating an artificial lake given the cosmically symbolic name of the Ocean of Milk. A pleasure house was built in the middle of the lake, connected by drawbridge to the palace. At last the city had taken virtually its present form.

Sights

The area with the Temple of the Tooth and associated buildings, a World Heritage Site is the chief focus of interest. Sadly, it was the target of a bomb attack on 26 January 1998, which left over 20 dead, and badly damaged the area near the entrance. Since then, security has been tightened around the temple area with a number of roadblocks restricting vehicular access. Consequently, traffic has to go via the south of the lake making the road difficult to cross for pedestrians at times. Repairs to the extensive damage of the temple were completed in 1999.

The Palace Area

The **entrance** to the complex is in Palace Square opposite the *Natha Devala*. The Cultural Triangle Permit does not cover the temple here.

The Central Highlands

● ●

Worship of the 'Tooth Relic'

*The eyewitness account of **Bella Sidney Woolf** in 1914 captures something of the atmosphere when the Tooth Relic could be viewed by pilgrims: "The relic is only shown to royal visitors, or on certain occasions to Burmese and other pilgrims. If the passenger happens to be in Kandy at such a time he should try to see the Tooth, even though it may mean many hours of waiting. It is an amazing sight. The courtyard is crammed with worshippers of all ages, bearing offerings in their hands, leaves of young coconut, scent, flowers, fruit. As the door opens, they surge up the dark and narrow stairway to the silver and ivory doors behind which lies the Tooth.*

The doors are opened and a flood of hot heavy scented air pours out. The golden 'Karandua' or outer casket of the tooth stands revealed dimly behind gilded bars. In the weird uncertain light of candles in golden candelabra the yellow-robed priests move to and fro. The Tooth is enclosed in five Karanduas and slowly and solemnly each is removed in turn; some of them are encrusted with rubies, emeralds and diamonds.

At last the great moment approaches. The last Karandua is removed – in folds of red silk lies the wondrous relic – the centre point of the faith of millions. It is a shock to see a tooth of discoloured ivory at least three inches long – unlike any human tooth ever known. The priest sets it in a golden lotus – the Temple Korala gives a sharp cry – the tom-toms and conches and pipes blare out – the kneeling worshippers, some with tears streaming down their faces, stretch out their hands in adoration.'

● ●

Temple of the Tooth (**Dalada Maligawa**) is a genuine place of worship. The original dated from the 16th century, though most of the present building and the **Patthiruppuwa** or Octagon (which was badly damaged in the 1998 attack), were built in the early 19th century. The gilded roof over the relic chamber is a recent addition. The oldest part is the inner shrine built by Kirti Sri after 1765. The drawbridge, moat and gateway were the work of Sri Wickrama Rajasinha. There is a moonstone step at the entrance to the archway, and a stone depicting Lakshmi against the wall facing the entrance. The main door to the temple is in the wall of the upper verandah, covered in restored frescoes depicting Buddhist conceptions of hell. The doorway is a typical *makara torana* showing mythical beasts. A second Kandyan style door leads into the courtyard, across which is the building housing the Tooth Relic. The door has ivory, inlay work, with copper and gold handles.

The **Udmale** – upper storey – houses the Relic. Caged behind gilded iron bars is the large outer casket (*karandua*), made of silver. Inside it are seven smaller caskets, each made of gold studded with jewels. Today the temple is controlled by a layman (the *Diyawadne*) elected by the high priests of the monasteries in Kandy and Asgiriya. The administrator holds the key to the iron cage, but there are three different keys to the caskets themselves, one held by the administrator and one each by the high priests of Malwatte and Asgiriya, so that the caskets can only be opened when all four are present.

The **sanctuary** is opened at dawn. Ceremonies start at 0530, 0930 and 1830. These are moments when the temple comes to life with pilgrims making offerings of flowers amidst clouds of incense and the beating of drums. The casket is displayed for only a part of the day. The relic itself, for many years, has only been displayed to the most important of visitors. You can join pilgrims to see the casket but may well have to overcome pushing and jostling by those desperate to see the holy object. There is a separate enclosure in front of the relic, which wealthy Sri Lankans pay to go into.

● ●

Ayurvedic healing

*Ayurveda (science of life/health) is the ancient Hindu system of medicine – a naturalistic system depending on diagnosis of the body's 'humours' (wind, mucus, gall and sometimes, blood) to achieve a balance. In the early form, gods and demons were associated with cures and ailments; treatment was carried out by using herbs, minerals, formic acid (from ant hills) and water, and hence was limited in scope. Ayurveda classified substances and chemicals compounds in the theory of **panchabhutas** (five 'elements'). It also noted the action of food and drugs on the human body. Ayurvedic massage using aromatic and medicinal oils to tone up the nervous system, has been practised for centuries.*

This ancient system which developed in India over centuries before the Buddha's

*birth was written down as a **samhita** by Charaka. It probably flourished in Sri Lanka up to the 19th century when it was overshadowed by the western system of allopathic medicine. However, with the renewed interest in alternative forms of therapy in the West, Sri Lanka too considers it a serious subject for scientific research and has begun exploring its wealth of wild plants. The island has seen a regerneration of special Ayurvedic herbal cure centres which are increasingly attracting foreign visitors.*

In addition to the use of herbs as cures, many are used daily in the Sri Lankan kitchen (eg chilli, coriander, cumin, fennel, garlic, ginger, onions, turmeric), some of which will be familiar in the West, and have for centuries been used as beauty preparations.

● ●

The hall behind the tooth relic sanctuary has a number of golden Buddha statues and and modern paintings depicting the Buddha's life and and the arrival of Buddhism on the island. It is also interesting for its collection of old documents. The museum above is accessed from the rear. Entry Rs 100.

The **Audience Hall** was rebuilt in the Kandyan style as a wooden pillared hall (1784). The historic document ending the Kandyan Kingdom was signed here, and the territory was handed over to the British. There is excellent carving on the pillars.

■ *Entry Rs 300. Still cameras, Rs 50 (videos sometimes allowed, Rs 300). Charges appear to vary and some travellers report that they were expected to take a guide for a fee. Wear a long skirt or trousers. Otherwise lungis (sarongs) must be worn over shorts. Remove shoes and hats before entering. It is best to visit early in the morning before it gets too busy with tourist buses and pilgrims.*

Across from the complex is a working monastery and beyond its walls is **St Paul's Church** which was built in 1843 although the earliest minister, George Bisset, was here in 1816. There are various interesting memorials from 1822 to the 1870s in the British Garrison **Cemetery**, which is up a hill behind the National Museum. The caretaker is there every day and is very helpful (a donation is expected). Behind the temple, in the area of the **Law Courts**, you can watch lawyers in black gowns and white wigs going about their business in open-sided halls.

The lake area

An attractive 4 km walk goes round the lake. There are some beautiful views, especially of the island pavilion. The Royal Palace Park (Wace Park), overlooks the lake and also has superb views. The lake is sacred so it is prohibited to enter it for any reason. ■ *A tour round the lake is available from the boat jetty, Rs 400.*

On the lakeside, **Ulpenge**, opposite the Temple of the Tooth, was the bathing place of former queens. The Cultural Triangle Fund has undertaken to

The Central Highlands

restore the Ulpenge which is open to visitors. Further along to the east, the **Buddhist Publications Society** which has information on courses about Buddhism and meditation (see below).

The 18th-century **Malwatte Vihara**, on the south side of the lake, where important annual ordination of monks take place in June, is decorated with ornate wood and metal work. Occasionally, a friendly monk shows visitors around the monastery and the small museum. This and the **Asigiriya Vihara** (northwest of town) are particularly important monasteries because of the senior position of their incumbents. The latter, which stands on a hill, has good wood carving and an impressive collection of old palm leaf manuscripts. There is a large recumbent Buddha statue and the mound of the old Royal Burial ground nearby.

Other sights

A large modern concrete Buddha statue at Bhairawakanda, overlooks the town

Udawattekele Sanctuary is the 'forbidden forest of the kings of Kandy'. Kande Veediya (Hill Street), past the post office leads to the entrance gate to the sanctuary. Lady Horton's Drive takes you into the tropical rain forest and further east offers good views of the Mahaweli River. ■ *Rs 250 for foreigners.*

Trinity College, which is approached from DS Senanayake Veediya, has a chapel with some beautiful paintings which makes a quiet diversion from the busy part of town.

Mahaweli Spice Garden is a small (1 acre) garden with a wide range of spices and an informative tour in a relaxed atmosphere. Mrs Kodituwakku is friendly and welcoming. There is no pressure to buy but check prices in the market beforehand. ■ *13/68 Lewella Rd. 2.5 km north of town. T222474.*

The **Elephant Bath** at Katugastota near the *Mahaweli Reach Hotel* had to be abandoned since a dam built in Pollgolla, a few kilometres below the hotel, resulted in raising the water level too high at that point. It has shifted about 4 km up river and is now sited opposite the War Cemetery on Deveni Rajasinghe Mawatha (southwest of town). Tame elephants work until about 1200. After this they are brought to the river where their *mahouts* brush, sponge and splash them with water (essential for the animals' health). There are around 60 elephants (mainly one to five years old) and it is well worth a visit. ■ *Rs 150.*

Museums

Archaeological Museum Good sculptures in wood and stone housed in what remains of the old King's Palace. Some architectural pieces, notably columns and capitals from the Kandyan Kingdom. Three dusty rooms, disappointing. ■ *0900-1700, closed Fri. Palace Sq. You can arrange to see the teaching collection at the University in Peradeniya, Dept of Archaeology. T388345, ext 518, T388301, ext 217.*

Kandy National Museum The collection traces a vivid history of the development and culture of the Kandyan Kingdom. Jewels, armaments, ritual objects, sculptures, metalwork, ivory, costumes, games, medical instruments,

Floral decoration, Asigiriya Vihara Source: LPT Manjusri's Design Elements

old maps – an enormous range of everyday and exceptional objects. There is much memorabilia, and the attendants will attempt to explain it all, pointing out the obvious, in expectation of a tip. ■ *0900-1700, closed Fri. Entrance Rs 55, children Rs 30, still camera Rs 135 (no videos). Within the Queen's Palace, behind the Temple of the Tooth, T223867.*

Tusker Raja Museum The much venerated elephant which carried the

Tooth Relic casket in the *Esala Perahera* for many years, was offered to the temple by a pious Buddhist family when he was very young. Raja was 85 when he died in 1988. He was stuffed and placed in this separate museum north (left) of the Temple of the Tooth which is more easily visited before entering the Temple.

Gemmological Museum has a private collection of gems and precious minerals attatched to a retail outlet. ■ *Ceygems International, 673 Peradeniya Rd.*

Essentials

It is best to reserve your accommodation before arriving here. Kandy is full of touts. Some board trains approaching Kandy. Others besiege newcomers at the bus and rail stations. They (and also some taxi and tuk-tuk drivers) can be very persistent and will try to put you off going to certain hotels/guesthouses and then direct you to one where they can get a large commission from your host, often demanding up to 20% of everything you spend (not just the room, but food and tours as well). Insist that you want to choose your own and have a confirmed reservation. Don't tell them which hotel you will be staying at (it is none of their business) and ignore stories that your hotel/guesthouse has closed or is no good. Some touts will follow you, if you are on foot, and pretend they have taken you to your hotel. Politely, but firmly ask them to leave you, but if they persist make it clear to your host that you chose the hotel of your own accord. Many guesthouse owners refuse to pay touts. These are the ones that the touts will tell you are closed or no good. Ignore them!

A con-man may stop you on the street, saying he recognizes you as he works in your hotel. Caught off-guard, you feel obliged to accept him as your guide for exploring the sights (and shops), and so are ripe for exploitation. Be polite, but firm, when refusing his offer of help.

Kandy touts

The following street names have changed: *Castle Hill Street* to Kotugodella Veediya, *Gregory Road* to Rajapihilla Mawatha. *Hill Street* to Kande Veediya. *Lady Blacke's Drive* to Devani Rajasinghe Mawatha. *Lady Horton's Drive* to Vihara Mahadevi Mawatha. *King Street* to Raja Veediya *Lady McCallum Drive* to Srimath Kuda Ratwatte Mawatha. *Temple Street* to Deva Veediya. *Trincomalee Street* to DS Senanayake Veediya.

Street names

Many wish to stay within a walking distance of the centre. Out-of-town hotels are sometimes off the main road and can mean an uphill climb, and involve high transport costs. Prices during *Perahera* are highly inflated and accommodation is difficult to find. Some visitors have complained about the size and cleanliness of swimming pools. If this will influence your choice, it is best to see the pool before you check-in.

Rates given here are for a standard double room in the high season. Unless otherwise specified, all bathrooms have hot water and rooms have mosquito nets.

Sleeping

Expensive A *Suisse*, 30 Sangaraja Mawatha, T233025, F232083, 100 a/c rooms. Best with balcony on lakeside. Limited views of lake but friendly and helpful staff, restaurant (some bored waiters), good pool (non-residents, Rs 100) but close to busy road, tennis, snooker, shopping arcade, good position, colonial style hotel (c1920s), was Lord Mountbatten's war time HQ. **A** *Swiss Residence* (Jetwing), 23 Bahirawakanda, near Buddha statue, T074-479055, F479057, www.jetwing.net 40 comfortable rooms (19 a/c with TV), variable views, best towards Buddha Statue, all with balcony, 1 **AL** stylish suite with jacuzzi, pool, nightclub Fri and Sat (Rs 350, ladies free). **A** *Topaz*, Anniewatta (1.6 km from town), T224150, F232073. 76 well kept rooms (45 a/c with TV and tub) in excellent location on high hill overlooking mountains, but rather remote, popular with package tours, all rooms with balconies, good pool shared with sister hotel slightly lower down, regular shuttle to town. Recommended. **A** *Tourmaline*, Anniewatte, sister hotel of Topaz, T224172, F232073. 29 a/c rooms with similar facilities.

Kandy

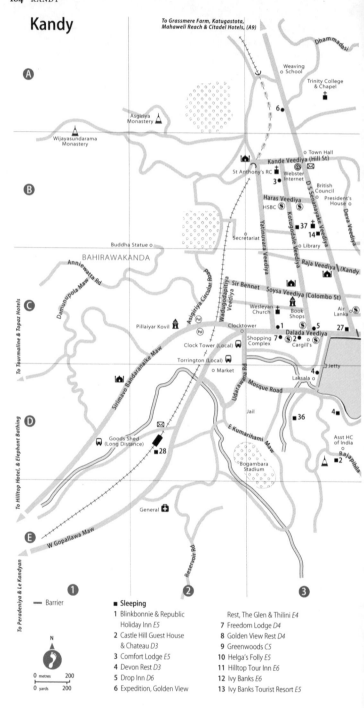

To Grassmere Farm, Katugastota, Mahaweli Reach & Citadel Hotels, (A9)

Dhammadasi

Weaving School

Trinity College & Chapel

6

Asgiriya Monastery

Wijayasundarama Monastery

Town Hall (Hill St)

Kande Veediya

St Anthony's RC

3

Webster Internet

British Council

President's House

Haras Veediya

HSBC

37

14

Buddha Statue

BAHIRAWAKANDA

Anniewatta Rd

Secretariat

Library

Raja Veediya (Kandy

Sir Bennet

Soysa Veediya (Colombo St)

Damunupola Maw

Pillaiyar Kovil

Clocktower

Wesleyan Church

Book Shops

Air Lanka

Clock Tower (Local)

1

Dalada Veediya

5

27

Torrington (Local)

Shopping Complex

7

2

Cargill's

Market

Laksala

Jetty

Sirimavo Bandaranaike Maw

Mosque Road

4

Udatalawana Rd

Jail

E Kumarihami Maw

36

4

Asst HC of India

Rajapihilla

2

Goods Shed (Long Distance)

28

Bogambara Stadium

General

W Gopallawa Maw

N

0 metres 200
0 yards 200

— Barrier

■ Sleeping
1 Blinkbonnie & Republic Holiday Inn *E5*
2 Castle Hill Guest House & Chateau *D3*
3 Comfort Lodge *E5*
4 Devon Rest *D3*
5 Drop Inn *D6*
6 Expedition, Golden View Rest, The Glen & Thilini *E4*
7 Freedom Lodge *D4*
8 Golden View Rest *D4*
9 Greenwoods *C5*
10 Helga's Folly *E5*
11 Hilltop Tour Inn *E6*
12 Ivy Banks *E6*
13 Ivy Banks Tourist Resort *E5*

The Central Highlands

To Tourmaline & Topaz Hotels

To Hilltop Hotel, & Elephant Bathing

To Peradeniya & Le Kandyan

The Central Highlands

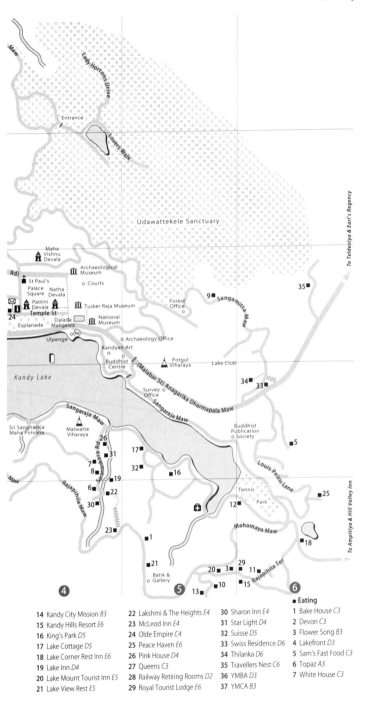

Maw

Lady Hortons Drive

Lovers Walk

Entrance

Udawattekele Sanctuary

To Teldeniya & Earl's Regency

Maha Vishnu Devala

Archaeological Museum

Rd)

St Paul's Palace Square

Natha Devala

Courts

Pattini Devala

24

Temple St

Tusker Raja Museum

National Museum

Esplanade

Dalada Maligawa

9

Sangamitta Maw

35

Forest Office

Archaeology Office

Ulpenge

Kandyan Art

Potgul Viharaya

Lake Club

Buddhist Centre

(Malabar St) Anagarika Dharmapala Maw

34

33

Kandy Lake

Survey Office

Sangaraja Maw

Sangaraja Maw

Buddhist Publication Society

Sri Sangharaja Maha Pirivana

Malwatte Viharaya

26

5

31

17

7

8

19

32

16

Louis Peiris Lane

Maw

6

22

Tennis Park

12

25

Rajapihla Maw

30

To Ampitiya & Hill Valley Inn

23

Mahamaya Maw

1

18

21

Batik & Gallery

20

29

3

11

10

15

Rajapihla Ter

13

4

5

6 ● Eating

14 Kandy City Mission *B3*
15 Kandy Hills Resort *E6*
16 King's Park *D5*
17 Lake Cottage *D5*
18 Lake Corner Rest Inn *E6*
19 Lake Inn *D4*
20 Lake Mount Tourist Inn *E5*
21 Lake View Rest *E5*

22 Lakshmi & The Heights *E4*
23 McLeod Inn *E4*
24 Olde Empire *C4*
25 Peace Haven *E6*
26 Pink House *D4*
27 Queens *C3*
28 Railway Retiring Rooms *D2*
29 Royal Tourist Lodge *E6*

30 Sharon Inn *E4*
31 Star Light *D4*
32 Suisse *D5*
33 Swiss Residence *D6*
34 Thilanka *D6*
35 Travellers Nest *E4*
36 YMBA *D3*
37 YMCA *B3*

1 Bake House *C3*
2 Devon *C3*
3 Flower Song *B3*
4 Lakefront *D3*
5 Sam's Fast Food *C3*
6 Topaz *A3*
7 White House *C3*

B *Helga's Folly*, (was The Chalet), 70 Frederick E de Silva Mawatha, T074-474314, F234571 chalet@sltnet.lk 40 rooms in eccentrically designed hotel full of character and quirkiness ('the Salvador Dali of hotels'), uniqueness of interior (and exterior) design has to be seen to be believed, set in quiet wooded hills, stylish restaurant, small pool (not well maintained), far from town but recommended for imagination and romance. **B** *Hill Top* Aitken Spence, 200/21 Bahirawakanda Peradeniya Rd, 2 km from centre, T224162, F232459 ashmres@lanka.ccom.lk 80 rooms (US$40), a/c US$5 extra, in attractively designed hotel, comfortable and striking rooms, beautiful restaurant, poolside rooms better. Recommended though attention to detail could be improved. **B** *King's Park*, 34 Sangaraja Mawatha, T/F223620 kingpark@sltnet.lk 20 rooms (5 a/c), fairly comfortable, TV in sitting area, smart restaurant, convenient quiet location but not quality finish, rather characterless, overpriced. **B** *Queens*,45 Dalada Veediya, T222813, F232079. 54 smallish but comfortable rooms, half a/c, but non-a/c rooms are better value, some with tub, avoid noisy front rooms, 2 reasonably priced restaurants, pool (non-residents, Rs 100). Despite age (established 1844) lacks colonial character, but good location. **B-C** *Thilanka*, 3 Sangamitta Mawatha T074 475200, F22549, thilanka@ids.lk 80 well furnished rooms, including 35 deluxe which are worth the extra, private balconies with lake views, good restaurant but Westernized menu (Rs 400 buffet lunch), good pool (non-residents, Rs 100), very clean, good service, retains parts of original house which began as a small guest house, helpful and friendly staff. Recommended.

Mid-range D *Castle Hill Guest House*, 22 Rajapihilla Mawatha, T224376. 4 large beautifully decorated rooms, 2 on garden-side, meals (breakfast included), good views over town. **D** *Comfort Lodge*, 197 Rajapihilla Mawatha, T/F074 473015 comfort@sri.lanka.net 6 rooms (Rs 1400 nett including breakfast), clean, modern rooms with TV, hot water, balconies, friendly and helpful staff. **D** *Kandy City Mission*,125 DS Senanayake Veediya, T223464. 12 large clean rooms (Rs 850; half price for singles), 2 a/c (Rs 1000), restaurant with good snacks, home made bread and cheese. **D** *Royal Tourist Lodge*, 93 Rajapihilla Mawatha, T222534, F233364. 3 good sized rooms (Rs 800-1,200) in family guest house, nets, clean, friendly. **D-E** *Lake Mount Tourist Inn*, 195a Rajapihilla Mawatha, T233204, F235522 hirokow@sltnet.lk 8 spotless, modern though smallish rooms (Rs 800 shared bath, Rs 1200 attached including breakfast), nets, meals, quiet, free pick up from station, friendly atmosphere but pricey compared to similar choices.

Cheap Many good-value rooms in private homes are available– the tourist office has a list of small guest houses. There are several by the lake with meals available. Most will offer transport from station on request. Some are within easy reach of the *Hotel Suisse* swimming pool which non-residents pay Rs 100 to use.

E *Blinkbonnie Tourist Inn*, 69 Rajapihilla Mawatha, 9 rooms with balcony and good views (Rs 650), breakfast included, will pay for tuk-tuk from the station. **E** *Expeditor Tourist Inn*, 58a Sarankara Road, T/F 238316. 3 comfortable rooms (Rs 500-600), hot water, nets, friendly, excellent food, no touts, excellent wildlife tours (see Tour companies below). Highly recommended. **E** *Freedom Lodge*, 30 Saranankara Rd T074 471589. 3 spotless rooms (Rs 550-650), super friendly and knowledgeable owners, Highly recommended. **E** *Ivy Banks Tourist Resort*, 68 Rajapihilla Mawatha, T234667. 4 large rooms (Rs 750) in another annexe of the original Ivy Banks, excellent views of lake and town from attractive and peaceful garden, meals on order but a bit isolated. **E** *Ivy Banks Annexe*, 62/5 Anniewatta Rd (opposite Kalutara Kade), southwest of town, T222875. 4 large rooms in modern house, immaculate garden overlooking lake, 'wonderful'. Recommended. **E** *Ivy Banks Guest House*, 52 Sangaraja Mawatha (opposite Kandy Gardens Club), T234667. 4 large rooms (Rs 750) in another annexe of the original Ivy. **E** *Lake Inn*, 43 Saranankara Rd, T222208, F232343 matsui@slt.lk 7 rooms with attached bath (Rs 700), 1 with bath opposite (Rs 500), most with balcony, restaurant, original guest house on this road but no longer the best. **E** *Lake View Rest*, 71A Rajapihilla Mawatha, T232034, F234484. 18 good sized clean rooms (Rs 700), most with balcony and good views, restaurant, cheaper rooms at the back but no-one ever chooses to stay in these! **E** *McLeod Inn*, 65a Rajapihilla Mawatha, T222832 T222832. 8 rooms with bath and hot water (Rs 650), 2 with excellent views, restaurant has the best view of any in this area (can be patronised by non-residents with advance warning), friendly. Recommended. **E** *Tourmaline Guest House*, Anniewatte, in same complex as Topaz and Tourmaline, T224172, F232073. 7 excellent value rooms with bath (US$10 for walk-ins) sharing facilities with big sister hotels. Recommended. **E** *Republic Holiday Inn*, 143 Rajapihilla Mawatha, T224231. 5 well furnished rooms, good views, but only cold water.

E-F *Lake Corner Rest Inn*, 9 Ampitiya Rd, T074-471444. 8 small rooms (Rs 300 common bath, Rs 400 attached), discounts for long stay, good cheap café next door (room service available), free pick up from station, good value for budget travellers and students. **E-F** *Sakura Hill Guest House*, Anniewatta Rd, Buddha statue hill, good rooms with balcony in a delightful guesthouse, meals (Rs 150), will collect from station (arrange in advance) saving a 15-min walk uphill. **E-G** *Travellers Nest*, 117/4 Anagarika Dharmapala Mawatha, T232174. 9 rooms (Rs 250-600), 1 dorm (Rs 100), upstairs better in very friendly guest house, homely atmosphere, excellent home cooking (owner will demonstrate recipes), quiet location, one of the first in Kandy, will pay for transport from station, recommended. **F** *Golden View Rest*, 40 Saranankara Rd, T224978. 3 rooms with attached bath (Rs 500), best is a rooftop room with light and airy views, separate bath (Rs 350), herbal treatment, restaurant, good value. Recommended. **F** *Greenwoods*, 34a Sangamitta Mawatha, T070-800674. Quiet and rural location on edge of Udawattekele Sanctuary, doubles plus 1 family room, attached bath, friendly family, good food. Recommended. **F** *Kandy City Mission*, 125 DS Senanayake Veediya, 150m from Dalada Maligawa, 12 good rooms, clean, comfortable, limited menu restaurant, good value for snacks, home made bread and cheese. **F** *Olde Empire Hotel*, 21 Temple Street, T224284. 6 clean rooms with common bath (Rs 396 nett), lovely verandah overlooking lake, excellent location close to Dalada Maligawa, cheap bar/restaurant, popular with backpackers, so book ahead. **F** *Peace Haven*, 47/10 Louis Pieris Mawatha, T232584. 2 simple rooms (Rs 400), 1 spacious but sparsely furnished apartment (Rs 20,000 per month) in quiet location, good food, especially the soup!. **F** *Star Light*, 15a Saranankara Rd, 5 rooms, attached bath, clean, good value, tasty food. **F** *Thilini*, 60 Saranankara Rd, T224975. 2 rooms with attached cold bath (Rs 350-400), homely atmosphere with charming family, very good food (owner formerly with Peace Corps), non-residents may eat here with advance notice, good value. Recommended. **F** YMCA, 90 Kotugodalle Veediya, T223529. 10 rooms, 4 double (Rs 480), 6 single (Rs 280), common bath (YMCA no longer has accommodation at the lake side).

G *The Glen*, 58 Saranankara Rd, T235342. 3 clean rooms, 1 attached (Rs 350), 2 common bath (Rs 300), nets, good food, pleasant garden, peaceful, friendly family home, good value. Recommended. **G** *Pink House*, 15 Saranankara Mawatha. 9 basic but clean rooms with shared bath (Rs 300), pleasant garden, home cooking, friendly motherly hostess, popular with backpackers. There are **G** dormitories with shared facilities which may not be too clean. Some have double rooms. *YMBA* (Young Men's Buddhist Assoc), 5 Rajapihilla Mawatha, near Wace Park, overlooks lake. *YMCA Sports Hall* will allow visitors to sleep there for Rs 30 during the *Perahera*, together with hundreds of mosquitoes. *Railway Retiring Rooms* at Kandy station. *Youth Hostel*, Trinity College, DS Senanayake Veediya.

The Central Highlands

Out-of-town **On Mahaweli River** **AL** *Earl's Regency*, 4 km east of city on A26, T422122, F422133 eregency@sltnet.lk Kandy's newest luxury hotel (opened Nov 1999), 100 rooms (US$130), 40 more planned, some with views overlooking Mahaweli River (and the road!) although the best views are to the rear, all facilities, good free-form pool although overall the site is rather characterless. **A** *Citadel* (Keells), 5 km west, 124 Srimanth Kuda, Ratwatte Mawatha, T234365, (Colombo T320862) utlres@keells.com 121 large, comfortable a/c rooms (24 deluxe) with attractive door paintings, river views, 2 restaurants, large pool, terrace gardens, popular with groups (surcharge Christmas to Apr). Recommended if you can cope with monkeys jumping on the roofs!

At Katugastota By river Mahaweli, 5 km north, **AL** *Mahaweli Reach*, 35 PBS Weerakoon Mawatha, by Katugastota Bridge, T232062, F232068, mareach@slt.lk 115 large, well-furnished a/c rooms in striking building overlooking river, tubs, TV, balconies with excellent river views, superb food (including good buffet choice), very attentive service, Kandy's biggest and best pool, ayurvedic health centre, extensive sports facilities, classic car collection in underground car park, family owned (started as a 4-room guesthouse!). Highly recommended. **G** *Travellers Halt,* 53/4 Siyambalagastenna. 25 beds, 4 km from centre (take bus from railway crossing to Katugastota where you cross the bridge to reach the hostel).

At Ukuwela 19 km north, **D** *Grassmere Farm*, Alupothuwala (between Km 5 and 6 posts, on Wattegama-Matale Rd, take Bus 636), T078 68329. 3 large rooms with bath (US$16) in a plantation bungalow, excellent (but not cheap) home cooked meals taken with hosts, large grounds, beautiful gardens (tea, coffee, fruit and spices), peaceful, homely, free pick-up from Kandy station (otherwise difficult to find). Recommended.

At Elkaduwa (27 km, 45 min drive from Kandy), higher in the hills, **A** *Hunas Falls* (Jetwing), T723630, F735134, or Colombo T345700, F345729, hunasfalls@eureka.lk 31 comfortable a/c rooms (3 suites, hot tubs, restaurant, bar, pool, boating, fishing, tennis, minigolf, games room for youths, many activities on offer, beautifully located in a tea garden by a waterfall with excellent walks, visits to tea estate, factory and spice gardens. Highly recommended.

At Heerassagala 7 km southeast (towards Peradeniya): **A** *Le Kandyan*, Mount Pleasant, T070 800560, F233948 lekandy@sltnet.lk 100 very comfortable rooms including 4 excellent split-level suites in the most stylish hotel in Kandy based on a traditional Kandyan palace (well produced hotel booklet is highly informative), excellent restaurant, tea room (40 varieties), good pool, superbly themed 'Le Garage' nightclub (Fri and Sat, Rs 400, ladies free), excellent views, well run. Highly recommended.

At Rajawella 14 km east, on Teldeniya Rd via Kundasale, **D** *Digana Village Resort*, T/F08 274255. 12 rooms in 4 villas, restaurant, tennis, squash, pool, not far from Victoria.

At Yahalatenna (11 km north, left off Kurunegala Rd at Barigama Junction) **A** *Tree of Life*, T499777, F499711 treelife@lanka.net 38 well-furnished 'cottages' with tubs, balconies in new building, in natural surroundings, built around a century old plantation bungalow, good restaurant, bar, pool, well kept gardens (wealth of plants, herbs, spices), ayurvedic health centre.

Avanhala Royal Garden, 72 Sangaraja Mawatha, is near the tourist office. *Devon*, 4E Dalada Veediya (1st floor), 0800-2000, serves excellent food at a reasonable price (rice and curry, 1100-1400, Rs 40-70 with 'refills'), also pleasant rooms with fan and shower. Bakery next door. *Flower Song*, 137 Kotugodalle Veediya (1st floor, a/c) serves excellent Chinese, good portions (Rs 140 per dish). *Topaz Hotel's* restaurant, opposite *Devon*, does good buffets (pricier). *Ram's*, 87 Colombo St, T471927. Excellent South Indian, first class service, attractive decor, immaculate. **Cheap** *Nawa Surasa*, 30 George de Silva Mawatha, southwest of town, does good continental and Chinese. *White House* Dalada Veediya, open during the day, slow service, but excellent coffee and good food. For breakfast and snacks try the good value *Lakeside Café* near *Olde Empire Hotel*. *Lyon's*, 27 Peradeniya Rd, near the main roundabout serves cheap snacks and some Chinese dishes.

Eating
The top hotels in the town are good but can be expensive

There are English style pubs at *Queens* and (*Lion* lager Rs 96) and *The Olde Empire* (*Lion* lager Rs 77). *The Pub*, Dalada Veediya, serves draught beer from the Ceylon Brewery. An alcohol shop at the south end of DS Senanayake Veediya, masquerades as *Lanka Medicinal Wine City*!

Bars

Kandyan dancing There are performances in several parts of the town, most starting between 1800 and 1900 most lasting 1 hr. Tickets Rs 200-250 (touts sell tickets around the lake but pay only the printed price. The shows are heavily geared towards the tourist market including snippets of several dances and the occasional fire walking. *Kandyan Arts Association*, 72 Sangaraja Mawatha, around 1930, 'touristy but still excellent and well worth seeing'. *Kandy Lake Club Dance Ensemble* performs dances of Sri Lanka, at 7 Sangamitta Mawatha (off Malabar St), T223505. Daily at 1900. Recommended. Performance at the *Red Cross Building*, includes fire dance, fire walk etc, simple but fine. *YMBA Hall*, Kandyan and Low Country dancing, at about 1900, 1 hr, good value.

Entertainment

End Jul/Aug: *Esala Perahera* for 10 days (see box on page 197).

Festivals

Batiks Good batiks from *Fresco*, 901 Peradeniya Rd. Also in curio shops on south Bandaranaike Mawatha, towards Botanical Gardens, just past railway station.

Shopping

Books *KVJ de Silva*, 86 DS Senanayake Veediya has a good selection of local history. *Lake House Bookshop* and *Vijitha Yapa Bookshop*, 5 Kotugodella Veediya, T070-800573. Stocks a good range of English titles. *The Wheel* by the Lake sells Buddhist literature.

Crafts and jewellery *Laksala*, near Lake Jetty, and *Kandyan Arts Association* (tourist office), 72 Sangaraja Mawatha, are government sales outlets where you can watch weavers and craftsmen working on wood, silver, copper and brass, and buy lacquer-ware and batik. There are several shops on Dalada Veediya near the Temple of the Tooth. *Kandyan Handicrafts Centre*, 10/4 Kotugodalle Veediya, has good metalwork. Also several antique shops, many along the lake and on Peradeniya Rd. The *Crafts village* set up with government help is at *Kalapuraya Nattarampota*, 7 km away (see Excursions above) where craft skills have been handed down from father to son.

Kandyan dancer

Markets   A visit to the *Municipal Market*, west of the lake is worthwhile even if you are not planning to bargain for superb Sri Lankan fruit and spices. *Cargill's Supermarket*, Dalada Veediya, is reasonable. **Photography**   *Midland Studio*, 46 King St. **Tailoring and textiles** *Junaid Stores*, 19 Yatinuwara Veediya. Outstanding made-to-measure western style clothes in quality fabrics, beautifully cut and sewn, and at reasonable prices. Shops along Colombo St sell material.

Sports   **Boating**   Motorised boats are available at the jetty for a 20 min round of the lake. Rs 100 per person, minimum Rs 500 per boat that holds up to 20 people. 0900-1830.

Golf *Victoria Golf Club*, Rajawella, 21 km east, off A26, T/F070-800249, victoria@sltnet.lk   Excellently maintained 6879 yd, par 73, course surrounded on 3 sides by Victoria Reservoir with the Knuckles Range providing a further attraction as a stimulating backdrop. A round, including green fees, caddy, club and shoe hire will cost around Rs 3,000 during the week, extra Rs 400 at weekends. Some larger hotels will provide free transfer for residents.

Riding *Victoria Saddle Club*, Rajawella, just before golf course, T072-245707, 08 421459 (evenings), offers lessons (Rs 350-750), pony rides for young children (Rs 150) and accompanied trail rides for experienced riders (Rs 1,000). Phone in advance for information and booking.

Swimming   *Hotel Suisse* has a large pool but during the peak season (Dec-Feb) it can be fairly crowded. The cleanest pool is at *Queens* (no chlorine). It is usually very quiet. *Tourmaline/Topaz*'s shared uncrowded pool, is worth visiting for an afternoon for the spectacular hill-top views. *Thilanka* has good views over town. Non-residents pay Rs 100 (includes use of towel) at these hotels. The best pool is at the *Mahaweli Reach*, but it is out of town.

Tour operators   **Wildlife-Nature Trekking Tours**, c/o *Expeditor Tourist Inn*, 58a Saranankara Rd, T/F238316, is run by Mr Sumane Bandara Illangantilake who has 40 years experience in leading small groups on tours of the island. Specialises in trekking, nature (he can recognise over 200 bird calls) and wildlife tours as well as rafting. Trips arranged according to experience ranging from 'smooth' to 'adventure' lasting 4-14 days. Highly recommended.

Transport   **Local**   **Bus**   the **Clock Tower Bus Stand**, and **Torrington Bus Stand** (between the Central Market and George E de Silva Shopping Complex), are for 'local' destinations (including places near Kandy). See below for long distance buses.

Taxis and tuk-tuk   These are available for transport to your hotel. A tuk-tuk should cost around Rs 60 (after bargaining) to the *Hotel Suisse* area. A/c **Radio cabs** are very convenient, safe and reliable, Rs 25 per km, min Rs 50. Phone T233322, giving exact location and allow 10 mins. See page 43 for details.

Train   See page 191.

Long distance   **Bus**: The **Goods Shed Bus Stand** near the railway station is for long distance buses. Frequent buses to **Colombo**: regular Rs 30, a/c Rs 70. A/c buses (*Intercity Expresses*) take 2½ hrs, Rs 100, but are often congested, nerve wracking and far less pleasant than the train – your life is in their hands – but so are the lives of many others on the road. To **Anuradhapura**: No 42 (1st bay on right), every 30 mins, 4 hrs, Rs 40 (Rs 75 for Express). Also to Nuwara Eliya, 4 hrs, and Polonnaruwa. **Car hire**: If time is very limited for sightseeing, it is possible to hire a car for the day to visit

The hill railway

*The train journey between **Colombo** and **Kandy** is far more comfortable, quieter and more scenic than going by road. From Colombo it is best if you sit on the left, facing the rear in the 1st class 'Observation Car' (seats 23 and 24 from Colombo, seats 11 and 2 from Kandy). The 1st class 'Car' or 'Saloon' is sometimes only available on the early morning departures in both direction. The last hour of the journey to Kandy is most memorable, climbing slowly into the mountains*

(thankfully away from road-fumes) through terraced paddy fields, lush home gardens and managed forests. Watch out for monitor lizards and flying squirrels; best seen at dusk if you take the 1530 train from Colombo. The journey to Nanu Oya and Ella is also recommended for the beautiful scenery.

Those who suffer from motion-sickness should note that you really get bounced around on this route, especially in the 'Observation Car'.

Trains from Kandy

To	1st Class	2nd Class	3rd Class	Train	Departure time	Journey
Badulla	*Rs 182	Rs 104	Rs 38	Mail	0855, 1015, 2310	7¾ hrs
Colombo (Fort)	*Obs Rs 122	Rs 72 §		Intercity Exp	0630, 1500	2½ hrs
Colombo (Fort)	120	Rs 69	Rs 25	Exp	0130, 0525, 0645, 1030, 1540, 1650	3¼ hrs
Hikkaduwa	Rs 213	Rs 123	Rs 45	Exp	0525	5¾ hrs
Matara (via Fort)	Rs 274	Rs 157	Rs 57	Exp	0525	fs7¼ hrs
Nanu Oya (for Nuwara Eliya)	Rs 98	Rs 57	Rs 21	Exp	0855, 2310	4¼ hrs

*Trains run daily unless otherwise indicated. **NB** *The 'Observation Car' should be reserved ahead; Reservation Fee Rs 50 each way. Return tickets are valid for up to 10 days. § Return tickets, valid for 10 days, Rs208 (1st Class), Rs108 (2nd Class)*

Dambulla, Sigiriya and Polonnaruwa (ask your hotel or guest house). While this is a very full day it can be most rewarding.

Airlines offices Sri Lanka Airlines, *Queens Hotel*, 19 Temple St, 2nd floor, T/F232494 (open Mon-Fri 0830-1700, Sat 0830-1230). **Banks** most are on Dalada and Katugodale Veediyas an. ANZ, Temple St, and HSBC, Haras Veediya, have ATMs that accept Visa and Mastercard. Sampath Bank, accepts Mastercard. **Communications** Post offices: opposite Railway Station and on Senanayake Veediya (crossing with Kande Veediya) and Poste Restante. Telecommunications: outside hotels are cheaper. Some, including *Matsui Communications, 3A Temple St, T232647, F232343. Will receive fax messages. There are plenty of Metrocard and Lanka payphones phonecard* boxes. **Courier:** *DHL Keell*, 7 Deva Veediya, T232215 tracing@cmb.co.lk.dhl.com See 'Essentials' for rates. **Internet:** *Webster*, Sinhaputhra Bldg, 11 Hill Street, T074 475267. Rs 75 per 15 min, charged in 15 min segments, 2 terminals, offline also possible, Rs 100 per hr. Open 0830-1800 except public holidays. **Embassies and consulates**: Assistant High Commissioner of India, 47 Rajapihilla Mawatha (open Mon-Fri 0830-1030), will issue Indian visas. It may take 1 week, though some travellers have got it in a day (usually one day in Colombo). Pakistan High Commissioner, 30 Colombo St, T232346. **Medical services**: *General Hospital*, T22261. Chemist: *New Kandy Dispensary*, Brownearigg St. **Libraries and cultural centres**: *Alliance Française*, 412 Peradeniya Rd, T224432. Has a library and also shows films (Mon-Sat, 1100-1700). *British Council* 178 DS Senanayake Veediya, T222410. Has a library plus 2-week old British papers (Tue-Sat, 0930-1700,

Directory

The Central Highlands

closed Sun, Mon and public holidays). Reading Rooms are open to non-members. **Buddhism and Meditation** *Buddhist Publication Centre*, 54 Sangharaja Mawatha, T223679, has a good library, a book shop and information on courses on Buddhism and meditation where serious visitors are welcome. South of Kandy *Theruwan Meditation Centre*, Uduwela (take Bus 655, then walk 2 km). *Nilambe*, is beyond Galaha. **Tourist offices**: Tourist Information Centre, Headman's Lodge, 3 Temple St (Deva Veediya), opposite entrance to Temple of the Tooth. T222661, 0900-1645 Mon-Fri. Closed weekends and public holidays.

Around Kandy

West of Kandy

Beyond the Botanic Gardens, 6 km southwest of town, is a group of 14th-century temples which display ancient artistic skills of the islanders. The traditions continue to be practised in the crafts villages nearby. You can combine a visit to the gardens and some temples with a visit to the Pinnawela Elephant Orphanage if you have your own transport. You will need to allow two days if you have to depend on public transport. ■ *Getting there: There are frequent buses along the congested road from Kandy to Peradiniya, and further west along the A1, which pass close to Gadaldeniya temple, but you will have to walk to reach the others nearby. Alternatively, hrly buses from Kandy also travel the 7 km from Peradeniya, southwest to Embekke village, where you can start your tour.*

Peradeniya

Colour map 2, grid C4
Altitude: 500 m

Famous for its magnificent Botanic Gardens, Peradeniya is also the home of the Sri Lanka University.

Botanic Gardens

Conceived originally in 1371 as the Queen's pleasure garden, Peradeniya became the residence of a Kandyan Prince between 1741-1782 where royal visitors were entertained. The park was converted into a 60 ha Botanical Garden in 1821, six years after the fall of the last Kandyan King.

There are extensive well-kept lawns, pavilions, an *Orchid House* with an outstanding collection, an *Octagon Conservatory, Fernery*, banks of bamboo and numerous flower borders with cannas, hibiscus, chrysanthemums, croton and colourful bougainvillaea. The *Tank* has water plants including the giant water lily and papyrus reeds. You will see unusual exotic species, especially palms (palmyra, talipot, royal, cabbage), and *Ficus elastica* (latex-bearing fig or 'Indian rubber tree' with buttress roots), an amazing avenue of drunken looking pines, and some magnificent old specimen trees. In all, there are about 4,000 labelled species. ■ *0800-1745 daily (last ticket at 1700). Entry Rs 150 (Sri Lankans Rs 15), students and child Rs 75, cars Rs 65, scooters/ motorbikes Rs 25, cycles Rs 10 (hire one in Kandy).*

If you drive yourself (minivans are not allowed) make sure you are not issued an extra entry ticket for 'the driver'. However, it is very pleasant to walk around. Even at midday there are walks under shady trees but it can be quite tiring. It is best to visit in the early morning or late afternoon– and take your binoculars. A notice says 'Indecent or disorderly behaviour specially of couples within the gardens is an offence'!

A signboard at the entrance, with a map, features a numbered circuit from 1-25. The corresponding numbers are placed at strategic points on the route, black on a yellow background. The suggested route below closely follows this.

Start at the *Spice Garden* (to the right of the entrance) which has many exotic spices (eg cardamom, cloves, pepper, vanilla). Follow the road to the right (east) to take in the *Orchid House*. Just off *Palmyra Avenue* there are *Javanese Almond* trees with amazing roots. The palmyra leaf was used for ancient manuscripts. The *Cabbage Palm Avenue* from South America was planted in 1905. You can then walk along the *Royal Palm Avenue* (1885) – you will notice the fruit bats in quite large colonies hanging in many of the trees. This meets the *River Drive* which follows the course of the Mahaweli Ganga.

A suggested walk
It is best to keep to the paths to avoid the invisible large holes in the rough grass

Follow the drive to the *Suspension Bridge* which is about half way around the River Drive and you can if you wish go back via the *Royal Palm Avenue*. This goes through a large grassy central area around which visiting dignitaries have planted further specimens. King George V and Queen Mary planted a *Cannon Ball Tree* on 14 April 1901. Their great-grand-daughter, Princess Anne, planted an *Asoka* tree (*saraca asoca*) in 1995. Between the **Great Circle** and the **Great Lawn** is the **Herbarium**.

Try not to miss one of the rarest plants in the gardens – the *Coco de Mer*. You will find it on the path leading to George Gardner's monument. This is on your right (West) as you return to exit (left, as you enter the park). This plant has the largest and heaviest fruit (or nut) in the plant kingdom, weighing on average some 10-20 kg. They take between five to eight years to mature and are surprisingly productive. It is not unusual to have over 20 nuts on a tree. They are all carefully numbered. Native *Coco de Mer* are only found Praslin, an island in the Seychelles. Carry on along this path to get to the Memorial, a dome shaped structure. George Gardner was Superintendent of the gardens from 1844-49. From here you overlook the lily tank which is surrounded by giant bamboo, some 40-m tall (it grows at 2-3 cm a day!).

Outside, a bridge across the Mahaweli river, takes you to the **School of Tropical Agriculture** at Gannoruwa, where research is carried out into various important spices and medicinal herbs as well as into tea, coffee, cocoa, rubber, coconuts and varieties of rice and other cash crops. The **Economic Museum** has botanical and agricultural exhibits.

The **university** (1942) is nearby, built in the old Kandyan style in an impressive setting of a large park with the Mahaweli Ganga running though it and the surrounding hillocks. It is worth visiting the small teaching collection **museum** in the Dept of Archaeology (call ahead, T388345 ext 518, T388301 ext 217).

D *Peradeniya Rest House*, 100 m east of the main entrance, T/F388299. 12 grubby, basic rooms (Rs 1,100 including breakfast), next to the noisy main road, more staff than guests, grossly overpriced. *Royal Park Cafeteria* in the garden, closes at 1700. Good lunches (reserve a table for the latter, on arrival). *Cool Spot*, near the ticket office, serves snacks and drinks.

Sleeping & eating

Bus Many buses from Kandy's Torrington Bus Station, stop outside the entrance, Rs 5. **Tuk-tuks** charge Rs 150 one way.

Transport

The Buddhist temple is in a beautiful hilltop setting, built on a rock, 1 km from the main road. Built of stone (showing influence of Indian temple architecture), it has lacquered doors, carvings and frescoes and a moonstone at the entrance of the shrine. The brick superstructure shaped like a stupa has an octagonal base. The inscriptions on the rock by Dharmakirti date it to 1344. The principal gilded image of the Buddha (18th century, which replaced the original destroyed by the Portuguese) is framed by elaborate *makara* decoration. Unusually, there is also a shrine to Vishnu here. Outside, there is a covered stupa and a Bodhi tree. ■ *Rs 25.*

Gadaladeniya Temple

The Central Highlands

At **Kiriwavula** village nearby, craftsmen cast brass ornaments by the ancient lost-wax (*cire-perdu*) process. Some are for sale.

Lankatilaka Mahaviharaya The second monument of the group, 4 km away in Hiripitiya, sits on top of the rock Panhalgala. King Bhuvanekabahu IV (ruled 1341-51) moved the Sinhalese capital from Kurunegala to Gampola nearby. When a monk reported the extraordinary vision of an elusive golden pot on the water of the tank here, the King saw this as a sign and had the temple built. He appears among the wall paintings.

The present two-storeyed white-washed brick 'structure was originally four storeys high. It was renovated and the tiled roof was added in 1845 after the two top storeys had fallen. You climb up a rock-cut stairway to the moonstone at the entrance, and the finely carved wooden doorway flanked by guardian *gajasinghas* (elephant-lions). The inner image house containing fine gold plated images of the Buddha is surrounded by a devale. The walls and ceiling have well preserved frescoes (some of the oldest and best examples of the Kandyan temple style. The west door has carved figures of Hindu gods (*Saman, Skanda, Ganapathi, Vibhisena* among others). ■ *Rs 25. Craftsmen can be seen carving wood at the base of the rock.*

Embekke Devale The Hindu devale, dedicated to God *Kataragama* or *Skanda*, is 1.5 km away along a track through pleasant cultivated fields. The temple with its sanctuary, Dancing Hall and the Drummers' Hall, is famous for its carved wooden pillars (which may have once adorned the Audience Hall in Kandy) with vibrant figures of soldiers, wrestlers, dancers, musicians, mythical animals and birds. You can see similar carved pillars at the remains of the old Pilgrim's Rest

Kandy excursions

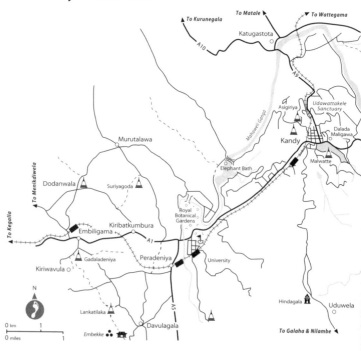

nearby. The patterned roof tiles are attractive too. The village has craftsmen working in silver, brass and copper. ■ *Getting there: There are hrly buses between Kandy and Embekke village, a short walk away from the devale.*

Suriyagoda Vihare

If you have your own transport and wish to visit the Suriyagoda Vihare, turn off north from the A1 at Kiribatkumbura, signed to Murutalawa. The present 18th-century vihara (on a 15th-century site) has striking Kandyan wall paintings, see over page.

North of Embiligama (Km 105 post), the 17th-century **Dodanwala Temple** was built by the Rajasinha II. It is where the king is believed to have offered the deity his crown and sword after defeating the Portuguese. From Embiligama, to reach the textile weaving village of **Menikdiwela**, after a short distance along the Murutalawa road take the left fork for 6 km.

Route

From Kandy, the A1 west goes towards Kegalle where a right turn towards Rambukkana leads to Pinnawela. En route, about 1 km after Mawanella, a sign points to the place where Saradial ('the local Robin Hood') lived. There is a small monument. You then pass Molagoda, a village devoted to pottery with both sides of the road lined with shops displaying a wide range of attractive pots. The trip can be extended to visit the Dedigama vihare, south of Kegalla, see page 195.

Maximus Elephant Foundation

The private charity at Samaragiri, Randeniya, Hiriwadunna near Kegalle (T65377, elefound@sltnet.lk) cares for five captive animals. There are three elderly elephants which worked in the timber industry and two younger ones. Visitors pay Rs 200 to help bath, or ride an elephant (disappointingly, 'only for a few minutes', 'overpriced') and learn more about them in a museum. A shop sells local crafts including handmade elephant dung paper.

Route

Alternatively, from Colombo to Pinnawela, take the A6 towards Kurunegala. At Polgahawella turn right (A19) and immediately left. The road begins to climb into the hills at Rambukkana (4 km north of Pinnawela) which is on the Colombo-Kandy rail line - some trains have to have an engine attached to push them up to Kadugannawa!).

Pinnawela
Colour map 2, grid C3

The government's **Pinnawela Elephant orphanage** (49 km from Kandy) is a must for most visitors. This was set up in 1975 to rescue seven orphaned baby elephants, whereas now there are over 60, the largest group of captive elephants in the world. Several dozen young animals, some only a few weeks' old, very hairy and 1 m high, are kept in parkland where they are nursed by adult elephants. The successful captive breeding project has succeeded in producing second generation births.

The Central Highlands

A special zoo is to open here in 2003. The place is pleasantly uncommercialized and there are no touts. The elephants, which roam freely in parkland, are 'herded' just before being taken to the feeding sheds, when they are very photogenic. They may occasionally 'charge', so to avoid getting hurt stand well back. The feeding (usually around 0915, 1315 and 1700) is done in a couple of large sheds. Each baby elephant is tied to a post and then bottle fed with copious amounts of milk. Adults, which need around 250 kg of food each day, are fed mainly on palm leaves. Two special farms run by the National Zoological Gardens meet part of their needs. After feeding they are driven across the road, down to the river. You can usually watch them bathing there for about an hour from 1000, 1200, 1400 and 1600, and sometimes being trained to work. ■ *0830-1800. Entry Rs 150 (Sri Lankans Rs 75), children Rs 40. Video camera Rs 200 (professional Rs 600). Retain your ticket as this is checked again on the way to the elephant bath.*

Pinnawela village becomes an oasis of natural quietness as calm descends when the tourist groups leave. Travellers who choose to spend a night are delighted by the peace and beauty of this place with its river and jungle orphanage.

Sleeping and eating There are a few guesthouses nearby: **C** *Green Land Guest House* Elephant Bath Rd, Pinnawela, T035-65668. 2 clean rooms with nets and attached bath (Rs 650 cold, Rs 700 hot), host family live nearby, excellent rice and curry dinner. Restaurant, just inside entrance of the orphanage is useful for breakfast, omelettes and snacks. Non-patrons however, must pay Rs 15 for use of the toilet! Others on Elephant Bath Road including one by the river with good view of elephants bathing.

Shopping The roads nearby are lined with souvenir stalls with a wide range of trinkets, not all elephant related. Bargaining is essential (a coconut shell animal priced at US$12 was bought for Rs 250!).

Transport Bus Regular service from Kandy (Goods Shed) to Kegalle (1 hr, Rs 11). Change at Keggale clock tower for bus to Pinnawela (30 mins, Rs 3.50). Some buses will drop you at the junction for Pinnawela on the A1. **Train** From Kandy to Rambukhana (short bus or tuk-tuk ride from the orphanage) at 0630 and 0655. Enquire at station for return times.

Route From Pinnawela, the B32 runs south to meet the A1 just east of Kegalla at Udamulla.

Kegalla This is a long straggling town in a picturesque setting. It is a useful junction for
(19 km) buses between Colombo and Kandy and for getting to Pinnawela.

Dedigama Dedigama is about 5 km south of Kegalla on the main road (A1). Turn off near the '70 km post', along B21. Two 12th-century dagobas built by King Parakramabahu I, who was born here, exist, one having 10 relic chambers, including one a lower level. A gem studded golden reliquary was found here. The **museum** nearby is worth visiting (closed Tuesday).

Route En route to Kandy, some beautiful hill scenery lies along the A1 between Kegalla and **Mawanella**, the latter surrounded by spice plantations. On either side the vegetation is stunningly rich. At the top of the **Balana Pass** is a precipice called **Sensation Point**. The railway goes through two tunnels to Peradeniya (10 km), where the road crosses the Mahaweli Ganga, Sri Lanka's longest river.

The festival of festivals

The **Esala Perahera** (procession), Sri Lanka's greatest festival is of special significance. It is held in the lunar month of Esala (named after the Cassia Fistula which blossoms at this time) in which the Buddha was conceived and in which he left his father's home. It has also long been associated with rituals to ensure renewed fertility for the year ahead. The last Kandy kings turned the Perahera into a mechanism for reinforcing their own power, trying to identify themselves with the gods who needed to be appeased. By focusing on the Tooth Relic, the Tamil kings hoped to establish their own authority and their divine legitimacy within the Buddhist community. The Sri Lankan historian Seneviratne has suggested that fear both of the king and of divine retribution encouraged nobles and peasants alike to come to the Perahera, and witnessing the scale of the spectacle reinforced their loyalty. In 1922, DH Lawrence described his experience as 'wonderful – midnight – huge elephants, great flares of coconut torches, princes ... tom-toms and savage music and devil dances ... black eyes ... of the dancers'.

Today the festival is a magnificent 10-day spectacle of elephants, drummers, dancers, Chieftains, acrobats, whip-crackers, torch bearers and tens of thousands of pilgrims in procession. Buddhists are drawn to the temple by the power of the Tooth Relic rather than by that of the King's authority. The power of the Relic certainly long preceded that of the Kandyan Dynasty. Fa Hien described the annual festival in Anuradhapura in 399 AD, which even then was a lavish procession in which roads were vividly decorated, elephants covered in jewels

and flowers, and models of figures such as Bodhisattvas were paraded. When the tooth was moved to Kandy, the Perahera moved with it.

Following the Tree Planting Ceremony (Kap), the first five days, Kumbal Perahera, are celebrated within the grounds of the four devalas (temples) – Natha, Vishnu, Skanda and Pattini. The next five days are Randoli Perahera. Torch light processions set off from the temples when the Tooth Relic Casket is carried by the Maligawa Tusker accompanied by magnificently robed templr custodians. Every night the procession grows, moving from the Temple of the Tooth, along Dalada Veediya and DS Senanayake Mawatha (Trincomalee St) to the Adahanamaluwa, where the relic casket is left in the keeping of the temple trustees. The separate temple processions return to their temples, coming out in the early morning for the **water cutting** ceremony. Originally, the temple guardians went to the lake with golden water pots to empty water collected the previous year. They would then be refilled and taken back to the temple for the following year, symbolizing the fertility protected by the gods. On the 11th day, a daylight procession accompanied the return of the Relic to the Temple. The Day Perahera continues, but today the Tooth Relic itself is no longer taken out.

You don't necessarily need to buy tickets to watch the processions since you can good views by standing along the street. A good vantage point is that opposite or near to the Queen's hotel as much of that area is slightly better lit (the Presidential vantage point is somewhere nearby) and can provide for slightly better photography.

The **Medawela Temple** (Madavala, 10 km) marking a Buddhist revival, was built in the 18th century, where an older 14th-century temple stood. Interesting features include the small image house built in wood and wattle-and-daub, raised above the ground on stone pillars, similar to the old Kandyan grain stores. The railed balcony forms the *pradakshina path*. Inside, the marble Buddha image sits in front of a decoratively carved and painted wooden panel with representations of a Bodhi tree, protective gods, disciples and dragons. The fine Kandyan paintings on the side walls show a line of saints and disciples

Northeast of Kandy

The Central Highlands

along the lower level, tales from the *jatakas* along the middle (unfolding from the back of the room, to the front). Above this, the murals on the left show the weeks after the Buddha's enlightenment, and the right, the 16 holiest places for Buddhists. Medawela, at the junction of B36 and B37, is a metalworkers village. The Kandyan Dance academy near **Amunugama** is 3 km south of Medawela. ■ *Getting there: Take bus 603 from the Clock Tower Bus Stop near the Central Market.*

East of Kandy   The unusual incomplete 14th-century **Galmaduwa Temple** on the Kundasala road, was an attempt to combine the features of Sinhalese, Indian, Islamic and Christian architectural styles.

Nearby at **Kalapuraya Craft Village**, Nattarampota (6 km east of Kandy), in the beautiful Dumbara Valley, you can watch traditional craftspeople and is worth a visit. Artisans work in village homes with brass, copper, silver, wood, leather etc. Prices are better than elsewhere but not fixed. Turn left (north) down a lane, off the Digana road to get there.

The **Degaldoruwa Cave Temple**, Gunnepana, 3 km away, has vivid wall paintings of *Jataka* stories dating from the 18th century. There is a Dance Academy here.

■ *Getting there: Bus No 655 from the Market Bus Stop drops you at the suspension bridge across the river from the temple.*

Dumbara Hills   The hills to the northeast were given the English name because of the distinc-
(Knuckles   tive clenched-hand profile seen from a distance. The altitude (with peaks
Range)   above 1,500 m) and the variation in the climate (annual rainfall range is 2,500-5,000 mm) allows a variety of forest types from Lowland Dry *patana* to Montane Wet Evergreen, with their associated trees, shrubs, plants and epiphytes to flourish.

These forests, in turn, harbour a number of wildlife species, eg leopard, sambhur, barking deer, mouse deer, wild boar, giant squirrel, purple-faced langur, toque macaque and loris, as well as the otherwise rarely seen otter. Over 120 bird species recorded here include many endemic ones including the yellow-fronted barbet, dusky-blue flycatcher, ceylon lorikeet, ceylon grackle, yellow-eared bulbul and layard's parakeet. In addition, endemic amphibians and reptiles include the *nannophrys* frog and pigmy tree-lizard, which are only found here.

The importance of the range as a watershed for the Mahaweli River and the Victoria reservoir has led the government to designate the area over 1,500 m as a Conservation area. Soil and water conservation have become critical issues because of the way the area has been exploited so far. Cardamom cultivation, the removal of timber and fuelwood, the use of cane in basket making and the production of treacle from *kitul* (*Caryota urens*) have all been sources of concern. For details of hiking in the Knuckles Range, contact Mr Sumane Bandara Ilangantilake (see page 206).

South of Kandy   The **Hindagala Temple**, along the Galaha road, has sixth-century rock inscriptions. The wall paintings date from different periods. ■ *Getting there: take Bus 655 from the Clock Tower bus stand.*

The Highlands

Kandy to Nuwara Eliya via Ramboda

Both the main routes from Kandy to Nuwara Eliya start by passing through Peradeniya to the former capital Gampola. The shorter 80 km route then takes the A5, crossing the Mahaweli Ganga and climbing southeast through some of the highest tea gardens in the island. The longer alternative, which runs close to the railway line for much of the way, is a full day's journey.

Tea estates It is worth visiting one while you are on the island. There are some near Ramboda, on the A5 (Nuwara Eliya Road, see page 199). It is possible to learn about the complete process of tea production and also buy excellent tea.

Route The shorter route on the A5 initially continues along the Mahaweli valley to **Gampola**, the former Sinhalese capital (mid-14th century), and now a pleasant town with most services. The Niyamgampaya which has some interesting stone carvings, is built on the original 14th-century temple which was mostly built of brick and wood and largely disappeared. Shortly after Gampola, the road crosses the river and starts the long climb of almost 1,000 m up to Nuwara Eliya passing through Pussellawa.

Pussellawa Pussellawa is a busy shopping centre and has a rest house where you can stop for a meal or a drink. Tea gardens begin just below Pussellawa. The craggy hill, Monaragala appears to the south. Legends tell that this is where King Dutthagamenu hid in a rock while escaping from his father, who had imprisoned him. Sleeping at **E** *Rest House* (CHC), in an attractive location, T08-78397, reservations T01-503497, F503504. Four rooms with bath in a colonial bungalow, rather dated but with pleasant though steep terrace garden at back with good views across the valley, seating under large permanent sun umbrellas covered with the exotic 'ladies slipper' vine. The road passes the Helbodda Oya (5 km) as the A5 continues to Ramboda.

Ramboda
Altitude : 1,000 m There is a fine 100-m waterfall with a twin stream on the Puna Ela, a tributary of the Mahaweli river, just off the road which can be seen from the Bazar. A tea estate recommended for a visit is the **Rang Budda** where the manager is particularly helpful and you will be made very welcome. You can also buy excellent 'BOP' (Broken Orange Pekoe) for Rs 250 per kg. Sleeping at **D** *Ramboda Falls*, 76 Rock Fall estate, T/F59582. Ten rooms with hot bath (US$17), restaurant, bar, pool.

Greeting, Degaldoruwa cave temple
Source: LPT Manjusri's Design Elements

Route After 54 km from Kandy the road climbs through a series of hairpins to the Weddamulla Estate with great views to the west over Kothmale Reservoir. The whole area is covered with pine trees and ferns. These slowly give way to another large tea estate.

Labookellie Tea Estate
Altitude: 1,570 m The estate follows the twisty road for miles along the hillside. Teams of women pluck the tea on fairly steep slopes, picking in all weathers – the

The Central Highlands (side margin)

women using plastic sacks as raincoats. The women labourers are all Tamils, descendants of the labourers who migrated from Tamil Nadu before independence. The women are keen to pose for photographs, and since they earn very little, tipping is customary.

The tea factory, an enormous corrugated iron building, welcomes visitors to drop in to the tea shop and sample a free cup of tea, and perhaps to buy a packet or two though there is no pressure to do so. The tour is quite informative – all stages of the process from picking, drying, oxidation and grading are shown if you go in the morning. ■ *Groups of visitors are taken on free guided tours of the factory, between 0900 and 1700 (you may need to wait in a queue on a busy day).*

Sleeping   Estate *bungalows* are available for hire at Rs 1,500 including a cook.

Transport   From Nuwara Eliya it is 15 km on the Kandy Road. Taxis Rs550-600.

Route   From the Labookellie Estate it is a short climb through more tea gardens to the narrow pass above Nuwara Eliya, and the road then drops down into the sheltered hollow in the hills now occupied by the town.

Nuwara Eliya

නුවර එළිය
Phone code: 052
Colour map 3, grid A5
Altitude: 1,990 m

Nuwara Eliya (pronounced Noo-ray-lee-ya), which sits in a little valley, is the highest town in Sri Lanka and a major hill resort. It offers a cool escape from the plains (the nights can be very cold) especially at long weekends and during school holidays. Some visitors are turned off by the town's lack of civic pride ('dirty and dangerous from disrepair') but despite its fading appeal, there are some pleasant reminders of its colonial past and some attractive walks. It is also a useful base for visiting Horton Plains and Adam's Peak.

Ins & outs   **Getting there** The train station is 6 km away at Nanu Oya, a short bus or taxi ride away (avoid the touts who will offer free transport provided you go to a hotel of their choice). Ask to be dropped near the Town Hall if you are planning to stay in the southern part of town where most of the hotels are clustered up the hillside opposite the racecourse. **Getting around** It is possilbe to get around town on foot but carry a torch at night to avoid holes in the pavement leading to the sewers.

The town & its origins   In 1846, when Samuel Baker first visited the semi-enclosed valley, surrounded by hills on the west and overlooked by Pidurutalagala, the island's highest peak (2,524 m, 8,281 ft), he singled it out as an ideal spot for a hill country retreat. Today, with its television aerials, the highest on the island, and modern hotels, golf course and country walks, his rural idyll is being brought increasingly into the modern world.

'The City of Light' was a favourite hill station of the British and it still retains some distinctive features. The main street is the usual concrete jungle of small shops with the pink post office being an obvious exception. One of the distinctive features of Baker's plans was the introduction of European vegetables and fruit. Flowers are extensively cultivated for export to Colombo and abroad. The road out of Nuwara Eliya towards Hakgala passes through intensively cultivated fields of vegetables and a short walk up any of the surrounding hillsides shows how far intensive cultivation methods have transformed Nuwara Eliya into one of Sri Lanka's most productive agricultural areas.

The key to Nuwara Eliya's prosperity lay in the railway connection from Colombo to the hills. The line was extended from Talawakele to Nanu Oya in

The refreshing cup

An ancient Chinese legend suggests that 'tay', tea, originated in India, although tea was known to have been grown in China around 2700 BC. It is a species of Camellia, Camellia thea. After 1833, when its monopoly on importing tea from China was abolished, The East India Company made attempts to grow tea in Assam using wild 'chai' plants found growing there and later introduced it in the Darjiling area and in the Nilgiri hills in the south. Some believe that plants were smuggled in from China. Certainly, Chinese experts had to be asked to advise on improving the method of processing the leaves in the early days while horticulturists at the Botanical Gardens in Calcutta worked on improving the varieties.

In Sri Lanka, the first tea bushes (possibly imported from Assam) were planted in 1849 by James Taylor on a cleared hill slope just southeast of Kandy. It was an attempt at experimenting with a crop which would replace the unfortunate diseased coffee. The experiment paid off and Sri Lanka today is one of the world's leading producers of tea (second only to India), exporting nearly 94% to countries across the world. The bushes now grow from sea-level to the highest slopes, though the lush 'low-grown' variety lacks flavour, colour and aroma which characterise bushes grown above 1,000m. The slow-growing bushes at greater heights produce the best flavour and aroma when handpicked carefully – just two leaves and bud.

The old 'orthodox' method of tea processing, produces the aromatic lighter coloured liquor of the Golden Flowery Orange Pekoe in its most superior grade. The fresh leaves are dried by fans on 'withering troughs' to reduce the moisture content and then rolled and pressed to express the juices which coat the leaves. These are then left to ferment in a controlled humid environment in order to produce the desired aroma. Finally the leaves are dried by passing them through a heated drying chamber and then graded – the unbroken being the best quality, down to the 'fannings' and 'dust'.

The more common 'crushing, tearing, curling' (CTC) method produces tea which gives a much darker liquor. It uses machinery which was invented in Assam in 1930. The process allows the withered leaves to be given a short light roll before engraved metal rollers distort the leaves in a fraction of a second. The whole process can take as little as 18 hours.

1885, and in those days, with a coach transfer up to Nuwara Eliya itself, the journey could be completed in under 9 hrs. A very steep narrow gauge line right into Nuwara Eliya was opened in 1910, but subsequently closed to passenger traffic in 1940 as buses began to provide effective competition.

Without the pretensions or political significance of the Raj hill stations in India, Nuwara Eliya nonetheless was an active centre of an English-style social life, with county style sports including a hunt, polo, cricket and tennis. It has retained all the paraphernalia of a British hill station, with its colonial houses, parks, an 18-hole golf course which runs through much of the centre of town, and trout streams (there are brown trout in the lake for anglers). The real clue to its past perhaps lies in its extensive private gardens: dahlias, snap-dragons, petunias and roses, all amongst well kept lawns. However, it is unfortunate that waste disposal has become a major problem– a mound of the town's rubbish in the middle of the racecourse greets visitors who arrive by rail from Nanu Oya and the lake is filthy.

There are attractive walks round the small town, which has lawns, parks, an **Sights** Anglican church and the nostalgic *Hill Club*. To the south of town is the racecourse with the Council Building unusually sited in the middle of the oval.

The Central Highlands

Lake Gregory (about 1 km from the town centre) has boats which can be hired from Chalet du Lake. **Galway's Land Bird Sanctuary** covers 60 ha sanctuary to the north of Lake Gregory. Victoria Park (Rs 6 entry) provides a pleasant escape from the congested New Bazar, but take care when walking along the outside of the park where the metal fence is in poor repair and has some sharp rusty spikes which can cause nasty cuts.

Pidurutalagala (Mount Pedro) is the island's highest peak (2,524 m, 8,281 ft) and is a two-hour climb up the track off Keena Road, north of town. In places still through dense forest, it is a steep but manageable climb when feasible. At present, visitors are not allowed to climb the peak for security of the island's first TV transmitter there.

Single Tree Hill (2,100 m, 6,890 ft) is an alternative. The path to it winds up from Haddon Hill Road, beyond *Haddon Hill Lodge* (southwest of town), towards the transmission tower, through cultivated terraces and woods. You then follow the ridge along towards the north, through Shantipura, a small village, eventually emerging close to the golf course. This walk gives excellent views across Nuwara Eliya and beyond, taking 3-4 hours.

Pedro Tea Estate, at Boralanda (3 km), which is open to visitors, is within easy walking distance from Nuwara Eliya. It is a very attractive walk or about a Rs 300-350 taxi ride. **The Tea Factory** at Kandapola (on B39 northeast of town, 30 minutes by taxi) which has been converted to an excellent hotel retains a small working unit and is well worth a visit. The original oil driven engine (now powered by electricity) is still in place and switched on occasionally.

Sleeping There are some hotels in the Raj style, well kept, with good restaurants and plenty of atmosphere and also a few good value 'budget' places. However, prices can rise by as much as 3 times during the Apr New Year rush while long weekends can see prices double even if demand is low. It always pays to bargain (and of course avoid the touts). Usually bathrooms have hot water and rooms have blankets provided.

Expensive A *St Andrews*, 10 St Andrews Drive, overlooking golf course, T22445, F23153, or Colombo T345700, F345729, standrew@eureka.lk 52 good rooms (US$70) in beautiful century old building retaining a more homely colonial atmosphere than its rivals, good restaurant with show kitchen, attractive and pleasant garden, tubs, English style country bar, good snooker room (and also fans of Sunderland Football Club!). Highly recommended. **A** *The Tea Factory*, Aitken Spence, at Kandapola, transport needed (see above), T23600, F070-522105 ashmres@lanka.com.lk 57 comfortable rooms (best on top floor) in excellent conversion of old British factory (retaining original features) amidst tea plantation with superb scenery, good restaurant (nightly Pasta Corner, a nice touch), golf, riding, gym. Highly recommended for location and originality. **A-B** *The Grand*, Grand Hotel Rd, T22881, F22265, (Colombo T343720, F434524) tangerinetours@eureka.lk 156 rooms, 2 restaurants (one ballroom sized catering for package tour buffets, dinner Rs 600), considerable colonial character in century old hotel, efficient but can lack personal touch.

Climate: Nuwara Eliya

B *Galway Forest Lodge*, 89 Upper Lake Drive, T23728, F22978, info@galway.lk 52 well-furnished, comfortable rooms in quiet location close to Galway Forest Reserve, public areas rather utilitarian, restaurant, bar, billiard room, popular with tour groups. **B** *Hill Club*, up path from *Grand Hotel*, T22653, F22664, 36 rooms, including 2 **A** suites in 'modernised' century old Coffee Planter's Club (1930s), comfortable rooms with fireplaces (hot water bottles in bed), tubs, formal restaurant (long sleeved shirts and tie for dinner, which can be borrowed!), 2 bars (women are now allowed in both as the Hill Club catches up with the 21st century), note the side entrance originally used by women who were banned from using the main entrance! Good public rooms, excellent snooker room, colonial atmosphere, full of character. Recommended. **B** *The Windsor*, 1 Kandy Rd, T22554, F22889. 50 comfortable rooms in the heart of town though quiet inside, tastefully refurbished, good restaurant though lacking ambience, modern hotel with attractive plant-filled inner garden. Recommended.

Mid-range **C** *Tree of Life Bungalow* Wedderburn Rd, T23685, F23127. 5 sparsely furnished rooms in offshoot of Tree of Life hotel in Kandy, primarily an ayurvedic health centre, nice building in quiet, attractive location, but prices are high for what you get **C** *Wedderburn Rest*, 23 Wedderburn Rd, T/F22395. 10 well furnished rooms in year old hotel already under new management (so renovated ahead of its time), hot bath with tubs, restaurant, worth a look. **C-D** *Alpen Tour Inn*, 4 Haddon Hill Rd, T23500, F34500. 20 rooms, completely renovated in 2000, tours (see below), friendly management, popular with backpackers. Rrecommended. **C-D** *Glendower*, 5 Grand Hotel Rd, overlooking the 2nd Tee of the golf course, T/F22749. 7 comfortable rooms (Rs 1300), plus 3 suites, stylishly decorated, attractive modern half-timbered bungalow-style hotel, pleasant lounge with good satellite TV, superb snooker table (Rs 120 per hr), excellent restaurant (big portions), friendly and efficient service, convenient for town. Recommended. **C-E** *Sun Hill*, 18 Unique View Rd, T22878, F23770. 20 good rooms (Rs 700-1500), upstairs with balcony, attached hot bath, TV, excellent Chinese food, laundry (non-residents may use this service if they ask nicely!), friendly and helpful management, jeep tours (Horton Plains Rs 1300), good value. Recommended.

D *Cey Bank Rest*, Badulla Road, opposite racecourse, T/F23053, (Colombo T447845). 20 musty rooms (Rs 1200) now rather shabby in this former British residence, in need if restoration. **D** *Chalet du Lake*, on Gregory lake, Badulla Rd, T34967. 10 rustic cottages in good location fronting onto the lake (Rs 1200 including breakfast), hot bath, electric blankets (extra Rs 100), boat shaped restauran, fishing (bring own equipment), boating (Rs 300 per hr), friendly. **D** *Collingwood*, Badulla Rd, T23550. 9 large rooms (Rs 800-950) in old planterís house with some old-world British character, some rooms with fire place, a few a little damp (inspect first), need a coat of paint, poor restaurant. **D** *Grosvenor*, 6 Haddon Hill Rd, T22307. 14 comfortable rooms (Rs 1000) in old colonial house, fireplaces or heaters, hot water, well furnished **D** *Oatlands*, 124 St Andrew's Drive, T22572. Charming old bungalow, and equally charming host, 2 rooms attached bath, 2 rooms shared bath, all with washbasins, plus 4 simple **E** rooms, dining room, lounge, peaceful location, homely atmosphere. Recommended.Also other similar guest houses up St Andrew's Drive.

Cheap **D-E** *Haddon Hill Lodge*, 29 Haddon Hill, T22345, (Colombo T/F595352) dholiday@sri.lanka.net 8 clean rooms (Rs 650-850), one with tub, excellent views from pleasant garden on the hill, good food, homely atmosphere. Recommended. T22708. 10 large but shabby rooms (Rs 500), restaurant. **E** *Ascot*, Badulla Rd, T22708. 10 large but shabby rooms (Rs 500), restaurant. **E** *Green Garden Inn*, 16 Unique View Road, T23609. 3 rooms (Rs 600-800) with hot bath, restaurant, family run guesthouse. T22708. 10 large but shabby rooms (Rs 500), restaurant. **E** *New Keena*, 122 Badulla Rd, T23821. 10 basic rooms (Rs 600), attached bath, rather musty, lots of stuffed animals around the place. **E** *Single Tree*, 1/8 Haddon Hill Rd, T23009 10 clean rooms (Rs 500-700), comfortably furnished, modern bathrooms, upstairs rooms with balcony, good food (dinner Rs 300), friendly, good value. Recommended. **E** *Wattles Inn*,

The Central Highlands

👉 A morning climb to Pidurutalagala

In 1911 Hermann Hesse wrote an evocative description of his climb to the top of Pidurutalagala at the end of a journey round India and Ceylon. He wrote 'To bid India a proper and dignified farewell in peace and quiet, on one of the last days before I left I climbed alone in the coolness of a rainy morning to the highest summit in Ceylon, Pidurutalagala.

The cool green mountain valley of Nuwara Eliya was silvery in the light morning rain, typically Anglo-Indian with its corrugated roofs and its extravagantly extensive tennis courts and golf links. The Singhalese were delousing themselves in front of their huts or sitting shivering, wrapped in woollen shawls, the landscape, resembling the Black Forest, lay lifeless and shrouded.

The path began to climb upward through a little ravine, the straggling roofs disappeared, a swift brook roared below me. Narrow and steep, the way led steadily upward for a good hour. The rain gradually stopped, the cool wind subsided, and now and again the sun came out for minutes at a time.

I had climbed the shoulder of the mountain, the path now led across flat country, springy moor, and several pretty mountain rills. Here the rhododendrons grow more luxuriantly than at home, three time a man's height, and there is a furry silvery plant with white blossoms, very reminiscent of the edelweiss; I found many of our familiar forest flowers but all were strangely enlarged and heightened and alpine in character.

I was approaching the last ascent of the mountain, the path suddenly began to climb again, soon I found myself surrounded once more by forest, a strange, dead, enchanted forest where trunks and branches, intertwined like serpents, stared blindly at me through long thick, whitish beards of moss; a damp, bitter smell of foliage and fog hung between.

Then the forest came to an end; I stepped, warm and somewhat breathless, out onto a gray heath, like some landscape in Ossian, and saw the bare summit capped by a small pyramid close before me. A high, cold wind was blowing against me, I pulled my coat tight and slowly climbed the last hundred paces.

What I saw there was the grandest and purest impression I took away from all Ceylon. The wind had just swept clean the whole long valley of Nuwara Eliya, I saw, deep and immense, the entire high mountain system of Ceylon piled up in mighty walls, and in its midst the beautiful, ancient and holy pyramid of Adam's Peak. Beside it at an infinite depth and distance lay the flat blue sea, in between a thousand mountains, broad valleys, narrow ravines, rivers and waterfalls, in countless folds, the whole mountainous island on which ancient legend places paradise.'

Police Station Rd, T22804. 10 dark but reasonable, wood panelled rooms (Rs 700), restaurant, bar, pleasant garden. **E-F** *Haddon Hill Inn*, Haddon Hill Rd, T23304. 10 basic but clean and comfortable rooms (Rs 450-750), hot water, reasonable value. **E-F** *Maggie's Cottage*, Haddon Hill Road, T23826. 5 rooms (Rs 400-600) in family guesthouse, food available. **F** *Carnation*, 1 Unique View Road, T34260. 5 clean rooms (Rs 350) with reliable hot shower in new family run guest house (but new to the business), cheapest in town (Sri Lankans pay more!), friendly, good value, meals on order, worth trying. **F** *Victoria Inn*, 15/2 Park Rd, T22321. 10 clean rooms (Rs 400-500), hot showers, restaurant, upstairs rooms lighter, good tours (ask for Santha, see below), friendly, good value. Recommended.

Eating *Milano*, central market, 'first Halal restaurant' here, upstairs a/c, tasty Chinese and Sri Lankan (about Rs 140), tempting *wattapalam* dessert, sales counter. **New Paris**, 10 New Bazar St. Good tasty snacks and short eats. **Star Bakery**, opposite *Food Lanka*, Old Bazar St, good cheap food, short eats. There are numerous cheap restaurants along Old and

Nuwara Eliya

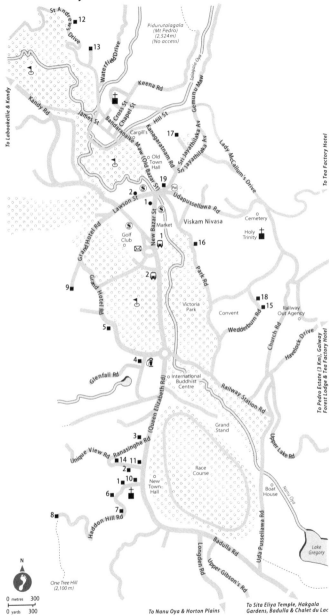

St Andrew's Drive

12

13

Waterfield Drive

Pidurutalagala
(Mt Pedro)
(2,524m)
(No access)

Keena Rd

To Labookellie & Kandy

Kandy Rd

James St

St Cross St

Chapel St

Bandaranaike Maw

Cargill's

Hill St

Kangaratnam Rd

Sri Jayathilaka Av

Sri Jayathilaka Av

Gemunu Maw

Talaipolai Oya

Lady McCallum's Drive

To Tea Factory Hotel

17

Old
Town
Hall

19

2 **1**

Lawson St

New Bazar Rd (Old Bazar St)

Udapussellawa Rd

Market

Viskam Nivasa

Cemetery

Holy
Trinity

Grand Hotel Rd

Golf
Club

1

2

16

Grand Hotel Rd

9

5

Park Rd

Victoria
Park

Convent

Wedderburn Rd

18

15

Railway
Out Agency

Church Rd

Havelock Drive

To Pedro Estate (3 km), Galway
Forest Lodge & Tea Factory Hotel

4

Glenfall Rd

International
Buddhist
Centre

(Queen Elizabeth Rd)

Railway Station Rd

Grand
Stand

Unique View Rd

Ranasinghe Rd

3

14 **11**

2

1 **10**

6

7

8

Haddon Hill Rd

New Town
Hall

Race
Course

Upper Lake Rd

Boat
House

Nanu Oya

Lake
Gregory

One Tree Hill
(2,100 m)

N

0 metres 300
0 yards 300

Badulla Rd

Longden Rd

Upper Gibson's Rd

Uda Pussellawa Rd

To Nanu Oya & Horton Plains

To Sita Eliya Temple, Hakgala
Gardens, Badulla & Chalet du Lac

The Central Highlands

Sleeping
1 Alpen
2 Carnation
3 Collingwood
4 Glendower
5 Grand
6 Grosvenor

7 Haddon Hill Inn
   & Single Tree
8 Haddon Hill Lodge
9 Hill Club
10 Maggies Inn
11 New Keena
12 Oatlands

13 St Andrews
14 Sun Hill
15 Tree of Life
16 Victoria Inn
17 Wattles Inn
18 Wedderburn Rest
19 Windsor

Eating
1 Milano
2 Lion Pub

Buses
1 CTB
2 Private

April in Nuwara

Around the April full moon, the town is invaded by the Colombo set. A banner across the road proudly announces 'Nuwara at 6,128 ft: Welcome to the salubrious climate of Nuwara Eliya: cultured drivers are welcomed with affection!'.

For about a week, prices become inflated (tripled) and it is virtually impossible to find accommodation. Stallholders, mostly selling food and drink, pay vast amounts of money to rent a pitch alongside the main road by Victoria Park. Most hotels run all night discos (the best is said to be at the Grand Hotel) and the crowds roam the streets for much of the night. During the day, horse races, hill climbs and other sporting events are held.

New Bazar Roads. *Hill Club* gets mixed reviews for its food, but it's a unique dining experience. Formal. *Grand Hotel*, usually offers quite good lunch time and dinner buffets (Rs 450). Good Chinese at *King Prawn* at *Glendower*. *Sun Hill's*, Chinese, is excellent.

Entertainment   **Bars** *Lion Pub*, Lawson St. Serves draught stout and lager (Rs 35 per mug) as well as bottled beer (Rs 55+). Inside is an English style pub whilst outside has a more European terrace feel. Snacks are also available, but check your bill carefully. Open 1100-2300, closed Poya Days.

Sports   **Golf** Beautiful and superbly maintained golf course. 5550 yds, par70. Rs 2300 including club hire etc. Rs 1750 for 6 holes if you are pushed for time. **Snooker** At the *Hill Club* (Rs 50 temporary membership, plus table fees), though those who play like Alex Higgins may like to note the '1 million rupees first tear' sign (presumably the 2nd one is free!). Also at *Glendower Hotel*. **Tennis** At the *Hill Club*, see above.

Tour operators   *Alpine Adventures*, Mr Mahindakumara, c/o *Alpen Tour Inn*, 4 Haddon Hill Rd, T072-226898. Established 16 years, jeep tours to Horton Plains (Rs 1500), camping trips, '12 waterfalls' tours, fishing, island tours, mountain bikes for hire (Rs 450-600 per day). Also night transport to Adam's Peak, pick up at 2300 and return or drop elsewhere (Rs 2500). friendly, honest deals (but unaccompanied women should ignore pointed personal questions asked by one of the drivers, Raja). Recommended. *Santha*, c/o Victoria Inn, 15/2 Park Road, T22321, is an excellent driver/guide, especially for the Hill Country although island tours also available. Safe, reliable and respectful. Highly recommended.

Transport   **Road Bus**: frequent buses to **Badulla** (via Hakgala) and to **Kandy** (4 hrs) from both bus stands. To **Colombo**: several a day to Colombo (6 hrs) including faster a/c Intercity buses (Rs 110). By **car** to Colombo, the most direct route is the A7 via Ginigathena and Avissawella. It is also possible to take the longer route via Ella, Bandarawela and Ratnapura, travelling round the southern flank of the Central Highlands. **Train** New arrivals are besieged by touts on the train and at the station and will offer free transport to the hotel of their choice. You will end up paying heavily for this service in commissions. Better to take the bus which often waits for the arrival of trains or take a taxi (if none at station walk a few hundred metres to the main road). Railway Out Agency in town sells tickets. To **Colombo**: *Uda Rakamenike*, 0935, 6 hrs. *Podi Menike Exp*, 1255, 7¼ hrs. *Mail*, 2140, 2305. To **Kandy** (via Hatton): 0600, Podi Menike Express 1255 (4 hrs 15 mins), 1730. To **Badulla** (via Haputale, Ella): 0255, 0510, 1000, 1300, 1540.

Directory   **Banks** *Bank of Ceylon*, near post office, accepts Visa. *Hatton National Bank*, just up from post office, accepts Mastercard. *Seylan Bank* which cashes TCs, and others are on Park Rd. **Communications** The post office is opposite the CTB bus station (Mon-Sat 0700-2000, Sun 0800-2000). *Salika Communications*, Old Bazar Rd, offers discount IDD calls (0730-2100). *TNT*

The Central Highlands

courier service, 36 Park Rd, T2697. **Medical services Chemists** *Cargills*, Kandy Rd. **Tourist offices** The local Hoteliers Association Information Centre. Close to the entrance to Victoria Park (in front of post office).

Around Nuwara Eliya

The **Horton Plains** can be visited on a day trip if you have a car, but involves an early start (breakfast at 0600) as the plains have a reputation for bad weather after midday (see below). A jeep costs around Rs 1,500. **Randenigala Reservoir** is good for bird-watching (and elephants in the early morning). It can easily be visited as a day trip, but is also a good camping spot. See page 266.

The Strict Natural Reserve (10 km), established in 1861, was once a Cinchona Plantation is now famous for its roses. The name *Hakgala* or 'Jaw Rock' comes from the story in the epic *Ramayana* where the Monkey god takes back a part of the mountainside in his jaw, when asked by Rama to seek out a special herb! There are monkeys here which are quite used to visitors. The different sections covering the hillside include a plant house, Japanese garden, wild orchid collection, old tea trails, arboretum, fruit garden, rock garden and oaks. ■ *0730-1800. Rs 150 (Sri Lankans Rs 15), students and children Rs 75.* **Hakgala Botanical Garden**

Sleeping and eating E *Humbugs*, 100 m beyond entrance to gardens, T22709, F23308 meenella@slt.lk 5 attractive rooms (Rs 600), beautiful location, carpeted, hot water, balconies, quiet. restaurant serves good snacks including strawberries and cream in season! Extensive views across the Uva basin, particularly attractive in the early morning mist.

Transport Several private and government buses from Nuwara Eliya, Rs 6.50.

A short distance before you reach the gardens you will pass the temple to Rama's wife which is thought to mark the spot where she was kept a prisoner by King Ravana. There are magnificent views. **Sita Eliya Temple**

Peaks and plateaus

The most scenically beautiful route from Kandy up into the hills runs through the great tea estates of the Hatton-Dikoya region to the popular holiday resort for Sri Lankans at Nuwara Eliya. As far as Hatton, it follows the upper reaches of the Mahaweli Ganga towards its source. This route is also followed by the train, which despite its snail-like pace offers a really relaxing alternative to the road journey.

From Kandy, the A5 goes south to Gampola where the B43 branches to the right for Nawalapitiya and the Ginigathena Pass (38 km) where it joins the A7 which comes up from Avissawella in the low country. There are magnificent views at the top, although they are often obscured by cloud, for the pass is in one of the wettest areas of Sri Lanka. From here on the road runs through tea country. **Ginigathena** is a small bazaar for the tea estates and their workers. **Routes**

The A7 winds up to **Watawala** (10 km) and nearby the **Carolina Falls**, spectacular in the wet season. The A7 follows the left bank of the Mahaweli Ganga up to Hatton (12 km), but this route can be quite slow. The alternative road from Nawalapitiya (B41) to Dimbula and A7 to Hatton is very poor and even slower, occasionally allowing only one Dikoya.

Hatton
Phone code: 0512

Hatton is one of the major centres of Sri Lanka's tea industry, and the base from which most pilgrims and tourists trek to the top of Adam's Peak but it lacks suitable places to stay or eat. The only reason to stay a night here would be before or after climbing Adam's Peak.

Sleeping At Dikoya **D** *Glencairn Bungalows*, 5 km south of Hatton on Maskeliya Rd, T2348, 9 rooms in two colonial estate bungalows among tea plantations with view of Adam's Peak, clean though dated, restaurant, bar. In Hatton **F** *Lanka Inn Tourist Rest*, 47/6 Dunbar Rd, 1 km from railway, T2647. 11 rooms, restaurant, bar. **D-F** *Hatton Rest House* is poor, 6 dirty rooms. Not recommended. **F** *Ajantha*, just across railway tracks (signed from A7), poor rooms. Not recommended.

Transport Road The car journey from Nuwara Eliya or Kandy takes at least 3 hrs as the surface is poor.

Adam's Peak ශ්‍රී පාදය

Colour map 3, grid B4
Altitude: 2,260m, 7,415ft

A steep footpath from Dalhousie leads to the peak sacred to three religious groups, which is one of the island's main centres of pilgrimage. The giant 'footprint' on the summit is believed to be an imprint left by either the Buddha hence Sri Pada or Siva (thus *Sivan Adipadham*) by Hindus, or Adam by Muslims. It is covered by a huge stone slab in which has been carved another print. A local Buddhist tradition promises any woman who succeeds in climbing by this route that she will be re-born in the next life as a man. The trek up, in the company of pilgrims, is particularly rewarding but it can be very crowded. You may notice the first-timers with white cloth on their heads.

Adam's Peak can be reached on a night trip from Nuwara Eliya or alternatively you can spend the night in Dalhousie and set off at around 0300. The more intrepid and fit could climb from this side and then walk down towards Ratnapura, a long but rewarding day. If returning to Dalhousie ask for breakfast at either the *Green House* or the *Yellow House*.

Ins & outs

Getting there Buses run the tortuously winding route from Hatton to Maskeliya (20 km, altitude 1,280 m) and on to the Dalhousie Estate. By car it takes about an hr, going through some of the most productive tea growing areas towards Norwood. Keep to the Maskeliya road up the pass before Norwood. The air is already strikingly fresh, and the higher road is lined with tropical ferns. The bus journey takes about 2 hrs to Dalhousie.

Dalhousie
There are tea shops in town & you can pick up some food for the climb though there are stalls along the way

This is where the climb starts. It takes about three hours to reach the top. The path is clearly marked throughout (lit up for pilgrims from January to April), beginning fairly easily but rapidly become steeper. Most people do the walk by moonlight, arriving in time to see the dawn when the conical peak, only 50 m square, forms an extraordinary shadow across the plains to the west. The climb is completely safe, even the steepest parts being protected, and steps and chains provided where necessary but avoid going alone. The route is ancient – **Marco Polo** commented on the chains provided for pilgrims in the 13th century. It is very cold on top of the peak until well after sunrise so it is essential to take warm clothing.

From **Ratnapura**, an alternative 11 km route, much steeper and more difficult, starts from the Carney Estate, and takes about seven hours. See page 167.

Sleeping **Dalhousie** **D** *Wathsala Inn*, 14 rooms with bath (hot water), good views. *There are only a few,*
E *Yellow House*, near the big mango tree, T051-23958. 5 comfortable rooms with *very basic, guesthouses*
attached hot bath (Rs 500), friendly, good food. Recommended. **F-G** *Green House*, *in Maskeliya*
near the first step, T051-23956. 11 rooms (Rs 150-400) with shared bath, hot water,
good food, very friendly. Recommended.

Routes

From Hatton the road crosses the railway line and winds up through the tea
estates of Dimbula to Talawakele (10 km). For much of the way it is above
2,000 m though it drops slightly between Dimbula and Talawakele. In
Talawakele, Sri Lanka's Tea Research Institute (sometimes open to visitors)
has played a major role in improving Sri Lanka's tea production. From
Talawakele to Nuwara Eliya the road runs through country in the rain shadow
of hills to the southwest and the northeast, the range halving the total rainfall. A
right turn after Talawakele in Lindula leads up a beautiful mountain road to
Agrapatana, but the A7 continues through Nanu Oya, and finally down into
Nuwara Eliya.

Nuwara Eliya to the Horton Plains

From the humid heat of Kandy itself, the freshness of the highlands comes as a
welcome relief, whether travelling by road or taking the slow winding railway
route via Ginigathena and Talawakele. The Horton Plains, Sri Lanka's highest
plateau, offers the chance to trek through an area rich in bird and animal life.

Route

The drive from Nuwara Eliya, much of it along poor road, takes about two
hours. Take the A5 out of town on the Badulla Road, past the racecourse
towards the Hakgala Gardens (10 km). This is the market garden area: carrots,
bean, brassicas and many other fresh vegetables are grown, much of it for
export to the Middle East. Take the road to **Ambewela** at the Warwick tea
estate sign. The road condition deteriorates sharply and it is very slow going.
Ambewela has the highest railway station in the country. You can see the occasional dairy herd here: the dairy marketed under the Highland Milk brand is
also based here. The road, climbing all the time, continues through Pattipola
and passes between Mount Totapola (2,357 m, 7,730 ft) and Mount
Kirigalpotta (2,396 m, 7,860 ft). Eventually the plains are reached with views of
the peaks all around. Keep an eye open for the pyramid shape of Adam's peak
in the west looking for all the world like the *Paramount Picture*'s logo.

Horton Plains National Park   හෝර්ටන් තැන්න

The island's highest and most isolated plateau forms a part of the Peak Wilder- *Colour map 3, grid B5*
ness Sanctuary. It is increasingly becoming popular with local day visitors since *Altitude: 2,130 m*
the area is now accessible by car though the drive is not for the faint hearted. *40 km from*
   If you wish to walk, it is best to get to **Ohiya** station, the nearest on public *Nuwara Eliya*
transport (see trains below), which has shops selling refreshments in the early
morning. You then follow the 8 km, fairly steep winding track to get to *Ander-*
son Lodge, and reaching *Farr Inn*, 3 km further across the plain, around
mid-day (about 3½ hours uphill, two hours downhill).

There is an alternative short-cut, though the trail can be hard to find. Head *If misty keep to the*
west along the railway line towards the first (Summit) tunnel, then turn up the *foopaths. A number of*
track to the left. It is quite a steep climb through the forest, followed by a walk *people go missing*
along hilly terrain towards *Farr Inn*. The short-cut takes 1½ to two hours, *each year*
depending upon how fit you are and how many times you get lost. From

The Central Highlands

Nuwara Eliya, it costs around Rs 1,200-1,500 per jeep. *Farr Inn*, just northwest of the park car park and 10 km from Pattipola railway station, T07-522042, now has the Information Centre. ■ *Best months to visit are Apr and Aug. The winter months, though dry, can be very cold. Entry Foreigners US$12 children under 12 and students with ISIC US$6, Sri Lankans Rs 20, at the Rangers' Hut just below the car park near Farr Inn which is open 0530-1600. Make sure you keep your tickets as they will be asked for at the park entrance about 100m away.*

Wear stout shoes. It is best to carry some food and drink though some are available (see below). It can get cold at night so come prepared.

The Horton Plains, which covers 3160 ha, was declared a national park in 1988. There is a mixture of montane temperate forest and wet *patana* grassland. The prominent canopy tree is *Keena* (*Callophylum*) with white flowers contrasting with the striking red rhododendrons lower down. In some ways this makes them quite like a Scottish moor. In other ways, the gently undulating grassland have an almost savannah-like feel with stunted forest on the hill tops. There is widespread concern in Sri Lanka about the condition of the forest which appears to be slowly dying. Blame seems to be attached to the many water irrigation schemes which are allegedly changing the climate.

The bleak and windswept area harbours many wild animals (though no longer the elephant or leopard). You should see plenty of sambhur (sambar) and some toque macaques, purple-faced leaf monkeys, bear monkeys and horned lizards. There is a rich variety of hill birds (including the Dusky blue flycatcher, Sri Lanka white-eyed arrenga, Yellow-eared bulbul) and a good range of butterflies. People have been disappointed by the lack of wildlife – particularly birds.

Horton Plains

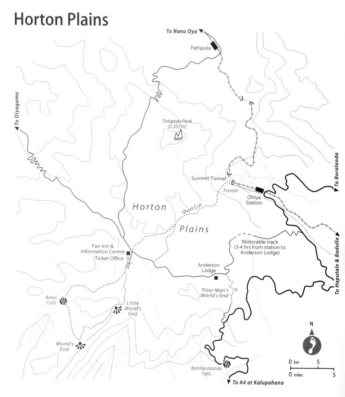

The best bet is to look out for bear monkey although these are not easy to see in the trees which are quite heavily leafed and also are covered in wispy ferns.

Jeep tracks allow you to visit the plains as a day excursion (see transport below) but it is worth spending a night there. Unfortunately, the plains are often covered in mist. Drivers often dissuade visitors from walking down to the falls but it can be exhilerating and rewarding. Just the last few metres at the bottom of the falls can be slippery.

World's End Most people will take the well-trodden path to World's End, a 4.5 km bridle path from *Farr Inn*. The walk takes about 40 minutes, and is quite pleasant, crossing a small stream with lots of croaking frogs before passing across the grassland and then descending a few hundred metres through the forest. You first come to Little (or Small) World's End, a mere 260 m cliff, overlooking a ravine (more a wide valley) with a tiny village 700 m below. You can look along the sheer cliff face to the big green rock which marks (Big) World's End about 1 km away which has a spectacular precipice with a 1,050m drop. This is best visited early in the morning.

On a clear day, you can apparently see the coast, but more realistically, it is the blue-green lake of the Samanala Wewa reservoir project. Once at Big World's End, take the small path up the hill. After only a few yards, there is a split in the rock which gives an excellent view of the valley below. A track to the right leads to *Baker Falls*.

If you object to paying US$12 to view World's End an alternative is to visit (free) what is now nicknamed *Poor Man's World's End*, reached by heading east along the track from *Anderson Lodge*.

Sleeping & eating **Mid-range** C *Anderson Lodge*, 3 km before *Farr Inn* Reservations, Wildlife Conservation Dept, T694241, sleeps 6 (US$24). Some travellers have been offered mattresses in *Rangers Huts* for Rs 250-400 (depending upon negotiating skills). They are very basic and you'll need your own sleeping bag and provisions. **Camping** Fees are US$5. Reservations, Wildlife Conservation Dept, T694241. Near the river close to *Farr Inn*. Recommended. If you camp inside the park, you'll have to pay for 2 days' admission. *Canteen*, near the entry gate does rotis for breakfast, tea and simple snacks at other times.

Transport **Road** Access by 4WD from Nuwara Eliya is through Hakgala and Pattipola (north) winding around Totapola Peak (2,357m. 7,730 ft) or via Agrapathna and Diyagama Estate (west). The best route is from Haputale or Welimada via Boralanda and Ohiya (about 2 hrs). It is another 11 km (¾ hr) to *Farr Inn* and the Park entrance. A jeep tour from Nuwara Eliya costs around Rs 1,200-1,500 per jeep. **Train** Walkers should travel to **Ohiya** station (on the Colombo-Badulla line). **Haputale** is the best base for visiting the Horton Plains on a day trip (train/walk). *Udarata Menike*, dep Ella, 0652, 1¾ hrs; dep Bandarawela, 0724, 1¼ hrs; dep Haputale, 0755, 40 mins. You can also do a day-trip and travel back to Colombo via Nanu Oya by the *Night Mail*, depart Ohiya, 2047, arriving Colombo 0540 (3rd class, Rs 40).

Route **Horton Plains to Bandarawela** From the plains a track winds down quite steeply through the Udeirva/Ohiya estate through wooded slopes where you might see bear monkeys. At **Borlanda**, the track joins the B805. A turn to the south allows approach to Bandarawela along the A4 through Haputale. Alternatively, the road to the north to Welimada joins the B810 which passes through pleasant countryside. You can sometimes see resin being collected from pine trees. There is a large school (St Thomas College) in a very attractive location at Gurutwala, just outside Welimada.

The Central Highlands

Uva Province

7

Uva Province

216 Badulla, Ella, Bandarawela
and Haputale

217 Badulla

219 Ella

223 Bandarawela

225 Haputale

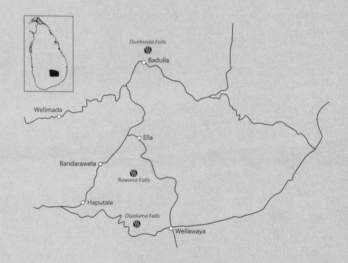

Uva Province, which forms the eastern part of the hill region, occupies a basin on the southeastern edge of the Central Highlands. It has sometimes been held to be the original home of the Kandyan civilization. The river valleys draining into the Mahaweli Ganga would have provided a natural route from the north and east Dry Zone for Sinhalese migrating up into the hills. The relatively bare landscape, with trees restricted to the rivers' edges, suggest the difficulty of cultivation, and Uva has witnessed ancient irrigation systems, including tunnels through hills.

Uva is associated by popular legend with the Buddha who is believed locally to have made two visits to the area. Buddhist pilgrims are drawn to festivals at Badulla and Mahiyangana while Kataragama to the south attracts thousands to the Hindu temple. In the east it has high waterfalls, spectacular 'gaps' in its precipitous ridges and some interesting wildlife. It is also famous for spices and Ayurvedic herbs which grow in the southwest of the province.

Badulla, Ella, Bandarawella and Haputale

A very pleasant circular route from Nuwara Eliya gives excellent views of the Southeast Highlands. It makes a rewarding day tour, although there are also some comfortable and very attractive places to stay if you don't want to rush. From Badulla it is possible to go east across the Dry Zone to Arugam Bay or Batticaloa, and from Ella two roads go south, one to Hambantota, and the other to Tissamaharama, Kataragama and Ruhuna-Yala National Park. These are thus within comfortable reach of a two or three days' excursion from Kandy or Nuwara Eliya after entering the Uva Province.

Route   From Nuwara Eliya, the A5 goes southeast across Wilson's Plains then east to Badulla. Just past the **Hakgala Gardens**, 10 km (see page 207), is a superb view southeast across the hills of Bandarawela and over the baked plains of the east coastlands. The road passes through Keppetipola as it drops rapidly through to Welimada on the Uma Oya River.

Central Highlands

Keppetipola Junction is southeast of Hakgala. The *Summer Place Restaurant* and *Travel Information Centre*, Forest Park, Haputale Road (3 km from Keppetipola Junction), T072-666608, is a useful place to stop for tea or typical homemade Sri Lankan food, good information about local walks, waterfalls plus simple accommodation. Part of the *Woodlands Network* (see Bandarawela).

Keppetipola

The caves north of Welimada are a pot-holer's delight. They are reached by a path from **Paranagama**, which is 10 km along the road north from Welimada. The maze of damp caves hold a large lake.

Istripura caves

From Welimada, a right turn on to the B51 leads to Bandarawela (see page 223), past terraced fields of paddy and across occasional streams. At **Hali-Ela**, the A5 goes to Badulla. This area is already in the rainshadow of the hills to the west, sheltered from the southwest monsoon and much drier than Nuwara Eliya. Rubber plantations cover some of the slopes before Badulla.

Route

Badulla බදුල්ල

The capital of Uva Province is surrounded by paddy fields along the banks of the river Gallanda Oya. It has an old fort against a backcloth of mountains and a small lake.

Colour map 3, grid A6
Phone code: 055
Altitude: 675m
45 km

Badulla is one of the oldest towns in Sri Lanka though there are no traces of the earlier settlement. The Portuguese once occupied it but set the town on fire before leaving.

At one time Badulla was an extremely active social centre for planters, with a racecourse, golf, tennis and cricket clubs, long since fallen into disuse. The park was once a small botanical garden. Notice the little stone grey Methodist church on the left. Major Rogers, an elephant hunter who died from a lightning strike is believed to have been buried in the cemetery. The clock tower celebrates the opening of a garment making factory by the late President Premadasa.

The **Muthiyangana Vihare** attributed to Devanampiya Tissa, the first Buddhist convert on the island, is thought to have a 2,000-year old ancient core. The Hindu **Kataragama Devale** was built in the 18th-century highland style in thanksgiving for King Vimaladharma's victory over the Portuguese. Note the plaster-on-wood statues and wooden pillars of the 'throne room'. There is also a revered Bo tree.

The town & its history

Uva Province

The island's original people

Uva today is also one of the few remaining homes for the **Veddas**, living in isolated pockets (in particular in the Nilgala and Dambane jungles), normally out of sight, though occasionally these aboriginal peoples can still be seen. Once hunter-gatherers, the matrilineal Veddas worshipped ancestral spirits, but most have lost their old hunting grounds and have been forced to find alternative methods of survival by adopting local Sinhalese ways, and with that many of their tribal beliefs and customs. Those in the Eastern Province, around Gal Oya, have become assimilated into the local Tamil community. The government's resettlement schemes have been strongly resisted by some, who have remained on the forest edge carrying out subsistence farming by the chena ('slash and burn') method, having abandoned their customary bow and arrow. Under increasing pressure to allow some Vedda groups to return to their old settlements, the government has set aside 'Reserved' areas for them and given them hunting rights.

Excursions

The road north out of town, lined stalls selling limes, rapidly descends before reaching the island's highest perennial waterfalls, 6 km away

Dunhinda Falls There is a small car park on a bend in the road about 2 km from the falls, north of town, which takes about 25 minutes on foot (you may have to pay for the car to be guarded). Buses also stop nearby (about 10 minutes walk away). The path to the falls is across the road from the car park. It is quite rough and steep in places, so take care and wear suitable shoes. The valley at this point is also quite narrow which can make it very hot. The humidity is also very high near the falls, which is noticeable if you have come down from the highlands. Numerous stalls sell cold drinks, herbs etc at the start of the walk and along it. As the falls are very popular with Sri Lankans, foreign travellers are not hassled too much.

Shortly after the beginning of the path you can see the lower falls (more of a cascade really), quite a long way down in the valley below. These are only about 15 m in height and much broader than the main falls. A ledge about 10 m from the top makes for a spectacular 'spurt' when the river is running high. At the main falls, the river plunges in two stages about 60 m through a 'V' in the rock which causes a misty haze (*dunhind*) which gives the falls its name. There are granite cliffs on either side and a large pool at the bottom. It is quite spectacular and well worth the effort. Here there is also a large, kidney shaped observation platform where concrete tables and benches have been built to give a pleasant picnic spot. It can, however, be very busy at times.

Bogoda This very peaceful place with a small monastery and rock temple is well off the beaten track, off the road to the north of Hali Ella, 13 km from Badulla. The attractive 16th-century wooden **bridge** across the Gallanda Oya which is built without nails (the original claimed to date from the 1st century). The only surviving one of its kind, it has an unusual tiled roof in the Kandyan style supported on carved pillars. The railings are painted with natural lacquer. The Raja Maha Vihare **rock temple** nearby has old murals and pre-Christian inscriptions.

Parks

Botanical Gardens A pleasant four-acre park away from the bustle of Badulla town. ■ *Rs 5.*

Sleeping

Dunhinda Rd is now Mahiyangana Rd

Cheap D-E *Dunhinda Falls Inn*, 35/11-1/1 Bandaranaike Mawatha, 1.5 km from town centre, T/F23028. 12 large rooms of varying standards (Rs 500 - Rs 1250), restaurant, bar, exchange, car/cycle hire, visits to tea gardens. **E** *Green Woods Holiday Inn*, 301 Bandarawala Rd, 2.5 km before town, T31358. 8 comfortable rooms (Rs 750) with hot bath in quiet location (although can get busy with local people), good restaurant, views would be good if you could open the childproof windows! **E** *Peace Haven Inn*, 18 Old Bede's Rd, opposite General Hospital, T22523. 8 rooms (Rs 550) quiet but a bit musty, restaurant. **E** *Rest House* (UDA), 800 m from railway station, T22299. 17 rooms (Rs 500) around central courtyard, simple meals, good value. **E** *Tourist Resort*, 97 Dunhinda Rd (ask at *Badulla New Tourist Inn*, opposite). 5 rooms (Rs 550) with hot water, quiet, good value. **E-G** *Riverside Holiday Inn*, 27 Lower King St, T22090, F23910. 16 rooms (Rs 300-750), upstairs better, restaurant, bar, 8 mins walk from railway station but no river here! **F** *Badulla New Tourist Inn*, 22 Mahiyangana Rd (towards Dunhinda Falls), T/F23423. 30 rooms (Rs 350 - Rs 500), variable so check first, restaurant, may see birds nesting in light fittings! Not bad value for the price.

Paying guests Local families take in guests and offer good home cooking. Some recommended: 5/2 Malla Gastenne, T2105, not too far from Railway and Bus Stand, and 28 Passara Rd, which is well kept with a garden.

Festivals **May-Jun:** *Wesak* and *Poson* full moon festivals with drummers, dancers and elephants. **Sep:** *Esala Perehera* at Muthiyangana Vihare when Veddas participate.

Tour operator *Namunkula Mountaineering*, T94762 (ask for Indika) for exploring the Namunkula (nine mountains) Range between Ella, Passara and Badulla.

Transport **Local Car hire:** from *Sugimal Fast Foods*, opposite Muthiyangana Vihare and Railway station or *Dunhinda Falls Inn*, T23028. **Long distance Road Bus:** frequent buses to Bandarawela, Colombo (several Intercity Express, Rs 110), Nuwara Eliya (2 hrs), and to Galle. Occasional buses to the east coast. **Train** To **Colombo** via Demodara (look out for the Loop!), Ella, Bandarawela, Haputale, Ohiya: *Udarata Menike*, 0555, 9¾ hrs. *Podi Menike Exp*, 0910, 11¼ hrs. *Mail*, 1745, 12 hrs. **Kandy:** *Podi Menike Exp*, 0910, 8 hrs.

Route From Badulla, the A5 goes through **Hali-Ela**, where the A16 turns south to **Demodara**. This is also tea country and there is a tea factory here. The road then reaches the beautiful gap town of Ella.

From the Bandarawela direction, travel northeast on the A16 and after 7 km turn right for Ella on the A23. The A16 continues to Badulla (20 km). Alternatively, it is a pleasant walk along the railway line. There are only a few trains and the route is well used by local people.

Ella ඇල්ල

Ella occupies a scenic vantage point. A traveller writes, 'The view through the Ella gap was probably the best in the entire island. It was quite early and the isolated hills on the plain popped up like islands in the mist.' Most visitors go to the rest house garden to get the best view.

Phone code: 057
Colour map 3, grid A6
13 km

Excursions **Rawana Ella Cave** The cave in the massive Ella Rock can be seen from the rest house, to the right of the Ella Gap. It is associated with the *Ramayana* story, in which the demon king of Lanka, Ravana, imprisoned Rama's wife Sita. The cave which is of particular interest to palaeontologists has a small entrance which scarcely lets light in and then a long drop to the floor. It is filled with water from an underground stream which has hindered exploration but excavations here have unearthed prehistoric remains of human skeletons and tools dating from 8000 to 2500 BC. The skeletons are believed to belong to *Homo Sapiens Balangodensis*. According to Deraniyagala, the finds show evidence of

Uva Province

a culture superior to that of the present-day Veddas. ■ *Getting there: Walk downhill beyond the Ella Rest House for 10 mins up to the road bridge then branch up the track to the right which climbs (good views) to a rock monastery where a young monk will happily show you the temple and hope for a few rupees' donation. There is often someone who will be pleased to accompany you on a very steep and difficult path up to the cave. He may not ask for payment but Rs 50 seems a fair reward for his trouble.*

Rawana Ella Falls Return to the main road near the bridge and continue downhill for 1½ hours (6.5 km) to the falls. The road is not too busy so it is a pleasant walk with views over fire-affected forest/savanna, of the small Rawana Ella Wildlife Sanctuary, and onwards to the plains to the southeast. The 9-m high Rawana Ella (or Bambaragama) Falls, are to the right (west) of the road just beyond a bridge. They are quite dramatic and you can climb over the rocks up the falls quite a way. *Bambaragama Restaurant* sells rather expensive snacks and drinks at the bottom. At the falls themselves there is an intriguing small business in coloured stones gathered from the foot of the falls. A few

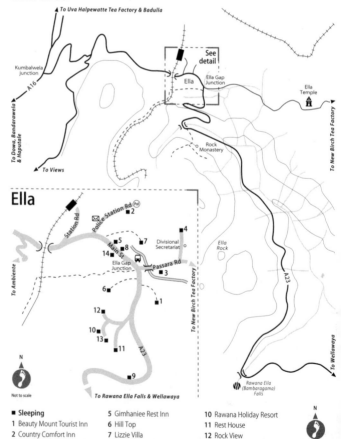

Ella area

Ella

Not to scale

■ **Sleeping**
1 Beauty Mount Tourist Inn
2 Country Comfort Inn
3 Ella Gap Tourist Inn
4 Forest Paradise

5 Gimhaniee Rest Inn
6 Hill Top
7 Lizzie Villa
8 Mount View Inn
9 Ravana Heights

10 Rawana Holiday Resort
11 Rest House
12 Rock View
13 Tea Garden Holiday Inn
14 Udayanga

0 metres 500
0 yards 500

enterprising vendors sell them to passing tourists. A handful of small stones should not cost much more than Rs 30 but a common method of transaction is to swap the stones for a foreign coin or coins. The stone seller then waits for the next tourist, hoping to exchange the foreign coins with a native of the relevant country at the prevailing exchange rate! ■ *Getting there: The falls are south of Ella on the A23 so you can get there by bus (towards Wellawaya). There is a small pocket of local opinion that disputes the name of the falls on the Wellawaya Road, claiming that it is in fact Bambaragama Falls, with the real Rawana Ella Falls being on the Ella Rock close to the railway line. However, it is widely accepted and agreed by a Tourist Board sign that the falls on the main road are the real ones.*

Sleeping

There is an undercurrent of animosity between the different guesthouse owners, and each may have a bad story to tell about one of the others. So many rumours fly around town that it's probably best not to believe any of them!

Mid-range C *Ravana Heights*, opposite 27 km post, Wellawaya Road, T31182. 3 classy rooms in new intimate guest house just outside town, classical music, personal attention, reasonable food. Recommended though a bit pricey. **C** *Rest House* (CHC), overlooking Ella Gap, 1 km south from railway station, T01-503497, F01-533504. 14 large rooms ($27) with hot water, completely refurbished in 2000, some new rooms but not all have good views, what it lacks in efficiency it makes up by the good views from the terrace verandah and garden, restaurant, popular in wedding season, overpriced. **D** *Ella Gap Tourist Inn*, near Ella Gap Junction, T22628. 7 clean rooms, good restaurant, friendly, one of the longest running guest houses in Ella backed up by a consistently favourable visitor book, a bit pricey but recommended. **D** *Ambiente*, Kitalella Road, 2 km up into tea plantations, T055-31666, F055-31667 kanta@telenett.net 5 very clean spacious rooms, 4 more planned, incredtble views, high above the town, laid-back young person's atmosphere, friendly, free pick up from station, day tours arranged, good food, friendly staff. Highly recommended.

Cheap D-E *Tea Garden Holiday Inn*, on top of the hill above the Rest House, T22915. 8 good, clean rooms (Rs 650-850), hot bath, good views of the gap, food available, starting price may depend on how wealthy you look, but otherwise all right. **E** *Country Comfort Inn*, Police Station Rd, T23132. 8 clean, well furnished rooms (Rs 750), plus 12 new in 2000, hot bath, good restaurant, modern hotel, reasonable but 'adds the highest service charge in Sri Lanka at 15%!' **E** *Rawana Holiday Resort*, T072-664094. 4 clean rooms (Rs 500), hot bath, nice terrace, good breakfast. **E** *Rock View Guest House*, T22661. 4 large rooms (Rs 600), warm bath, friendly. **E-F** *Gimhaniee Rest Inn* Main St, T22127. 5 large, clean rooms (Rs 400 cold bath, Rs 500 hot bath), restaurant, good value. **E-F** *Hill Top Guest House*. off Main St, T30080. 8 good, clean rooms (Rs 350-700), better upstairs with excellent views, good food, useful returnable walking maps, not a bad choice. **F-G** *Lizzie Villa Guest House*, signposted path off Main St, T23243. 7 clean rooms (Rs 250-350 cold bath, Rs 500 hot bath) in quiet location in attractive spice garden, very quiet, friendly, one of Ella's first guesthouses, well run. Recommended. **G** *Forest Paradise Guest Home*, Passara Rd, T23507. 5 clean rooms (Rs 250 shared bath, Rs 350 attached hot bath), nets, friendly, quiet location, JP Wimalasooriya (T072-658823, ask for J.P.). Here is a good local guide. Recommended.

Eating

Ella Gap Tourist Inn. Unimpressive surroundings, expensive but tasty food, smallish servings but can be topped up. *Rest House*. Limited menu, reasonable food, excellent setting and views.

Shopping

Shops on the main street near the rest house are overpriced. walk up the street and pay half the price for water and provisions.

● ●

🖝 Trains from Ella

To	1st Class	2nd Class	3rd Class	Departure time	Journey
Badulla	Rs 71	Rs 12	Rs 5	0528, 0755, 1446, 1508, 1809	1 hr
Colombo	Rs 318 (Obs)*	Rs 154	Rs 56	0652	8¾ hrs
Colombo (via Kandy)	Rs_318 (Obs)*	Rs_154	Rs 56	1007	10½ hrs
Colombo		Rs 154 (berth)	Rs 65 (sleeperette)	1844, 2013	11 hrs
Haputale	Rs 74	Rs 14	Rs 6	Colombo trains	1 hr
Hatton (for Adam's Peak)		Rs 55	Rs 20	Colombo trains	5 hrs
Kandy			Rs 34	1007 (direct), 1651, 1307 (change at Gampola)	6¼ hrs
Nanu Oya (for Nuwara Eliya)	Rs 115	Rs 37	Rs 14	Colombo trains	3½ hrs
Ohiya (for Horton Plains)		Rs 55	Rs 20	Colombo trains	2 hrs

* Reserve `Observation Car' (well in advance); Trains run daily unless otherwise specified

● ●

Tour operators *Travel Information Service*, Main Street. Advises on walks and treks in the area and has souvenirs for sale. Part of the Woodlands Network (see Bandarawela).

Transport Persistent hotel touts besiege those arriving by train or changing buses at Wellawaya. Ignore them and go to the hotel of your choice, preferably with an advance reservation. **Bus** For the south coast resorts, you have to usually change buses at **Wellawaya**. Several early morning buses go to **Okkampitiya** (for Maligawila, see page 199). There are buses to **Bandarawela** (change for **Haputale** - by car the journey takes 45 mins). For **Badulla** you may have to go to Kumbalawela Junction, 3 km north on the Haputale-Badulla road.

Route From Ella, the A23 runs due south to Wellawaya past the Rawana Ella Falls. The road is scenic but of poor quality. Local people sell *Kitul* palm syrup (jaggery) in bottles which is excellent, especially when poured over thick buffalo milk yoghurt sold in clay pots along the south coast.

Wellawaya
Phone code: 055

Wellawaya is a major transport junction with many buses coming from the Hill Country terminating here. The A4 here is the main road connecting the southwest and southeast coasts and the Central Highlands, while the A2 goes to Hambantota on the south coast. You may well see wild elephants from the bus around this area.

Excursions There is a very attractive road to the site of Buduruvagala, south of town, past a dammed lake, which is good for bird watching. The turn off for the rock carvings of the Mahayana Buddhist period is to the right (west) about 5 km along the Tissa road (ask in town for directions). The 3 km road, now accessible by car, leads to the massive rock to your left. It is a short walk away to the sanctuary. Of the seven rock-cut figures in high relief, the 16-m high Buddha in the centre (painted white, and the tallest standing figure in Sri Lanka) is flanked by possibly *Avalokitesvara* (to his right) who in turn has his consort *Tara* by his side, and an attendant. To the Buddha's left, the figure is believed to be *Maitreya* who too is accompanied. The *vajra* (thunderbolt) held by one, symbolizes *Vajrayana* the Tibetan Tantric Buddhist sect. Some find these sculptures a little disappointing. The site itself is very peaceful and often deserted although unfortunately a pair of ugly concrete posts carrying lights have been erected in front of the carvings making photography of all seven images difficult. ■ *Rs 100.*

Sleeping E *New Rest House*, Ella Rd, T74899. 5 reasonable, clean rooms (Rs 500), nets, restaurant, knowledgeable manager used to work for the Archeological department, reasonable overnight halt. **E** *Saranga Holiday Inn*, off Ella Road, 1 km north of town, T74904. 9 rooms (Rs 550) including 1 a/c (Rs 750), quiet, restaurant, a bit grubby but all right for a night, some good comments in the visitors book.

Transport Since this is the major transport junction for buses travelling between the Hill Country and the southeast, it attracts touts from the hill towns who may tell you that there are no more buses for the hills that day. They will offer to find you a taxi instead plus get a commission on their choice of your room! It is best to ask the resident peanut or vadai sellers at the bus stand whether there are buses to your destination since they have nothing to gain from giving false information. **Road** An important **bus** terminus, you change here for **Matara** (via Tissamaharama, Hambantota and Tangalla). For buses east to **Pottuvil** (for Arugam Bay), you may have to change at **Monaragala**. For the hills, there are connections for **Badulla** (via Haputale and Ella).

Route The B53 from Buttala (which is east of Wellawaya on the A4) goes due south to Yala National Park and Kataragama (also in Uva, see page 161). It is not shown on all maps, but is a well-made and relatively quick route.

From **Ella** the A23 west joins the A16 for Bandarawela. The railway line hugs the contours on the opposite hillside. The valley widens and paddy fields become more apparent before the road climbs steadily to Bandarawela.

Bandarawela බණ්ඩාරවෙල

The town is pleasantly small, with a reputation for a very good climate and is a good base for walks and for exploring the Uva basin. The rain shadow of the Central Highlands gives the place a drier southwest monsoon than the hills immediately to the west. The area is most renowned for tea and growing fruit. The straggling town however has little of interest to see. Its long wide main road slopes quite steeply down with lots of shops lining each side. It has a bustling market-town feel and is good for picking up supplies.

Colour map 3, grid A5
Phone code: 057
Altitude: 1,230 m

Excursions **Bindunuwewa**, some 3 km east, has an Ayurvedic herbal treatment centre which travellers visit for exercise routines and herbal massages. See *Himalie* and *Queens* under sleeping. The *Suwamadhu Ayurvedic Centre*, T/F22504 is a popular herbal treatment centre for those wishing to be pampered. A short programme taking a couple of hours involves a body massage, herbal steam bath and a sauna bath. ■ *0800-2000. Rs 1500. Longer courses also available. Getting there: There are buses from town or tuk-tuk (about Rs 60).*

Dowa Rock Temple Taking the Badulla road out of town, shortly after the Sewamadhu Ayurvedic Centre, 4 km, you pass the Dowa temple squeezed between the road and the stream in the bottom of the valley. The cliff face has an incomplete carving of a large standing Buddha, while inside the cave there are murals and first century BC inscriptions. It is a pleasant walk if you follow the attractive valley down.

The **Bogoda Bridge** and **Dunhinda Falls** are nearer Badulla (see page 218).

Sleeping **Expensive B** *Bandarawela Hotel* (Aitken Spence), 14 Welimada Rd, on a hill overlooking main street near Cargill's supermarket at top end of town, T22501, F22834, (Colombo T304604, F433755) ashmres@lanka.ccom.lk 36 rather cramped rooms, including 1 deluxe and 1 suite with attached hot tubs in old tea planters club (1893), retaining period furniture, rooms built around central courtyard (look for tortoises), good gardens, passable restaurant, popular with groups, atmospheric colonial air.

Mid-range C *Orient*, 10 Dharmapala Mawatha, 500 m from railway station, T22377, F22407 orient@eureka.lk 50 comfortable rooms, half of them deluxe with hot tub, attractive rooms, restaurant, billiard room, fitness centre, beer garden, more facilities in the pipeline. **D** *Ventnor Guest House*, 23 Welimada Rd, T22511. 4 large, carpeted rooms (Rs 1000), well furnished, hot tub, restaurant, a bit pricey.

There are several others along Welimada Rd, as well as Tea Estate Bungalows out-of-town (worth looking out for if you have your own transport)

Cheap E *Himalie Guest House*, off Badulla Rd, Bindunuwewa, 3 km east (8 km from Ella), T22362. 7 large, furnished rooms (Rs 500-650), attached hot bath, quiet, attractive bungalow in a tea estate, excellent views, restaurant, good value. **E** *Rest House*, Rest House Road, just beyond Orient Hotel, T22299. 9 large, simple rooms (Rs 750) in pleasant location, nets, restaurant. **E** *Sandella Holiday Inn*, 50/5 Welimada Rd, T22593. 9 variable rooms (Rs 750) close to sports ground, inspect first. **F** *Mount View Guest House*, 35/2 Welimada Rd, T31480. 10 basic rooms (Rs 450) in Christian run place, meals available. **F-G** *Chinese Union*, 8 Mt Pleasant Rd, T22502. 5 rather dark rooms (Rs 250-450), attached hot bath.

Bandarawela

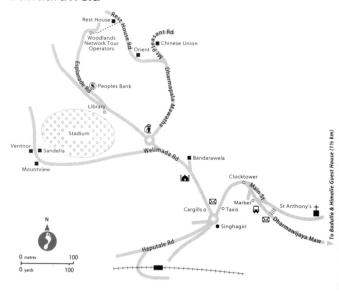

Woodlands Network, 30/6 Esplanade Road, T/F22735 haas@personal.is.lk **Tour operators**
A co-operative women's group which provides advice and information on alternative
tourism in Uva Province. Ideas for walks, treks, information about home stays plus
food culture (recipe books for sale) and fair trade tea and spices. *Woodlands Hostel*,
Rs 350 per double room, meals Rs 50-150, knowledgeable guides Rs 500 per day for a
group of 5. Recommended for those who wish to explore the culture and landscape
of Uva in more depth. Open 0800-1800 weekdays.

Road Bus: Frequent services to Haputale, Badulla, Ella and Wellawaya. Direct bus to **Transport**
Nuwara Eliya takes just over an hr. There is also an hrly intercity bus to Matara via
Wellawaya, 6 hrs, Rs 100. **Train** To **Colombo**: *Udarata Menike*, 0720, 8 hrs. *Podi Menike
Exp* (via Kandy), 1015, 9¾ hrs (6¼ hrs); Mail, 1920, 10 hrs.

Banks *Peoples Bank* changes up to US$200 only. *Seylan Bank* is very efficient. **Directory**

From Bandarawela the road crosses the railway line and climbs before **Route**
descending into Haputale.

Haputale   හපුතලේ

Haputale, from its ridge-top position, has magnificent views at dawn over the   *Colour map 3, grid B5*
Low Country to the east. On a clear day you can see the salt pans at   *Phone code: 057*
Hambantota to the south, and the horizon is the sea. To the north, in magnifi-   *Altitude: 1,400 m*
cent contrast, are the hills. It is a good area for walking with the town providing
a base with a choice of cheap guest houses. Most of the owners can advise on
good walks in the surroundings.

A small town with a busy shopping street, Haputale has quite a lively
Sunday morning market. To see a curious sight, walk down the main street
from the Station Road crossing, and watch the apparent disappearance of the
road over the cliff!

The **Dambetenne Road** from the town towards the Kelburne Tea Estate must   **Walks**
rate as one of the most spectacular in the whole island with breathtaking views
across several tea plantations down to the plains. It is possible to walk the
length of the road, which is not busy, or alternatively take the regular bus from
town to the Dambetenne (Lipton) Tea Factory (10 km). Along the way you will
pass a number of tea factories including the Greenfield Bio Plantations (see
Sleeping below), one of the few organic tea producers in the country, where
you can ask for a tour demonstrating the various processes involved (phone
first, T/F 68102). A tour of the more traditional Dambetenne Tea Factory will
cost Rs 100 per head (before 1100). At the end of the road it is a short uphill
walk following a clear trail up to Lipton's Seat from where, on a clear day, it is
possible to see up to 60% of the island. This walk is highly recommended.

Adisham monastery, 3 km, on the hill to the west, bordering the Tangamalai
bird sanctuary which is good for spotting jungle and highland species, is certainly worth walking up to. A quirky stone-built anachronism dating from the
1930s, it houses a Benedictine novitiate which has interesting period features.
Modelled on Leeds Castle (Kent, England), it has attractive rose gardens and
orchards. A few spartan rooms (cold water) in an annexe are open to visitors
(reserve ahead by post or T8030).■ *Open on Sat and Sun, Rs 60.*

Uva Province

Tea estates If you wish to visit a tea factory just stop and ask. The manager is usually happy to show you around. The estates sometimes have accommodation for visitors (see *Kelburne* below).

Excursion **Horton Plains** If using public transport, Haputale is probably a better base than Nuwara Eliya for visiting Horton Plains National Park and World's End since you can make a round trip by train/on foot, in one day. However, by the time you arrive the plains will be covered in cloud, which normally sweep up the valleys by midday. For details see page 209.

Sleeping From the railway station, take a 'short cut' for Temple Rd and nearby guest houses by walking west along tracks, up steps to Temple Rd, then following signposts down steps on the other side. Most places have hot water available.

Mid-range **C** *Kelburne Mountain View Cottages*, Dambetenne Road, 2 km south-east of railway station, T68029, (Colombo T573382, F573253). 3 wonderfully furnished cottages (Rs 3500-4000), sleeping 4 or 6, two with fireplaces, at least 2 bathrooms in each, meals on order, spectacular views, unique hand-painted open-air visitors book! Superb place to unwind. Highly recommended. **D** *Greenfield Cabanas*, Dambetenne Road, T/F68102 durk@sri.lanka.net 5 new eco-cabanas being built above the tea factory using local materials, with plans for a restaurant, herbal clinic, information centre, meditation centre, superb location.

Cheap **E** *New Rest House*, 100 Bandarawela Rd (1 km), T68099. 6 simple but comfortable rooms (Rs 550) with hot bath although a bit musty, could do with a lick of paint, nets, good food in quiet location. **E** *Queen's Rest Inn*, 68 Badulla Road, T68268. 6 rooms (Rs 550), hot water, restaurant but nothing special. **E-F** *Amarasinghe Guest House*, Thambapilla Ave (see 'short cut' above, or take Bus 47), T68175. 7 good, clean rooms (Rs 600) in family house including some new on first floor with excellent views

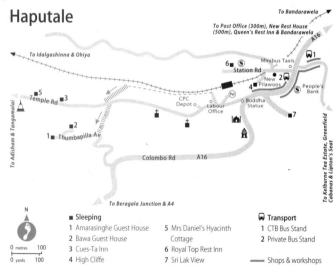

Haputale

To Bandarawela
To Post Office (300m), New Rest House (500m), Queen's Rest Inn & Bandarawela
A16
To Idalgashinna & Ohiya
Minibus Taxis
6 (S)
Station Rd
New Pilawoos
People's Bank
Temple Rd 3
5
CPC Depot
Labour Office
Buddha Statue
7
To Adisham & Tangamalai
2
1 Thumbapilla Av
Colombo Rd A16
To Beragala Junction & A4
To Kelburne Tea Estate, Greenfield Cabanas & Lipton's Seat

N
0 metres 100
0 yards 100

■ **Sleeping**
1 Amarasinghe Guest House
2 Bawa Guest House
3 Cues-Ta Inn
4 High Cliffe
5 Mrs Daniel's Hyacinth Cottage
6 Royal Top Rest Inn
7 Sri Lak View

Transport
1 CTB Bus Stand
2 Private Bus Stand
— Shops & workshops

Trains from Haputale

To	1st Class	2nd Class	3rd Class	Journey	Departure time
Badulla	Rs 95	Rs 26	Rs 10	0535, 1509, 1713	1¾-2 hrs
Bandarawella				Badulla trains	25 mins
Colombo	Rs 295	Rs 141	Rs 50	0755, 1052, 1959	7½ to 10 hrs
Ella				Badulla trains	1 hr
Kandy	Rs 187	Rs 80	Rs 30	1052, 1959 (change)	6 hrs
Nanu Oya for Nuwara Eliya		Rs 25	Rs 9	Colombo trains	2 hrs-2½ hrs
Ohiya for Horton Plains		Rs 10	Rs 4	Colombo trains	40 mins

Trains run daily unless otherwise specified

which will be the best in town, plus 2 rooms in separate block (Rs 350), good food, friendly and knowledgeable owner. Recommended. **F** *Cues-Ta Inn*, Temple Rd, T68110. 5 clean rooms (Rs 450) although a bit run down, hot water, excellent views, restaurant. **F** *Sri Lak View Holiday Inn*, 48 Sherwood Rd, 200 m from bus stand, T68125. 8 clean rooms in new guest house (Rs 400-500), hot water (although a small problem with dampness), restaurant, excellent views, free pick up from station. **F** *Royal Top Rest Inn*, 22 Station Rd, T68178. 5 clean but musty rooms (Rs 400 shared bath, Rs 500 attached), good restaurant, close to buses and trains, inspect first. **G** *Bawa Guest House*, 32 Thambapilla Mawatha, above *Amarasinghe Guest House*, T68260. 6 simple rooms (Rs 250 shared bath, Rs 350 attached), in family guest house, friendly owners 'urging you to eat more and more!', recommended. **G** *Mrs Daniel's Hyacinth Cottage*, Temple (Welimada) Rd, T68283. 2 basic rooms (Rs 200) and a small dorm (Rs 150) in Haputale's original guest house, now sadly becoming very run down ('even my driver wouldn't stay here!'), however a friendly welcome and a Scrabble challenge partly compensates for the poor state of the rooms.

Eating Home cooking at most of the guesthouses is hard to beat. No real restaurant here but you can buy rotties and snacks in food stalls, and good groceries along the road between the rail and bus stations. *The Bakery* at the bus station does plenty of hot milk tea.

Transport **Road** **Bus** There are separate CTB and Private bus stands with several early morning buses for **Colombo** (6 hrs), and some to **Nuwara Eliya**, but you may have to change at **Welimada**. To get to the south coast usually means changing buses. There may be an early morning express bus to **Matara** (via **Hambantota** and **Tangalla**), though you usually have to change at **Wellaway**. The more scenic route via Balangoda is awkward. bus reaches Pelmadulla at 1030, leaves for Matara early next morning. **Train** See table for times and destinations.

Directory **Banks** *Bank of Ceylon*, and *People's Bank* Station Rd, changes currency and TCs.

Route From Haputale the A16 goes west to Beragala (10 km) where it joins the A4. This has some of the most rugged scenery in Sri Lanka. Black rocks tower above the road as it goes towards Belihuloya (see page 172). Much of the route is very windy, not steep but with many blind bends. The A4 continues

Uva Province

west to Ratnapura or east to Koslande, past the Diyaluma waterfall to Wellawaya (see above).

Diyaluma Falls If you want to get to the waterfall without having to walk, the easiest way is to take this diversion off the A4 near Wellawaya. The minor road to the falls which winds through rubber plantations, turns off just before the sign for the *New Resthouse* in Haputale. The 170-m Diyaluma which drop in two stages over a huge convex outcrop, are not as spectacular as the Dunhinda falls mainly because the stream is much smaller. It is quite peaceful here and although there are no official picnic areas, there are several large rocks to sit on. Beware of the monkeys though! You can buy drinks at a store nearby.

Route From Wellawaya you can either take the A23 north to Ella and Nuwara Eliya, or the A2 south to Hambantota, or the A4/B53 to Ruhunu-Yala and Kataragama. If you wish to return to Nuwara Eliya from Haputale, the B48 goes directly through Boralanda and Nawela with fruit orchards, and Welimada, where it rejoins the A5 to Nuwara Eliya.

Uva

Ancient cities - Cultural Triangle

8

Ancient cities – Cultural Triangle

232 Sites north of Kandy
233 Nalanda and Dambulla

238 Anuradhapura and Mihintale

238 Anuradhapura
239 Sights
245 Essentials
247 Mihintale

251 Sigiriya
255 Essentials

257 Pollonaruwa
259 Sights
263 Essentials
265 Mahiyangana

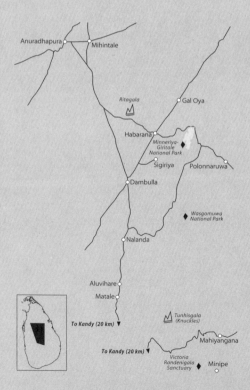

At the three corners of the "Cultural Triangle" are the ancient capitals of Anuradhapura (5th century BC – 10th century AD) and Polonnaruwa (10th – 12th centuries AD) and Kandy (16th – 19th centuries AD). These ancient cities represent the two early phases of cultural development in Sri Lanka. Anuradhapura was the capital over 2,500 years ago, and the north was the major centre of political power and of the first Buddhist sites for a thousand years. Polonnaruwa represented the last major centre of northern power before the Dry Zone economy fell into catastrophic decline and the Sinhalese pushed south into the Wet Zone.

The cultural wealth of the region is indicated by the presence of five of the island's World Heritage sites, containing treasures ranging from the exquisite paintings high of Sigiriya's rock face to the recumbent monolithic Buddha in Polonnaruwa.

Ancient cities - Cultural Triangle

Sites north of Kandy

The most famous cultural and archaeological sites in Sri Lanka can easily be visited in a short tour from Kandy. The development of a new road network accompanying the huge irrigation and colonization plans of the Mahaweli Ganga scheme in the Dry Zone to the northeast of the highlands, has opened up the possibility of making a circular tour. The route described follows the one most commonly used: Kandy to **Dambulla** – **Sigiriya** – **Polonnaruwa** – **Anuradhapura** – **Mihintale** (then often on to Colombo). Note that from Polonnaruwa there is an alternative way back to Kandy (via Mahiyangana), but this means a separate excursion to Anuradhapura.

Kandy to Dambulla   A very attractive road, the A9, runs north from Kandy through Matale (24 km), to Nalanda and Dambulla. Unfortunately, the road is in a very poor state of repair up to Matale, after which there is a miraculous transformation into a 'carpet road' for the rest of the Cultural Triangle areas.

Matale
Phone code: 066

The small, but bustling town surrounded by hills has some interesting short walks as well as some longer treks into the Knuckles Range (see under Kandy). The British built a fort here at the beginning of the 19th century (of which only a gate remains) while the branch railway line opened in 1880. There are a number of banks in town. There are also a large number of **spice gardens** which line the road out of Matale towards Dambulla, and plantations of coffee, cocoa and rubber. Some so-called spice gardens which are open to visitors have very few plants and are primarily there to sell commercially grown spices and ayurvedic herbal products.

Sleeping   Mid-range   D *Clover Grange*, 95 King Street, T31144, F30406. 7 comfortable rooms (Rs 1200), good restaurant, friendly and knowledgeable owner can advise on walking and trekking in the area. Recommended. **E** *Rest House*, Park Road, T22299, F32911 thilanka@ids.lk 13 rooms (Rs 750), 1 a/c (Rs 1,200), now run by the owners of *Thilanka Hotel* in Kandy.

Transport   Train   Several slow trains run between Kandy (Plat 1) and Matale, daily except Sun.

Directory   Banks   There is a *Bank of Ceylon* in town.

Aluwihare
8 km N of Matale

Well worth a visit

Aluwihare has the renovated ruins of ancient shrines carved out of huge boulders. The spot is very quiet and a welcome change from Dambulla nearby, for those jaded by the tourist route.

In the first and second century BC, the site was associated with King Vattagamani Abhaya (103-77 BC). The *Mahavansa* (Buddhist chronicle of the island) was inscribed here in Pali. The original manuscript, inscribed on palm leaves prepared by 500 monks, was destroyed in the mid-19th century, and replacements are still being inscribed today. With the expectation of a contribution to the temple (for which you are given a receipt) you are shown the technique of writing on palmyra palm.

Four of the 10 caves have ancient inscriptions. The curious 'Chamber of Horrors' has unusual frescoes vividly illustrating punishments doled out to sinners by eager demons, including spearing of the body and pouring of boiling oil into the mouth. The sculptures in another cave show torture on a 'rack' for the wrongdoer and the distress of having one's brains exposed by the skull

Palm leaf manuscripts

The palmyra palm strips were prepared for manuscripts by drying, boiling and drying again and then flattened and coated with shell. A stylus was used for inscribing; held stationary while the leaf was moved to produce the lettering or illustration (the rounded shape of some South Asian scripts was a result of this technology). The inscribed grooves would then be rubbed with soot or powdered charcoal while colour was added with a brush. The leaves would then be stacked and sometimes strung together and sometimes 'bound' between decorative wooden 'covers'.

being cut open. The impressive painted reclining Buddhas include one about 10 m long. The stupa on top of the rock just beyond the cave temples gives fine views of the Dry Zone plains and pine covered mountains.

Sleeping E-F *Aluwihare Kitchens By The Road*, 833 Dambulla Rd, about 300 m south of entrance to Aluwihare temple, T22343. 3 simple colourful rooms with shared or attached bath (Rs 400- 550) attached to restaurant, good value.

Eating *Aluwihare Kitchens*, The Walauwe, 33 Aluwihare, up hill *from Kitchens By The Road*, T22404. For parties of 6 or more, the promise of 'the biggest rice and curry in Sri Lanka' (25 separate curries). Superb location next to the home of Ena de Silva with stunning views of the surrounding countryside. Booking essential. *Aluwihare Kitchens By The Road*, 833 Dambulla Rd, Aluwihare, T22343. Co-operative restaurant offering breakfasts, lunches and dinners customised for the western palate (if you like your food spicy you may be disappointed). Also jams, chutneys, pickles and sweets for sale. Recommended.

Shopping *The Walauwe*, 33 Alu Vihare, T22404. For those with a serious interest in tapestries, batiks, furniture, brassware and a genuine desire to see the work in this community based enterprise. Much of the work is used by architects. Phone in advance.

Transport Buses between Matale and Dambulla stop on the main road. The caves are to the west of the road.

Nalanda and Dambulla

These two small but ancient sites are considered part of the 'triangle'. The older of the two, the richly painted cave temple at Dambulla, about 2,000 years old, and now a World Heritage site (designated in 1991), is no longer included in the Cultural Triangle ticket however. Closer to Kandy is the small Buddhist temple of Nalanda, sharing some features in common with Hindu temples of southern India with the earliest parts dating from the 7th century AD. A little distance off the main road north are other sites such as the massive rock cut Buddha at Aukana and the nearby monastery of Sasseruwa.

Nalanda has a small *gedige* (Buddha image-house) built with stone slabs, originally dating from the 7th-10th centuries. The reconstructed temple stands on the raised *bund* of a reservoir. Some tantric carvings have been found in the structure which combines Hindu and Buddhist (both Mahayana and Theravada) features. It is the only extant Sri Lankan *gedige* built in the architectural style of the seventh-century Pallava shore temples at Mamallapuram near Madras in India. The place is very atmospheric and has few visitors, so is particularly recommended. ■ *Entrance to the gedige is covered by the Cultural*

Nalanda
නාලන්ද
49 km N of Kandy

Ancient cities – Cultural Triangle

Triangle Ticket. Otherwise US$5. The staff here tend to be more friendly than at other sites and also speak some English.

Sleeping A mediocre **F** *Rest House*, T46199. 5 basic, poorly maintained rooms (Rs 350-450) with attached bath.

Transport Many **buses** between Dambulla and Kandy stop near the turn off for the gedige opposite the rest house. From here there is a 1 km gravel track to the site east of the road.

Route The A9 continues 19 km to Dambulla in an area known for its mangoes, where there are famous rock caves and temples only 15 km from the magnificent and dramatic site of Sigiriya.

Dambulla ⟨𝕰𝒸𝒸

Colour map 2, grid B4
Phone code: 066

Dambulla is sited on a gigantic granite outcrop which towers more than 160 m above the surrounding land. The rock is more than 1.5 km around its base and the summit is at 550 m. The caves were the refuge of King Valagambahu (Vattagamani Abhaya) when he was in exile for 14 years. When he returned to the throne at Anuradhapura in the first century BC, he had a magnificent rock temple built at Dambulla. The site has been repaired and repainted several times in the 11th, 12th and 18th centuries. The temple authorities are currently in the process of constructing the largest Buddha in the world.

The caves have a mixture of religious and secular painting and sculpture. There are several reclining Buddhas, including the 15-m long sculpture of the dying Buddha in Cave 1. The frescoes on the walls and ceilings date from the 15th-18th centuries. The ceiling frescoes show scenes from the Buddha's life and Sinhalese history. Cave 2 is the largest and most impressive, containing over 150 statues, illustrating the Mahayana influences on Buddhism at the time through introducing Hindu deities such as Vishnu and Ganesh. A large white Buddha statue (similar to the ones in Kandy and Mihintale) is planned for Dambulla.

There is little evidence of monks who are housed in monasteries in the valley below where there is a monks' school. Some monasteries and sacred sites receive large donations from Buddhists overseas (particularly Japan) and so are not dependant on government sponsorship. Gifts have provided the monks here with a four-wheel drive and other comforts not available to others of similar calling.

Approach
There are panoramic views from the terrace of the surrounding jungle & lakes, & of Sigiriya, 19 km away

From the car park, it can be a hot and tiring climb. It is quite steep first, almost 100 m across the bare granite and then there are about 200 steps in a series of 18 terraces some longer and steeper than others. It is not too difficult to get to the top but try to avoid the heat in the middle of the day (it is best visited in the early morning). The caves are about half way up the hill and now form part of a temple complex.

The Caves There are five overhung cliff caves. Monastic buildings have been built in front, complete with cloisters, and these in turn overlook a courtyard which is used for ceremonial purposes and has a wonderful view over the valley floor below.

Cave 1 (Devaraja-Viharaya) Contains the huge lying *Parinirvana* Buddha which is 14 m long and is carved out of solid rock. The frescoes behind the Arahat Ananda (a disciple) are said to be the oldest in the site. 'Devaraja' refers to the Hindu god Vishnu. The deity may have been installed here in the Kandyan period though some believe it is older than the Buddha images. There is a Vishnu temple attached.

Cave II (Maharaja-Viharaya) This cave is about 24 sq m and 7-m high and was named after the two kings whose images are here. To the left as you enter is a wooden painted statue of Vattagamini Abhaya (Valagambahu) who founded the temple here. The principal Buddha statue facing the entrance is in the *Abhaya mudra*, under a makara torana or 'dragon arch'. The cave has about 1,500 paintings of the Buddha – almost as though the monks had tried to wallpaper the cave. The paintings of his life (near the corner to the right) are also interesting you can see his parents holding him as a baby, various pictures of him meditating (counted in weeks, eg cobra hood indicates the sixth week): some have him surrounded by demons, others with cobras and another shows him being offered food by merchants. The other historical scenes are also interesting with the battle between Dutthagamenu and Elara particularly graphic the decisive moment when the defeated falls to the ground, head first from an elephant. Here, in the right hand corner, you can see the holy pot which is never empty. Drips are collected into a bucket which sits in a wooden fenced rectangle and is used for sacred rituals by the monks.

You will notice that some paintings clearly show other older ones underneath

Cave III (Maha Alut Viharaya) This cave is about 30 sq m and 18-m high. It was rebuilt in the 18th century and has about 60 images (some under 'dragon arches') and more paintings of thousands of the seated Buddha on the ceiling. This cave was a former storeroom and the frescoes are in the Kandyan style.

Cave IV (Pascima Viharaya or 'western' cave) The smallest cave and the westernmost. It had the fifth cave constructed later to its west and contains about 10 images. Unfortunately the stupa here was damaged by thieves who came in search of Queen Somawathie's jewels. One image in particular, at the back of the cave, needed restoration. Unfortunately it is now painted in a very strong yellow which jars with the rest of the cave.

Cave V (Devana Alut Viharaya) The newest, it was once used as a store-room. The images here are built of brick and plaster and in addition to the Buddha figures, also includes the Hindu deities, Vishnu, Kataragama and Bandara (a local god).

Some of the other subsidiary caves which were occupied by monks contain ancient inscriptions in Brahmi.

■ *0600-1100. 1400-1900. Ticket, Rs 200 (no student concession) from the office at the bottom of the hill. Go prepared with the correct amount: change for large denomination notes is sometimes not available and you may be told 'no change, no ticket'. Bags, shoes and hats are not allowed into the complex but they can all be left with the 'shoe keepers' who will also 'hire out' a lungi (sarong) to anyone wearing shorts. Get this from the same person otherwise you will be tipping repeatedly. Alternatively, wear trousers or a longish skirt. Carry a torch. It is diffi-cult to dodge the touts and beggars who line the steps leading to the caves and the guides as they stand in the temple doorway. You can feel rather pressurized to pay various people providing services (guide, shoe keeper, sarong provider) and also make a donation to the temple.*

Ancient cities - Cultural Triangle

Photography is allowed of the exterior of the complex but is strictly prohibited inside the temples (postcards are available). It appears that the ban was imposed after a foreign magazine used the site as a location for offensive photos.

Further reading *Golden rock temple of Dambulla* by A Seneviratna, Sri Lanka Central Cultural Fund, 1983. A good booklet in English and German is on sale, Rs 250.

Excursions **Aukana**, west of the large Kala Wewa Tank, is best visited early in the morning. There is a remarkable, undamaged 12 m high free-standing statue of the *Abhayamudra* Buddha carved out of a single rock. It has been ascribed to King Dhatusena (459-477) who was responsible for the building of several tanks including the one here. However, JC Harle dates it to the eighth or ninth century by the stylized quality of the face. Sadly, an ugly brick-built shelter in the style of an early image house, now protects the statue. ■ *Entry Permit, available at the entrance, Rs 20. Photography is not allowed. Getting there: Just before Kekirawa, turn left (west) and continue for 10 km on the minor road that skirts the north of the tank (or take the B64 at Kekirawa and turn left at Ihalagama), and then south along the causeway on the west side of the tank past Kala Wewa. At Aukana village (4 km), a minor road to the right (west) leads to the statue (3 km). You can also get to Kala Wewa by train and walk. only a few trains stop at Aukana station. Alternatively, get a direct bus from Dambulla or from Kekirawa (20 km north of Dambulla) on the A9. Finding Aukana can be difficult as signposts are lacking.*

Sasseruwa, about 13 km west of Aukana, has an ancient monastery site with over 100 cave cells, remains of stupas, moonstones and inscriptions, dating back to the 2nd century BC. Here too, there is a similar standing Buddha framed by the dark rock, but not quite as impressive in workmanship. It was possibly carved at the same time as the Aukana, although some believe it to be a later copy. Its location, halfway up a rocky hillside, requires climbing nearly 300 steps. ■ *Getting there: The minor road from Aukana continues to the Sasseruwa via Negampaha. The surface is poor.*

Sleeping **Expensive AL-A** *Kandalama* (Aitken Spence), head along Kandalama Rd for 4.5 km, take right fork, follow road, then

Dambulla

To Anuradhapura & Mihintale

To Sigiriya

Mirisgoni Junction

Mirisgoni Oya

Tammana Ela

Clocktower Colombo Junction

Matala Rd

To Kandalama Hotel (10 km) & Culture Club (9 km)

To Kurunegala & Colombo

Missaka Rd

Dambulla Rock

Viharaya (Site entrance)

To JC Village (1 km), Matale & Kandy

0 metres 500
0 yards 500

N

■ **Sleeping**
1 Chamara Tourist Inn
2 Dambulla Rest House
3 Freddy's Holiday Inn
4 Gimanala Transit Hotel
5 Katapathpaura
6 Laxapana
7 Sena Tourist Inn
8 Sunray Inn

● **Eating**
1 Apayuna Bar & Restaurant
2 Visaka Food Centre

cinder track for 8 km, T84100, F84109 (Colombo T304604, F433755) kandala@slt.lk 162 plush a/c rooms in uniquely designed hotel by Geoffrey Bawa, excellent baths (glass picture windows with illusion of taking a shower among the tree tops!), resort style complex with restaurants (excellent European cuisine) and full facilities, 3 pools including one of the most spectacularly sited swimming pools in the world î with crystal clear water (filtration system based on ancient Sri Lankan technology), billed as offering 'the aura of ancient hermit caves', but obviously much more luxurious, whole site is camouflaged within the jungle so nature is never far away. Highly recommended. **A** *Culture Club Resort*, follow Kandalama Rd for 4.5 km, take left fork, then follow lake around for 4.6 km, T31822, F31932, (Colombo T683378, F685555) cdchm@eureka.lk 92 very attractive, comfortable split-level a/c chalets in sister hotel to Le Kandyan, this time with a village theme, many local touches (village drum beat beckons you to breakfast, wooden flute and songs serenade at sundown from tree houses), good pool in large gardens, restaurant, ayurvedic health centre, very attractive setting on edge of lake, bullock cart trips (a welcome change from the ubiquitous elephant rides!), very relaxing. Highly recommended.

Mid-range C *Gimanhala Transit*, 754 Anuradhapura Rd, 1 km north of Colombo Junction, T84864, F84817. 8 clean a/c rooms, good restaurant overlooking lovely large and very clean pool, pleasant grounds, 2 deer (now behind bars for eating too many of the guests breakfasts!), friendly horse, bar, best of the town hotels, good value. Highly recommended. **D** *Dambulla Rest House*, Matale/Kandy Rd, T84799. 4 dark rooms, breakfast included, reasonable restaurant, poorly maintained despite staff of 15. **D** *Pelvehera Village*, Bullagala Junction, off A6, 5 km northeast of Dambulla. 4 bungalows, spotless bath, hot water, excellent food. Highly recommended. **D** *Sunray Inn*, 156 Kandy Rd,T84769. 10 clean rooms (Rs 800), restaurant.

Cheap E *Chamara Tourist Inn*, 121 Matale/Kandy Rd, T84088, 5 cheap, simple rooms (Rs 750), attached bath, overpriced. **E-F** *Laxapana Inn*, Matale/Kandy Rd, 500 m south of site entrance, T/F84803. 5 clean rooms (Rs 450-550), although they can get hot, good food in open-air restaurant, friendly. **E-F** *Sena Tourist Inn*, Matale/Kandy, Rd T84421. 6 rooms (Rs 350-550) of varying sizes, all with attached bath although some with squat toilet, food available, friendly. **F** *Freddy's Holiday Inn*, 62 Missaka Rd, opposite Police Station, T84780. Clean, basic rooms (Rs 400), friendly elderly owners, not bad value. **F** *Sparrows*, 44th mile post, 6 rooms along pleasant verandah, fan, attached bath (squat toilet), good food, good value, friendly.

Eating

Rockside Restaurant, Matale/Kandy Rd. *Visaka Food Centre*, Anuradhapura Rd.

Transport

Road Bus: most long distance buses stop at Colombo Junction, about 2.5 km north of the cave site. local buses run to the site entrance, as do Kandy buses. Regular services from Colombo (takes 4 hrs), Anuradhapura, Kandy and Polonnaruwa (about 2½ hrs each) and frequent to/from Sigiriya (30 mins).

Directory

Banks *Bank of Ceylon*, Kandy-Jaffna Rd (A9). **Useful addresses** Petrol Station: Kandy-Jaffna Rd (A9). **Police**: Missaka Rd.

To Anuradhapura & Mihintale

From Dambulla the road to Anuradhapura is reasonably quiet and has a good surface. It passes through Kekirawa near the large Kalawewa tank where you can see the magnificent Buddha colossus at **Aukana** (see above). The road crosses the flat plain, interspersed by occasional boulders of granite breaking the surface, with rice fields appearing from time to time as pockets of bright green in the widespread forest.

Routes From Dambulla, the **A9** northwest to Anuradhapura (65 km) forks left at Mirisgoni Junction and enters the town on the A13. Alternatively, the right fork (**A6**) eventually goes to Trincomalee. From the junction, 7 km along the A6 (at Inamalawa), a road heads northeast towards Sigiriya (15 km, see page 251). From there it is possible to go to Habarana (14 km) or Minneriya (37 km) and on to Polonnaruwa in another 45 km (see page 257).

Anuradhapura and Mihintale

Buddhism found its first real home in Sri Lanka at Anuradhapura and Mihintale, and they thus contain some of Sri Lankan Buddhism's most sacred sites. The Ambasthala Dagoba in Mihintale, where King Tissa received the Emperor Asoka's son Mahinda and converted to Buddhism, and the Sri Maha Bodhi tree in Anuradhapura, planted from a cutting from the original Bo under which the Buddha received enlightenment, continue to draw thousands of Buddhist pilgrims from around the world.

Anuradhapura අනුරාධපුර

Colour map 2, grid A3

Anuradhapura is Sri Lanka's most sacred town. From origins as a settlement in the sixth century BC, it was made capital in 377 BC by King Pandukhabhaya (437-367 BC) who started the great irrigation works on which it depended, and named it after the constellation *Anuradha*. Although the city has remained a symbol of Sinhalese regal power and of Buddhist orthodoxy its period as a centre of real political power had ended by the 12th century AD though for 500 years before that it had suffered widely fluctuating fortunes. By the 19th century it was completely deserted. 'Re-discovered' in the early 19th century by Ralph Backhaus, archaeological research, excavation and restoration have been going on ever since. In 1988, it was designated a World Heritage Site. The new town was started in the 1950s. At its height Anuradhapura may have stretched 25 km. Its ruins and monuments today are widely scattered, which makes a thorough tour time consuming, but it more than repays the effort.

Ins & outs
Be prepared for several security checks in the site

Getting there There are several alternatives. Many visitors arrive from Dambulla to the southeast, along the A9/A13 (see above). Others may come from Colombo via Kurunegala (see page 104). From Trincomalee, the route is via the A12 (see page 269), and there is also an approach from the west, along the A12 from Puttalam (see page 102). **Getting around** A bicycle (available from guest houses) is the best way since the ruins and monuments are spread out but be prepared to park it and walk when told to. There is a free bus service from the road block next to the Dakhini Dagoba to and from the Sri Maha Bodhi or alternatively, use the main car park next to the Thuparama and walk around the central sites. Simplified hand-drawn maps can be purchased at the Archaeological Museum ticket office. **Admission** There are 3 ticket offices for the site. One is at the Archaeological Museum (north of the Tissawewa Rest House), one to the east of the Brazen Palace and a further one towards the Dalada Maligawa. The site is covered by the 'Cultural Triangle Round Ticket' (US$32.50, see page 84) though it does not cover all places within this site, eg the Issurumuniyagala charges Rs 50. Single ticket, US$15 (no student discount). **Facilities** Guides are Rs 300 for 3-4 hrs. Ask at the ticket office or museum. There are lots of little drink stalls around but the ones near the dagobas tend to be expensive. The souvenir sellers can be very persistent and unpleasant, so be firm.

The first era of religious building followed the conversion of King **History** Devanampiya Tissa (ruled 250-210 BC). In his 40-year reign these included the Thuparama Dagoba, Issurumuniyagala, and the Maha Vihara with the Sri Maha Bodhi and the Brazen Palace. A branch of the **Bodhi tree** (see below) under which the Buddha was believed to have gained his enlightenment was brought from Bodhgaya in India and successfully transplanted. It is one of the holiest Buddhist sites in the world.

Anuradhapura remained a capital city until the 9th century AD, when it reached its peak of power and vigour. After the 13th century it almost entirely disappeared, the irrigation works on which it had depended falling into total disuse, and its political functions taken over first by Polonnaruwa, and then by capitals to the south. The earliest restoration work began in 1872, and has continued ever since. The town is now the headquarters of the Sri Lanka Archaeological Survey.

Sights

The **Archaeological Museum** (see below) is central to the site and makes a *The authorities & army* good starting point for a tour. Immediately to its west is the **Basawak Kulam** *have made entry to the* **Tank**, the oldest artificial lake in the city, built by King Pandukabhaya in the *different sites difficult* 4th century BC. The dried-up southern side is good for walks and *unless you follow a* bird-watching, and there are excellent sunset views from the east shore. *prescribed route*

It was begun by King Dutthagamenu (Dutugemunu) to house relics. Priests **Ruvanwelisiya** from all over India were recorded as being present at the enshrinement of the **Dagoba** relics in 140 BC. A huge dagoba, it is surrounded by the remains of lots of *Opposite the museum* buildings. You can see the columns often no more than 500 cm in height dotted around in the grass underneath huge rain trees where monkeys play. The dome is 80 m in diameter at its base and 53-m high. A small passage leads to the relic chamber. At the cardinal points are four 'chapels' which were reconstructed in 1873, when renovation started. The restoration has flattened the shape of the dome, and some of the painting is of questionable style, but it remains a remarkably striking monument. Today, you may find watching the dagoba being 'white washed' an interesting spectacle.

Ancient cities - Cultural Triangle

Moonstone

• •

☛ *An alternative cycle route around Anuradhapura*

- *Issurumuniyagala, Royal Park, Mirisawetiya dagoba.*
- *Archaeological and Folk Museums.*
- *Park bike in main car park and then walk to Thuparama, Ruvanwelisiya.*
- *Dagoba, Brazen Palace and Sri Maha Bodhi.*
- *Return to car park and cycle to Lankarama Dagoba from where you*

could explore the old ruins to the northwest.
- *Follow signs to Abhayagiriya Dagoba and the moonstone.*
- *Pass Samadhi Buddha statue towards the 'twin' ponds.*
- *Return to New Town (Nuwarawewa) via Jetavanarama Dagoba.*

• •

Mirisawetiya Dagoba
Near the Tissawewa Rest House, 1 km to the SW

Originally from the second century BC, it was completely rebuilt during the reign of King Kasyapa V in 930 AD. Surrounded by the ruins of monasteries on three sides, there are some superb sculptures of *Dhyani* Buddhas in the shrines of its chapels. Renovation work on the dagoba started in 1979 with support from UNESCO.

Tissawewa lake & Royal Park

To the south, this lake was built by King Devanampiya Tissa. You can walk/jog on the east and south sides along the raised tank *bund* and continue all round using local tracks on the west and a tarmac road on the north. The **park** just below the lake is very pleasant as it has few visitors. You can wander undisturbed across large rocks among ruined buildings and remains of bathing pools.

Issurumun-iyagala

This small group of striking black rocks is one of the most attractive and peaceful places in town. It also has some outstanding sculpture. The temple, carved out of solid rock, houses a large statue of the seated Buddha. You can climb up steps to the top of the rock above the temple to get a good view of the countryside. There is a cleft in the rock which is full of bats which are fascinating to watch. On the terraces outside is a small square pool. There are also some beautifully carved elephants, showing great individual character. Note the carvings beside the main entrance just above the water level. The small **museum** is to the left of entrance. Some of the best sculptures in Anuradhapura are now housed here, including a horse's head on the shoulders of a man, the superbly executed '*Kapila*' and perhaps the most famous of the sculptures – 'the lovers'. ■ *0800-1930. Rs 50. Ask for permission to take photos.*

King Elara's tomb

From Issurumuniyagala return east to the road and back towards the centre, passing after 1 km, the tomb also known as **Dakkhina dagoba** (Southern dagoba). The Chola Tamil king had captured Anuradhapura in 205 BC, setting up a Tamil Kingdom which lasted over 40 years. Sinhalese kingdoms in the south eventually rose against him, and he was killed in a single-handed duel by King Dutthagamenu, who gave him full battle honours.

Sri Maha Bodhi tree
800 m to the N
This is one of Sri Lanka's most sacred sites

The 'Bo' ('Bodhi') tree or Pipal (*Ficus religiosa*) was planted as a cutting brought from India by Emperor Asoka's daughter, the Princess Sanghamitta, at some point after 236 BC. Guardians have kept uninterrupted watch over the tree ever since. There are other Bo trees around the Sri Maha Bodhi which stands on the highest terrace. In April a large number of pilgrims arrive to make offerings during the *Snana Puja*, and to bathe the tree with milk. Every 12th year the ceremony is particularly auspicious.

A broad, paved path leads from the point you leave your shoes. It is shaded by a tent like structure – tasselled ropes crossing the path coloured yellow, blue, red, white and orange. Groups of drummers in the courtyard may approach visitors and demand payment for performing. You can only see the top of the Bo tree which is supported by an elaborate metal structure and is surrounded by brass railings which are bedecked with colourful prayer flags and smaller strips of cloth which pilgrims tie in expectation of prayers being answered.

Anuradhapura

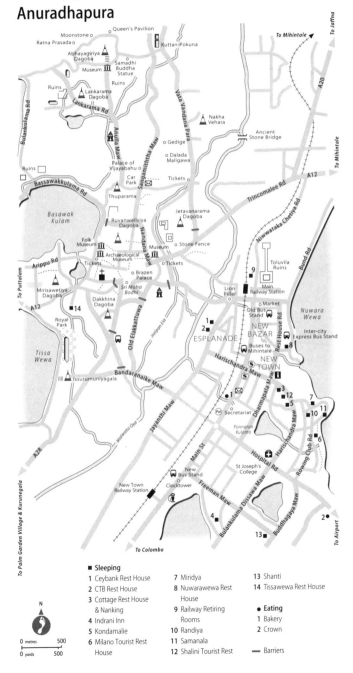

■ **Sleeping**
1 Ceybank Rest House
2 CTB Rest House
3 Cottage Rest House
   & Nanking
4 Indrani Inn
5 Kondamalie
6 Milano Tourist Rest
   House

7 Miridya
8 Nuwarawewa Rest
   House
9 Railway Retiring
   Rooms
10 Randiya
11 Samanala
12 Shalini Tourist Rest

13 Shanti
14 Tissawewa Rest House

● **Eating**
1 Bakery
2 Crown

— Barriers

Dutthagamenu: Battle with Elara

AL Basham gives a flavour of the Mahavansa's account of the battle between Putthagamenu and Elara's forces:

The city had three moats, And was guarded by a high wall.
　　Its gate was covered with iron, Hard for foes to shatter.
The elephant knelt on his knees, and battering with his tusks
　　stone and mortar and brick, he attacked the iron gate.
The Tamils from the watch-tower, threw missiles of every kind,
　　balls of red hot iron and vessels of molten pitch.
Down fell the molten pitch upon Kandula's back.
　　In anguish of pain he fled and plunged in a pool of water.
'This is no drinking bout!' cried Gothaimbara.
　　'Go, batter the iron gate! Batter down the gate!!'
In his pride the best of tuskers took heart and trumpeted loud.
　　He reared up out of the water and stood on the bank defiant.
The elephant-doctor washed away the pitch, and put on balm.
　　The King mounted the elephant and rubbed his brow with his hand.
'Dear Kandula, I'll make you the lord of all Ceylon!' he said,
　　and the beast was cheered, and was fed with the best fodder.
He was covered with a cloth, and he was armoured well
　　with armour for his back of seven-fold buffalo hide.
On the armour was placed a skin soaked in oil.
　　Then, trumpeting like thunder, he came on, fearless of danger.
He pierced the door with his tusks. With his feet he trampled the threshold.
　　And the gate and the lintel crashed loudly to earth.

The Brazen Palace

Opposite the Bodhi tree Take the eastern gate & walk out over a moon stone

The name refers to the first monastery here and its now-disappeared roof, reputedly made of bronze. It is the most remarkable of many monastic buildings scattered across the site. Described in the *Mahavansa* as having nine storeys, there are 600 pillars laid out over an area 70 m sq. The pillars, just under 4-m high, supported the first floor but you need imagination to visualize the scale of the building as it may have been as there is no hint of its structural style or decoration. The walls between the pillars were made of brick while the upper floors were wooden. Built originally by Dutthagamenu, it was the heart of the monastic life of the city, the Maha Vihara. Rebuilt several times, much of what is visible today is the reconstruction of King Parakramabahu I in the last quarter of the 11th century, making use of the remnants of former buildings.

Nuwarawewa

The road east between the Brazen Palace and the Bo tree goes to this new town, the railway station and the largest of Anuradhapura's artificial lakes (1,000 ha) completed about 20 BC. Going east from the Brazen Palace (along the Mihintale/Trincomalee Road), a left fork after 800 m goes north to the ruined Jetavanarama Dagoba. Along the Malwatu Oya, north of the road are ruins of ancient stone bridges – these may have been used as elephant crossings.

Jetavanarama Dagoba

Jetavanarama Dagoba was named after the first Buddhist monastery (names of the Jetavanarama and Abhayagiriya dagobas are sometimes reversed). The largest dagoba in Anuradhapura (considered by some to be the highest in the world) it is also being renovated with help from UNESCO. Started by King Mahasena (AD 275-292), its massive scale was designed in a competitive spirit to rival the orthodox Maha Vihara. The paved platform on which it stands covers more

Gleaming white bells

Dagobas are one of the striking features of the land. They are everywhere and range in size from tiny village structures to the enormous monuments at Ruvanwelisiya in Anuradhapura and Maheseya at Mihintale. Even in nature the stone of the canonball tree fruit is a perfectly formed white dagoba.

There are of course many reasons why they stand out in a landscape – partly for their position, partly their size but mostly for their colour – a dazzling white. Most are beautifully maintained and are often repainted before important festivals.

It is no easy job to paint a large dagoba. A lime whitewash is used. Elaborate bamboo scaffolding cocoons the spire linked to the base by rickety bamboo ladders. Bamboo is ideal as it can be bent to conform to the shape of the dome and the lightness makes the ladders easily

moveable. A team of about five painters assembles on the ladder which is about 20 m in height. Four men are deployed with ropes attached at the top and midpoints to give it some form of stability. At each stage, a painter is responsible for about 3 m of the surface in height, and an arm's width. The topmost 1.5 m of the painter's patch is covered first. Then he takes three steps down the ladder to cover the bottom 1.5 m. Once completed, the bamboo structure is moved an arm's width round and the whole process starts again.

The end result is a gleaming white bell standing out majestically against the green of the countryside and the blue of the sky. Sadly not all the dagobas have yet been restored, their red brick or plain plastered suface still dull in comparison with those that have been returned to their original condition.

than 3 ha and it has a diameter of over 100 m. In 1860 Emerson Tennet, in his book *Ceylon*, calculated that it had enough bricks to build a 3-m high brick wall 25 cm thick from London to Edinburgh, equal to the distance from the southern tip of Sri Lanka to Jaffna and back down the coast to Trincomalee!

Thuparama Continuing north from the Jetavanarama Dagoba, turn left at the crossroads to the site's oldest dagoba to house the right collar-bone of the Buddha. Built by Devanampiya, the 19-m high dagoba has retained its beautiful bell shape, despite restoration work. It is surrounded by concentric circles of graceful granite monolithic pillars of a Vatadage which was added in the 7th century, possibly originally designed to support an over-arching thatched cover. It is a centre of active pilgrimage, decorated with flags and lights. Immediately to its northeast was the original Dalada Maligawa where the Tooth Relic was first enshrined when it was brought to Ceylon in AD 313. Fa Hien gave a vivid description of its display, but only the stone columns remain.

Samadhi Buddha The road north (Sanghamitta Mawatha) goes 1.5 km through the site of the 11th-century palace of **Vijayabahu I** to the superb statue of the serene Buddha with an expression depicting 'extinction of feeling and compassion'. Some think the expression changes as the sun's light moves across it. Roofed to protect it from the weather, it probably dates from the 4th century AD. It is one of the more active religious sites it is adorned with lotus buds and payer flags.

Kuttan-Pokuna Across the Vatavandana Para, a little to the north, you turn right for the two ponds – recently restored eighth and ninth-century ritual baths with steps from each side descending to the water. They were probably for the use of the monastery or for the university nearby. Though called **'twin' ponds**, one is over 10 m longer than the other. You can see the underground water supply channel at one end of the second bath.

Ancient cities – Cultural Triangle

Forest hermitages with pretty carved latrines!

The Pansukulika or Tapovana sect of ascetic Buddhist hermits who lived a simple life of deep meditation in forests and caves are associated with Arankale, Mihintale and Ritigala, around the 7th to the 11th centuries. The monks were expected to wear ragged clothing and to immerse themselves in seeking the Truth, devoid of ritualistic forms of worship associated with Buddha images, relics and relic chambers. Such communities often won the admiration and support of Kings, Sena I (831-851).

The sites had certain features in common. There was a porched entrance, ambulatories, a water pool for cleansing and the **padhanaghara**. One was an open terrace, possibly intended as a 'chapter house' connected to a smaller section which was usually roofed. These 'double platforms' were aligned east to west, the two raised stone-faced platforms were connected by a narrow walkway or bridge. An interesting contradiction of the austere life was the beautifully carved latrines or urinal stones the monks used, examples of which can be seen in the Anuradhapura Archaeological Museum, see page 245.

Abhayagiriya Dagoba
Left from the crossroads

It is 400 m round and was supposedly 135 m high in its original form (part of the pinnacle has disappeared). It is now about 110-m high. Built in 88 BC by Vattagamani (and later restored by Parakramabahu I in the 12th century), it has two splendid sculpted *dwarapalas* (guardians) at the threshold. The dagoba and its associated monastery were built in an attempt to weaken the political hold of the Hinayana Buddhists and to give shelter to monks of the Mahayana school. It was considered an important seat of Buddhist learning and the Chinese traveller/monk Fa Hien visiting it in the 5th century noted that there were 5,000 monks in residence. South of the Abhayagiriya Dagoba is the fairly new **Abhayagiriya** (Fa Hien) **Museum** (see Museums below).

Ratna Prasada

To the west of the Abhayagiriya Dagoba are the ruins of the monastery. The area had once been the 'undesirable' outskirts of Anuradhapura where the cremation grounds were sited. In protest against the King's rule, an ascetic community of monks set up a *tapovana* community of which this is an architectural example. Though they lived an austere life, the buildings here were superbly crafted and curiously, contained elaborately carved lavatories (examples in the Archaeological Museum)! This type of monastery typically had two pavilions connected by a stone bridge within a high-walled enclosure which contained a pond. The main entrance was from the east, with a porch above the entrance. Here the Ratna Prasada did not remain a peaceful haven but was the scene of bloody massacres when a rebellious group took refuge with the monks and were subsequently beheaded by the King's men. Their turn to have their heads roll in the dust followed another bloody revolt.

Mahasena Palace

The nearby Mahasena Palace has a particularly fine carved stone tablet and one of the most beautifully carved moonstones, see page 311, though the necessary protective railing surrounding it makes photography a little tricky. Note also the flight of steps held up by miniature stone dwarfs! You can return to the museums by taking the Lankarama Road to the south.

Museums

Abhayagiriya (Fa Hien) **Museum**, south of the Abhayagiriya Dagoba, was built by the Chinese. The collection includes further examples of latrine plinths as displayed in the Archaeological Museum. There is also an extensive display detailing the excavation of the Abhayagiriya site.

Archaeological Museum in the old colonial headquarters. An excellent small museum, with a large collection including some beautiful pieces of sculpture and finds from Mihintale. It is well laid out, with occasional informative labels and some fascinating exhibits. There are statues from several sites, moonstones (see note in introduction), implements, and outside in the garden, beautifully sculpted guard stones and meticulously designed latrines. Separate latrine plinths were used for urinals, solid waste and bidets. Under each immaculately carved platform was a succession of pots containing sand, charcoal and limestone to purify the waste. Mr KS Pereira is very knowledgeable and will act as your guide (a voluntary payment, eg Rs 100, is gratefully received). ■ *0800-1700, closed Tue.*

Folk Museum, nearby. The collection reflects rural life in the North Central Province with a large display of vessels used by villagers in Rajarata, and handicrafts. ■ *0900-1700, closed Thu. Rs 40, camera Rs 135 (not strictly enforced).*

A **museum** beyond the Brazen Palace has a small collection of exhibits (fragments from the site, gem stones, jewellery etc) few are labelled. ■ *Entry free.*

Essentials

Anuradhapura has a reasonable selection of hotels and guest houses, but is rather lacking at the top end. The main cluster is around the junction of Harishchandra Mawatha and Rowing Club Rd. The guesthouses on Freeman Mawatha are much closer to the 'New' bus station and the 'New Town' railway station. Nearly all rent out bicycles (usually Rs 100-150 per day) and can arrange guided tours. Alternatively opt for the new rest house in Mihintale, see page 247.

Sleeping
JR Jaya Mawatha is Rowing Club Rd

Mid-range A *Palm Garden Village*, Puttalam Rd, Pandulagama, 2.5 km from the sites, T23961, F21596 pgvh@pan.lk 50 a/c rooms in upmarket hotel, full facilities including pool, good restaurant. C *Miridya*, Rowing Club Rd, T22112, F22519. 35 rooms including 21 a/c (US$31), some with view over Nuwara Wewa, restaurant, bar, exchange, pool (non-residents pay Rs 100), pleasant atmosphere and attractive gardens, most comfortable hotel here, popular with groups. C *Nuwarawewa Rest House*, Rest House Rd, near New Town, T22565, F23265, (Colombo T583133, F587613). 70 a/c rooms (Rs 2129 nett) though no views, modern bathrooms, public areas rather shabby, good restaurant, bar, clean pool (non-residents pay Rs 100, and the occasional monkey has a dip too!), attractive garden, friendly and helpful staff. C *Tissawewa Rest House*, near the tank, T22299, F23265. 25 clean, simple rooms including 5 a/c, inspect first as some are rather small and dark, upstairs better, charming former Dutch Governor's house with some period furniture, beautifully situated in secluded parkland with lots of monkeys, restaurant, bike hire (Rs 150 per day), guests can use pool at Nuwarawewa Rest House, reasonable value, closest to archaeological sites. Recommended. D *Randiya*, off Rowing Club Rd, T22868, F22071. 10 rooms in modern house (Rs 975) including 2 a/c (extra Rs 225), hard beds, restaurant. D-E *Shalini Tourist Inn*, 41/388 Harishchandra Mawatha (opposite Water Tower Stage 1), T/F22425. 7 large, clean, comfortable rooms in modern house (Rs 550-850), some with hot bath, good food in attractive restaurant, well kept, keen owner, cycle hire, free transfer from/to station. Highly recommended.

Cheap E *Ceybank Rest House*, Jayanthi Mawatha, T/F35520, (Colombo T/F447845). 20 large rooms with small balconies (Rs 500) including 4 a/c (Rs 700) and some family rooms, clean, not too bad. E *Cottage Tourist Rest* 388/38 Harishchandra Mawatha, T35363. 5 rather poorly maintained small rooms (Rs 500), restaurant. E *Kondamalie*

Trains running daily from Anuradhapura

To	1st Class	2nd Class	3rd Class	Departure time	Journey
Colombo	Rs 202	Rs 116	Rs 45	0500, 0855, 1411, 1430, 2310	4¾-5 hrs
Colombo	Rs 277	Rs 116	Rs 45	1115, 1430	4½ hrs
Colombo (Intercity Express)		Rs 150	Rs 120	0640	3¼ hrs
Galle via Colombo		Rs 184	Rs 66	0500, 1411	
Kandy	Colombo trains: change at Polgahwela				
Matara (via Colombo), Galle		Rs 184	Rs 66	0500, 1411	9¼ hrs

Guest House, 388/42 Harishchandra Mawatha, T22029. 12 clean rooms (Rs 500- 650), another 22 being added, now in hands of original owner, good verandah restaurant, bike hire, worth a try. **E** *Samanala Tourist Guest House*, 4N/2 Wasala Daththa Mawatha, T072 621384. 4 new, clean rooms (Rs 600-700) in new guest house run by former manager of Kondamalie, quiet location next to lake (boating can be arranged), pleasant garden, cycle hire, excellent home cooking. Recommended. **E-F** *Milano Tourist Rest*, 596/40 Rowing Club Rd, T22364. 10 clean rooms (Rs 400-600), good restaurant, bar, good value, Recommended.

F *Ceylon Tourist Board Rest House*, Jayanthi Mawatha, T22188. Set in extensive grounds, 29 large rooms, fan, attached bath, reasonable value though service rather slow, popular in the pilgrimage season, restaurant.**F-G** *Shanti Guest House*, 891 Mailagas Junction, Freeman Mawatha, T35876. 10 basic but large rooms of varying standards (Rs 200-400) although 5 are occupied by long-stay guests, friendly, good food, tour and bike hire arranged, popular with backpackers, free pick up from station. **G** *Indrani Inn*, 745 Freeman Mawatha, along a lane south, 1 km from New bus stand, T22478. 2 clean rooms (Rs 300), cycle hire. **G** *Railway Retiring Rooms*, T22271. 10 basic rooms (Rs 300), not too clean but only one train at night so quiet, security-conscious caretaker, rooms available for non-passengers **F** *Lake Side*, Rowing Club Rd, T23111. 10 rooms, a little run down though attached bath clean and modern, fan, restaurant.

Eating

The north end of town lacks restaurants but has some friendly food stalls

You can get cheaper meals at numerous eating places in town – some of these have a couple of rooms to take in guests during the festival season. There is a varied choice of menu at the following hotels: *Miridya* and the 2 *Rest Houses*, which need prior notice, offer reasonable food and pleasant seating (no alcohol at *Tissawewa*). *Kondamalie Guest House*, has pleasant, open-air seating (take mosquito repellent!), popular with budget travellers. *Milano Tourist Rest* (rice and curry Rs 150, Western dishes slightly more, *Lion* lager Rs 100) is also recommended. *Winter House*, Bandaranaike Mawatha, opens 1900 for good cheap hoppers and curry. *Lee's Chinese Guest House* (see above), has a Chinese cook. Recommended. *Nanking*, also on Harishchandra Mawatha, offers a reasonable selection. *Swan* upstairs, good food, generous portions, spotlessly clean, reasonable prices.

Festivals

Apr: *Snana piya* at Sri Maha Bodhi. **Jun**: at the full moon in *Poson*, the introduction of Buddhism to Sri Lanka is celebrated with huge processions when many pilgrims visit the town. **Jul-Aug**: *Esala Perahera* celebrations, less spectacular than the one at Kandy.

Local Bus: frequent service between Old and New Bus Stands. **Cycle hire**: from Transport most guesthouses and hotels in the New Town (about Rs 100-150 per day). Sometimes, **motorbike** (Rs 400 per day) and **car hire** (Rs 500 per day). **Train**: See table for times and destinations. Some hotels are closer to the New Town station which is south of the main station. Services to **Jaffna** and **Talaimannar** may be disrupted. **Tuk-tuks**: from station to Bank Site about Rs 25, and to Freeman Mawatha hotels Rs 60. From Archaeological Museum to Bank Site Rs 60-70. From Bus station to Freeman Mawatha Rs 30, and to Bank Site, about Rs 50.

Long distance Road Bus: there are 3 bus stations in Anuradhapura. **New Bus Station**, Main St, south end of town, has departures for **Polonnaruwa** (frequent service from 0515 to 1400, 3 hrs; **Trincomalee** (0510, 3½ hrs); **Mihintale** (frequent, 30 mins). **Old Bus Station**, Rest House Rd, has CTB buses to **Colombo** (hrly, Rs 50, 5 hrs). **Kandy** via **Dambulla** (hourly, Rs 40, 4 hrs). **Intercity Express Bus Station** is diagonally opposite the *Old Bus Station*, and offers a/c express services to **Colombo** (hrly, Rs 90, 4 hrs), **Kandy** (hrly, Rs 75, 3½ hrs) and to **Kurunegala** and **Negombo**. **Cycle/motorbike**: Mihintale: 11 km easy ride along a flat road. A **tuk-tuk** charges about Rs 350 for a half day trip.

Take the A12 out of Anuradhapura to Mihintale

Banks some in New Town, near Bank Site roundabout including: *Hatton Bank* is on Main St, Directory opposite the Police Station. *People's Bank*, open 0900-1600, accepts TCs and sterling but not credit cards for cash, exchange facilities at correct rate, tourists are sometimes offered special treatment.

Mihintale මිහින්තලේ

Mihintale (pronounced Mihin-taalay) named as Mahinda's hill, is revered as *11 km E of* the place where Mahinda converted King Devanampiya Tissa to Buddhism in *Anuradhapura* 243 BC, thereby enabling Buddhism to spread to the whole island. The legend tells how King Tissa was chasing a stag during a hunting expedition. The stag *It is a beautiful,* reached Mihintale and fled up the hillside followed by the King until he *peaceful site* reached a place surrounded by hills, where the animal disappeared and the frustrated King was astonished to find a gentle person who spoke to him the Buddha's teachings. It was Mahinda, Asoka's son, who had come to preach Buddhism and was able to convert the King with 40,000 followers. As well as being important historically, it is an important religious site and is well worth visiting as it is a pleasant place to just stroll around away from the crowds at the more famous ancient sites.

Mihintale is close to the Anuradhapura-Trincomalee Road. The huge dagoba *Sights* can be seen from miles around. At the junction with the village road there are statues of six of the principle characters of the site. The minor road leading to the site has evidence of a **quincunx vihara** to the left and has ruins of a **hospital** on the right. The ninth-century hospital appears to have had an outer court where medicines were ground and stored, and stone tanks for oil and herbal baths. The inner court appears to have had small treatment rooms. A 10th-century stone inscription mentions the use of leeches in treatment. There is a small museum nearby which has erratic opening times.

Approach There are about 1,840 granite steps to the top but they are very *The site* shallow and it is much less of a climb than it first looks. About half the steps can be avoided if you have your own transport, by driving around the back of the lower car park. An old road leads to flat area at the refectory level (Rs 15 to park at this 'upper' car park). There are drinks kiosks nearby. The climb starts

Ancient cities - Cultural Triangle

gently, rising in a broad stairway of 350 steps shaded by frangipani trees which lead to the first platform. Further steps to the right take you up to an open area with Kantaka Chetiya.

Kantaka Chetiya is the earliest *stupa* here. A board at this point states that it was built by King Lajji Tissa at the improbably early date of 424-434 BC, more than 200 years before Buddhism was brought to Sri Lanka. Excavated in 1932-35, it had been severely damaged. Over 130 m in circumference, today it is only about 12-m high compared with its original height of perhaps 30 m. There is some fine carving: note the beautiful sculptures at the four cardinal points geese, dwarves, and a variety of animals and several rock cells around it.

The second terrace Returning to the first platform, steeper steps lead to a large refectory terrace. As you climb up you can see the impressive outer cyclopean wall of the complex (it takes under 10 minutes from the car park, at a gentle pace). As an alternative to the steps to get to the refectory level, take a faint footpath to the left between the second and third flights. This crosses an open grassy area. Walk to the end and you will see the lake, green with algae. A path to the left takes you towards the **Giribandhu Chetiya Kiri Vehara**. Largely ruined and grassed over on the north side, it is not really worth a visit. You can look down on the lower car park and the quincunx. To the right, the path approaches the refectory from the rear and you pass a massive stone trough.

The Refectory Immediately on the left is the Relic House and the rectangular **Bhojana Salava** (Monks' refectory). There is a stone aqueduct and a trough which may have been used for storing water.

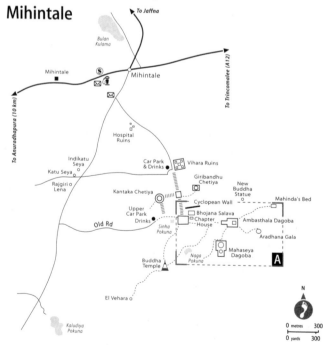

Mihintale

To Jaffna

Bulan Kulama

To Anuradhapura (10 km)

To Trincomalee (A12)

Mihintale
Mihintale

Hospital Ruins

Indikatu Seya
Katu Seya
Rajgiri Lena

Car Park & Drinks
Vihara Ruins

Giribandhu Chetiya

New Buddha Statue

Mahinda's Bed

Kantaka Chetiya

Cyclopean Wall

Upper Car Park Drinks

Old Rd

Bhojana Salava
Chapter House

Ambasthala Dagoba

Aradhana Gala

Sinha Pokuna

Naga Pokuna

Mahaseya Dagoba

A

Buddha Temple

El Vehara

Kaludiya Pokuna

Related map
A Mihintale sacred
centre, page 250

Ancient cities - Cultural Triangle

N

0 metres 300
0 yards 300

The square **Chapter House**/'Conversation Hall' with signs of 48 pillars and a 'throne' platform, immediately to the north, is where the monks and lay members met. This has the bases of a series of evenly spaced small brick dagobas. At the entrance, stone slabs covered in 10th-century inscriptions on granite give detailed rules governing the sacred site.

The flat grassy terrace which can also be approached by car from the south up the old paved road or steps down from the Kantaka Chetiya, is dotted with trees and the outlines of three small shrines.

Sinha Pokuna (Lion Bath) To the south of the terrace is about 2 m sq and 1.8-m deep and has excellent carvings in the form of a frieze around the bottom of the tank, of elephants, lions and warriors. The finest, however, is the 2-m high rampant lion to the west whose mouth forms the spout. Water was gathered in the tank by channelling and feeding it through the small mystic gargoyle similar to the one that can be seen at Sigiriya.

The main path up to the Ambasthala Dagoba up the long flight of steps, starts by the 'Conversation Hall' in the square. After a five-minute climb a path leads off to the right, round the hillside. Take this and walk through cool forest to the **Naga Pokuna** (Snake Pond) with a five-headed cobra carving which you can still make out. It is a 40-m pool carved out of solid rock which stored water for the monastery and, some believe, where King Tissa would have bathed. At one end is a very small tank, now without water. Apparently this was where the Queen would bathe. It is a peaceful and beautiful place which you might like to visit after climbing to the sacred centre of Mihintale, which is another two-minute climb.

Ambasthala Dagoba Straight ahead at the heart of the complex is the 'mango tree' dagoba, the holiest part of the site, built at the traditional meeting place of King Tissa and Asoka's son Mahinda. Foreigners are charged Rs 50 entry fee and shoes must be removed. The monk in his office makes frequent loud-speaker announcements for donations from pilgrims – these donations have funded the erection of a large white Buddha statue overlooking the central area in 1991. The bronze Buddhas are gifts from Thailand.

Sela Cetiya A rock stupa at the site of the original mango tree has a replica of the Buddha's footprint. It is quite small and is surrounded by a double circle of crowned pillars – there is a gilt railing covered in prayer flags and with a scattering of pilgrims' coins.

Mahinda's cave A path leads out of the northeast corner of the compound between a small cluster of monks' houses down a rough boulder track to the cave, less than a 10-minute walk away. A stall selling local herbal and forest product remedies (including 'a cure for arrack!') is sometimes set up halfway to the cave which is formed out of an extraordinary boulder, hollowed out underneath to create a narrow platform at the very end of a ridge above the plain below. From the stone 'couch', known as **Mahinda's bed**, there are superb views to the north across the tanks and forested plains of the Dry Zone. You have to retrace your steps to the Ambasthala compound.

Aradhana Gala From the northwest corner of the compound a path with rudimentary steps cut in the bare granite rock leads to the summit of the Aradhana Gala (Meditation Rock). It is a very steep climb, and if you have no socks, very hot on the feet. A strong railing makes access quite secure. There is nothing

Mihintale sacred centre

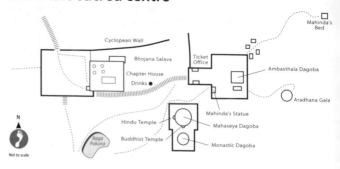

much to see on the rock but there are superb views from the top, especially across the compound to the Mahaseya Dagoba, which is at the same height.

Mahaseya dagoba A short flight of steep steps from the southwest corner of the compound, just beyond a small temple with a modern portrayal of Mahinda meeting King Tissa at the mango tree, leads up to the summit (310 m) with the Mahaseya Dagoba. According to legend this was built on the orders of King Tissa as a reliquary for a lock of the Buddha's hair or for relics of Mahinda. The renovated dagoba which dominates the skyline, commands superb views back towards Anuradhapura to the southwest. Another monk will ask for donations here (anything above Rs 100 is recorded in a book). On the south side of the main dagoba is a smaller brick dagoba while abutting it on its south side is a small Buddhist temple. To the west side is a Hindu temple with modern painted images of four Hindu deities, *Ganesh, Saman, Vishnu* and *Kataragama*. After collecting your shoes, look out for a rock inscription (showing the allocation of land in the area). Immediately below this and opposite a lime-washed building is a small path which leads to the Naga Pokuna, mentioned above.

■ *Open 24 hrs. Rs 100. Rathu, a licensed guide, offers in-depth information of the site, Rs 350 for 2½ hrs. There are basic rooms available in the monks' quarters for those who wish to learn more.*

Sleeping **B-C** *Hotel Mihintale*, Anuradhapura Rd, near crossroads, 10 km from Anuradhapura, 1 km from the sacred site, T66599. 10 well furnished a/c rooms (US$31), those upstairs far lighter (extra US$10), 2 good-value family rooms (US$51), pleasant atmosphere, good value but no credit cards or TCs accepted. **F** *Railway Retiring Rooms*, 8 modest rooms, fans, attached baths, a well designed modern block.

Festivals **Jun**: *Poson* at full-moon in Jun is of particularly importance to Buddhists who commemorate the arrival of Buddhism on the island. The width of the steps indicate the large number of pilgrims who visited the sacred site on special occasions in the past. Today tens of thousands flock to climb to the sacred spot, chanting as they go: *Buddham saranam gachchaami. Dhammam saranam gachchaami. Sangam saranam gachchaami,* meaning 'In the Buddha I seek refuge, In Dhamma I seek refuge, In the Sangha I seek refuge'.

Transport **Road** **Bus**: Regular buses run between Mihantale and Anuradhapura's New Bus Station (Rs 5). **Cycle/motorbike**: easy ride of 11 km along a flat road from Anuradhapura. **Train** Mihintale has a modern well designed station. The new line to Mihintale branches east at Mihintale Junction (13 km from Mihintale), 3 times daily (more frequently during Jun *Poson*).

The A6 runs east to the coast at Trincomalee but due to the uncertain political situation this is not often used. Buses may run in the daytime but hire car drivers are extremely reluctant to take the road until the political climate improves.

An ancient **stone bridge** (21-m long and over 3-m wide) on the *Mahakanadarawa tank* (northeast of Mihintale) in the direction of *Rambewa* was recently discovered accidentally. It suggests a road once linked Anuradhapura with the ancient harbour at Gokanna (Trincomalee).

Mihintale
to Sigiriya
*The journey takes
about 1½ hrs*

From Mihintale the A9, which has a good surface, goes south (to join the Kandy-Jaffna road A13) and continues as far as Maradankadawala. Here, the A11 turns left and passes the ancient site of **Ritigala** (on left, after 10 km) to join the A6 (Kurunegala-Trincomalee road) at Habarana (see page 256). Go south along the A6 and turn left at **Inamalawa**, to see the rock fort at Sigiriya, 11 km away.

Sigiriya සිගිරිය

The vast flat-topped 200-m high Lion Rock (Sinha-Giri) stands starkly above the surrounding countryside of the central forest with magnificent views over the Dry Zone and south to the Central Highlands. It was an exceptional natural site for a fortress, which gets its name from the lions which were believed to occupy the caves. For many visitors, this impressive site is their favourite in the whole of Sri Lanka. There are stunning views from the top. In addition to the rock fortress with its palace and famous frescoes, there are extensive grounds at the base and the whole is enclosed by an outer moat which contains water. The rewards of Sigiriya (pronounced See-gee-ree-ya) justify the steep climb. It was designated a World Heritage Site in 1982.

Getting there The main bus stop is close to the bridge by the South Entrance but those without a Cultural Triangle Permit have to walk round to the main West Entrance to buy their ticket (the track is signposted off the road 2 km west from the village, past the rest house). Those visiting by car may avoid the long walk from the ticket office to the rock by continuing to the South Entrance (where guards are sometimes reluctant to let visitors in). There is an unofficial car park inside the inner moat.
Getting around Very early morning is beautiful – the site still very quiet until 0730, but the late afternoon light is better for the frescoes. There can be long queues on public holidays and the rock can be very crowded from mid-morning. If you wish to make an early start (avoiding groups which start arriving by 0800) buy your ticket on the previous day if you arrive in time. The round ticket (see page 311) is only for a single entry at each site. There are over 60 licensed guides here so competition is fierce. It is worth getting one. Charge, about Rs 300 for 2 hrs. **Admission** There is a new car park at the South Entrance where it is possibly to buy the Cultural Triangle Permit (US$32.50). Tickets for the site itself are US$16 (half price for ISIC holders). The ticket office is open from around 0700, but those holding the round ticket can enter as soon as it is light.

Ins & outs
*Allow at least 2 hrs
for a visit*

*Evenings bring out
armies of mosquitoes
so take adequate
precautions &
cover up well*

Hieroglyphs suggest that the site was occupied by humans from very early times, long before the fortress was built. The royal citadel built between 477-485 AD was surrounded by an impressive wall and a double moat. The city had the palace and quarters for the ordinary people who built the royal pavilions, pools and fortifications. When the citadel ceased to be a palace, it was inhabited by monks until 1155, and then abandoned. It was rediscovered by archaeologists in 1828.

Water, a scarce commodity in the Dry Zone, was conserved and diverted cleverly through pipes and rock-cut channels to provide bathing pools for the palace above, and enhance the gardens below with pools and fountains. The water pumps are thought to have been powered by windmills. On the islands in the two pools in the water garden near the entrance, stood pavilions, while the shallow marble pools reflected the changing patterns of the clouds. Excavations have revealed surface and underground drainage systems.

Approach Entering the site from the west, you will pass the fifth-century **water gardens** (restored by the Central Cultural Fund with UNESCO sponsorship) with walks, pavilions, ponds and fountains which are gravity fed from the moats as they were 1,500 years ago. You can see the secret changing room doors! The water gardens and moat are very pleasant, not least because they give the visitor more room to move around before facing the crush to climb the rock.

A straight path leads through the group of four fountain gardens with small water jets (originally fifth-century), some with pretty lotuses attracting a number of water birds. Finally the flower garden with colourful beds and flowering trees including *azedirachta indica* (bearing red flowers and flat seed pods), *cassia siamea* and yellow-flowered *nerium oleander*. To the right as you walk up to the rock is a **miniature water garden**. The whole area (including the moat and drive) is immaculate. It is difficult to visualize the winter palace as there are no visible foundations.

Sigiriya

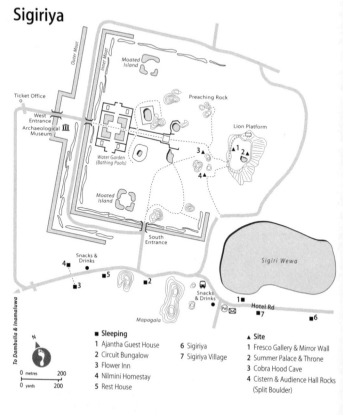

■ Sleeping
1 Ajantha Guest House
2 Circuit Bungalow
3 Flower Inn
4 Nilmini Homestay
5 Rest House
6 Sigiriya
7 Sigiriya Village

▲ Site
1 Fresco Gallery & Mirror Wall
2 Summer Palace & Throne
3 Cobra Hood Cave
4 Cistern & Audience Hall Rocks
(Split Boulder)

To rival the God of Wealth

It was King Kasyapa's intention to reproduce on earth the legendary palace of Kubera, the God of Wealth, and so had it decorated lavishly with impressive gardens, cisterns and ponds. For the famous frescoes he gathered together the best artists of his day. Apart from these exceptional frescoes, it is worth noting that the entire site was built over a period of seven years and effectively abandoned after 18 years. The engineering skills required for the water and fountain gardens as well as lifting water by a series of bamboo lifts to the top

of the rock, were remarkable for the time.

The Mahavansa records that King Kasyapa, having killed his father to gain the throne, lived in terror that his half-brother, who had taken refuge in India, would return to kill him. He did come back, after 18 years, to find that Kasyapa had built a combination of pleasure palace and massive fortress. Kasyapa came down from the hill to face his half brother's army on elephant back. Mistakenly thinking he had been abandoned by his supporters, he killed himself with his dagger.

It is easy to forget that the site was in fact developed as a massive defensive fortress. Lookout points were located on ledges clinging to the rock and as you climb up you will see there is a massive rock, close to the Guard House, wedged with stone supports which could be knocked out to enable it to crash on the enemy far below.

The Rock
The top of the rock has a surface area of 1.5 ha

Base of the rock Before reaching the steps the path goes through the boulder garden where clusters of rocks, including the **preaching rock** with 'seats', are marked with rows of notches and occasional 'gashes'. These may have been used for decorating the area with lamps during festivals. To the right at the start of the climb, under a natural overhang is the **Cobra Hood** rock which has a drip ledge inscription in Brahmi script dating from the second century BC. The floor and ceiling have lime plaster, the latter is decorated with paintings and floral patterns. A headless Buddha statue is placed horizontally. It is thought to have been a monk's cell originally. The **Cistern** and the **Audience Hall** rocks are parts of a single massive boulder which had split, and half of which had fallen away. The exposed flat surface had a 'throne' at one end and came to be called the Audience Hall while the upper part of the standing half, retained the rectangular cistern.

The climb Beginning in earnest with steps leading through the Elephant Gate on well-maintained brick-lined stairways and up to the second checkpoint immediately below the gallery containing the frescoes. Steps lead up to the **Fresco gallery**, painted under an overhanging rock and reached by a spiral staircase which was made in 1938. Don't rush: the steps are not really adequate for the numbers visiting at certain times of the day. Of the original 500 or so frescoes, which vie with those in Ajanta in Western India, only 21 remain. They are remarkably well preserved, as they are sheltered from the elements in a

The apsara frescoe

Ancient cities - Cultural Triangle

niche. In the style of Ajanta, the first drawing was done on wet plaster and then painted with red, yellow, green and black. The figures are 'portraits' of *apsaras* (celestial nymphs) and attendants above clouds – offering flowers, scattering petals or bathing. Here, guides are keen to point out the girl with three hands and another with three nipples. Some paintings were destroyed by a madman in 1967 and you can see pictures of this in the small museum. ■ *0800. You may photograph the frescoes but a flash is not permitted. A 'fast' film (ISO 400), or a steady hand, is recommended. Avoid the high sun around noon and mind the aggressive monkeys.*

Mirror Wall Immediately beyond the foot of the spiral staircase the path is protected on the outer side by the 3-m high, highly polished plaster wall believed to have been coated with lime, egg white and wild honey. After 15 centuries it still has a reflective sheen. Visitors and pilgrims between (mostly seventh and 11th century) wrote verses in Sinhalese – 'graffiti' prompted by the frescoes and by verses written by previous visitors. Some, today, find this section a little disappointing. It is also difficult to stop and look at the graffiti because of the pressure of people when the rock is 'busy'.

Lion Terrace This marks the half way point of the climb where there is welcome shade and welcome cool drinks (expensive at Rs 50). The wire cage is apparently to protect people from wild bees. You can see their nests under the metal staircase.

Final stairway The main path takes you to the top of the rock up the steep west and north sides. The final stage of the ascent on the north ledge leads through the giant plaster-covered brick paws of the lion (the remainder of the animal has disappeared). The size of the paws gives some clue to the height of the lion's head. It is worth studying the remaining climb to the summit. You can clearly see the outline of small steps cut into the granite. The king was apparently scared of heights so these steps would also have been enclosed by a 3-m high mirror wall. Here was the lion's gate after which the place is named: *Si* (shortened form of *Sinha*, lion) *Giriya* (throat). The stairway of 25 flights is mostly on iron steps with a small guard rail and is steep (particularly in one place where a small flight resemble a ships ladder!). Small children can find this quite frightening.

Summer Palace At the top are the ruins of the palace – the foundations reveal the likely size which appears very small especially when compared with the size of the stone throne underneath it. There was the granite throne, dancing terraces, a small pool fed by rain water, drinking water tanks, sleeping quarters of the concubines, a small flower garden and precariously positioned platforms for guards. If you walk to the sign on the west, there is a very good birds-eye view of the winter palace and its surrounding moat. Retrace your steps to the second checkpoint. Just below this, the path splits to the left from where you can get a view of the king's audience chamber and his anteroom. Once again, there is a huge throne in a semicircle where his advisors would sit – justice was swift and often brutal. Immediately below the audience chamber was another granite slab: this was the place of execution. Again to the left is the ante-chamber which was cooled by a tank of water cut into the rock above the ceiling. It too would have been covered in frescoes. Much of the construction is in brick, faced with lime plaster but there are sections built with limestone slabs which would have been carried up. The upper structures which have disappeared were probably wooden. Finally you exit through the cobra gate – a huge, overhanging rock. All around this area you can see steps cut into the rock for soldiers to guard the palace. The King apparently feared attack not only from his half-brother but also from enemies within his palace.

The **Mapagala Rock** with evidence of dressed stone work, a dagoba and other **Other sights** ruins on the roadside just over a km away. The **Pidurangala Royal Cave Temple** and Buddhist Meditation centre (1.5 km) is signposted from the car park. The cave on the rock Pidurangala where there had been an ancient monastery still has a stupa with a 10th century reclining Buddha and an inscription dating from the first century BC. These, and other finds of early settlement in **Rama Kale** nearby point at the ancient nature of the spot chosen by Kasyapa for his palace fortress. The small **Archaeological Museum** has been rather badly neglected and is not particularly impressive.

Further reading *Sigiriya*, by RH De Silva, Ceylon, Department of Archaeology, 1971.

Essentials

Expensive A-B *Sigiriya Village*, near the rock, T23502, F84716, (Colombo T381644, **Sleeping** F381645), www.sigiriyavillage 120 tastefully furnished rooms with small terraces, including 50 a/c, good open-sided restaurants and theme clusters of cottages, each with its own colour scheme and accessories, very good ayurvedic centre, friendly and efficient management. Recommended. **B** *Sigiriya*, 1 km from entrance to rock, T31821, F84811, (Colombo T332155, F438933) serenlti@sri.lanka.net 80 well decorated, comfortable a/c rooms, started as a small guest house, arranged around 2 terraces, reasonable food, large pleasant garden, organised bird watching walks, attractive wooded setting, cultural shows, good pool, good value. Recommended. **Mid-range C** *Sigiriya Rest House*, close to site entrance, T31899. 17 rooms, including 4 a/c, clean though rather musty and smelly, pleasant dining area and terrace, swimming pool to come. **Cheap E** *Flower Inn*, 200m from entrance to rock, 3 very clean rooms (Rs 600, negotiable), table fans, attached bath, good food, friendly owner. Recommended. **F-G** *Nilmini Home Stay*, opposite *Flower Inn*, T33313. 2 simple rooms (Rs 200 shared bath, Rs 400 attached), good restaurant, very friendly. Recommended. **G** *Ajantha Guest House*, near the rock, 1 very basic room (Rs 200) on the side of a family house.

At Inamaluwa (3 km) **C** *Eden Garden*, Sigiriya Road, T/F84635. 20 large, clean *Regular buses leave* rooms, including 15 a/c, restaurant. **E** *Ancient Villa*, Sigiriya Road, 2 km from *to the site from early* Inamaluwa, T072-627854. 5 good-sized, clean cabanas (Rs 670), 7 more to be added, *morning onwards* private balconies, nets, 12 acre site in natural surroundings, excellent for nature walks, reasonably priced restaurant, friendly. Highly recommended. **E** *Inamaluwa Inn*, T84533. 10 overpriced rooms (Rs 800 including breakfast), pricey restaurant.

There are shops selling bottled water and film but no eateries other than very basic **Shopping** hopper shops.

Road The journey by car from **Colombo** takes about 3 hrs and from **Kandy** about **Transport** 2½ hrs, the latter on a good surface between Matale and Dambulla. you might stop at a spice garden on the way or at Aluwihare just north of Matale (see page 232). **Bus**: The main bus stop is close to the southern entrance to the site. Non-stop bus from **Colombo** to **Dambulla** (3 hrs, Rs 100). Then hrly local buses to **Sigiriya** (30 mins, Rs 14) or a tuk-tuk/taxi, Rs 300. Daily bus between **Kandy** and Dambulla or Matale and connections to Sigiriya (total 3½-4 hrs). Fewer in the afternoon. From Kandy, one

Ancient cities - Cultural Triangle

direct morning bus to Sigiriya, 3 hrs. From **Sigiriya**, there is a direct bus to **Colombo** at 0415, at least 2 buses to **Kandy** (0830 1145), and buses to **Dambulla** (30 mins, Rs 14) about every 30 mins (last at about 1830). **Train** Inter-city to **Dambulla** from **Colombo**, a/c, Rs 300. Taxi from there to Sigiriya.

Directory **Useful addresses** **Tourist Police**: Sigiriya Village, Hotel Rd.

To Ritigala From Sigiriya, most visitors continue north along the reasonably good B294 road. After 12 km, at Moragaswewa, it meets the A11. Some 2 km west (left) is **Habarana**, whilst a right (east) turn leads to Minneriya (25 km) and then Polonnaruwa, 45 km, see page 257. From Habarana, continue west on the A11. A road up to Ritigala goes north (right) at the village of Galapitagala.

Ritigala
රිටිගල
The marked Ritigala hills can be seen clearly to the N from the main rd

To experience something of the thrill of 'discovering' a remote site in a jungle, Ritigala is well worth visiting though the trip can be very exhausting. It is very humid and airless and involves climbing through dense forest.

The wildlife in this Strict Nature Reserve includes leaf-eating monkeys, elephants, sloth bear and leopard and varied bird life. The area, rich in unusual plants and herbs, is associated with the *Ramayana* story in which Hanuman dropped a section herb-covered Himalaya here (see page 137).

The forest hermitage complex which has been proposed for listing as a World Heritage Site, was occupied by *Pansakulika* monks (see page 284). This is where Brahmi inscriptions in the caves date the site from the third and second centuries BC. The structures found here include the typical double platforms joined by stone bridges, stone columns, ambulatories, herbal baths filled by rain water, sluices and monks' cells (see page 106).

■ *US$8. Covered by the Cultural Triangle Permit. There is a local guide (Rs 200) but he speaks no English so it helps to have your own guide. Getting there: From the A11, follow the road (which was re-laid in 2000) for 5 km into the forest, then turn left (west) along a track (4WD) for about 3 km where an ancient rock-cut path leads to the site.*

Habarana
හබරන
Phone code: 066

Habarana is an important crossroads, though apart from a scattering of hotels and rest houses and its accessibility, it has little to offer. It is the quality of the accommodation and the central location which make this an excellent place to stay if you are travelling by car (groups often spend one night here). Visitors are also offered a wide choice of elephant 'safaris'. There is an attractive Buddhist temple with excellent paintings. Behind the tank, next to the temple, you can climb a rock for superb views over the forest to Sigiriya.

Sleeping **Expensive** **A** *The Lodge* (Keells), Colombo T320862, F447087) htlres@keells.com 150 tastefully decorated a/c rooms in bungalows, some deluxe with tubs and TV, excellent facilities and lush grounds with woods, good pool, good service. Highly recommended. **A-B** *Village Habarana* (Keells), T70046, (Colombo T421101, F447087), htlres@keells.com 106 'rustic' cottages including 20 a/c, on the banks of the lake, extensive gardens, small boomerang shaped pool, excellent food although reception can be inefficient. **C** *Habarana Rest House*, Polonnaruwa Crossroads, T70003, (Colombo T503497, F503504). 4 dirty rooms (breakfast included), reasonable food but grossly overpriced. **Mid-range** **F** *New Habarana Inn*, Dambulla Rd, south of Habarana Junction, T70010. 4 clean enough rooms (Rs 450), restaurant, near busy road so can be noisy.

Eating *Acme Transit Hotel*, 30 Magaswewa. Excellent Sri Lankan meals. Also good clean rooms, delightful family.

Ancient cities - Cultural Triangle

Transport Habarana Junction is a good place to pick up buses heading north to Trincomalee (85 km northeast along the A6).

The A11 east from Habarana skirts the Minneriya-Giritale sanctuary en route to Polonnaruwa. Stands of gum trees line the road in the valley bottom, with low forest clad hills. Alternatively, the A11 northwest goes to Maradankadawala (24 km), and from there the A9-A13 continues northwest to **Anuradhapura** (see page 238).

Here is King Mahasena's magnificent Minneriya Tank (fourth century AD) covering 3,000 ha. At the end of the dry season there is little evidence of the tank which gets covered in weeds. However, you may spot some wildlife along the road, eg giant monitor lizards, or, if you are lucky, see Ceylon fish-owl and the large white-bellied sea-eagle hovering over the water. At the north end of the tank the *Anusha Curio Factory* has carvings and masks, where many tour buses stop. A further 12 km away is the Giritale Sanctuary with a tank dating from the seventh century AD.

Minneriya-Giritale Sanctuary
මින්නේරිය ගිරිතලේ
Phone code: 027
26 km from Polonnaruwa
Keep a look out for wild elephants on the Mineriya-Giritale rd

Sleeping Expensive These upmarket hotels overlook the lake in beautiful settings, and can make a convenient base for Polonnaruwa: **A** *Deer Park*, overlooking Giritale Tank, T46272, (Colombo T448850, F448849) jinasena@sri.lanka.net 76 cottages, plus 4 suites with open-air showers, upmarket facilities, business centre, gym, herbal health centre, split-level pool. Highly recommended. **B** *Giritale Hotel*, high above the Giritale tank, T46311, F46086. 42 good a/c roomssmall pool, unattractive public areas but good facilities and superb views from the restaurant and terrace. Recommended. **B** *Royal Lotus* T46316, (Colombo T448850, F448849). 56 comfortable a/c rooms plus 4 cottages, fine views over Giritale Tank, pool, good food, friendly and efficient staff. Recommended. **Cheap E** *Hemalee*, Polonnaruwa Rd, T46257. 18 large, basic rooms (Rs 700), helpful staff but overpriced. **E** *Woodside Tour Inn*, Polonnaruwa Rd, T46307. 10 grubby, basic rooms (Rs 600), restaurant.

Eating *Hotel The Village*, Polonnaruwa Road (10 km before Polonnaruwa), T47275. Good roadside halt for lunch. Authentic rice and curry with over 11 curries, Rs 250, very good service, clean toilets, 5 rooms planned. Recommended.

Transport Frequent bus service to Polonnaruwa.

Polonnaruwa   පොළොන්නරුව

Polonnaruwa, the island's medieval capital between the 11th and 13th century, flowered principally during 89 years of the reign of three kings. Today, the ruins stand witness to a lavish phase of building alongside the vast artificial lake. The ancient capital enclosed within its three concentric walls, palaces, stupas, image-houses, monasteries and bathing pools. In its imperial intentions, and the brevity of its existence, it may be compared to the great Mughal emperor Akbar's city of Fatehpur Sikri, near Agra in India.

Phone code: 027
Colour map 2, grid B5
Polonnaruwa is 13 km E from the sanctuary along the A11

The Sinhalese kings of Anuradhapura in 369 AD used Polonnaruwa as their residence but it did not rank as a capital until the eighth century. The Cholas from South India destroyed the Sinhalese Kingdom at the beginning of the 11th century, and taking control of most of the island, they established their capital at Polonnaruwa. In 1056 King Vijayabahu I defeated the Cholas, setting up his own capital in the city. It remained a vibrant centre of Sinhalese culture

Polonnaruwa

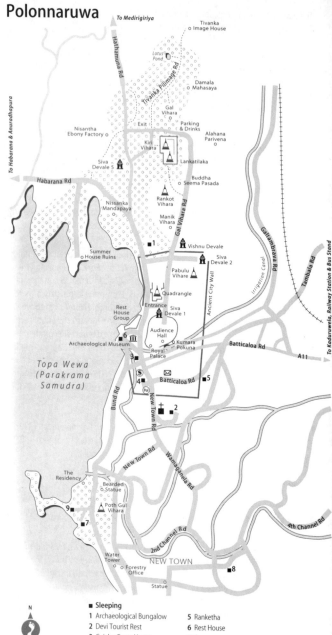

To Medirigiriya

To Habarana & Anuradhapura

Hathamuna Rd

Tivanka Pilimage Rd

Gal Vihara Rd

Galkambava Canal

Irrigation Canal

Tambala Rd

To Kaduruwela, Railway Station & Bus Stand

Tivanka
Image House

Lotus
Pond

Damala
Mahasaya

Gal
Vihara

Parking
& Drinks

Alahana
Parivena

Exit

Nisantha
Ebony Factory

Kiri
Vihara

Lankatilaka

Buddha
Seema Pasada

Siva
Devale 5

Habarana Rd

Rankot
Vihara

Nissanka
Mandapaya

Manik
Vihara

Vishnu Devale

Siva
Devale 2

Summer
House Ruins

Pabulu
Vihare

Ancient City Wall

Quadrangle

Entrance

Siva
Devale 1

Rest House
Group

Audience
Hall

Kumara
Pokuna

Batticaloa Rd

A11

Archaeological Museum

Royal
Palace

Topa Wewa
(Parakrama
Samudra)

Bund Pil Rd

New Town Rd

Batticaloa Rd

The
Residency

Bearded
Statue

Poth Gul
Vihara

New Town Rd

Wamagarela Rd

4th Channel Rd

2nd Channel Rd

Water
Tower

Forestry
Office

NEW TOWN

Statue

N

0 metres 500
0 yards 500

■ **Sleeping**

1 Archaeological Bungalow
2 Devi Tourist Rest
3 Gajaba Guest House
4 Orchid, Samudra &
   Dharshani Guest Houses

5 Ranketha
6 Rest House
7 Seruwa
8 Sri Lanka Inns
9 Village

under his successors, notably Parakramabahu I (1153-1186) who maintained very close ties with India, importing architects and engineers, and Nissankamalla (1187-1196). The rectangular shaped city was enclosed by three concentric walls, and was made attractive with parks and gardens. Polonnaruwa owes much of its glory to the artistic conception of King Parakramabahu I who planned the whole as an expression and statement of imperial power. Its great artificial lake provided cooling breezes through the city, water for irrigation and at the same time, defence along its entire west flank. The bund is over 14 km long and 1-m high, and the tank irrigates over 90 sq km of paddy fields. Fed by a 40 km long canal and a link from the Giritale tank, it was named after its imperial designer, the Parakrama Samudra (Topa Wewa).

Sights

After Parakramabahu, the kingdom went into terminal decline and the city was finally abandoned in 1288, after the tank embankment was breached. Fortunately, many of the remains are in an excellent state of repair though several of the residential buildings remain to be excavated. In 1982, it was designated a World Heritage Site. The restoration at the site is by the UNESCO sponsored Central Cultural Fund. Today it attracts numerous water birds, including cormorants and pelicans.

Entrance The entrance to the main site from the main road is just north of the Royal Palace. There is a one-way route through the sacred site that is generally quite well signed. You don't need a ticket for the Southern or the Rest House Groups. For **guides**, ask at the ticket office (or they will find you!). You can cover part of the tour (ie the main site) by car/taxi, and part on foot. Under a hot sun, walkers find visiting the whole site, which is very spread out, extremely tiring. If you are not visiting by car or a tour bus, cycling makes a very pleasant alternative (Rs 75 per day, available from most hotels) though the tracks are rough in places.

■ *0600-2000. Allow at least 3 hrs. A whole day is better to get some impression of this ancient site (and a further day cycling along the canals is also recommended). The ticket office (open 0800-1700) is to the right of the approach road to the Rest House (see map). A Cultural Triangle Round ticket, US$32.50 (combined ticket, only worthwhile if visiting all the sites), is valid.Single ticket US$15. Children under 12 and students with ISIC card, half price.*

Southern Group If you are staying at the lakeside rest house, or nearby, you can start by going 1.5 km south. A walk along the raised route on the east bank of the tank can be very pleasant. You will first see the giant 3.5-m high **statue** of a bearded figure, now believed to be King Parakramabahu himself, looking away from the city he restored, holding in his hand the palm leaf manuscript of the 'Book of Law' (some suggest it represents 'the burden of royalty' in the shape of a rope). Sadly, the statue is surrounded by rusty corrugated iron and barbed wire.

To its south is the now restored **Pothgul Vihara**, a *gedige* (image house) type building which is circular (instead of being corbelled from two sides), with four small solid *dagobas* around. The central circular room, with 5-m thick walls, is thought to have housed a library.

Rest House Group Nissankamalla built his own 'New' Palace close to the water's edge, in a beautiful garden setting. Today, the ruins are sadly in a poor state of repair. Just north of the rest house, beyond the sunken **royal baths**, are a stone 'mausoleum', the **Audience Hall**, and lastly the interesting **Council Chamber** which had the stone Lion throne (now housed in the Colombo National Museum). The four rows of 10 sculpted columns have inscriptions indicating the seating order in the chamber – from the King at the head, with the princes, army chiefs and ministers, down to the record keepers on his right. While to his left, were placed government administrators, and representatives of the business community. Across the water, to the northwest, the mound on the narrow strip of land which remains above flood water, has the ruins of the King Parakrama-

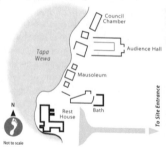

Polonnaruwa Rest House Group

bahu's 'Summer House' which was decorated with wall paintings.

Royal Citadel Group

Across the main road to the east of the rest house, is the entrance to the main site. Just south of the entrance, stands King Parakramabahu's Palace (Vejayanta Pasada). It is described in the Chronicles as originally having had seven storeys and 1,000 rooms, but much of it was of wood and so was destroyed by fire. The large central hall on the ground floor (31m x 13m) had 30 columns which supported the roof. you can see the holes for the beams in the 3-m thick brick walls. It has porticoes on the east and west and a wide stairway.

The **Council Chamber** (sometimes called Audience Hall) is immediately to its east. It has fine octagonal granite pillars and friezes of elephants, lions and dwarves, which follow the entire exterior of the base. Nearby, outside the palace wall, is the stepped **Kumara Pokuna** (Prince's Bath), restored in the 1930s. You can still see one of the spouts where the water is channelled through the open jaws of a crocodile.

Ancient City

The 'Quadrangle' is immediately to the north of the Citadel covering a huge walled area. The structures are comparatively modest in size but are carved in fine detail. To the east of the entrance is the **Siva Devale I**, a Hindu Temple (one of the many Siva and Vishnu temples here) built in about 1200 AD which has lost its brick roof. An example of the Dravidian Indian architectural style, it shows exceptional stone carving, and the fine bronze statues discovered in the ruins have been transferred to the Colombo Museum. This is still regarded as a sanctuary and shoes and hats have to be removed.

The **Vatadage** ('hall of the relic') near the entrance is a circular building with a dagoba on concentric terraces with sculptured railings, the largest with a diameter of 18 m. A superbly planned and executed 12th-century masterpiece attributed to Nissankamalla (1187-1196), the Vatadage has modest proportions but remarkably graceful lines. It was almost certainly intended to house the Tooth Relic. There are impressive guard stones at the entrances of the second terrace and wing stones with *makaras* enclosing lion figures. The *moonstone* to the north entrance of the top terrace is superb. The dagoba at the centre has four Buddhas (some damaged) with a later stone screen.

The **Hatadage** (also known as the Atadage – 'house of eight relics, built in 60 Sinhalese hours' which made up a day'. With extraordinary *moonstones* at its entrance (see page 311), the sanctuary was built by Nissankamalla and is also referred to as the Temple of the Tooth, since the relic may have been placed here for a time. See the Buddha statue here framed by three solid doorways, and then look back at one of the Buddha statues in the Vatadage, again beautifully framed by the doorways.

Gal Pota, to the east of the Hatadage, is 'Book of Stone' which is to the side of the path and can easily be missed. According to the inscription it weighs 25 tons, and was brought over 90 km from Mihintale. It is in the form of a palm leaf measuring over 9 m by 1.2 m, over 60 cm thick in places, with Sinhalese inscriptions praising the works of the King Nissankamalla including his conquests in India. The **Chapter House** nearby dates from the seventh century. The ziggurat-like Satmahal Prasada (originally seven-storeyed) in the northeast corner, decorated with stucco figures, has lost its top 'storey'. The 9-m sq base decreases at each level as in Cambodian *prasats*.

The **Bo Tree shrine** is to the west of the main Vatadage. The **Nissankalata** (**Lotus Mandapa**) nearby was built by King Nissankamalla (1187-96) for a dagoba. This small pavilion has remains of a stone seat (from which the King listened to chanting of scriptures), steps and a stone fence imitating a latticed wooden railing with posts. The ornamental stone pillars which surround the dagoba are in the form of thrice-bent lotus buds on stalks, a design which has become one of Sri Lanka's emblem. A statue of a *Bodhisattva* is to its east.

The **Thuparama**, in the south of the Quadrangle, is a small *gedige* which was developed as a fusion of Indian and Sinhalese Buddhist architecture. This has the only surviving vaulted dome of its type and houses a number of Buddha statues. It has very thick plaster-covered brick walls with a staircase embedded in them, now usually locked.

The **Hindu temples** belong to different periods. If you walk past the **Pabulu Vihare**, a squat stupa up to the north wall of the ancient city, you come to one of the earliest temples with Tamil inscriptions, **Siva Devala 2**. Built of

Polonnaruwa Quadrangle

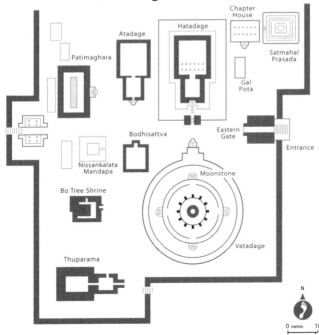

Ancient cities - Cultural Triangle

stone by the Indian Cholas in a style they were developing in Tamil Nadu (as at Thanjavur) but using brick rather than stone.

Northern monuments

Another group of scattered monuments is further north. The **Alahana Parivena** (Royal Crematory Monastery) Complex was set aside by Parakramabahu and is worth exploring. The UNESCO restoration project is concentrated in this area.

To the left of the path, beyond the ancient city wall, is the **Rankot Vihara**. The fourth largest dagoba on the island with a height of 55 m, it was built by Nissankamalla in the 12th century. Note the perfection of the spire and the clarity of the statues round the drum.

The tall **Buddha Seema Pasada** was the Chapter House or convocation hall where you can still make out the central throne of the chief abbot, which was surrounded by monks' cells.

The large *gedige* **Lankatilaka** ('ornament of Lanka'), the image house with a Buddha statue, had five storeys. It has walls which are 4-m thick and still stand 17-m high, although the roof has crumbled. The design illustrates the development in thinking which underlay the massive building, for it marks a turning away from the abstract form of the dagoba to a much more personalized faith in the Buddha in human form. The building is essentially a shrine, built to focus the attention of worshippers on the 18-m high statue of the Buddha at the end of the nave. Though built of brick and covered in stucco, the overall design of the building shows strong Tamil influence. The exterior bas relief sculpture, most of which is in very impressive, sheds light on contemporary architectural styles. To the south of the Lankatileke is a *mandapa* with carved columns.

Queen Subhadra is believed to have built the 'milk white' **Kiri Vihara** stupa next to it, so named because of its unspoilt white plaster work when it was first discovered. It remains the best preserved of the island's unrestored dagobas. The plasterwork is intact although the whitewash is only visible in place, eg around the relic box. There are excellent views from the Chapter House which has the foundations only just visible.

A short walk from the car park in front the Kiri Vihara alongside a small tank

The **Gal Vihara** (Cave of the Spirits of Knowledge) is rightly regarded as one of the foremost attractions of Sri Lanka and has great significance to Buddhists. It forms a part of Parakramabahu's monastery where a gigantic Buddha seated on a pedestal under a canopy was carved out of an 8-m high rock. On either side of the rock shrine are further vast carvings of a seated Buddha and a 14-m recumbent Buddha in *Parinirvana* (rather than death), indicated by the way the higher foot is shown slightly withdrawn. The grain of the rock is beautiful as is the expression. Near the head of the reclining figure, the 7-m standing image of banded granite with folded arms was once believed to be his grieving disciple Ananda but is now thought to be of the Buddha himself. The foundation courses of the brick buildings which originally enclosed the sculptures, are visible. Sadly, the presentation of the magnificent carved Buddhas is rather disappointing. An unattractive, protective canopy now shields the seated Buddha, which is caged in with rusty metal bars and a scratched plastic 'viewing window' making clear viewing and photography impossible. There are plans to raise further protective roofings above the reclining and standing Buddha statues.

A path continues north to rejoin the road. The **Lotus Pond** a little further along, is a small bathing pool with five concentric circles of eight petals which form the steps down into the water.

The road ends at the **Tivanka Image House** where the Buddha image is in the unusual 'thrice bent' posture (shoulder, waist and knee) associated with a female figure, possibly emphasizing his gentle aspect. This is the largest brick-built shrine here, now substantially renovated (though work continues). There are remarkable frescoes inside depicting scenes from the *Jatakas*, though not as fine as those in Sigiriya. Under the 13th-century frescoes, even earlier original paintings have been discovered. The decorations on the outside of the building are excellent with delightful carvings of dwarves on the plinth. The image house actually has a double skin, and for a small tip the guardian will unlock a door about half way inside the building. You can then walk between the outer and inner walls. The passage is lit from windows high up in the wall. It is an excellent way of seeing the corbel building technique. The guardian may also unroll the painted copies of the frescoes, which eventually will be repainted onto the walls.

Archaeological Museum, on the edge of Parakrama Samudra, 1 km from the **Museum** *Rest House*. Well presented exhibits, statues found on site, very informative, with scaled down reconstructions. ■ *0800-1730. Tickets are on sale here for the site. Guides expect around Rs 350.*

Essentials

Mid-range C *Rest House*, Lake Bund (by Parakrama Samudra), T22299, F01-503504. **Sleeping** 10 clean rooms with modernised bath extended for Queen Elizabeth's visit in the 1950s, some austere with black floor, fine bar area, popular restaurant (busy at lunchtime), sun deck with superb views, excellent location.

Hotels west of the Poth Gul Vihara by the lakeside are 3 km from the old town, so transport is essential. Bikes are available. **C** *Seruwa*, T22411. 40 rather dark, cramped rooms (Rs 1500) including 6 a/c (extra Rs 416), all with private lake-facing balcony, restaurant, bar, pool, popular with tour groups. **C** *Village Polonnaruwa*, T23366. 30 a/c rooms (US$5 reduction if a/c is turned off!), including some cheaper noisier rooms around courtyard, small pool, restaurant, bar, unattractive building (dark public areas), may be rowdy on public holidays but reasonable value given the amenities.

Cheap E *Gajabha Guest House*, Kuruppu Garden, Lake Bund, near Rest House, T22394. 23 very clean, comfortable rooms (Rs 600-700) including some a/c with hot bath (Rs 1000), TV lounge, good restaurant, bike hire, very friendly, welcoming and knowledgeable host (Mr Srikanth), excellent choice, best in this class. Highly recommended. **E** *Gama Guest House*, Habarana Rd, T23101. 5 new clean rooms (Rs 500) including 1 a/c (Rs 700), restaurant. **E** *Ranketha*, 160 Kaduruwela Rd, T22080. 12 rooms (Rs 600), some a/c (Rs 800) in rural style guesthouse refurbished in 2000, open-air restaurant overlooking rice fields, upmarket ambitions mean prices may rise. Recommended. **E-F** *Devi Tourist Home*, Lake View Garden Rd, off New Town Rd, T23181. 5 rooms of varying age and size (Rs 350-650), 4 with attached bath, very clean, extremely welcoming family, excellent home cooking, bike hire (Rs 100/day), free pick-up from Old Town, peaceful location. Highly recommended. **E-G** *Orchid Guest House* Habarana Rd, T25253. Choice of 6 clean enough rooms (Rs 250-600), reasonable value. **G** *Samudra Guest House*, Habarana Rd, T22817. 6 variable rooms (Rs 200-300), inspect first, some larger with private terrace, popular with backpackers, restaurant.

For hotels near the New Town you can get a bus from the railway station or the Old Town bus stop, and take the path signposted beyond the Statue, for 1 km to the east: **D** *Sri Lankan Inns*, 2nd Channel Rd, T22403. 17 pricey rooms (Rs 800), around a pleasant courtyard, meals to order, beautiful walks along waterways, clean but showing signs of decline.

Eating If you are in the Old Town, the *Gajabha Hotel* offers the best food with many guests from other hotels dining here. There are several cheap eating places (Chinese/Sri Lankan) in the Old Town, along Habarana Rd.

Shopping *Nishantha Ebony Factory*, No 3, 26th Post, Hathamuna Rd, expects tourists to call where craftsmen can be seen carving, large stock on sale but make sure you bargain hard though.

Transport **Road Bus**: the out-of-town bus stop is near the railway station, in Kuduruwela. Several buses daily to **Colombo** (6 hrs), via **Dambulla** (2 hrs). Minibuses to/from **Anuradhapura** (3 hrs), **Kandy** (4 hrs), and **Batticaloa**. For **Sigiriya**, travel to Sigiriya Junction in Inamaluwa, and change to a CTB/private bus (Rs 7-10). For **Trincomalee**, travel to Habarana Junction and change. **Train** The Station is in Kuduruwela, 4 km east of the Old Town on Batticaloa Rd. **Colombo**: *Udaya Devi*, 1225, 6 hrs. *Mail*, 2147, 8 hrs.

When leaving Polonnaruwa, it pays to get on at Kuduruwela to get a seat

Directory **Banks** *Seylan Bank*, corner of Habarana Rd and road to *Rest House*, offers foreign exchange at good rates (including TCs) with no commission (1% stamp duty). **Useful addresses Tourist Police**: junction on Habarana Rd, Batticaloa Rd, New Town Rd, T23099.

Medirigiriya
 මැදිරිගිරිය

About 30 km north of Pollonoruwa, the Mandalagiri Vihara is a 7th-8th century vatadage. The circular image house with concentric pillared terraces (similar to the one at Pollonoruwa) is on a hilltop site which is covered by the Cultural Triangle round ticket. ■ *Getting there: the site is reached via Giritala or Minneriya on the Habarana Rd. Buses and tuk-tuks from both places can get you to Medirigiriya.*

Routes From Polonnaruwa there are several choices. You can return to Habarana Junction (45 km west) and then either head south via Sigiriya and Dambulla towards Kandy. Go northwest towards Anuradhapura or travel northeast to Trincomalee. Alternatively you can return to Kandy via Mahiyangana.

Polonnaruwa to Kandy via Mahiyangana

This is a quiet road with a good surface and beautiful scenery, only 15 km longer than the route via Dambulla. The A11 goes east through Polonnaruwa crossing the Mahaweli Ganga on a road/rail bridge. The road to Mahiyangana (via Siripura) is signed to the right. There is a good chance of seeing elephants feeding near the road.

The road turns back towards the hills with one of Sri Lanka's most recent reserves, **Wasgomuwa National Park** to the right. The old entrance was via Handungamuwa, scheduled to be replaced by an entrance near Polonnaruwa on completion of a bridge). Call the Wildlife Department first (T433012). There is some pricey accommodation in the park. There is a belt of woodland on both sides of the river but otherwise the vegetation consists of grass, scrub and low bushes.

The **Maduru Oya National Park** is to the left. It was designated a national park in 1983 to protect the catchment of the reservoirs in its neighbourhood and also to conserve the natural habitat of the large marsh elephant which is found particularly in the Mahaweli flood plain. Deer, sambhur and the rarer leopard or bear are present, in addition to a large number of bird species.

The area to the east of Mahiyangana is one of the few areas left where **Veddas**, the original inhabitants of Sri Lanka are found. They live on the edge of the Maduru Oya National Park and have rights to hunt in the Park (though bows and arrows may have been superseded by the gun) and to sell the meat to local people. Their numbers are shrinking.

There are wonderful views of spectacular mountains of central Sri Lanka in the distance and rice fields and forest in foreground before the A26 turns right into Mahiyangana town.

Mahiyangana

This is a bustling town with a long history. In legend it is associated with a visit by the Buddha, and the new temple which the late Premadasa had built to resemble the famous Buddhist temple at Bodhgaya in Bihar, India.

Colour map 2, grid C5
Phone code: 055

The centre is busy with a bazar with shops of all kinds, curiously even a dealer in elephant tusks! The Mahaweli Ganga Project has added to the town's importance and there are obvious signs of prosperity in the modern office buildings.

Mahiyangana Dagoba, 500 m south from the main Kandy road, is of special importance since the Buddha was supposed to have visited the spot and preached to the tribal people. Unfortunately it is not so well kept as those in the north, possibly because it is slightly out of the way now that the east coast cannot be visited. The area though is very attractive – the park with the dagoba in it is well kept and is overlooked by the hills on the far bank of the Mahaweli.

Sorabora Wewa is just on the outskirts of Mahiyangana on the road to Bibile. According to legend a giant is said to have created the dam. You will probably have to ask someone to find the road for you. You can see two enormous outcrops (the Sorabora Gate) through which the run off from the lake is channelled.

Cheap D *Rest House* (UDA), west of Clocktower Junction, 1 km south of the A26, T7099. 10 rooms with bath, 2 a/c (Rs 500-1,200), restaurant serving good food (meals Rs 150), rooms are large but not of a particularly good standard, nice position overlooking the river, pleasant garden, quiet (the river is dangerous for bathing). A smaller **F** *Rest House*, closer to the main road, 3 rooms at the back, meals in dining room, fairly clean, basic but good value for the price. Ask the bus to drop you at the *Old Rest House* stop for both rest houses.

Sleeping
For eating the best is at the UDA Rest House. Small food stalls and 'bakeries' in the bazar

Ancient cities - Cultural Triangle

Road Bus: buses to/from Kandy, several between 0500 and 1530. To Kandy takes 3 hrs, from Kandy about 2¾ hrs, Rs 21.

Transport

Mahiyangana

▲ **Sri Lankan Leaders**

1 Devanampiya Tissa
2 King Dutugemunu, 161-137
3 Parakrama Bahu VI, 1412-1467
4 Kirti Sri, 1747-1780
5 Don S Senanayake, 1948-52
6 Dudley Senanayake, 1952-56, 1965-70

Not to scale

Directory **Banks** *People's Bank*, opposite the New Temple, where, with special treatment for foreign visitors you can get exchange against TCs within 15 mins.

Mahiyangana to Kandy
There are 3 possible routes

The A26 passes through several small hamlets – **Udadumbara** (46 km), **Hunnagiriya** (40 m) and **Teledeniya** (23 km). There are superb views of the Victoria Lake, created in the late 1970s as part of the British Aid sponsored Mahaweli Project. It then runs west through Pallewatta and Hasalaka (with an entrance to the national park) into the hills before climbing through a series of 18 hairpin bends between 62 and 57 km from Kandy. This road is often described locally as Sri Lanka's most dangerous road. For anyone familiar with mountain roads in the Himalaya the relatively gentle climb and forested slopes present little sense of hazard but buses often take the bends too fast for safety. There are spectacular views across the plains of the Dry Zone, now irrigated by the Mahaweli Ganga Project. Don't forget to stop near the top to look back on the glistening Mahaweli crossing the plains below.

Approaching Kandy the road passes the dolomite quarries of Rajooda and the Kandy Free Trade Zone before crossing to the west bank of the Mahaweli Ganga. The roads in and out of Kandy can all be very congested, particularly at festival times.

These two pleasant alternatives to the A26 go through the **Randenigala Sanctuary**. The slightly shorter route crosses the Mahaweli Ganga at Mahiyangana and then goes due south to Weragantota immediately after crossing the river. The road climbs to the south side of the Randenigala Reservoir, then crosses the Victoria Dam to rejoin the A26 about 20 km from Kandy. There is no fuel available on this route.

The road offers a typical example of Sri Lankan life

To take the second alternative, you have to take the B road out of Mahiyangana to the southeast to **Pangarammana**, then join the road which also climbs to the southern edge of the Randenigala Reservoir.

The irrigation development has created an area of intensive rice production. During the *maha* harvest (April-May) you will come across farmers winnowing and the stalks being constructed into quite large circular walls. Water is so important that it is very rare indeed to travel without seeing people washing clothes and themselves in rivers, streams or other water courses.

Wild country where elephants can often be seen roaming along the shores of the lake

After passing through **Minipe** the road follows the 30-km long Minipe Right Bank Canal, then slowly starts to rise. It crosses the river at the base of the Randenigala Reservoir Dam, which straddles the last gorge before the Mahaweli Ganga plunges to the plains. Its crest is 485-m long and 94-m high. The road then winds spectacularly around the southern side of the upper lake. Notice too the 'contour lines' on the lake side as the water level drops during the dry season. The road continues to climb over a small pass – you see paddy fields in the valley below. Once over the pass you can see the **Victoria Dam**. There are a couple of vantage points from which you can take photographs. Over 120-m high, the dam is a massive structure, even bigger than the Randenigala Dam. There is a restaurant and look out place on the dam's north side. Not surprisingly both dams are quite heavily guarded and there are several checkpoints.

Eastern Region

9

Eastern Region

270 Eastern Province (North)

270 Trincomalee
271 Sights
273 Essentials
273 Beaches north of Trincomalee

275 Eastern Province (South)
275 Batticaloa
276 Gal Oya National Park
277 Arugam Bay
279 Lahugala National Park
279 Monaragala

280 Jaffna and the Northern Provinces

The eastern province is located entirely within the Dry Zone. Comparatively sparsely populated, the coastline is dotted with fishing hamlets along the lagoon fringed shore. Inland are some of Sri Lanka's largest wildlife parks, soon to be joined together by a corridor which it is hoped will allow elephants a free passage right across the region. But the dry interiorhas also seen some of Sri Lanka's most ambitious re-colonisation projects, including the 1950s Gal Oya scheme.

In the early 1980s the coastal fringe from Batticaloa through Trincomalee to Kuchchaveli was designated one of Sri Lanka's five Tourist Development Zones. It was hoped to capitalize on the superb beaches and underwater opportunities of diving and snorkelling, and on the distinct climatic regime which makes June to August the best season, just when the southwest beaches of the southwest are being lashed by the southwest monsoon. However since 1983 the province, with the strategically important port of Trincomalee and Batticaloa, its largest towns, has been devastatingly affected by the civil war. Many of the large hotels completed before 1983 have been unoccupied since, and many have become derelict.

Eastern Province (North)

This part of the east coast, particularly the beautiful deserted beaches just north of Trincomalee, held much promise for development as attractive tourist destinations but the civil war made it impossible to travel freely in this region. The area did however begin to see a rise in foreign visitors in 2000, with most heading for Nilaveli, just north of Trincomalee. Although travel to and from Trincomalee is relatively safe, there are many checkpoints on the way so progress may be slow. The situation could change at any time so ask advice from your embassy before travelling. The northeast monsoon between October and January can bring strong winds and heavy downpours when the sea can get rough.

Route The direct route to Trincomalee along the A12 from Anuradhapura and Mihintale runs northeastwards across the Dry Zone. Few people use this route which was closed for long periods during the civil war though it is now considered safe during daylight hours. Buses run regularly along this road (except when it is unpassable due to flooding) although there are frequent police checks. The journey from Mihintale (in spite of the occasionally poor surface) is at least an hour shorter than the more widely used alternative via Habarana.

The route itself runs through one of Sri Lanka's least populated regions. Abandoned irrigation tanks and marshy ground are interspersed by forest and occasional fields of paddy land. Most of the journey is across the flat plain, broken by a few isolated granite blocks, giving way to the low range of hills just inland of the coast.

Trincomalee ත්‍රිකුණාමලය

Colour map 4, grid A1
Phone code: 026

The main points of interest in Trincomalee today are the harbour and Fort Frederick (the latter is out of bounds). At any one point it is only possible to see sections of the magnificent bay which gives Trinco its reputation as one of the finest natural harbours in the world. The harbour has often been fiercely contested, and it was a crucial naval base for the British during the Second World War. The town itself holds little of interest and is rather depressing.

Background The town itself is a remarkable exception to the typical pattern of colonial ports which, once established, became the focal points for political and economic development of their entire regions. In India Madras, Calcutta and Bombay each owed their origin to colonial development and succeeded in re-orienting the geography and economy of their entire regions. However, Trincomalee was established as a colonial port purely for its wider strategic potential, the finest natural harbour in Asia, dominating the vital navigation lanes between Europe and Asia, especially significant from the late 19th century when steam power saw a massive increase in the size and draught of naval ships. Trincomalee was home to the South East Asia Command of the British Navy during the Second World War, and its bombing by the Japanese in 1942 was seen as a major threat to the Allies lifeline to Australasia and the Pacific.

Despite the port's global strategic importance it had virtually no impact on its immediate hinterland. Barren and thinly populated, the region around the city saw no development, and economically Trincomalee District remained one of Sri Lanka's most backward regions. The town itself has never been very important, but that reflects its location in Sri Lanka's dry northeastern region, where the interior has been difficult to cultivate and malaria-infested for

History of Fort Frederick

1623	Built by Portuguese	1800	Duke of Wellington stayed at
1639	Captured by Dutch		lodge: missed boat which sank
1672	Attacked by French		losing all hands
1782	Captured by British (Jan)	1803	Renamed Fort Frederick after
	Recaptured by French (Aug)		Duke of York
1783	Treaty of Paris transferred from	1842	St Stephens Church built
	French to British and finally	1905	Dismantled
	Dutch	1942	Trincomalee bombed by Japanese
1795	Captured by British	1946	Reservoir completed

centuries. Only today, with the completion of the Victoria Dam and the re-settlement scheme of colonizers using irrigation from the Mahaweli Ganga Project, is the area inland developing into an important agricultural region.

However, it is also torn by political strife. The civil war since 1983 destroyed the tourism which offered one of the few opportunities for increasing revenue, and the possibility of a return to peace remains the best hope of stimulating significant economic development in its hinterland. Future development is wholly dependent on a permanent improvement in the political situation. The town had miserable connections by narrow and badly surfaced road to the rest of the country and only a skeleton train and bus service.

Sights

The main town is built on a fairly narrow piece (perhaps 700 m wide) of land between Back Bay and the inner harbour. Nearer the centre, there is a thriving shopping area. Small single-storey shops selling all sorts of goods, as well as several pawn brokers, line Central Street. Many shops are Muslim run (a mosque is halfway up on the west side of the street). The north end of Central Street is more residential. Ravages of the civil war, however, are evident – some homes have clearly been destroyed, while the Mother Teresa Home for the Destitute on Colombo Road does its share to alleviate the condition.

Fort Frederick When open to visitors, bear left around the stadium near the bus stand to reach the fort. This is still an active army base but visitors may enter to go up to the Swami Rock and the Hindu temple built on the cliffs high above the sea. The magnificent harbour gave 'Trinco' a huge strategic importance. It was fought over many times. The fort was originally built by the Portuguese who destroyed the original and ancient Siva temple. The gatehouse dates from 1676. Outside are two cannons, a howitzer and a mortar. Inside, apart from Wellesley house (closed to visitors) you can see some classic British Army colonial buildings (the design seems to have been used in all tropical locations for the British army) and the parade ground. Part of the area has been given over to a deer park. Don't take photos though.

At times the whole of the Fort Frederick promontory is 'out of bounds'

Konesvaram Temple This modern temple, dedicated to Siva (one of five most sacred Saivite sites), stands at the farthest end of the rock in the place of the original. It has a lingam, believed to be from the original shrine, which was recovered by a diver. Only a couple of stone pillars from the original temple have survived. The new temple is highly decorated and painted. A tree on a precarious ledge on the cliffside has typical strips of coloured cloth tied on its branches, left there by devotees in the hope to have their prayers answered.

Regular services are held. The one on Fri evening is particularly colourful

Eastern Region

Go behind the temple to find the so-called 'Lovers Leap' memorial, apparently after the legend according to which the daughter of a Dutch official, Francina van Rhede, threw herself from the rock after her lover sailed away. The truth seems to be more prosaic than the fiction, however, for according to government archives she was alive and well when the Dutch memorial was placed here! The memorial stands on an old temple column.

The terrace around the temple offers fine views to the north across Black Bay and the Inner Harbour and from vantage points on the rock cliff, you can sometimes see turtles swimming in the transparent blue-green sea over a 100 m below.

British War Cemetery On the north outskirts of town, at **Sampalthivu**, is the British War Cemetery, just before the road crosses the Uppveli creek. A number were killed as a result of the Japanese air raid on the harbour in 1942. HMS Hermes was sunk off Kalkudah and Passekudah, just south of Trinco. However, the island was a recuperation centre and many more died as a result of their wounds. The cemetery was damaged by bombing during Sri Lanka's civil war in the late 1980s. The damaged headstones have now been replaced and the garden is beautifully maintained in the tradition of Commonwealth War cemeteries. It has great sentimental value for many in Britain whose families were stationed at the naval base. The custodian has a register of the graves and will show the visitor some interesting documents relating to Trincomalee.

Other sights St Mary's cemetery is opposite the stadium. On Inner Harbour Road you get a good impression of this huge harbour with Powder Island just off it. Ferries leave from here for Mutur on the far side of the bay.

Trincomalee

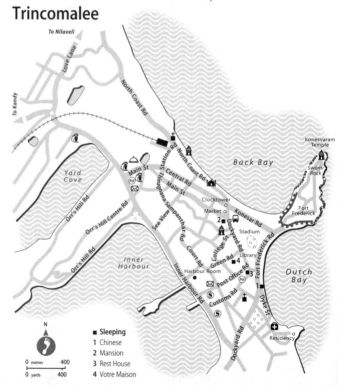

■ **Sleeping**
1 Chinese
2 Mansion
3 Rest House
4 Votre Maison

Eastern Region

Other buildings of interest, eg Admiralty House, the British Dockyard are not open to visitors. There is little left of the British naval days apart from picturesque names on the map: Marble Bay, Sweat Bay, Yard Cove, Deadman's Cove, Powder and Sober Islands. French Pass marks the passage where the French fleet escaped.

The **Archaeological Museum** has some Buddhist finds from the coast.

Museum

Essentials

Cheap E *Rest House*, corner of Dockyard and Post Office Rds, T22562. 8 rooms with fan, two **D** with a/c (overpriced), attached bath, cheap restaurant, bar (*Lion* beer Rs 90), not particularly well maintained but better than most of the competition. **F** *7 Islands*, Orr's Hill, T22373. 25 a/c rooms (Rs 500), some facing the harbour. **F** *Railway Retiring Rooms* on 1st floor, 6 rooms with fan, shower, some with nets, all share a sitting area with balcony, short eats downstairs.

Sleeping
The uncertain political climate has left the traveller with a pretty poor choice

There are a number of cheap restaurants near the bus station, and at the junctions of Post Office and Court Roads. The *Rest House* serves cheap, if bland, rice and curry (Rs 75) and breakfasts (Rs 100). Meals and short eats are available during the day at the *Harbour Room* at the *Elephant Soft Drinks* factory on Inner Harbour Rd.

Eating

Air The airport is at China Bay, 10 km southwest but domestic services remain suspended. **Road** The A12 between Anuradhapura and Trincomalee may be open during daylight hours only. **Bus**: the CTB and private bus stations are adjacent to each other at the junction of Dockyard Rd, North Coast Rd and Main St. To **Colombo**: private buses (via Habarana and Dambulla) depart when full during the morning and early afternoon (5-6 hrs, Rs 120 for Intercity Express). CTB buses go at 0730, 0800, 0830, 0900, 1000, 1400 (5½-7 hrs, Rs 55). To **Anuradhapura** (4 hrs). **Batticaloa** at 0700. **Dambulla**, 3 hrs. **Kandy** at 0700, 1030, 1230 (5 hrs, Rs 35). **Vavuniya** at 0850. **Train** To **Colombo** (Fort), 1600, 8 hrs (2nd class Rs 168, 3rd class Rs 61). To **Gal Oya Junction**, 1230 (2 hrs). Check departure times.

Transport

Banks *Bank of Ceylon* on Inner Harbour Rd, near Customs Rd. **Communications** Post Office: corner of Power House and Kachcheri Rds. Also, plenty of *Metrocard* and *Lanka Payphones* cardphones around town, or make discount IDD calls at *Votre Maison*. **Useful addresses** *UNHCR*, Main St. *International Committee of the Red Cross (ICRC)* Orr's Hill Rd.

Directory

Eastern Region

Beaches north of Trincomalee

The road from Trincomalee to Nilaveli runs inland for much of the way, occasionally close to the lagoon. Several of the hotels closed during the troubles but a few have re-opened.

Nilaveli, 16 km north of Trincomalee, is a small village but its attraction is the inviting fine 'white' sand beach which is safe for swimming outside the period of the northeast monsoons. Screw pines/palms (*Pandanus* pedunculatus) with their prop-like roots grow securely in the sand and provide some shade. The lack of large numbers of tourists means there is the added bonus of the absence of persistent hawkers on the beach.

Nilaveli
Phone code: 026

The narrow **Pigeon island**, just a few hundred metres off-shore, is covered with rocks but has some sandy stretches and offers worthwhile snorkelling to view corals and fish. It has potential for good diving too. The island is apparently named after Blue Rock pigeons which were found here. Their eggs are prized by Sri Lankans. There are boat trips organized by the resort hotel which charges around Rs 600 for six in a boat for a half day trip. There are no facilities and little shade, so go prepared.

Sleeping and eating Expensive A *Nilaveli Beach Resort*, 800m off road, 15 km north of Trinco, T22071, F32297. 101 rooms, choice of furnished standard a/c rooms (US$40), deluxe a/c with carpets, mini-fridge, and closer to beach (US$50), some good value non-a/c rooms (US$33), plus 2 very good a/c suites with minibar, sitting area, hot water, great views and private sun deck, pleasant open-sided restaurant serves reasonable meals (Rs 250+), bar quite pricey (lime-soda Rs 80), good pool, attractive hotel with densely-shaded beach-front garden, excellent location, very quiet, very good value. **Mid-range D** *Club Oceanic*, Alles Garden, T22307. 600 m off road, 3.3 km north of Trinco (and 300 m before the Second World War cemetery), only 36 of the 98 rooms still functioning, set in blocks of 4, a/c, fan, attached hot bath, small private balconies, rooms considerably better than rest of the hotel (public areas in ruins), potentially excellent site right on curved bay with superb sandy beach, small pool, nightclub closed (though signs still reads 'Holy Mass at 1600 in the nightclub'!). **Cheap F** *Shahira*, '10th mile', 1 km off road, 13.5 km north of Trinco, T32224. 28 rooms with fan around shady garden, attached bath, restaurant (meals Rs 200-250), bar, exchange, 200m from beach, boat to Pigeon Island (about 30 mins), friendly, good value. **G** *French Garden Pragash*, 3 km north of Trinco, T21705, 10 basic but cheap chalets, excellent location right on the beach, fan, no nets, attached bath not to clean, seafood restaurant, will probably improve as more guests visit.

Transport Crowded public buses run to Uppuveli and Nilaveli, or you may be able to get a tuk-tuk (Rs 250 to Nilaveli).

Trincomalee area

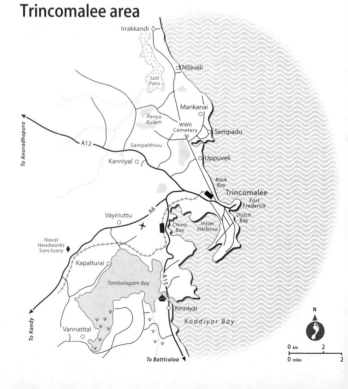

From Trincomalee the road passes through the heart of the Dry Zone and shifting '*chena*' cultivation across the gently sloping plain to **Habarana** (85 km). Irrigated rice is interspersed with extensive tracts of mixed jungle, including teak, bamboo and eucalyptus.

Trincomalee to Habarana
The A6 goes SW to Habarana passing Kantalai

Since the outbreak of the civil war, there have been few places suitable for travellers to stop along the route. There has been obvious clearance of bush on each side of the road to provide a clear firing zone for military bunkers. The road may also be subject to a dusk to dawn curfew and a journey has frequently been interrupted by many checkpoints, both police and army. At the check-points, bus passengers must dismount, walk through, then get back on the bus, while tourists travelling by car are often waved on without questioning. Do, however, slow right down and make sure that the guards have acknowledged you and indicated that you may go through). In spite of this, the journey along the A6 can be quite a pleasant drive. For the first 20 km the road is narrow and the surface very poor. There are, however, some attractive areas such as the Devil's Bends around the Kandurukanda peak and as the countryside changes when the road passes through pleasant forested hills. In the last part of the route the landscape has a more 'domesticated' feel, with fruit trees, coconut, mango, tamarind and palmyra palms. It is possible to visit the Minneriya-Giritale Sanctuary, just off this route (see page 257).

Kantalai (Kantale) has fuel and a few shops. It is the centre of a very intensive farming area made possible from the irrigation provided by the huge Kantalai Tank, originally dating from the seventh century, which provides water to extensive rice fields to the southeast of the main road. The restored tank bund (retaining dam) was breached in 1987 with hundreds killed. Kantalai is also the Headquarters for the second Battalion Sri Lanka National Guard. There is a rest house in a beautiful position by the lake, particularly appreciated by those with an interest in water birds, but in the present political situation visi-tors cannot stay. There is not much evidence of the Somawathie National Park which comes quite close to the road for a few kilometres just before the Kantalai Tank, nor of the Naval Headworks Sanctuary.

Kantalai

Eastern Province (South)

From Trincomalee, the A15 hugs the east coast all the way south to Batticaloa, sometimes between the sea itself and shallow lagoons. There are numerous ferry crossings. This coastal road is affected by cyclones from time to time making it a desolate journey. During the present political situation it is inac-cessible to tourists.

Trincomalee to Batticaloa

This old Dutch town is called the 'town of tamarinds' by its predominantly Tamil population. The Dutch fortified the town in 1602, the remains of which can be seen near the present day rest house, but today it is famous for its sing-ing fish, heard in the middle of the lagoon on still nights. The centre of the lagoon bridge is reputed to be the best place for listening to the extraordinary resonating sounds. Batticaloa has been the centre of repeated violent fighting between the Tamil Tigers and the army. Check locally whether it is possible and safe to visit.

Batticaloa
මඩකලපුව

Sleeping and eating **Mid-range C** *Lake View Inn*, 6 Lloyd's Rd, T065 2593. 3 rooms, restaurant with good seafood. The following may be available: near the Dutch Fort on Arugam Bay side, the rebuilt **D** *Resthouse*. **E** *Beach House Guesthouse*, Bar Rd, near

Eastern Region

Lighthouse, quiet, good food. **E** *Sunshine Inn*, 118 Bar Rd, on the other side of the rail-way track from the station, clean, in a pleasant garden. **F** *Railway Retiring Rooms*, T065 2271, 8 rooms.

Batticaloa The route from Batticaloa to Badulla leaves the coastal lagoons and goes due
to Badulla & southwest across the heart of the Dry Zone along the A5 for 70 km to the junc-
the Central tion with the A26. This then climbs low outliers of the Central Highlands
Highlands before dropping down again to Mahiyangana on the banks of the Mahaweli
Ganga. The road then climbs through the Highlands to Kandy.

The A15 leaves Batticaloa to the northwest, running 10 km to its junction
with the A5 at Chenkaladi. The A5 then goes southwest across the Dry Zone
through Maha Oya. 35 km beyond Maha Oya the road passes southeast of the
687m hill Kokagala before being joined by the A26 to Waywatta. This is the
shortest route into the Central Highlands, going via Mahiyangana. For alternative routes from Mahiyangana to Kandy, see page 266.

An alternative route to the Central Highlands continues south down the A5
through Bibile and climbs steeply to Lunugala and Tennugewatta. The A5
continues to Badulla.

Batticaloa to The coastal route south of Batticaloa is no easier than that to Trincomalee. A
Arugam Bay & succession of tiny fishing hamlets line the coast, but the A4 has had little work
Nuwara Eliya on it for years and it runs through an area subject to periodic violence. At
Karativu, the A31 goes inland to **Ampara**, a district headquarters. A minor
road then goes to **Inginiyagala** where you can stay to visit the Gal Oya
National Park early in the morning.

Sleeping A *Inginiyagala Safari Inn*, superbly situated, T063 2499 or in Colombo
T91805. 22 comfortable rooms, restaurant, 10 min walk brings you to the lake, picturesque at sunset, the hotel will organize tours into the park.

Gal Oya The park was stablished in early 1950s around the huge lake, Senanayaka
National Park Samudra, which was created when a dam was built across the Gal Oya.
ⓒ ⓓ It extends over 540 sq km of rolling country most of which is covered in tall
grass (*illuk* and *mana*) with a sizeable area of dry evergreen forest which
escaped being submerged. The Veddas lived in the forests and certain areas of
the park still harbour medicinal herbs and plants which are believed to have
been planted centuries ago.

The park is famous for its elephants and a variety of water birds which are
attracted by the lake. It is best visited in the early morning for watching elephants
and white buffaloes which come down to the lake, the crocodiles in the water and
the birds including the white-bellied sea-eagle (*haliaeetus leucogaster*). You can
take motor-boat tours on the lake, lasting two to three hours.

Sleeping There is a simple *Lodge* outside the park at Ekgal Oya, 20 km which has 3
rooms. Elephants may be seen nearby.

Route From the Gal Oya National Park you can rejoin the A25 which runs south past
the 558m hill known as Westminster Abbey to the east of the road. It joins the
A4 at **Siyambalamduwa**. If you don't wish to visit the Gal Oya National Park
you can continue south from **Karativu** on the A4 towards Pottuvil and
Arugam Bay.

The bay with its beautiful beach is particularly interesting for not only those keen on watersports (it's surf is so good that the bay is often referred to as 'Little Australia'!), and underwater photography but also offers exciting possibilities for divers keen to explore wrecked ships. The lagoon here attracts water birds. Take a sailing boat at dawn or dusk. You can also visit old temple ruins by walking over the dunes.

Although Arugam Bay itself has not seen political violence in recent years the surrounding area is not free from trouble. Barbed wire fences and machine guns are evidence of the earlier military presence with a curfew imposed from 1800-0800. However, in 2000, Arugam Bay is considered safe by some foreign visitors though there are still several army checkpoints on the Monaragala-Pottuvil road. It is possible to hire a bicycle and go south as far as **Panama**.

Arugam Bay
ආරුගම්බේ
15 km passing through Pottuvil

Take advice before travelling here & don't go further S than because of military activity

Sleeping For much of the last 7 years, since Arugam Bay was considered to be 'off limits', many of the hotels and guest houses closed down. Some have reopened but many are run down as their owners lack sufficient funds to renovate them properly. **Mid-range D** *Stardust Beach Hotel*, just on south edge of mouth of lagoon, 3 km south of Pottuvil, T/F072-286482. 20 well-furnished thatched roof chalets and cabanas, most with attached bath, some **E** rooms with shared bath, very clean, pleasant beach garden, good restaurant (dinner Rs 400, breakfast Rs 150), cycle hire,

The lack of tourists makes prices very competitive. You may get a simple room for under Rs 100

Eastern Province (south)

beautiful location, attentive service, Danish run. Highly recommended. **Cheap E** *Siam View Beach Hotel*, 2 a/c **D** rooms, 1 with a water-bed (!), several carpeted doubles, clean, good value if you can bargain price down. **G** *Beach Hut*, down alley from main road towards beach, simple rooms in 3 chalets in garden of family house, plus 1 cabana, shared bath in house, very cheap (Rs 50-100). **G** *Mermaid's Village Beach Resort*, once one of the most popular budget places, a lot of work needs doing when funds become available, run by friendly Mr Ghaffar. **G** *Sooriyah's Beach Hut*, several tree houses, a few cottages, 1 family house with 4 rooms, restaurant, shop, bike hire, a few surfboards available, very cheap (Rs 75-100), surfers' favourite, mainly for long-stay guests (months rather than days).

Transport Road Most visitors to Arugam Bay arrive from the west, on the A4. There are buses between Pottuvil and **Wellaway**, though generally you have to change at **Monaragala** (which can also be reached from Badulla). You can either walk between Pottuvil and Arugam Bay, or take a tuk-tuk (Rs 50).

Directory Communications A small post office in Pottuvil is the only place from which international calls can be made (must be booked, allow up to 2 hrs).

Route In normal political circumstances the coastal road south of Arugam Bay takes you to Kumana (40 km) via Okanda in a four-wheel drive.

Kumana Bird Sanctuary or Yala East National Park Kumana, to the northeast of the larger Yala National Park, is visited for its resident and migratory aquatic birds including flamingoes, ibis, herons, pheasants, particularly impressive in May and June when many nest in the mangrove swamps. You may see the endemic red-faced malkoha or the blue magpie in the forested areas. Herds of elephants can be spotted, although leopards and bears are more elusive. **Sleeping** There are two simple **G** *Bungalows* at Tunmulla and Okanda, with warden/cook, bring your bedding and food. Reservations: Wildlife Conservation Dept, T694241.

Magul Mahavihara
8 km W of Pottuvil along the A4

The ruins here, of various religious buildings in a jungle setting which have been dated from the first to the 10th centuries, include a vatadage and a dagoba (with impressive moonstones and guard stones), a large Buddha, a few pavilions and an elephant stable.

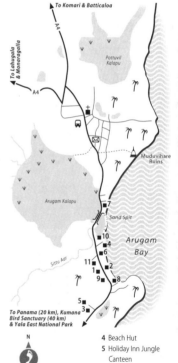

Pottuvil & Arugam Bay

To Komari & Batticaloa

To Lahugala & Monaragala

A4

Pottuvil Kalapu

Muduvihare Ruins

Arugam Kalapu

Sand Spit

Arugam Bay

Sittu Aar

To Panama (20 km), Kumana Bird Sanctuary (40 km) & Yala East National Park

N

Not to scale

■ **Sleeping**
1 Arugam Bay Hideaway
2 Arugam Bay Hilton
3 Bamburi Beach
4 Beach Hut
5 Holiday Inn Jungle Canteen
6 Mermaid's Village
7 Rest House
8 Siamview Beach
9 Sooriya's
10 Stardust
11 Tri Star Beach

Eastern Region

A walk through the parks

Elephants are both the most striking of the mammals and the most economically important, for there are many areas where they are put to work. The Asian elephant (Elephas maximas), smaller than the African, is the world's second largest land mammal. Compared to the African elephant, the male rarely reaches a height of over 3 m; it also has smaller ears. Other distinguishing features include the rounded shape of the back and the smooth trunk with a single 'finger' at the end. Unlike the African, the female is often tuskless or bears small ones called tushes, and even the male is sometimes tuskless (makhnas). The **Lahugala National Park** is the best place for viewing elephants. The Mahaweli basin has the larger marsh elephant. There is a plan to create an elephant 'corridor' of contiguous national parks and sanctuaries in the south east of the island in order that they may move freely over a large area as needed, throughout the year.

Lahugala National Park ලාහුගල

14 km W of Pottuvil The area has been politically unstable from time to time

This small national park (15 sq km) is good for watching birds and large elephant herds. It was established in 1980 and in theory is open throughout the year. Lying between Gal Oya and Ruhunu-Yala, the park is part of the government's endeavour to provide a connected parkland 'corridor' for the elephant population to move freely across the southeastern part of the island.

The Lahugala Mahawewa and Kitulana tank here attract numerous species of water birds. Sometimes the elephant herds number over a hundred, especially in the dry season (August-October) when they come down to the water. They are attracted by the *beru* grass that grows in the shallow tanks and the best time to watch them is in the late afternoon. The climbing Perch (*anabas testudineus*) fish is said to slither across from the Mahawewa to Kitulana tanks when the former runs dry! You might also catch sight of the colourful Ceylon blue magpie (*cissa ornata*) or the red-faced malkoha (*phaenicophaeus pyrrhocephalus*) in the woodland near the tanks. **Sleeping** Report at the *Park Lodge* on the edge of the park on arrival. There are some rooms for overnight stay.

The small town and district headquarters at Monaragala ('Peacock Rock') can be used as a halfway stop on the way between Arugam Bay and the Hill Country , or alternatively as a base to explore the surrounding countryside, including Jeelon Mount. There are some simple roadside places serving local food near the bus stand as well as some accommodation including *Victory Inn* on Wellawaya Road. For further advice about accommodation and guide, contact *Kanda Landa*, 500 m from the bus stand, almost opposite the Roman Catholic Church which is part of the Woodlands Network.

Monaragala *71 km from Pottuvil*

From here, the A22 goes west to Tennugewatta and into the Hills, while along the A4, about 10 km south of Monaragala, there is an interesting diversion off the road from Kumbakkana. Here a road heads south towards **Okkampitiya** and continues to the ancient site of Maligawila. There is open-pit garnet and sapphire mining at Okkampitiya.

Route

Maligawila is noted for its 10.5-m high, 3-m wide, monolithic standing Buddha statue (circa seventh century). The statue which had been installed here many centuries earlier on a lotus pedestal within a monastic complex which had a gateway, pillared hall and terraces, had fallen and been 'lost'. It was rediscovered and restored in 1991. There is another statue at Dambegoda, nearby. ■ *Getting there: there are direct buses to the site from Wellawaya, at least one of which originates in Ella.*

Maligawila

Eastern Region

Jaffna and the Northern Province

The Jaffna Peninsula and the offshore islands have a highly distinctive physical environment, deriving from the combination of its limestone geology, Dry Zone rainfall pattern and centuries of Tamil Hindu culture.

Travel to this part of the island is not advisable. In the absence of authentic and up to date information it has been decided not to publish a guide section to Jaffna and the northern Province. Since 1983 it has been impossible for visitors to go freely either to the town of Jaffa or its surrounding villages. Although Jaffna town is now re-occupied by its Tamil inhabitants and the LTTE no longer controls it the peninsula remains unsafe.

Background
See page 288 for the political history

Jaffna's proximity to India ensured that when Tamil settlers came to Sri Lanka as much as 2,000 years ago Jaffna was one of their earliest homes. Over the centuries they built a wholly distinctive culture. Despite the unsuitability of much of the thin red soil for agriculture, Tamil cultivators developed techniques of well irrigation which capitalized on the reserves of groundwater held in the limestone, making intensive rice cultivation the basis of a successful economy. Diversity was provided by coconut and palmyra palms, tobacco and a wide range of other crops, but the Tamil population was also in a real sense international in its outlook. It maintained trading links with the Tamil regions across the Palk Straits but also with southeast Asia. From the mid-19th century Jaffna Tamils took up the educational opportunities which came with an extended period of British rule, and rapidly became numerically dominant in a range of government services and jobs both inside and outside Sri Lanka.

The ability to cope with the harsh environment of the peninsula and their specific adaptation to its own regional character isolated the Jaffna Tamil community just as much as cultural distinctiveness from the regions to the south. The colonial period widened the geographical divide between the peninsula and the economically productive areas of southern Sri Lanka. In addition to the disasters that had overtaken the complex irrigation works of the Dry Zone after the 13th century, the northern part of the Dry Zone around Vavuniya, known as the *Wanni*, was laid waste by a succession of wars with the Dutch and the British, contributing to its present character as an almost uninhabited wasteland.

Through the 19th and 20th centuries the Wanni had the reputation of being one of the poorest areas of the island. The routes from Jaffna town to the rest of the island have to cross through the Wanni. The main road south goes through Vavuniya to Anuradhapura, following the route of the railway line (currently closed). One road runs east to Trincomalee, while another goes southwest to Mannar and Talaimannar, formerly the port for crossings to India.

Background

10

282

Background

283 **History**
283 Settlement and early history
285 Political developments in
pre-colonial Sri Lanka
286 The Sinhalese move south
286 The Kandyan Kingdom
287 Colonial power
288 The moves to independance

288 **Modern Sri Lanka**
289 Government
290 Economy

293 **Culture**
293 Religion
309 Architecture
314 Art
315 Language

316 **Land and environment**
316 Geography
317 Climate
318 Wildlife
326 Vegetation

History

Sri Lanka has a rich cultural history. In this sense it is no different to much of South Asia where religion and the migraton of people are interlocked. What makes it so interesting to the traveller is its accessibility. Few will fail to imagine the great battle involving kings atop elephants as they look over the plains from the heights of the fortress at Sigirya. Others will be moved as they watch the sun set over the Sun and Moon bastions at the colonial fortification in Galle. Surely this must be one of the most atmospheric places on the island. We hope that this brief history of the island will help your understanding and hence enjoyment of the great sites.

Settlement and early history

Stone tools from the Middle Palaeolithic Age have been found in several places, evidence of settlement in Sri Lanka perhaps as much as 500,000 years ago. Recent genetic research however suggests that *Homo sapiens* may not have evolved until very much later, and spread from Africa in the last 100,000 years.

The early record of settlement in Sri Lanka is scanty. Archaeologists believe today that the first *Homo sapiens* arrived perhaps 75,000 years ago, bringing with them a life of hunting and gathering centred on open-air campsites. Evidence of their activity has been found in a variety of habitats. However, no Neolithic tools have been found, and no tools from the Copper Age, which is so well represented in peninsular India from the second millennium BC.

The picture changes with the arrival of the Iron Age, for the megalithic graves, associated with black and red pottery, suggest that Sri Lanka had direct contact with South India well before the Aryans immigrated from North India from around 500 BC. Sri Lanka's archaeological record remains comparatively sparse, with barely any evidence with which to date the development of Stone Age cultures or the later spread of domesticated animals and cultivation. At some point in the first millennium BC rice cultivation made its appearance, though whether as a result of migration from either North India or South East Asia remains controversial.

The earliest aboriginal settlers, of Australoid, Negrito and Mediterranean stock, have now been almost entirely absorbed in the settled populations. The earliest named culture is that of **Balangoda**, distributed across the whole island between 5000 and 500 BC. The **Veddas** are the only inhabitants today whose ancestors were in Sri Lanka before the Aryan migrations. Related to the Dravidian jungle peoples in South India, they dwelt in caves and rock shelters, and lived by hunting and gathering. They practised a cult of the dead, communicating with ancestors through reincarnated spirits. Today the Veddas have been largely absorbed into the Sinhalese community and have virtually ceased to have a separate existence. In the mid 1960s their numbers had shrunk to under 800, from over 5,000 at the beginning of the century.

The overwhelming majority of the present population of Sri Lanka owes its origins to successive waves of migration from two different regions of India. Most people are of Indo-Aryan origin and came from North India. The earliest migrations from North India may have taken place as early as the fifth century BC. Although these migrants brought with them a North Indian language which had its roots in the

Migration from India

Background (side margin)

Sanskrit tradition, they were not yet Buddhists, for Buddhism did not arrive in Sri Lanka until the third century BC. It is most likely that the Sinhalese came from India's northwest, possibly Punjab or Gujarat, and it seems probable that Gujarati traders were already sailing down India's west coast by this time. The origins of Tamil settlement are unclear, but are thought to go back at least to the third century BC, when there is clear evidence of trade between Sri Lanka and South India.

Today the **Sinhalese** make up 74% of the total population. Sri Lanka's **Tamil** population comprises the long settled Tamils of the north and east (12.6%) and the migrant workers on the tea plantations in the Central Highlands (5.5%) who settled in Sri Lanka from the late 19th century onwards. By the middle 1990s over 340,000 adults from this Tamil community had been repatriated to India. The so-called '**Moors**', Tamil speaking Muslims of Indian-Arab descent, were traders on the east coast and now number over 1.1m (7.7%). A much smaller but highly distinct community is that of the **Burghers**, numbering about 50,000. The Dutch (mainly members of the Dutch Reformed Church), and the Portuguese intermarried with local people, and their descendants were urban and ultimately English speaking. There are similar numbers of Malays and smaller groups of Kaffirs. The Malays are Muslims who were brought by the Dutch from Java. The Kaffirs were brought by the Portuguese from Mozambique and other parts of East Africa as mercenaries.

A literate society With the development of agriculture came the origins of a literate and complex society. Tradition associates the founding of Sri Lanka's first kingdom with Devanampiya Tissa (250-21 BC), who the *Mahavansa* suggests was converted to Buddhism by Mahinda, son of the great Indian emperor Asoka. Myth and legend are bound up with many of the events of South Asian history, but the Sri Lankan historian KM de Silva has noted that the historical mythology of the Sinhalese 'is the basis of their conception of themselves as the chosen guardians of Buddhism.' The basic text through which this view of the island's history has been passed on by successive generations of Buddhist monks is the *Mahavansa* (the *Great Dynasty* or *Lineage*), which de Silva suggests possibly goes back to the sixth century AD, but is probably much more recent. It is the epic history from Prince Vijaya, the legendary founder of Sri Lanka, to King Mahasena (died 303 AD) and is a major source on early history and legend. It was continued in the 13th-century text the *Culavansa*, which gives a very full account of the medieval history of the island. These works were compiled by **bhikkus** (Buddhist monks) and inevitably they have the marks of their sectarian origins.

Interpretation of Sri Lanka's early history does not depend entirely on the writings of the Buddhist monks who ultimately wrote the Mahavansa. The first known writings are inscriptions discovered near caves in several parts of the island. Written in the Brahmi script (which was also used in India on the great inscriptions of the Emperor Asoka to express his principles of government and to mark out the limits of his territorial power), in Sri Lanka the inscriptions are brief epigraphs, testifying to the donation of caves or rock shelters to Buddhist monks. Written in an early form of Sinhala, rather than in the Prakrit which was the language used by Asoka, they give vivid testimony to the existence of prosperous, literate agricultural societies. The alphabet and the language were common right across the country, and even from early times it is clear that wet rice cultivation using sophisticated irrigation technology was the basis of the economy. As the map shows, settlement spread steadily right through to the 13th century. A notable feature of this early settlement and culture was its restriction to the Dry Zone and to altitudes below 300 m.

From the origins of this agricultural civilization in the third century BC there was a progressive economic and social evolution. The economy and the culture developed around the creation of extraordinarily sophisticated irrigation systems, using the rivers flowing from the Central Highlands across the much drier northern and eastern plains. Traditional agriculture had depended entirely on the rainfall brought by the retreating monsoon between October and December. The developing kingdoms of North Sri Lanka realized the need to control water to improve the reliability of agriculture, and a system of tank irrigation was already well advanced by the first century BC. This developed into possibly the most advanced contemporary system of hydraulic engineering in the world by the end of the fifth century AD. Many of these developments were quite small scale and today it is impossible to identify their creators. Others however were of a previously unparalleled size and are clearly identified with powerful kings. Thus King Mahasena, for example (274-302 AD) the 15-m high dam which impounded the Kantalai Tank, covering 2,000 ha and served by a 40-km long canal. King Dhatusena (460-478 AD) constructed the Kalawewa Lake in Anuradhapura, then by far the largest tank in Sri Lanka, to be surpassed in the late 12th century by King Parakramabahu's Parakrama Samudra ('Sea'), retained by an embankment 14-km long.

Political developments in pre-colonial Sri Lanka

Proximity to India has played a permanent part in Sri Lanka's developing history. Not only have the peoples of the island themselves originated from the mainland, but through more than 2,000 years, contact has been an essential element in all Sri Lanka's political equations.

According to the *Mahavansa* the Buddha commanded the king of the gods, Sakra, to protect Lanka as the home in which Buddhism would flourish. In recent years, much has been read into both the text and to more recent history to suggest that Sinhalese have always been at war with the Tamils. The truth is far more complicated. The earliest settlement of the island took place in the North-east, the area now known as the Dry Zone. Until the 13th century AD this was the region of political and cultural development for Sinhalese and Tamil alike.

The political history of the island after the establishment of the first recorded kingdom was not as smooth as might be inferred from the steady expansion of settled agriculture and the spread of sophisticated irrigation technology. Before the 13th century AD three regions played a major role in the island's political life. **Rajarata** in the north-central part of the island's plains grew into one of the major core regions of developing Sinhalese culture. To its north was **Uttaradesa** ('northern country'), while in the southeast, **Rohana** (Ruhunu) developed as the third political centre.

Periodically these centres of Sinhalese power came into conflict with each other, and with Tamil kings from India. The *Mahavansa* records how the Rohana Sinhalese King Dutthagamenu defeated the Chola Tamil King Elara, who had ruled northern Sri Lanka from Anuradhapura, in 140 BC. Dutthagamenu's victory was claimed by the chroniclers as a historic assertion of Buddhism's inalienable hold on Sri Lanka. In fact it is clear that at the time this was not a Tamil-Sinhalese or Buddhist-Hindu conflict, for the armies and leadership of both sides contained Sinhalese and Tamils, Buddhists and Hindus. By that time Buddhism had already been a power in the island for two centuries, when the king Devanampiya Tissa (307-267 BC) converted to Buddhism.

Buddhism became the state religion, identified with the growth of Sinhalese culture and political power. The power of the central kingdom based at Anuradhapura was rarely unchallenged or complete. Power was decentralized, with a large measure of local autonomy. Furthermore, provincial centres periodically established their independence. Anuradhapura became one of Asia's pre-eminent cities, but from the 11th century AD, Polonnaruwa took over as capital.

Background

The Tamil Although Buddhist power was predominant in Sri Lanka from the first century BC,
involvement Sri Lankan kings often deliberately sought Tamil support in their own disputes. As a
result Sri Lanka was affected by political developments in South India. The rise of the
expansionist Tamil kingdoms of the Pandiyas, Pallavas and Cholas from the fifth
century AD increased the scope for interaction with the mainland. In de Silva's
words, 'South Indian auxiliaries became in time a vitally important, if not the most
powerful element in the armies of the Sinhalese rulers, and an unpredictable,
turbulent group who were often a threat to political stability. They were also the
nucleus of a powerful Tamil influence in the court.'

It was not a one way flow. Occasionally the Sinhalese were themselves drawn in to
attack Tamil kings in India, as in the ninth century when to their enormous cost they
joined with their beleaguered allies the Pandiyans and attacked the Cholas. The Chola
Emperor **Rajaraja I** defeated them in India and then carried the war into Sri Lanka,
adding Jaffna and the northern plains, including Anuradhapura, to his empire.

The Cholas ruled from Polonnaruwa for 75 years, finally being driven out by the
Rohana king **Vijayabahu I** in 1070 AD. He established peace and a return to some
prosperity in the north before civil war broke out and disrupted the civil
administration again. Only the 33 year rule of **Parakramabahu I** (1153-1186)
interrupted the decline. Some of Sri Lanka's most remarkable monuments date from
his reign, including the *Parakrama Samudra* at Polonnaruwa. However, it was the
collapse of this kingdom and its ultimate annihilation by the Tamils in the 13th
century that left not only its physical imprint on the North Sri Lankan landscape but
also an indelible psychological mark on the Sri Lankan perception of neighbouring
Tamil Hindus.

The Sinhalese move south

Other factors, such as the spread of malaria which occurred with the deterioration in
maintenance of the irrigation system, may have led to the progressive desertion of
the northern and eastern plains and the movement south of the centre of gravity of
the Island's population. Between the 12th and 17th centuries Sinhalese moved from
the dry to the wet zone. This required a change in agriculture from irrigated to rain
fed crops. Trade also increased, especially in cinnamon, an activity controlled by the
rising population of Muslim seafarers. A **Tamil Kingdom** was set up in Jaffna for the
first time, briefly coming back under Sinhalese power (under the Sinhalese king
Parakramabahu VI, 1412-67, based in his capital at **Kotte**), but generally remaining
independent, and a frequent threat to the power of the Sinhalese kingdoms to the
south. Other threats came from overseas. As early as the 13th century, a Buddhist
king from Malaya invaded Sri Lanka twice to try and capture the tooth relic and the
Buddha's alms bowl. In the early 15th century the island was even invaded by a fleet
of Chinese junks sent by the Ming Emperors.

The Kandyan kingdom

Between the southern and northern kingdoms, Kandy became the capital of a new
power base around 1480. Established in the Central Highlands, it became fully
independent by the end of the 15th century. By the early 16th century the Sinhalese
kingdom of Kotte in the south was hopelessly fragmented, giving impetus to
Kandy's rise to independent power. Its remote and inaccessible position gave it
added protection from the early colonial invasions. Using both force and diplomacy
to capitalize on its geographical advantages, it survived as the last independent
Sinhalese kingdom until 1815. It had played the game of seeking alliances with one
colonial power against another with considerable success, first seeking the help of
the Dutch against the Portuguese, then of the British against the Dutch. However,

this policy ran out of potential allies when the British established their supremacy over all the territory surrounding the Central Highlands in 1796, and by 1815 the last Kandyan King, a Tamil Hindu converted to Buddhism, was deposed by his Sinhalese chiefs, who sought an accord with the new British rulers in exchange for retaining a large measure of their own power.

Colonial power

The succession of three colonial powers, the Portuguese, Dutch and the British, finally ended the independent Sinhalese and Tamil rule. Expanding Islam, evidenced in the conversion of the inhabitants of islands on the Arab trading routes such as the Maldives and the Laccadives as well as significant numbers on the southwest coast of India, had also been making its presence felt. The Portuguese arrived in Sri Lanka in 1605 and established control over some of the island's narrow coastal plains around Colombo. They were responsible for large-scale conversions to Roman Catholicism which today accounts for 90% of the island's Christians, leaving both a linguistic legacy and an imprint on the population, evidenced today in many names of Portuguese origin. During this period the rest of the island was dominated by the rulers of Sitavaka, who overpowered the Kotte Kingdom in 1565 and controlled the whole of the southwest apart from Colombo. For 10 years they occupied Kandy itself, nearly evicted the Portuguese and came close to reasserting Sinhalese power in the far north.

By 1619 the **Portuguese** had annexed Jaffna, which thereafter was treated by the **Dutch**, and more importantly the **British**, as simply part of the island state. They were less successful in subjugating Kandy, and in 1650 the Portuguese were ousted by the Dutch. The Dutch extended their own colonial control from Negombo (40 km north of Colombo) south, right round the coast to Trincomalee, as well as the entire northern peninsula, leaving the Kandyan Kingdom surrounded in the Central Highlands. Because the Portuguese and Dutch were interested in little other than the spice trade, they bent most of their efforts to producing the goods necessary for their trade. The British replaced the Dutch in 1795-6 when British power was being consolidated in South India at the expense of the French and the Mysore Muslim Raja, Tipu Sultan. Their original purpose was to secure the important Indian Ocean port of Trincomalee. Initially the British imported administrators and officials from Madras, but as BH Farmer points out, by 1802 'it was apparent that Madras-trained officials were, apart from other disabilities, quite unable to understand the language and customs of the Sinhalese, and Ceylon became a Crown Colony.'

When the **British** came to control the whole island after 1815 they established a quite distinctive imprint on the island's society and economy. This was most obvious in the introduction of plantation agriculture. During the British period coffee took over from cinnamon, but by the beginning of the 20th century, even though coffee had largely been wiped out by disease, plantation agriculture was the dominant pillar of the cash economy. Rice production stagnated and then declined, and Sri Lanka became dependent on the export of cash crops and the import of food. In 1948 it was only producing about 35% of its rice needs.

The colonial period also saw major social changes take place. Under the Portuguese and then the Dutch the development of commercial activity in the coastal lowlands encouraged many 'low-country' Sinhalese to become involved in the newly emerging economic activity. In a process which continued in the early British colonial period, the Low Country Sinhalese became increasingly westernized, with the widespread adoption of an English education and the rise of an urban middle class, while the Kandyan Sinhalese retained far stronger links with traditional and rural social customs. Despite British reforms in 1833 which introduced a uniform administrative system across the whole of Ceylon, wiping out the Kandyan political system, a contrast between Kandyan and Low-Country Sinhalese persisted into the modern period.

However, an even more significant change took place in the 19th century. British commercial interests saw the opportunities presented for the cultivation of cash crops. Cinnamon and coconuts had been planted by the Dutch and become particularly important, but after 1815 coffee production was spread to the Kandyan hills. Despite ups and downs production increased dramatically until 1875, when a catastrophic attack of a fungus disease wiped out almost the entire crop. It was replaced, particularly in the higher regions by tea.

Labour had already begun to prove a problem on the coffee plantations, and as tea spread the shortage became acute. Farmer has shown how private labour contractors were recruited to persuade labourers to come to Ceylon from the Tamil country of South India. between 1843-1859 over 900,000 men women and children migrated to work as indentured labour. The cost of their transport was deducted from their wages after they had arrived, and they could not leave until they had repaid their debt. Immigration on that scale created a massive change in the ethnic mix of the Highlands, with a particularly significant effect on the Kandyan farmers, whose land was increasingly hemmed in by the spread of estates. The Indian Tamils however remained entirely separate from the Sinhalese, returning to South India whenever possible and sending cash remittances home.

The moves to independence

Dominated by Buddhists and Sinhalese in its early stages, no one in the Independence movement at the beginning of the 20th century would have believed that British rule would end within 50 years – nor would many have wanted it to. The **Ceylon National Congress**, formed in 1919, was conservative and pragmatic, but the pressures of imminent democratic self-rule made themselves felt throughout the 1930s, as minority groups pressed to protect their position. Universal suffrage came in 1931, along with the promise of self-rule from the British Government. It had the positive benefit of encouraging the development of welfare policies such as health care, nutrition and public education. However, it also had the immediate impact of encouraging a resurgence of nationalism linked with Buddhist revivalism.

Independence came with scarcely a murmur on 4 February 1948, six months after that of India and Pakistan. Ceylon's first Prime Minister was **Don Stephen Senanayake**. His son **Dudley Senanayake**, who followed, was identified with a pragmatic nationalism. The heart of his programme was the re-colonization of the deserted Sinhalese heartlands of the Dry Zone. It was a programme deliberately calculated to recapture the glories of the past while laying the groundwork for post-Independence prosperity. In the event, its results have proved far more complex than even its critics fully recognized.

Modern Sri Lanka

Sri Lanka's image as one of the most peaceful and progressive of the modern South Asian countries has been overshadowed in recent years by repeated outbreaks of violence. Yet despite the continuing failure to find a solution to the conflicts which have threatened to tear its society apart, Sri Lanka has continued to see rapid economic and social change. The old plantation economy remains important though no longer as dominant as it was during the colonial period, while newer industries, including tourism, have taken on the prime role.

Government

The administrative divisions which the British inherited in 1796 underwent changes in definition during the next century to bring the island under a uniform system of revenue collection. The five provinces set up in 1833 were increased to nine in the following decades. The Sri Lankan government has further subdivided the provinces into 25 administrative district.

In its first 30 years of Independence Sri Lanka held eight general elections, sometimes accompanied by radical changes in political direction. Between 1956 and 1977 the governing party always lost. Power alternated between the socialist **Sri Lanka Freedom Party** (SLFP), and the free-market **United National Party** (UNP), which had formed the first government after Independence. Neither succeeded in achieving a degree of economic success which could keep pace with the growing demands of an increasingly young and literate population, struggling for jobs. Education has been one of the triumphs, with the country achieving high adult literacy figures. It has the sixth highest pupil-teacher ratio in the world, with 14 primary pupils per teacher (*Asiaweek*).

There has been a series of moves to turn away from British institutions and styles of government. Both parties competed in the search for more and more potent symbols of national identity, largely Buddhist and Sinhalese. The last 20 years has seen the divisions worked out in ethnic conflict of these two fundamental aspects of political development.

Since July 1983, when an anti-Tamil pogrom devastated many Tamil areas of Colombo and led to the loss of hundreds of Tamil lives, Sri Lanka has been locked in a bitter conflict between the government forces and Tamil guerrillas. Over 150,000 Tamils fled as refugees to India, many ultimately finding new homes in Europe and North America. In the north and east, Tamil militancy rapidly gained ground, and between 1983 and 1987 the **Liberation Tigers of Tamil Eelam** (LTTE or just 'the Tigers') waged an increasingly successful battle for control of what they regarded as the Tamil homeland, both against rival Tamil groups and against the Sri Lankan armed forces. Indian intervention at Rajiv Gandhi's initiative in July 1987 failed to achieve a peaceful solution and instead the Indian army became bogged down in a conflict with the Tigers themselves. At the same time the presence of the Indian forces roused fierce opposition from the Sinhalese, and the angry upsurge of support among young people for the fiercely anti-Tamil **JVP party** (Janatha Vimukhti Peramuna, People's Liberation Army) in the south of the island was accompanied by escalating violence and disruption. Many people 'disappeared' (presumed dead) at this time.

In November 1989 the JVP was crushed as a militant force. The Indian Peace Keeping Force finally completed

Administrative provinces & districts

PROVINCE

District

Not to scale

its withdrawal in March 1990 but in the seven years since successive governments have failed to find either a military or a political solution to the conflict. An independent estimate in 2,000 claimed that over 50,000 lives had been lost in 10 years of conflict, mainly in the north and east, and the victims claimed by the Tigers violent campaign have included the former Indian Prime Minister Rajiv Gandhi, the former Sri Lankan President Premadasa, and a series of other high ranking politicians in Sri Lanka.

In 1994 the governing United National Party lost heavily in District elections. Mrs Bandaranaike's daughter Chandrika took up the mantle of her mother's chosen successor, leading the SLFP at the head of a rather loose grouping of parties in the anti-UNP **People's Alliance**. In the Parliamentary elections the Alliance gained a narrow 49% to 44% majority over the UNP, but in the Presidential elections which followed **Chandrika Kumaratunga** gained over 62% of the vote. Her mother, Mrs Sirimavo Bandaranaike who became the world's first woman prime minister in 1960 (after her husband was assassinated in 1959) was again chosen as Prime Minister, a post she held until just before the recent elections. She passed away on 11 October 2000 and her ashes were buried next to her husband's.

Successive attempts by Mrs Kumaratunga's government to achieve a constitutional and political solution to the confrontation with the Tamil Tigers have met with repeated failure. Offers of talks have run alongside military attempts to curb Tamil military attacks and the use of terrorist bomb blasts any high level figure who opposes them. Mrs Kumaratunga herself lost an eye in a suicide bomb attack on the eve of the last elections, and in early 2000 the Tigers caused a series of bomb explosions at bus stands.

Parliamentary elections in October 2000, the latest in a run of elections were held against the backdrop of the continuing civil war. On this occasion they took place in the context of the widest ranging political debate about a new constitution, which if adopted would give a far greater degree of autonomy to Tamil majority regions than ever previously contemplated, but the Tiger leadership seemed wholly unwilling to compromise on their basic demand for independence for the North and East.

The People's Alliance formed the new government with 116 members. Mr Ratnasiri Wickremanayake was sworn in as the new Prime Minister.

Economy

Key statistics Main agricultural products in 2000: tea 265,000 tonnes, rubber 110,000 tonnes, paddy three million tonnes, coconut three billion nuts. Major exports: textiles and garments US$2 billion, tea US$500 million, rubber US$100 million, coconuts US$100 million, petroleum products US$85 million, gems US$85 million.

Agriculture & fishing About 25% of Sri Lanka's area is cultivated by sedentary farmers or under cultivated forests, a further 15% being under shifting cultivation. About half is under forest, grassland, swamp and waste land. In the Wet Zone virtually all the cultivable land is now taken up.

Sri Lanka has not produced enough food to meet the needs of its population since the 18th century, yet in many respects it has been the most obviously prosperous state in South Asia. In the 1970s more than half the money earned from the export of tea, rubber and coconuts was spent on importing food grains, leaving little for investment. In 1999, for the first time for over a decade, agriculture grew as fast as the rest of the economy, but a high proportion of Sri Lanka's farmers remain poor, and 25% of the total population is below the Government's poverty line.

The indispensable coconut

The coconut, so much a part of the coastal scene on the island, particularly to the west, is the country's third most important crop.

The inland palm is often short enough to be harvested by cutting bunches of mature nuts with a sharp knife tied to the end of a long bamboo pole which the 'picker' skilfully manipulates from the ground. The coastal palm is too tall to be harvested this way so the nuts must be collected by climbing each tree.

Every bit of the palm is put to use. The green fruit produces an excellent refreshing 'milk' which is on tap when the top is cut off. The 'shell' is split open to expose the soft white kernel which is edible. The outer fibrous coir, just under the skin, is removed and soaked in tanks before being woven into mats, twisted into rope or used as mattress filling and even

exported for agricultural and garden use to improved soil texture.

The dry, older nut yields a white layer of 'flesh' or kernel (copra) is grated or pounded for cooking while some of the best is turned into desiccated coconut (a small industry which employs women) for use at home and abroad.

The fresh sap which is 'tapped' from a proportion of trees is prized by most Sri Lankans who drink the fermented toddy or the more alcoholic arrack. The sweet juice is also turned into jaggery or treacle. See also 'The Sap Tappers' on page 114.

Palm oil and cattle feed in the shape of oil cakes are products in demand. The shell itself ends up as fuel, the leaves as thatch or for basket weaving throughout the year, and finally (when the tree dies) the strong trunk is cut up for building.

Rice Sri Lanka has two main rice growing seasons. The *Maha* crop is harvested between January and March, the *Yala* crop between August and September. Attempts to increase rice production have ranged from land reform to the introduction of high yielding varieties (hyv). By the early 1980s there was virtually a 100% take-up of new varieties. Yields have increased significantly, and by 2000 Sri Lanka was producing over 80% of its domestic needs despite the speed of population growth. In addition to the intensification programme the government has also carried out major colonization schemes, bringing new land under rice cultivation. This has been expensive and certainly not always cost effective, but in part has been a response to political pressures to reclaim land for Sinhalese cultivators.

The **cash crops** of tea, rubber and coconuts continue to contribute the lion's share of Sri Lanka's foreign exchange earnings. In 2000, approximately 20% of foreign exchange earnings still came from these three products alone. The **Coconut** palm (*Cocos nucifer*) grows easily along the south and west coast and in the Kurunegala District. Kernel products rather than fresh nuts remain more important for export. See page 291. **Tea** suffered for many years from inadequate investment and fierce competition from expanding production in other countries of cheaper, lower quality tea. The area cropped under tea fell steadily, though production improved between 1948 and 1965, only to decline again. Since the mid-1980s there has been a remarkable turnaround. In 2000 Sri Lanka was expected to produce over 280,000 tonnes of tea. World tea prices were rising in the wake a poor crops among other major world producers, notably Kenya, and surging demand from Russia and the Middle East.

The commercially important **rubber** tree (*Hevea brasiliensis*), a native of Brazil, is cultivated in plantations in areas of high rainfall. New clones have been developed which are disease resistent and high yielding. See page 170.

Spices (cinnamon, pepper, clove, nutmeg/mace and cardamom), **coffee** and **cocoa** also contribute a significant 8% of earnings from export.

Background

Fact file

Official name *Sri Lanka Prajatantrika Samajawadi Janarajaya (Democratic Socialist Republic of Sri Lanka)*
Capital *Jayawardanapura Kotte (Legislative); Colombo (Commercial)*
National anthem *Namo Namo Matha (namo = greetings, matha = mother). All are expected to stand when this is sung.*
National flag *On a dark red field, within a golden border, a golden lion passant holds a sword in its right paw with a representation of a bo-leaf at each corner. To its right are two vertical saffron and green stripes (representing Hindu and Muslim minorities), also within a golden border.*

Statistics *Population: 19.3 million (UN projection for 2000).*
Annual growth rate: 1.6%.
Crude birth rate: 2.4%.
Crude death rate: 0.8%.
Urban population: 21%.
Life expectancy at birth: 74.2 (F), 69.5 (M).
Infant mortality: 2.9% of live births.
Adult literary: M 93%; F 84% (in comparison to India M 66%; F 38%, 1995).
Area: 66,000 sq km.
Population density: 292 per sq km.
GDP per capita: US$620 (UN real GDP per capita: US$3,000).
Average annual growth rate: 6%, 1996-7.
Annual per capita income: US$730.

The potentially rich **fishery resources** have yet to be fully developed. Fresh water stocking programmes have increased the yield of rivers and lakes, and brackish water fishing is becoming increasingly commercialized. However, nearly 40% of households which depend on fishing have no boats or equipment, and despite the potential of the export market production does not meet domestic demand. An easing of the situation in the East allowed the resumption of fishing in 1999, but political uncertainty continues to be a major barrier to expansion.

Resources & industry Sri Lanka has few fossil fuels or metallic minerals. Gemstones, graphite (crystalline carbon) and heavy mineral sands are the most valuable resources, though clays, sands and limestones are abundant. Gemstones include sapphires, rubies, topaz, zircon, tourmaline and many others. Gem bearing gravels are common, especially in the southwest around the appropriately named Ratnapura (City of gems). Other minerals are also concentrated in the southwest. The greatest concentration of heavy mineral sands – ilmenite, rutile and monazite – is north of Trincomalee, where deposits are 95% pure. Monazite is found on the west coast. There are scattered deposits of iron ore in the southwest, and some veins of magnetite in the northwest interior. High evaporation rates make shallow lagoons suitable for salt manufacture. The most important salterns are at Puttalam and Elephant Pass in the north and Hambantota in the south.

Due to the lack of fossil fuel resources, 95% of the island's electricity is now generated by hydro power. The first HEP project was opened in the 1930s, but firewood still accounts for over half of all energy used. Supplies are under increasing pressure, and the Mahaweli Project undertaking has meant that most of the HEP is now developed.

Sri Lanka had very little industry at Independence, manufacturing accounting for less than 5% of the GDP. By 1996 a number of new industries had been developed – cement, mineral sands, ceramics, cloth. These were all planned originally in the state controlled sector. The socialist government under Mrs Bandaranaike envisaged public ownership of all major industries, but the United National Party government elected under President Jayawardene's leadership in 1977 reversed this policy, moving towards a free trade economy.

Among the leading sectors of the new policy was tourism, with particular efforts to exploit the superb beaches and equable climate. Sealife and the opportunities for watersports have made some beaches particularly attractive along the south and southwest of the island. Although tourism has been seriously affected by the political unrest, it was staging a significant recovery and by 2000 was showing a strong recovery.

In the late 1990s the overall economic performance has been remarkably strong in view of the continuing difficulty faced in resolving the underlying political crisis. Tea production has grown rapidly in the last five years. Industrial output has been growing at over 7% a year. Services, which account for about half of the GDP, also grew by just over 6%, and overall growth continued at over 5% per annum through 2000. In 1999-2000 inflation dropped to under 5%, having been in double digits for over a decade.

Export performance has continued to be strong, but the 1990s have seen a major change in the composition of Sri Lanka's exports. At the beginning of the decade, tea (27% of the total) was still nearly as important an export as manufactured goods, notably textiles and garments (32%), but by 2000 textiles accounted for over 60% compared with tea's 15%. The change partly reflected the rapid increase in foreign investment in the manufacturing sector which has continued into the mid-1990s. The government is now paying particular attention to the improvement of productivity through technology transfer and research and development.

As Sri Lanka reaches the end of the millennial year most people are hoping desperately for a resolution of the conflict which has brought grief to thousands and massive economic strain to the economy. A recent trade agreement with India, part of a widening package of agreements within South Asia, hints at the potential for rapid improvement, but there are no solid grounds for optimism yet that the civil strife will be ended soon.

Culture

Religion

The gleaming white stupas of Anuradhapura and the serene stillness of the Buddha's image captured in stone across the island testify to the interweaving of Buddhism with Sinhalese life. Yet Sri Lanka has always been a diverse society. Hinduism has been the dominant religion of Tamils in the north for over two thousand years and of many of the tea plantation workers today. Islam arrived with the Arab traders across the Indian Ocean over a thousand years ago, and the three main colonial powers – the Portuguese, Dutch and British – brought Catholicism and Protestant Christianity to the island from the 17th century onwards. In Colombo these religions all have a visible presence, and Buddhists, Christians and Muslims live peacefully side by side in many parts of the island, despite present-day political conflicts. Statistically the population is split: Buddhists 69%; Hindus 15%; Christians 7.5%; Muslims 7.5%; Others 1%.

Buddhism

In Sri Lanka Buddhism is the most widespread religion of the majority Sinhalese community. Although India was the original home of Buddhism, today it is practised largely on the margins of the sub-continent, and is widely followed in Ladakh, Nepal and Bhutan as well as Sri Lanka.

Background

Buddha's life Siddharta Gautama, who came to be given the title of the Buddha – the Enlightened One – was born about 563 BC in the Nepal/India foothills of the Himalaya. A prince in a warrior caste, he was married at the age of 16 and his wife had a son. When he reached the age of 29 he left home and wandered as a beggar and ascetic. After about six years he spent some time in Bodh Gaya in the modern Indian state of Bihar. Sitting under the Bo tree, meditating, he was tempted by the demon Mara, with all the desires of the world. Resisting these temptations, he received enlightenment.

These scenes are common motifs of Buddhist art. The next landmark was the preaching of his first sermon on 'The Foundation of Righteousness' and set in motion the *Dharma Chakra* (Wheel of the Law), in the deer park at Sarnath near Benaras (Varanasi) to his first five disciples. This was followed by other sermons during his travels when he gathered more disciples. Ananta (his closest disciple) was a cousin. Another cousin, Devdutta opposed the Buddha and made three attempts to have him killed but failed – a hired assassin was converted, a boulder rolled downhill split in two and finally the wild elephant sent to crush the Buddha underfoot was calmed by his sermon.

By the time he died the Buddha had established a small band of monks and nuns known as the *Sangha*, and had followers across North India. The male monks were divided into *sramana* (ascetics), *bhikku* (mendicants), *upasaka* (disciples) and *sravaka* (laymen); the nuns were known as *bhikkuni*.

On the Buddha's death or *parinirvana* (Parinibbana or 'final extinction') at the age of 80, his body was cremated, and the ashes, regarded as precious relics, were divided up among the peoples to whom he had preached. Some have been discovered as far west as Peshawar, in the northwest frontier of Pakistan, and at Piprawa, close to his birthplace.

After the Buddha's death From the Buddha's death – to the destruction of Nalanda (the last Buddhist stronghold in India) in 1197 AD, Buddhism in India went through three phases. These are often referred to as Hinayana, Mahayana and Vajrayana, though they were not mutually exclusive, being followed simultaneously in different regions. The *yana* ('Way' or vehicle) derives from the imagery of the seeker being conveyed in a vessel across the ocean of the world to *nirvana*.

Hinayana The Hinayana, or 'Little Way', insists on a monastic way of life as the only path to achieving *nirvana* (see page 295). Divided into many schools, the only surviving Hinayana tradition is the **Theravada Buddhism** (*thera*, wise man) or

The Buddha in Dhyanamudra - meditation

The Buddha in Bhumisparcamudra - calling the earth goddess to witness

Background

The Buddha's Four Noble Truths

The Buddha preached Four Noble Truths: that life is painful; that suffering is caused by ignorance and desire; that beyond the suffering of life there is a state which cannot be described but which he termed nirvana; and that nirvana can be reached by following an eightfold path.

The concept of nirvana is often understood in the West in an entirely negative sense – that of 'non-being'. The word has the rough meaning of 'blow out' or 'extinguish', meaning to blow out the fires of greed, lust and desire. In a positive sense it has been described by one Buddhist scholar as 'the state of absolute illumination, supreme bliss, infinite love and compassion, unshakeable serenity, and unrestricted spiritual freedom'. The essential elements of the eightfold path are the perfection of wisdom, morality and meditation.

School of Elders, which was taken to Sri Lanka by Mahinda, Emperor Asoka's son. It became the state religion under King Dutthagamenu in the 1st century AD.

Mahayana The followers of the Mahayana school, 'the Great Way', believed in the possibility of salvation for all. They practised a far more devotional form of meditation, and new figures came to play a prominent part in their beliefs and their worship – the **Bodhisattvas**, saints who were predestined to reach the state of enlightenment through thousands of rebirths. They aspired to Buddhahood, however, not for their own sake but for the sake of all living things. The Buddha is believed to have passed through numerous existences in preparation for his final mission. One of the most notable Mahayana philosophers was the 2nd/3rd century saint, Nagarjuna. Mahayana who was noted for asserting a form of nihilism, saying reality was an illusion and, thus, incomprehensible.

Vajrayana The Diamond Way resembles magic and yoga in some of its beliefs. The ideal of Vajrayana Buddhists is to be 'so fully in harmony with the cosmos as to be able to manipulate the cosmic forces within and outside himself'. It had developed in the north of India by the 7th century AD, matching the parallel growth of Hindu Tantrism, and periodically also exercised some influence in Sri Lanka.

Buddhism became dominant over most of South Asia, and its influence is evidenced in Buddhist art from Sigiriya in Sri Lanka to Ajanta in central India and as far as Gandhara in northern Pakistan.

The decline of Buddhism in India probably stemmed as much from the growing similarity in the practice of revivalist Hinduism from seventh to 12th centuries in North India and Mahayana Buddhism with its reverence for Bodhisattvas and its devotional character. In South India the Chola Empire contributed to the near extinction of Buddhism, while the Muslim conquest of North India was accompanied by large scale slaughter of monks and the destruction of monasteries. Without their institutional support Buddhism in India gradually faded away, retreating to the regions peripheral to India. The nature of Buddhism's decline in mainland India may well have contributed to the powerful sense in Sri Lanka that militant Hindu expansionism was a major threat to the security of Sri Lanka's Buddhists.

India still has many sites of great significance for Buddhists around the world: **Lumbini**, the Buddha's birthplace, near the border, in Nepal, **Bodh Gaya**, where he attained 'supreme enlightenment' in Bihar; **Sarnath**, where he preached his first sermon, just outside Varanasi; and **Kushinagara**, where he died, 50 km east of Gorakhpur. In addition there are remarkable monuments, sculptures and works of art, from Gandhara in modern Pakistan to Sanchi and Ajanta in central India, to the

Background

Buddhism's
decline in India

treasures in ancient sites in Sri Lanka where it is still possible to see the vivid evidence of the flowering of Buddhist culture in South Asia.

Sri Lankan Buddhism The recent history of Sri Lanka's **Theravada** Buddhism may conceal the importance of the cultural and historical links between Sri Lanka and India in the early stages of its development. The first great stupas in Anuradhapura were built when Buddhism was still a religious force to be reckoned with in mainland India, and as some of the sculptures from Sigiriya suggest there were important contacts with Amaravati, another major centre of Buddhist art and thought, up to the 5th century AD.

The origins of Buddhism in Sri Lanka are explained in a legend which tells how King Devanampiya Tissa (d 207 BC) was converted by Mahinda, widely believed to have been Asoka's son, who was sent to Sri Lanka specifically to bring the faith to the Island's people. He established the Mahavihara monastery in Anuradhapura. Successors repeatedly struggled to preserve Sri Lankan Buddhism's distinct identity from that of neighbouring Hinduism and Tantrism. It was also constantly struggling with Mahayana Buddhism, which gained the periodic support of successive royal patrons. King Mahasena (276-303AD) and his son Sri Meghavarna, who received the famous 'tooth of the Buddha' when it was brought to the island from Kalinga in the 4th century AD, both advocated Mahayana forms of the faith. Even then Sri Lanka's Buddhism is not strictly orthodox, for the personal character of the Buddha is emphasized, as was the virtue of being a disciple of the Buddha. *Maitreya*, the 'future' Buddha, is recognized as the only *Bodhisattva*, and it has been a feature of Buddhism in the island for kings to identify themselves with this incarnation of the Buddha.

The Sinhalese see themselves as guardians of the original Buddhist faith. They believe that the scripture in Pali was first written down by King Vattagamani Abhaya in the 1st century BC. The Pali Theravada canon of scripture is referred to as *Tipitakam Tripitaka* (three 'baskets'), because the palm leaf texts on which they were written were stored in *pitakas* (baskets). They are **conduct** (*vinaya*), consisting of 227 rules binding on monks and nuns; **discourses** (*sutta*), the largest and most important, divided into five groups (*niyakas*) of basic doctrine which are believed to be the actual discourses of the Buddha recording his exact words as handed down by word of mouth; and **metaphysics** (*abhidhamma*) which develop the ideas further both philosophically and psychologically. There are also several works that lack the full authority of the canon but are nonetheless important. Basham suggests that the main propositions of the literature are psychological rather than metaphysical. Suffering, sorrow and dissatisfaction are the nature of ordinary life, and can only be eliminated by giving up desire. In turn, desire is a result of the misplaced belief in the reality of individual existence. In its Theravada form, Hinayana Buddhism taught that there is no soul and ultimately no god. *Nirvana* was a state of rest beyond the universe, once found never lost.

The cosmology Although the Buddha discouraged the development of cosmologies, the Hinayana Buddhists produced a cyclical view of the universe, evolving through four time periods.

Period 1 Man slowly declines until everything is destroyed except the highest heaven. The good go to this heaven, the remainder to various hells.

Period 2 A quiescent phase.

Period 3 Evolution begins again. However, 'the good *karma* of beings in the highest heaven' now begins to fail, and a lower heaven evolves, a *world of form*. During this period a great being in the higher heaven dies, and is re-born in the world of form as Brahma. Feeling lonely, he wishes that others were with him. Soon other beings from the higher heaven die and are reborn in this world. Brahma interprets these people as his own creation, and himself as The Creator.

Period 4 The first men, who initially had supernatural qualities, deteriorate and become earthbound, and the period fluctuates between advance and deterioration.

The four-period cycles continue for eternity, alternating between 'Buddha cycles' – one of which we live in today – and 'empty cycles'. It is believed that in the present cycle four Buddhas – *Krakucchanda*, *Kanakamuni*, *Kasyapa*, and *Sakyamuni* – have already taught, and one, *Maitreya*, is still to come.

In Sri Lanka the scriptures came to be attributed with almost magical powers. Close ties developed between Buddhist belief and **Sinhalese nationalism**. The Sinhalese scholar *Buddhaghosa* translated Sinhalese texts into Pali in the fifth century AD. At the beginning of the 11th century Sri Lankan missionaries were responsible for the conversion of Thailand, Burma, Cambodia and Laos to Theravada Buddhism. Subsequently, in the face of continued threats to their continued survival, Sri Lanka's Buddhist monks had to be re-ordained into the valid line of Theravada lineage by monks from Southeast Asia. Buddhist links with Thailand remain close.

Buddhist practice

By the time Buddhism was brought to Sri Lanka there was a well developed religious organization which had strong links with secular authorities. Developments in Buddhist thought and belief had made it possible for peasants and lay people to share in the religious beliefs of the faith. As it developed in Sri Lanka the main outlines of practice became clearly defined. The king and the orders of monks became interdependent; a monastic hierarchy was established; most monks were learning and teaching, rather than practising withdrawal from the world. Most important, Buddhism accepted a much wider range of goals for living than simply the release from permanent rebirth.

The most important of these were 'good rebirth', the prevention of misfortune and the increase in good fortune during the present life. These additions to original Buddhist thought led to a number of contradictions and tensions, summarized by Tambiah as: the Buddha as a unique individual, rather than a type of person (*Bodhisattva*) coming into the world periodically to help achieve release from *samsara* (rebirth), or rebirth into a better life; Buddhism as a path to salvation for all, or as a particular, nationalist religion; Buddhism as renunciation of the world and all its obligations, in contrast with playing a positive social role; and finally, whether monasteries should be run by the monks themselves, or with the support and involvement of secular authorities. These tensions are reflected in many aspects of Buddhism in Sri Lanka today, as in debates between monks who argue for political action as against withdrawal from the world.

Sects Until the 16th century Buddhism in Sri Lanka enjoyed the active support of the state. It remained longest in Kandy, but was withdrawn steadily after the British took control in 1815. The 18th-century revival of Buddhism in the Wet Zone was sponsored by the landowning village headmen, not by royalty, and castes such as the *Goyigama* and *Salagama* played a prominent role. Through the 19th century they became the dominant influence on Buddhist thought, while the remaining traditional Buddhist authority in Kandy, the *Siyam Nikaya*, suffered permanent loss of influence.

The *Siyam Nikaya*, one of the three sects of Sri Lankan Buddhism today, originated in the 18th mission of the Kandyan kings to Ayuthya in Thailand (Siam) to re-validate the Buddhist clergy. By a royal order admission to the sect's two branches was restricted to high caste Sinhalese. Today their monks are distinguished by carrying umbrellas and wearing their robe over one shoulder only. The exclusion of lower castes from this sect however bred resentment, and in 1803 a new sect, the

Background

Amarapura Nikaya was established to be open to all castes, while in 1835 the third contemporary sect, the *Ramanya Nikaya*, was set up in protest at the supposedly excessive materialism of the other two. Both these sects wear robes which cover both shoulders, but while the *Amarapura* sect carry umbrellas the *Ramanya* carries a traditional shade. Sri Lankan monks wear orange robes and take the vows of celibacy and non-possession of worldly wealth, owning only the very basic necessities including two robes, begging bowl, a razor, needle and thread. They do not eat after mid-day and spend part of the day in study and meditation. The order of nuns which was introduced in Sri Lanka in the early days was shortlived.

This new, independent Buddhism, became active and militant. It entered into direct competition with Christians in proselytising, and in setting up schools, special associations and social work. After Independence, political forces converged to encourage State support for Buddhism. The lay leadership pressed the government to protect Buddhists from competition with other religious groups. The Sinhalese political parties saw benefits in emphazising the role of Buddhism in society.

Buddhist worship

The Buddha himself refuted all ideas of a personal God and of worshipping a deity, but subsequent trends in Buddhism have often found a place for popular worship. Even in the relatively orthodox Theravada Buddhism of Sri Lanka personal devotion and worship are common, focused on key elements of the faith. Temple complexes (*pansalas*) commonly have several features which can serve as foci for individual devotion. Stupas or dagobas, which enshrine personal relics of the Buddha, are the most prominent, but Bodhi or Bo trees and images of the Buddha also act as objects of veneration.

Sri Lankan Buddhists place particular emphasis on the sanctity of the relics of the Buddha which are believed to have been brought to the Island. The two most important are the sacred **Bo tree** and the tooth of the Buddha. The Bo tree at Anuradhapura is believed to be a cutting from the Bo tree under which the Buddha himself achieved enlightenment at Bodh Gaya in modern Bihar. The Emperor Asoka is recorded as having entrusted the cutting to Mahinda's sister Sanghamitta to be carried to Sri Lanka on their mission of taking Buddhism to the island. As the original Bo tree in Bodh Gaya was cut down, this is the only tree in the world believed to come directly from the original tree under which the Buddha sat, and is visited by Buddhists from all over the world. Many other Bo trees in Sri Lanka have been grown from cuttings of the Anuradhapura Bo tree.

The tooth of the Buddha, now enshrined at the Dalada Maligawa in Kandy, was not brought to Sri Lanka until the 4th century AD. The Portuguese reported that they had captured and destroyed the original tooth in their attempt to wipe out all evidence of other religious faiths, but the Sinhalese claimed to have hidden it and allowed a replica to have been stolen. Today pilgrims flock from all over the island, queuing for days on special occasions when special access is granted to the casket holding the tooth in the Dalada Maligawa.

In ordinary daily life many Buddhists will visit temples at least once a week on **poya** days, which correspond with the four quarters of the moon. Full moon day, a national holiday, is a particularly important festival day (see page 50). It is also an opportunity for the worship of non-Buddhist deities who have become a part of popular Buddhist religion. Some have their origins explicitly in Hinduism. The four Guardian Deities seen as future Buddhas, include Natha, Vishnu, Skanda and Saman. **Skanda**, described below, the Hindu god of war, is worshipped as Kataragama, and **Vishnu** is seen as the island's protector. It is not surprising, therefore, to see the Hindu deities in Buddhist temples. Other deities have come from the Mahayana branch of Buddhism, such as **Natha**, or *Maitreya*, the future Buddha. Thus in worship as in many other aspects of daily life, Sinhalese Buddhism shares much in common with Hindu belief and practice with which it has lived side by side for over 2,000 years.

A final feature of Buddhist worship which is held in common with Hindu worship is its individualism. Congregational worship is usually absent, and individuals will normally visit the temple, sometimes soliciting the help of a *bhikku* in making an offering or saying special prayers. One of the chief aims of the Buddhist is to earn merit (*punya karma*), for this is the path to achieving nirvana. Merit can be earned by selfless giving, often of donations in the temple, or by gifts to bhikkus, who make regular house calls early in the morning seeking alms. In addition merit can be gained by right living, and especially by propagating the faith both by speech and listening.

Some elements of the caste system were probably present in pre-Buddhist Sri Lanka, with both the priestly caste of Brahmins and a range of low caste groups such as scavengers. Although Buddhism encouraged its followers to eradicate distinctions based on caste, the system clearly survived and became a universal feature of social structures among Buddhists and subsequently Christians, despite their beliefs which explicitly condemn such social stratification. However, the complexities and some of the harsh exclusiveness of the caste system as practised in India was modified in Sri Lanka.

Caste in Sri Lankan Buddhism

Sinhalese Buddhism has no Brahmin or Kshatriya caste, although some groups claim a warrior lineage. The caste enjoying highest social status and the greatest numbers is the *Goyigama*, a caste of cultivators and landowners who are widely seen as roughly equivalent to the *Vellala* caste among Jaffna Tamils. The *Bandaras* and the *Radalas* comprise a sub-caste of the Goyigamas who for generations have formed a recognizable aristocracy. Among many other castes lower down the social hierarchy come fishermen (*Karavas*), washermen (*Hena*), and toddy tappers (*Durava*).

Some caste groups, such as the **Karava**, have achieved significant changes in their status. Ryan suggests for example that the original Karava community came from South India and converted to Buddhism and began to speak Sinhalese while retaining their fishing livelihoods. Subsequently many converted to Roman Catholicism, located as they were in the heart of the coastal region just north of modern Colombo controlled by the Portuguese. Through their conversion many Karavas received privileges reserved by the Portuguese for Christians, enabling them to climb up the social ladder. Thus today, unlike the fishing communities of Tamil Nadu who remain among the lowest castes, the Karava are now among Sri Lanka's upper caste communities.

Hinduism

Hinduism in northern Sri Lanka was brought over by successive Tamil kings and their followers. It has always been easier to define Hinduism by what it is not than by what it is. Indeed, the name Hinduism was given by foreigners to the peoples of the sub-continent who did not profess the other major faiths, such as Muslims, Christians or Buddhists. The beliefs and practices of modern Hinduism began to take shape in the centuries on either side of the birth of Christ. But while some aspects of modern Hinduism can be traced back more than 2,000 years before that, other features are recent. Hinduism has undergone major changes both in belief and practice. Such changes came from outside as well as from within. As early as the 6th century BC the Buddhists and Jains had tried to reform the religion of Vedism (or Brahmanism) which had been dominant in some parts of South Asia for 500 years.

A number of ideas run like a thread through intellectual and popular Hinduism, some being shared with Buddhism. Some Hindu scholars and philosophers talk of Hinduism as one religious and cultural tradition, in which the enormous variety of belief and practice can ultimately be interpreted as interwoven in a common view of the world. Yet there is no Hindu organization, like a church, with the authority to

Modern Hinduism

●●

 ### *Karma – an eye to the future*

According to karma, every person, animal or god has a being or self which has existed without beginning. Every action, except those that are done without any consideration of the results, leaves an indelible mark on that self. This is carried forward into the next life, and the overall character of the imprint on each person's 'self' determines three features of the next life. It controls the nature of his next birth (animal, human or god) and the kind of family he will be born into if human. It determines the length of the next life. Finally, it controls the good or bad experiences that the self will experience. However, it does not imply a fatalistic belief that the nature of action in this life is unimportant. Rather, it suggests that the path followed by the individual in the present life is vital to the nature of its next life, and ultimately to the chance of gaining release from this world.

●●

define belief or establish official practice. Although the Vedas are still regarded as sacred by most Hindus, virtually no modern Hindu either shares the beliefs of the Vedic writers or their practices, such as sacrifice, which died out 1,500 years ago. Not all Hindu groups believe in a single supreme God. In view of these characteristics, many authorities argue that it is misleading to think of Hinduism as a religion at all.

Be that as it may, the evidence of the living importance of Hinduism is visible among Hindu communities in Sri Lanka as well as in India. Hindu philosophy and practice has also touched many of those who belong to other religious traditions, particularly in terms of social institutions such as caste.

Four human goals For many Hindus there are four major human goals; material prosperity (*artha*), the satisfaction of desires (*kama*), and performing the duties laid down according to your position in life (*dharma*). Beyond those is the goal of achieving liberation from the endless cycle of rebirths into which everyone is locked (*moksha*). It is to the search for liberation that the major schools of Indian philosophy have devoted most attention. Together with *dharma*, it is basic to Hindu thought.

Dharma *Dharma* (dhamma to Buddhists) represents the order inherent in human life. It is essentially secular rather than religious, for it doesn't depend on any revelation or command of God but rather has 10 'embodiments': good name, truth, self-control, cleanness of mind and body, simplicity, endurance, resoluteness of character, giving and sharing, austerities and continence. In *dharmic* thinking these are inseparable from five patterns of behaviour: non-violence, an attitude of equality, peace and tranquillity, lack of aggression and cruelty, and absence of envy.

Karma The idea of *karma* 'the effect of former actions' – is central to achieving liberation. It is believed that 'Every act has its appointed effect, whether the act be thought, word or deed. If water is exposed to the sun, it cannot avoid being dried up. The effect automatically follows. It is the same with everything. The cause holds the effect, so to say, in its womb. If we reflect deeply and objectively, the entire world will be found to obey unalterable laws. That is the doctrine of karma'.

Rebirth The belief in the transmigration of souls (*samsara*) in a never-ending cycle of rebirth has been Hinduism's most distinctive and important contribution to the culture of India and Sri Lanka. The earliest reference to the belief is found in one of the Upanishads, around the seventh century BC, at about the same time as the doctrine of karma made its first appearance. By the late Upanishads it was universally accepted, and in Buddhism there is never any questioning of the belief.

The duty of tolerance

One of the reasons why the Hindu faith is often confusing to the outsider is that as a whole it has many elements which appear mutually self-contradictory but which are reconciled by Hindus as different facets of the ultimate truth. S Radhakrishnan suggests that for a Hindu 'tolerance is a duty, not a mere concession. In pursuance of this duty Hinduism has accepted within its fold almost all varieties of belief and doctrine and accepted them as authentic expressions of the spiritual endeavour.' Such a tolerance is particularly evident in the attitude of Hindus to the nature of God and of divinity. C Rajagopalachari writes that there is a distinction that marks

Hinduism sharply from the other monotheistic faiths such as Christianity or Islam. This is that 'the philosophy of Hinduism has taught and trained the Hindu devotee to see and worship the Supreme Being in all the idols that are worshipped, with a clarity of understanding and an intensity of vision that would surprise the people of other faiths. The Divine Mind governing the Universe, be it as Mother or Father, has infinite aspects, and the devotee approaches him or her, or both, in any of the many aspects as he may be led to do according to the mood and the psychological need of the hour.'

Ahimsa

AL Basham pointed out that belief in transmigration must have encouraged a further distinctive doctrine, that of non-violence or non-injury – *ahimsa*. Buddhism campaigned particularly vigorously against the then-existing practice of animal sacrifice. The belief in rebirth meant that all living things and creatures of the spirit – people, devils, gods, animals, even worms – possessed the same essential soul.

Hindu philosophy

It is common now to talk of six major schools of Hindu philosophy. The best known are yoga and vedanta. Yoga is concerned with systems of meditation that can lead ultimately to release from the cycle of rebirth. It can be traced back as a system of thought to at least the third century AD. It is just one part of the wider system known as Vedanta, literally the final parts of the Vedantic literature, the Upanishads. The basic texts also include the Brahmasutra of Badrayana, written about the first century AD, and the most important of all, the Bhagavadgita, which is a part of the epic Mahabharata.

Hindu worship

The sacred in nature Some Hindus believe in one all-powerful God who created all the lesser gods and the universe. The Hindu gods include many whose origins lie in the Vedic deities of the early Aryans. These were often associated with the forces of nature, and Hindus have always revered many natural objects. Mountain tops, trees, rocks and above all rivers, are regarded as sites of special religious significance. They all have their own guardian spirits. You can see the signs of the continuing lively belief in these gods and demons wherever you travel. Thus trees for example are often painted with vertical red and white stripes and will have a small shrine at their base. Occasionally branches of trees will have numerous pieces of thread or strips of coloured cloth tied to them – placed there by devotees with the prayer for fulfilment of a favour. Hill tops will frequently have a shrine of some kind at the highest point, dedicated to a particularly powerful god. Pilgrimage to some important Hindu shrines is often undertaken by Buddhists as well as Hindus.

Puja For most Hindus today worship (often referred to as 'performing puja') is an integral part of their faith. The great majority of Hindu homes will have a shrine to one of the gods of the Hindu pantheon. Individuals and families will often visit shrines or temples, and on special occasions will travel long distances to particularly holy places such as Kataragama.

Acts of devotion are often aimed at the granting of favours and the meeting of urgent needs for this life – good health, finding a suitable wife or husband, the birth of a son, prosperity and good fortune. In this respect the popular devotion of simple pilgrims of all faiths in South Asia is remarkably similar when they visit shrines, whether Hindu, Buddhist or Jain temples, the tombs of Muslim saints or even churches.

Performing puja involves making an offering to God, and darshan – having a view of the deity. Although there are devotional movements among Hindus in which singing and praying is practised in groups, Hindu worship is generally an act performed by individuals. Thus Hindu temples may be little more than a shrine in the middle of the street, housing an image of the deity which will be tended by a priest and visited at special times when a darshan of the resident God can be obtained. When it has been consecrated, the image, if exactly made, becomes the channel for the godhead to work.

Images The image of the deity may be in one of many forms. Temples may be dedicated to Vishnu or Siva, for example, or to any one of their other representations. The image of the deity becomes the object of worship and the centre of the temple's rituals. These often follow through the cycle of day and night, as well as yearly life cycles. The priests may wake the deity from sleep, bathe, clothe and feed it. Worshippers will be invited to share in this process by bringing offerings of clothes and food. Gifts of money will usually be made, and in some temples there is a charge levied for taking up positions in front of the deity in order to obtain a darshan at the appropriate times.

Hindu sects Today three Gods are widely seen as all-powerful: Brahma, Vishnu and Siva. Their functions and character are not readily separated. While Brahma is regarded as the ultimate source of creation, Siva also has a creative role alongside his function as destroyer. Vishnu in contrast is seen as the preserver or protector of the universe. There are very few images and sculptures of Brahma, but Vishnu and Siva are far more widely represented and have come to be seen as the most powerful and important. Their followers are referred to as Vaishnavite and Saivites respectively, the majority in Sri Lanka today being Saivites.

Sarasvati Seen by some Hindus as the 'active power' of Brahma and popularly thought of as his consort, Sarasvati has survived into the modern Hindu world as a far more important figure than Brahma himself. In popular worship Sarasvati represents the goddess of education and learning, worshipped in schools and colleges with gifts of fruit, flowers and incense. She represents 'the word', which began to be deified as part of the process of the writing of the Vedas, which ascribed magical power to words themselves. Unlike Brahma Sarasvati plays an important part in modern Hindu worship. Normally shown as white coloured and riding on a swan, she usually carries a book, and is often shown playing a vina.

Vishnu Vishnu is seen as the God with the human face. From the second century a new and passionate devotional worship of Vishnu's incarnation as Krishna developed in South India. For Vaishnavites, God took 10 different forms in order to save the world from impending disaster. These include Rama and Krishna, in which he was believed to take recognizable human form. In the earliest stories about Rama he was not regarded as divine. Although he is now seen as an earlier incarnation of Vishnu than Krishna, he was added to the pantheon very late, probably after the Muslim invasions of India in the 12th century AD. The story has become part of the cultures of southeast Asia. Krishna is worshipped extremely widely as perhaps the most human of the gods. His advice on the battlefield of the

Vishnu's ten incarnations

Name	Form	Story
1 Matsya	Fish	Vishnu took the form of a fish to rescue Manu (the first man), his family and the Vedas from a flood.
2 Kurma	Tortoise	Vishnu became a tortoise to rescue all the treasures lost in the flood, including the divine nectar (Amrita) with which the gods preserved their youth. The gods put Mount Kaila on the tortoise's back, and when he reached the bottom of the ocean they twisted the divine snake round the mountain. They then churned the ocean with the mountain by pulling the snake, raising the nectar, the other treasures, and the Goddess Lakshmi, Vishnu's consort.
3 Varaha	Boar	Vishnu appeared again to raise the earth from the ocean's floor where it had been thrown by a demon, Hiranyaksa. The story probably developed from a non-Aryan cult of a sacred pig.
4 Narasimha	Half-man, half lion	Having persuaded Brahma to promise that he could not be killed either by day or night, by god, man or beast, the demon Hiranyakasipu then terrorized everybody. When the gods pleaded for help, Vishnu burst out from a pillar in the demon's palace at sunset, when it was neither day nor night, in the form of a half man and half lion and killed Hiranyakasipu.
5 Vamana	A dwarf	Bali, a demon, achieved supernatural power by asceticism. To protect the world Vishnu appeared before him in the form of a dwarf and asked him a favour. Bali granted Vishnu as much land as he could cover in three strides. Vishnu then became a giant, covering the earth in three strides. He left only hell to the demon.
6 Parasurama	Rama with the axe	Vishnu (Parasurama) was incarnated as the son of a Brahmin, Jamadagni. Parasurama killed the wicked king for robbing his father. The king's sons then killed Jamadagni, and in revenge Parasurama destroyed all male kshatriyas, twenty one times in succession.
7 Rama	The Prince of Ayodhya	As told in the Ramayana, Vishnu came in the form of Rama to rescue the world from the dark demon, Ravana. His faithful wife Sita is the model of patient faithfulness while Hanuman, is the monkey-faced god and Rama's helper.
8 Krishna	Charioteer for Arjuna. Many forms	Krishna meets almost every human need.
9 The Buddha		Probably incorporated into the Hindu pantheon in order to discredit the Buddhists, dominant in some parts of India until the 6th century AD. An early Hindu interpretation suggests that Vishnu took incarnation as Buddha to show compassion for animals and to end sacrifice.
10 Kalki	Riding on a horse	Vishnu's arrival will accompany the final destruction of this present world, judging the wicked and rewarding the good.

Mahabharata is one of the major sources of guidance for the rules of daily living for many Hindus today. In Sri Lanka, Vishnu appears in Buddhist temples since he is considered to be one of the four 'Guardian Deities', destined to become a future Buddha. He is seen as the protector of Buddhism on the island.

Commonly represented as Vishnu's wife, **Lakshmi** is widely worshipped as the goddess of wealth. **Hanuman** is the faithful monkey who helped Rama search of Sita. The Ramayana tells how he went at the head of his monkey army in search of the abducted Sita across India and finally into the demon Ravana's forest home of Lanka. He used his powers to jump the sea channel separating India from Sri Lanka and managed after a series of heroic and magical feats to find and rescue his master's wife. Whatever form he is shown in he remains almost instantly recognizable.

Background

Siva Is interpreted as both creator and destroyer, the power through whom the universe evolves. He lives on Mount Kailasa with his wife **Parvati** (also known as Uma, Sati, Kali and Durga) and two sons, the elephant-headed Ganesh and the six-headed Karttikeya, known in Sri Lanka and South India as Subrahmanya, Kataragama or Skanda. To many contemporary Hindus Siva and Parvati and their sons form a model of sorts for family life. In sculptural representations Siva is normally accompanied by his 'vehicle', the bull (*nandi or nandin*).

Siva is also represented in Shaivite temples by the linga, literally meaning 'sign' or 'mark', but referring in this context to the sign of gender or phallus and *yoni*. On the one hand a symbol of energy, fertility and potency, as Siva's symbol it also represents the yogic power of sexual abstinence and penance. The linga has become the most important symbol of the cult of Siva. **Nandi**, Siva's vehicle, the bull, is one of the most widespread of sacred symbols of the ancient world. Strength and virility are key attributes, and pilgrims to Siva temples will often touch the nandi's testicles on their way into the shrine. **Ganesh** is one of Hinduism's most popular gods. He is seen as the great clearer of obstacles. Shown at gateways and on door lintels with his elephant head and pot belly, his image is revered among Hindu communities across the world. Meetings, functions and special family gatherings will often start with prayers to Ganesh.

Skanda (Kataragama) The name Skanda means 'attacker', and he is seen as the God of War. Kataragama, one of the sons of Siva and Parvati, is one of Sri Lankan Hinduism's most important deities. One legend suggests that he was conceived by the Goddess Ganga from Siva's seed, and he is seen as the bringer of disease and the robber of good health. Different aspects of Kataragama are worshipped in several major Hindu temples on the island. His vehicle is the cock which was sacrificed to him. In Sri Lanka Kataragama carries the trident, known as the *vel*, in India the weapon of Siva himself, and he is the presiding deity at the great Kataragama Festival.

Kataragama is one of the four Guardian Deities who appear in Buddhist art as future Buddhas, and is hence a figure venerated by Buddhists. His power is associated with the fight by the Sinhalese in ancient times, against Hindu Tamil dominance. His colour is red.

Caste One of the defining characteristics of South Asian societies, caste has helped to shape the social life of most religious communities in South Asia. Although the word caste (meaning 'unmixed' or 'pure') was given by the Portuguese in the 15th century AD, the main features of the system emerged at the end of the Vedic period. Two terms – *varna* and *jati* – are used in India itself, and have come to be used interchangeably and confusingly with the word caste. In Sri Lanka the Tamils of Jaffna have a modified form of the caste social structure typical of neighbouring Tamil Nadu.

Varna Literally meaning colour, had a fourfold division. By 600 BC this had become a standard means of classifying the population. The fair-skinned Aryans distinguished themselves from the darker skinned earlier inhabitants. The 4th-century 'Laws of Manu' suggested that the priestly varna, the Brahmins, were seen as coming from the mouth of Brahma; the Kshatriyas were warriors, coming from Brahma's arms; the Vaishyas, a trading community, came from Brahma's thighs, and the Sudras, classified as agriculturists, from his feet. Relegated beyond the pale of civilized Hindu society were the untouchables or outcastes, who were left with the jobs which were regarded as impure, usually associated with dealing with the dead (human or animal) or with excrement.

Jati The great majority of Sri Lankan Hindus (and Indians) do not put themselves into one of the four varna categories, but into a jati group. All are part of local or regional hierarchies, not organized in any institutional sense, and traditionally with no formal record of caste status. While individuals found it impossible to change caste or to move up the social scale, groups would sometimes try to gain recognition as higher caste by adopting practices of the Brahmins such as becoming vegetarians. Many used to be identified with particular activities, and occupations used to be hereditary. Caste membership is decided simply by birth. Although you can be evicted from your caste by your fellow members, usually for disobedience to caste rules such as over marriage, you cannot join another caste, and technically you become an outcaste.

Among Jaffna Tamils Brahmins occupy the same priestly position that they hold in India, and have also played an important role in education. Beneath them in ritual hierarchy but occupying a dominant social and political position, until recent times at least, were the cultivating and landlord caste known as the *vellalas*. Below them in rank was a range of low and outcaste groups, filling such occupations as washermen, sweepers and barbers, such as the Pallas and Nallavas. The tea plantation workers are all regarded as low caste.

Jaffna was subject to Christian missionary work, especially through education, from the early 19th century. It produced a Hindu response, and a Hindu renaissance took place in the late 19th century under the leadership of *Arumuga Navalar*. Setting up an extensive network of schools, he was anxious to strengthen orthodox Saivism, on the one hand through restoring temples and on the other by publishing religious texts.

Virtually all Hindu temples in Sri Lanka were destroyed by the Portuguese and the Dutch. Those that have been rebuilt never had the resources available to compare with those in India, not having had their lands restored in the post colonial period, so they are generally small. However, they play a prominent part in Hindu life. De Silva suggests that Arumuga Navalar's failure to argue for social reform meant that caste – and untouchability – were virtually untouched. The high caste **Vellalas**, a small minority of the total Hindu population, maintained their power unchallenged until after Independence. Removal of caste disabilities started in the 1950s. The civil war over the demand for a separate Tamil state, Tamil Eelam, during which the Liberation Tigers of Tamil Eelam (LTTE) have taken complete control of social and political life in Jaffna and the north, may have changed the whole basis of caste far more thoroughly than any programme of social reform. Such changes will only be open to scrutiny when peace has returned.

Islam

Islam was brought to Sri Lanka by Arab traders. Long before the followers of the Prophet Mohammad spread the new religion of Islam Arabs had been trading across the Indian Ocean with southwest India, the Maldives, Sri Lanka and South East Asia. When the Arab world became Muslim so the newly-converted Arab traders brought Islam with them, and existing communities of Arab origin adopted the new faith. However, numbers were also swelled by conversion from both Buddhists and Hindus, and by immigrant Muslims from South India who fled the Portuguese along the west coast of India. The great majority of the present Muslim population of Sri Lanka is Tamil speaking, although there are also Muslims of Malay origin. Both in Kandy and the coastal districts Muslims have generally lived side by side with Buddhists, often sharing common interests against the colonial powers. However, one of the means by which Muslims maintained their identity was to refuse to be drawn into colonial education. As a result, by the end of the 19th century the Muslims were among the least educated groups. A Muslim lawyer, *Siddi Lebbe*, helped to change attitudes and encourage participation by Muslims.

The five pillars of Islam

In addition to the profession of faith that there is no God but Allah, there are four further obligatory requirements imposed on Muslims. Daily prayers are prescribed at daybreak, noon, afternoon, sunset and nightfall. Muslims must give alms to the poor. They must observe a strict fast during the month of Ramadan. They must not eat or drink between sunrise and sunset. Lastly, they should attempt the pilgrimage to the Ka'aba in Mecca, known as the Hajj. Those who have done so are entitled to the prefix Hajji before their name.

Islamic rules differ from Hindu practice in several other aspects of daily life. Muslims are strictly forbidden to drink alcohol (though some suggest that this prohibition is restricted to the use of fermented grape juice, that is wine, it is commonly accepted to apply to all alcohol). Eating pork, or any meat from an animal not killed by draining its blood while alive, is also prohibited. Meat prepared in the appropriate way is called Halal. Finally usury (charging interest on loans) and games of chance are forbidden.

In 1915 there were major Sinhalese-Muslim riots, and Muslims began a period of active collaboration with the British, joining other minorities led by the Tamils in the search for security and protection of their rights against the Sinhalese. The Muslims have been particularly anxious to maintain Muslim family law, and to gain concessions on education. One of the chief of these is the teaching of Arabic in government schools to Muslim children. Until 1974 Muslims were unique among minorities in having the right to choose which of three languages – Sinhala, Tamil or English – would be their medium of instruction. Since then a new category of Muslim schools has been set up, allowing them to distance themselves from the Tamil Hindu community, whose language most of them speak.

Muslim beliefs The beliefs of Islam (which means 'submission to God') could apparently scarcely be more different from those of Buddhism or Hinduism. Islam has a fundamental creed; 'There is no God but God; and Mohammad is the Prophet of God' (*La Illaha illa 'Ilah Mohammad Rasulu 'Ilah*). One book, the Qur'an, is the supreme authority on Islamic teaching and faith. Islam preaches the belief in bodily resurrection after death, and in the reality of heaven and hell.

The idea of heaven as paradise is pre-Islamic. Alexander the Great is believed to have brought the word paradise into Greek from Persia, where he used it to describe the walled Persian gardens that were found even three centuries before the birth of Christ. For Muslims, Paradise is believed to be filled with sensuous delights and pleasures, while hell is a place of eternal terror and torture, which is the certain fate of all who deny the unity of God.

Islam has no priesthood. The authority of Imams derives from social custom, and from their authority to interpret the scriptures, rather than from a defined status within the Islamic community. Islam also prohibits any distinction on the basis of race or colour, and there is a strong antipathy to the representation of the human figure. It is often thought, inaccurately, that this ban stems from the Qur'an itself. In fact it probably has its origins in the belief of Mohammad that images were likely to be turned into idols.

Muslim sects During the first century of its existence Islam split in two sects which were divided on political and religious grounds, the Shi'is and Sunni's. The religious basis for the division lay in the interpretation of verses in the Qur'an and of traditional sayings of Mohammad, the Hadis. Both sects venerate the Qur'an but have different *Hadis*. They also have different views as to Mohammad's successor.

Calculating the Hijra year

Murray's *Handbook for travellers in India* gave a wonderfully precise method of calculating the current date in the Christian year from the AH date: 'To correlate the Hijra year with the Christian year, express the former in years and decimals of a year, multiply by .970225, add 621.54, and the total will correspond exactly with the Christian year.'

The **Sunnis** – always the majority in South Asia – believe that Mohammad did not appoint a successor, and that Abu Bak'r, Omar and Othman were the first three caliphs (or vice-regents) after Mohammad's death. Ali, whom the Sunni's count as the fourth Caliph, is regarded as the first legitimate Caliph by the Shi'is, who consider Abu Bak'r and Omar to be usurpers. While the Sunni's believe in the principle of election of Caliphs, Shi'is believe that although Mohammad is the last prophet there is a continuing need for intermediaries between God and man. Such intermediaries are termed Imams, and they base both their law and religious practice on the teaching of the Imams.

From the Mughal emperors in India, who enjoyed an unparalleled degree of political power, down to the poorest fishermen in Sri Lanka, Muslims in South Asia have found different ways of adjusting to their Hindu or Buddhist environment. Some have reacted by accepting or even incorporating features of Hindu belief and practice in their own. Akbar, the most eclectic of Mughal emperors, went as far as banning activities like cow slaughter which were offensive to Hindus and celebrating Hindu festivals in court.

Muslim year

The first day of the Muslim calendar is 16 July 622 AD. This was the date of the Prophet's migration from Mecca to Medina, the Hijra, from which the date's name is taken (AH = Anno Hijrae). The Muslim year is divided into 12 lunar months, alternating between 29 and 30 days. The first month of the year is *Moharram*, followed by *Safar, Rabi-ul-Awwal, Rabi-ul-Sani, Jumada-ul-Awwal, Jumada-ul-Sani, Rajab, Shaban, Ramadan, Shawwal, Ziquad* and *Zilhaj*.

Significant dates

New Year's Day – 1st of *Moharram*
Anniversary of the killing of the Prophet's grandson Hussain, commemorated by Shi'i Muslims – 9th and 10th of *Moharram*
Birthday of the Prophet (Milad-ul-Nabi) – 12th of *Rabi-ul-Awwal*
Start of the fasting month – 1st of *Ramadan*
Night of prayer (Shab-e-Qadr) – 21st of *Ramadan*
Three-day festival to mark the end of Ramadan – 1st of *Shawwal: Id-ul-Fitr*
Two-day festival commemorating the sacrifice of Ismail; the main time of pilgrimage to Mecca (the Haj). An animal (goat) is sacrificed and special meat and vermicelli dishes are prepared – 10th of *Zilhaj: Id-ul-Ajha*

Christianity

Christianity was introduced by the Portuguese. Unlike India, where Christian missionary work from the late 18th century was often carried out in spite of colonial government rather than with its active support, in Sri Lanka missionary activity enjoyed various forms of state backing. One Sinhalese king, Dharmapala, was converted, endowing the church, and even some high caste families became Christian. When the Dutch evicted the Portuguese they tried to suppress Roman Catholicism, and the Dutch Reformed Church found some converts. Other Protestant denominations followed the arrival of the British, though not always with

Background

official support or encouragement. Many of the churches remained dependent on outside support. Between the two World Wars Christian influence in government was radically reduced. Denominational schools lost their protection and special status, and since the 1960s have had to come to terms with a completely different role in Sri Lanka.

Christian beliefs   Christian theology had its roots in Judaism, with its belief in one eternal God, the Creator of the universe. Judaism saw the Jewish people as the vehicle for God's salvation, the 'chosen people of God', and pointed to a time when God would send his Saviour, or Messiah. Jesus, whom Christians believe was 'the Christ' or Messiah, was born in the village of Bethlehem, some 20 km south of Jerusalem. Very little is known of his early life except that he was brought up in a devout Jewish family. At the age of 29 or 30 he gathered a small group of followers and began to preach in the region between the Dead Sea and the Sea of Galilee. Two years later he was crucified in Jerusalem by the authorities on the charge of blasphemy – that he claimed to be the son of God.

Christians believe that all people live in a state of sin, in the sense that they are separated from God and fail to do his will. They believe that God is personal, 'like a father'. As God's son, Jesus accepted the cost of that separation and sinfulness himself through his death on the cross. Christians believe that Jesus was raised from the dead on the third day after he was crucified, and that he appeared to his closest followers. They believe that his spirit continues to live today, and that he makes it possible for people to come back to God.

The New Testament of the Bible, which, alongside the Old Testament, is the text to which Christians refer as the ultimate scriptural authority, consists of four 'Gospels' (meaning 'good news'), and a series of letters by several early Christians referring to the nature of the Christian life.

Christian   Although Christians are encouraged to worship individually as well as together,
worship   most forms of Christian worship centre on the gathering of the church congregation for praise, prayer the preaching of God's word, which usually takes verses from the Bible as its starting point. Different denominations place varying emphases on the main elements of worship, but in most church services today the congregation will take part in singing hymns (songs of praise), prayers will be led by the minister, priest or a member of the congregation, readings from the Bible will be given and a sermon preached. For many Christians the most important service is the act of Holy Communion (Protestant) or Mass (Catholic) which celebrates the death and resurrection of Jesus in sharing bread and wine, which are held to represent Christ's body and blood given to save people from their sin. Although Christian services may be held daily in some churches most Christian congregations in Sri Lanka meet for worship on Sunday, and services are held in Sinhala and Tamil as well as in English. They are open to all.

Denominations   Between the second and the fourth centuries AD there were numerous debates about the interpretation of Christian doctrine, sometimes resulting in the formation of specific groups focusing on particular interpretations of faith. One such group was that of the Nestorian Christians, who played a major part in the theology of the Syrian Church in Kerala. They regarded the Syrian patriarch of the east their spiritual head, and followed the Nestorian tradition that there were two distinct natures in Christ, the divine and human. However, although some believe that St Thomas and other early Christians came to Sri Lanka as well as South India the early church left no real mark on the island.

Today Roman Catholics account for 90% of the Island's Christians. The Roman Catholic church believes that Christ declared that his disciple Peter should be the first spiritual head of the Church, and that his successors should lead the Church on earth. Modern Catholic churches still recognize the spiritual authority of the Pope and cardinals.

The reformation which took place in Europe from the 16th century onwards resulted in the creation of the Protestant churches, which became dominant in several European countries. They reasserted the authority of the Bible over that of the church. A number of new denominations were created. This process of division left a profound mark on the nature of the Christian church as it spread into South Asia. The Dutch brought with them their Dutch Reformed faith and left a number of churches, and subsequently during British colonial period the Anglican Church (Church of England) also became established, and several Protestant missionary denominations including Baptist and Methodist, established small churches. The reunification of the Protestant Christian churches which has taken significant steps since 1947 has progressed faster in South Asia than in most other parts of the world.

Architecture

Sri Lankan architecture has many elements in common with Buddhist and Hindu Indian traditions, but the long period of relative isolation, and the determined preservation of Buddhism long after its demise in India, have contributed to some very distinctive features. In order to understand the distinctiveness of Sri Lanka's Buddhist architecture, however, it is helpful to trace its origins in early Indian architectural developments.

Over the 4,000 years since the Indus Valley civilization flourished art and architecture developed in India with a remarkable continuity through successive regional and religious influences and styles.

The Buddhist art and architecture of the third century BC left few remains, but the stylistic influence on early Hindu architecture was profound. From the 6th century AD the first Hindu religious buildings to have survived into the modern period were constructed in southern and eastern India, alongside a continuing development of the Buddhist tradition elsewhere. Although Hindu buildings across India had many features in common, regional styles began to develop.

Coming into India as vanquishing hordes, the early Muslims destroyed much that was in their path. Temples that had been encrusted with jewels were left bare. Mosques were built out of the stones of destroyed temples. To the east, the Muslims finally completed the decline of Buddhism in India by destroying the last remaining Buddhist monasteries, notably the great monastery at Nalanda.

Introducing concepts of religious building from a faith completely different from that of the Hinduism into which it was transplanted, the new Islamic rulers also brought alien cultural concepts – notably from Persia. Yet the greatest flowering of Islamic architecture India ever saw under the Mughals, was not simply a transplant from another country or region. It grew out of India's own traditions as a new and distinctive architecture, yet with recognizable links to the culture which surrounded it. That continuity reflected many forces, not least the use made by the great Mughal emperors of local skilled craftsmen and builders at every stage of their work. Constantly in contact not just with Hindu religious buildings, but with the secular buildings of the Rajputs to their south and west, the Mughal emperors took up themes present in the Hindu traditions of their time, and bent them to a new purpose.

Painting, sculpture, inlay work, all blended skills from a variety of sources, and craftsmen – even occasionally from Europe. These were sometimes employed to embellish the great works. What emerged was another stepping stone in a tradition of Indian architecture, which, far from breaking the threads of Hindu tradition actually wove them into new forms.

Sinhalese stupas

The Sinhalese classify the domes into six different types, such as bell-shaped, or bubble-shaped. On top of the dome is a small square enclosure (hataraes kotuwa), which contained valuable offerings, surrounded by a railed pavilion. Above it is the ceremonial umbrella (chatta). The Sri Lankan parasols are furled into a staff-like shape (see page 309). Percy Brown suggests that they are more reminiscent of the totem poles of the Veddas, and may be derived from aboriginal symbols. Originally the cubical box housed the sacred relics themselves. However, the post left little room for the relics and offerings. A compartment was then hollowed out of the brickwork immediately below the staff.

Into it was lowered the 'mystic stone', a granite block carved with nine recesses to contain the relics and offerings. The finial staff then sealed and surmounted the relic stone and the whole dagoba.

Many of these buildings are immense, and enormous effort went into ensuring that they would last. The Mahavansa records how King Dutthagamani prepared their foundations. The base was laid of round stones, crushed by pounding and then trampled by huge elephants with leather shoes to protect their feet. Clay was then spread over the hard core, followed by a layer of iron, another layer of stones and then a layer of ordinary stone.

These developments left Sri Lankan Buddhist architecture virtually untouched, thereby widening the gap between the two traditions. It is a distance which can be seen even in 19th- and early 20th-century architecture, for whereas the British encouraged an attempt to revive what they regarded as Islamic and Rajput ideals in some of their most ambitious building works, Sri Lanka's modern buildings make no attempt to recall such styles.

Sri Lankan buddhist architecture

Buddhist and Hindu architecture probably began with wooden building, for the rock carving and cave excavated temples show clear evidence of copying styles which must have been developed first in wooden buildings. The 3rd-2nd century BC caves of the Buddhists were followed in the 7th and 8th centuries AD by free standing but rock-cut temples such as those at Mamallapuram.

Stupas Stupas were the most striking feature of Buddhist architecture in India. Originally they were funeral mounds, built to house the remains of the Buddha and his disciples. The tradition of building stupas was developed by Sri Lanka's Sinhalese kings, notably in golden age of the fourth and fifth centuries AD, and the revival during the 11th-12th centuries. In Sri Lanka, a stupa is often referred to as 'dagoba' (from Sanskrit *dhatu* – relic, *garbha* – womb chamber) and sometimes named 'saya' (from *cetiya* – funeral mound) or 'wehera' (from *vihara* – monastery)). Some of the stupas (*dagobas*) are huge structures, and even those such as the fourth century *Jetavana* at Anuradhapura, now simply a grassed-over brick mound, is impressively large.

Few of the older Buddhist monuments are in their original form, either having become ruins or been renovated. Hemispherical mounds built of brick and filled with brick and rubble, they stand on a square terrace, surmounted by three concentric platforms. In its original or its restored form, the brick mound is covered with plaster and painted white. Surrounding it on a low platform (*vahalakadas*) is the ambulatory, or circular path, reached from the cardinal directions by stone stairways. Around some of the dagobas there are fine sculptures on these circular paths at the head of each stairway.

The design is filled with symbolic meaning. The hemisphere is the dome of heaven, the axis of the cosmos being represented by the central finial on top, while the umbrella-like tiers are the rising heavens of the gods. Worshippers walk round the stupa on the raised platform in a clockwise direction (*pradakshina*), following the rotational movement of the celestial bodies.

Many smaller stupas were built within circular buildings. These were covered with a metal and timber roof resting on concentric rows of stone pillars. Today the roofs have disappeared, but examples such as the *Vatadage* at Polonnaruwa can still be seen. King Parakramabahu I also built another feature of Sri Lankan architecture at Polonnaruwa, a large rectangular hall in which was placed an image of the Buddha. Most of Sri Lanka's early secular architecture has disappeared. Made of wood, there are remnants of magnificent royal palaces at both Anuradhapura and Sigiriya.

Moonstones

Sri Lanka's moonstones (not the gem) are among the world's finest artistic achievements. Polished semi-circular granite, they are carved in concentric semi-circular rings ('half-moons', about 1 m in radius) portraying various animals, flowers and birds, and normally placed at the foot of flights of steps or entrances to important buildings. There are particularly fine examples in Anuradhapura and Polonnaruwa.

The moonstones of pure Buddhist art at Anuradhapura comprise a series of rings and are often interpreted in the following way. You step over the flames of fire, through which one must pass to be purified. The next ring shows animals which represent the four stages of life: **1** Elephant – birth; **2** Horse – old age; **3** Lion – illness; **4** Bull – death and decay. These continue in an endless cycle symbolizing the continuous rebirths to which one is subject. The third row represents the twisting serpent of lust and desire, while the fourth is that of geese carrying lotus buds, representing purity. The lotus in the centre is a symbol of nirvana.

Guard stones The steps have on either side beautifully carved guard stones with *makaras* designed to incorporate features from eight symbolically significant creatures: the foot of the lion, the crocodile's mouth and teeth, an elephant's tusk, the body of a fish, the peacock's feather, the serpent inside the mouth and the monkeys eyes.

Sri Lankan hindu architecture

Hindu temple building

The principles of religious building were laid down in the *Sastras*, sets of rules compiled by priests. Every aspect of Hindu and Buddhist religious building is identified with conceptions of the structure of the universe. This applies as much to the process of building – the timing of which must be undertaken at astrologically propitious times – as to the formal layout of the buildings. The cardinal directions of north, south, east and west are the basic fix on which buildings are planned. The east-west axis is nearly always a fundamental building axis.

Hindu temples were nearly always built to a clear and universal design, which had built into it philosophical understandings of the universe. This cosmology, of an infinite number of universes, isolated from each other in space, proceeds by imagining various

Doorframe from Galapata Vihara in the Galle district Source: Godakumbura, CE (1982) Sinhalese Doorways, Archaeological Department, Colombo

Background

possibilities as to its nature. Its centre is seen as dominated by **Mount Meru** which keeps earth and heaven apart. The concept of *separation* is crucial to Hindu thought and social practise. Continents, rivers, and oceans occupy concentric rings around the mountain, while the stars encircle the mountain in another plane. Humans live on the continent of **Jambudvipa**, characterized by the rose apple tree (*jambu*).

The *Sastras* show plans of this continent, organized in concentric rings and entered at the cardinal points. This type of diagram was known as a **mandala**. Such a geometric scheme could then be subdivided into almost limitless small compartments, each of which could be designated as having special properties or be devoted to a particular deity. The centre of the mandala would be the seat of the major god. Mandalas provided the ground rules for the building of stupas and temples across India, and provided the key to the symbolic meaning attached to every aspect of religious buildings.

Temple design Hindu temples developed characteristic plans and elevations. The focal point of the temple lay in its sanctuary, the home of the presiding deity, known as the womb-chamber (*garbhagriha*). A series of doorways, in large temples leading through a succession of buildings, allowed the worshipper to move towards the final encounter with the deity himself and to obtain *darshan* – a sight of the god. Both Buddhist and Hindu worship encourages the worshipper to walk clockwise around the shrine, performing *pradakshina*.

The elevations are designed to be symbolic representations of the home of the gods the tallest towers rising above the *garbagriha* itself, symbolizing the meeting of earth and heaven in the person of the enshrined deity. In both, the basic structure is usually richly embellished with sculpture. When first built this would usually have been plastered and painted, and often covered in gems. In contrast to the extraordinary profusion of colour and life on the outside, the interior is dark and cramped. Here is the true centre of power.

Hindu architecture on the island bears close resemblances with the Dravida styles of neighbouring Tamil Nadu. Although all the important Hindu temples in Sri Lanka were destroyed by the Portuguese, the style in which they have been re-built continues to reflect those southern Indian traditions.

Tamil Nadu has been at the heart of southern Indian religious development for 2,000 years. Temple building was a comparatively late development in Hindu worship. Long before the first temple was built shrines were dotted across the land, the focus of **pilgrimage**, each with its own mythology. Even the most majestic of South Indian temples have basic features in common with these original shrines,

and many of them have simply grown by a process of accretion around a shrine which may have been in that spot for centuries. The **myths** that grew around the shrines were expressed first by word of mouth. Most temples today still have versions of the stories which were held to justify their existence in the eyes of pilgrims. There are several basic features in common. David Shulman has written that the story will include 'the (usually miraculous) discovery of the site and the adventures of those important exemplars (such as gods, demons, serpents, and men) who were freed from sorrow of one kind or another by worshipping there'. The shrine which is the object of the story nearly always claims to be supreme, better than all others. Many stories illustrate these claims of superiority: for example, we are often told that the Goddess **Ganga** herself is forced to worship in a South Indian shrine in order to become free of the sins deposited by evil-doers who bathe in the river at Benares.

Through all its great diversity Hindu temple architecture repeatedly expresses these beliefs, shared though not necessarily expressed, by the thousands of Sri Lankan Hindus who make visiting temples such a vital and living part of their life. In architecture as in religious philosophy, South India has derived much from its northern Hindu relations. The Buddhist *chaitya* hall with its apsidal plan had been the common form of most religious shrines up to the time of the Chalukyans in Karnataka, who in the sixth century started experimenting with what the Guptas in the north had already achieved by elaborating the simple square plan of earlier shrines. In the north, the *sikhara* was a smooth pyramidal structure, rising to a rounded top with a pointed end, while in the South the *vimana* was more like a stepped pyramid, usually square in plan and had at its top a rounded cupola.

The **Dravida** or Dravidian style underwent several changes for about 1,000 years from the time of the Pallavas who laid its foundations. In Mamallapuram, just south of Chennai (Madras), rock-cut cave temples, *mandapas* or small excavated columned halls and the *rathas* or monoliths in the shape of temple chariots, were carved out by the early Pallavas in the seventh century. These were followed by structural temples and bas relief sculptures on giant rocks, which added another dimension (eg eighth century Shore Temple).

Various dynasties fought for the Tamil lands until the **Cholas** gained supremacy in the ninth century and established their kingdom in the Kaveri River valley later extending their realm to become rulers over a vast area from the Ganga to Sri Lanka. They did away with the rampant lion pilasters, introduced high relief, half-size sculptures of deities and the gryphon motifs. The Cholas are also remembered for the fine bronzes which adorned their temples.

Today the most striking external features of Hindu temples in Sri Lanka as in South India are their elaborately carved towering gateways (*gopurams*). These were first introduced by the **Pandiyas**, who succeeded the Cholas a century later. The *gopuram* took its name from the 'cow gate' of the Vedic village, which later became the city gate and finally the monumental temple entrance. This type of tower is distinguished from the *vimana* by its oblong plan at the top which is an elongated vaulted roof with gable ends. It has pronounced sloping sides, usually 65°C, so that the section at the top is about half the size of the base. Although the first two storeys are usually built solidly of stone masonry, the rest is of lighter material, usually brick and plaster.

By the 15th century the Vijayanagar kings established their empire across much of South India. Their temples were built on an unprecedented scale, with huge gopurams studding the outside walls. None of the Sri Lankan temples were built on a scale anywhere near that of the 16th and 17th-century Vijayanagar temples of South India. Furthermore, all Hindu temples were destroyed by the Portuguese during the period in which Vijayanagar architecture was flourishing across the Palk Straits. Thus contemporary Hindu temples in Sri Lanka, while retaining some of the elements common to Hindu temples in Tamil Nadu, are always on a much smaller scale.

Background

Art

Sculpture Early Sri Lankan sculpture shows close links with Indian Buddhist sculpture. The first images of the Buddha, some of which are still in Anuradhapura, are similar to second and third century AD images from Amaravati in modern Andhra Pradesh. The middle period of the fifth to 11th centuries AD contains some magnificent sculptures on rocks, but there is a range of other sculpture, notably moonstones. There are decorated bands of flower motifs, geese and a variety of animals, both Anuradhapura and Polonnaruwa having outstanding examples. While the moonstones are brilliant works in miniature, Sri Lankan sculptors also produced outstanding colossal works, such as the 13-m high Buddha at Aukana, now dated as from the 9th century, or the 13th-century reclining Buddha at Polonnaruwa.

Painting Sri Lanka's most famous art is its rock paintings from Sigiriya, dating from the sixth century AD. The heavenly nymphs (*apsaras*), scattering flowers from the clouds, are shown with extraordinary grace and beauty (you may notice the absence of the black pigment). Polonnaruwa saw a later flowering of the painting tradition in the 12th and 13th centuries. The Thivanka murals depict tales from the *Jatakas* and the Buddha's life, some elaborating and extending the strictly religious subject by introducing scenery and architectural elements. The wall paintings of Dambulla are also noteworthy (although many of the original paintings were covered by later ones), but thereafter classical Sri Lankan art declined though the folk tradition of scroll painting carried on.

The mid-18th century saw a new revival of painting in the Kandyan Kingdom, this time based on folk art which were inspired by traditional tales instead of religious themes. Many survive in temples around Kandy and elsewhere in the southwest.

Crafts Local craft skills are still practised widely in households across the country. Pottery, coir fibre, carpentry, handloom weaving and metalwork all receive government assistance. Some of the crafts are concentrated in just a few villages. **Brasswork**, for example, is restricted to a small area around Kandy, where the 'city of arts', Kalapura, has over 70 families of craftsmen making superb brass, wood, silver and gold items. Fine **gold and silver chain work** is done both in the Pettah area of Colombo. **Batiks**,

Hamsa (goose) found at Panduvasnuwara. Terracota tiles were often used as decoration on the walls of buildings. This ancient art was practised as recently as 1965 by craftsmen in the Kandy district.

from wall hangings to *lungis* (sarongs), and a wide range of cotton **handloom**, in vibrant colours and textures are widely available. **Silver jewellery** (also from Kandy), trays, ornaments and inlay work is a further specialization. **Masks** are a popular product in the southwest of the island, especially around Ambalangoda, based on traditional masks used in dance dramas, while Galle is famous for pillow **lace** and crochet. **Reed, cane, rattan** are fashioned into attractive household goods, while fine **wood-carving** and colourful **lacquer ware** can reach a high standard.

Language

Sinhala (or Sinhalese) the language of the Sinhalese, is an Indo-European language with North Indian affinities, unlike the Dravidian language, Tamil. The language brought by the North Indian migrants, possibly in the fifth century BC, can be traced from inscriptions dating from the second century BC onwards which show how it had developed away from the original Sanskrit. The spoken language had changed several vowel sounds and absorbed words from the indigenous races and also from Tamil. The Sinhala language had acquired a distinct identity by the beginning of the first century.

Sinhala

Although at first glance the **script** might suggest a link with the South Indian scripts, it developed independently. The rounded form was dictated by the use of a sharp stylus to inscribe on palm-leaf which would later be filled in with 'ink' instead of the North Indian technique of writing on bark.

Literature The early verse and later prose literature were religious (Buddhist) and apart from inscriptions, date from the 10th century although there is evidence of some existing 300 years earlier. Non-religious texts only gained prominence in the last century.

Like Sinhala, Tamil is also one of South Asia's oldest languages, but belongs to the Dravidian language family. It originated on the Indian mainland, and although Sri Lankan Tamil has retained some expressions which have a 'pure', even slightly archaic touch to them, it remains essentially an identical language both in speech and writing to that found in Tamil Nadu.

Tamil

Literature The first Tamil literature dates approximately the second century AD. At that time a poets' academy known as the **Sangam** was established in Madurai. The poetry was devoted to religious subjects. From the beginning of the Christian era a development began to take place in Tamil religious thought and writing. Krishna became transformed from a remote and heroic figure of the epics into the focus of a new and passionate devotional worship – *bhakti*. Jordens has written that this new worship was 'emotional, ardent, ecstatic, often using erotic imagery'. From the seventh to the 10th century there was a surge of writing new hymns of praise, sometimes referred to as 'the Tamil *Veda*'. Attention focused on the 'marvels of Krishna's birth and infancy and his heroic and amorous exploits as a youth among the cowherds and cowherdesses of Gokula'. In the ninth century Vaishnavite Brahmans produced the *Bhagavata Purana*, which, through frequent translation into all India's major languages, became the vehicle for the new worship of Krishna. Its tenth book has been called 'one of the truly great books of Hinduism'. There are over forty translations into Bengali alone. These influences were transmitted directly into Hindu Tamil culture in Sri Lanka, which retained intimate ties with southern Tamil region.

Background

Land and environment

Geography

Sri Lanka is practically on the equator so there is little difference between the length of night and day, both being about 12 hours. The sun rises around 0600 and it is completely dark by 1900. Its position has meant that Sri Lanka is at the heart of the Indian Ocean trading routes. The opening of the route round the Cape of Good Hope by Vasco da Gama in 1498 brought the island into direct contact with Western Europe. The opening of the Suez Canal in 1869 further strengthened the trading links with the West.

Origins Only 100 million years ago Sri Lanka was still attached to the great land mass of what geologists call 'Pangaea', of which South Africa, Antarctica and the Indian Peninsula were a part. Indeed, Sri Lanka is a continuation of the Indian Peninsula, from which it was separated less than 10,000 years when sea level rose to create the 10-m deep and 35 km wide **Palk Straits**. It is 432 km long and at its broadest 224-km wide. Its 1,600 km of coastline is lined with fine sandy beaches, coral reefs and lagoons.

Many of the rocks which comprise over 90% of Sri Lanka and the Indian Peninsula were formed alongside their then neighbours in South Africa, South America, Australia and Antarctica. Generally crystalline, contorted and faulted, the **Archaean** rocks of Sri Lanka and the Indian Peninsula are some of the oldest in the world.

The fault line which severed India from Africa was marked by a north-south ridge of mountains. These run north from the Central Highlands of Sri Lanka through the Western Ghats, which form a spine running up the west coast of India. Both in Sri Lanka and India the hills are set back from the sea by a coastal plain which varies from 10 km to over 80 km wide while the hills are over 2,500-m high.

Sri Lanka 200 million years ago

The oldest series are the **Charnockites**, intrusive rocks named after the founder of Calcutta and enthusiastic amateur geologist, Job Charnock. These are between 2,000 and 3,000 million years old. In Sri Lanka they run like a broad belt across the island's heart, important partly because they contain most of Sri Lanka's minerals, including gems, though these are found largely in the gravelly river deposits rather than in their original rocks.

Unlike the central Himalaya to their north which did not begin to rise until about 35 million years ago the highlands of Sri Lanka have been upland regions for several hundred million years. The island has never been completely covered by the sea, the only exception being in the far north where the Jaffna peninsula was submerged, allowing the distinctive Jaffna limestones to be deposited in shallow seas between seven million and 26 million years ago.

Today the ancient crystalline rocks form an ancient highland massif rising to its highest points just south and southwest of the geographical centre of the pear-shaped island. The highlands rise in three dissected steps to *Piduratalagala* (Sri Lanka's highest mountain at 2,524 m) and the sacred *Adam's Peak* (2,260 m). The steps are separated from each other by steep scarp slopes. Recent evidence suggests that the very early folding of the ancient rocks, followed by erosion at different speeds, formed the scarps and plateaus, often deeply cut by the rivers which radiate from the centre of the island. Even though the origin of these steps is not fully understood the steep scarps separating them have created some beautiful waterfalls and enormous hydro-electric power potential. Some of this has now been realized, notably through the huge Victoria Dam project on the Mahaweli Ganga, but in the process some of the most scenic waterfalls have been lost.

Rivers lakes & floods

By far the largest of the 103 river basins in Sri Lanka is that of the Mahaweli Ganga, which covers nearly one fifth of the island's total area. The river itself has a winding course, rising about 50 km south of Kandy and flowing north then northeast to the sea near Trincomalee, covering a distance of 320 km. It is the only perennial river to cross the Dry Zone. Its name is a reference to the Ganga of North India, and in Sri Lanka all perennial rivers are called Ganga, while seasonal streams are called *oya* (Sinhalese) or *aru* (Tamil). A number of the rivers have now been developed both for irrigation and power, the Victoria project on the Mahaweli Ganga being one of the biggest in Asia – and one of the most controversial. It has created Sri Lanka's largest lake, the Victoria Reservoir.

The short rivers of Sri Lanka's Wet Zone sometimes have severe floods, and the Kelani, which ultimately reaches the sea at Colombo, has had four catastrophic floods in the last century. Others can also be turbulent during the wet season, tumbling through steamy forests and cultivated fields on their short courses to the sea.

Background

Climate

Sri Lanka's location just north of the equator places it on the main track of the two monsoons which dominate South Asia's weather systems. Derived from the Arabic word *mausim* (meaning season), the 'monsoon' is now synonymous with 'rains'. Strictly however it refers to the wind reversal which replaces the relatively cool, dry and stable northeasterlies, characteristic from October to May, with the very warm and wet southwesterlies from May to October. However, the northeasterlies, which originate in the arid interior of China, have crossed over 1,500 km of the Bay of Bengal by the time they reach Sri Lanka, and thus even the northeast monsoon brings rain, especially to the north and east of the island.

Rainfall

Nearly three quarters of Sri Lanka lies in what is widely known as the 'Dry Zone', comprising the northern half and the whole of the east of the country. Extensively forested and with an average annual rainfall of between 1,200-1,800 mm, much of the region does not seem unduly dry, but like much of southeast India, virtually all of the region's rain falls between October and January. The rain often comes in relatively short but dramatic bursts. Habarana, for example, located between Polonnaruwa and Anuradhapura received 1,240 mm (nearly 50 in) of rain in the three days around Christmas in 1957. These rains caused catastrophic floods right across the Dry Zone.

The Wet Zone also receives some rain during this period, although the coastal regions of the southwest are in the rain shadow of the Central Highlands, and are much drier than the northeast between November and January. The southwest corner of Sri Lanka, the Wet Zone, has its main wet season from May to October, when the southwest monsoon sweeps across the Arabian Sea like a massive wall of warm moist air, often over 10,000 m thick. The higher slopes of the Central Highlands receive as much as 4,000 mm during this period, while even the coastal lowlands receive over 500 mm.

Agriculture in the north and east suffers badly during the southwest monsoon because the moisture bearing winds dry out as they descend over the Central Highlands, producing hot, drying and often very strong winds. Thus June, July and August are almost totally rainless throughout the Dry Zone. For much of the time a strong, hot wind, called *yal hulunga* by the Sinhalese peasantry and *kachchan* by the Tamils, desiccates the land.

From late October to December cyclonic storms often form over the Bay of Bengal, sometimes causing havoc from the southern coast of India northwards to Bangladesh. Sri Lanka is far enough south to miss many of the worst of these, but it occasionally suffers major cyclones. These generally come later in the season, in December and January and can cause enormous damage and loss of life.

The Wet Zone rarely experiences long periods without rain. Even between the major moonsoon periods widespread rain can occur. Convectional thunderstorms bring short cloudbursts to the south and southwest between March and May, and depressions tracking across the Bay of Bengal can bring heavy rain in October and November.

Temperatures Lowland Sri Lanka is always relatively hot and humid. On the plains temperature reflects the degree of cloud cover. Colombo has minimum of 25°C in December and a maximum of 28°C in May. At Nuwara Eliya, over 2,000 m up in the Central Highlands, the average daytime temperatures hover around 16°C, but you need to be prepared for the chill in the evenings. Only the northeast occasionally experiences temperatures of above 38°C.

Humidity The coastal regions have humidity levels above 70% for most of the year. In the southwest it is rare for levels to fall below 80%, which can be very uncomfortable. However, sea breezes often bring some relief on the coast itself.

Wildlife

For one small island Sri Lanka packs an enormous variety of wildlife. This is largely because in that small space there is a wide range in altitude. The Central Highlands rise to over 2,500 m with damp evergreen forests, cool uplands and high rainfall. Within 100 km there are the dry coastal plain and sandy beaches. The climatic division of the island into the larger, dry, mainly northern and eastern region, and the smaller, wet, southwestern section is of importance to observers of wildlife. In the Dry Zone remnants of evergreen and deciduous forests are interspersed with cultivation, and in the east of this region the savanna grasslands are dominated by the metre high grass, Imperata cylindrica, widely regarded as a scourge. The whole vegetation complex differs sharply from both the Central Highlands and the Wet Zone of the southwest. These different areas support very different species. Many species occur only in one particular zone, but there are some, often the ones associated with man, which are found throughout. See the booklist on page 57.

Sri Lanka's 24 wildlife reserves are home to a wide range of native species, eg elephants, leopard, sloth bear, the unique small loris, a variety of deer, the

Wildlife reserves

National parks & sanctuaries

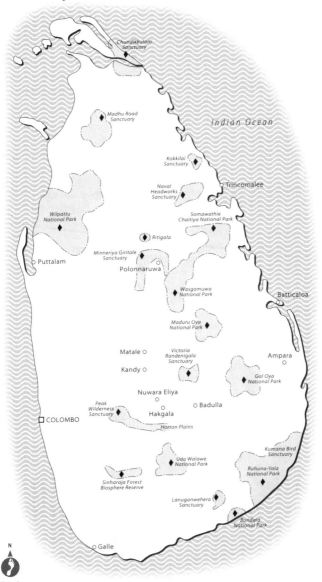

Chundikkulam
Sanctuary

Madhu Road
Sanctuary

Indian Ocean

Kokkilai
Sanctuary

Naval
Headworks
Sanctuary

○ Trincomalee

Wilpattu
National Park

Somawathie
Chaitiya National Park

◆ Ritigala

Minneriya Giritale
Sanctuary

○ Puttalam

Polonnaruwa

Wasgomuwa
National Park

Batticaloa ○

Maduru Oya
National Park

Matale ○

Victoria
Randenigala
Sanctuary

Ampara
○

Kandy ○

Gal Oya
National Park

Nuwara Eliya
○

Peak
Wilderness
Sanctuary

○ Badulla

Hakgala

□ COLOMBO

Horton Plains

Kumana Bird
Sanctuary

Uda Walawe
National Park

Ruhuna-Yala
National Park

Sinharaja Forest
Biosphere Reserve

Lanuganwehera
Sanctuary

Bundala
National Park

N

○ Galle

Not to scale

purple-faced leaf monkey, the endangered wild boar, porcupines and ant-eaters. Reptiles include vipers and the Marsh and Estuarine crocodiles. Among the 16 amphibians unique to the island are the Nanophrys frogs in the hills. Most of the fish are river or marsh dwelling – the trout, introduced by the British, are found in the cool streams of the Horton Plains.

All the reserves are for the protection of wildlife and plants though the categories differ. A few 'Strict Natural Reserves' are set aside for wildlife exclusively so that only those with permits from the Director of Wildlife Conservation may enter in order to carry out research or official work. 'National Parks' are open to anyone issued with a permit, to observe or study. 'Nature Reserves' provide suitable habitat for wildlife but allow limited human activity, while 'Sanctuaries' allow human activity alongside wildlife.

The three largest reserves are the national parks at **Ruhuna-Yala**, **Gal Oya** and **Wilpattu**. Ruhuna-Yala is the most accessible, the elephants of Lahugala and Gal Oya are famous while Wilpattu (which continues to be closed to visitors because of the difficult political situation) still harbours a sizeable number of leopards. The **Sinharaja Biosphere Reserve** (a World Heritage Site) and the highland **Peak Wilderness** and **Adam's Peak** attract enthusiasts. The Wildlife Conservation programme is undertaken by the government with an office in Colombo. Entrance fees for all national parks are US$12 for foreigners (Rs 20 for Sri Lankans), US$6 for children under 12.

Mammals

The **Asiatic elephant** *(Elephas maximus)* has a sizeable population, some wild which can be seen in several of the national parks. The animals come down to the water in the evening, either in family groups or herds of 20 or so. The 'Marsh Elephants', an interesting sub-species significantly larger, are found in the marshy basin of the Mahaweli River. Wild elephants are increasingly come into contact with humans in the growing settlements along their traditional migration routes between the northwest and southeast of the island and so the Wildlife Conservation Department is attempting to protect migration corridors from development. Visitors travelling away from the coast may get a chance to see domesticated animals being put to work or watch them at Pinnawela near Kandy.

The solid looking **Asiatic wild buffalo** *(Bubalus bubalis)*, with a black coat and wide-spreading curved horns, stands about 170 cm at the shoulder. When domesticated, it is known as the **water buffalo**.

The **leopard** or **panther** *(Panthera pardus)*, the only big cat in Sri Lanka, is found both in the dry lowland areas and in the forested hills. Being shy and elusive, it is rarely seen. The greyish **fishing cat** *(Felis viverrina)* with dark spots and dashes with somewhat webbed feet search for prey in marshes and on the edge of streams.

The **sloth bear** *(Melursus ursinus)*, about 75 cm at the shoulder, can be seen in areas of scrub and rock. It is distinguished by it's black unkempt shaggy black coat, the yellowish V shaped mark on the chest and a long and pendulous lower lip.

Leopard (panther)

Sloth bear

Chital

Purple-faced Langur

Sambhur

The **deer** on the island are widespread. The commonest, the **chital** (or spotted) **deer** *(Axis axis)*, only about 90 cm tall, is seen in herds of 20 or so in grassy areas. The bright rufous coat spotted with white is unmistakable. The stags carry antlers with three tines. The magnificent **sambhur** *(Cervus unicolor)* (150 cm tall) with its shaggy coat varying from brownish grey to almost black in older stags, is seen in wooded hillsides. The stags carry large three-tined antlers and have a mane-like thickening of the coat around the neck. The **muntjac** or **barking deer** *(Muntiacus muntjak)*, is small and shy (60 cm at the shoulder). It is brown with darker legs with white underparts and chest. The stag carries a small pair of antlers. Usually found in pairs, their staccato bark is heard more often than they are seen.

The **wild boar** *(Sus scrofa)* is easily identified by its pig-like head, its mainly black body sparsely covered with hair except for a thick line along the spine; the young are striped. Only the male bears tusks. Commonly seen in grass and light bush, near water, it can do great damage to crops.

The interesting **purple-faced langur** *(Presbytis senex)* is only found in Sri Lanka. A long-tailed, long-legged monkey about 125 cm in length (nearly half of it tail) it has a dark coat contrasting with an almost white head. Hair on the head grows long to form swept back whiskers, but the face itself is almost black. Usually seen in groups of a dozen or so, it lives mainly in the dense, damp mountain forests but is also found in open woodland.

Apart from animals that still live truly in the wild, others have adapted to village and town life and are often seen near temples.

The most widespread of the **monkeys** is the **common** (or Hanuman) **langur** *(Presbytis entellus)*, another long-tailed monkey with a black face, hands and feet. The **tocque macaque** *(Macaca sinica)* 60 cm, is a much more solid looking animal with shorter limbs. It varies in colour from grey to brown or even reddish brown above, with much paler limbs and underparts. The pale, sometimes reddish, face has whorls of hair on the cheeks. On top of the head the hair grows flat and cap-like, from a distinct parting!

You can't fail to notice the small squirrels. These **five-striped palm squirrels** *(Funambulus pennanti)*, are about 30 cm long, about half of which is tail.

Background

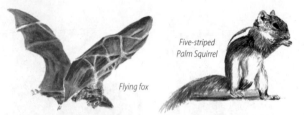

Five-striped Palm Squirrel

Flying fox

Look out for the **flying fox** *(Pteropus giganteus)* which has a wing span of 120 cm. These are actually fruit-eating bats, found throughout, except in the driest areas. They roost in large, sometimes huge, noisy colonies in tree tops, often in the middle of towns or villages, where they look like folded umbrellas hanging from the trees. In the evening they can be seen leaving the roost with slow measured wing beats.

The **common mongoose** *(Herpestes edwardsi)* usually found in scrub and open jungle, can also be seen in gardens and fields. Tawny with a grey grizzled tinge, it is about 90 cm long, of which half is the tail with a pale tip. It is well known as a killer of snakes, but it will also take rats, mice, chickens and birds' eggs.

Birds

Sri Lanka is also an ornithologist's paradise with over 250 resident species, mostly found in the Wet Zone, including the grackle, whistling thrush, yellow-eared bulbul, malkoha and brown-capped babbler. The winter migrants come from distant Siberia and western Europe, the reservoirs attracting vast numbers of water birds (stilts, sandpipers, terns and plover, as well as herons, egrets and storks). The forests attract species of warblers, thrushes, cuckoo and many others. The endemic jungle fowl *(Gallus lafayetti)* is Sri Lanka's national bird. (It is common to see large ornaments topped by a brass jungle fowl which has an honoured place in the home on special occasions). The **Kumana** sanctuary in the southeast, and **Bundala** (famed for flamingoes), **Kalametiya** and **Wirawila** sanctuaries between Tissamaharama and Hambantota in the south, all with lagoons, are the principal bird sanctuaries.

Town & village birds Some birds are seen in almost every town and village. The ubiquitous **house sparrow** *(Passer domesticus)* 15 cm, is almost world-wide in its distribution. The smart looking but noisy **house crow** *(Corvus splendens)* 45 cm, has a grey body and black tail, wings, face and throat. You may see them congregating in groups, as though at a conference. Two members of the **pigeon** family are often seen in built-up areas. The slaty grey **blue rock dove** or feral pigeon *(Columba livia)* 32 cm, with two dark bars on the wings, is found everywhere, while the **spotted dove** *(Streptopelia chinensis)* 30 cm, frequents gardens and parks and is often seen feeding on the ground. It is recognized by its speckled dark back and wide half-collar of white spots; its head and underparts are pale pink.

The **red-vented bulbul** *(Pycnonotus cafer)* 20 cm, is widespread in parks and gardens. The brown bird has a slight crest and a bright red patch under the tail.

The **common myna** *(Acridotheres tristis)* 22 cm, is often spotted feeding on lawns, especially after rain. Look for the white under the tail and the bare yellow skin around the eye, yellow bill and legs, and in flight, the large white wing patch.

The lively **magpie-robin** *(Copsychus saularis)* 20 cm, is a delightful songster. The wings, head and upperparts of the male are mainly black, but with a noticeable white wing bar. The long black and white tail is often held cocked up. The female has similar colouring but is greyish.

The **white-headed babbler** *(Turdoides affinis)* 23 cm, an inhabitant of gardens and bushy country, is basically brown, with a scaly throat and breast. The top of the head is creamy white, which contrasts with the darker brown at the sides of the head.

Pariah Kite

Brahminy Kite

Malabar Pied Hornbill

The mainly yellow weaver birds build remarkably intricate nests. The commonest is the **baya weaver** *(Ploceus philippinus)* 15 cm, which nests in large colonies, often in palm trees. The male in the breeding season has a black face and throat and contrasting yellow cap and breast band. At other times, the male and female are both brownish sparrow-like birds.

Some of the town birds perform a useful function by scavenging and clearing refuse. The common **pariah kite** *(Milvus migrans)* 65 cm, is a brown bird with a longish tail. It has buoyant flight and swoops down boldly to pick up scraps of food. The more handsome **brahminy kite** *(Haliastur indus)* 48 cm, is largely confined to waterside places such as docks and the coastal strip. Its chestnut and white plumage is unmistakable.

The **white-breasted kingfisher** *(Halcyon smyrnensis)* 27 cm, is frequently found away from water, when it is perched on wires and posts. The rich chestnut of its body plumage contrasts with the brilliant blue of its wing feathers as it swoops down to capture its prey. The red bill and white front make it unmistakable.

Bird-watching is rewarding in this zone as the birds are plentiful and easily seen in the open countryside.

Lowland dry zone birds

The **malabar pied hornbill** *(Anthracoceros coronatus)* 90 cm, is seen in small noisy flocks, often in fruiting trees. The plumage is black and white and the long tail has white edges. The massive bill is mainly yellow and carries a black and yellow protuberance known as a casque, along the top.

The **rose-ringed parakeet** *(Psittacula krameri)* 40 cm, with a long tail, found in the dry North-east and the coastal strip, gather in large noisy flocks as they come to roost in coconut groves. Females lack the collar. They can be very destructive to crops, but are attractive and so are frequently kept as pets.

The all black **drongo** *(Dicrurus adsimilis)* 30 cm, is almost invariably seen perched on telegraph wires or bare branches. Its marked forked tail makes it easy to identify. The related **racquet-tailed drongo** *(Dicrurus paradiseus)* 35 cm, with a tufted crest, has a distinctive tail which ends in long streamers with broadened tips.

The **paradise flycatcher** *(Terpsiphone paradisi)* frequents woods and gardens in the Dry Zone and lower hills in pursuit of insects. The head is a shiny metallic black with a noticeable crest, which contrasts with the white of the underparts. The wings and tail are white or chestnut. The male has particularly long tail feathers.

The **little green bee-eater** *(Merops orientalis)* is usually seen in pairs, perched on posts and dead branches. The green of its plumage contrasts with the bluish throat and chestnut top of the head.

The **peafowl** *(Pavo cristata)* is common in the extreme southeast of the Dry Zone. The male peacock with the elegant tail can be over 2m, the plain female 100 cm.

Dry zone tank birds A feature of the Dry Zone is the presence of shallow, man-made reservoirs (tanks) which form an important habitat for birds.

One of the largest and most easily identified is the **spot-billed pelican** *(Pelecanus philippensis)* 150 cm, with the characteristic fleshy pouch below the beak. It is often seen soaring overhead. It breeds colonially in trees.

The **painted stork** *(Mycteria leucocephala)* 100 cm, which is also mainly white, but has a pinkish tinge on the back and greenish black marks on the wings and a broken black band on the lower chest. The bare yellow face and yellow down-curved bill are conspicuous.

The **little egret** *(Egretta garzetta)* 62 cm, and the **cattle egret** *(Bubulcus ibis)* 50 cm, are pure white in the non-breeding season but have different coloured bills: black in the little egret, yellowish in the cattle egret. The little egret with black legs and yellow toes (not easy to see).is taller and more elegant looking. In the breeding season the cattle egret develops golden or buff plumes on its head and back.

The **red-wattled lapwing** *(Vanellus indicus)* 33 cm, gives the impression of being a black and white bird with long yellow legs and a red bill. It is a noisy, neurotic bird given to calling out loudly at real or imagined danger.

Among the floating vegetation in the tanks you will see the lovely and very distinctive brown and white **pheasant-tailed jacana** *(Hydrophasianus chirurgus)*.

Wet & highland zone birds The bird life of the Central Highlands and the southwest of the country includes many of the common species associated with man throughout the island, but in addition has a rich variety of species found only in this area. Many of the 21 birds endemic to Sri Lanka are found here, including two members of the parrot family.

The **ceylon lorikeet** *(Loriculus beryllinus)* 14 cm, is a bright green short tailed parrot-like bird, seen in small flocks in wooded areas in fruiting and flowering trees. The bill, top of the head and the rump are bright red, and there is a patch of orange on the back which shades into the red on the head. The male has a blue throat. The endemic **layard's parakeet** *(Psittacula calthorpae)* 32 cm, is long tailed with a soft grey head and back, green wings and underparts and a mainly black collar. The male has a red bill, and the female a black one. It is seen in noisy flocks, especially in hilly forests.

The **grackle** or hill myna *(Gracula religiosa)* 28 cm, is often kept as a pet as it is an excellent 'talker'. In the wild, noisy flocks are found in highland forests, in fruiting trees. The **Ceylon grackle** *(Gracula ptilogenys)* 25 cm, found only in Sri Lanka, also lives on the wooded hillsides in noisy flocks. Both Grackles are black with white wing patches and can be distinguished from each other by the wattles on the head. The Ceylon Grackle has only two small yellow wattles on the back of the head, whereas those in the Grackle are more extensive.

The species described above tend to be found high in the tree canopies, the next four are usually found in the lower branches of trees or in bushes.

The endemic **yellow-eared bulbul** *(Pycnonotus penicillatus)* 20 cm, common in the highland forests, is usually seen in pairs or in small flocks. It is olive green above, with the underparts being more yellow. The head is dark brown with a white throat, and white eyebrow. It gets its name from the prominent tuft of yellow feathers on the side of the head.

The **dusky blue flycatcher** *(Muscicapa sordida)* 14 cm, is an attractive and noticeable blue-grey bird with a brighter blue forehead and a black patch in front of the eye. It occurs in scrub, bush and gardens and in forest undergrowth in the hills. It behaves in typical flycatcher fashion, capturing its prey by flying out from a look-out post or branch.

The **grey tit** *(Parus major)* 13 cm (widespread in Europe) is common in hills and lowland areas in gardens and light woodland. Grey above with a black head it has large white cheek patches. Below, the white underparts have a broad black stripe running down the middle.

The restless **black-headed babbler** *(Rhopocichla atriceps)* 13 cm, constantly on the move, is found in small flocks on the forest floor or in thick undergrowth. The rich brown upperparts, and the black head with the pale yellow eyes contrasts with the clear white of the throat and chest.

Reptiles

Two species of crocodile are found in Sri Lanka. The rather docile **mugger** (or marsh) **crocodile** *(Crocodilus palustrus)*, 3-4 m in length, lives in freshwater rivers and tanks in many parts of the island. The **estuarine** (or saltwater) **crocodile** *(Crocodilus porosus)* prefers the brackish waters of the larger rivers where it can grow to 7m. Among the lizards, the large **monitor** *(Varanus)* (up to 2 m long), greyish brown with black and yellow markings, is found in a variety of habitats. They have become quite widespread and tame and can even be seen scavenging in the rubbish dumps and market places.

Seashore and marine life

The sandy beaches of Sri Lanka are a paradise for wildlife with a fantastic variety of fish, shells and corals which abound in the shallow warm waters, the sand banks and the reefs. The off-shore coral reefs harbour rich marine life, making snorkelling and diving particularly popular along the South-west coast.

Corals are living organisms and consist of two basic types: the typical hard coral (eg Staghorn) and the less familiar soft corals which anchor themselves to the hard coral – one form looks like the greyish pink sea anemone.

Fish

Among the living coral swim a bewildering variety of colourful fish. There are shoals of silvery **sardinella** and stately, colourful **angelfish** *(Pomacanthus)* often with noticeable mouths in a different colour. Butterfly fish *(Chaetodontidae)* are similar to small angelfish but their fins are rounded at the end. The **surgeon fish** *(Acanthuridae)* get their name from the sharp blades at the base of their tails. Rounded in outline, with compressed bodies and pouting lips, they are often very brightly coloured (eg 17 cm **blue surgeon**). Striped like a zebra, the **scorpion fish** *(Pteriois)* is seen among live coral, and sometimes trapped in pools of the dead reef by the retreating tide. Although it has poisonous dorsal spines it will not attack if you leave it alone.

Shells

The commonest are the **cowries** which you can find on the beach. The **ringed cowrie** *(Cypraea annulus)* has a pretty grey and pinkish white shell with a golden ring while the **money cowrie** which was once used as currency in Africa, varies from greenish grey to pink, according to its age. The big and beautiful **tiger cowrie** *(Cypraea tigris)* (up to 8 cm), has a very shiny shell marked like a leopard. The spectacular **spider conch** *(Lambis)* and the common **murex** *(Chicoreus)* can grow 15-20 cm. **Sea urchins** *(Echinoidea)*, fairly common on sandy beaches and dead coral, are extremely painful to tread on, so be sure to wear shoes when beach combing.

Turtles

Of the seven species of marine turtle in the world, five return to lay their eggs on Sri Lankan beaches but all are on the endangered list. One of the rarer species is the giant **leather-back turtle** *(Dermochelys coriacea)* which grows to 2 m in length, has a ridged leathery skin on its back instead of a shell. The smaller **olive ridley turtle** *(Lepidochelys olivacea)* has the typical rows of shields along the shell. The Turtle Conservation Project is carrying out a very worthwhile programme near Tangalla on the south coast, see page 156.

Background

Vegetation

From tropical thorn forest in the driest regions of the southeast and northwest, (generally with a rainfall of less than 1,200 mm) the vegetation ranges through to montane temperate forest of the Central Highlands and then to mangroves of some stretches of the coast. Today mangroves are restricted almost exclusively to a stretch of the west coast, north of Puttalam. and of the southeast coast, east of Hambantota.

None of the original forest cover has been unaffected by human activity, and much has now been either converted to cultivated land, or given over to a range of tree cash crops, notably coconut and rubber at low altitudes and tea at higher levels. Indeed most of the forest cover is now restricted to the Dry Zone. Here dry evergreen forest, with trees generally less than 12 m in height, and moist deciduous forest, whose canopy level is usually up to 20 or 25 m, provide an excellent habitat for wildlife, and continue to cover extensive tracts of land. Even here the original forest has been much altered, most having re-colonized land which was extensively cultivated until 500 years ago. Sri Lanka also has four different types of grassland, all the result of human activity.

Common trees In addition to the endless lines of coconut palms (*Cocos nucifer*) along the coastal belt and the Kurunegala district, the **sago** or **fish-tail palm** (*Caryota urens*), locally called 'kitul', is a regular feature on the island. The leaves are large and distinctive consisting of many small leaflets, each shaped like a fish tail while the flowers hang down like horses' tails. Sago comes from the pith, toddy and jaggery from the sap and the fibres are used to make bristles in brushes, as well as rope.

The **rain tree** (*Enterlobium saman*) is a large tree from South America, with a spreading canopy, often planted as a roadside shade tree. The dark green feathery leaves are peculiar in that they become horizontal in the daytime, thus maximizing the amount of shade thrown by the tree. At night time and in the rain they fold downwards. The flowers are pale pink, silky looking tufts.

The **eucalyptus** or **gum tree** (*Eucalyptus grandis*), introduced from Australia in the 19th century, is now widespread and is planted near villages to provide both shade and firewood. All the varieties have characteristic long, thin leaves and the colourful peeling bark and fresh pleasant smell.

Bamboo (*Bambusa*) strictly speaking is a grass which is found almost everywhere. It can vary in size from small ornamental clumps to the enormous wild plant whose stems are so strong and thick that they are used for construction and as pipes for irrigation in small holdings.

The **banyan** (*Ficus benghalensis*), featured widely in eastern literature, is planted by temples, in villages and along roads. Curiously its seeds germinate in crevices in the bark of other trees. It sends down roots to the ground as it grows until the original host tree is surrounded by a cage-like structure which eventually strangles it. So a single banyan appears to have multiple 'trunks' which are in fact roots.

Related to the banyan, the **peepal** (*Ficus religiosa*) is distinguishable by the absence of aerial roots, and pointed heart shaped leaves which taper into a pronounced 'tail'. It too is commonly found near temples and shrines where it cracks open walls and strangles other trees with its roots. The purplish figs it bears in abundance are about 1 cm across.

Flowering trees Visitors to Sri Lanka cannot fail to notice the many flowering trees planted along the roadside. The **gul mohur** (*Delonix regia*), a native of Madagascar, grows throughout the island. A good shade tree, it grows only to about 8 or 9 m in height and has spreading branches. The leaves are an attractive feathery shape, and a bright light green in colour. The fiery coloured flowers which appear after it has shed its leaves, make a magnificent display.

Holy but not wholly efficacious!

The sal tree is one of the most widespread and abundant trees in the tropical and sub-tropical Ganges plains and Himalayan foothills; it was the tree under which Guatama Buddha was born. Like the pipal (ficus religiosa), under which the Buddha was enlightened, the sal is greatly revered in Sri Lanka. It is often planted near temples, for example on the lawn close to the Temple of the Tooth Relic in Kandy. However, the sal in Sri Lanka is very different to the one found in northern South Asia, and the difference has been known to have serious consequences since extracts from the tree are widely used for medicinal preparations. The sal tree proper is shorea robusta (dipterocarpaceae), whereas the sal of Sri Lanka is the tree

known all over the tropics as the cannon ball tree (couroupita surenamensis). Unfortunately, the difference is not widely known and it is not unknown for Auyurvedic medicinal preparations using the Sri Lankan sal but following recipes of Indian origin, to have been taken without any positive effect!

The distinctive shape of the flowers on c. surenamensis which appear at the end of extraordinarily long stems which cascade down the full length of the trunk is of special significance. These stems are large and have a hooded structure which overhangs the reproductive organs of the flowers in a form reminiscent of the way the cobra is depicted as having protected the Buddha when he resided in the forest alone.

The **jacaranda** (Jacaranda mimosaefolia), originally from Brazil, though rather straggly in shape, has attractive feathery foliage. The purple-blue thimble-shaped flowers (up to 40 mm long) make a striking splash of colour.

The **tamarind** (Tamarindus indica) is an evergreen with feathery leaves and small yellow and red flowers which grow in clusters in its spreading crown. The noticeable fruit pods are long, curved and swollen at intervals.

The large and dramatic **silk cotton tree** (Bombax ceiba) can be up to 25m in height. The bark is often light grey with conical spines; the bigger trees have noticeable buttress roots. The wide spreading branches keep their leaves for most of the year, the cup-shaped fleshy red flowers appearing only when the tree is leafless. The dry fruit pod produces the fine silky cotton which gives it its name.

The **ceylon ironwood** (Mesua ferrea) is often planted near Buddhist temples. Its long slender leaves, reddish when young set off the white four-petalled flowers with yellow centres.

Background

Coffee flower

Rain Tree flower

Tamarind flower & fruit

Silk Cotton Tree flower

The beautiful flowering **rhododendron** is common in the highland regions. It grows as either a sprawling shrub or a tree up to 12-m high. In the wild, the flowers are usually crimson or pale purple.

Fruit trees The **mango** (*Mangifera indica*), a fairly large tree ranging from 6-15-m high or more, has spreading branches forming a rounded canopy. The dense shade it casts makes it a very attractive village meeting place. The distinctively shaped fruit is quite delicious and unlike any other in taste.

The **jakfruit** (*Artocarpus heterophyllus*) is one of the most remarkable trees. A large evergreen with dark green leathery leaves, its huge fruit can be as much as 1-m long and 40 cm thick, growing from a short stem directly off the trunk and branches. The skin is thick and rough, almost prickly. The strong smelling fruit of the main eating variety is sickly sweet and an acquired taste.

The **banana** plant (*Musa*) is actually a gigantic herb arising from an underground stem. The very large leaves grow directly off the trunk which is about 5 m in height. The fruiting stem bears a large purple flower, which yields up to 100 fruit.

The **papaya** (*Carica papaya*) which often grows to 4 m has distinctive palm-shaped leaves. Only the female tree bears the shapely fruit which hang down close to the crown.

The **cashew nut** (*Anacardium*) tree, a native of tropical America, was introduced into Sri Lanka, but now grows wild as well as being cultivated. Usually less than 7 m in height, it has bright green, shiny, rounded leaves. The nut hangs from a fleshy bitter fruit called a cashew apple.

Originally from tropical America, the **avocado pear** (*Persea*) grows well in the Wet Zone. The broad-leaved tree up to 10m in height, with oval, pointed leaves, bear the familiar fruit at the ends of the branches.

Flowering plants Many flowering plants are cultivated in parks, gardens and roadside verges. The **frangipani** (*Plumeria acutifolia*) is particularly attractive with a crooked trunk and regular branches which bear leaves with noticeable parallel veins which taper to a point at each end. The sweetly-scented waxy flowers are usually white, pale yellow or pink.

The **bougainvillea** grows everywhere as a dense bush or a strong climber, often completely covered in flowers of striking colours from pinks to purples, oranges to yellows, and brilliant white. If you look carefully you will see that the paper-thin colourful 'petals' are really large bracts.

The trumpet-shaped flowers of the **hibiscus** too, come in brilliant scarlet, pink and yellow or simply white.

Orchids abound but sadly most go unnoticed because of their tiny flowers. The large flowered, deep mauve *Dendrobium macarthiae* can be seen around Ratnapura in May. From spring to summer you may find the varicoloured, sweet-scented *vanda tessellata* in bloom everywhere.

Papaya

Footnotes

11

330

Footnotes

331   Glossary

335   Useful words and phrases -
Sinhalese

337   Useful words and phrases -
Sri Lankan Tamil

339   Eating out - food and menus

341   Sri Lankan specialites

342   Index

346   Shorts

347   Map index

348   Advertisers

359   Colour maps

Glossary

Words in *italics* are common elements of words, often making up part of a place name.

A

aarti (arati) Hindu worship with lamps
abhaya mudra Buddha posture signifiying protection; forearm raised, palm facing outward fingers together
ahimsa non-harming, non-violence
ambulatory processional path
amla/amalaka circular ribbed pattern (based on a gourd) on top of a temple tower
Ananda the Buddha's chief disciple
anda lit `egg', spherical part of the stupa
antechamber chamber in front of the sanctuary
apse semi-circular plan, as in apse of a church
arama monastery (as in Tissamaharama)
architrave horizontal beam across posts or gateways
Arjuna hero of the Mahabharata, to whom Krishna delivered the Bhagavad Gita
arrack spirit distilled from palm sap
aru river (Tamil)
Aryans lit 'noble' (Sanskrit); prehistoric peoples who settled in Persia and N India
asana a seat or throne; symbolic posture
ashram hermitage or retreat
Avalokiteshwara Lord who looks down; Bodhisattva, the Compassionate
avatara 'descent'; incarnation of a divinity, usually Vishnu's incarnations

B

banamaduwa monastic pulpit
Bandaras sub-caste of the Goyigama caste, part of the Sinhalese aristocracy
bas-relief carving of low projection
basement lower part of walls, usually adorned with decorated mouldings
bazar market
beru elephant grass
Bhagavad-Gita Song of the Lord from the Mahabharata in which Krishna preaches a sermon to Arjuna
bhikku Buddhist monk
bhumi 'earth'; refers to a horizontal moulding of a shikhara (tower)
bhumisparasa mudra earth-witnessing Buddha posture
Bo-tree Ficus religiosa, large spreading tree associated with the Buddha; also Bodhi
Bodhisattva Enlightened One, destined to become Buddha
Brahma universal self-existing power; Creator in the Hindu Triad. Often represented in art, with four heads

Brahman (Brahmin) highest Hindu (and Jain) caste of priests
Brahmanism ancient Indian religion, precursor of modern Hinduism and Buddhism
Buddha The Enlightened One; founder of Buddhism who is worshipped as god by certain sects
bund an embankment; a causeway
Burghers Sri Lankans of mixed Dutch-Sinhalese descent

C

cantonment large planned military or civil area in town
capital upper part of a column or pilaster
catamaran log raft, logs (*maram*) tied (*kattu*) together (Tamil)
cave temple rock-cut shrine or monastery
chakra sacred Buddhist Wheel of Law; also Vishnu's discus
chapati unleavened Indian bread cooked on a griddle
chena shifting cultivation
chhatra, chatta honorific umbrella; a pavilion (Buddhist)
Chola early and medieval Tamil kingdom (India)
circumambulation clockwise movement around a stupa or shrine while worshipping
cloister passage usually around an open square
coir coconut fibre used for making rope and mats
copra dried sections of coconut flesh, used for oil
corbel horizontal block supporting a vertical structure or covering an opening
cornice horizontal band at the top of a wall
crore 10 million
Culavansa Historical sequel to Mahavansa, the first part dating from 13th century, later extended to 16th century

D

dagoba stupa (Sinhalese)
darshan (darshana) viewing of a deity
Dasara (dassara/dussehra/dassehra) 10 day Hindu festival (Sep-Oct)
devala temple or shrine (Buddhist or Hindu)
Devi Goddess; later, the Supreme Goddess; Siva's consort, Parvati
dhal (daal) lentil 'soup'
dharma (dhamma) Hindu and Buddhist concepts of moral and religious duty
dharmachakra wheel of 'moral' law (Buddhist)
dhyana meditation

dhyani mudra meditation posture of the Buddha, cupped hands rest in the lap

distributary river that flows away from main channel, usually in deltas

Diwali festival of lights (Sep-Oct) usually marks the end of the rainy season

Dravidian languages – Tamil, Telugu, Kannada and Malayalam; and peoples mainly from S India

Durga principal goddess of the Shakti cult; rides on a tiger, armed with weapons

dvarpala doorkeeper

E

eave overhang that shelters a porch or verandah

eri tank (Tamil)

F

finial emblem at the summit of a stupa, tower or dome; often a tier of umbrella-like motifs or a pot

frieze horizontal band of figures or decorative designs

G

gable end of an angled roof

garbhagriha literally `womb-chamber'; a temple sanctuary

gedige arched Buddhist image house built of stone slabs and brick

gopura towered gateway in S Indian temples

Goyigama landowning and cultivating caste among Sinhalese Buddhists

H

Haj (Hajj) annual Muslim pilgrimage to Mecca (Haji, one who has performed the Haj)

hakim judge; a physician (usually Muslim)

Hanuman Monkey hero of the Ramayana; devotee of Rama; bringer of success to armies

Hari Vishnu

harmika the finial of a stupa; a pedestal where the honorific umbrella was set

Hasan the murdered eldest son of Ali, commemorated at Muharram

howdah seat on elephant's back

Hussain the second murdered son of Ali, commemorated at Muharram

I

illam lens of gem-bearing coarse river gravel

imam Muslim religious leader in a mosque

Indra King of the gods; God of rain; guardian of the East

Isvara Lord (Sanskrit)

J

jaggery brown sugar made from palm sap

jataka stories accounts of the previous lives of the Buddha

JVP Janatha Vimukhti Peramuna (People's Liberation Army) – violent revolutionary political movment in 1970s and 1980s

K

kadu forest (Tamil)

kalapuwa salty or brackish lagoon

Kali lit `black'; terrifying form of the goddess Durga, wearing a necklace of skulls/heads

kalyanmandapa (Tamil) hall with columns, used for the symbolic marriage ceremony of the temple deity

kapok the silk cotton tree

kapurala officiating priest in a shrine (devala)

karandua replica of the Tooth Relic casket, dagoba-shaped

Karavas fishing caste, many converted to Roman Catholicism

karma present consequences of past lives

Kataragama the Hindu god of war; Skanda

Kartikkeya/Kartik Son of Siva, also known as Skanda or Subrahmanyam

katcheri (cutchery, Kachcheri) public office or court

khondalite crudely grained basalt

kolam masked dance drama (Sinhalese)

kovil temple (Tamil)

kitul fish-tailed sago palm, whose sap is used for jaggery

Krishna 8th incarnation of Vishnu; the cowherd (Gopala, Govinda)

Kubera Chief yaksha; keeper of the earth's treasures, Guardian of the North

kulam tank or pond (Tamil)

L

laddu round sweet snack

lakh 100,000

Lakshmana younger brother of Rama in the Ramayana

Lakshmi Goddess of wealth and good fortune, consort of Vishnu

lattice screen of cross laths: perforated

lena cave, usually a rock-cut sanctuary

lingam (linga) Siva as the phallic emblem

Lokeshwar 'Lord of the World', Avalokiteshwara to Buddhists and of Siva to Hindus

LTTE Liberation Tigers of Tamil Eelam, or "The Tigers", force rebelling against Sri Lankan Government

lungi wrap-around loin cloth

M

maha great; in Sri Lanka, the main rice crop
Mahabodhi Great Enlightenment of Buddha
Mahadeva lit 'Great Lord'; Siva
Mahavansa Literally "Great Dynasty or Chronicle", a major source on early history and legend
Mahayana The Greater Vehicle; form of Buddhism practised in East Asia, Tibet and Nepal
Mahesha (Maheshvara) Great Lord; Siva
mahout elephant driver/keeper
Maitreya the future Buddha
makara crocodile-shaped mythical creature
malai hill (Tamil)
mandapa columned hall preceding the sanctuary in a Jain or Hindu temple
mandir temple
mantra sacred chant for meditation by Hindus and Buddhists
Mara Tempter, who sent his daughters (and soldiers) to disturb the Buddha's meditation
mawatha roadway
maya illusion
Minakshi lit 'fish-eyed'; Parvati, Siva's consort
Mohammad 'the praised'; The Prophet; founder of Islam
moksha salvation, enlightenment; lit 'release'
moonstone the semi-circular stone step before a shrine; also a gem
mudra symbolic hand gesture and posture associated with the Buddha
Muharram period of mourning in remembrance of Hasan and Hussain, two murdered sons of Ali

N

Naga (nagi/nagini) Snake deity; associated with fertility and protection
Nandi a bull, Siva's vehicle and a symbol of fertility
Narayana Vishnu as the creator of life
Nataraja Siva, Lord of the cosmic dance
Natha worshipped by Mahayana Buddhists as the bodhisattva Maitreya
navagraha nine planets, represented usually on the lintel of a temple door
navaratri lit '9 nights'; name of the Dasara festival
niche wall recess containing a sculpted image or emblem,
nirvana enlightenment; (lit 'extinguished')

O

ola palm manuscripts
oriel projecting window
oya seasonal river

P

pada foot or base
paddy rice in the husk
padma lotus flower. Padmasana, lotus seat; posture of meditating figures

pagoda tall structure in several stories
Pali language of Buddhist scriptures
pankah (punkha) fan, formerly pulled by a cord
pansukulika Buddhist sect dwelling in forest hermitages
parapet wall extending above the roof
Parinirvana (parinibbana) the Buddha's state prior to nirvana, shown usually as a reclining figure
Parvati daughter of the Mountain; Siva's consort
pilimage Buddhist image house
potgul library
pradakshina patha processional passage or ambulatory
puja ritual offerings to the gods; worship (Hindu)
pujari worshipper; one who performs puja
punya karma merit earned through actions and religious devotion (Buddhist)

R

raj rule or government
raja king, ruler; prefix 'maha' means great
Rama seventh incarnation of Vishnu; hero of the Ramayana epic
Ramayana ancient Sanskrit epic
Ravana Demon king of Lanka; kidnapper of Sita
rickshaw 3-wheeled bicycle-powered (or 2-wheeled hand-powered) vehicle
Rig Veda (Rg) oldest and most sacred of the Vedas
rupee unit of currency in Sri Lanka, India, Pakistan and Nepal

S

sagar lake; reservoir
Saiva (Shaiva)the cult of Siva
sal hardwood tree of the lower mountains
sala hall
salaam greeting (Muslim); lit 'peace'
samadhi funerary memorial, like a temple but enshrining an image of the deceased; meditation state
samsara eternal transmigration of the soul
samudra sea, or large artificial lake
sangarama monastery
sangha ascetic order founded by Buddha
Saraswati wife of Brahma and goddess of knowledge; usually seated on a swan, holding a veena
Shakti Energy; female divinity often associated with Siva; also a name of the cult
shaman doctor/priest, using magic
Shankara Siva
sharia corpus of Muslim theological law
shikhara temple tower
singh (sinha) lion
Sita Rama's wife, heroine of the Ramayana epic.
Siva The Destroyer among Hindu gods; often worshipped as a lingam (phallic symbol)
Sivaratri lit 'Siva's night'; festival (Feb-Mar) dedicated to Siva
Skanda the Hindu god of war
sri (shri) honorific title, often used for 'Mr'
stucco plasterwork

stupa hemispheric funerary mound; principal votive monument in a Buddhist religious complex

Subrahmanya Skanda, one of Siva's sons; Kartikkeya in S India

sudra lowest of the Hindu castes

svami (swami) holy man

svastika (swastika) auspicious Hindu/ Buddhist emblem

T

tale tank (Sinhalese)

tank lake created for irrigation

Tara historically a Nepalese princess, now worshipped by Buddhists and Hindus

thali S and W Indian vegetarian meal

torana gateway with two posts linked by architraves

tottam garden (Tamil)

Trimurti Triad of Hindu divinities, Brahma, Vishnu and Siva

U

Upanishads ancient Sanskrit philosophical texts, part of the Vedas

ur village (Tamil)

V

Valmiki sage, author of the Ramayana epic

varam village (Tamil)

varna `colour'; social division of Hindus into Brahmin, Kshatriya, Vaishya and Sudra

Varuna Guardian of the West, accompanied by Makara (see above)

vatadage literally circular relic house, protective pillard and roofed outer cover for dagoba

Veda (Vedic) oldest known religious texts; include hymns to Agni, Indra and Varuna, adopted as Hindu deities

vel Skanda's trident

Vellala Tamil Hindu farming caste

verandah enlarged porch in front of a hall

vihara Buddhist or Jain monastery with cells opening off a central court

villu small lake (Sri Lanka)

Vishnu a principal Hindu deity; creator and preserver of universal order; appears in 10 incarnations (Dashavatara)

vitarka mudra Buddhist posture of discourse, the fingers raised

W

Wesak Commemoration day of the Buddha's birth, enlightenment and death

wewa tank or lake (Sinhalese)

Y

yala summer rice crop

yoga school of philosophy concentrating on different mental and physical disciplines (yogi, a practitioner)

yoni female genital symbol, associated with the worship of the Siva Linga (phallus)

Useful words and phrases: Sinhalese

Pronunciation
ah is shown $\bar{a}$ as in car
ee is shown $\bar{i}$ as in see
oh is shown $\bar{o}$ as in old

These marks, to help with pronunciation, do not appear in the main text

Useful words and phrases

General greetings	*Ayubowan*
Thank you / No thank you	*Es-thu-thee / mata epa*
Excuse me, sorry	*Samavenna*
Pardon?	*Ah?*
Yes/no	*Ou/nā*
Nevermind/that's all right	*Kamak na*
Please	*Karunakara*
What is your name?	*Nama mokakda?*
My name is …	*Mage nama …*
How are you?	*Kohamada?*
I am well thanks	*Mama hondin innava*
Not very well	*Wadiya honda ne*
Do you speak English?	*Ingirisi kathakaranawatha?*

Shopping

How much is this?	*Mīka kīyada?*
That will be 20 rupees	*Rupial wissai*
Please make it a bit cheaper	*Karunakara gana adukaranna*

The hotel

What is the room charge?	*Kamarayakata gana kiyada?*
May I see the room please?	*Kamaraya karnakara penvanna?*
Is there an a/c room?	*A/c kamarayak thiyenawada?*
Is there hot water?	*unuwathura thiyenawada?*
… a fan/mosquito net	*… fan/maduru delak*
Please clean the room	*Karnakara kamaraya suddakaranna*
This is OK	*Meka hondai*
Bill please	*Karunakara bila gaynna*

Travel

Where is the railway station?	*Dumriyapola koheda?*
When does the Colombo bus leave?	*Colombata bus eka yanne kīyatada?*
How much is it to Colombo?	*Colombota kīyada?*
Will you go for 10 rupees?	*Rupiyal dahayakata yanawada?*
Left/right	*Wama/dakuna*
Staight on	*Kelin yanna*
Nearby	*Langa*
Please wait here	*Karunakara mehe enna*
Please come here at 8	*Karunakara mehata atata enna*
Stop	*Nawathinna*

Time and days

right now	*dang*	week	*sathiya*
morning	*ude*	month	*masey*
afternoon	*dawal*	Sunday	*irrida*
evening	*sawasa*	Monday	*sanduda*
night	*raya*	Tuesday	*angaharuwada*
today	*atha*	Wednesday	*badhada*
tomorrow	*heta*	Thursday	*brahaspathinda*
yesterday	*īye*	Friday	*sikurada*
day	*dawasa*	Saturday	*senasurada*

Numbers

1	*eka*	9	*namaya*
2	*deka*	10	*dahaya*
3	*thuna*	20	*wissai*
4	*hathara*	30	*thihai*
5	*paha*	40	*hathalihai*
6	*haya*	50	*panahai*
7	*hatha*	100/200	*sīayaī/desiyai*
8	*ata*	1000/2000	*dāhai/dedāhai*

Basic vocabulary

Some English words are widely used such as airport, bathroom, bus, embassy, ferry, hospital, stamp, taxi, ticket, train (though often pronounced a little differently).

bank	*bankuwa*
café/food stall	*kamata kadyak*
chemist	*beheth sappuwa*
clean	*sudda*
closed	*wahala*
cold	*sī thai*
dirty	*apirisidui*
doctor	*dosthara*
excellent	*hari honthai*
ferry	*bottuwa*
food/to eat	*kanda/kāma*
hospital	*rohala*
hot (temperature)	*rasnai*
hotel	*hōtalaya*
open	*arala*
police station	*policiya*
restaurant	*kāmata*
road	*pāra*
room	*kamaraya*
shop	*kade*
sick (ill)	*asaneepai*
station	*istashama*
this	*meka*
that	*araka*
water	*wathura*
when?	*kawathatha?*
where?	*koheda?*

Useful words and phrases: Sri Lankan Tamil

general greeting	*vanakkam*
Thank you/no thank you	*nandri*
Excuse me, sorry, pardon	*mannikkavum*
Yes/no	*ām/illai*
never mind/thats all right	*paruvai illai*
please	*thayavu seithu*
What is your name?	*ungaludaya peyr enna*
My name is...	*ennudaya peyr*
How are you?	*ningal eppadi irukkirirgal?*
I am well, thanks	*nan nantraga irrukkirain*
Not very well	*paruvayillai*
Do you speak English?	*ningal angilam kathappirgala*

Shopping

How much is this?	*ithan vilai enna?*
That will be 20 rupees	*athan vilai irupatha rupa*
Please make it a bit cheaper!	*thayavu seithu konjam kuraikavuam!*

The hotel

What is the room charge?	*arayin vilai enna?*
May I see the room please?	*thayavu seithu arayai parka mudiyama?*
Is there an a/c room?	*kulir sathana arai irrukkatha?*
Is there hot water?	*sudu thanir irukkuma?*
...a bathroom?	*oru kuliyal arai...?*
...a fan/mosquito net?	*katotra sathanam/kosu valai...?*
Please clean the room	*thayavu seithu arayai suththap paduthava*
This is OK	*ithuru seri*
Bill please	*bill tharavum*

Travel

Where's the railway station?	*station enge?*
When does the Chennai bus leave?	*eppa Chennai bus pogum?*
How much is it to Madurai?	*Madurai poga evalavu?*
Will you go to Madurai for 10 rupees?	*paththu rupavitku Madurai poga mudiyami?*
left/right	*idathu/valathu*
straight on	*naerakapogavum*
nearby	*aruqil*
Please wait here	*thayavu seithu ingu nitkavum*
Please come here at 8	*thayavu seithu ingu ettu*
stop	*nivuthu*

Time and days

right now	*ippoh*
morning	*kalai*
afternoon	*pitpagal*
evening	*malai*
night	*iravu*
today	*indru*
tomorrow/yesterday	*nalai/naetru*
day	*thinam*
week	*vaaram*
month	*maatham*

Sunday	gnatruk kilamai
Monday	thinkat kilamai
Tuesday	sevai kilamai
Wednesday	puthan kilamai
Thursday	viyalak kilamai
Friday	velli kilamai
Saturday	sanik kilamai

Numbers

1	ontru	10	pattu
2	erantru	20	erupathu
3	moontru	30	muppathu
4	nangu	40	natpathu
5	ainthu	50	ompathu
6	aru	100/200	nooru/irunooru
7	aelu	1000/2000	aiyuram/iranda
8	ettu		iuram
9	onpathu		

Basic vocabulary

Some English words are widely used, often alongside Tamil equivalents, such as, airport, bank, bathroom, bus, embassy, ferry, hospital, hotel, restaurant, station, stamp, taxi, ticket, train (though often pronounced a little differently).

airport	agaya vimana nilayam
bank	vungi
bathroom	kulikkum arai
café/food stall	unavu kadai
chemist	marunthu kadai
clean	suththam
closed	moodu
cold	kulir
dirty	alukku
embassy	thootharalayam
excellent	miga nallathu
ferry	padagu
hospital	aspathri
hot (temp)	ushnamana
hotel/restaurant	sapathu
juice	saru/viduthi
open	thira
road	pathai
room	arai
shop	kadi
sick (ill)	viyathi
stamp	muththirai
station	nilayam
this	ithu
that	athu
ticket	anumati situ
train	rayil
water	thannir
when?	eppa?
where?	enge?

Eating out - food and menus

Cooking in Sri Lanka remains distinctive in the frequent use of some ingredients such as coconut in various forms, *umbalakada* the powdered dry Maldive fish used to flavour curries as well as the different ways in which rice is prepared like *appa* and *pittu*.

The Dutch and Portuguese have also influenced Sri Lankan food. Festive *lamprais* and *frikkadels*, the small, crumbed and fried meat or fish balls. The influence is more obvious in confectionary and desserts using eggs, as in *breudher* the 'Christmas cake' or *wattapallam*, as well as flaky pastries like *foguete* or the cashew-filled *bolo folhado*.

A typical Sri Lankan '**rice and curry** meal' would include a couple of different curries and *sambols*, some chutney and pickles, and would be eaten with the fingers of the right hand, however, you may get a spoon to eat the meal. It is quite usual to ask for second helpings of whatever you fancy. For variety rice may be replaced by hoppers, pittu or rotty on occasions.

Here is a rough guide as to how hot the curry is: *Kiri* are fairly mild 'white' curry prepared with coconut milk; *Badun* prepared with freshly roasted spice are drier, 'black' and hotter; *Rathu* the 'red' curries are hottest, with plenty of dried red-chilli (rathu miris) powder added.

Spices which are grown locally and which attracted sea-faring traders to the island, are liberally used in the kitchen - cardamom, cinnamon, cloves, fenugreek and pepper etc, as well as the typical cumin, coriander and turmeric.

Coconut is plentiful and appears in various forms or during cooking or serving - coconut oil, coconut 'milk' (strained infusion) to cook with or prepare a batter, grated coconut, small pieces of kernel - even the shell is used as a ladle. Molee are mild curries with a creamy coconut milk gravy. As a drink, King Coconut water (*thambili*) is safe and refreshing. The unfermented palm sap produces thelija, the fermented toddy and the distilled arrack.

Footnotes

Pronunciation
ā as in ah
ī as in bee

ū as oo in book
ō as in oh

These marks to help with pronunciation do not appear in the main text.

Basic vocabulary	Sinhalese	Tamil
bread	pān	rotti/pān
butter		butter/vennai
(too much) chilli	miris wadi	kāram
drink	bīma	kudi
egg	biththara	muttai
fish	malu	min
fruit	palathuru	palam
food	kama	unavu

jaggery	*hakuru*	*sini/vellam*
juice	*isma*	*sāru*
meat	*mus*	*iraichchi*
oil	*thel*	*ennai*
pepper	*gammiris*	*milagu*
pulses (beans, lentils)	*parippu*	*thāniyam*
rice	*buth*	*arisi*
salt	*lunu*	*uppu*
savoury		*suvai*
spices	*kulubadu*	*milagu*
sweetmeats	*rasakevili*	*inippu pondangal*
treacle	*pani*	*pāni*
vegetables	*elawalu*	*kai kari vagaigal*
water	*wathura*	*thanneer*

Fruit

avocado	*alkigetapera*	
banana	*keselkan*	*valaippalam*
cashew	*cadju*	*muruthivi*
coconut	*pol*	*thengali*
green coconut	*kurumba*	*pachcha niramulla thengai*
jackfruit	*(jak) kos ambul*	
mango	*amba*	*mangai*
orange	*dodam*	
papaya	*papol*	*pappa palam*
pineapple	*annasi*	*annasi*

Vegetables

aubergine	*vambatu*	*kathirikai*
beans (green)	*bonchi*	*avarai*
cabbage	*gowa*	*muttaikosu*
gourd (green)	*pathola*	*pudalankai*
mushrooms		*kalān*
okra	*bandakka*	*vendikkai*
onion	*luunu*	*venkayam*
pea		*pattani*
pepper	*miris*	*kāram*
potato	*ala*	*uruka kilangu*
spinach	*niwithi*	*pasali*
tomato	*thakkali*	*thakkali*

Meat, fish and seafood

chicken	*kukulmas*	*koli*
crab	*kakuluvo*	*nandu*
pork	*ōroomas*	*pantri*

Ordering a meal in a restaurant: Sinhalese

Please show the menu	*menu eka penwanna*
No chillis please	*miris nathuwa*
sugar/milk/ice	*sini/kiri/ice*
A bottle of mineral water please	*drink botalayak genna*
do not open it	*arinna epa*
sweet/savoury	*sweet/rolls*
spoon/fork/knife	*handa/garappuwak/pihiya*

Order a meal in a restaurant: Tamil

Please show the menu	*thayavu seithu thinpandangal patti tharavum*
No chillis please	*kāram vendām*
sugar/milk/ice	*sini/pāl/ice*
A bottle of mineral water please	*oru pothal soda panam tharavum*

Sri Lankan specialities

amblulthial sour fish curry

kaha buth kaha rice (yellow, cooked in coconut milk with spices and saffron/turmeric colouring)

kiri rice is similar but white and unspiced, served with treacle, chilli or pickle

biththara rotti rotti mixed with eggs

buriyani rice cooked in meat stock and pieces of spiced meat sometimes garnished with boiled egg slices

hoppers (āppa) cupped pancakes made of fermented rice flour, coconut milk, yeast, eaten with savoury (or sweet) curry

lamprai rice cooked in stock parcelled in a banana leaf with dry meat and vegetable curries, fried meat and fish balls and baked gently

mellung boiled, shredded vegetables cooked with spice and coconut

pittu rice-flour and grated coconut steamed in bamboo moulds, eaten with coconut milk and curry

polos pahi pieces of young jackfruit (tree lamb) replaces meat in this dry curry

rotty or rotti flat, circular, unleavened bread cooked on a griddle

sambol hot and spicy accompaniment usually made with onions, grated coconut, pepper (and sometimes dried fish)

sathai spicy meat pieces baked on skewers (sometimes sweet and sour)

'short eats' a selection of meat and vegetable snacks (in pastry or crumbled and fried) charged as eaten.

string hoppers (indiāppa) flat circles of steamed rice flour noodles eaten usually at breakfast with thin curry

thosai or *dosai* large crisp pancake made with rice and lentil-flour batter

vadai deep-fried savoury lentil dough-nut rings

Sweets (rasakavilis)

curd rich, creamy, buffalo-milk yoghurt served with treacle or jaggery

gulab jamun dark, fried spongy balls of milk curd and flour soaked in syrup

halwal aluva fudge-like, made with milk, nuts and fruit

kadju kordial fudge squares made with cashew nuts and jaggery

kaludodol dark, mil-based, semi solid sweet mixed with jaggery, cashew and spices (a moorish delicacy)

rasgulla syrup-filled white spongy balls of milk-curd and flour

thalaguli balls formed after pounding roasted sesame seeds with jaggery

wattalappam set 'custard' of coconut, milk, eggs and cashew, flavoured with spices and jaggery

Indian specialities

A typical meal in an Indian restaurant would include some 'bread' (roti, chapāti or nān) and/or rice, a vegetable curry and/or a meat curry, lentils (dāl), raita (yogurt with shredded cucumber or fruit) and pāpadam (deep-fried pulse flour wafer rounds).

do piaza with onions (added twice during cooking)

dāl makhani lentils coated with butter

dum aloo potato curry with a spicy yogurt, tomato and onion sauce

kebab skewered (or minced and shaped) meat or fish; a dry spicy dish cooked on a fire

kima mattar mince meat with peas

korma in a fairly mild rich sauce using cream/yoghurt

matar panīr curd cheese cubes with peas and spices (and often tomatoes)

mughlai rich north Indian style

murgh massallam chicken in a rich creamy marinade of yoghurt, spices and herbs with nuts

rogan josh mutton/beef pieces in a rich creamy, red sauce

tandoori baked in a tandoor (special clay oven)

tikka marinated meat pieces baked quite dry

Index

A

accommodation 38
Adam's Peak 167
Ahangama 141
ahimsa 301
AIDS 54
air ticket agents 31
air travel 30
air travel, domestic 41
air-conditioning 40
airport information 31
airport transfer 81
alcohol 48
Aluthgama 116
Aluwihare 232
Amaduwa 162
Ambepussa 104
Amunugama 198
Ananta 294
angelfish 325
animals 320
Anuradhapura 238
Arankele 106
archaeological sites 33
architecture 309
  Buddhist 310
  Hindu 311
Arugam Bay 277
Asiatic elephant 320
Asiatic wild buffalo 320
athlete's foot 55
ATMs 29
Aukana 236
Avissawella 165
ayurvedic medicine 181

B

Badulla 217
Bakr-Id 51
Balangoda 171, 283
Bambarakanda (Bam- baragala)
  Falls 173
bamboo 326
banana 328
Bandaranaike 103
Bandaranaike, Sirimavo 290
Bandarawela 223
banyan 326
barking deer 321
batik 112
Batticaloa 275
Bawa, Bevis 117
Bawa, Geoffrey 69
begging 36

Belihuloya 172
Bentota 117
Beruwela 114
Bhagavata Purana 315
bhakti 315
bhikkus 284
Bhuvanekabahu I 107
bikes 43
birds 322
bird-watching 154, 157
black-headed babbler 325
blue rock dove 322
blue surgeon 325
Bo tree 298
boat travel to Sri Lanka 32
boat trips 119
Bodhi tree 240, 298
Bodhisattvas 295
booklist 56
Botanic gardens 192
  Hakgala 207
  Heneratgoda 103
  Peradeniya 192
bougainvillea 328
brahminy kite 323
Brief Garden 117
British, The 287
Buddha's life 294
Buddhism 293
  architecture 310
  cosmology 296
  Hinayana 294
  Mahayana 295
  practice 297
  Sri Lankan 296
  Theravada 296
  Vajrayana 295
Buddhism & meditation courses
  192
budget hotels 38
budgeting 30
Buduruvagala 222
Bundala 159
Bundala, NP 157
Burghers 284
bus travel 41

C

canals 91
car 41
car hire 42
card phone 46
cashew nut 328
Caste 299, 304

caves, prehistoric 219
cell phones 46
Ceylon Grackle 324
Ceylon Hotels Corporation 39
Ceylon Ironwood 327
Ceylon Lorikeet 324
Ceylon National Congress 288
Ceylon Tourist Board overseas 25
changing money 28
charities 36
charter flights 31
checklist, health 51
Chilaw 102
children, travelling with 35
Chital 321
Cholas 313
cholera 52,54
Christianity 307
climate 317
collect calls 46
Colombo
  centre 62
  directory 81
  eating 73
  essentials 70
  parks and zoos 70
  shopping 75
  sleeping 70
  sports 77
  tours 77
  transport 78
common langur 321
common mongoose 322
common myna 322
communications 45
conduct 36
confidence tricksters 37
con-men 37
corals 325
cosmology, Buddhist 296
costs 30
couriers 45
courtesy 36
cowries 325
credit cards 29
crocodiles 325
cuisine 47
Culavansa 284
Cultural Triangle
  Anuradhapura 238
  Kandy 177
  permit 84
  Polonnaruwa 257
  round tickets 33
currency 28
customs 28,36
cycles 43

D

Dalada Maligawa, Kandy 180
Dalhousie 208
Dambadeniya 107
Dambulla 234
dancing, kandyan 189
Dedigama 196
Deepavali 50
dengue fever 55
departure tax 32
Deraniyagala 219
Devanampiya Tissa 285,296
Devdutta 294
dharma 300
diarrhoea 53
Dikwella 147
diving 127,151
Diyaluma Falls 228
Dodanduwa 129
Dondra 147
Dravida 313
drink 48
Dudley Senanayake 288
Dumbara Hills 198
Dunhinda Falls 218
Durga 304
Dutch canals 91
Dutch, The 287
Dutthagamenu 106
duty free allowances 28

E

Eastern Province 275
economy 290
Elephant Orphanage,
  Pinnawela 195
elephants 279, 320
Elkaduwa 188
Ella 219
email 46
embassies, Sri Lankan 26
Embekke 194
Embilipitiya 173
Esala Perahera, Kandy 189, 197
etiquette 36
Eucalyptus 326
exchange 28
export 28

F

fax 46
festivals 197
  Muslim 307
  Sri Lanka 50
fire-walking 163
fish 325
flag 292
flying fox 322
food 47
forest hermitage, cave 106
Fort Frederick 271

frangipani 328
fruit 48
fruit bat 322
fruit trees 328
further reading 56

G

Gadaladeniya Temple 193
Gal Oya National Park 276
Galle 130
Gampaha 103
Ganesh 304
Ganga, Riv 313
gay travellers 34
gem mining 122
gem testing 76
geography 316
getting around 41
getting there 30
gopurams 313
guard stones 311
guesthouses 38
Gul Mohur 326
Gum Tree 326

H

Habaraduwa 141
Habarana 256
Hakgala Gardens 207
Hambantota 155
Hanuman 303
hanuman langur 321
Hanwella 164
Haputale 225
Hatadage 260
Hatton 208
health 51
  before travelling 51
  further information 52
  other risks and more serious
    diseases 54
  staying healthy 53
  when you get home 56
heat stroke 54
Heerassagala 188
Heneratgoda 103
hepatitis 52
herbal cures 181
hermitage, cave 106
hibiscus 328
Hikkaduwa 122
Hill Myna 324
Hinayana 294
Hinayana cosmology 296
Hindagala Temple 198
Hindu sects 302
Hindu temple architecture 311
Hinduism 299
hire charges 42
history 283
holidays 50
homosexuality 34
Horana 164

Horton Plains 207
hotels 38
humidity 318

I

Ibn Batuta 130
Id-ul-Fitr 51
Id-ul-Zuha 51
immunisations 51
import 28
Inamaluwa 255
Independence 288
Induruwa 119
influenza 55
insect pests 40
insects 54
international phone calls 45
Internet 46
intestinal upsets 53
Intestinal worms 56
Islam 305
Istripura Caves 217

J

jacaranda 327
Ja-ela 88
jakfruit 328
Jambudvipa 312
Japanese B Encephalitis (JVE) 52
Jati 305
Jayawardenepura 68
JVP 289

K

Kaduwela 164
Kalametiya Bird Sanctuary 154
Kali 304
Kalutara 112
Kandyan Kingdom 286
Kantalai 275
Karava 299
karma 300
Kataragama 162, 304
Katugastota 188
Kegalla 196
Kelaniya 67
Keppetipola 216
King Kasyapa 253
King Nissankamalla 69
King Valagambahu 234
Kirinda 159
Kirivehera 163
Kirti Sri 179
Kitulgala 165
Knuckles Range 198
Koggala 141
Konesvaram Temple 271
Kosgoda 120
Kotte 68
Kotte Kingdom 286
Kubera 253

Kudawella 148
Kumana Bird Sanctuary 278
Kumarakanda Rajamahavihara 129
Kumaratunge 290
Kurunegala 104
Kuruwita 165
Kushta Raja 141

L

Labookellie Tea Estate 199
Lahugala National Park 279
lakes 317
Lakshmi 303
language 315
Lankatilaka Mahaviharaya 194
leopard 320
lesbian travellers 34
Liberation Tigers of Tamil Eelam 289
linga 304
Lion Rock 251
literature 57

M

Madampe 171
Madungala 154
Magul Mahavihara 278
Maha Saman Dewale 166
Maha Vihara 242
Mahavansa 284
Mahaweli River 188
Mahayana 295
Mahinda 247
Mahiyangana 265
Maho 107
Maitreya 296
Malala Lewaya 157
malaria 55
mammals 320
mandala 312
mango 328
manuscripts, palm 233
maps 58
Marawila 97
marsh crocodile 325
Maskeliya 208
Matale 232
media 46
medical care 51
medicines 51
Meetiyagoda 122
Meningococcal Meningitis 52
Midigama 141
Mihintale 247
Minneriya-Giritale
  National Park 257
Mirissa 143
Monaragala 279
money 28
money transfer 29
monkeys 321
moonstone (gem) 122
moonstones 311

Moors 284
Moragalla 114
Moratuwa 112
mosques 34
motorcycles 43
Mount Lavinia 84
mountain railway 191
Mount Meru 312
mugger crocodile 325
Muharram 51
Mulgirigala 151
Munneswaram 102
Muntjac 321
Murex 325
Muslim
  beliefs 306
  calendar 307
  festivals 307
  Sects 306
Mythology 303, 312

N

Nalanda 233
Nandi 304
national anthem 292
national holidays 50
national parks
  Gal Oya 276
  Horton 209
  Kumana Bird Sanctuary 278
  Lahugala 279
  Uda Walawe 173
  Yala East 278
Negombo 89
newspapers 46
Nilaveli 273
Nissankamalla 259
Northern Province 280
Nuwara Eliya 200

O

Olive Ridley Turtle 325
orchids 328

P

painting 314
Paiyagala South 113
Palace Area 179
Palatupana 161
Palk Straits 316
palm manuscripts 232
Panadura 112
Pandiyas 313
Panther 320
papaya 328
Parakrama Samudra, Lake 259
Parakramabahu I 259, 286
Parakramabahu II 107
Parakramabahu VI 68
parinirvana 294
Parvati 304

Pasgama 103
pay phone 46
Peradeniya 192
Perahera, Kandy 189, 197
personal security 37
Pettah, the 65
phone 45
photography 36
pilgrimage 312
Pinnawela Elephant Orphanage 195
Polhena 144
police 37, 38
polio-myelitis 52
Polo, Marco 208
Polonnaruwa 257
Portuguese 287
poste restante 45
Pothgul Vihara 259
poya days 298
prehistory 219
prohibited items 28
puja 301
Pussellawa 199
Puttalam 102

R

rabies 52
radio 46
radio cabs 43
rail travel 43
railway retiring rooms 40
railway, mountain 191
rainfall 317
Rajaduwa 188
Rajaraja I 286
Rajarata 285
Rama 302
Ramadan 51, 306
Ramayana 163, 303
Ramboda 199
Randenigala Reservoir 207
Ravana 163
Rawana Ella Cave 219
Rawana Ella Falls 220
reading list 56
rebirth 300
religion 293
religious sites, visiting 34
reptiles 325
respiratory diseases 55
Rest House Group 259
resthouses 39
restricted areas 37
restricted items 28
Ridigama Vihara 106
Ritigala 256
rivers 317
road 41
Rohana 285
route plans 19
Royal Citadel Group 260
rubber 103, 291
Ruhunu 285
Rumassala 137

S

safety 37
Sago 326
Sakra 285
sal 327
salmonella infections 54
saltwater crocodile 325
sambhur 321
samsara 300
Sanghamitta 240
sanni 121
Sapugaskanda 103
Sarasvati 302
Sardinella 325
Sati 304
sculpture 314
sea life 325
sea urchins 325
sects 297
security 37
Seenigama 122
shells 325
shopping 48
Sigiriya 251
silk cotton tree 327
Sinhalese 315
Sinhalese nationalism 297
Sinharaja Biosphere Reserve 169
Sita 163
Sita Eliya Temple 207
Siva 304
Siva Devale I 260
Sivarathri 50
Skanda 304
sloth bear 320
small-pox 52
snake bite 55
soft drinks 48
Sri Jayawardenepura 68
Sri Lanka Freedom Party 289
Sri Vikrama Rajasinha 179
statistics 292
stupas 310
sunburn 54
sunnis 307

T

Talahena 94
Talawakele 209
Talpe 138
tamarind 327
Tamil 315
Taprobane 141
tax, airport 32
taxis 43
TCs 29
tea 201, 291
telephone 45
television 46
Telwatta 123
temperatures 318
Temple architecture 311
temple design 312

Temple of the Tooth, Kandy 180
temples, visiting 34
tetanus 52
Theravada 294
Theravada Buddhism 296
three-wheelers 43
Thuparama, Anuradhapura 243
time 33
tipping 36
Tissa, Devanampiya 239,296
Tissamaharama 158
Tissawewa 159
tocque macaque 321
toilets 40
Tooth Relic 178
tour operators 24
tourist offices overseas 25
train travel 43
transport to Sri Lanka 30
travel 41
travel permits 26
travellers cheques 29
Trincomalee 270
tuk-tuks 43
Turnour, George 151
Turtle Conservation Project 153
turtle hatchery 120
Turtle Research Project 119
turtles 119, 156, 325
typhoid 52

U

Uda Walawe National Park 173
Ukuwela 188
Uma 304
Unawatuna 137
United National Party 289
useful addresses 25
Uttaradesa 285

V

vaccinations 51
Vajrayana 295
Varna 304
Vatadage 260
Vattagamani Abhaya 296
Vedanta 301
Veddas 218, 283
vegetarians 47
vegetation 326
vel 304
Vellalas 305
Vijayabahu I 257,286
Vijayanagar 313
Vimala Dharma Suriya 178
visas 26
Vishnu 302
voluntary work 156

W

Waikkal 97
Warakapola 104
water buffalo 320
water cutting 197
watersports 95
Weherahena 147
Weligama 141
Wellawaya 222
western shrines 192
Wewurukannala 147
what to take 27
when to go 24
where to stay 38
wild boar 321
wildlife 318
women travellers 34
work permits 35
World End, Horton Plains 211

Y

Yala 159
Yapahuwa 107
yellow fever 52
yoga 30

Shorts

62	A foot in the door		327	Holy but not wholly efficacious!
204	A morning climb to Pidurutalagala		300	Karma – an eye to the future
279	A walk through the parks		53	Leeches
240	An alternative cycle route around Anuradhapura		233	Palm leaf manuscripts
206	April in Nuwara		170	Rubber
181	Ayurvedic healing		158	Salt of the earth
163	Barefoot over hot coals		310	Sinhalese stupas
307	Calculating the Hijra year		65	Slave Island
63	Colombo Harbour		77	Sports mad Sri Lanka
79	Colombo's straggling suburbs – a traveller's woe		295	The Buddha's Four Noble Truths
78	Cricket crazy		301	The duty of tolerance
121	Dance of the sorcerers		47	The email explosion
242	Dutthagamenu: Battle with Elara		197	The festival of festivals
35	Eco travelling: a few tips		306	The five pillars of Islam
156	Endangered Turtles		191	The hill railway
91	European influences: catholicism and canals		291	The indispensable coconut
292	Fact file		218	The island's original people
244	Forest hermitages with pretty carved latrines!		95	The lure of the underwater world
40	Full Moon Poya days		201	The refreshing cup
20	Gems of Sri Lanka		114	The Sap Tappers
243	Gleaming white bells		168	The sparkle of romance
271	History of Fort Frederick		169	To drink or not to drink
			253	To rival the God of Wealth
			42	Unwritten rules of the road
			303	Vishnu's ten incarnations
			180	Worship of the 'Tooth Relic'

Map index

289   Administrative provinces
       & districts
118   Aluthagama & Bentota
241   Anuradhapura
172   Balangoda
74   Bambalapitiya
224   Bandarawela
115   Beruwela
216   Central Highlands
64   Colombo
236   Dambulla
277   Eastern Province (South)
220   Ella area
66   Fort & Pettah
133   Galle
68   Galle Face and Union Place
155   Hambantota
226   Haputale
126   Hikkaduwa & Wewala beach
123   Hikkaduwa area
210   Horton Plains
184   Kandy
194   Kandy excursions
72   Kollupitiya & ward place
105   Kurunegala

106   Kurunegala area
265   Mahiyangana
146   Matara & Polhena
248   Mihintale
250   Mihintale Sacred Centre
85   Mount Lavinia
129   Narigama & Thirangama
319   National parks & sanctuaries
92   Negombo Beach
90   Negombo Town
205   Nuwara Eliya
258   Polonnaruwa
261   Polonnaruwa Quadrangle
260   Polonnaruwa, Rest House Group
278   Pottuvil & Arugam Bay
167   Ratnapura
252   Sigiriya
316   Sri Lanka 200 million years ago
149   Tangalla
152   Tangalla to Hambantota
160   Tissamaharama
272   Trincomalee
274   Trincomalee area
139   Unawatuna
142   Weligama

Footnotes

Advertisers

Colour section
Jetwing Hotels, Sri Lanka

86   Berjaya Mount Royal Beach
         Hotel, Sri Lanka
25   Exodus Travels, UK
24   Gateway to India & Asia, UK

Will you help us?

We try as hard as we can to make each Footprint Handbook as up-to-date and accurate as possible but, of course, things always change. Many people write to us - with corrections, new information, or simply comments.

If you want to let us know about an experience or adventure - hair-raising or mundane, good or bad, exciting or boring - we would be delighted to hear from you. Please give us as precise information as possible, quoting the edition number (you'll find it on the front cover) and page number of the Handbook you are using.

Your help will be greatly appreciated, especially by other travellers. In return we will send you details about our special guidebook offer.

email Footprint at:
sri3_online@footprintbooks.com

or write to:
Elizabeth Taylor
Footprint Handbooks
6 Riverside Court
Lower Bristol Road
Bath BA2 3DZ
UK

Footprint travel list

Footprint publish travel guides to over 120 countries worldwide. Each guide is packed with practical, concise and colourful information for everybody from first-time travellers to travel aficionados . The list is growing fast and current titles are noted below. For further information check out the website **www.footprintbooks.com**

Andalucía Handbook
Argentina Handbook
Bali & the Eastern Isles Hbk
Bangkok & the Beaches Hbk
Bolivia Handbook
Brazil Handbook
Cambodia Handbook
Caribbean Islands Handbook
Chile Handbook
Colombia Handbook
Cuba Handbook
Dominican Republic Handbook
East Africa Handbook
Ecuador & Galápagos Handbook
Egypt Handbook Handbook
Goa Handbook
India Handbook
Indian Himalaya Handbook
Indonesia Handbook
Ireland Handbook
Israel Handbook
Jordan Handbook
Jordan, Syria & Lebanon Hbk
Laos Handbook
Libya Handbook
Malaysia Handbook
Myanmar Handbook
Mexico Handbook
Mexico & Central America Hbk
Morocco Handbook
Namibia Handbook
Nepal Handbook
Pakistan Handbook

Peru Handbook
Rio de Janeiro Handbook
Scotland Handbook
Singapore Handbook
South Africa Handbook
South American Handbook
South India Handbook
Sri Lanka Handbook
Sumatra Handbook
Thailand Handbook
Tibet Handbook
Tunisia Handbook
Venezuela Handbook
Vietnam Handbook

In the pipeline – Turkey, London, Kenya, Rajasthan, Scotland Highlands & Islands, Syria & Lebanon

Also available from Footprint
Traveller's Handbook
Traveller's Healthbook

Available at all good bookshops

Sales & distribution

Footprint Handbooks
6 Riverside Court
Lower Bristol Road
Bath BA2 3DZ England
T 01225 469141
F 01225 469461
discover
@footprintbooks.com

Australia
Peribo Pty
58 Beaumont Road
Mt Kuring-Gai
NSW 2080
T 02 9457 0011
F 02 9457 0022

Austria
Freytag-Berndt Artaria
Kohlmarkt 9
A-1010 Wien
T 01533 2094
F 01533 8685

Freytag-Berndt
Sporgasse 29
A-8010 Graz
T 0316 818230
F 3016 818230-30

Belgium
Craenen BVBA
Mechelsesteenweg 633
B-3020 Herent
T 016 23 90 90
F 016 23 97 11

Waterstones
The English Bookshop
Blvd Adolphe Max 71-75
B-1000 Brussels
T 02 219 5034

Canada
Ulysses Travel Publications
4176 rue Saint-Denis
Montréal
Québec H2W 2M5
T 514 843 9882
F 514 843 9448

Europe
Bill Bailey
16 Devon Square
Newton Abbott
Devon TQ12 2HR. UK
T 01626 331079
F 01626 331080

Denmark
Nordisk Korthandel
Studiestraede 26-30 B
DK-1455 Copenhagen K
T 3338 2638
F 3338 2648

Scanvik Books
Esplanaden 8B
DK-1263 Copenhagen K
T 3312 7766
F 3391 2882

Finland
Akateeminen Kirjakauppa
Keskuskatu 1
FIN-00100 Helsinki
T 09 121 4151
F 09 121 4441

Suomalainen Kirjakauppa
Koivuvaarankuja 2
01640 Vantaa 64
F 09 852751

France
FNAC – major branches

L'Astrolabe
46 rue de Provence
F-75009 Paris 9e
T 01 42 85 42 95
F 01 45 75 92 51

VILO Diffusion
25 rue Ginoux
F-75015 Paris
T 01 45 77 08 05
F 01 45 79 97 15

Germany
GeoCenter ILH
Schockenriedstrasse 44
D-70565 Stuttgart
T 0711 781 94610
F 0711 781 94654

Brettschneider
Feldkirchnerstrasse 2
D-85551 Heimstetten
T 089 990 20330
F 089 990 20331

Geobuch
Rosental 6
D-80331 München
T 089 265030
F 089 263713

Gleumes
Hohenstaufenring 47-51
D-50674 Köln
T 0221 215650

Globetrotter Ausrustungen
Wiesendamm 1
D-22305 Hamburg
T040 679 66190
F 040 679 66183

Dr Götze
Bleichenbrücke 9
D-2000 Hamburg 1
T 040 3031 1009-0

Hugendubel Buchhandlung
Nymphenburgerstrasse 25
D-80335 München
T 089 238 9412
F 089 550 1853

Kiepert Buchhandlung
Hardenbergstrasse 4-5
D-10623 Berlin 12
T 030 311 880
F 030 311 88120

Greece
GC Eleftheroudakis
17 Panepistemiou
Athens 105 64
T 01 331 4180-83
F 01 323 9821

India
India Book Distributors
1007/1008 Arcadia
195 Nariman Point
Mumbai 400 021
T 91 22 282 5220
F 91 22 287 2531

Israel
Eco Trips
8 Tverya Street
Tel Aviv 63144
T 03 528 4113
F 03 528 8269

For a fuller list, see www.footprintbooks.com

Italy
Librimport
Via Biondelli 9
I-20141 Milano
T 02 8950 1422
F 02 8950 2811

Libreria del Viaggiatore
Via dell Pelegrino 78
I-00186 Roma
T/F 06 688 01048

Netherlands
Nilsson & Lamm bv
Postbus 195
Pampuslaan 212
N-1380 AD Weesp
T 0294 494949
F 0294 494455

Waterstones
Kalverstraat 152
1012 XE Amsterdam
T 020 638 3821

New Zealand
Auckland Map Centre
Dymocks

Norway
Schibsteds Forlag A/S
Akersgata 32 - 5th Floor
Postboks 1178 Sentrum
N-0107 Oslo
T 22 86 30 00
F 22 42 54 92

Tanum
Karl Johansgate 37-41
PO Box 1177 Sentrum
N-0107 Oslo 1
T 22 41 11 00
F 22 33 32 75

Olaf Norlis
Universitetsgt 24
N-1062 Oslo
T 22 00 43 00

Pakistan
Pak-American Commercial
Hamid Chambers
Zaib-un Nisa Street
Saddar, PO Box 7359
Karachi
T 21 566 0418
F 21 568 3611

South Africa
Faradawn CC
PO Box 1903
Saxonwold 2132
T 011 885 1787
F 011 885 1829

South America
Humphrys Roberts
Associates
Caixa Postal 801-0
Ag. Jardim da Gloria
06700-970 Cotia SP
Brazil
T 011 492 4496
F 011 492 6896

Southeast Asia
APA Publications
38 Joo Koon Road
Singapore 628990
T 865 1600
F 861 6438

In Hong Kong, Malaysia,
Singapore and Thailand:
MPH, Kinokuniya, Times

Spain
Altaïr
C/Balmes 69
08007 Barcelona
T 933 233062
F 934 512559

Altaïr
Gaztambide 31
28015 Madrid
T 0915 435300
F 0915 443498

Libros de Viaje
C/Serrano no 41
28001 Madrid
T 01 91 577 9899
F 01 91 577 5756

Il Corte Inglés – major
branches

Sweden
Hedengrens Bokhandel
PO Box 5509
S-11485 Stockholm
T 08 611 5132

Kart Centrum
Vasagatan 16
S-11120 Stockholm
T 08 411 1697

Kartforlaget
Skolgangen 10
S-80183 Gavle
T 026 633000
F 026 124204

Lantmateriet Kartbutiken
Kungsgatan 74
S-11122 Stockholm
T 08 202 303
F 08 202 711

Switzerland
Office du Livre OLF
ZI3, Corminboeuf
CH-1701 Fribourg
T 026 467 5111
F 026 467 5666

Schweizer Buchzentrum
Postfach
CH-4601 Olten
T 062 209 2525
F 062 209 2627

Travel Bookshop
Rindermarkt 20
Postfach 216
CH-8001 Zürich
T 01 252 3883
F 01 252 3832

Tanzania
A Novel Idea
The Slipway
PO Box 76513
Dar es Salaam
T/F 051 601088

USA
NTC/ Contemporary
4255 West Touhy Avenue
Lincolnwood
Illinois 60646-1975
T 847 679 5500
F 847 679 2494

Barnes & Noble, Borders,
specialist travel bookstores

Jetwing Hotels

West Coast

* **Royal Oceanic Hotel**, NEGOMBO †
* **Blue Oceanic Beach Hotel**, NEGOM
* **Seashells Hotel**, NEGOMBO
* **Hotel Sunset Beach**, NEGOMBO
* **Sea Garden Hotel**, NEGOMBO

South Coast

* **The Blue Water**, WADDUWA †
* **Tropical Villas**, BERUWELA
* **The Villa Riviera**, BERUWELA
* **Kosgoda Beach Resort**, KOSGODA
* **Lighthouse Hotel**, GALLE

Hill Country

* **The Swiss Residence**, KANDY
* **Hunas Falls Hotel**, KANDY
* **St Andrew's Hotel**, NUWARA ELIYA

Safari &
Adventure

* **Ella Adventure Park**, ELLA
* **Yala Safari Beach Hotel**, YALA †

Transit

* **The Tamarind Tree**, KATUNAYAKE †

† Pictured

Jetwing Travels

JETWING TRAVELS OFFER A FLEET OF VEHICLES FROM CARS TO COACHES AND ORGANISE
GUIDED TOURS AND TRAVEL WITHIN AND OUT OF THE COUNTRY.

"JETWING HOUSE", 46/26 NAVAM MAWATHA, COLOMBO 2, SRI LANKA   TEL: 94-1-345700, 94-75-545
E-mail: jethot@sri.lanka.net ● jettrav@sri.lanka.net ● www.jetwing.net   FAX: 94-1-345729

Sri Lanka

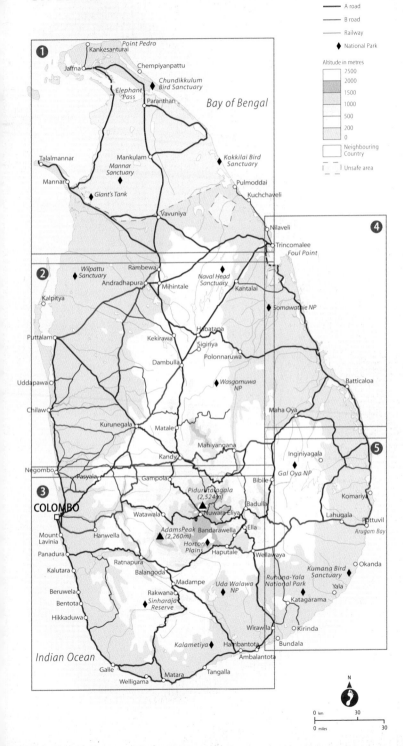

1

Point Pedro
Kankesanturai
Jaffna
Chempiyanpattu
Elephant Pass
Chundikkulum Bird Sanctuary
Paranthan

Bay of Bengal

Talalmannar
Mankulam
Mannar Sanctuary
Mannar
Kokkilai Bird Sanctuary
Giant's Tank
Pulmoddai
Vavuniya
Kuchchaveli

4

Nilaveli
Trincomalee
Foul Point

2
Wilpattu Sanctuary
Rambewa
Andradhapura
Mihintale
Naval Head Sanctuary
Kantalai
Somawathie NP
Kalpitya
Puttalam
Kekirawa
Habatana
Sigiriya
Polonnaruwa
Dambulla
Uddapawa
Wasgomuwa NP
Batticaloa
Chilaw
Kurunegala
Matale
Maha Oya
Mahiyangana
Kandy
Negombo
Pasyala
Gampola
Bibile
Gal Oya NP
Inginiyagala

5

Komariya
3
COLOMBO
Watawala
Pidurutalagala (2,524m)
Nuwara Eliya
Badulla
Lahugala
Pottuvil
Mount Lavinia
Hanwella
Adams Peak (2,260m)
Bandarawella
Ella
Arugam Bay
Panadura
Horton Plains
Haputale
Wellawaya
Kalutara
Ratnapura
Balangoda
Kumana Bird Sanctuary
Okanda
Beruwela
Madampe
Uda Walawa NP
Ruhuna-Yala National Park
Bentota
Rakwana
Sinharaja Reserve
Yala
Hikkaduwa
Katagarama
Wirawila
Kirinda
Kalametiya
Hambantota
Bundala
Galle
Matara
Ambalantota
Welligama
Tangalla

Indian Ocean

A road
B road
Railway
National Park

Altitude in metres
2500
2000
1500
1000
500
200
0

Neighbouring Country
Unsafe area

N

0 km 30
0 miles 30

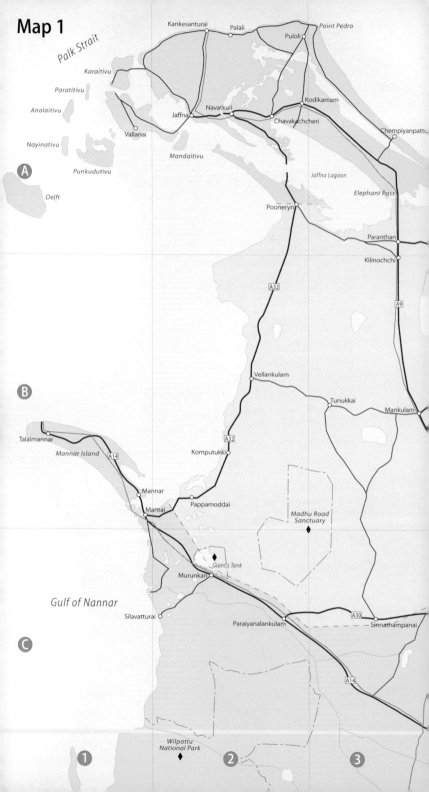

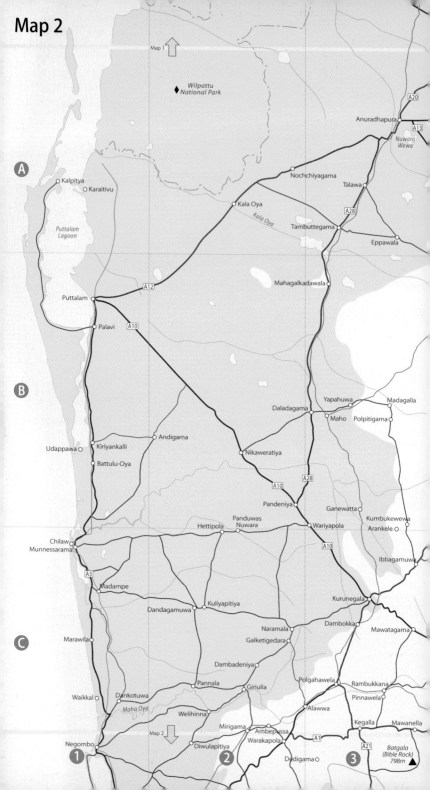

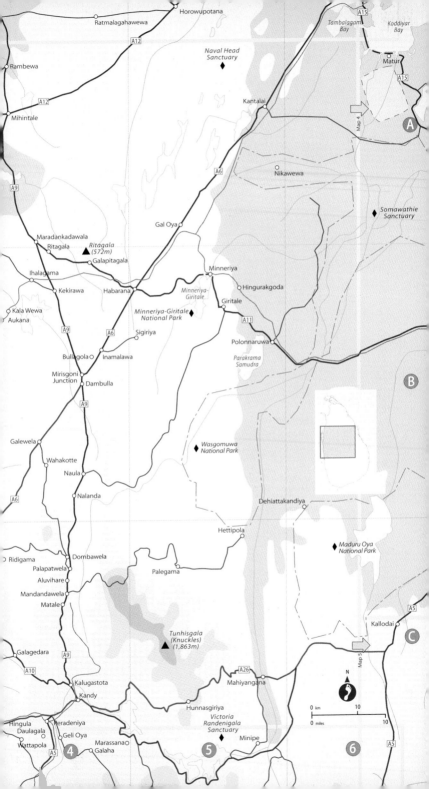

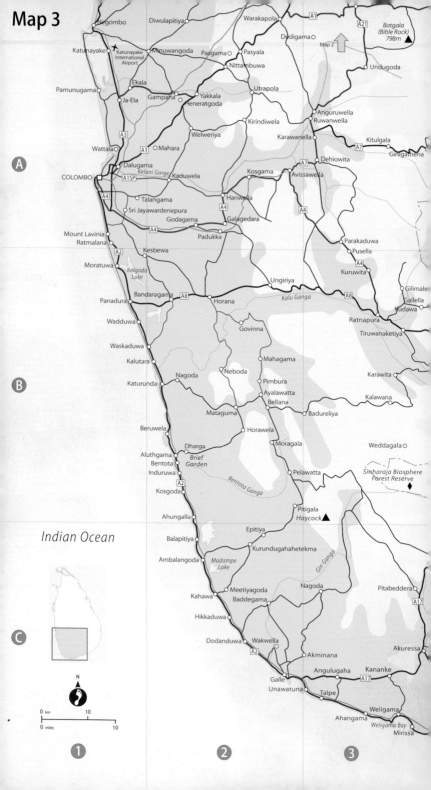

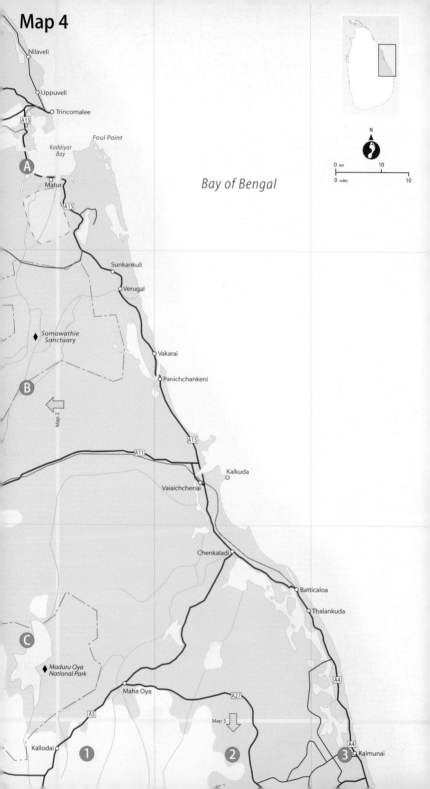

Map 5

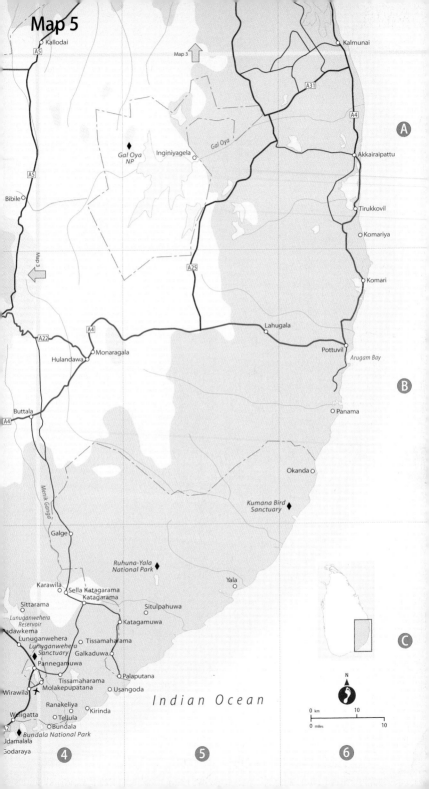

Kallodai
A5

Map 3

Kalmunai

A31

A4

Gal Oya NP

Inginiyagela

Gal Oya

A

Akkairaipattu

Bibile
A5

Tirukkovil

Komariya

Map 3

A25

Komari

A22
A4

Lahugala

Hulandawa

Monaragala

Pottuvil

Arugam Bay

B

Buttala

A4

Panama

Menik Ganga

Okanda

Kumana Bird
Sanctuary

Galge

Ruhuna-Yala
National Park

Karawila

Yala

Sella Katagarama
Katagarama

Sittarama

Situlpahuwa

Lunuganwehera
Reservoir

Katagamuwa

C

Kadawkema

Lunuganwehera

Lunuganwehera
Sanctuary

Panneganuwa

Galkaduwa

Tissamaharama

Wirawila

Tissamaharama

Palaputana

Molakepupatana

Usangoda

A2

Ranakeliya

Weligatta

Tellula

Kirinda

Indian Ocean

Bundala

Jdamalala

Bundala National Park

N

Godaraya

0   km   10

0   miles   10

4   5   6

"If 'the essence of real travel' is what you have been secretly yearning for all these years, then Footprint are the guides for you."
Under 26

"Footprint can be depended on for accurate travel information and for imparting a deep sense of respect for the lands and people they cover."
World News

"The guides for intelligent, independently minded souls of any age or budget."
Indie Traveller

"Intelligently written, amazingly accurate and bang up-to-date. Footprint has combined nearly 80 years' experience with a stunning new format to bring us guidebooks that leave the competition standing."
John Pilkington, writer and broadcaster

Mail order

Available worldwide in bookshops and on-line. Footprint travel guides can also be ordered directly from us in Bath, via our website **www.footprintbooks.com** or from the address on the imprint page of this book.

Acknowledgements

We are greatly indebted to Ian Large who was the chief researcher for this new third edition. Ian spent several hectic weeks from December 1999 to February 2000 travelling around the island checking out most of the areas covered by the handbook. He would particularly like to thank Nalini and Sarath de Alwis, Kandy for treating him as one of the family and invaluable assistance in the Kandy area, Anna Kartalski, Antwerpen, Belgium, for her support, encouragement and additional research and Sabri Khan and family, Galle, for in-depth local information and WM Wijesinghe (Santha), Nuwara Eliya, for being an excellent guide, driver and friend.

We also wish to thank the Sri Lanka Tourist Board in London for supplying the Sinhala place names with the assistance from the Sri Lanka Educational, Cultural and Welfare Foundation, Kingsbury, England and Jeevan Thiagarajah from Colombo provided the Sinhala and Tamil phrases.

We are most grateful to travellers and friends of the Handbook who have written in with their comments and updates:

Colin Anderson, Winchester, UK; K & G Ansell, Winchester, UK; Chris Carruthers; Barry Copping, London, UK; Naja Dalbøl, Brussells, Belgium; Dr DK Edussuriya, Kandy, Sri Lanka; Lorraine Green, Essex, UK; Pietro Guarldi, Italy; Bridget Harris, Wisbech, Cambs, UK; Jim and Pat Hutchins, Trevissome, Cornwall, UK; Jaz, Australia; Olivier Jaylet, France; Paul J Kastin, Atlanta, USA; Kenneth McKenzie, Aberdeen, UK; Mary Macpherson, Exeter, Devon, UK; Regine Nonnenmacher; Roth Neil , UK; Richard Phillips; Ian Plumley, London, UK; Roger Tebb; BL Underwood, Colchester, UK; Jenny Vaysse; Juan Pedro Villanueva, Brussels, Belgium.

Robert and Roma Bradnock and Ian Large

Born near Delhi, Robert went to India overland as a research student at Cambridge to spend a year in South Asia. That journey was the first of many visits, living and working throughout the sub-continent. Since joining the School of Oriental and African Studies, where he is now Head of the Department of Geography, he has carried out and supervised research covering the whole region. An international authority on Sri Lanka and its neighbours, Robert broadcasts frequently about the region on networks across the world, and lectures extensively in Britain and Europe.

A Bengali by birth, Roma was brought up in Kolkata (Calcutta) where, after graduating, she worked as a librarian. Her travels across the subcontinent had started early but to widen her horizons she went to Europe, and England subsequently became her home.

In addition to this new edition, she and her husband write the India and Goa Handbooks and the handbooks on South India, Indian Himalaya, and Rajasthan and Gujarat. They have returned to Sri Lanka twice to update this edition.

Ian first visited Sri Lanka in 1992 as part of an 18 month tour of Asia undertaken to escape the institutionalization of working for the BBC. Since then he has returned to India frequently on research trips for Footprint. He has relished the opportunity to re-explore it's island neighbour. In between trips Ian keeps himself busy ruling ancient kingdoms (on his PC!), watching yo-yos (due to his irrational passion for Sunderland AFC), and indulging his enthusiasm for photography.